W9-DGN-155

marriage and
family development

fifth editio

marriage and family development

Evelyn Millis Duvall

J. B. Lippincott Company PHILADELPHIA · New York· San Jose ·Toronto

Fifth Edition

Copyright © 1977, 1971, 1967, 1962, 1957 by J.B. Lippincott Company

ISBN 0-397-47362-1

Library of Congress Catalog Card Number 76-30744
Printed in the United States of America
3579864

Library of Congress Cataloging in Publication Data

Duvall, Evelyn Ruth Millis, 1906–
  Marriage and family development.

  First-4th ed. published under title: Family development.
  Bibliography: p.
  Includes index.
  1. Family. 2. Family—United States. I. Title.
HQ734.D9588   1977   301.42'0973   76-30744
ISBN 0-397-47362-1

contents

introduction

This new edition recognizes the many forms that marriage and family life take in the United States today. It takes into account those who never marry, those who marry and have no children, and those who have children without marrying. It deals first with the fundamental fact of the generative potentials in human sexuality, proceeds through the myriad facets of the societal settings in which families develop, continues with profiles of individual and family development throughout the life cycle, and concludes with the crises and satisfactions that come at somewhat predictable stages of the family life cycle.

The thesis of the book is that developmental stages can be predicted and identified as the family moves through its life cycle and can be understood in terms of the development of individual family members and of the family as a whole. The concepts set forth have been in the process of formulation for many years and represent the contributions of hundreds of researchers.

The Fifth Edition is new in focus and content in that it reflects such contemporary emphases as the equal rights movement; flexible gender roles; the several marital options open to husbands and wives today; varieties of sexual attitudes and expression before, during, and after marriage; ethnic and racial differences among American families; the rising divorce rate; dying; and death with dignity.

Current census data and projections into the twenty-first century have been shared for this edition by the senior demographer of the United States Bureau of the Census, Dr. Paul C. Glick. Many other colleagues have contributed further advances in family theory and research which are cited throughout the text.

The developmental task
concept—a personal history

When I returned to the University of Chicago in 1941-1942 to complete my residency for a Ph.D. in human development, I was fresh from seven years' active community work with teenage youth and their parents. At that time "impulses" and "drives" were popular ways of interpreting adolescent behavior. Such concepts appeared to remove responsibility for their behavior from young people, and to make it seem to them and to those who worked with them that adolescents were, as one writer in a book for youth put it, "human puppets on an invisible string." Such a point of view—interpreting human behavior mainly in terms of biological drives—was unacceptable to me.

Another concept that had gained considerable acceptance was that of "needs." This had the advantage of recognizing that people, like all other growing organisms, have needs that must be met if they are to grow satisfactorily. It had the disadvantage of being ambiguous. Even more serious from my point of view was that so often "the needs of youth" were discussed in terms of the limitations and inadequacies of schools, families, and community agencies in meeting these seemingly inexhaustible requirements. Youth was too often seen as an empty cup impatiently waiting for someone or something to fill it. Problems were seen as reflecting unmet needs. The growth of young people was likened to that of a tomato plant, which, given the proper amounts and kinds of nutrients, sunshine, moisture, and other requirements, would flower and bear fruit in due time. Again, the person himself had little responsibility for his behavior, development, or destiny.

It was with this immediate background that I found members of the Committee on Human Development exploring the possibilities of the concept of the developmental task. Work in classes, seminars, and professional workshops with Daniel Prescott, director of the Division of Child Study of the Commission on Teacher Education of the American Council on Education and a member of the faculty of the University of Chicago, first introduced me to the developmental task concept. Study with Robert J. Havighurst, who had just come to the University of Chicago as chairman of the Committee on Human Development, acquainted me with the history of the developmental task concept up to that time. Dr. Havighurst credits Lawrence K. Frank with first using the term in his hearing about 1935, at one of the many meetings of the staff of the Progressive Education Association's "Adolescent Study" under the direction of Caroline Zachry.[1] It is probable that the original idea came from Frankwood Williams, who several years earlier had published essays stressing what young people must do to work through their developmental problems.[2]

Peter Blos of the Adolescent Study Staff referred briefly to adolescent adjustment problems as "tasks" in his book that appeared in 1941[3] as one of several volumes published by members of the staff. In these studies adolescence was increasingly recognized as a time of life in which certain essential tasks must be mastered if the young person is to emerge into effective adulthood.

The first published work giving a central place to the developmental task concept was a chapter written collaboratively by Robert J. Havighurst, Daniel Prescott, and Fritz Redl for the North Central Association's *General Education in the American High School* in 1942.[4]

The developmental task concept satisfied my search for a frame of reference that dealt dynamically with the challenges of human development, keeping responsibility in the hands of the developing persons, and still allowing room for the helping roles that family members, school personnel, and community workers might play. It satisfactorily met the objections raised by the use of "impulse," "drive," and "needs," and yet covered the realities implied in each of these concepts. Further, it seemed adequate to cover effectively not only the developmental sequence of the teen years, but that of the entire life cycle.

In 1943 the American Council on Education undertook, through a committee chaired by T.R. McConnell, to prepare an outline of objectives and courses in general education that would be appropriate for members of the armed forces. Ernest W. Burgess of the University of Chicago chaired the subcommittee (of which Reuben Hill, Oliver Ohmann, and I were members) that had been commissioned to draw up an outline of a course in marriage and family adjustment.[5]

As a result of this assignment Reuben Hill and I were appointed by the United States Armed Forces Institute to prepare a workbook on marriage and the family for the use of members of the armed services. This eventu-

[1] Robert J. Havighurst, *Human Development and Education* (New York: Longmans, Green and Company, 1953), p. 328.
[2] Frankwood Williams, *Adolescence-Studies in Mental Hygiene* (New York: Farrar and Rinehart, 1930).
[3] Peter Blos, *The Adolescent Personality* (New York: Appleton-Century, 1941), p. 275. (This reference was mainly illustrative, with developmental task still to be recognized as a key concept.)
[4] B.L. Johnson, ed., *General Education in the American High School* (Chicago: Scott, Foresman, 1942), chap. 4.
[5] American Council on Education, *A Design for General Education* (Washington, D.C.: American Council on Education, 1944), pp. 74-84.

ated in the text *When You Marry*,[6] written with a functional emphasis to satisfy student interests and readiness—from "first date through last baby." It was during this collaboration that the life cycle approach, well known among sociologists, and the developmental task concept, then emerging in human development, began to be seen as a series of developmental tasks continuing throughout the life cycle.

In 1947 Reuben Hill and I were asked to work together in the preparation of background papers for the National Conference on Family Life to be held in Washington in May, 1948. As cochairmen of the Committee on the Dynamics of Family Interaction, Dr. Hill and I prepared a two-dimensional outline for plotting the developmental tasks of children and of parents for each stage of the family life cycle and anticipating the probable need for services arising out of the challenges, hazards, and problems involved in the achievement of each developmental task in our culture. Eight subcommittees of specialists at the various developmental levels were appointed by the cochairmen to prepare reports on the various life cycle stages, as noted in Chapters 9 through 16.

In referring to this committee's work, Dr. Havighurst credits it with creatively contributing to the development of the concept.

> This committee made a step forward in the use of the concept by showing how each member of the younger, middle, and older generations in the family has his own developmental tasks, and how the successful achievement of one person's tasks is dependent on and contributory to the successful achievement by others in the family of their appropriate tasks.[7]

The work of the Committee on the Dynamics of Family Interaction appeared in several hundred pages of mimeographed working papers used as background study material for the National Conference on Family Life.[8] Many years have come and gone since the report first appeared. In that interval, faculty members of various university and specialized research centers have generously shared criticisms, questions, and further elaborations of the original materials that have helped to bring the concept to its present state of development.

Family development tasks— conceptual origins

The idea that the family as a whole has developmental tasks of its own

---

[6] Evelyn Millis Duvall and Reuben Hill, *When You Marry* (Boston: D.C. Heath and Company; New York: Association Press, 1945).

[7] Havighurst, *Human Development and Education*, p. 331.

[8] Evelyn Millis Duvall and Reuben Hill, "Report of the Committee on the Dynamics of Family Interaction," mimeographed (Washington, D.C.: National Conference on Family Life, 1948).

was evolved during the first interdisciplinary workshop on marriage and family research at the University of Chicago during the summer of 1950. As executive for the National Council on Family Relations, I called and directed this family research workshop. One of its subgroups set itself the task of carving out a multidisciplinary way of studying families that would stimulate creative research in family development. This 1950 Work Group in Family Development research was the first to formulate the concept of family developmental tasks as such. In its report it defined family developmental tasks as "those which must be accomplished by a family in a way that will satisfy (a) biological requirements, (b) cultural imperatives, and (c) personal aspirations and values, if the family is to continue and grow as a unit."[9] Using the structure-function approach, this work group compiled an outline of family developmental tasks for stage one of the family life cycle. Since then, this outline has been greatly elaborated and extended to cover the entire family life cycle—and has developed into this book.

The fifth edition

The findings of recent longitudinal studies from a number of disciplines provide substantive materials that further expand the scope of the book. Timeless concepts as well as the outlines of developing trends may thus be viewed in the light of current data. The text in its previous editions has proven useful in such university departments as adult education; child development and family relations; home and family; home economics; human development; nursing; social work; sociology; and general education, as well as in preprofessional and paraprofessional courses. Since the book is designed for students from many disciplines, the use of unnecessarily technical terminology from any one field has been avoided. The student who has a particular professional orientation may find in the *Glossary* quick working definitions of terms from other fields related to family development in some way.

My gratitude to the many scholars to whom both student and author owe so much. Their creative thinking and basic research in the fields of individual, marriage, and family development study continue to deepen our understanding of this ever-intriguing and important field. I salute them all.

Evelyn Millis Duvall, Ph.D.

Sarasota, Florida
August 1976

[9] Quoted by Reuben Hill in his report of the workshop—Reuben Hill, "Interdisciplinary Workshop on Marriage and Family Research," *Marriage and Family Living* 13, no. 1 (February 1951): 21-22.

generative potentials in
human sexuality

part one

*Breathes there a man with soul so tough
Who says two sexes aren't enough?*

Samuel Hoffenstein

Sex differences and gender roles

chapter one

The differences between the sexes have always been of interest. Human sexuality in general and the roles of the two sexes are being widely discussed today. Men and women talk over what they expect of one another in terms of dating, courtship, marriage, family life, the working world, and world affairs. Hundreds of articles on gender roles appear in popular magazines and professional journals. Learned papers are given at conferences of scholars; and books on the subject proliferate in ever-increasing numbers.

Biological differences between the sexes

Males and females differ in every cell of their bodies. There are essential differences in their anatomy and physiology. Members of each sex have specific capacities and limitations that correspond to their basic form

3

and function. These biological differences are a fundamental fact of life, with which each person must come to terms in his or her own way.

Sex determination

The sex of each individual is determined at the moment of conception. If an x-bearing sperm unites with the x-bearing ovum, a female is conceived. When a y-bearing sperm fertilizes the x-bearing ovum, a male begins to develop. From that moment on the miracle of growth and development is underway. The basic genetic differences between the girl (xx) and the boy (xy) are influenced by female and male hormones that begin to be produced in both sexes months before birth.

Sex differences before and after birth

Male and female embryos look very much alike during the first three months of development in the uterus. Both have a tiny genital tubercle in the area of the external genitalia. This is the precursor of the penis in the male, or of the clitoris in the female. Rolling back from this small protuberance is a double fold of tissue that surrounds the central cleft, or slit. By the third or fourth prenatal month the genital areas of the two sexes show different patterns of development. In the female fetus, the tiny labial swellings sweep back from clitoris to anus on either side of the slit that is to become the opening to the vagina. In the male, the genital tubercle is now seen as the head of the penis at the end of the shaft being formed by the urethral folds that unite behind the penis, while the swelling on either side is enlarging to become the scrotum (Mahan and Broderick 1969:175–220).

Male hormones (androgens) and female hormones (estrogens) are produced in both the male and the female early in the course of prenatal development. Male hormones stimulate the growth and maintenance of the male reproductive systems, whereas estrogens influence the development of female structures and functions. Without an adequate supply of the androgen testosterone the male fetus becomes feminized. Estrogens in the mother's body normally supplement any estrogen deficiency occurring during the female's fetal development. Studies at Johns Hopkins University find that prenatal androgens predispose boys to compete for dominance and to be more active than girls. Females, lacking high levels of androgens in utero, tend to expend less energy, to compete less for dominance, and to be more nurturant, even as little children (Money and Ehrhardt 1972).

At birth the external genitals distinguish the male; the penis lies over the scrotum, in which hang the testes of the boy baby. In the girl child the outer and inner labia surround the opening to the vagina, with the clitoris at their forepoint. The female's ovaries at birth contain all of the half million or so ova the girl (and woman) will ever have. The male testes are capable of producing millions of sperm daily from puberty on.

Puberal development of male and female

Between birth and puberty, male and female hormones are at low levels in both boys and girls. The puberal growth spurt is triggered by pituitary hormones that stimulate the sex glands (testes and ovaries) to greatly increase the levels of androgens in the boy and of estrogens in the girl.

Maturing girls rapidly increase in height and weight, breasts develop, hips broaden, and dark, curly hair appears in a triangle in the pubic area low on the pelvis, as well as under the arms. By twelve years of age, more or less, the girl begins to menstruate in the monthly cycle of menstruation and ovulation that continues in mature females until menopause.

Boys start to mature a year or more later than do girls. They become taller and gradually stronger as their bones and muscles develop. Male voices change to a deeper register during puberty. Hair gradually appears in the typical male pattern in the pubic region, under the arms, on face, chest, arms, and legs. Spontaneous release of semen occurs by ejaculation at intervals from pubescence on, throughout most of the life of the male.

Biological differences between men and women

The mature male is taller and heavier than the grown woman. His shoulders are broader, his chest is larger and his hips narrower than are the female's. His muscles are larger, stronger, and more pronounced than those of the woman, whose body is rounded with a subcutaneous fatty layer. Both sexes have pubic and underarm hair, but only the male normally has hair on face and body. Male breasts are rudimentary; female breasts are rounded and potentially capable of lactation. The man's hands and feet are larger, and his fingers and toes are heavier than are the woman's. Male sex cells (sperm) are produced in the testes and ejaculated through the penis at frequent intervals throughout the life of the man. Female sex cells (ova) mature at the rate of one each month or so in the process of ovulation that alternates with menstruation in the maturing girl and woman. The female's paired ovaries deep within her pelvis release one ripened ovum monthly into one of the paired Fallopian tubes that connect with the uterus (womb). The cervical (lower) end of the uterus hangs into the upper portion of the vagina, which extends to the opening between the labia. Only the male sex cell can impregnate the female and fertilize the egg. Only the female can ovulate, gestate, give birth, and breast-feed the human infant. Each sex has its own essential biological role in the miracle of creation. A summary of biological sex differences in the male and female is found in Table 1–1.

Individual differences

Differences among individuals of the same sex are quite as remarkable as those between members of the two sexes. There are women who are taller and stronger than many men. There are men who are smaller and more graceful than many women. A wide range of characteristics usually associated with one sex can be found in members of the other, all within

Table 1-1
Normal Biological Sex Differences

Male	Female	Characteristic
XY sex chromosomes	XX sex chromosomes	Sex is determined by X-bearing sperm to form female (XX), or Y-bearing sperm to form male (XY) chromosome
Androgens (testosterone)	Estrogens	Male and female sex hormones
Penis	Clitoris	Erectile external genitals
Scrotum, in which hang paired testes	Vulva (major and minor labia)	Sensitive, soft external gentialia
Testes (testicles) paired gonads	Ovaries (paired gonads in the pelvis)	Gonads produce male and female hormones and sex cells from puberty (or before) through adulthood
Sperm (spermatazoa) millions at frequent intervals puberty on	Ovum (egg cell) one each 28± days puberty through menopause	Sex cells contain tiny packets of chromosomes made up of DNA and RNA molecules, determining genetic makeup of each new individual
Vas deferens	Fallopian tubes	Paired tubes in which sperm and ova travel
Prostate (gland surrounding upper urethra)	Glands of Bartholin lubricating glands of vulva and vagina	Moisture-producing glands of genital tracts of male and female
Ejaculation	Menstruation (menses) Ovulation Labor and delivery (birth) Lactation	Release of products of reproductive organs of each sex
Facial and body hair	Underarm and pubic hair	Characteristic adult skin and hair patterns of each sex
Narrow hips, broad shoulders	Broad hips, sloping shoulders	Distinctive body shape of each sex from puberty on
Strong, heavy muscles relative to female	Fatty layer beneath skin over smaller muscles	Distinctive body shape of each sex from puberty on
Rudimentary breasts and nipples	Well-developed breasts and nipples from puberty on	Distinctive body shape of each sex from puberty on
Larynx enlarges at puberty	Larynx smaller relative to male	Male voice deepens at puberty, female voice remains relatively higher
Taller, heavier, stronger on the average than the female	Shorter, lighter, not as powerful, usually, as the male	Great variations within each sex in height, weight, and muscular strength

Generative potentials in human sexuality

the range of the normal. Any of these can be accentuated or played down in the way they are expressed by a given individual.

Masculinity and feminity

Masculinity and femininity are those behavioral characteristics that are usually associated with members of either sex. Concepts of masculinity and femininity vary widely from society to society and from time to time. Traditionally, masculinity in the Western world meant strength, bravery, and ambition; whereas femininity was thought of in terms of gentleness and dependence. A man was expected to be strong, silent, and capable, while a woman was considered feminine when she was weak and dependent. These definitions of what it means to be masculine or feminine have undergone significant changes and are still changing rapidly.

Behavioral differences between the sexes

Psychological studies over many years have revealed the existence of a multitude of myths concerning differences between the sexes. Unfounded beliefs are (1) that girls are more "social" than boys; (2) that girls are more "suggestible" than boys; (3) that girls have lower self-esteem; (4) that girls are better at rote-learning and simple repetitive tasks, whereas boys excel in the higher cognitive processes; (5) that boys are more "analytic"; (6) that girls are more affected by heredity, and boys more affected by environment; (7) that girls lack achievement motivation; and (8) that girls are auditory, boys visual.

Four differences between boys and girls are "fairly well established" according to recent research:

1. Girls have greater verbal ability than boys
2. Boys excel in visual-spatial ability
3. Boys excel in mathematical ability
4. Boys are more aggressive

Still to be confirmed are such possible differences between the sexes as tactile sensitivity; fear, timidity and anxiety; activity level; competitiveness; dominance; compliance; and nurturance and "maternal behavior" (Maccoby and Jacklin 1975). There are athletically active and competitive women, just as there are sensitive boys and nurturing, gentle men. Wide variations are found in intellectual, emotional, social, and behavioral expression in members of both sexes.

Maleness and femaleness are innate, genetically determined "givens" operating within each individual. Masculinity and femininity are learned through action and interaction with others from birth onward throughout life. A boy is born male—he becomes masculine; a girl is born female—she learns to be feminine.

Boys and girls are reared differently from birth

The announcement "It's a boy!" or "It's a girl!" starts each new individual down the road to masculinity or femininity. A growing awareness of gender will be an essential part of his or her life from then on. Doctors Mollie and Russell Smart (1972:329) share this personal illustration:

> Once we gave a pink sweater before a baby was born. When the baby turned out to be a boy, the mother expressed regrets that she would have to save the sweater until she had a girl. That little boy's color scheme was to leave no doubt in him or anybody else as to what sex he was! He soon received a wealth of trucks, cars, and erector sets but no dolls. His father played boisterously with him, stimulating vigorous motor play, being casual about bumps, discouraging tears. And what happened when someone came along to occupy our pink sweater? She received dolls and homemaking toys. She was held tenderly. Her father stroked her curls, tickled her chin, and taught her to bat her long eyelashes at him. Big Brother stroked her curls, tickled her chin, and elicited eye-batting also. The mother applauded when Brother was aggressive, active and courageous, and when Sister was nurturant, beguiling, and sensitive. Often the parents' techniques of influence were subtle—a pat, a shove, a smile, a frown, a tight voice, a song. At other times they were direct—"Don't do that, Brother. Be a big man, like Daddy" or "I was so proud of my girl, acting like a regular little lady."

Long before Big Brother or Little Sister were old enough to talk or walk or go to nursery school, their education in what it means to be a boy or a girl was already well begun.

Throughout the preschool years, little girls usually are allowed more flexibility than are boys. Both boys and girls may wear jeans and knit shirts, but only girls may wear dresses and hair ribbons. Boys are pressured to avoid anything that smacks of femininity and to limit their behavior to what is clearly masculine while they are still preschoolers. Even in nursery school, it is more acceptable for a girl to be a "tomboy" than for a boy to be a "sissy" (Fling and Manosevitz 1972). Girls of kindergarten age are allowed to "amble gradually in the direction of 'feminine' patterns for five more years" (Hartley 1959) Udry observes (1974:52–53):

> Any contemporary four-year-old boy who was allowed to wear female clothing would be a neighborhood curiosity, and it is likely that both he and his parents would be considered in need of psychiatric attention. On the other hand, American culture is not nearly so restrictive in eliminating masculine items from the behavioral repertoire of the young girl.

Generative potentials in human sexuality

It might be interesting to speculate on the reasons for the apparent shift to very early sex-role emphasis, especially for boys. It might indicate that contemporary parents are not as confident of their boys growing up to become "masculine men" as previous generations were. Perhaps the general unclarity of sex roles in modern American society, abetted by frightening articles in popular magazines, leads anxious parents to work with great attention to getting boys to be boys.

A summary of research measuring degree of masculinity in boys reports remarkably stable levels from childhood through adulthood. Warm, supportive fathers, encouraging mothers, older brothers, and peers to grow up with—all are positively related to the adoption of masculine roles by boys (Biller 1967). The girl who grows up in a loving family that encourages her development as a person enters adolescence with a secure sense of her femininity. Differential treatment of boys and girls throughout childhood is to be expected, although it is less prevalent now than it used to be.

Socialization

Gender role-learning is an important facet of the socialization of the members of both sexes. Children must be socialized in order to become truly human. At birth they are bundles of potentials yet to be developed. Although their prenatal life readied them for living without the umbilical attachment to their mothers, infants are far from being independent. They must rely on others as they learn to be members of one gender or the other in the years that lie ahead.

Socialization is the process by which individuals acquire the knowledge and develop the skills, attitudes, and competence that enable them to function in society (in family, community, or the world at large). Socialization continues throughout life as new roles are played in each new situation or group that the individual enters. Socialization always takes place in interaction with others. Social pressures mold the newcomer so that he conforms to the expectations and the customs of the particular culture he is entering. Socialization is the process by which individuals are helped to

1. become acceptable members of the group
2. develop a sense of themselves as social beings
3. interact with other persons in various roles, positions, and statuses
4. anticipate the expectations and reactions of other persons
5. prepare for future roles that they will be expected to fill.

Positions and gender roles in the family

Each member of a family occupies a number of particular positions in that family (Chapter 6). Each person's position differentiates him or her from others in the family. Some positions are sequential: one is first an infant, then a schoolchild, a teenager, a young adult, a husband or wife, a parent, and a grandparent. Other positions are concurrent: a woman may be a daughter, a sister, a wife, a mother, and a business woman all at the same time. Each position has its accompanying roles.

Roles are expectations of behavior, obligations, and rights that are associated with a given position in a family or social group. Sex roles (gender roles) are behavioral expectations specific to members of either sex. Christensen (1975:3) defines the terms in this way:

> Usually the term *sex* is used to designate biological differences (male or female), *gender* to designate personality differences (with respect to identity and the accompanying attributes of masculinity and femininity), and *role* to designate differences in behavioral expectations lodged within the social structure. To me, the sex role/gender role labels are synonomous and equally acceptable. The important thing to keep in mind is that we are talking about a *role* that is differentiated according to sex and/or gender . . .

Sociologist Reuben Hill makes the point that roles are plural—not "*the* woman's role" but "the many roles of women"; not even "*the* mother's role," but the many roles built into the mother's position. He sees all gender role changes within the family context as paired role changes. "If there are changes in the roles of wife, there follow changes in the counter-roles of husband; just as changes in father roles bring changes in child roles and coordinately changes in mother roles" (Hill 1975:2).

Theories of sexual differentiation

Scholars of many disciplines are working on the question, How different are the two sexes—and why? Reports of studies of many kinds in various populations and from different theoretical stances are currently available (see Table 6-1, Chapter 6). Five theories of the nature of masculinity and femininity are often cited.

1. *Anthropological.* For instance, Margaret Mead emphasizes the great cultural differences that are reflected in the ways in which the roles of the two sexes are defined in various societies around the world.
2. *Biogenetic.* Dr. John Money's work at Johns Hopkins University, for example, alerts students of sexuality to the importance of hormonal influence on genetic males and females in utero.
3. *Psychoanalytic.* Followers of Sigmund Freud talk of oral, anal, and oedipal stages of psychosexual development in which the little boy competes with his father for his mother's love, and the little girl, feeling incomplete because of penis envy, adapts by being subserviently "feminine."

4. *Sociological.* Spokespersons too numerous to list consider the main differentiating factor to be socialization through direct interaction with others in the environment who serve as models of masculinity and femininity.

5. *Cognitive-developmental.* Erik Erikson, Jean Piaget, and Jerome Kagan identify stages in children's development over the years in which boys and girls gradually perceive and internalize patterns of masculinity and femininity within a particular society.

Theories and research in the several disciplines have focused so intently on significant differences between the sexes that even greater similarities may have been obscured. A University of Michigan research team reports:

> One result of this obsession is an overemphasis on differences and a corresponding underemphasis on similarities between groups. For example, if one studies the reactions of men and women to 100 words, and they react very similarly to 80 of them, and significantly differently to 20, then it is likely that only the differences will get published—often without even a mention that the similarity of 80 responses existed. (Hefner, Meda and Oleshansky 1975:7)

While scholars refine their theories and research deals with the rapid changes in the many expressions of human sexuality, students can study the parts of the puzzle available to them, without question.

How sex roles are learned

Child development specialists would not expect infants who have yet to discover their own toes to be aware of their gender. Babies spend the first two years or so responding to the many stimuli within and beyond themselves. It is not until they begin to speak and to understand the words for things that they can make much sense of the multitude of details that pertain to them.

Boy and girl babies are remarkably similar in their behavior. Professor Kagan (1975:2) observes,

> In the first two years of life there is a dramatic similarity in the activities of boys and girls. There are sex differences, but they're subtle, they're not overwhelming. There's an enormous overlap. Boys play with tea cups and doll houses. Girls play with bicycles and guns. And the differences are quite trivial in the first two years of life. It's after that that you begin to see boys and girls go off, following different pipers.

Sometime after the second year of life, children normally begin to realize that there are two sexes and that each person belongs to either one sex or the other. Gender identity is being established as a tiny tot begins to understand that he is a male, or that she is a female. Each responds appropriately when called "a boy" or "a girl." Each discovers his or her own genitals and those of members of the same and of the other sex. In time the child comes to associate these differences with boyness or girlness. It takes a while for a boy to find out that someday he will be a man, and for the girl to learn that she will one day be a woman. Two basic distinguishing learnings are now underway: (1) maleness and femaleness, and (2) young and mature forms of boy/man and girl/woman. Once children recognize that they belong to one gender and not to the other, they try to become masculine or feminine as they see these attributes modeled for them and expected of them by the persons around them. Children find models of masculinity and of femininity in their parents, in other adults in the family, in their brothers, sisters, and playmates of both sexes, and—from very early ages—in the programs and commercials they see on television. It is estimated that preschoolers spend more time watching television than in any other activity (Bronfenbrenner 1970). The establishment of identity is a creative process in which

> the child synthesizes these three sources of information (parents, children and television) and creates what some psychologists call an ego-ideal, an ideal standard which will be remarkably similar in members of one particular culture. Once he has crystallized that, he starts to mold his behavior, his thoughts, his attitudes, his beliefs so that they will come as close as possible to that ideal . . . It's important to appreciate that these sex differences pertain to behavior within a particular society. (Kagan 1975:2-3)

A child's first and most lasting impression of society is found within his or her own family, which mirrors and personifies the larger society of which it is a part.

Sex roles are learned in the family

It is in the family that the little girl and boy have intimate day-to-day association with members of both sexes and of two or more generations. Parents consciously or unconsciously teach their children by such everyday comments as, "That's a good girl," or "What a big, brave boy you are," or "Girls don't do that," or "Don't be a sissy." By a much subtler process, children learn what is expected of them through a multitude of often-repeated rituals, customs, and situations. They are exposed daily to masculine and feminine conduct appropriate to members of the neighborhood, social class, and racial and ethnic group to which their families belong. They pick up the speech inflections, body stance and posturing, emotional expressions (or repressions), clothing and grooming, likes and dislikes, and other attributes of both sexes of persons of their own and older ages. All this takes place as "naturally" as learning how to hold a spoon, or to drink from a cup—by observation, imitation, identification, and practice.

Families determine the gender roles of their members. Reuben Hill (1975:2) reflects the views of social scientists when he says,

> In virtually all societies, the family is the institutional structure for the protection, physical maintenance, socialization and social placement of the young, involving a division of labor by gender among family members.
>
> Moreover, in fulfilling these functions, the family has tended to monopolize the shaping of the basic personality make-up of junior members including the development of the important component, gender identity.

Imitation and identification

Three-year-old Jane mirrors her mother's every move as the two "women" prepare a meal. A casual observer might say "Isn't that sweet? Jane is imitating her mother." Actually, Jane is working hard at *being* her mother—in her food preparation roles and in all of her other activities and behaviors. Jane's twin brother Jim, meantime, lights his imaginary pipe and sits with one leg across the other scowling at the papers before him, just as his father does. Both children are identifying with the parent of the same sex, by internalizing what they see their parents doing. They talk over toy telephones in the same inflections and with the same words they hear their parents use. They play house and go through the same dialogues and routines their mother and father have modeled for them only hours before.

Identification in the family is more difficult for boys than for girls for a number of reasons:

> 1. Girls identify with their mothers, boys with a culturally defined male role. But mothers are home more than are fathers, usually.
> 2. Both girls and boys identify more closely with the mother than with the father.
> 3. Boys have more trouble achieving same-sex identification than do girls.
> 4. More boys than girls fail to achieve same-sex identification.
> 5. Boys, more than girls, identify with the opposite sex.
> 6. Boys are more anxious than girls about sex role identification.

7. Boys tend to be more hostile toward girls than girls are toward boys.
8. Boys identify more firmly with the masculine role as they grow older.
9. More girls than boys prefer the role of the opposite sex.
10. More girls than boys adopt aspects of the roles of the other sex. (Lynn 1966:470)

Same-sex identification is easier for the girl because she does not have to shift from mother to father as her role model, as does the boy. The mother's activities are more explicit in the typical family than are the father's, whose work tends to be out of the home and beyond the comprehension of little children. Furthermore, a boy has to actively express his masculinity, whereas the girl simply *is* a feminine person. She thereby is freer to be a "tomboy" than is the boy to be a "sissy" in many a family or neighborhood. The student is reminded that these speculations are only hypothetical at the moment. In the meantime, they are food for thought and discussion, while they await confirmation or modification by more intensive research than is yet available.

Older brothers and sisters in the family serve as role models, as the younger children in the family identify with them. Orville Brim (1973: 43–46), following Helen Koch's extensive research (Koch 1955, 1956), concludes that cross-sex siblings tend to adopt traits of the other sex, with the greater effect for the younger child. These studies are of two-child families. In families with many children, older sisters tend to serve as "little mothers" in helping to rear the young ones. Their influence might then be expected to be not only that of an older sibling, but of a substitute mother as well.

Kindergarten and first grade children often identify with their teachers, and in playing school they vie to "be the teacher." In early adolescence, boys identify with some local hero or national figure; while adolescent girls try out the hair styles, grooming aids and postures affected by the glamorous women they see in the mass media. These identifications are relatively short-lived compared with the long-standing identifications with more influential family members.

Stages in sex role identity development

Children progress from one stage to another in the development of their sex role identity. First comes the undifferentiated stage of infancy, discussed earlier in this chapter. The second stage is one of active sex role differentiation, in which children of both sexes accept conventional sex roles for themselves and for members of the other sex. Boys may then vigorously reject feminine associations and attributes as they conform to what is expected of them as "big guys." This stage is one of polarization, in which femininity and masculinity are at opposite poles in the eyes of youngsters.

By adolescence, boys are urged to do well in school and to plan for their careers; whereas achievement by girls is discouraged (Horner 1972; Shaw and McCuen 1971). During the teen years, girls try to become attractive to boys (Laws 1976) and play down the intellectual and academic excellence that might threaten the teenage boys' egos. These are the years when young adolescent males tend to be especially restrictive in what they expect of girls (Meixel 1976). Young women tend to lower their career aspirations as they approach womanhood (Schwenn 1970). Gagnon and Simon (1973) state that both males and females follow their own sexual scripts that label, elicit, and form human sexuality; and that this general consciousness of sexuality in turn gives meaning to gender roles and sexual behavior. Only after the individual develops a sense of his or her own sexual identity as a person, is a third stage of sex-role transcendence possible.

Conventional sex-role stereotyping

Conventional sex roles are the usual behaviors traditionally expected of males and females in most societies. Lee and Groper (1974) list such areas of sex-typed differences as:

1. Communication—different patterns of speech and emotional expression
2. Physical gestures—sitting, walking, stance styles of the two sexes
3. Naming—last names patronymic, first names male or female
4. Group affiliations—sex-segregated children's and adult organizations
5. Dress and grooming—lipstick, earrings, long dresses (female only)
6. Cultural artifacts—sex-typed toys, needlework (female), woodworking
7. Occupations and tasks—many jobs in home and community sex-typed
8. Games and avocations—team sports (more male than female)

Stereotyping rigidly fixes sex roles at opposite poles, without regard for individual talents and interests. The slender young man with an artistic bent is made to feel somewhat less a "real man" because he falls short of the macho ideal. The athletically active girl finds herself at a disadvantage in the male-dominated sports world. Since both sexes are limited in the full range of behavior of which they are capable, society is denied their maximum contribution, and the individuals are limited in their personality development and fulfillment.

Problems in gender polarization

Polarization of gender roles poses particular problems in marriage and family life:

> If a woman can achieve herself solely through the male, what it amounts to is that she is living her life through him. This may be great for the male ego; it's also a fairly awesome responsibility. Many a marriage is broken up when the man, who in his younger years delighted in taking care of a highly dependent wife, eventually grew to resent her dependency and buckled under the strain in middle age. (Brenton 1966:54)

Husbands are often limited in their emotional expressiveness in the family because they were brought up to be "strong, silent" men. Adults of both sexes must be able to relate sensitively to others, to care for the dependent members of the family, and to receive affection easily from their loved ones. These are the very things that men find difficult if they have been taught that these traits are feminine. Fathers able to develop warm, intimate relationships with their wives and children know how much some of their colleagues miss by standing on their dignity as males. So too, the "helpless little woman" who must await her husband's homecoming to make some simple repair of an essential piece of household equipment is not only delayed by the breakdown, but misses the opportunity of finding personal satisfaction in doing all she can to keep the home running smoothly.

In the modern world, an adult of either sex has to be self-reliant, independent and assertive at times. However, the restrictions traditionally associated with femininity make it difficult for women to learn and to express such attitudes. Competent wives and mothers are passed over in the world of work and are straitjacketed into housewifery at home. With such stereotyping, everyone loses—the wife-mother, the husband-father, the children, the family, and society as a whole. Using census figures, Bernard (1975:211–221) estimates that if sexism were eliminated, women's earnings would be increased by 74.5 percent and their unemployment substantially decreased.

Avoiding sexism

Sexism is prejudicial restriction of individual roles by gender. This bias has the general effect of casting girls and women in inferior, submissive roles, and of discouraging their participation in the more prestigious areas of life, while assigning dominant roles in family and society to males (regardless of competence, in many cases). Except for reproductive functions, both males and females of all ages are capable of a wide diversity of roles and accomplishments that remain unrecognized and undeveloped because of sexist thinking. During the 1970s there was a mass movement in the direction of affirming equal rights to members of both sexes. This meant recognizing and dealing with sexist influences in the society that affect people from early childhood on throughout life.

Title IX of the National Education Act focused on equal opportunities for women on the payrolls of schools receiving federal funds and prohibited sexism in textbooks. Major textbook publishers instructed their editors and writers to avoid allusions, statements, and illustrations that perpetuate sex role stereotyping. One such publisher's guide says:

> Many people today share a determination to create a world in which all young people shall be *free to choose* patterns of life, work, study, and recreation consistent with their innermost aspirations, interests, talents, resources, and energies, and to do so unhampered either by overt discrimination or by an equally limiting tyranny of the norm. Such a tyranny seeks to enforce upon individuals previously unchallenged but often irrelevant, inaccurate, and outdated stereotypes about what it means to be: male or female, black or white, young or old, rich or poor. (Macmillan Guidelines for Creating Positive Sexual and Racial Images in Educational Materials 1975:v)

Illustrative sexist terms in common usage are listed in Table 1–2; and more acceptable alternatives for sexist language are found in Table 1–3. These listings only hint at the prevalence of sexist ideas in today's society.

Such offensive terms as "nigger," "kike," "Polack," and other disparaging names for members of ethnic and racial groups have all but disappeared in recent decades, as they met with general disapproval. Now that Americans are becoming aware of the prejudicial nature of sexist

Table 1-2
Sexist Words and Phrases in Common Usage

Male	Female
Sissy	Tomboy
A fine big fellow	A lovely little girl
Gay bachelor	Spinster; old maid
Lucky devil	She got her man
Henpecked husband	Ball and chain
Casper Milquetoast	She wears the pants
Just like a man	Woman driver
The man on the street	Feminine intuition
He took it like a man	Girls (when referring to women)
He acted like a woman	Women can't . . . (with few exceptions)
He is all man	Ladylike
Bully	Hussy
That's a man's job	Woman's work
Pantywaist	Petticoat politician

Table 1-3
Acceptable Alternatives for Sexist Language

Sexist language	Acceptable alternatives
Man's achievements	Human achievements
The man on the street	The average person
Man and wife	Husband and wife
Lady athlete	Athlete
Hen doctor	Doctor (regardless of gender)
Male nurse	Nurse
Coed	Student
Working man*	Worker
Salesman	Salesperson
Postman	Letter carrier
Chairman	Chairperson, moderator, "the chair"
Manpower	Human resources
Manmade	Handmade, manufactured, machine-made
Foreman	Supervisor

Source: Adapted from *Macmillan Guidelines for Creating Positive Sexual and Racial Images in Educational Materials*. Macmillan Publishing Co., Inc., pp. 18–23, 1975.

terms, ridicule, and jokes, they may be expected to abandon these terms and attitudes too. Other possibilities for dealing with the problem of sexism in society are (1) androgyny, and (2) sex-role transcendence.

Androgyny

The word androgyny comes from the Greek *andro* (male) and *gyn* (female) and means literally, male-female. The term is used in biology to refer to individuals with both male and female genitalia (hermaphrodites). In recent years, the term androgyny has been used to refer to persons with both male and female psychological characteristics. It represents the capacity of any one person of either sex to embody the full range of human character traits, despite the fact that some traits may be labeled "feminine" and others "masculine" (Heilbrun 1973; Secor 1974).

The concept of androgyny implies that a person may be gentle or tough, yielding or assertive, weak or strong as occasion demands, and enjoy thereby a greatly expanded range of behavior. Thus individuals of both sexes could cope more effectively with a wide variety of situations, with a greater degree of emotional and psychological health (Bem 1975).

Summarizing the literature on the subject, a University of Michigan team see androgyny as "a combination of male and female qualities in all people; and clearly for some people it means a uniform, unisexual integration of society" (Hefner, Meda, and Oleshansky 1975:10). Unisex trends in clothing, grooming, and behavior suggest that young people are moving away from rigid male-female polarization, and toward a life-style that is not determined by gender. Applied throughout society, a unisexual approach could have the effect of obscuring sex differences in one homogeneous mass.

Sex-role transcendence

Instead of masking the differences between the sexes, sex-role transcendence encourages the expression of differences in human beings of whichever sex.

> Thus sex-role transcendence implies flexibility (over time, over situation, and over personal moods), plurality, personal choice, and the development of new or emergent possibilities once we move away from the present oppressor-oppressed sex-roles. In essence, we would all be human beings first and males and females second. (Hefner, Meda, and Oleshansky. 1975:10)

Sex-role transcendence offers a pluralistic view of human society in which genuine options are available to everyone, in any situation that may arise. The transcendent person is free to do what is appropriate at the time without regard for masculine-feminine labeling. The young father is free to tenderly comfort the crying baby while his wife tackles a competitive examination for a fellowship, because this is their mutual choice at the time. Somewhere along the line, the same couple may redefine their notion of success and realign their roles accordingly. "The neo-macho male is strong enough to reveal his vulnerabilities, confident enough to be sensitive, successful enough to be proud of his mate's career, virile enough to wash dishes, fearless enough to take care of the children" (Mariani 1975:5).

A person who transcends stereotyped sex roles and traditional demands for conventional gender conformity becomes a self-actualized person according to Maslow; a productive person according to Fromm; a fully-functioning person according to Rogers; and a productive personality according to Gilmore. "None of these theories focuses on sex differences or on a different potential for growth dependent on the sex of the person. They state that the human being has certain potentials for becoming fulfilled and that if this goal is not realized then one must look to the restraints placed by the culture on the person" (Feldman and Feldman 1975:6).

American Council on Education surveys of freshmen entering college and university provide evidence that some young women have achieved a degree of sex-role transcendence in that they

1. Have argued with teachers
2. Want administrative responsibility
3. Want to become authorities in their fields
4. Do not want to be obligated to anyone
5. Believe that large families should be discouraged.

"They are aggressive, ambitious, achievement-oriented, independent, and not interested in full-time domesticity. . . . they actually did transcend polarity in the values they viewed as very important or essential; they were more "feminine" than other women and also more "masculine" than were the men" (Bernard 1975:49–50).

Professor Christensen proposes that women be given equal access to the more prestigious roles within society, that traditional female tasks be made more prestigious, and that both men and women be given a choice in what they do, and in how and where they do it. He sees sex roles as necessary, because of biological differences, to avoid ambiguity and to increase efficiency. "But it is not necessary that these roles cover everything, nor that they be arbitrarily imposed, nor that they give either sex an overall advantage. I do not believe that equality requires the elimination of the sex-role structure, only its alteration" (Christensen 1975:13).

Historically, the family has moved through three stages. In preindustrial societies economic production was the task of the family as a whole. In the second, or distribution stage, most productive work was done outside the home for wages, and the father provided for his wife and children from his earnings. Most American families remain in this stage for the greater part of their lives. The third stage, which many American families are now entering, is the consumption stage in which both husband and wife pool their incomes, personal resources, and services for the maintenance of their home and family (Sawhill, Ross, and MacIntosh 1973). This type of family life calls for the kind of flexibility in male-female roles that is promoted by the concept of sex-role transcendence.

As gender roles become more flexible, girls may be less likely to have to prove themselves by rushing into early marriage. More of them can be expected to continue their education, to develop their talents, to pursue their interests, and to enter careers of interest to them as persons. Meanwhile boys and men may become more interested in homemaking and child-rearing—areas in which they can freely express the gentler, less competitive aspects of their personalities without censure. It is possible then, that as rigid polarity disappears the two sexes may rediscover one another in new patterns of intimate association. This holds the promise of greater companionship within marriage and family life.

The thing that takes up the least amount of time and causes the most amount of trouble is Sex.

John Barrymore

Sexual attitudes and behavior in the United States

chapter two

Sexual behavior is the overt expression of one or more sexual attitudes in response to physical, emotional, or social stimuli. The sexual attitudes and conduct of individuals change with their personal and collective experience. Economic and social conditions affect the feelings that the two sexes have for one another, and the many ways in which these feelings are expressed, from one period of time to another.

Sex in the nineteenth and twentieth centuries

Sexual advice in American literature throughout the nineteenth century was offered mainly in collections of sermons and in books written specifically as marriage manuals. A review of such material gives one the sense that sex was considered dangerous, but necessary for procreation.

23

Marriage was seen as a prerequisite to sex relations, but even then restraints were necessary. Rational conduct rather than spontaneous expression of emotion was recommended, and frequent warnings about the dangers of sexual indulgence were added (Gordon and Bernstein 1970).

Magazine articles published in the United States between 1825 and 1850, dealing with man-woman relationships, have been analyzed for content. The sexual misconduct of females before and after marriage received twice as much attention as that of males. The prevailing attitude was that both males and females should be punished or ostracized for premarital or extramarital sexual relations—although sympathy was expressed for the female whose misconduct was beyond her control, or due to her trust of her man (Lantz, Keyes, and Schultz 1975). Romantic love and personal happiness were beginning to emerge as important factors in mate selection even before the middle of the nineteenth century.

Recognition of woman's sexuality and of her right to be satisfied sexually appeared early in the twentieth century. As a combined effect of the aftermath of World War I, Prohibition, bathtub gin, the speakeasy, and the Flapper, Puritanism was routed and sexual attitudes took a giant leap toward freedom of expression. During the World War II years, women went to work to replace men in military service and to fill orders in the booming economy. Women workers wore slacks, bobbed their hair, rode in car pools, and relaxed with their fellow workers over coffee cups and in cocktail bars. They had money in their pockets and a new spirit of independence in their attitudes. Contraceptives were widely available, so women could escape the "tyranny of pregnancy" if they wished. More girls and women had premarital and extramarital relations, divorces increased, and satisfaction in the marriage bed was expected by wives as well as by husbands.

The Vietnam war in the 1960s brought a similar kind of social, economic and sexual upheaval, as well as widespread disenchantment with government. As the military establishment came under attack, other institutions were openly criticized. The cake of custom crumbled, and militant demands for personal freedom replaced former values of loyalty and service. Parents who had brought up their children to be autonomous found their young people turning on with drugs, turning away from middle-class values, and turning to one another for intimacy and security.

In the fifty years between World War I and America's involvement in Vietnam, sexuality dominated discussions in the press, popular magazines, and professional journals; mass media humor; and conversation in the community. Sex talk went beyond the blush and giggle in home, school, shop, and public forum. Recreational sex became a multimillion dollar business, visible in Playboy Clubs, topless waitresses, and Go-Go bars across the country. Scholarly efforts to study sexual attitudes and behavior were underway, led by such investigators as Kinsey and his staff,

Masters and Johnson, SIECUS, and others engaged in research on many campuses. Researchers investigated intimate pairing, both normal and atypical, from sociological, psychological, medical, anthropological and human development points of view. Ira Reiss (1973:7-9) suggests that it was the change in attitudes toward sex occurring between 1915 and 1965 that laid the foundation for the changes in sexual behavior that followed.

By the mid-1970s candor had replaced guilt and pretense throughout America. The First Lady was only mildly criticized when she said publicly that she would not be surprised if her unmarried 18-year-old daughter should tell her someday that she was having an affair. The general shift from sacred to secular values replaced asceticism with hedonism and prudery with "naturalness." Hypocrisy and guilt about sex, sexual feelings, and sexual behavior were waning, but confusion and contradictions remained (Spock 1971; Duberman 1974; Skolnick 1973).

Is there a sexual revolution?

The mass media have made much of the sexual revolution in the 1960s and 1970s. They frequently quote rising divorce rates and the higher incidence of premarital intercourse as evidence of a real revolution in sexual behavior. Some scholars do not concur that a sexual revolution is underway. One authority says that some Americans are going in a more permissive direction and that this does not represent a sudden change, but rather a broadening of our concepts of masculinity and femininity (Reiss 1969:117).

A study of 2,064 Illinois teenagers found that the incidence of male adolescent premarital intercourse has declined substantially since the Kinsey data were published in 1953 (Miller and Simon 1974:58-76). Comparison of recent data on the premarital activity of college students with those collected more than twenty years ago, shows relatively stable rates of premarital coitus. The researchers feel that prolonged reporting of a sexual revolution only intensifies the anxieties of young people.

> The heralding of impending sexual liberation may ultimately be more generative of increased anxiety, self-alienation, and doubt than anything else. As some young people might express it, we have no right to lay our trip on them. (Simon, Berger, and Gagnon 1972:221)

Some change in the sexual attitudes of university students did occur in the period between the Kinsey studies and 1965. Over the next five years (1965-1970) there was a liberalization of female college students' behavior, according to sequential studies at a southern university. There is evidence too that while some coeds have become more permissive, male students have become more conservative as they increasingly assume responsibility for upholding standards traditionally expected primarily of females (Robinson, King, and Balswick 1972).

Other social scientists say that there has been a real sexual revolution. Professor John Cuber points out that there is a profound difference between a person who breaks the rules and one who does not accept the rules. The first is a transgressor, the second is a revolutionary. In Cuber's view, a sizable minority of previous generations broke the rule of premarital chastity with a great sense of guilt; whereas many of the present generation no longer accept the rule. "They challenge the validity of the law—and *that* is revolution" (Cuber 1971:176). Whereas formerly students saw an act as "right" or "wrong" with no questions asked, they now qualify their responses and object to making judgments without knowing pertinent facts about the situation, the persons, and their interpersonal relationships (Cuber 1971:173).

Psychiatrists seeing individuals who have been hurt by sexual attitudes and behavior are often concerned about the damage done by changing sexual mores. Dr. Herbert Hendin, Director of Psycho-Social Studies at the Center for Policy Research, sees the sexual revolution taking on a threatening aspect in the anger, cynicism, and bitterness he finds among young middle-class men and women. What others view as casual camaraderie between the sexes, he interprets as fear of involvement that is profound and pervasive. To him, the relations between the sexes on campus are often the result of an uneasy truce between enemies, with men and women exploiting one another in their lust for experience. This pressure to experiment turns many people into "rapacious consumers of each other, often leaving them in the position of dissatisfied customers." His thesis is that the sexual revolution that began in the 1950s as a protest against the work ethic has ended in a revolution against intimacy. Thus, "In a culture that institutionalizes lack of commitment, it is very hard to be committed; in a nation that seems determined to strip sex of romance and tenderness, it is very hard to be a tender and faithful lover" (Hendin 1975:20–27).

The old codes are relaxing, allowing people more freedom to choose their own patterns of behavior. Contraception separating coitus from childbearing leaves both sexes free of the burden of parenthood in their sex expression. The IUD, the Pill, and "Band-Aid sterilization" do not necessitate planning or premeditation on the part of male or female for full intimacy. Open discussion lessens guilt so that "everything is possible and anything goes." The positive side of the massive freeing of sexual attitudes and behavior from the taboos of the past is the greater potential for marital satisfaction and the possibility of bringing sex home from the brothel (Hill 1975:5).

Premarital sex

Sexual activity before marriage is nothing new; but much of what is known about it has come from research done in recent decades. Young people are widely studied, partly because they are so easily available in the schools and colleges where researchers work, and partly because they are considered to be barometers of change. They will form the marriages and found the families of the immediate future. What they do today often reflects latent trends in the larger society. Premarital sexual attitudes and behavior are of general interest in portraying what young people are thinking, feeling, and doing in intimate interaction—data no longer quite so available in more committed and established adults.

During the 1960s and 1970s there was a withering of the double standard that had allowed men to sow their wild oats while expecting women to remain virginal until marriage. During this period the premarital activity of teenage and college males changed little (as noted above) but the behavior of females became more permissive. A government study of a national probability sample of females aged 15 to 19 found that by the early 1970s, 2.35 million (27.6 percent) were no longer virgins; that twice as many blacks were sexually active as compared to whites; and that the older the girl, the more likely she was to have had intercourse, (Table 2-1).

This survey found that premarital intercourse among teenagers is increasing and that it is also starting at younger ages. The sexually experienced teenage girls are not necessarily promiscuous, but appear to have relatively stable relationships. At least half the girls have intercourse only with the men they intend to marry. The lowest proportion of females with coital experience live in families headed by their own fathers. Among both blacks and whites, those who say they subscribe to no religion have the highest proportions of coital experience (Kantner and Zelnik 1972:18).

Teenage girls are less reluctant to talk about their sexual experience now than formerly. The researchers attribute this greater freedom to the change in public attitudes that has taken place in recent years. Today, when formerly tabooed topics are widely discussed by millions of Americans, feelings about sexuality are more relaxed, and sexual behavior once frowned upon is now more generally accepted or at least tolerated (Zelnik and Kantner 1972b :341).

Being in love, dating, going steady, getting engaged, and planning to marry are significantly related to young women's kissing, petting, and sexual intercourse, according to research studies in several states (Mirande and Hammer 1974; Miller and Simon 1974). Teenage boys who are alienated from their parents, close to their peers, and delinquency-prone are those most likely to have premarital sexual experience. The least sexually active boys are more religious, aspire to higher levels of education, are close to their parents, and have little dating and love experience

Table 2-1
Never-Married Females Who Have Had Intercourse, by Age and Race

Age	Percent			Number		
	Black	White	Total	Black	White	Total
15	32.3	10.8	13.8	88,181	181,824	270,005
16	46.4	17.5	21.2	113,503	286,971	400,474
17	57.0	21.7	26.6	138,606	325,422	464,028
18	60.4	33.5	37.1	129,370	461,990	591,360
19	80.8	40.4	46.1	156,444	471,683	628,127
Total	53.6	23.4	27.6	626,104	1,727,890	2,353,994

Source: Melvin Zelnik and John F. Kantner, *Sexuality, Contraception and Pregnancy Among Young Unwed Females in the United States* Commission on Population Growth and the American Future, Research Reports, Vol. 1, of Charles Westoff and Robert Parke, Jr., eds., *Demographic and Social Aspects of Population Growth*, 1972[a], Table 1, p. 360.

(Simon, Berger, and Gagnon 1972). More than one out of four senior men on an Ivy League campus are still virgins, although they do not boast about their lack of sexual experience (Komarovsky 1976).

Dr. Joseph Katz (1974), Director of Research for Human Development and Educational Policy at the State University of New York at Stony Brook, says that he is not dismayed at the increased acceptance of coeducational living on college campuses. He is quoted as saying, "This college generation, as it matures, may well be pioneers in relationships characterized by mutual care, respect, joint learning, and the most elusive yet most needed emotion, love" (Katz 1974:4-E).

Change in attitudes toward premarital intercourse

The way people feel about premarital sex is closely linked to what youth does about it. That attitudes toward sexual activity before marriage have become more permissive in recent years is beyond question. As with any rapid social change, the trend toward accepting sexual permissiveness is not the same for all groups. Female attitudes have changed much more than those of their male counterparts. More liberal sexual attitudes and behavior have been significantly more prevalent among college women than among college men (Robinson, King, and Balswick 1972; Bell and Chaskes 1970; Christensen and Gregg 1970). Interesting shifts in attitudes toward the morality of premarital sexual relationships also occurred between 1965 and 1970. The greatest change observed is in the movement of females' attitudes closer to those of males, as shown in Table 2-2.

Adults' attitudes have also become more permissive, to a degree comparable to that reported for students, according to national adult samples (Table 2-3).

Married men and women are more conservative and family-minded

Table 2-2
1965 and 1970 Student Responses Regarding Sexual Morality

Statement		Percentage of college students strongly agreeing	
		Male students	Female students
I feel that premarital sexual intercourse is immoral:	1965	33%	70%
	1970	14	34
Some people feel that sexual behavior is a moral and public issue	1965	39	43
	1970	52	49
Sexual behavior is a concern of the community	1965	32	34
	1970	35	29
Sexual behavior is a concern of a person's friends	1965	21	43
	1970	37	36
Sexual behavior is a person's own business	1965	85	75
	1970	96	94

Source: Adapted from Ira E. Robinson; Karl King; Jack O. Balswick, "The Premarital Sexual Revolution Among College Females," *The Family Coordinator*, vol. 21, no. 2, April 1972, pp. 191–192.

than single adults, but both groups are becoming more permissive. In 1963, 44 percent of the single adults and 18 percent of the married adults in a national sample held highly permissive views. By 1970, percentages had increased to 74 percent for the single and 50 percent for the married adults (Reiss 1973:19). A larger sample of 340,374 (mainly middle-class, married women) answered questionnaires in the February and March 1972 issues of *Better Homes and Gardens* (1972:70). In response to the question, "Do you approve or disapprove of two people living together before they get married?" 75 percent of the wives and 72 percent of the husbands said they disapproved—a strikingly more conservative attitude than that found in the national probability sample of adults noted above. More than three out of four (76 percent) said yes to the question, "Is open discussion of sex in our society good for a marriage?" suggesting that even among more conservative adults, there is approval of the opening up of sexual attitudes, although disapproval of premarital intercourse continues.

Consequences of premarital intercourse

The ways in which premarital coitus affects a given individual differ greatly, according to the person's early conditioning, current experience and competence, attitudes of friends, family and significant others, level

Sexual attitudes and behavior in the United States 29

Table 2-3
Percentage of American Adults Who Accept Premarital Intercourse as Proper under Some Conditions

National adult sample by race and sex	Percent highly permissive	
	N = 1,399	N = 2,917
	1963*	1970**
White men	30%	61%
White women	7%	35%
Black men	65	82
Black women	29	66
Total	21	52

Source: *Ira L. Reiss, *The Social Context of Premarital Permissiveness.* Holt, Rinehart and Winston, p. 36, 1967. **Ira L. Reiss; Albert Klassen; and Eugene E. Levitt, "Premarital Sexual Relationships, 1963–1970. Unpublished manuscript (1972) reported in Ira L. Reiss, *Heterosexual Relationships Inside and Outside of Marriage.* Morristown, N.J.: General Learning Press, 1973, p. 16.

of commitment, and other individual factors. The result of increasing premarital permissiveness in society as a whole is a combination of potentials, negative and positive. Some possible effects, both helpful and harmful, are summarized in Table 2–4, from sources within this chapter.

Sex in marriage

The sexuality of both men and women is widely accepted as a part of life today. Guilt, embarrassment, and reluctance to admit sexual desire no longer block sexual expression in many marriages. Both partners tend to be more experienced in sexual stimulation and satisfaction, and to respond more readily to one another than marriage partners of an earlier age. Widely publicized research findings in recent decades have raised the level of understanding of the nature of human sexual behavior. What once was alluded to with smirks and giggles is now openly and candidly discussed. Sex has emerged from the era of hush and pretend, and marriage is the better for it.

Sexual satisfaction in marriage

There is more sexual activity within marriage than in any other relationship. Opportunities are limited only by a couple's schedule and inclinations. Expectations of the pair, their families, friends, and neighborhood affirm their right to privacy. Legal and moral questions are no longer relevant even for the conservative individual. Caring for and being committed to one another enhances the marital union. Husband and wife come together to celebrate their oneness, to relieve normal tensions, to

Table 2-4
Effects of Increasing Premarital Permissiveness

Potentially harmful	Potentially helpful
More unplanned, unwanted pregnancies	More babies for adoption
Less effective contraception among teenagers	Wider acceptance of birth control
Increase in abortions in young unmarried women	Increase in acceptance of abortion
More neglected babies of unwed girls	Encouragement of childcare facilities
More exploitation of girls by aggressive boys and men	Increased protection through more specific sex education
More exploitation of boys by aggressive girls and women	More boys specifically prepared to protect themselves
More venereal disease, already at epidemic rates among teenagers	Increased public support of venereal disease campaigns
Increased impotence among boys and men	Increased sexual liberation of females
Guilt and shame in some young people of both sexes	Guilt and shame reduced in general
Suicides increasing among youth (more than doubled recently)	Fewer young people depressed as sexual activity is more widely accepted
More fear of couple involvement	Increased couple fulfillment
Increasing alienation of youth	Reduced preoccupation with sex in personal and corporate life
More pressures to experiment in unsatisfying ways	More freedom in personal sexuality
Greater strain between the generations	Some relaxation of adult anxieties about premarital sex expression
Increase in numbers of girls who drift into prostitution	Prostitution declines as coitus between peers increases
More confusion in moral codes with fewer guidelines	Increase in realism and honesty in acceptance of human sexuality
More anxiety and anguish among puzzled youth and adults	Greater knowledge and understanding as sex research and education proliferate
Increase in have-to marriages	Both sexes better prepared for marriage
More marital instability and divorce	Stronger families among those who mature and fulfill potentials

express their gratitude to one another, to put their love into action, to make up after an argument, to lift their spirits when they are depressed, and for myriad other personal reasons that punctuate an ongoing marriage.

Happiness and sexual satisfaction

No one is happy all of the time. But out of a group of 100,000 women surveyed in 1975, 84 percent of the wives who said they were "mostly

Sexual attitudes and behavior in the United States   31

happy" described the sexual side of their marriages as good/very good. Conversely, the majority (53 percent) of the wives who reported a poor sexual relationship in the marriage were "mostly unhappy" (Levin and Levin 1975:57). The women's responses showed little embarrassment even in the most sensitive areas such as masturbation, intercourse after smoking marijuana, oral-genital sex, etc. It is safe to assume that those who were ill at ease about their sexuality did not respond; neither did many of those over 50 years of age, in low income, and in nonwhite groups. Earlier sex research has had similar sampling limitations, along with narrower representation of women in the mainstream of life and less sophisticated questions and response analysis.

Sexual satisfaction is related to satisfaction with marriage

Sexual satisfaction and a good marriage go together. It is possible to have one without the other, but it is less likely. Eight out of ten wives with good marriages enjoy good sex lives, but only 14 percent of those who rate their marriages as poor describe them as sexually satisfying. The more at ease husbands and wives are in confiding their real feelings to one another, the more able they are to express sexually the deep, hidden urges within them. Thus, nine out of ten wives who always confide in their husbands have fulfilling sex lives, while almost half of the wives who never discuss their sexual feelings and desires with their mates are miserably unsatisfied sexually (Levin and Levin 1975:57–58; see also Bernard, Jessie, *The Sex Game* 1968).

Sexually active wives

The outmoded notion that a good woman is a passive recipient of her husband's advances in the marital bed is hard to find among today's young wives. The great majority (78 percent) of married women responding to the 1975 survey are always or usually active sexual partners with their husbands. Practically all the rest say they are active partners sometimes to half of the time. When one considers how much a young wife has on her mind—the children, household problems, tight scheduling, chronic fatigue, and conflicting demands on her—it is remarkable that so many participate so actively in marital coitus (Levin and Levin 1975:57).

Once a good sexual relationship has been established in marriage, it continues to be satisfying. Most brides married less than one year (82 percent) rate their sex lives as good. After the first year of marriage the percentage levels off; however, 67 percent of those married more than ten years still find marital sex good or very good (Levin and Levin 1975:54).

Do children curtail marital sex?

Sunday supplements supported by research in recent years have focused on how hard children are on marriage. This may be so, but it is not reflected in what young mothers themselves report. They tell their best friends and confidantes how hard it is to plan for privacy with little children in the home. They put in long days of work with a busy household. Their husbands are busy trying to get ahead and support the family. The couple come together after the children are in bed, on a visit to friends, or with their grandparents. But in spite of all this, mothers are just as likely to be sexually satisfied as women without children. Couples with two children have sex lives as good as those of couples with only one child. The conclusion is that "children make no appreciable difference" (Levin and Levin 1975:55). The reason may be what one mother of several children told us—"When you really want to, you find a way, even with kids."

Frequency of coitus in marriage

Marital happiness is not told in numbers. But there is a significant relationship between the number of times married couples have intercourse and the way wives rate their sex lives. The more frequently coitus occurs each month, the more likely wives are to say that sex is "good" or "very good." When intercourse occurred 16 or more times a month, nine out of ten wives in a *Redbook* survey said they had a good sexual relationship with their husbands (Table 2-5). It is important to remember that those quoted were mostly women under 30 years of age. It is possible that older couples have intercourse less frequently and that many enjoy it more. Note too, that 44 percent of the wives who described the sexual side of the marriage as good to very good reported little or no coitus. Marriage is an elaborate complex of two interacting personalities. No two

Table 2-5
Frequency of Intercourse and Marital Sex Satisfaction

Wives' estimates of monthly frequency of marital coitus	Satisfaction with marital sex (percent)		
	Good/Very good	Fair	Poor/Very poor
None at all	9%	8%	83%
1 to 5 times	35	34	31
6 to 10 times	72	23	5
11 to 15 times	86	11	3
16 to 20 times	91	7	2
More than 20 times	93	5	2

Source: Robert J. Levin and Amy Levin, "Sexual Pleasure: The Surprising Preferences of 100,000 Women," *Redbook*, September 1975, p. 55.

Sexual attitudes and behavior in the United States   33

marriages are alike, and all are difficult to evaluate even with extensive or intensive study.

Does religion put a damper on marital sex?

The answer to the question is a resounding *no*. In spite of all the talk about religious women being inhibited and cold, the evidence is that the more religious a wife, the more she enjoys the pleasures of sex with her husband. Three out of four who say they are strongly religious describe their marital sex as good to very good. Wives who are not at all religious are far more likely to be dissatisfied with their sex life. This significant relationship between interest in religion and enjoyment of marital sex had not surfaced in earlier studies. It may be one result of recent efforts by clergymen to prepare young couples for the sexual side of marriage, and to endorse sexual satisfaction within marriage (Levin and Levin 1975: 53-54).

Myths about sex in marriage

"Men are sexier than women" is a popular belief. The idea is that men are male animals interested in any available female at any time. Men are supposed to measure their sexual success by the number of females they have had, or by the number of times they could have intercourse in a single instance. This "marks on the wall" rating system assumes that men are interested solely in their own physical prowess and only secondarily interested, if at all, in their partners. Actually, females are found to have greater orgasmic capacity than men (Masters and Johnson 1966). As far as sexual response is concerned, men and women are more alike than different (Masters and Johnson 1975b:51).

The double standard was supposed to give men the freedom they needed as males. Masters and Johnson found that the double standard, which left men free to roam while women were expected to remain faithful, instead left men with deep psychological scars, "Under the double standard men floundered and sexual dysfunction increased alarmingly" (Masters and Johnson 1975b:52).

The myth about premature ejaculation held—and led many women to believe erroneously—that if a man really cared about a woman he would postpone his own satisfaction to coincide with hers. There are many reasons for coming too soon, but not wanting to hold off is not one of them. A man can try too hard to please his sex partner; and his fear of failure is a frequent factor in his inability to hold his erection (Masters and Johnson 1975b:52).

Husbands are turned off by sexually assertive wives—so the old wives' tale goes. Actually, just the opposite is true in many cases. Most men are pleased when their wives find them sexually attractive and let them know it. As wives become more active in initiating and in participating with their husbands in their sexual union, their pair performance is enhanced. An eager and available wife is stimulating to her husband more often than not (Masters and Johnson 1975[b]:42).

If a couple is unable to have children, it is the wife that is barren, is an unfortunate myth that goes back to Bible times. Modern experts do not speak of "barren" women, or of sterile couples, but rather of infertility in the marriage. In at least 60 percent of the cases that have been clinically reviewed it is the male rather than the female who is infertile (Masters and Johnson 1975[b]:42). Many cases of infertility are being successfully treated in family planning clinics and by physicians in private practice in the United States today.

Extramarital sex

Some wives and husbands are intimate with others at one time or another in their marriages, for a number of reasons:

1. As revenge for what the mate is allegedly doing
2. As a means of relieving sexual frustration
3. As a means of "proving" oneself still young and sexually attractive
4. For the excitement of escaping humdrum routines
5. As part of a continuing pattern of permissive sexuality
6. For variety in sexual partners
7. For emotional satisfaction and enrichment
8. For idiosyncratic reasons within the individual or the situation

As sex is freed from traditional restraints, some increase in extramarital sex can be expected, whatever the "reasons."

Who the unfaithful are

Infidelity is found at every level of society. One study of 437 business executives, government officials, and professional men and their wives found that most of them were responsible parents who believed in marriage and had no interest in changing mates, and yet condoned extramarital sexual relationships. Some were quite open about violating their marriage vows; others attempted concealment by pretenses of one kind of another (Cuber and Harroff 1965).

In the early 1950s Dr. Kinsey and his colleagues reported that "29 percent of the females with histories of premarital coitus had had extramarital coitus by the time they contributed their histories to this study, but only 13 percent of those who had not had premarital coital experience [had had extramarital coitus]" (Kinsey et al. 1953:427). Twenty-five years later the *Redbook* survey found 30 percent of the married women reporting some extramarital sexual experience. Most of these (26 out of 30) had had premarital intercourse. However, of the 70 percent of the wives who had *not* been unfaithful more than half (55 percent) had had premarital experience. The researchers conclude that "premarital sex . . . does not necessarily lead to extramarital sex—it simply increases the odds that it will" (Levin 1975:40).

The odds are especially great for those females who began their premarital experience at early ages. Only 16 percent of the women who were over 21 when they had their first premarital experience (in contrast to 48 percent of those whose first experience was at age 15 or younger) reported extramarital coitus. The younger the girl at the time of her first sexual experience, the more likely she is to have extramarital sex (and with more men) during her marriage (Levin 1975:40). Other factors associated with wives' extramarital sex are: little interest in religion, little education (especially among young wives), and employment outside the home. Edwards and Booth (1976) find severe marital strain is related both to less frequent marital coitus and to increased likelihood of extramarital involvement.

Masters and Johnson (1975[a]) discuss ways in which the traditional double standard continues to influence modern men and women. They point out that men have much to gain from the crumbling of the double standard. They envisage sex not as something one person does to another, but rather as what happens when two persons are honestly and completely united. They describe the one-to-one relationship that waxes strong when weakness is admitted and triumphs in mutual surrender. Articulation of such values into the new sexual freedom may do much to strengthen the man-woman relationships of the future.

Effect of extramarital sex

Infidelity may be personally gratifying and may enrich a marriage in some cases, but there is evidence that most husbands and wives react to it emotionally in ways that damage the marriage. Analysis of court cases, survey data, and clinical evidence indicates that not only are opportunities for extramarital experience more prevalent, but their effects can be surprisingly violent. Emotions "run the gamut from shocked amazement to utter lack of control and violent responses leading to the death of the spouse" (Whitehurst 1971:685).

Responses to extramarital sex on the part of the spouse range widely: (1) righteous indignation—wrath, vindictiveness, punishment, scorn, and hostility are heaped upon the wrongdoer in ways that may be culturally acceptable, but that are in effect generally destructive; (2) physical or psychological separation—this, accompanied by some sense of being wounded and wronged, does little to improve the marriage; (3) recruitment of allies (relatives, the church, employers, lawyers, etc.) to fight the unfaithful spouse—of questionable help in reintegrating the marriage; (4) intellectual acceptance of the wandering spouse—the offended partner remains cool and aloof emotionally, deepening the alienation; (5) sincere efforts to reintegrate the marriage—feelings are recognized and dealt with rationally, at least with lip service; (6) real dialogue with a sense of commitment to one another as married partners—this most difficult but most promising course calls on all available resources within the couple and the community (Whitehurst 1971). When sexual experimentation by either partner elicits jealousy and self-doubt, as it often does, it becomes a threat to the marriage.

Militant sexuality—issues and rights

Open discussion has brought sexual problems to the surface, where they can be viewed collectively. Individuals who have felt the sting of discrimination now tend to band together to demand their rights. Dr. Herbert Hendin, psychoanalyst, observes, "Treating feeling as a political issue permits one to make the enemy external, to turn pain into anger and avoid the conflicts within" (Hendin 1975:26). This process is seen in the efforts of the women's bloc to gain their share of power in personal, social, economic, and political life, and in other areas as well.

Woman's right to be autonomous and equal

Modern woman struggles against traditional inequities laid down by biblical pronouncements, legal restrictions, an outmoded system of morality, and male-dominated controls that have kept her in a subservient role for centuries. Even liberal-minded men who favor equalitarian treatment of women in general, still may choose wives who are content to devote themselves to furthering their husbands' careers (Reiss 1973:12). Female sexuality also has its militant aspect—as expressed in nude male centerfolds in women's magazines, in topless waiters in tearooms, in picketing by retired "Bunnies" in support of their right to continued employment in Playboy Clubs, and in the demand for satisfaction in the marriage bed. More men and women feel that the movement for women's rights is a force for the better, but only one in five report any specific effect of the women's rights movement on the marriages they know (*Better Homes and Gardens* 1972:41, 43). More younger than older women have emancipated themselves from traditional restrictions, which suggests that the effects of the women's rights movement may be cumulative, with full effects still to come.

Birth control—a modern issue

From a historical perspective, the prevention of pregnancy is a relatively new concern. The condom was introduced in 1870 and was followed by the pessary, the cervical cap, the diaphragm, and the spermicidal foam or jelly. It was not until the middle of the twentieth century that reliably safe and effective contraceptives—the Pill and the IUD—became widely available as a means of separating coitus from childbearing.

Conservative religious groups following the Biblical injunction to "be fruitful and multiply" joined in fighting the use of contraceptives. At the other pole, ecologists, conservationists, and futurists were concerned about the dangers of overpopulation due to the limited resources aboard "spaceship earth." Meanwhile, public attitudes joined private practice in the widespread acceptance of contraceptives. Limiting the number of children in a family to that which a couple could care for was seen as an attempt to have "every child a wanted child" and to remove the fear of pregnancy from husband-wife intimacy. By 1972 the majority of Americans (85 percent) felt that improved birth control methods had contributed to better sexual adjustment in marriage, and 78 percent felt that birth control methods and information should be available to anyone, including unmarried teenagers (*Better Homes and Gardens* 1972:68, 84). Premarital contraceptive usage is found to be an expression of a university woman's acceptance of her own sexuality (as indicated by her belief that she has a right to make such a choice), and to be associated with her courtship involvement of going steady, being engaged, or planning to marry (Reiss, Banwart, and Foreman 1975).

Abortion and the right to life

Studies show that persistent misinformation about the risk of pregnancy, a great deal of unprotected intercourse, and many unplanned and unwanted pregnancies, especially among young unwed girls, are still major problems (Zelnik and Kantner 1972a:373). On one side of the issue of aborting an unwanted fetus is the woman's right to her own body, and on the other the unborn's right to life. At the liberal pole is the planned parenthood movement; at the other pole are conservative churches that attempt to block abortion reform on theological grounds (Planned Parenthood of New York City, 1973; Richardson and Fox 1975). Abortion is still a live political issue, of concern to millions of Americans. A nationwide sample of married and unmarried adult women conducted sequentially in 1963 and 1972 by the National Opinion Research Corporation found that the number of women supporting abortion had increased in the eight years between the two surveys for such reasons as:

> 1. Inability of families to support another child (from 18 percent in 1965 to 49 percent in 1973)

2. Unwillingness of unwed mothers to marry the child's father (from 13 percent in 1965 to 46 percent in 1973)
3. Unwillingness of married women to have more children (from 11 percent in 1965 to 41 percent in 1973) (Ryser, Cutler, and Grice 1974; see also Zelnik and Kantner 1975; and Pilpel, Zuckerman, and Ogg 1975).

In 1976, a national plebiscite on abortion found that three out of four of thousands of respondents supported the 1973 Supreme Court decision to legalize abortion (Katz 1976:1).

Venereal disease tracing and the right to privacy

Public Health officials urge venereal disease patients to reveal the names of those with whom they have had sexual congress, so that these contacts may be found and treated. Physicians are expected to report the names of private patients whom they are treating for venereal disease. Both efforts have been relatively unsuccessful to date. The chief reason appears to be the strong conviction on the part of young people, among whom venereal infection is rampant, that what they do is their own business and that their privacy is being invaded by infection-tracing. Doctors avoid reporting VD patients under treatment in order not to violate the code of professional confidence. Meanwhile both gonorrhea and syphilis rates continue to rise, especially among teenagers and young adults, both in heterosexual and homosexual contacts.

"Gay Lib"—homosexuals vs. societal norms

Homosexuality in this country has been forbidden, thought to be sinful, considered a mental illness, considered dangerously linked to other sexual perversions, and until recently was a felony punishable by imprisonment. Militant members of the Gay Liberation movement insist that this punitive attitude has deprived the homosexual of his rights to earn a living, to get married, to be a member in good standing in the military establishment, and to enjoy his full status as a citizen. Voices have been raised in legislative halls, churches, schools, and public forums in efforts to secure for homosexuals of both sexes their rights, as citizens, to live as they choose, without penalties or loss of status. Uncertain about the nature and causes of homosexuality, about the activities of homosexuals, and especially about the potential harm (if any) they might represent with regard to children and heterosexual adults, the public has been slow to grant full status to acknowledged homosexuals (Hooker 1961:166–183; Simon and Gagnon 1967; Moore 1969). This attitude has resulted in discrimination, say members of the Gay Liberation Front and other blocks of homosexuals, who cite as examples of biased treatment police harassment, dishonorable military discharge, housing problems, and social ostricism. The lines are drawn and the fight continues between those who would protect "public morals" and those who fight for the rights of homosexuals as citizens ("The Homosexual . . ." 1969; Smothers 1975:33).

Pornography vs. civil rights

Pornography and the sale of lurid, salacious, and prurient pictures, films, and written material of all kinds surfaced in the latter half of the twentieth century. Responding to the relaxation of taboos, many adults prided themselves on being unshockable. "Adult" bookstores catering to sophisticated tastes sprang up in residential neighborhoods, often close to schools and youth centers. Movies became increasingly blatant in depicting all kinds of sex practices—often coupled with brutality. By the 1970s the pendulum had swung from pride in propriety toward tolerance of anything and everything. Shocked leaders, concerned over the effect of such rampant lewdness on morality in general and on children in particular, took the question to court, where it ran into the rights of free speech, a free press, and free enterprise.

The civil libertarian objection to censorship and obscenity laws was argued on a number of points:

> 1. There is no evidence that obscenity ever hurt anyone.
> 2. Parents are responsible for protecting their children's morals.
> 3. Obscenity and decency are not absolute concepts, but relative ones that reflect the attitudes and taste of people at a given time and place.
> 4. It is difficult to distinguish between moral and immoral intent. (Spock 1971:82–88)

Judges, caught between the polar principles of civil rights and public morality, used as their criteria the "appeal to prurience" and "utter lack of social significance." The decision whether a given piece of material would be allowed or banned was left to the local community. Mass-produced media such as commercial films and network television programs were subject to the rating systems of the industries, with particular emphasis on their suitability for children and youth.

The public strongly supports strict laws on pornography. In the 1969 Gallup Poll, 85 percent of American adults favored stricter laws on obscene literature sent through the mails; and 76 percent wanted stricter state and local laws regulating the kinds of magazines and newspapers available at newstands (Gallup 1969). The question is still being discussed in many a community, in many instances with more heat than light.

Sex education—sensitive issue of the sixties

Sex education was headline news in the 1960s. School and community leaders were worried about a group of steadily worsening problems—high incidence of teenage sex activity and of venereal disease; widespread misinformation and ignorance among children and youth; rising numbers of unwed mothers; and the inability of many parents to give their children the needed knowledge, skills, and values to cope with the massive sensual pressures exerted by exploitative elements in the society. Educators and physicians recommended that "the schools accept appropriate responsibility for reinforcing the efforts of parents to transmit knowledge about the values inherent in our family system, and about the psychic, moral and physical consequences of sexual behavior . . ." (Joint Committee on Health Problems in Education, 1964).

Endorsement of sex education in the schools came from professional associations in education, family life, health, parent-teachers, and religion. Elementary, junior, and senior high schools quickly augmented their course offerings in sex and family life education to meet the growing demand. The sudden burgeoning of sex instruction in the schools created urgent needs—sometimes unmet—in such areas as effective teacher training, selection of adequate materials, and sufficient involvement of parents and other responsible adults (Somerville 1971:11-35).

Violent attacks against sex education came from such right wing groups as the John Birch Society and its MOTOREDE Committees, Gordon Drake and the Christian Crusade, Dan Smoot, and a plethora of militant citizen action groups (Kerckhoff and panel 1970). In the heat of the battle, pages were torn from textbooks, books were burned, and vitriolic attacks were made on prominent leaders and spokesmen for sex education (Silver 1970:30).

SIECUS (Sex Information and Education Council of the U.S.) rallied support in its defense of sex education and wholesome sexuality. The National Education Association blasted the opponents of sex education. The National Congress of Parents and Teachers circulated a special guide on how to deal with the venomous attacks of extremist groups. In time the hostility subsided, schools reevaluated their programs, mature teachers were trained, leaders saw that goals could be more modest than those originally proposed, and the atmosphere cleared (LeMasters, Lewis, Burt, Osmond, and Smith 1970:2-5).

Of all adults interviewed in the 1969 Gallup Poll, 71 percent were in favor of sex education in the schools (Gallup 1969). By 1972, four out of five American adults said yes to the question, "Should sex education be taught in school?" (*Better Homes and Gardens* 1972:75). In 1975, the responses of 100,000 American women strongly suggested a desperate need for the sexual guidance of girls at an early age (Levin 1975).

Sexual attitudes and behavior have changed throughout the twentieth century in the United States. Sex has come out into the open, and old restraints and taboos have all but disappeared. The challenging of formal moral codes of conduct has brought freedom to some and confused anxiety to others. Potentials for sex-related pain and pleasure are greater than they have ever been before. Sexuality remains a complex tangle of personal, social, and political strands. Great as the changes in sexual attitudes and behavior have been, there are more yet to come as gains are consolidated and as new values emerge freeing men and women for fuller lives as persons, as couples, and as members of American society.

And step by step, since time began,
I see the steady gain of man.

John Greenleaf Whittier

societal settings for
marriage and family

part two

*All things must change to something
new, to something strange.*
Henry Wadsworth Longfellow

Changing families in a changing world

chapter three

Families have survived war, peace, prosperity, panic, depression, and recession, in various forms and combinations. Families cope with the pressures exerted on them by changing to meet new conditions. In relatively quiet times, family life remains stable. In times of rapid social change, families will break under the strain unless they acquire the flexibility needed to explore new ways of living in their world.

In the twentieth century social change has occurred with a rapidity unparalleled in human history. Socio-economic specialists trace families through four great transitions in the history of the human race. The first took place ten thousand years ago, when families shifted from hunting and food-gathering and settled in farming villages. Five thousand years later, the growth of cities marked a second transition period. The third—

within the memory of living persons—saw the emergence of a world culture based on scientific technology. The fourth, now underway, is the "crisis of closure" on spaceship earth.

Our awareness, in the space age, that our resources are finite, has brought about profound changes in technology, political systems, moral principles, attitudes, and beliefs. Moon walks and exploration of nearby planets have convinced moderns that emigration to some other spot fit for human habitation is not a realistic expectation. The only frontiers left are those within people themselves—human resources to be released through adaptability, ingenuity, and education.

Families change as their world changes

Times are changing so fast that no one today can expect to live out his life in the world in which he was born, nor to die in the world in which he matured. Change in itself is neither good nor bad, but it makes demands upon families and family members. Social changes in this century have brought families face to face with new conditions, possibilities, problems, promises, and challenges. That families have responded so well and adapted so quickly to the new situations and potentials they have met bears witness to their amazing flexibility and creative capacity. There was a time when family members spent most of their time together. They worked side by side on the old home place. They played together or with their closest neighbors from nearby farms. Today family members are scattered, and their work and play activities are more individual than family-based.

The roles of family members have become more complex and flexible. Men, women, and children worked hard on the old family farm in bygone years. But they knew what was expected of them, and they had been prepared rather specifically for the roles they played. A woman had to be a good cook, since her family would depend upon her food throughout its lifetime. A man had to be a good, steady provider, as it was not possible for his wife to get a job to supplement his earnings. Both men and women had learned their roles in their own homes before they married. Children had their place in the scheme of things and knew what was expected of them from the beginning. The whole neighborhood agreed on what was man's work and what was woman's work and what was to be expected of a child. The family lived according to relatively rigid rules traditionally established and maintained by social and moral pressures of the entire society.

Today both men and women expect a wide variety of roles of each other. These expectations differ from couple to couple and from family to family. In one family a woman is expected to work outside the home; in another her place is seen to be in the home. In one household a man is expected to be a companion to his wife and children; in another his roles are more traditionally defined. In general, the trend is for both husbands and wives to expect each other to fill the intangible and more demanding roles of understanding companion, stimulating colleague, and loving, sympathetic parent.

The challenge of democratic interaction between family members—husband and wife, parent and child, close and extended family members—imposes new tasks and responsibilities upon all members of the family. Now that the authority of the father-head in many families has been taken over by family discussion, decisions are not reached as quickly, nor plans as easily made. Now, when the social pressures of church and neighborhood have declined, every member of every family faces innumerable choices and possibilities.

When a home is seen as a good place to grow up in—not as merely a "roof over our heads"—life there is lived at a much deeper level. The potentialities of such a home are tremendous, but its problems, especially for transitional generations, are felt in the very warp and woof of family living. The family, freed at last from the burden of producing things, faces as its primary task today the development of sturdy, wholesome personalities. Such a shift does not come all at once, however. Every step in the new direction is taken slowly, and sometimes painfully or laboriously, as every member of the family learns his new roles and adapts to the innovations that are appropriate in today's family.

It is much harder to raise a child according to the sound child development principles recommended today than it used to be when anyone with any "common sense" knew what was good for a child. Being a warmly sympathetic and companionable spouse is more difficult than baking a light biscuit or mending a harness. The arts and skills of human interaction that are expected of family members today open new social and emotional frontiers for which few have been adequately prepared by previous experience. Today's family becomes a laboratory at work on the world's most challenging problem—how to live together in creative peace, build harmony out of differences, and make democracy work.

Today's American families have a level of conscious aspiration unknown in other times and places. The big change in family life in recent decades is in the family's dreams and ambitions. It is no longer enough to make ends meet, nor to feed and clothe a child. Present-day families in ever-increasing numbers seek a quality of life for all of their members that is truly something new in the history of mankind.

Americans value education today

Few families in earlier centuries saw any reason for keeping children in school after they had received an elementary, basic education. There was much the young could do around the house and on the farm, and they learned in action how to do a man's or a woman's work. With industrialization, families moved off farms, and children—no longer an economic asset—had to have more education to cope with the complexities of modern living.

Families rarely question the value of an education today. Each generation of Americans throughout this century has taken pride in the fact that its children have gone further in school than their parents did. One study of married children (21 to 30 years of age), their parents (aged 46-55), and grandparents (71-80 years old) found that each successive generation had had more education than its predecessors. Grandparents who did well to get through grade school early in this century, in most cases saw that their children went to high school and went on to see their grandsons and granddaughters graduate from high school and go on to college (Table 3-1).

The nation as a whole reached higher levels of education with each succeeding generation (Figure 3-1). By the mid-1970s nearly half (47 percent) of all white girls finished high school, and 33 percent had some college education. Comparable figures for white boys showed 38 percent with a high school diploma and 44 percent with one to three years of college (U.S. Bureau of the Census December 1974).

Signs of a leveling off in school attendance had become apparent by the mid-1970s. More than three million fewer children were enrolled in grade school in 1975 than had been enrolled in 1970, and high school growth was also slowing (Table 3-2). The percentage of young men going to college had already begun to level off in the early 1970s. During the 1960s, each year found a higher percentage of students entering college. In the 1970s, however, the Census Bureau reported that the percentage of

Table 3-1
Education of Husbands and Wives in Three Generations

Years of school	Grandparents		Parents		Married children		All three generations	
	H	W	H	W	H	W	H	W
7 or less	56%	49%	16%	6%	—	—	23%	17%
8	28	33	31	26	6%	1%	21	19
9-11	7	10	21	25	20	24	16	20
12	4	5	23	35	44	55	24	32
13-15	5	3	8	8	15	16	9	9
16-17 or more	—	—	2	1	15	6	6	2
Total	100%	100%	100%*	100%*	100%	100%*	100%*	100%*

Source: Reuben Hill, *Family Development in Three Generations* (Cambridge, Mass.: Schenkman Publishing Company, 1970), Chap. 2, Table 2.03.
*Due to rounding of figures, the columns may not total 100%.

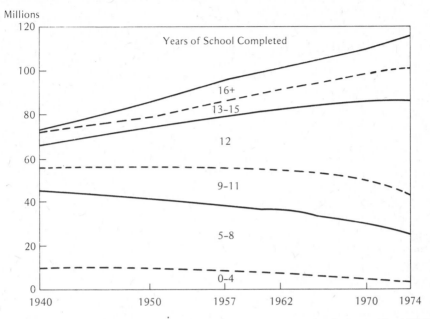

Figure 3-1

Years of School Completed by Persons 25 Years Old and Over in the United States:
1940 to 1974

Millions

Years of School Completed

16+

13-15

12

9-11

5-8

0-4

1940   1950   1957   1962   1970   1974

Source: U.S. Bureau of the Census, "Educational Attainment in the United States: March 1973
and 1974," *Current Population Reports*, Series P-20, no. 274, December, 1974a, (cover).

Table 3-2

School Enrollments 1970, and Estimates for 1975 and 1980

Students enrolled	1970	1975 (est.)	1980 (est.)
Elementary school	36,677,000	33,600,000	31,200,000
High schools	14,632,000	15,600,000	15,600,000
College, graduate and professional schools	7,920,000	9,300,000	9,600,000*

Source: National Center for Education Statistics: American Association of University Professors, in
U.S. News & World Report, September 1, 1975, p. 45.
*College enrollments are expected to start a slow decline in the early 1980s.

college men had dropped six percent (from 52 percent in 1970 to 46
percent in 1972), while enrollments of female students were off by one
percent (43 percent in 1970 to 42 percent in 1972).

Costs of education

Education costs put a heavy burden on taxpayers. By the mid-1970s,
many school systems faced insolvency. Federal financing of elementary

and secondary schools had risen from 26.7 billion dollars in 1965 to $68.2 billion in 1975, an increase of 155 percent. Federal spending for college and university education rose from 12.9 billion dollars in 1965 to $39.5 billion in 1975 (up 206 percent). In that decade the cost per pupil had increased from $484 to $1,255 in public schools, and from $1,236 to $3,045 in colleges and universities. Teachers' salaries had risen more than 80 percent in the same decade (National Center for Education Statistics 1975:44), and prices for everything else (educational materials, fuel, food, utilities, building costs and maintenance) were skyrocketing. College-bound students paid more for tuition, room, and board than in any previous year. By the mid-1970s going to a good private American college for four years could cost as much as $25,000.

Families looked for scholarships for their college-bound sons and daughters; public community colleges became more popular; student loan programs were widely used; and working one's way through college was once again acceptable. Widely circulated 1975 census data reported that heads of households with college degrees had higher annual median incomes than those with less education (college graduates $17,554; high school graduates $12,036; less than eight years of schooling $5,356 [Gribbin 1975]. However, the difference between high school and college graduates' median annual income had narrowed since 1968, when college graduates made 59 percent more a year than high school graduates (Wattenberg 1974).

While millions of families struggled to help their young people get more education than their parents had had, some hardheaded students and their families began to wonder if college was worth all it cost. They saw college graduates taking jobs unrelated to their major fields of study and interest. They watched the differences in pay between college and high school graduates narrow sharply during the 1970s. In many places, the possibilities of getting work were greater for carpenters and factory workers than for recent college graduates. The prediction was that the percentage of young Americans going to college would never again be as high as it had been during the 1960s. "For the first time in American history, there will be a considerable downward generational mobility as many young persons will obtain less schooling than their parents (Freeman and Hollomon 1975).

The American dream of climbing the educational ladder to success no longer looked so rosy. Millions of young people and adults continued their schooling, but their choice of courses was more highly selective, more realistic, and possibly more related to changing conditions in the world. As unemployment rates rose, many a man took specialized courses in the hope of getting a more promising job. Women went back to school to upgrade their salable skills so that they might ease the financial strains at home. Adult and vocational education programs flourished as American families tightened their belts in response to the economic doldrums of the period.

Families are immediately affected by changes in the nation's economy. In prosperous times jobs are plentiful, pay is good, and families raise their standards of living by moving into better homes, buying more things on credit, and "living it up." When depressed periods come, men are laid off work. Gone are the salaries and wages they counted on to pay monthly installments on automobiles, household equipment, and the home itself. As a result, poorer jobs paying less attract the wage-earner, his wife, and other relatives as a way of meeting the family's financial squeeze.

Family incomes over the years

Family incomes increased throughout the twentieth century, as is seen in Table 3-3. In the immediate postwar period of 1947, some 57 percent of American families had incomes under $5,000 a year; by 1967 only 26 percent were this low; and by 1985 only 12 percent are expected to fall below the $5,000 annual income level. At the other end of the income scale, some 9 percent of American families received over $15,000 in annual income in 1947; by 1985, 44 percent will be getting at least this much.

The trend toward higher incomes is illustrated in the responses of members of three-generation families. The married-child generation reports a greater number of adequate family incomes than either their parents or grandparents. Whereas 28 percent of the grandparents do without many needed things, only 4.7 percent of the parents and 1.2 percent of the married children do. On the item, "Have the things we need and a few of the extras," 30.5 percent of the grandparents, 61 percent of the parents, and 76 percent of the married children responded affirmatively (Hill et al. 1970:41).

Table 3-3
Median Family Income, 1947–1985 (Estimated)

1967 dollars	1947 $4,531	1957 $5,889	1967 $7,974	1985 $13,800
Under $3,000	27%	20%	13%	6%
$3,000 to $4,999	30	19	13	6
$5,000 to $6,999	21	24	16	8
$7,000 to $9,999	14	22	24	12
$10,000 to $14,999		11	22	25
$15,000 and over	9	4	12	44
Total	100%*	100%	100%	100%*

Source: "The Changing Income Distribution," *Family Economics Review*, June 1969, p. 14.
*Due to rounding of figures, the columns may not total 100 percent.

Changing families in a changing world 53

Rising costs, shrinking dollars

The mid-1970s were a strange mix of high incomes, high prices, high unemployment, and inflated dollars that gave the illusion of plenty to many a family and brought economic distress to many others. In August, 1975 the U.S. Bureau of the Census released figures showing that the median income of all American families had been $12,840 in 1974, an increase of 7 percent over the $12,050 median family income of 1973 (Table 3-4).

The catch was that while family incomes had risen 7 percent, prices had gone up 11 percent that year. Thus, what looked like a higher income actually bought less than it would have the year before. Increases in medical, hospital, and dental bills; in local, state, and federal taxes; rising fuel costs due to the energy crisis; higher utility rates, housing costs, and interest payments; spiraling prices for food and practically everything else families consume meant that with each succeeding year more of a family's income went for necessities. Discretionary income (money spent for what is *wanted* rather than for what is *needed*) dropped as inflation ate away at the family's available dollars. A 1970 dollar was worth only 72 cents in 1975, because of the rise in prices during each intervening year. By 1980, that 1970 dollar will amount to 51 cents if costs continue to rise at an average rate of 6.9 percent a year (*U.S. News & World Report* 1975[c]:62).

Inflation has become a way of life. With few exceptions, the consumer price index has risen every decade for more than a hundred years (*Statistical Abstract Supplement* 1960:124-127 and *Statistical Abstract of the United States* for more recent years). The rise in the mid-1970s was especially sharp (Table 3-5) and there is little chance of reaching a plateau in rising prices in the foreseeable future. Inflation is seen as "the economic trick by which the mass of people have been forced to accept a lower standard of living even though their pay packet remains the same or even goes up" (*Forbes Magazine* 1975).

Government social welfare expenditures designed to lift the poor out

Table 3-4
Percentage of American Families in Four Income Groups

Annual family income	1973	1974	
Over $25,000	9.4%	11.5%	(6,400,000 families)
$15,000-$25,000	26.2	28.3	(15,800,000 families)
$10,000-$15,000	25.5	24.4	(13,600,000 families)
$ 5,000-$10,000	24.3	22.7	(12,700,000 families)
Under $5,000 (poverty level)	14.6	13.1	(7,300,000 families)
Total	100.0%	100.0%	(55,800,000 families)

Source: U.S. Bureau of the Census, August 1975 release.

Table 3-5
Rising Prices, 1965–1975 (Index: 1967 = 100)

Year	Wholesale prices	Consumer prices
1965	96.6	94.5
1966	99.8	97.2
1967	100.0	100.0
1968	102.5	104.5
1969	106.5	109.8
1970	110.4	116.3
1971	113.9	121.3
1972	119.1	125.3
1973	134.7	133.1
1974	160.1	147.7
1975 (August)	176.7	162.8
Total increase	83%	72%

Source: U.S. Department of Labor data in John O'Riley, "Prices . . . Putting the High Cost of Living in Perspective," *The National Observer*, October 1, 1975.

of poverty have grown enormously since 1965. Benefit programs providing goods and services—mainly food and medical care—have grown substantially in recent years, so that a smaller proportion of the population is living in poverty. Yet many poor families are farther away from being able to support themselves at levels typical of American standards of living than they were in 1965 (Jondrow 1976:11).

Cost of living pacts tie automatic boosts in pay to the consumer price index. By 1975 half of all private workers under major contracts had such escalator protection (a total of 5,100,000, up from 4,000,000 in 1960). Some drawbacks associated with such inflation cushions are:

1. Time lags between the time when inflation cuts into the worker's paycheck and the time he gets a cost of living raise
2. Limits specified in union contracts on amounts workers can get from escalator clauses
3. Lack of coverage for millions of workers not under union contracts
4. Lack of protection for millions on fixed incomes (retirees, for instance)
5. Prolongation of inflationary periods due to continued high wages
6. Unemployment (*U.S. News & World Report* 1975[a]:89)

The specter of unemployment

When millions of workers are unemployed, families worry about how long their income will continue. "No one who lived through the Great Depression can doubt the searing personal costs of unemployment, the tragedy that strikes when an able-bodied head of a family cannot find a job that will enable him to discharge his responsibilities and maintain his self-respect. The recession has certainly increased the number of persons who suffer this tragedy and there is no gainsaying the great harm it has done. . . ." (Friedman 1975:63). This economist goes on to say that the specter of 8 million Americans out of work in 1975 is not as frightening as it might at first appear, since most people receive some income even when they are unemployed. Families themselves soften the blow by having more than one wage-earner to count on, and by searching out and holding another position after being laid off. The net effect of the recession of the mid-1970s was to lengthen the time it takes to find a job—from an average of 10 weeks in 1973 to about 15 weeks in 1975 (Friedman 1975:63).

How families cope

A 1975 study of a national probability sample of 2,502 families found many concerned about money. Family worries focused on actual or feared unemployment (28 percent); on savings being eroded by inflation (35 percent); on not being as well off as expected (32 percent); on having to draw out savings to meet current expenses (22 percent); and on debts (16 percent) (Yankelovich, Skelly, and White 1975:19). Most families were actively trying to cope with inflation in many ways (Table 3-6).

Despite their efforts to cut spending, family members spent substantially more on such things as insurance, utilities, car repairs and gasoline,

Table 3-6
Family Adjustments to Inflation

Life-style adjustment	Percentage of families
Minimizing use of electricity	65%
Spending time at home instead of going out	54
Not buying so many clothes	44
Shopping more at discount stores	44
Cutting back on gifts	43
Bargain hunting	38
Not eating out at restaurants	37
Repairing things normally thrown out	34
Cutting back on beauty shop/barber shop	25
Using less prepared foods	24
Cutting out newspapers/magazines	21
Giving up hobbies/sports which cost money	21
Buying less liquor/beer	19
Doing without meat at some meals	19
Postponing medical/dental checkups	18
Looking for tips on money managing	17
Entertaining less	12
Working overtime/moonlighting	11
Cutting back on charities	9
Wife taking a job	9
Not giving the children extra money	8
Not having seconds at meals	6
Letting life insurance lapse	2

Source: Yankelovich, Skelly, and White, 1975:83-84.

meat, and other food in 1975 than they had previously (Yankelovich, Skelly, and White 1975:79).

Families tend to pull together to meet their financial crises. They see themselves as becoming wiser shoppers (70 percent); less wasteful (59 percent); more sympathetic and understanding of the poor (45 percent); satisfied with less (42 percent); going back to basic values (33 percent); enjoying an increase in family togetherness (25 percent); and having a greater sense of neighborliness (15 percent) (Yankelovich, Skelly, and White 1975:103).

Close to 23 million husband-wife families had more than one family member in the labor force by the mid-1970s. The number of wives who were gainfully employed increased until by March 1974, 43 percent of wives were working. More than half a million wives went to work in the year 1973-1974 alone; many of these were mothers of young children (U.S. Department of Labor 1975[a]:60-62). More than half of all mothers of schoolage children were working then, as were more than a third of all mothers of preschool children. Some held part-time jobs, but 69 percent were working full time. Almost 27 million children in the United States (42 percent of those under age 18) had mothers who were working or looking for work in early 1974. One out of every four of these children (6,100,000) were preschoolers, requiring some kind of care in their working mother's absence (Waldman 1975:64-65).

Mothers of young children do not find it easy to work outside their homes. Reliable childcare workers are hard to find; good day care centers are scarce and expensive; and housework awaits the mother's homecoming at an hour when she, the children, and her husband are tired. Many a husband resents his wife's working (21 percent in one survey). The same study showed that most of the working wives themselves believed that mothers with small children should not work (Yankelovich, Skelly, and White 1975:77). Why do women work under such circumstances? Because they have to to support their families, to augment their husbands' earnings, or to provide their families with the good things of life they could not otherwise afford.

Family assets

American families have the highest standard of living in the world today. They view as necessities things considered luxuries in much of the rest of the world. Even rather humble American homes have running water, indoor plumbing, refrigerators, heating systems, radios, television sets, and other household equipment. They take for granted their family cars and the freedom to travel with few restrictions. They have an abundance of food distributed daily to their local markets. They believe that every family has a right to privacy and a place of its own, and they consider doubling up a hardship. Aging parents and young couples expect to live by themselves rather than with relatives.

Today's families live better than their parents, grandparents, or other forebears did. One national survey of representative American families in 1975 found that 97 percent had television sets, 93 percent owned cars (51 percent had more than one car in the family), and most of them have assets they can count on in the future (Table 3-7).

Housing and equipment are acquired sooner

Practically all married couples over 20 years of age have established their own households. The younger generation today have better housing than their parents and grandparents. Improvement has been progressive, each succeeding generation being better housed than former ones. The present married-child generation is more comfortably housed—and sooner—than their forebears within specific families. (Hill 1970: Chapter 5).

Families today have equipment unknown to "the old-fashioned family" at the turn of the century. Many grandparents who married in the first decade of the twentieth century have not acquired in a lifetime what young people start out with today. Grandparents, most of whom have celebrated their golden wedding anniversaries, had been married forty years or more before they acquired their first electric coffee maker, electric frypan, food freezer, gas or electric clothes dryer, garbage disposer, dishwasher, electric blanket, air conditioner, or television set. All of these items were owned by young generation couples within the first five years of marriage, on the average. The generation between, married during the depression, did better than the old folks, but fell short of their

Table 3-7
American Family Assets by Income Groups, 1975

Families own	Total	Yearly income			
		Under $10,000	$10,000–$14,999	$15,000–$19,999	$20,000 and over
Health insurance	82%	70%	88%	91%	96%
Own home	74	64	76	84	88
Savings account (adult)	72	54	79	86	92
Real estate holdings	38	27	36	49	63
Children's savings	34	18	36	53	55
Government bonds	29	19	30	34	47
Stocks	21	9	15	31	50
Special savings (education)	11	3	11	18	21
Second home	5	4	5	5	12

Source: Yankelovich, Skelly, and White, Inc., *The American Family Report: A Study of the American Family and Money.* General Mills, Inc., 9200 Wayzata Blvd., Minneapolis, MN 55440, 1975, pp. 94-95.

married children in the speed with which they equipped and furnished their homes. During the year when the three-generation study was being made, the differential rate of acquiring household possessions continued. The grandparents that year acquired 52 new pieces of equipment (seven regrigerators, five gas ranges, five electric frypans, five electric blankets, and sundry other items) to increase their household inventories by 5 percent. The parents increased their family inventories by 9 percent with the acquisition of 14 radios, 14 television sets, 13 electric frypans, and a variety of other items that their married children had had since they were first married. That same year, the youngest generation further outstripped its parents and grandparents with 132 new pieces of equipment (12 television sets, 11 wall-to-wall carpets, 11 vacuum cleaners, and other items) to upgrade their household inventories by 12 percent (Hill 1970: Chapter 5).

In the early years of the century, when most families lived on farms, and the economy had not yet commenced its rapid development through industrialization, a couple learned to do without, or to "make do." Those husbands and wives who married during the depression of the 1930s knew deprivation too, and only after World War II did they begin to have many of the things their children were to take for granted when they married. Couples marrying now have more to begin with, expect more, and acquire more faster.

Families are smaller than they used to be

There was a time when raising many children was an economic advantage. In the old farm family the more sons and daughters there were, the more land the family could till, the more stock they could raise, and the more canned food they could process. In 1890, 64 percent of Amercia's families lived on farms. In the decades that followed there was a steady migration from farms into cities and suburbs. By the 1970s less than five percent of all American families were those of farmers.

Now, when the vast majority of families live and work in town, where less space and fewer roles for children are available, it is not surprising that families have grown smaller over the years. In 1700, the average mother had borne 7.4 children by the age of forty-five. By 1910, the number had shrunk to 4.7; by 1940 to 2.9; by 1960 to 2.7. In 1970 the average number of children was 3.3; from that time on, the number of births has dropped sharply. By the mid-1970s parents were barely replacing themselves (*Statistical Bulletin* 1975:8–9). The two-child family was then seen as ideal, partly in response to the urgings of environmentalists concerned with counteracting the worldwide population explosion, and partly in response to the shifting plans of families in the changing economic scene.

Fewer births, more people

The United States had a rapidly growing population from 1850 through to 1975. In the middle of the nineteenth century there were less than 25 million people; by mid-1975 the population had grown to 212 million and was still growing. Despite fewer births, the total number of people was increasing, although at a slower rate than in earlier decades. The numbers of deaths and of immigrants had remained fairly constant, so that the net growth paralleled the numbers of babies born (Figure 3–2).

Census experts predict that there will be a larger proportion of 18- to 44-year-olds (the reproductive years) and a proportional decrease in the number of persons in the 45 to 64 year range in the near future. These are reliable estimates, since the individuals expected to reach these ages are already here. "By 1990, depending on future fertility levels, between 39 percent and 43 percent of all persons are likely to fall in the young adult ages, as compared with 36 percent now. At the

Figure 3–2
United States Population, 1930–1974

(Annual Levels of Net Growth, Births, Deaths, and Net Immigration)

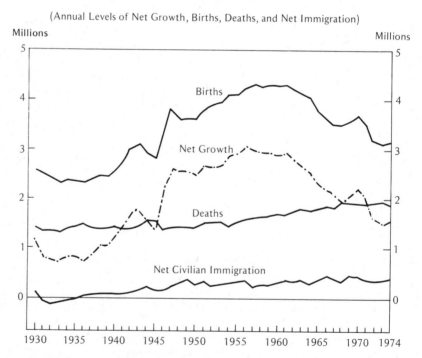

Source: U.S. Bureau of the Census, "Population Estimates and Projections," *Current Population Reports*, Series P-25, no. 545 (Washington, D.C.: U.S. Government Printing Office, April 1975a), Figure 1 (cover).

same time, the proportion of aged persons (65 years old and older) is very likely to continue for some time, with the proportion increasing from 10.0 percent in 1972 to between 10.4 percent and 11.6 percent in 1990" (U.S. Bureau of the Census May, 1974:179). If these projections are realized, the closing decade of the twentieth century will see proportionally fewer children and more adults in the population than at present. The total population of the United States is expected to increase by only 24 percent in the last quarter of the twentieth century to 264,400,000 in the year 2,000, compared with the 40 percent growth between 1950 (when there were 152,300,000 Americans) to 1975, when the population was 213,700,000 (*U.S. News & World Report* 1975b:35).

Marriage reflects the mood of the nation

The age at which Americans marry, and the proportion of them who do marry has varied from one period to another throughout our history. At the turn of the century, a man typically left school at 14 and worked a dozen years before he took a wife—usually a girl considerably younger than he was. Young adults today are more inclined to marry within their own age group, typically in the early to mid-twenties. Teenage marriages, so popular after World War II and into the 1950s, have declined in numbers and percentages since then.

"By the late 1960s and early 1970s the marriage rate among single persons under 45 years of age was as low as it had been at the end of the Depression . . . the average age at marriage was close to a year higher than it had been in the 1950s, and the proportion of women who remained single until they were 20 to 24 years old had increased by one-third since 1960. . . . For the first time since soon after World War II the marriage total for a 12-month period was significantly smaller (by 68,000) than it had been the preceding year" (Glick 1975a:16).

Young women in the mid-1970s were marrying much later than their mothers had in the late 1940s and early 1950s. Sociologists cite a combination of factors delaying marriage for women:

1. More young women going to college (3 times as many in 1972 as in 1960)
2. More marriageable women than men (the "marriage squeeze" resulting from the baby boom after World War II)
3. More young women in paid employment
4. Increasing scope of women's involvement in community life
5. Women's new sense of identity, highlighted by the women's movement

The tendency for the best educated and most highly paid women to postpone marriage or to remain single by preference may continue, since these women enjoy their independence and prefer it to marrying the men they know (Bernard 1972). This tendency could change as more boys and men come to feel less threatened by able, intelligent girls and young women and to value them as persons, and to appreciate the new partnership roles of which they are capable.

Fewer marriages last a lifetime

Until the twentieth century marriages were more often broken by death than by divorce. Mothers died in childbirth, men were killed in accidents—life was short and strenuous. Husbands and wives needed one another to survive on frontier and farm. A man had to have a wife to cook and sew, to bear and rear the children, and to help with the crops, quite as much as a woman needed a husband for support and protection. As industrial production picked up, farmers got jobs in town and farming became mechanized, electrified, and later automated, so that all of the nation's food and fiber could be produced by relatively few large agricultural units.

Couples who had once worked side by side in family farms and businesses worked apart when they moved to cities and suburbs. Working wives became more independent and also less essential to their husbands for goods and services now commercially available. Marriage, a partnership once held together by necessity, was now bound by ties of companionship or not at all. Demands for personal happiness and individual freedom increased as more marital options became available. The wonder is that so many millions of marriages do continue "till death do us part."

Marriages are more liable to break in some periods than in others. During the depression of the 1930s, few couples could afford to separate. Jobs were scarce, family incomes dropped, and married couples struggled to make ends meet. Wartime marriages in the 1940s and 1950s had high failure rates. By the mid-1970s some 37 percent of all first marriages were ending in divorce, and an even larger percentage (59 percent) of second marriages were expected to dissolve (Westoff 1975). Some of the reasons why so many marriages break today can be found within the changing social scene (Table 3-8).

More remarriage

Americans divorce, but they still believe in marriage. When a marriage fails, more often than not the tendency is to marry again. Four out of five divorced women and five out of six divorced men eventually remarry (Glick 1975a:17, 19). Divorced persons tend to marry divorced persons, often within three years of the dissolution of the previous marriage. Women delay longer in marrying again, if they remarry at all, partly

Table 3-8
Social Factors in Marital Dissolution in the Late Twentieth Century

Societal phenomena	Factors favoring marital instability
Romanticism	Disillusionment when realities do not match dreams of marital bliss
Sexual freedom	More exposure to other possibilities
Individualism	Personal freedom replaces duty
Higher levels of education	Horizons broadened, mates outgrown
More women working	Wives independent of husbands for support
Rising family incomes	Unhappy couples can afford to divorce
Urbanization	Less concern for "what the neighbors think"
Secularization	Sacredness of marriage challenged
Relaxation of churches' stand against divorce	Less guilt in breaking marriage vows
Legal reforms and legal aid	Divorcing easier
Social disruption and unrest	Disenchantment spreads to marriage
Economic inequities	Disadvantaged demand better lives

because there are fewer available men within their age range. Men tend to seek mates not only in their own age groups but also in those that are much younger, so they have more possibilities from which to choose than do divorcees.

Remarried individuals tend to believe that their first marriages failed because of poor judgment in the choice of a partner, or because of their immature approach to handling the complicated adjustments of marriage. When they remarry, they find themselves enmeshed in even more complicated family relationships, with two sets of in-laws and old habits that are hard to break. The excitement of love the second time around subsides in time, and the second marriage proves to be no more lasting than the first.

Changes in child-rearing

"Tell us of the olden days when you were young, Grandma," is often a modern child's request for accounts of old-fashioned discipline—of punishment by shaving strop or hairbrush meted out for the misdeeds of the young in an earlier day. Changes in child-rearing practices over the decades reflect the parents' shifting conceptions of themselves, of their children, and of their relationships with one another.

From entrepreneurial to bureaucratic child-rearing

A typical member of the "old middle class" (banker or small entrepreneur) grew up with a strong inner sense of direction that was implanted early in life by his elders. The new, outer-directed person has learned to look to others for guidance as a result of his early childhood experience of a flexible, responsive, nurturing approach to child-rearing (Riesman, Glazer, and Denney 1950). Entrepreneurial and bureaucratic parents use significantly different child-rearing methods, which are summarized in Table 3-9. The increase in the size and complexity of large corporations is reflected in an increase in the number of bureaucratically-oriented families that encourage their children to be accomodative and adaptive in ways compatible with contemporary values in American life (Miller and Swanson 1958).

From strict to permissive child-rearing

A review of 60 years of child training practices reports, "Three different schools of thought have prevailed with regard to how children should be raised. The 1890s and 1900s saw a highly sentimental approach to child-rearing; 1910 through the 1930s witnessed a rigid disciplinary approach; the 1940s have emphasized self regulation and understanding the child. These 60 years have also seen a swing from emphasis on character development to emphasis on personality" (Stendler 1950:134). A critical review of recent revisions of popular child-rearing manuals concludes that the permissiveness of the 1950s continued into the late 1960s (Gordon 1968). Since then there has been a shift in emphasis, and concern is now focused more on development.

More emphasis on development

Interest in the wholesome development of human personality has increased in recent years. Traditionally, parents defined their gender and

Table 3-9
Entrepreneurial and Bureaucratic Child-rearing Methods

Entrepreneurial	Bureaucratic
Stress self-control and internalization in control of impulses	Child is taught to fit in with others, to be a "nice guy," affable, unthreatening, adaptive, and to seek direction
Train child to change the situation	
Stress activity and independence	
Encourage mastery	Child learns to go to parents for wisdom in social skills, even as adult
Prefer sharp differences between sex roles	
More likely to:	Person is trained to be cautious, precise, rational, secure, and unaggressive
Feed babies on schedule	
Begin toilet training early	New levels of comfort and security with lessening psychic pressures are sought
Use symbolic punishment	
Let babies cry	New sense of participation in a responsible, moral community is emerging
Training is by suppression of impulsive drives	Loyalty to the group is central
Egocentricity and hostility are more frequent	Child and adult are free to enjoy themselves and to express their feelings
	Individual should be warm, friendly, supportive of others

marital roles relatively rigidly (Chapters 1 and 4), and expected their children to obey them without question. Developmentally-oriented parents today are more concerned with a child's development than with his blind obedience. They value development and encourage growth in their children and in each other. These new role definitions and the mental images that parents have of themselves and of their children are revealed in their verbatim responses to such questions as "What are five things a good mother does?" "What are five things a good child does?" etc. (Table 3-10).

Developmentalism does not imply unrestrained permissiveness, but rather the establishment of relationships conducive to optimal development, along with the freedom and the controls that promote growth in both parents and children. The principles of developmentalism are more widely accepted among young parents than among older ones, and this acceptance bears a positive relationship to the amount of education the parents have had (Duvall 1946; Staples and Smith 1954; Kell and Aldous 1960). The grandparent generation is found to be more traditional, fatalistic, and past-oriented, in contrast to young parents who are more flexible, companionable, and communicative (Hill 1970).

Since developmentalism is associated with education and comfortable levels of living, it can be expected to increase. In time, higher standards of living and of education may narrow the gap between the haves and the have-nots in society, so that the developmental may one day become the traditional. Modern child-rearing requires a firm set of family values and the willingness to pursue them diligently. The rights of each member of the family, regardless of age or sex, are protected. Responsibilities are shared by all family members according to their capacities. Neither laissez-faire anarchy nor unrestricted license are fostered; on the contrary, self-disciplined and goal-directed individuals and families are valued.

New freedoms, new values

New personal, marital, and family options have freed both men and women from traditional restraints (Chapters 4 and 6). New values and concerns are emerging that penetrate deep into American life. The energy crisis turned attention to new sources of power within the United States— the atom, the earth, the sea, the sun, the wind, and the tides. The recycling of materials of all kinds is a concern of millions of families. Maintaining a stable population is an objective that modern multitudes take seriously. There is a growing tendency to pursue individualistic personal goals, especially among modern youth. Such values as individual freedom, independence, autonomy, a sense of accomplishment and achievement, the confidence that comes from being good at something

Table 3–10
Parents' Traditional and Developmental Conceptions

Traditional conceptions	Developmental conceptions
A good child:	*A good child:*
Keeps clean and neat, is orderly, is clean, keeps himself neat, etc.	Is healthy and well, eats and sleeps well, grows a good body, has good health habits, etc.
Obeys and respects adults, minds his parents, does not talk back, respects teachers, etc.	Shares and cooperates with others, gets along with people, is developing socially, etc.
Pleases adults, has good character traits, is honest, truthful, polite, kind, fair, etc.	Is happy and contented, is a cheerful child, is emotionally well adjusted, etc.
Respects property, takes care of his things, is not destructive, hangs up his clothes, etc.	Loves and confides in his parents, responds with affection, has confidence, etc.
Is religious, goes to Sunday school, loves God, prays, follows Jesus, etc.	Is eager to learn, shows initiative, asks questions, expresses himself, accepts help, etc.
Works well, studies, goes to school, is dependable, takes responsibility, etc.	Grows as a person, progresses in his ability to handle himself, enjoys growing up, etc.
Fits into the family program, has an interest in his home, does his share, helps out, etc.	
A good mother:	*A good mother:*
Keeps house, washes, cooks, cleans, mends, sews, manages the household, etc.	Trains for self-reliance, encourages independence, teaches how to adjust to life, etc.
Takes care of the child physically, feeds, clothes, bathes him, guards child safety, etc.	Sees to emotional well-being, keeps child happy and contented, helps child feel secure, etc.
Trains the child to regularity, establishes regular habits, provides a schedule, etc.	Helps child develop socially, provides toys and companions, supervises child's play, etc.
Disciplines, corrects child, demands obedience, rewards good behavior, is firm, etc.	Provides for child's mental growth, reads to child, provides stimulation, educates, etc.
Makes the child good, instructs in morals, builds character, prays for, sees to religion, etc.	Guides with understanding, gears life to child's level, interprets, answers questions, etc.
	Relates lovingly to child, enjoys and shares with child, is interested in what child says, etc.
	Is a calm, cheerful, growing person oneself, has a sense of humor, smiles, keeps rested, etc.
A good father:	*A good father:*
Is a strong individual, always right, and the child is his ward	Is an individual, as is his child
"Knows" what the child "should" be, so does not seek to understand child as an individual	Seeks to understand the child and himself Places emphasis on the growth of the child and himself
Is interested only in activities which he determines are his responsibility for child's "good"	Is interested in child's determining and attaining child's own goals
Places emphasis on giving things to and doing things for the child	Finds satisfaction in child's becoming a mature individual
Is interested in child's accepting and attaining goals set by the father	Feels that parenthood is a privilege which he has chosen to assume
Finds satisfaction in child's owing father a debt which can be repaid by child's obedience	
Feels parenthood is a duty which the church and/or society expect him to discharge	

Source: Traditional and developmental conceptions of a good child and a good mother are categories of verbatim responses of 433 mothers reported in Evelyn Millis Duvall, "Conceptions of Parenthood," *American Journal of Sociology* 52, no. 3 (November 1946): 195–196. Traditional and developmental conceptions of a good father are derived from constructed father types emerging from Rachel Ann Elder, "Traditional and Developmental Conceptions of Fatherhood" (Master's thesis, Iowa State College, 1947), p. 21.

one enjoys, and of having an exciting life, are all being openly explored today (Fendrich 1974; Laufer and Bengtson 1974; Bengtson 1975).

Family members are taught to express their feelings more openly than was allowed in earlier generations (Chapters 2 and 4). Rage, defiance, assertiveness, and fear are acknowledged and accepted as freely as are the gentler emotions of love, compassion, and tenderness. The Sexual Revolution shook sex loose from its hiding places deep within human beings, and since that time some men and women have made almost frenetic efforts to throw off their earlier restraints. As a result of the relaxation of controls on sexual behavior, sex has suffered from over-exposure and has moved off center stage as a source of passion "to return as a form of play—as a parallel to gourmet cooking. . .sexuality played out in a new key, less important, less central, less over-determined" (Gagnon and Simon 1973). The revolution still raging is one of broad, deep social change that is altering the nature of marriage, the meaning of children, and the functioning of families.

Revolutionary social change

The revolutionary social changes of recent decades have blasted relatively stable families out of old ways of living that have persisted for many hundreds of years. New forms and functions with far-reaching repercussions are arising. According to the eminent historian Arnold Toynbee, "The vital revolution of our time is the emancipation of women, workingmen and 'natives'. . . The women are the most important contingent of the three because, in the long run, their emancipation is going to affect everybody's life. Above all, it is going to demand an immense and disturbing psychological adjustment on the part of men, because it implies a revolutionary change in the traditional relations between the sexes" (Toynbee 1955).

Marriage is that relation between man
and woman in which the independence
is equal, the dependence mutual, and
the obligation reciprocal.

L.K. Anspacher

Marital roles and conjugal options

chapter four

Marital roles may be defined as the behavioral expectations of husbands and wives (Aldous 1974:60–89). A husband is generally expected to be adequate as a provider, sex partner, companion, confidant, decision-maker and accountant. The husband's role performance is enforced by society at large. If a man does not provide the basic essentials for the support of his family, social workers from community agencies step in to investigate. If he squanders his resources in drink, drugs, or gambling, rehabilitative services may be brought to bear. When he does not file an income tax return, IRS calls him to account. Should his wife be dissatisfied because of his sexual demands or his neglect of her emotional needs, marriage and family counselors may be consulted. The husband who performs his marital roles well earns the respect of his wife and the admiration of those who know the couple well.

A wife is expected to perform acceptably her roles as housekeeper, shopper, cook, laundress, seamstress, sex partner, confidante, companion, social secretary, and family planner. Her husband, neighbors, and others in the community criticize her if she flagrantly neglects her family. She may be called to account for failure to perform her wifely roles. As a simple illustration, if she fails to pay the electric bill the power may be shut off. If she does not reply to invitations, she and her husband are not invited again. When she plays her marital roles well, her husband, her family, and their friends approve of her as a good wife.

Marital roles vary

Many marital roles are sequential as a marriage continues over the years. A man is first a husband; when his children arrive, he is a father; as the children grow up and marry he becomes a father-in-law; then a grandfather, and finally a widower, if his wife dies before he does. Each of these positions has its cluster of concurrent roles. Similarly, a married woman occupies a series of positions as wife, mother, mother-in-law, grandmother and widow. Her child-rearing roles as wife-mother-grandmother change as her sons and daughters grow up—from childbearer to infant-caretaker, to young child disciplinarian, to older child guide, to teenager counselor, to young adult emancipator, to interdependent in-law facilitator, and then around the cycle again as her grandchildren arrive (Chapter 7).

Marital roles are reciprocal. Each partner has rights and responsibilities that are necessary for the continuation of the marriage. Reciprocity is based on an exchange in which each spouse receives from and gives to the other. The partners monitor each other's role performance, rewarding satisfying service ("A good dinner, dear," or "Congratulations on the raise you earned"); and punishing defaults ("Do you have to be so messy?" or "Don't come near me until you apologize"). Standards of performance vary according to the expectations of the individuals. Perfectionists demand more of their mates than do more easygoing people. Rigid individuals have more difficulty adjusting to crises and change than do those who have learned to take life philosophically.

Husband/wife roles vary greatly from marriage to marriage and from time to time. Marital roles are shaped by at least four basic factors:

1. Historical setting (peace or war, economic and social conditions)
2. Socioeconomic level (affluent, comfortable, getting-by, poor)
3. Unforeseeable situations and special requirements (special expenses or extraordinary services needed in illness, etc., periods of unusual need or of unexpected affluence)
4. Personal aspirations (the wife's wish to continue her education, the husband's wish to change his career, etc.)

All or any of these factors influence what is expected of married people throughout their life together, Marital roles are dynamic and ever-changing in all but the most stable periods in history.

Traditional husband/wife roles

Throughout history, in most of the societies of the world, a man has been responsible for supporting his wife and children. The wife in turn has been expected to keep house, provide regular meals, and to care for children and other dependent members of the family. Throughout the centuries preceding our own, a woman needed a husband's support. A man had to have a wife to look after his household, prepare his food, bear his children, and serve as his companion, sex partner, and nurse. Today, however, many housekeeping and other services are commercially available.

Housewife/working husband roles are still preferred by millions of today's married couples. Many a girl has so internalized the homemaker role that she is interested in no other. From the time she played with dolls she has looked forward to having children and taking care of her family. A boy reared by a domestically inclined mother unconsciously looks for "a good old-fashioned girl" when he marries and is content to support her and their children as his part of the bargain, without question. Men and women college students still are found to hold traditional husband/wife attitudes—members of both sexes accepting a sharp division of labor in marital roles and assigning primary responsibility for home and childcare to the wife (Osmond and Martin 1975).

Some men are so career-oriented that they need full-time wives. Physicians, politicians, clergymen, and many small-businessmen count on their wives to keep house, rear the children, serve as hostess, take phone messages, keep the accounts, and help them fulfill their work schedules and obligations. Such a wife is not hard to find among the many women who still aspire to the status assured them by the husband's career. As a young woman with this outlook nears the age of marriage, her fear of success interferes with her academic progress (Horner 1971; Deckard 1975). Such a young woman would rather have a man's approval than his job. She prefers running his house to running her own life as an independent woman. In Israel today, the founding mothers look with disappointment at young women in the kibbutz. They thought they had modeled female independence and sexual equality for their daughters. They now look on with dismay as joy in domesticity replaces fierce interest in feminism (Hazleton 1976).

Millions of American women enjoy being homemakers. They find creative outlets in cooking, sewing, and decorating their homes, and take special pleasure in caring for their husbands and children. Three out of four say they find all the fulfillment they need in their homemaking. This is especially true of women with less than college-level education. But four out of five college-educated wives say that an outside job is *not* necessary to give a woman satisfaction. Few such wives (25 percent) want to switch jobs with their husbands except to help out in a pinch. The majority (52 percent) say they show their love for their husbands in the effort they put into family meals (*Better Homes and Gardens* 1972:21-27).

The money value of a housewife's production

The lifetime value of a wife's household production may exceed what a mother with children would earn in the labor force (Gage 1975:127). Calculating her home production at $2.20 an hour for an eight-hour day, a full-time mother of two to four children puts in over three thousand hours a year for a total estimated monetary value of more than seven thousand dollars a year (Walker 1973). At the going rate for her specific services, the Chase Manhattan Bank of New York observes that the typical wife fills 12 well-defined occupations worth a minumum of $257.53 a week, or $13,391.56 a year (Table 4-1).

The bank does not attempt to put a money value on the service performed by the wife in counseling a disturbed child or a depressed husband, in planning or administering the family's social life, in being the hostess for her husband's colleagues and for the couple's friends, or on the other complicated roles a wife and mother fills routinely. It goes without saying that the homemaker works overtime without question, plans her vacation with the family's interests in mind, has no retirement or sickness

Table 4-1
Money Value of Typical Housewife's Work, 1972 Dollars

Housewife's work	Hours/Week	Rate/Hour	Value/Week
Nursemaid	44.5	$2.00	$ 89.00
Housekeeper	17.5	3.25	56.88
Cook	13.1	3.25	42.58
Dishwasher	6.2	2.00	12.40
Laundress	5.9	2.50	14.75
Food buyer	3.3	3.50	11.55
Chauffeur	2.0	3.25	6.50
Gardener	2.3	3.00	6.90
Maintenance man	1.7	3.00	5.10
Seamstress	1.3	3.25	4.22
Dietician	1.2	4.50	5.40
Practical nurse	0.6	3.75	2.25
Total	99.6		$257.53

Source: The Chase Manhattan Bank of New York, quoted in Sylvia Porter, "Housewife: 12 Occupations," Syndicated column, February 14, 1972.

benefits, and is not covered by social security. Her compensation is her satisfaction in doing something she feels is important—maintaining a pleasant home, looking after her husband, rearing their children. These and other "fringe benefits" are not measured in dollars.

Women's emancipation and working wives

Women's emancipation took a giant leap in the second decade of the twentieth century with the appearance of the leaders of the birth control movement, of the militants who pushed through the right to vote for women, and of the freedom-loving Flappers who followed World War I. Fifty years later, medical advances in family planning and relaxed attitudes about childbearing freed women from involuntary motherhood. By 1974, the all-male Supreme Court had legalized the right of women to abortion. Birthrates and family size fell, and more and more wives and mothers worked to augment the family income.

The first objective of the United Nations proclamation declaring 1975 International Women's Year was "to achieve full equality before the law in all fields where it does not yet exist." Title IX of the Higher Education Act, approved by Congress in 1972, was implemented in July 1975 by the U.S. Department of Health, Education, and Welfare. This act requires all schools to end discrimination against girls and women in the areas of administration, financial aid, employment, vocational counseling, and athletics. Schools can no longer exclude students from classes or set separate curfews for females and males without losing federal aid. In 1975 the Rhodes Scholarship Trust for the first time allowed females to apply on an equal footing with men for the prestigious scholarships (Fiske 1975). The Equal Rights Amendment to the U.S. Constitution (now in the process of being ratified by the states) provides that "equality of rights under the law shall not be denied or abridged by the United States or by any state on account of sex."

Working wives and mothers

Since 1967 children have been entitled to benefits based without discrimination on the work records of either parent. In 1975, the Supreme Court ruled that widowed fathers were entitled to survivors' benefits on the same basis as widowed mothers. This decision provided women workers with the same survivors' insurance protection as men. This ruling further officially recognized the impact that loss of a mother's earnings can have on a family.

At least 40 percent of the civilian work force are women. Most wives work at least part of their adult lives. Most college girls plan to have both jobs and children, according to assessments made in two recent time intervals (Parelius 1975). The usual pattern is that a woman works until she marries and continues to work until her first child comes, at which time she may drop out of the labor market until her children are schoolagers. She then returns to work (part time or full time) as often as not until retirement. Marriage and the number of children she has are significantly related to the extent of a woman's gainful employment (Table 4-2).

Jobs and salaries available to working wives vary greatly. Some questions a mother may well ask before seeking employment outside the home include:

1. What her salable skills are worth in the labor market
2. How much it will cost to work: in lunches, transportation, higher tax bracket, clothing, replacement at home, etc.
3. What help she can count on for the necessary homemaking tasks
4. How her husband feels about her working
5. What effects her working may have on the children
6. What employment means to her as a person
7. What local jobs are available in her areas of competence

Working mothers still face five to six hours of housework and child-care at home after their working day on the job. A study of 1400 families in Syracuse, N.Y. finds that the time spent in housework is related to a mother's outside employment as well as to the number of children at home (Table 4-3).

Presumably the same household tasks are performed in the homes of both working and nonworking wives (marketing, care of children, food

Table 4-2
Worklife Expectancy and Lifetime Earnings of American Women
by Marital Status and Number of Children

Marriage and family status	Worklife expectancy in years	Lifetime earnings in stenographic jobs (1973 dollars)
Never married	45 years	
Married		
No children	35 years	$204,085
One child	25 years	145,781
Two children	22 years	128,282
Three children	20 years	116,620
Four or more children	17 years	99,127

Source: Elizabeth Waldman, "Changes in the Labor Force Activity of Women," *Monthly Labor Review*, vol. 93, June 1970, pp. 10–17 and M. Geraldine Gage, "Economic Roles of Wives and Family Economic Development," *Journal of Marriage and the Family*, vol. 37, no. 1, February 1975, pp. 121–128.

Table 4-3
Wives' Time Spent in Housework by Employment and Number of Children

Number of children	Not employed		Employed	
	Hrs./Day	Hrs./Year	Hrs./Day	Hrs./Year
0	5.7	2080	3.7	1351
1	7.4	2701	5.1	1862
2	8.4	3066	5.9	2154
3	8.1	2957	6.0	2190
4	9.0	3285	6.3	2299
All families	8.0	2680	5.3	1934

Source: Kathryn Walker, "Household Work Time: Its Implication for Family Decisions," *Journal of Home Economics*, vol. 65, no. 1, October 1973, p. 11.

preparation, cleaning, etc.). Working wives must become more efficient and enlist more help from others than full-time homemakers. Mothers in well-paid positions may hire outside help for some of the housework. Most working wives carry both their jobs and their homemaking responsibilities, with the help of their husbands and children. Husbands have few such problems because they usually do not consider homemaking their responsibility after "a hard day's work."

Wives earn less than husbands

Wives typically earn only half as much as their husbands, only partly because they work less for fewer years. The great difference in income of husbands and wives is due to a combination of factors—discrimination against women in the labor force, less specialized education and job experience, fewer opportunities for married women to work, family demands on wives and mothers, and negative attitudes on the part of members of the family and the community (Bernard 1975; Treiman and Terrell 1975). Men hold the most prestigious professional positions, as they always have. Professional women are employed largely as nurses, librarians, teachers, and social workers (Table 4-4).

Women workers are paid less than men, whatever the job. As full-time managers and administrators, they earn 58 percent of the amount that men in comparable positions are paid; as clerical workers, 65 percent; as professional and technical personnel, 73 percent. Between 1955 and 1975, some 17 million women joined the labor force, as compared with less than 12 million men. Yet women lagged further behind men in pay in the mid-1970s than they did in 1956 (U.S. Bureau of the Census and other agencies 1975).

Women work for the same reasons men do—to support themselves and their families. More than seven million of America's families are headed by women, up 44 percent between 1965 and 1975. By 1975, both husband and

Table 4-4
Men Dominate the Professions

Professions	Percentage of men			
	1940	1950	1960	1970
Architects	97.7	96.6	97.7	96.5
Lawyers and judges	97.6	96.7	96.2	95.2
Physicians and surgeons	95.4	93.8	93.0	90.8
Photographers	86.3	82.7	88.0	86.2
College presidents and faculty	73.5	76.8	78.1	71.6
Authors	63.9	61.2	74.4	70.7
Religious workers	25.4	30.4	37.5	44.3
Social and welfare workers	35.7	30.8	37.2	37.3
Teachers	24.3	25.4	28.3	29.8
Librarians	10.5	10.9	14.3	18.1
Nurses and student nurses	2.1	2.4	2.5	2.7

Source: U.S. Bureau of the Census data, adapted from J. Richard Udry, *The Social Context of Marriage* (Philadelphia, Pa.: J.B. Lippincott Company, 1974), Table 3-1, p. 31.

wife were working in the typical American family. The proportion of working wives had increased from 36 percent in 1950 to 49 percent in 1975 (UPI release 1976). Wives typically work to supplement their husbands' earnings, and to increase their opportunities for a new home, a new career, more education, or a better life for themselves and their children. A professional woman married to a man in the same profession is more apt to get her Ph.D. degree, to hold a better job, and to have a longer professional career than other professional women. Possibly this is because "the marital pair share cues, clues, opinions, etc. relevant to occcupational success" (Martin, Berry, and Jacobsen 1975:742).

Opportunities increase conjugal options

A greater number of better-paid positions are opening up for women. Between 1960 and 1970 women held 28.6 percent of the new jobs in management. Throughout the 1970s and 1980s women are expected to be hired for an even larger proportion of the 413,000 job openings for managers and administrators across the country. One hopeful sign is the greater number of coeds studying business administration. Dr. Martha Peterson, president of Barnard College, feels hopeful about the prospects of the growing numbers of women college graduates in schools of business, and she finds most companies earnest in their efforts to move women upward in the corporate hierarchy ("More Women to Become Executives" 1973).

More women are delaying marriage and continuing their education and professional training now than in the past. The number of female law students climbed from 4 percent in 1960 to 19 percent in 1974. In medicine, the number of women students rose from 6 to 18 percent; in optometry, from 1 to 10 percent; and in pharmacy, from 12 to 32 percent in the same period (U.S. Bureau of the Census and other federal agencies 1975). See also, "Women Graduate Students Increasing" (1975).

Conjugal options are increasing for both wives and husbands as opportunities for both sexes open up in education, work, and family life. No longer does a girl have to marry right out of high school, nor a boy before he has found himself. No longer is a woman expected to be "just a housewife," unless that is her preference. No longer is a man fully responsible as the sole provider for his wife and children, unless that is what he wants. As women are allowed more latitude in developing their talents outside and inside the home, men too have more freedom to choose the life styles they wish.

Men's liberation means more freedom for both partners

The liberation of women has bestowed on men some new freedoms that are often overlooked. No longer are males held so responsible for the girls they date, the young women they get involved with, or the wives they marry. Girls and women today are increasingly capable of taking care of themselves, and are thus less dependent on the men in their lives. Females increasingly take the initiative in their relationships with males at every age level in the personal, social, and sexual aspects of their lives. These new relationships free men from the "masculine mystique" that had forced them into the "macho" bind of acting tough and aggressive whether they felt that way or not.

As styles in femininity change, there is a parallel shift in patterns of masculinity (Komarovsky 1976). This may puzzle, even frighten, the man who is no longer sure of what is expected of him. The man who has had some experience in relating to autonomous women—one, for instance, who has grown up in a home with a capable working mother—is better prepared for the new options he now has. The man with a clear sense of his own identity often finds real challenge in the many alternatives open to him.

Options open to husbands today

A man today is free to choose whom he wishes as his wife, to marry when he is ready, to elect fatherhood or not, to relate to his wife as an equal partner or to cast her in roles with which he is more comfortable—often the conscious or unconscious basis of his mate selection in the first place. More husbands today feel that they can express their emotions openly without fear of losing face. They can be tender or tough as their mood dictates. They can discipline their children gently or with vigor. They can rave in anger or cuddle with compassion. They can lean at times on their wives' strength, or play the strong supportive role when that is appropriate. They no longer have to be the strong, silent father figures whose word was law. They are free to discuss and question, to argue and work for a consensus in family decisions. Such freedom is heady stuff, but for the man who can take it, it has its rewards.

Men are more at home in their own families now than they used to be. Do-it-yourself tools for households are a multimillion dollar business. Electric and electronic household equipment fascinates most men. Outdoor cooking has lured millions of husbands into experimentation with grilling, baking, and gourmet cookery. Men tend to have closer personal relationships with their wives and children than they did in the past. Their recreation often is with their families. Families travel millions of miles each year on vacation trips with Father at the wheel, often alternating with Mother as navigator. Family groups made up most of the 45 million Americans who visited national parks in 1975. Campus family programs bring parents and children together for play-study vacations. Cornell University, for instance, opened its ninth alumni season with 747 adults and 347 children from toddlers to teenagers enrolled in four one-week sessions (Dullea 1975:24). Many a husband joins his wife for additional courses in a local college either for enrichment or for career advancement or change. One such man says, "It would never have occurred to me to take a course in classical literature or in computer programming, but, so help me, my wife got so interested, I just had to tag along. Now I'm tooling up for a better position, all in the local adult education section of the public schools."

Husbands of working wives

Men react in a variety of ways to their wives' working. A man with a low self-image may resent his wife's job and be jealous of her earning capacity. Husbands who have had less education are less willing to share the housework than better-educated men (Farkas 1975). Women who live their lives entirely through their husbands boost the male ego for a while, but become burdensome in time. "Many a marriage is broken up when a man who in his younger years delighted in taking care of a highly dependent wife, eventually grows to resent her dependency and buckles under the strain in middle age" (Brenton 1966:54).

When a man's wife has to work to eke out the family budget, the husband may feel that this reflects on his competence as breadwinner. But the wife's working causes no strain in those families in which the woman has a free choice, according to studies in metropolitan areas across the country. Men whose wives work are relieved of the pressures that go with being the family's sole provider. When both spouses are working, they are freer to go out and eat at a restaurant, to attend sporting events, to entertain, and to travel as a family (Orden and Bradburn 1969). Occasionally one hears of a couple switching roles for a while. The wife brings home the paycheck while the husband goes back to school, prepares for another job, writes a book, or simply stays home as "househusband." How successful such role-reversal is depends on the versatility of the pair, who must now function in unfamiliar roles (McGrady 1976:13).

Many men feel that the time and effort their wives devote to volunteer work or to busy social schedules might just as well be spent working in paying jobs. More wives who work outside the home on a part-time basis report that their marriages are happy than do those who are employed full time or not at all. In general, husbands of working wives have more freedom, greater happiness, and more friends with whom to socialize. The researchers conclude that as better educational opportunities become available and as more women work, marriages will be more rewarding for both wives and husbands (Orden and Bradburn 1969:394).

Fathers in families where both parents work

Traditionally, men have been trapped in their jobs quite as much as women. With marriage they assumed a lifetime commitment to support their wives and children, and faced severe penalties if they defaulted. Their children arrived as a matter of course, and they accepted each additional mouth to feed as a duty, if not a joy. However tedious or humdrum their jobs might be they took the daily stint "like a man" year after year.

Family planning relieves a man of overwhelming burdens of child-support. The conscious choice of parenthood has set a new style of family living that allows both parents to choose from the many options open to them today. "The father may be delighted, indifferent, or annoyed at the idea of being a parent, and if he is not too enthralled there are often escape hatches through which he can keep his parental involvement to a minimum—longer hours at work, a second job to help with the increased expenses of rearing a family, or perhaps more time spent with his male peer group" (LeMasters 1970:146). He may turn to alcohol to assuage his distress, but when he drinks too much, his drinking is a strain on the family budget, the marriage suffers, his children are adversely affected, and their attitude toward him sours (Trice 1966). When a couple bring into the world only as many children as they feel they can care for, and when the wife works at least part-time, a father is under less strain.

Some jobs take a father away from his family for days or weeks at a time. Some fathers have irregular hours that limit their participation in the lives of their children. One study found that afternoon shift work is detrimental to the father-child relationship, whereas night shift work adversely affects a man's marriage (Mott 1975). Jobs with little intrinsic interest tend to make men look to their families as havens from boredom on the job. Their homes provide them with satisfactions they lack at work. They participate with their wives in rearing the children, and may take great interest in their growth and development. They often admire their wives' job competence and the ease with which they manage the household. Such positive attitudes make them more willing partners in childcare than might otherwise be the case.

Fathers make good parents, especially when they are active family participants. A Cornell University study compared father-absent with father-present children in the same junior high school. A father who interacted with his children helped to improve their attitudes toward school as well as their relationships with peers, parents, and siblings (Feldman and Feldman 1975). Children become attached to their fathers if they are able to spend time with them. Child development specialists say that a child does not need to be cared for by his mother all of the time; he profits from contact with others—especially his father (Freeman 1973; Green 1976; Bronfenbrenner 1973; Smart and Smart 1972: 559–568).

The quality of the husband/wife relationship is enhanced as both share in the care of the children and of the household. A man is free to relax and to enjoy his home when he has a helpmate on whom he can rely regardless of what happens. The wife-mother is under less strain when her husband is available as a partner in their family living. Whatever the options chosen by a particular pair, they are less likely to be shackled today by marriage roles they find inappropriate.

Marital power

A husband may dominate his wife or she may "wear the pants"; they may make decisions jointly, or each may exercise control in different areas. Husband/wife power is exercised by the one who is in charge, who controls the other person, and who is considered to have the right to make decisions affecting their lives. Power is "the ability of persons or groups to impose their will on others despite resistance through deterrence either in the forms of withholding regularly supplied rewards or in the form of punishment" (Blau 1964:117). According to Blau's exchange theory, the right to make decisions is related to the goods and services one contributes to the family. A husband who is a "good provider" tends to have high marital power, and his wife tends to follow his lead. When a man loses his job, some of the power he held is assumed by the outside agency that now supports his family; or by his wife who, when she gets a job, begins to have more to say about what happens to the family's money.

Wives of well-educated husbands in important, highly paid jobs tend to accept husband-dominance (Scanzoni 1976:318). An executive who is used to making decisions at the office continues to make them at home (Aldous 1969). In equalitarian marriages of equally competent persons power is shifted as conditions change. Either partner is able to take charge in a crisis and to help make the necessary decisions. Egalitarian marriages have a flexible power structure that facilitates power change and interchange (Bahr and Rollins 1971).

One spouse may have a high degree of control in one area and low control in another—the degree based on relative competence and commitment in a given role. Examining control in five family role areas, Bahr (1975) found that among 216 couples studied in a systematic random sample of parents of third graders, most agreed on which mate exercised authority in various family roles. They concurred that the husband was in control as provider and that the wife was the authority as housekeeper. Most of the couples assigned the children's socialization and recreational roles to both parents (Table 4-5).

Most American marriages are partnerships. According to a national probability sample of 2,502 families, 61 percent of the husbands and wives were "partners"; the other 39 percent were considered "macho" families. The macho group feels that it is important for the husband to be the main provider and decision-maker, and that wives should not work unless it is absolutely necessary. In over half the families surveyed, one spouse makes the major decisions about money. The financial decision-maker is twice as likely to be the husband as the wife, according to both spouses (Yankelovich, Skelly, and White 1975:78).

Lewis (1972) traced husband-wife power throughout the marriage, using as a standard Duvall's eight-stage family life cycle (Chapter 7). He found that husbands and wives held similar views on the decision-making power of wives throughout the marriage (Figure 4-1). This descriptive study further suggests that wives yearn not so much for more power vis-à-vis their husbands, as for more equalitarian decision-making in the marriage. Since wives are found to want to make more decisions, and husbands would like to make fewer than they do, increasingly equalitarian

Table 4-5
Couple Agreement on Authority by Family Roles

| Family role | Authority assigned to: | | | |
	Husband	Both equally	Wife	Total agreement
Child socialization	1%	75%	2%	78%
Child care	1	38	15	54
Provider	83	1	1	85
Housekeeper	0	1	85	86
Recreation	3	78	1	82

Source: Stephen J. Bahr, "Competence, Authority, and Conjugal Control," paper presented at Annual Meeting of the American Sociological Association, August 1975.

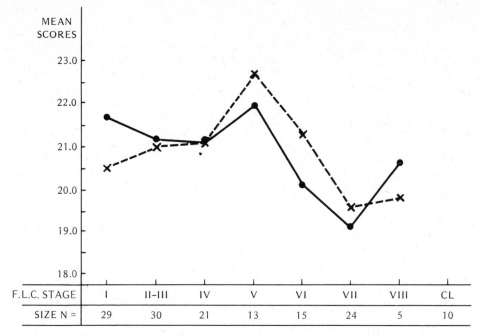

Figure 4-1

Perception of Wives' Decision-making by Husbands and Wives by Stage of the Family Life Cycle

F.L.C. STAGE	I	II–III	IV	V	VI	VII	VIII	CL
SIZE N =	29	30	21	13	15	24	5	10

LEGEND:

●——————● WIVES' PERCEPTIONS OF THEIR OWN DECISION-MAKING

✕－－－－✕ HUSBANDS' PERCEPTIONS OF THEIR WIVES' DECISION-MAKING

STAGE I	BEGINNING FAMILIES
STAGE II	CHILDBEARING
STAGE III	PRESCHOOL
STAGE IV	SCHOOL AGE
STAGE V	TEENAGERS
STAGE VI	LAUNCHING
STAGE VII	MIDDLE YEARS
STAGE VIII	AGING

CL CHILDLESS COUPLES

Source: Lewis, Robert A., "Satisfaction with Conjugal Power over the Family Life Cycle," paper presented at the National Council on Family Relations, Portland, Oregon, October 31, 1972.

marital decision-making might well reduce role strain and lead to more satisfying marriages (Lewis 1972).

Observing the interaction within family units consisting of husband, wife, and ninth grade child in a laboratory game situation, Kolb and Strauss (1974) counted the number of directive acts of each family member that resulted in change in behavior of the one to whom the act was directed. Some association was found between marital happiness (as evaluated by the ninth grader) and high husband power. "However, since low husband power was found to be associated with low problem-solving ability, part of the low happiness ratings of families with low-power husbands probably reflects dissatisfaction with competence rather than low power of the husbands" (Kolb and Strauss 1974:756).

Unemployed men tend to withdraw from their families, according to studies dating back to the Great Depression. The loss of his job may carry with it an added hardship for the husband/father—loss of status in the family. His importance as the breadwinner and his influence on the actions of his wife and children are challenged and diminished, especially if one or more of them, or some outside agency, takes over the support of the family. The father's role as provider is fundamental to his performance in other family roles (Cavan and Ranck 1938; Aldous 1969). Conversely, wives who work are less dependent on their husbands, usually less subservient, and more apt to assume greater power in the family.

Definitive studies of power in the family have yet to be made. At the present time, research projects are directed mainly to conceptual, theoretical, and methodological issues in the study of family power (Cromwell and Olson 1975; Turk and Bell 1972). It is wise to conclude only that husband-wife power varies greatly from marriage to marriage. From time to time within a given marriage one spouse may have the greater power, depending on his or her relative competence, the area of life in which the decision is being made, the time and emotion invested in the issue, and the way in which the pair view their marital options.

Growing acceptance of conjugal options

Throughout the twentieth century the movement away from the traditional gender roles and toward more open conjugal options has been gaining momentum (Table 4-6). As more and more women took jobs outside the home, members of both sexes came to recognize and accept the reality of the situation. Husbands whose wives worked and men who had grown up with working mothers could respond more positively to the idea of women's equality (Axelson 1963; Meier 1972). Husband-wife partnership in the home, on the job, and in the marketplace became widely accepted.

Surveys find that high school and college students as well as adults have swung away from traditional attitudes toward more varied options for members of both sexes. Between 1967 and 1973, percentages of male and female college freshmen who believed that women should be restricted to the career of home and family dropped significantly each year (Table 4-7). Graduating seniors in 1971, who had entered college in 1967, had

Table 4-6
Trend Toward More Open Options in Marriage

From traditional marital roles	Toward more open conjugal options
Husband dominant, wife submissive	Potential marital partnership
Rigid assignment of wives to housework and husbands to provider roles	Wives free to work as pair decide; men more at home with their families
Few wives in prestigious positions and paid less than husbands	Equality of compensation on the basis of merit advocated
Sex stereotyping restrictions on personal choices	Members of both sexes develop talents and interests with less stigma
Girls encouraged to marry early, and boys to compete for success	Both sexes encouraged in educational, social, and economic fields
Babies come "at the will of God"	Pregnancies planned by responsible parents
Abortions illegal	Legal right to limit children to those who can be loved and cared for
Childcare the mother's role; child support the father's	Child-rearing mutually assumed responsibility of both parents
Romanticism involves young of both sexes, often prematurely	Love developed in lasting relationships fosters maturity
Divorce is seen as failure	Marriage can be dissolved without guilt
Alimony is expected and accepted	Alimony is questioned as unfair to both
Anger is repressed by females, and tenderness by males	Honest expression of feelings increases understanding and empathy
Discrimination on the basis of gender widely practiced	Sexism decried as deprivation of rights and opportunities of both sexes

Table 4-7
Fewer Freshmen See Wives' Place Solely in the Home

Nationwide Surveys in 4 Recent Years (Acceptance of the statement, "The activities of married women are best confined to the home and family.")

	1967	1970	1971	1972
Freshmen men	61%	50%	43%	39%
Freshmen women	38	28	23	18

Source: American Council on Education Annual National Surveys of College Freshmen, 1967, 1970, 1971, 1972.

become even more equalitarian in their views, but 24 percent of the men and 11 percent of the senior women believed that women's place was solely in the home (Bayer, Royer, and Webb 1973).

Studies on one college campus found that: (1) 94 percent of the senior women felt that women should be allowed to compete for any job they wish; (2) 76 percent believed that men and women were equally competent except in physical strength; (3) 67 percent would advise women to try for the best jobs they could get even though it meant earning more than their husbands; and (4) 51 percent considered husbands and wives to be equally responsible for supporting the family (Parelius 1974).

Nationwide surveys of outstanding high school students in 1974 showed that the majority of teenagers of both sexes believed that husbands and working wives should share equally in household responsibilities (Educational Communications 1975). In response to a 1975 mail survey of families throughout the nation, 57 percent of the men queried reported that they regularly helped with the housework. By contrast, a similar survey in 1970 had shown that only 38 percent of the men responding were willing to admit to lending a helping hand around the house ("Taking Homemakers' Pulses" 1975:2).

The 340,374 readers of *Better Homes and Gardens* who responded to a poll by that magazine might well have been expected to endorse traditional roles. But even among this group, 79 percent said that the dominant role of the American husband is declining in importance; 64 percent of the men felt that a husband should share responsibility for cooking and cleaning up; 91 percent of these middle-Americans believed that children should be planned; and 85 percent of the men and women felt that improved birth control methods had contributed to better sexual adjustment in marriage. The editors conclude, "One thing is clear from the above findings: the American family is far from static. Much is happening to change the goals and values on which family life is built. The ways family members relate to each other—and the expectations they have—also are changing" (Better Homes and Gardens 1972:4).

Effects of increasing marital options

Men and women have never had more options than they do today. They may marry when they will and as they wish, with few to praise or blame them. They may select from an assortment of life styles the one that best suits them. They enjoy new freedom in the expression of love and sex, of gentleness and joy, of real feelings and candid opinions. A wide variety of relationships is available to them, both before and after marriage. They have the benefit of recent shifts of power in the family and community. They may have children or not, may bear or adopt and rear as many children, or as few, as they wish, at the times that suit them best. They can stay married for the rest of their lives—or leave when marriage no longer satisfies with less guilt and sense of failure than ever before. The potential satisfactions of marriage and family life have never been greater for the millions of men and women ready for them.

Yet, such great freedom to live as one chooses is a mixed blessing. Confusion and anxiety about what is expected of a man or woman, husband or wife, father or mother abound when marital roles are no longer clearly defined. The societal controls that traditionally limited an individual's opportunities also provided protection from abandonment, exploitation, or other serious damage. Because of more flexible marital roles it is possible for a person of either sex to act impulsively in ways that can endanger himself and others. Experiments in unconventional sexual behavior, drug use, gang "families", and other forms of deviancy tend to be unrewarding personally and harmful to marital and social relationships. On the other hand, there are more opportunities now to develop one's talents, to continue one's education, and to train or retrain for a promising career than have ever before existed for men and for women, for husbands and for wives.

When divorce is easy, a potentially good marriage can be broken in one impetuous moment—or a potentially tragic marriage can be ended before the couple is destroyed by it. A husband may no longer assume that his wife will accept a subservient role, now that she is free to develop herself and become more mature and self-supporting on her own. A wife no longer can expect that she has a meal ticket for life when she marries, so she is wise to prepare herself for autonomy and independence both before and after she marries. Questions arising out of today's uncertainty about marital roles are currently causing distress and discussion in marriages. The outcome may well be a greater number of divorces and also of strong marriages, depending on how well married couples handle their many marital options.

On balance, the family profits from more open conjugal options. Families are not the stable, secure cocoons they once purportedly were. Today's families are dynamic, changing, adapting to the realities of life within and outside themselves. This approach demands courage and maturity, but the rewards to the individual and to the whole family unit outweigh the difficulties involved (Table 4-8).

When viewed in a broad social context, the multiple options now available in marriage, family life, and the world beyond the family, are seen as potentials that will in fact be realized only by some individuals. "As societies modernize, societal complexity increases, the more options are available for work, leisure, group association, membership, health care and education. The mere presence of options, however, does not necessarily mean that individual members of societies have equal access to them" (Cogswell and Sussman 1974:23).

Many are deprived of options that others enjoy in modern communities. Unrest, protest, disappointment, and despair continue among the lonely, the disadvantaged, and the personally handicapped. Happiness has never been a universal right, but the pursuit of happiness continues to be part of the American dream.

More options mean greater possibilities for pain and for pleasure, for challenge and for commitment to a way of life that has been personally chosen, for as long as it is valued. When the potentials implicit in modern

Table 4-8
Family Benefits in Flexibility of Husband-Wife Roles

1. Family income increased with two pay checks
2. Husband under less strain with wife's help as provider
3. Wife less isolated as husband and children share homemaking
4. Husband-wife enjoyment greater as wife's interests expand
5. Wife's growth as a person increases her satisfaction and fulfillment
6. Family horizons broadened as more members become active in community
7. Husband-wife communication enhanced by more shared decisions
8. Children enriched by increased exposure to life around them
9. More democratic child-rearing methods with both parents involved
10. Mother's outside interests encourage children's growth
11. Children less indulged when given more family responsibilities
12. More family recreation with higher standard of living
13. Whole-family activities raise family morale and interaction
14. Improved ability to cope with change as marital roles overlap
15. More acceptable divorce frees miserable mates from poor marriage bonds
16. Increased remarriage possibilities encourage rebuilt marriages
17. More education for girls and women develops more latent talent
18. Fewer wives entirely dependent on husbands' support and life style
19. More autonomy and mature interaction possible in marriage
20. Fewer poor marriages as options increase
21. Later age at marriage related to marital success
22. More husbands free to train for first and second careers
23. Increased opportunities for personal, marital, and family development
24. Control and power decentralized on the basis of family member competence

marriage are realized to the full, the horizons of family life can be expanded far beyond their present limits. The way in which marital options are exercised can determine, in large measure, the outcome of a marriage—and of a life. Multiply the one by millions, and the future of family life in America is being shaped.

Inferiors revolt in order that they may be equal, and equals that they may be superior.

Aristotle

E thnic, racial, and social class differences

chapter five

Families from all of the world's continents and from the islands of the seven seas have come to live in the United States in wave after wave of migration over hundreds of years. They brought with them their own cultures, histories, and life-styles, which are still reflected in their families today. There is no such thing as *the American family*—only families of many backgrounds, each different from the others in discernible, fascinating ways.

Difference is desirable

Efforts at Americanization have helped newcomers acquire the knowledge, language, and skills they need to become productive citizens. But the melting pot produces an amalgam of different elements, not a homogeneous mass. Many families and cultural groups remain distinguishable entities in the crucible for one of four or more reasons:

1. Family pride
2. Apartness by cultural preference
3. Maintenance of identity
4. Involuntary separation

Pride in family line traced back through generations accounts for the solidarity of many old families (Malloy 1976). Apartness by preference is observed in the orthodox Jewish family, the Amish, many Asians, and to some extent in the American Indian. A school board member of a Navaho reservation is quoted as saying, "We want our children to be proud of being Navajos. We want them to know who they are. . . In the future they will have to be able to make many choices and do many different things. They need a modern education to make their way, but they have to know both worlds—and being Navajo will give them strength" (Fuchs and Havighurst 1972:246).

By maintaining a sense of their own identity, many foreign-born American citizens strengthen their own families and the nation as a whole. "More and more, I think in family terms. . .The differences implicit in being Slovak, and Catholic, and lower-middle class seem more and more important to me. Perhaps it is too much to try to speak to all peoples in this very various nation of ours. . . (but) by each of us becoming more profoundly what we are, we shall find greater unity in those depths in which unity irradiates diversity, than by attempting through the artifices of the American 'melting pot' and the cultural religion of science to become what we are not" (Novak 1971:50). The separatist movements and some of the communes on the current scene (Chapter 6) are further evidence of the clustering together of ethnic and racial groups.

The involuntarily separate tend to be those who have been the victims of discrimination and inequities in their struggle for a good life. For instance, Jews tend to be concentrated in cities, and to work at traditionally urban occupations—notably as small merchants and as professionals. They tend to be familistic, with close ties to kinfolk, to whom they look for security. When interviewed, 17 out of 20 Jewish wives in a Chicago suburb said that if anything happened to them, they would want their children to be reared by relatives (Winch, forthcoming: Chap. 2).

In solidarity there is strength

Many minority familes are disadvantaged economically, educationally, culturally, and politically. The inner city has been the scene of the struggle for equality by blacks and Spanish Americans in recent years. It is the hub of a wheel the spokes of which are action programs that fight for civil rights and racial justice, make "war on poverty," do battle for fair employment practices, and demand equal education for all. The impetus for the riots of the 1960s and 1970s was a surge of strength that grew out of a new awareness of racial solidarity and of a collective yearning for equal opportunity.

The walls of segregation crumbled noticeably between the mid-1960s and the mid-1970s when there was more frequent cross-racial contact in neighborhoods, schools, working places, and among friends. The number of whites who favored "strict segregation" declined from about one-quarter to one-tenth of those interviewed between 1964 and 1974. The number who felt that blacks should have the right to move into any neighborhood they could afford increased from 65 to 87 percent in that decade (Institute for Social Research 1975).

Millions are minorities

The majority of Americans are members of minority groups, in terms of privilege and power. The largest "minority" are females, who outnumber males by more than five million (108,455,000 vs 103,454,000), and yet are disadvantaged in many areas of life. Blacks and other nonwhites, who make up 13 percent of the total population (U.S. Bureau of the Census September 1974), grow in numbers and proportion with each succeeding decade. In the 1950s, immigrants accounted for 11 percent of the total population (1 in every 9 additional Americans); in the 1960s, for 16 percent (1 in every 6 additional Americans); in the 1970s immigrants contributed 21 percent, or 1 in every 5 new Americans. Between 1965 and 1975, the number of newcomers from Asia increased by 532 percent; from southern and eastern Europe by 53 percent; and from Latin America (especially Mexico and the West Indies) by 39 percent (U.S. Immigration and Naturalization Service 1975). Newcomers tend to settle near people of similar language and culture, usually in inner city ghettos where living conditions are poor and choices are limited. Those with special talents in sports, music, and other fields who "get the breaks" advance rapidly; most remain in lower socioeconomic levels.

Family social class

Social class position influences every facet of family life. Few other factors are so potent in determining where a family lives—and on what—what its members do, how much education they get, and how they fare generally. A child at birth is assigned a place in society according to the social status of his parents. He may remain in that social class, or he may become upward-mobile or downward-mobile from his original status.

Occupational prestige is the best indicator of a family's social status in modern industrial societies (Sewell, Haller, and Ohlendorf 1970; and Otto 1975). Other important factors are education, income, neighborhood, and religious and social affiliations. Most Americans (52 percent) consider themselves middle-class; another 41 percent say they are "working-class"; 4 percent lower-class; and 2 percent place themselves in the upper-class (Wattenberg 1974:57).

Families who have similar life styles, who have entrée into the same social circles, and who accept each other as equals, are generally of the same social class. A family is usually aware of its status in the community. It identifies others as having similar ("our kind of folks"), higher ("better than we are"), or lower ("not the kind of people we associate with") social class status. These social class positions are well known; in recent years they have been studied widely.

The quality of life is better at the higher social status levels, where more education, better jobs, and higher levels of income provide what Americans think of as "the good life." The incomes of some well-educated people (nurses, social workers, missionaries) are lower than those of some people who prosper with little schooling (entrepreneurs and those with exceptional talents for "making it"), as researchers point out (Andrews and Withey 1976). But, in general, families differ by status levels in ways listed in Table 5-1.

Table 5-1
Social Class Differences in Marriage and Family Life

Distinguishing factors	Lower-class	Middle-class	Upper-class
Where most live	Inner cities	Suburbs	Exclusive areas in exurbia
Space occupied	Small, crowded	Comfortable	Luxurious
What they live on	Wages, welfare	Salaries	Investments and salaries
What they do	Manual work	Business and professional	Administrative and executive positions
Who works for money	Husband and/or wife	Husband and often wife, too	Husband
Education	Gradeschool, highschool	College, plus	Prep schools and best colleges
Family size	Large	Small	Small units in kin network
Marriage, usually	Poor/good	Satisfying	Varies widely
Instability patterns	Desertion, divorce	Separation, divorce	Annulment, separation, divorce
Conjugal power	Male in some; female in black	Egalitarian	Male
Leisure	Sex-segregated (television)	Joint interests (community)	Separate and joint (clubs, trips)
Reading	Little	Books, magazines newspapers	Varies widely

Sources: References for Chapter 5.

Poor nonwhites

More nonwhites than whites are disadvantaged. Blacks, Spanish-speaking migrants from Latin America, and Asian newcomers crowd big city ghettos where living conditions are poor and unemployment is high (Laufer and Bengston 1974). Years ago Moynihan warned that the problems of blacks were compounded by the rapid growth of their population. As a rule, black women start bearing children at an earlier age and have larger families than whites. There are proportionally more unwed black mothers, many of whom rear their children without husbands. This leads, Moynihan said, to "an unconcealable crisis in Negro unemployment," so that the cycle of poverty and disadvantage continues (Moynihan 1965).

Absence of the husband-father is usually associated with poverty and with the unemployment and underemployment of males. Under existing economic conditions, the amount of money that a man is able to contribute to the family's support often cannot equal the amount available in welfare payments to mothers and children. Thus, when a poor young black woman becomes pregnant she finds more security for her baby and for herself in her parental home than she could expect from marrying the baby's father (Stack 1974). Barely half (50.7 percent) of black children live with two parents, in contrast to the 86.7 percent of white children who have this advantage (U.S. Bureau of the Census March 1974; Carter and Glick 1976:416–419).

"It appears that where conditions are unfavorable for the establishment of the nuclear triad (father-mother-child), the standby arrangement is the maternal consanguine family, which is able to function stably and reasonably efficiently under such adverse circumstances" (Winch, forthcoming: 8–14). The poor black family headed by the mother is not manless so much because it is black as because it is poor.

Minority workers find it hard to get work during an economic slowdown, and the jobs they do find pay less than those held by whites. When business slowed down in the 1970s unemployment rates rose faster among black workers than among whites, until by 1975 black unemployment was double that of whites (Table 5-2).

The jobless rate for workers of Spanish origin is consistently lower than that of blacks. Both black and Spanish workers are in occupations that characteristically have high unemployment rates, Table 5-3.

Advancement is slower for blacks than for white workers. Comparing workers of both races over fifteen years of their work experience, one study found that fewer blacks had jobs and that fewer of those employed advanced to more prestigious positions than did white workers. Great disparities exist in the opportunities open to the two races in terms of advancement or of changing jobs (Sørensen 1975).

Table 5-2
Unemployment Rates Among Blacks and Whites

	Percentage of workers unemployed	
	1970	1974
Blacks	8.2%	12.8%
Whites	4.5	6.4

Source: U.S. Bureau of the Census, "Social and Economic Status of the Black Population," quoted in "How Blacks Are Faring: Latest Official Report," *U.S. News & World Report*, August 11, 1975, p. 27; and Paul O. Flaim; Thomas F. Bradshaw; and Curtis L. Gilroy, "Employment and Unemployment in 1974," *Monthly Labor Review*, February 1975, pp. 3–14.

Table 5-3
Jobs of White, Black, and Spanish-origin Workers by Major Occupation Groups, 1974

Occupation	Percent distribution			
	Total	White	Black	Spanish origin*
White-collar workers	48.6%	50.6%	28.9%	31.5%
Professional and technical	14.4	14.8	8.8	7.0
Managers and administrators, except farmers	10.4	11.2	3.4	5.7
Sales workers	6.3	6.8	1.9	3.5
Clerical workers	17.5	17.8	14.8	15.3
Blue-collar workers	34.7	33.9	42.1	47.6
Craft and kindred workers	13.4	13.8	9.5	12.4
Operatives	16.2	15.5	23.2	26.7
Nonfarm laborers	5.1	4.6	9.4	8.5
Service workers	13.2	12.0	26.3	16.5
Farm workers	3.5	3.6	2.8	4.5
Total percent	100.0	100.0	100.0	100.0
Total number employed (thousands)	85,936	76,620	8,112	3,609

Source: Paul O. Flaim; Thomas F. Bradshaw; and Curtis L. Gilroy, "Employment and Unemployment in 1974," Monthly Labor Review, February 1975, reprinted in *Special Labor Force Report* 178 (Washington, D.C.: U.S. Department of Labor, Bureau of Labor Statistics, 1975), p. 13.
*Data on persons of Spanish origin are tabulated separately regardless of race or color, which means that persons included in this group are also included in the totals for both white and negro workers. According to the 1970 census, approximately 98 percent of the Spanish-origin population was white.

Differences in family incomes

Earnings comprise the largest source of family income. In one recent year, a third of all families in the United States reported that their only source of income was from earnings (wages, salaries and/or self-employment income). More than half (56 percent) had other types of income in addition to their earnings, in the form of interest, dividends, unemployment compensation, pensions, and social security. The remaining 11 percent reported income only from nonearned sources, such as investments among the well-to-do and government benefits for those in need (U.S. Bureau of the Census January 1975).

Husband-wife families have higher median incomes than others, mainly because in many cases both spouses are working. Wives' earnings are an important source of income, especially for black families. Thirty-one percent of the income of black families is earned by wives, whereas only 25 percent of the family income is earned by white wives. Even so, black husband-wife families have median incomes amounting to only 73 percent of those of comparable white families (U.S. Bureau of the Census January, 1975:5).

The rich and the poor

Family incomes have increased over the past quarter century, those of rich families most of all. Figure 5-1 shows graphically that between 1947 and 1973 family incomes of the poor rose moderately in comparison with the steep angle of increase recorded by the top 5 percent of families. Translating these data into percentages: the top 5 percent of America's families get 15.5 percent of the aggregate income, while all families below the median family income ($12,050 in 1973) receive 25 percent. The highest fifth of all families get 41.1 percent; the next to the top fifth receive 17.5 percent; the next to the bottom fifth receive 11.9 percent; while the lowest fifth of families ranked by size of their 1973 income get 5.5 percent of the aggregate money income of all families. Among those who have not benefited from recent economic gains are many members of minority groups, families headed by females, the elderly who live on income from social security and inadequate pensions, and the poorly educated.

Gross inequities afflict the poor, the inner cities where they are concentrated, and the entire society. As one social worker says, "A significant proportion of the United States lives in various conditions of poverty, ranging from dire poverty to relative deprivation. A vastly larger proportion lives in affluence ranging from moderate comfort to extreme wealth. From a humanistic viewpoint, the extremes are grossly unjust. A more hardheaded consideration suggests that the situation endangers the social, economic, and political well-being of all of us who live in our technological, highly inter-dependent society" (Levin 1975:312).

Differences between the rich and the poor can be seen in the discretionary income available for what they *want* as well as for what they *need*. One study of census data and of consumer expenditures prepared by the Bureau of Labor Statistics found that families of four with annual incomes under $6,000 have no money for anything but their essential needs. A four-member family with an annual income of $9,000 has about $1,000 discretionary income, enough for a color television and a short camping trip. Four-person families with incomes over $25,000 a year have some $16,091 to spend as they wish (Wattenberg 1974:54).

A man's economic condition is reflected in his marriage status. Men between the ages of 45 and 54 who earn a good income are more likely to be married than are those whose earnings are meager in the middle years of life. Men with "everything going for them" in terms of good education, jobs, and income were nearly all married at the time of the last census. This was true for both whites (95.4 percent) and blacks (91.6 percent). At the lower end of the socioeconomic ladder, significantly fewer men in the 45 to 54 year age range of their race were married—76.8 percent of the white men and 79.5 of the black men (Carter and Glick 1976:404–405).

The massive middle class

Most American families are neither extremely rich nor very poor. Until a few generations ago, most people struggled to make ends meet, and only a few at the top got rich. Now, 58 percent of our households have annual incomes over $10,000. After discounting the effects of inflation, real family income doubled in one generation—a remarkable financial improvement in which most families participated. The United States today is predominately a middle-class society with resources unknown to millions in the underdeveloped world.

In countries where the masses of people are very poor, with a few very wealthy families at the top, there is chronic poverty and underdevelopment. Only when a strong middle class emerges is there real personal, social, and economic progress. The large and growing American middle class has been denigrated in the recent struggle for equal opportunity and civil rights. The "Establishment"—the target of many militant groups—is largely middle class in developed countries. It is the middle class whose vision and industry have made possible economic progress, scientific achievements, and the many aspects of the society that moderns think of as personal and national development. The middle class is the burden-bearer of the culture. Middle-class men and women build, maintain, and staff the nation's schools, churches, youth-serving agencies, professions, and to a large extent its art and culture, through their support of theater, concert hall, opera house, art gallery, museum, and library.

Splinter groups of alienated middle-class youth (Keniston 1968) occasionally rebel from what they see as middle-class materialism and hypocrisy and demand immediate solutions to the age-old problems of poverty and inequality. Student uprisings have occurred throughout the centuries and around the world (Feuer 1969; Hechinger and Hechinger 1975). At times, small minorities of American middle-class youth

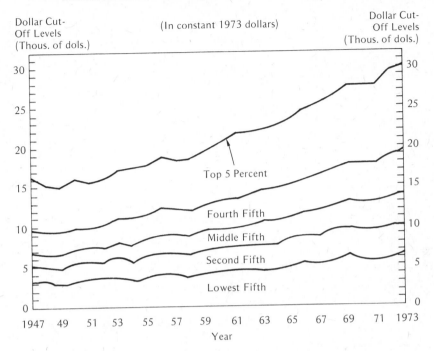

Figure 5-1

Incomes for Each Fifth and Top Five Percent of Families, 1947–1973

Dollar Cut-
Off Levels
(Thous. of dols.)

(In constant 1973 dollars)

Dollar Cut-
Off Levels
(Thous. of dols.)

Top 5 Percent

Fourth Fifth

Middle Fifth

Second Fifth

Lowest Fifth

Year

Source: U.S. Bureau of the Census, "Money Income in 1973 of Families and Persons in the United States," *Current Population Reports*, Series P-20, no. 97, January 1975 (cover).

repudiate their society, but the overwhelming tendency is for the young to support the way of life they have learned in their families, more of which belong to the middle class with each succeeding generation.

The narrowing education gap

The gap between levels of education reached by members of the black and white races in America is rapidly closing. If the proportion of those who have completed high school continues to increase at a higher rate for blacks than for whites, it may not be long before the racial gap in high school attainment is closed (Gatlin 1974:2). Figure 5-2 shows the increase since 1940 in percentages of persons completing high school, with the curves for blacks steeper than those for whites, especially since 1970.

A larger percentage of blacks than of whites were enrolled in 1974 than were in 1970 at all levels of education from kindergarten through college. The four-year increase in the number of black college students is

Ethnic, racial, and social class differences   97

Figure 5-2
Percent of Persons Who Have Completed High School, by Race and Sex: 1940-1974;
25 to 34 Year-olds

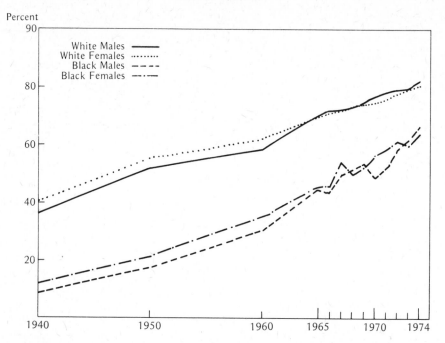

Source: U.S. Bureau of the Census, "Educational Attainment in the United States," *Current Population Reports*, Series P-20, no. 274, December 1974, p. 3.

especially noteworthy—male students 66.8 percent and female students 45.7 percent (Table 5-4).

Americans of Spanish origin do not fare so well in the educational system. "The median educational attainment of labor force members of Spanish background is lower than that of all persons. A much higher proportion of Spanish American workers had completed no more than elementary school—35 percent compared with 13 percent of all workers. At the other end of the spectrum, about 45 percent of the Spanish workers had completed four years or more of high school, including 6 percent who were college graduates—much smaller proportions than for all workers" (McEaddy 1975:64).

Many Spanish-speaking Americans are migrant workers who follow the ripening crops north each season. The geographical mobility of these families is detrimental to the education of their children. When a child is frequently uprooted he has no time to adjust to any one school. His is a hand-to-mouth world that offers little to look forward to in the future (Coles 1970).

Table 5-4
School Enrollment of the Population 3 to 34 Years Old by Level of
School and Race: October 1974 and October 1970

Level of school and race	(Numbers in thousands. Civilian noninstitutional population)		
	1974	1970	Percent change, 1970 to 1974
All Races			
Total enrolled	60,259	60,357	-0.2
Nursery school	1,607	1,096	46.6
Kindergarten	3,252	3,183	2.2
Elementary school	31,126	33,950	-8.3
High school	15,447	14,715	5.0
College	8,827	7,413	19.1
Male	[1]4,926	4,401	11.9
Female	[1]3,901	3,013	29.5
White			
Total enrolled	50,992	51,719	-1.4
Nursery school	1,340	893	50.1
Kindergarten	2,745	2,706	1.4
Elementary school	26,051	28,638	-9.0
High school	13,073	12,723	2.8
College	7,781	6,759	15.1
Male	4,367	4,066	7.4
Female	3,413	2,693	26.7
Negro			
Total enrolled	8,215	7,829	4.9
Nursery school	227	178	27.5
Kindergarten	463	426	8.7
Elementary school	4,585	4,868	-5.8
High school	2,125	1,834	15.9
College	814	522	55.9
Male	422	253	66.8
Female	392	269	45.7

[1]In addition 1,025,000 persons 35 years old and over were enrolled in college, including 476,000 males and 548,000 females.
Source: U.S. Bureau of the Census, *Current Population Reports*, Series P-20, No. 278., in "Population Profile of the United States: 1974," *Current Population Reports*, Series p-20, No. 279, March 1975, p. 15.

Educational aspirations of minorities

Many young people from minority groups are highly motivated to get a good education. A nationwide study of adolescent boys concludes that "black students'. . .aspirations are often found to be relatively higher than those of whites" (Bachman 1970:6). Ghetto blacks have many of the

Ethnic, racial, and social class differences   99

same goals and aspirations as middle-class whites, so their frustration is great when their opportunities are limited (Rainwater 1970; Dornbusch, Massey, and Scott 1975:48).

Does education mean more income?

This is a chicken and egg question: does education go with affluent family life-style—or does education lead to better jobs with more income—or both? One syndicated writer points out that the higher the family income, the higher the educational level; and she has the statistics to prove it. Only 20 percent of below-average income household heads have had any college education; 40 percent of those earning $15,000–$25,000 have had some college education; 45 percent of those in the $25,000–$50,000 bracket have college degrees; and "among the rich, an exceptionally high 54 percent of all household heads have college degrees and 90 percent are white-collar workers. You can't miss it! The tie is undeniable. The message is clear" (Porter 1975:6).

Other students of the question say that it is not quite that simple. Catherine Chilman writes, "An overly simplistic assumption was made that because poor people were especially apt to have little education, then more education would lead to more income. . . . A high level of education is only one of a complex of factors that leads to employment. The nation's general push for higher levels of educational achievement for the total population during the sixties and early seventies has resulted in a surplus of youth with advanced training. . .educational enrichment programs, alone, cannot significantly prevent or reduce poverty. . .nor can they importantly promote the intellectual and educational development of those people whose lives are severely disrupted by the ravages of poverty and environment" (Chilman 1975:58; see also Jencks 1972).

Family factors in children's education

The socioeconomic level of a child's family has a pervasive influence on a child's development. Poor family background in terms of slum neighborhoods, broken homes, and low or sporadic family income prevents many children from completing their schooling. A child of a working-class family may receive little help or encouragement at home. He may feel rejected by his middle-class teacher who he feels does not understand a lower-class child. Middle-class families' insistent pressure on their children to form good work habits and to advance in school makes middle-class children work harder than do children from less privileged families (Davis 1951:87).

The better a boy's relationship with his parents, the higher his self-esteem, his self-concept as a good student, his social values, his faith in others, and his trust in government. Poor family relations are related to more aggressive impulses, delinquency, rebellious behavior in school, test anxiety, negative school attitudes, and other problems (Bachman 1970:3,6).

Lower-class children are not as socially acceptable as are their middle-class classmates. Minority children are less often chosen as friends even by children of their own social class. Middle-class children in the fifth and sixth grades are considered better-looking than their lower-class classmates in significant percentages (Neugarten 1943). Distinctions based on social class and racial group are felt by these children throughout the first two decades of their lives and influence the way they feel, as young people, about school and about themselves. Parents who value achievement both for themselves and for their children encourage their children's academic success by their teaching and example in the areas of reading, learning, questioning, exploring, discussing, and problem-solving, as well as by their direct interest in school work. These are all practices difficult for poverty-stricken parents whose constricted lives foster apathy or discouragement, and whose negative memories of schooling lead to distrust of the school system (Chilman 1966:42–43).

A recent analysis of the 1966 Coleman Report of data on 570,000 students in 4,000 schools reaffirms its central finding that academic achievement depends far more on family background than on what happens in the classroom. Differences in early childhood learning caused by varied home backgrounds are so crucially important that improving the jobs and incomes of lower-class blacks may do more to raise the levels of their children's educational achievement than spending more on schools or integration (Mosteller and Moynihan 1972).

Social class difference in child-rearing

Studies over the years have shown that significant differences exist in the ways parents of different social classes see themselves and their children. Working-class mothers and fathers hold more traditional conceptions of parenthood than do middle-class parents, among whom the concept of developmentalism is more widely accepted (Chapter 3). Some reasons for this, suggested years ago, may be that "traditional conceptions of parenthood remain in the lower-middle and upper-lower class levels, where recent migration, household drudgery, cramped living, and infrequency of opportunity to meet other modes of adjustment keep both parents and children in line with traditional concepts of role. The effort to achieve respectability so evident in the two lower class levels and among minority racial groups tends further to perpetuate conformity" (Duvall 1946: 202–203).

Families of minority ethnic and racial groups tend to enjoy their children and to believe them to be an asset. One study found that 70 percent of the black, 58 percent of the Chicano, and only 28 percent of the white parents who were questioned felt that their children contributed to their marital stability (Heath, Roper, and King 1974). Higher proportions of black than of white high school students report:

1. Above average closeness to their mothers
2. Frequent praise during childhood
3. Most affection from their mothers
4. Freedom to talk with parents
5. Less influence and disciplinary control wielded by their fathers (Stinnett, Talley, and Walters 1973). Fatherlessness is the plight of roughly half of all black children in the United States (Malloy 1975:1). Many parents without partners do a good job of child-rearing, but harassed mothers without husbands and with a brood of children to support can be overwhelmed in the perpetual battle with poverty that characterizes their effort to survive.

Child-rearing is difficult in poor families

Impoverished parents love their children and would like to care for them as well as other families do, in many cases. But all too often poor families cannot feed, clothe, or educate their children as they would like. Overburdened mothers are worn out by and discouraged fathers often flee their day-to-day struggle to provide the bare essentials for survival, their crowded living conditions, and their crime-ridden neighborhoods.

Chilman's searching analysis of vast amounts of data on child-rearing shows that it is extremely difficult for very poor families to bring up their children in ways conducive to healthy personality development (Table 5–5). Children reared in conditions of poverty are more likely than others to be undereducated and to engage in delinquent behavior, and in general to be rejected by society. As time goes on, they run a disproportionate risk of mental illness, drug abuse, and marital failure. (Chilman 1966:2). Hope for them, and for the future of America, lies in a combination of intangible and tangible elements—the love of impoverished parents for their children, their aspirations for their children's education and development, and opportunities for rising out of the culture of poverty themselves. Only when family incomes rise, employment is equalized, discrimination against minorities declines (Chapter 3), and members of all ethnic, racial, and social class groups have a better chance to earn a good living and to become productive citizens will the age-old cycle of poverty from generation to generation at last be broken.

The present limited knowledge about child-rearing methods in the nation's many ethnic, racial, and social class groupings does not include much data about the great individual differences within any one subcul-

Table 5-5
Child-rearing Patterns Related to Emotionally Healthy Personality Development

Conducive (In families at any level)	Unfavorable (Characteristic of poor families)
1. Respect for child as individual whose behavior is caused by a multiplicity of factors. Acceptance of own role in events that occur.	1. Misbehavior regarded as such in terms of concrete pragmatic outcomes; reasons for behavior not considered. Projection of blame on others.
2. Commitment to slow development of child from infancy to maturity; stresses and pressures of each stage accepted by parent because of perceived worth of ultimate goal of raising "happy," successful son or daughter.	2. Lack of goal commitment and of belief in long-range success; a main object for parent and child is to "keep out of trouble"; orientation toward fatalism, impulse gratification, and sense of alienation.
3. Relative sense of competence in handling child's behavior.	3. Sense of impotence in handling children's behavior, as well as in other areas.
4. Discipline chiefly verbal, mild, reasonable, consistent, based on needs of child and family and of society; more emphasis on rewarding good behavior than on punishing bad behavior.	4. Discipline harsh, inconsistent, physical, makes use of ridicule; based on whether child's behavior does or does not annoy parent.
5. Open, free, verbal communication between parent and child; control largely verbal.	5. Limited verbal communication; control largely physical.
6. Democratic rather than autocratic or laissez-faire methods of rearing, with both parents in equalitarian but not necessarily interchangeable roles. Compansionship between parents and children.	6. Authoritarian rearing methods; mother chief child-care agent; father, when in home, mainly a punitive figure. Little support and acceptance of child as an individual.
7. Parents view selves as generally competent adults and are generally satisfied with themselves and their situation.	7. Low parental self-esteem; sense of defeat.
8. Intimate, expressive, warm relationship between parent and child, allowing for gradually increasing independence. Sense of continuing responsibility.	8. Large families; more impulsive, narcissistic parent behavior. Orientation to "excitement." Abrupt, early yielding of independence.
9. Presence of father in home and lack of severe marital conflict.	9. Father out of home (under certain circumstances).
10. Free verbal communication about sex, acceptance of child's sex needs, channeling of sex drive through "healthy" psychological defenses, acceptance of slow growth toward impulse control and sex satisfaction in marriage; sex education by both father and mother.	10. Repressive, punitive attitude about sex, sex questioning, and experimentation. Sex viewed as exploitative relationship.
11. Acceptance of child's drive for aggression but channeling of it into socially approved outlets.	11. Alternating encouragement and restriction of aggression, primarily related to consequences of aggression for parents.
12. Favorable attitude toward new experiences; flexibility.	12. Distrust of new experiences. Constricted life; rigidity.
13. Happiness of parental marriage.	13. High rates of marital conflict and family breakdown

Source: Catherine S. Chilman, *Growing Up Poor*, Welfare Administration Publication, no. 13 (Washington, D.C., 1966), pp. 28–29.

ture or family. The authors of a critical reappraisal of ten previous studies of the ways in which parents in various cultural groupings rear their children conclude that there is not yet sufficient evidence to warrant making general deductions. "Although future research could still confirm the class or ethnic generalizations, it is much more likely that class and ethnic differences in technique are relative, not absolute, and that the practices of parents in different groups greatly overlap" (Erlanger 1974:84).

Sex and culture

Although sex is a universal human attribute, the manner of its expression is learned from the culture in which an individual develops. In a country of many cultures sexual standards and practices vary widely from group to group. Similarities and differences in sexual expression among members of racial and social class groups have been studied in recent years. One important dual finding is that highly permissive persons may be found in all social classes, and that sharp differences exist within any one social class (Reiss 1973:18-19).

Premarital experience

In ethnic and religious groups in which premarital chastity is highly valued, responsible adults protect their unmarried girls from sexual exposure until they marry. Permissive attitudes are gradually becoming more widespread, but much more slowly among groups with strong religious roots. For instance, 100 percent of Danish males and females approve of premarital coitus, whereas only 38 percent of the males and 24 percent of the females in a church-centered culture in the United States do. The premarital permissiveness of young people in more cosmopolitan secular states falls between that of the Scandinavian and of church-oriented cultures (Christensen and Gregg 1970).

Educational and vocational aspirations delay sexual involvement. Lower-class boys are seven times more likely to have premarital intercourse than are college-educated males. Furthermore, lower-class boys with personal goals of education and upward mobility tend to delay sexual experience in pursuit of their objectives. Racial minorities with little to look forward to tend to be present-oriented and to get what sexual pleasure they can from an early age on. Two-thirds of the black females in one study were highly permissive in contrast to the white females, only 35 percent of whom would consider premarital intercourse proper under some circumstances (Reiss 1973:16). Black males are also significantly more permissive premaritally than white males.

White senior men on an Ivy League campus feel that sexual promiscuity is more reprehensible in women than in men, and are anxious about such premarital problems as jealousy of former lovers of their mate, pregnancy, infidelity, and jealousy or guilt in affairs. In addition, they view premarital sex as a source of strain with parents and community. These otherwise liberal college men believe that females should not take the sexual initiative in words or gestures in the early stages of a relationship and that infidelity is more permissible for males than for females (Komarovsky 1976:29).

Religion makes a difference in whether or not teenage girls are sexually active. A national probability sample study of 15-to 19-year-old females found that "for both blacks and whites, those who say they subscribe to no religion have the highest proportions with coital experience. This holds true for blacks and whites at every age, especially for ages 16 and younger where the proportion who had intercourse among those who claim no religious affiliation is about twice the average proportion at those ages. . . .Among those who attended church four or more times a month preceding the interview, the proportions sexually experienced were exceptionally low. . .that is, the more regular church attendance, the lower the proportions sexually experienced" (Kantner and Zelnik 1972:15).

Black girls in poor families are more likely to have had sexual experience in their teens than are girls from black families with higher incomes (Table 5-6). The differences between blacks and whites in this study are great at every age and income level, but the poor black girls are more likely to have had premarital experience than are those with higher family incomes.

A number of other factors are related to the premarital experience of teenage girls. Early experience is more prevalent among girls from families headed by mothers—"for whites, the proportion who have had intercourse is on the order of 60 percent higher for those in families headed by the mother rather than the father. . .for blacks 16 and younger. . .the proportion who have had coitus is a third to a half higher when the natural father is not around." The extent to which a girl confides in her family is signifi-

Table 5-6
Premarital Sexual Experience by Race and Family Income

Family income (annual)	Percent of sexually experienced girls 15–19 years old	
	Black	White
Less than $3,000	60.0%	28.5%
$3,001–$6,000	53.9	23.4
$6,001–$10,000	56.3	22.1
$10,001–$15,000	49.3	23.6
More than $15,000	44.7	25.6

Source: John F. Kantner and Melvin Zelnik, "Sexual Experience of Young Unmarried Women in the United States." Reprinted with permission from *Family Planning Perspectives*, vol. 4, no. 4, October 1972, p. 11.

cant; good rapport is associated with relatively low proportions of sexual experience. Another factor is that some girls are better informed than others. More white girls (42 percent) than blacks (18 percent) have knowledge of the period of greatest risk of pregnancy in the monthly cycle (Kanter and Zelnik 1972:16).

Unplanned teenage pregnancies

More black unmarried girls than white have unplanned pregnancies. A national study supported by the National Institute of Child Health and Development reports, "One-fifth of all never-married black females (the sexually active as well as the virgins) between the ages of 15 and 19 have experienced a pregnancy, a figure almost ten times the proportion of whites who have ever been pregnant" (Zelnik and Kantner 1972:371).

Most of these pregnancies were not only unplanned but unwanted. The girls became pregnant because although sexually active, (1) they were misinformed about when and how to protect themselves from becoming pregnant. "Vastly more whites than blacks have a generally correct notion about the period of greatest risk. Moroeever, among the whites, under-standing of the process improves significantly with age"—but this is not so for black girls (Zelnik and Kantner 1972:361). (2) They failed to use a contraceptive—only 19.6 percent of 15-year-old black girls always use a contraceptive, 27.3 percent never do, and 49.5 percent do so only sometimes. By the age of 19, only 8.9 percent of the black girls and 26.4 percent of the white girls always use a contraceptive, and the majority do so only sometimes—76.1 percent of the black girls, 59.1 percent of the whites (Zelnik and Kantner 1972:366). (3) They did not object to be-coming pregnant. "Twice as many blacks as whites were either trying to become pregnant or did not mind if that were the result" (Zelnik and Kantner 1972:370).

Roughly three out of four currently pregnant black and white teenage girls have no plans or intentions of getting married before their baby is born (Zelnik and Kantner 1972:372). However, "white teenagers who do not marry prior to the outcome of a premarital pregnancy are seven times more likely to terminate the pregnancy by induced abortion than blacks" (Zelnik and Kantner 1974:79).

Illegitimacy

Among all unwed mothers bearing illegitimate babies, proportionally more are black. "About two-thirds of all premarital pregnancies of black teenagers result in illegitimate births; only one-fifth of premarital first pregnancies of whites have such an outcome" largely because of the white girls' greater tendency to terminate premarital pregnancy by induced abortion (Zelnik and Kantner 1974:79). There are significant differences in what happens to illegitimate babies of unwed teenage girls. White girls tend more than blacks either to marry or to put their babies up for adoption. Most of the girls who marry after an illegitimate birth wed the man who fathered their child. More than nine out of ten of the black illegitimate firstborns were living in the mother's household, as were 72.2 percent of the white babies born to unwed teenage girls at the time of this study (Zelnik and Kantner 1974).

Another study of illegitimate firstborn children of black and white mothers in North Carolina found that 80 percent of the black mothers and 73 percent of the white mothers were not married. Most of the girls of both races wanted to keep their babies, even though they were not planning to be married. The black mothers kept their babies more often than the whites (95 percent vs 62 percent). Among the whites, the higher the girl's socioeconomic level the more likely she was to have her baby adopted. The researcher suggests that blacks have a lesser commitment to the norm of legitimacy than do whites, and that black women see marriage as no solution to their problems, especially at lower income levels (Pope 1969).

The first official survey of premarital childbirth by the United States Bureau of the Census found that of one million mothers who had never married, 561,141 were black and 414,704 were white. More than half of the first children born to black mothers in 1969 were illegitimate (Table 5-7).

Black social scientists find that lower-class blacks consider sex to be a natural human function, so that the designation of sexual attitudes as permissive or nonpermissive is not a major consideration. The greatest concern about premarital sex among blacks has been its possible outcome (pregnancy) rather than the act itself (Staples 1972:184). Illegitimacy is so linked to poverty and to low social status (Iutaka, Bock, and Berardo 1975), that there is hope that as conditions improve for poor girls, fewer will bear babies without fathers, and that such children may have opportunities beyond those available today.

Table 5-7
Illegitimacy among Blacks and Whites in the United States

Out of wedlock births reported	Percentage	
	Blacks	Whites
Illegitimate firstborns	52.6%	10.1%
15–20 year-old women bearing first child out of wedlock	71.0	22.0
25–30 year-old women reporting first child born out of wedlock	38.2	6.4
45–50 year-old women reporting first child born out of wedlock	18.1	5.7

Source: U.S. Bureau of the Census, "Census Studies Premarital Childbirth," AP release in *Sarasota Herald-Tribune*, August 18, 1976, p. 16–A.

Sex and social status

Sexual behavior as well as marriage, divorce, and family patterns vary according to ethnic, racial, and social class placement in society. Higher levels of stability and satisfaction are found most often among the better-educated, higher strata of the nation. An individual is born into the social class and culture of his or her family, but may, in the process of growing up (1) conform; (2) become upwardly mobile through education, occupational success, sports, special talents, etc.; or (3) become downwardly mobile through educational inadequacy, dissipation, delinquency, incompetence, or other factors. Rising standards of living, increases in the assimilation of ethnic and racial groups, differential birth rates that create a middle-class vacuum to be filled by upward-mobile lower-class youth, the high valuation of education, and the influence of labor unions in upgrading workers' compensations—all are associated with upward social mobility in the United States. This nation may be seen as having an open social class system, in which the lower classes include the largest number of poor families. There are a large and growing middle class and a small but influential upper class. A family's social class and mobility patterns greatly affect its members in many aspects of their lives, throughout their entire life cycle.

The family is the nucleus of civilization.

Will Durant

Families and family study

chapter six

Most Americans grow up in families and establish their own soon after they become adults. Leaders in business, political, and social life are family-oriented, as are the mass media through which they speak. Historians trace the evolution of the family throughout human history. Anthropologists describe regional and national variations in family groups and customs. This text examines the processes of development and change in families as they form, grow, contract, and age in the United States today.

What is a family?

Everyone "knows" what a family is, but few can define the term in ways acceptable to others. Social scientists study families from many angles and try to define them by describing the many forms, functions and conditions of family life in contemporary society. Theorists agree that "the family" is an elusive concept, defying definition, since it encompasses so many variant forms and meanings today. Is a family a nuclear unit of husband, wife and children living at home? If so, does this definition exclude those children who are college students living on campus? What position in the family is held by other relatives, living elsewhere (grandparents, aunts, uncles, cousins, etc.)? Are dead kinfolk part of a family? Is an unmarried couple living together on campus a family? Are communes and group marriages to be considered family units? Because of the "astonishing variance" that exists among American families, psychiatrists, sociologists and other scholars hesitate to define a "typical" family. (Aldous 1974; Spiegel 1971:144). One frequently quoted definition of a family is that

> The family is a group of persons united by ties of marriage, blood, or adoption; constituting a single household; interacting and communicating with each other in their respective social roles of husband and wife, mother and father, son and daughter, brother and sister; and creating and maintaining a common culture. (Burgess and Locke, 1953:7-8)

These sociologists are obviously describing the nuclear family, since they do not attempt to include other kinfolk in the extended family. Anthropologists point out that this concept of family does not include the many other family members who may not be present in the home.

> We've never adequately differentiated between a household, a biological nuclear family and whatever else people think a family really is . . . the ideal biological family makes a unit wherever it is; even if the father is in San Francisco, the mother remarried with stepchildren. It doesn't matter—you have to count all of them in—even including dead fathers and dead mothers. (Mead 1975:8)

Seventeen-year-old Future Family Leaders define "family" as,

> A unit of people, usually related, usually living together at least part of their lives, working together to satisfy their necessities and relating to each other to fulfill their wants.

> A family does not have to exist within the confines of the traditional legal concepts of marriage and parenthood, but every family has one or two adults who accept the responsibilities of parenthood and children who receive the guidance of the parents.

> The family is a small social unit consisting usually of husband, wife, and children, but sometimes excluding one of these

members, or including grandparents, other relatives, even non-related friends. The only real qualification for belonging to a family is a willingness to love and to try to understand its other members, to stand by them in times of stress and also in times of happiness. The family is the unit which gives the individual his strongest sense of community, and which, more than any other institution, lends stability and security to his life. (McCormack 1974)

Nuclear families, kin networks, and households

The nuclear family is universal. George Murdock's study of 250 representative cultures finds that everywhere husband, wife, and immature children are a clearly identifiable unit of society, sharing a common residence, economic participation, socially approved sexual relationships, reproduction, and child-rearing (Murdock 1949:2-3). Studies of American families find kin networks between nuclear families and their relatives linking at least three generations into a viable system of interdependence. Members of a kin network maintain close contact with each other and depend upon one another for help (Hill et al. 1970; Sussman and Burchinal 1962; Litwak 1965; Aldous 1967; Winch, forthcoming). The conclusion drawn from these studies is that the small nuclear family is generally secure within a network of interested relatives who keep in touch and are available to receive and to give assistance as needed.

Households consist of relatives and/or unrelated persons who live together in a common residence. The U.S. Bureau of the Census uses the following definitions as a basis for its population enumeration and analysis,

> *Household.* A household consists of all persons who occupy a housing unit. A house, an apartment, or other group of rooms, or a single room, is regarded as a housing unit when it is occupied or intended for occupancy as separate living quarters . . .
>
> A household includes the related family members and all the unrelated persons, if any, such as lodgers, foster children, wards or employees who share the housing unit. A person living alone in a housing unit, or a group of unrelated persons sharing a housing unit as partners, is also counted as a household.
>
> *Family.* The term "family" as used here, refers to a group of two persons or more related by blood, marriage, or adoption and residing together.
>
> *Married couple.* A married couple, as defined for census purposes, is a husband and his wife enumerated as members of the same household. The married couple may or may not have children living with them. (U.S. Bureau of the Census 1975:6)

Since Bureau of the Census data are used throughout this book, that agency's definitions of family, marriage, and household are applicable. Beyond these is assumed the kin network of relatives of three or more generations who interact within most nuclear families. Relatives living apart from the nuclear family are counted by census takers at their place of residence. In practice, these relatives are considered members of the family through frequent mention, telephone contact, visiting, family celebrations, exchange of gifts and services, and bequests, and are generally recognized as kin. This relationship is legally recognized under the "next of kin" designation regardless of where the relatives live.

Functions of modern families

Many functions formerly performed within families are now shared with others in the modern community. The production, preparation, and preservation of food is now Big Business. The education and religious training of children are now to some extent entrusted to schools, colleges, and churches. Protective services are furnished families by police and fire departments. Medical attention is provided by clinics, hospitals, doctors, nurses, and back-up teams of technicians. What functions are left for the family itself to perform? What, indeed, but the most important of all—those that contribute to producing human beings capable of living competently in a world their fathers never knew.

Emergent family functions

Modern families fulfill at least six emergent, nontraditional functions:

1. *Generating affection* between husband and wife, between parents and children, and among members of the generations. Love is a product of family living. Men and women marry for love and usually beget their children as an expression of their love for one another. Their children have to have love in an emotional climate of ongoing affection in order to thrive. The family stays together through the years not because it has to, but because the members want to, out of enduring affection for one another. Happiness is gauged by the strength of family love. Most wives feel that their families are more closely knit than "most other families" they know, and that this attests to the love they feel for and generate in their families (Blood 1964:8–9). Ideally, both parents and children grow in a climate of mutual affection that assures their healthy development.

2. *Providing personal security and acceptance.* Most people look to the family for the security and acceptance they need to live lives of dignity and worth. Within the family individuals can make mistakes and learn from them in an atmosphere of protective security. The family is one of the few remaining places where complementary rather than competitive

relationships can be fostered and enjoyed. Thus the family provides a home base, whose stability and continuity allow its members to develop naturally—each in his own way, each at his own pace.

3. *Giving satisfaction and a sense of purpose.* These are basic needs in an industrial age. The unskilled worker may derive only minimal satisfaction from his job, and the person in more challenging work may find it fraught with anxiety, conflict, and struggle. The family gives human beings a sense of basic satisfaction and worth that the industrial world can only occasionally provide. It is in the family setting that adults and children enjoy life and each other—in family gatherings and celebrations, around the family table, in family rituals, on family trips, and in many other activities that family members find satisfying. The parents feel that essentially they live for one another, and for the children for whom they are responsible.

4. *Assuring continuity of companionship.* Perhaps only within the family group can this need be met today. The expectation of permanence means much to modern man. Friends, neighbors, colleagues, teachers, clergy, and others may or may not remain close by for more than a few years. Jobs change, neighborhoods shift, children are promoted and graduate from school. In most cases, family associations alone can be expected to endure. The continuing presence of sympathetic companions encourages family members to relate the happenings of the day, to share the disappointments and the satisfactions of life as they occur, in ways not expected outside the family. Who but members of one's family can delight so fully in the flush of success, or share so completely the burden of failure? Companionship lasting over the years ranks high as a function of family life.

5. *Guaranteeing social placement and socialization.* In any society these are essential family functions. Because of the complexity of modern life they are imperative. At birth, a child automatically acquires his family's status by virtue of the genetic, physical, ethnic, national, religious, cultural, economic, political, and educational heritage unique to his parents and their kin. The family acts as the transmitter of the cultural heritage of the race from one generation to the next. It performs the task of interpreting to all of its members the meaning of the many situations of which they are a part. Elder family members serve as role models for the younger ones, as boys identify with their fathers, and girls with their mothers through the formative years of personality development.

> It is also generally recognized that lifelong patterns of behavior, values, goals and attitudes of children are strongly associated with the characteristics of their parents, especially as these are expressed in childrearing and family life styles. Although later experiences outside the home also have important influences on the developing child, the availability of

these experiences to him and the ways in which he uses them . . . are strongly affected by what he has learned in his home. (Chilman 1966:2)

6. *Inculcating controls and a sense of what is right.* Within the family, individual members can best learn the rules, rights, obligations, and responsibilities essential for the survival of a society. Family members feel free to criticize, to correct and to order, to praise or to blame, to reward or to punish, to entice or to threaten each other in ways that would be unthinkable elsewhere. "In all these ways, the family is an instrument or agent of the larger society; its failure to perform adequately means that the goals of the larger society may not be attained effectively" (Goode 1964:5). The kinds of praise and punishment experienced by a child in his earliest years instill in him the sense of right and wrong that he will carry into adulthood in his moral values and in his definitions of the good, the right, and the worthy. The family, functioning as a "choosing agency," evaluates and selects from among many ways of life, and so is the primary source of human values that spread outward into society as a whole.

Families are urgently needed because they meet the basic needs of individuals better than any other group now known. Families are expected to bear and to rear good citizens who will be capable of carrying the responsibilities of today's complex society. "Without a family unit to deal with the idiosyncrasies of aged parents, the emotional needs of adults, or the insecurities of children, very likely not enough adequately functioning people would be produced to man the industrial system" (Goode 1964:109). The family is the main source of mental and emotional health in society and in its members.

Family roles

Family functions are performed by the members of the family through their continuing interaction. Family interaction is the process through which one member's action is stimulated by the behavior of other members within the family. Family interaction is the sum total of all the family roles being played within a given family. The roles of each family member are directly related to the roles played by others in the family.

Positions, norms, roles, and role behavior

Each family member holds positions in relationship to others in the family. These positions are paired, i.e., "husband and wife," "father and child," "mother and daughter." Thus each family member occupies two or more positions, e.g., both husband and father, as well as son, brother, etc.

Roles of family members are part of the social positions they occupy within the family. For instance, a wife-mother plays many roles—those of homemaker, sex partner, companion, childbearer, and so forth. These concurrent roles may be thought of as a role cluster (Aldous 1974:11–12). Each of these roles is defined by the norms, or the expectations, the group has for it. The way in which a given family member plays his roles is termed his role behavior—for example, a mother's competence as a homemaker, or a father's actual performance as a provider. When role behavior deviates too widely from what is expected (the norms), negative sanctions in some form of punishment are applied to press the person to measure up to group expectations. Role behavior that conforms to the norms may elicit positive sanctions in the form of rewards from the group.

Each family member is a changing, developing person—biologically, intellectually, and socially—throughout his or her lifetime. As a person develops, he is expected to take on new roles and to abandon old ones, so that the role content of the positions he or she holds changes as time goes on. What might be acceptable role behavior at one stage of a family's life is unacceptable at another. Family members are expected "to act their age"—to behave in a manner appropriate to their time of life and to that of others in the family. If the individual is to be an acceptable member of his family, he must play those roles expected of him at any given time by virtue of his position in the family.

Marriage contracts

Few married men and women realize that their roles are already rigidly prescribed by the marriage contract under which they live. Each of the fifty states has laws regulating marriage. The rationale is that society has the responsibility of protecting at least four essentials through the regulation of marriage:

1. Public morality
2. Family stability
3. Support of dependents
4. Responsibility for children

These concerns are so crucial that they continue as basic assumptions in the legal and social system. Since they are implicit rather than explicit, the traditional marriage contract binding all married persons in each state is rarely understood either before or after marriage. As one legally trained sociologist says,

> The marriage contract is unlike most contracts: its provisions are unwritten, its penalties unspecified, and the terms of the contract are typically unknown to the "contracting" parties. Prospective spouses are neither informed of the terms of the contract nor are they allowed any options about these terms.

> In fact one wonders how many men and women would agree to the marriage contract if they were given the opportunity to read it and to consider the rights and obligations to which they were commiting themselves. (Weitzman 1974:1170)

In spite of recent trends toward more flexible and increasingly equalitarian family roles, the legal contract covering marriage in most states assumes that the husband is head of the family and provider, and that the wife acts as his companion and as a housewife, and is responsible for bearing and rearing his children. Dr Weitzman goes on to say,

> The discrepancy between legal reality and social reality is great and the law on the books is widely divergent from the law in action. The law on the books is archaic: it is the 200-year-old vestige of an extinct social structure. The law in action is a patchwork attempt to stretch the old law to deal with modern realities. (Weitzman 1974:1176–1277)

Inequities in the traditional contract

When a woman marries, she loses her full legal and social identity. She takes her husband's name, his social and economic status, and his place of residence as her own. If she chooses to live elsewhere during her marriage, she can be proved guilty of desertion. In many states she may not sell her own property without her husband's written permission. In some places she may not have a charge account without her husband's signature, since he is liable for her debts and responsible for her support. Should they divorce, the wife usually is entitled to alimony and child support, if she can collect it from her former husband. If and when either remarries, the new spouse is immediately endowed with a fixed share of the estate, regardless of the hardship this may bring to the children and to the spouse of the original marriage. For these and other reasons, many couples today consider drafting their own marriage contracts.

Marriage contracts reflecting a couple's interests

Advocates of personally designed marriage contracts try to avoid future conflict by spelling out the roles they expect of one another. Rights and responsibilities of husband and wife are defined according to the agreements the pair have reached through discussion. Marriage contracts may provide for periodic review and renewal (or nonrenewal) of the spousal agreements (Etzioni 1975).

When a couple fashion their own marriage contract, they write into it those items about which they feel strongly, so that it reflects their current needs, interests, resources, and life-style. They may specify such things as their aims and expectations; the duration of the contract (for a specified term or for an unlimited one, renewable in so many years, etc.); the inventory, management, and control of their property; plans for income and disbursement of individual and joint funds; responsibility for individual, community, and children's debts; household arrangements and responsibilities; relationships within and outside of marriage; plans for bearing or adopting and for rearing children of the contracting pair as well as others for which one or both feel responsible; agreements about religious practices and about the education of children; provisions for the inheritance and division of property; recommendations for resolving disagreements and the use of counseling and arbitration; and any other items of concern to the two persons. Outlines of suggested items for marriage contracts as well as illustrative examples are available (Weitzman 1974:1249–1288; Sussman 1975).

Some difficulties with personally drafted marriage contracts follow:

1. The legal status of such a contract can be called into question. Any portion of a personal marriage contract contrary to the laws of the state has no legal standing.
2. Feelings, values, and attitudes of the two spouses can change during marriage from what had been anticipated prior to the wedding.
3. Actual conflict areas in marriage are difficult to anticipate.
4. A highly detailed marriage contract may be too inflexible for comfort.
5. Marriage contracts tend to be based on anticipation of the worst that may befall the union, rather than on the expectation of success so important for permanence (Wells 1976:33–37).

Alternatives to legal marriage

The mood of Americans is such that anything that frees the individual from governmental control appears to merit consideration. The push for freedom is felt in many quarters. The voices of youth, minorities, ethnic groups, the Women's Liberation movement, and the "sexual revolution" focus on freeing individuals from the traditional roles of the sexes. Alternatives to legal marriage are many, varied, and highly publicized. They represent but a small proportion of all unions (Streib 1973:3), but their very atypicality is of interest to students and family specialists alike. Some of the most frequently discussed alternatives are summarized below.

Living together

Male and female college students live together for a number of reasons: economy, unrestricted intimacy, sexual access, and possibly more involvement than casual dating (Lyness, Lipetz and Davis, 1972:305). Living together without being married is easily begun, requires no blood tests, no papers, no waiting, and no disclosure to family and friends unless a couple wishes it. Families that would disapprove if they were informed about the situation may or may not be told. Some coeds have marriage in mind; more of the men do not (Lyness, Lipetz, and Davis 1972:311). Students agree that couples who are cohabitating are less committed to each other than they would be if they were legally married (Edwards and Stinnett 1974).

Living together is seen as a temporary arrangement, a substitute for marriage, or as preparation for marriage. The student couple's determination to stay together depends on the quality of their relationship (Lewis, Spanier, Storm, and LeHecka 1975). Some cohabiting students are found to be less apt to attend church and more likely to prefer liberal life-styles; some are drug users (Henze and Hudson 1974).

Cohabitation may be defined as sharing a bed with someone of the opposite sex to whom one is not married for four or more nights a week for three or four months. Between a fourth and a third of state university students, and one in ten or more students in small liberal arts colleges report one or more such experiences. Cohabiting college students say their most common emotional problems are:

1. Tendency to become overly involved (62 percent)
2. Overdependence on the relationship
3. Loss of personal sense of identity
4. Lack of opportunity to participate in other activities
5. Less chance to be with other friends
6. Jealousy of the partner's involvement in other relationships (57 percent)
7. Feeling trapped at times

Two thirds of the cohabiting Cornell students told researchers they felt no guilt about living together (Macklin 1974:57). Getting married after graduation is still a popular choice among students who live together, but others see cohabitation as a preferred long-term arrangement (Peterman, Ridley, and Anderson 1974:354).

A man whose business takes him away from home for extended periods of time may have a "love nest" with some willing girl. Some of these liaisons are quite open and generally recognized. Bigamy is not a problem because the man's "second home" is not legally sanctioned. Retirees sometimes live together without marriage to share expenses and companionship without risking loss of Social Security income or children's and grandchildren's inheritance. Such adult arrangements are easy to dissolve, with little property to divide, no family, and no ties (McWhirter 1973:207).

Informal living together is widely publicized and discussed, but largely escapes official enumeration. Dr. Paul C. Glick of the United States Bureau of the Census (1976:12) reports that "only a fraction of one percent of all couples have been identified as living together and maintaining a quasi-family relationship outside of marriage."

Trial marriage

Trial marriage was first seriously proposed by Judge Ben B. Lindsay in the 1920s under the term "companionate marriage" for the couple who did not want to have children, or who preferred to postpone having them (Lindsay 1926). Forty years later Margaret Mead (1966) advocated "marriage in two steps" the first to begin with a simple ceremony and to end if need be with an easy divorce. The second step came when the couple felt ready to assume responsibility for having children. Students tend to feel more positively toward trial marriage than toward other alternative life styles, although somewhat fewer of them would find it personally acceptable (Edwards and Stinnett 1974:150). The legal and social status of the trial marriage remains uncertain.

Singlehood

Some 7 percent of American women never marry—the proportion has not changed appreciably over the past 80 years (Glick 1976:7). There are more unmarried young adults in the population now than formerly primarily because more of them are postponing marriage until a later time. The number of never-married women over the age of 24 has doubled in recent years. When teenage marriages were taking place in large numbers, there was widespread concern about their high failure rate. So, later marriage ages may augur well for future marital stability. Some of today's singles will never marry. But, many more young adults opt for a period of personal freedom before settling down to the responsibilities of marriage and family life. College girls today may continue their education; they get better jobs at higher pay scales than in the past; and they enjoy seeing what they can do on their own before they marry (Spreitzer and Riley 1974; Stein 1975).

Single young adults have contributed importantly to the recorded jump in the number of households formed (6,800,000) since the beginning of the decade. "Today's singles constitute a vast market for a wide variety of goods and services, ranging from single-occupancy dwellings to coed apartment house complexes, to dating services, concert tickets, travel clubs, not to mention one-cup percolators and TV dinners" ("Singleness Is On the Rise Among Women," 1975:1). Moving into a singles' apartment complex offers a measure of safety from big city crime for the young adult who can afford the high rent (Hagestad 1975:68). Loneliness is a growing threat to the unmarried adult who finds being single not as satisfying as it had once appeared (Gordon 1976).

Communes

Communes are not new. Their history in the United States goes back many years. Some have lasted but a few months, others are successful over the years. One comparative study found that the following elements were common to the life-styles of all of the successful communes: practice of either free love or of celibacy; property signed over to the community upon admission; community-owned furniture and tools; no compensation for labor; no charge for community services; and fixed daily routines. By contrast, significantly lower percentages of these practices existed in the twenty-one unsuccessful communes studied (Kanter 1970:78; Cavan 1976).

At this time, communes unified by religion are more enduring than those with a secular base. Communes range in size of membership from a few individuals to several hundred adults and children. Many have strong charismatic leaders who fill the role of father figure. Others are designed to help former dope addicts, alcoholics, or mental patients to reenter society (Brozan 1975:34). Most communes fail eventually because of the conflict between individual freedom and community responsibility. Power struggles and disputes over communal property arise and the sense of family is weakened as newcomers arrive (Zablocki 1971). Even in the Israeli communes, strong family bonds currently threaten the solidarity of the kibbutz (Hazleton 1976; Rabkin 1976). Emotional ties to kinfolk, individualism, and a pervasive attitude of self-assertion tend to erode many a modern commune in time (Veysey 1974).

Sexual practices in communes vary from (1) celibacy, (2) exclusive monogamy, (3) intimate friendship, (4) group marriage, to (5) free love—the free love groups being especially short-lived (Ramey 1972:450). Religious communes tend to be highly structured, to be withdrawn from the larger society, and to have a strong family base and a work ethic. A new type of commune is springing up in metropolitan areas. Ramey (1972) calls these "evolutionary communes" and reports that they are made up of highly mobile, upper-middle-class high-achievers, over the age of 30. The members hold straight jobs and share a desire to provide better schooling for their children; to pool resources for investment, housing, and purchasing; and to provide luxuries otherwise unavailable. Although they concede that communal living offers possibilities for personal growth and close human relationships, most students would not find it an acceptable life-style for themselves (Edwards and Stinnett 1974:150).

Group marriage

A group marriage is one in which three or more individuals are pairbonded with at least two others (Ramey 1972:451; Constantine and Constantine 1971). Pair-bonded persons are mates, and in a group marriage each is married to all of the others. Pair bonds increase with each additional person, so the group marriage optimally consists of no more than six or seven. The triad (made up of one man and two women, or two men and one woman) is easy to form and offers twice as many pair bonds as does a couple. A group marriage of four persons has six pair bonds; five persons have ten pair bonds, and six have a possible fifteen mates. Titillating as this may sound, group marriage is not destined to replace the married pair. The type of person attracted to group marriage tends to be peculiar, emotionally disturbed, and freedom-loving—not the type who takes easily to the self-discipline, responsibility, and restraints of marriage (Ellis in Streib 1973:82).

Mate-swapping or swinging

Swinging is a married couple's willingly swapping sexual partners with another couple or going to a swinging party where both have sexual intercourse with strangers. Swingers find congenial pairs through friends, at swinging bars and socials, and in personal columns and advertisements in certain magazines and papers. Many would-be swingers try it once or twice and decide it is not for them (Ramey 1972:435–456). Enthusiasts who remain swingers find in it elements of variety, recreation, therapy, and couple revitalization. Husbands are reported to suggest swinging most often and they are most often eager to get out of it—partly because mate-swapping promotes the wife's independence. Swingers tend to be educated (some in the professions), white-collar suburbanites (Denfield and Gordon in Streib 1973:87–94).

A swinging suburban party resembles a cocktail party except for two distinguishing features—the exchange of sex partners and the absence of children. One study finds that "although the sexual deviance of the swingers may meet with disapproval in the population at large, it is a mutual or consensual form of adultery, engaged in with the agreement of the spouse . . . in what some of them called "faithful adultery" (Gilmartin 1975:58). Eight out of ten students say that extramarital sexual relations with mutual consent would not be acceptable to them personally (Edwards and Stinnett 1974:149). Sociologist Betty Yorburg reports, "The incidence of group forms of 'transmarital sex' is presently declining sharply" (1975: 396).

Same sex couples

The popular Broadway play and movie *The Odd Couple* makes the point that two men living together may have many of the same problems that they once had with their wives. In addition, it is difficult if not impossible for two persons of the same sex to be legally married, to adopt a child, or to enjoy certain other rights in most states. Same sex couples are more acceptable in most communities than they once were. Both the

American Psychological Association and the American Psychiatric Association have removed homosexuality from their lists of mental diseases (Hooker 1975:99). Still, homosexuality is not a preferred life-style. Nearly two thirds (64.98 percent) of the college students in one study said that they would not want to be closely associated with a marriage between homosexual persons—for example, by living next door to a homosexual couple (Edwards and Stinnett 1974:149).

Single-parent families

A single adult man or woman may adopt one or more children who then are reared in a single-parent family. More general are families of unwed or divorced mothers and their children. Ninety percent of the population of the United States live with their relatives. Of these, 85 percent are husband-wife families; 12 percent are female-headed; and 2 percent are male-headed, without a resident wife or mother (U.S. Bureau of the Census 1975).

A mother attempting to raise her children alone faces many problems: financial limitations, overwork at home and on the job she takes to support her family, inadequate childcare facilities, the effort to be both mother and father to her children, the struggle for complete acceptance, and the maintenance of healthy social and emotional relationships as a woman. Children make it hard for an unwed mother to meet and to date suitable men. Should the mother marry, she and her husband must work out new marital, familial, and parental roles that are comfortable to both, if their marriage is to succeed. A father living alone with his biological or adopted children faces many of the same problems. He may, in addition, encounter difficulties in housekeeping and childcare, as well as unwelcome interference on the part of solicitous women friends and neighbors.

One sociologist estimates that between 25 and 35 percent of all American parents live alone with their children at one time or another (LeMasters in Streib 1973:56). This does not include the millions of cases in which the husband and father is away on business or in military service, or when one of the parents is hospitalized or otherwise out of the home. These problems are similar to many of those experienced in some marriage-alternative situations (Brazelton 1975; Mead 1976).

Marriage is the norm

Experimental marriages represent only a minority among family groups—estimated at less than one percent (Glick 1976) to about eight percent (Cogswell and Sussman 1972:507). Atypical forms of marriage arise out of unusual situations or personal inclinations. But there is growing evidence that family life continues much as it always has (Barthel 1976; Glick 1976). Family flexibility allows the unit to change to fit new conditions and times. "The family today is very much alive. It is extremely sensitive, but it is also malleable so that it can withstand the pains of change and stress" (Billingsley 1975). Anything is possible in marriage and family living—and this is both its strength and its challenge.

The great majority of college students (70 percent in one study) feel that traditional marriage is the most fulfilling type of man-woman relationship. Family roles learned in childhood tend to be continued in adulthood; and it is in marriage and family life that most basic human needs are satisfied. "Marriage American-style is alive and well. In the foreseeable future it will probably remain essentially as we know it today. The majority of people who marry will stay married" (Hudson 1975).

Conventional young adults prefer marriage with legal ties; whereas students with radical attitudes are most liberal in their acceptance of new family life-styles (Yost and Adamek 1974). Thus it may be expected that the several traditional and emergent forms of marriage and the family will continue to be interesting areas for discussion and study.

Family studies

If everyone "knows" about family life from his own experience, why is family study needed? The answer is tenfold:

1. To get a broader view of family life than that afforded by experience in any one family
2. To correct the fallacies and distortions that prevail on the subjects of personal and family living
3. To focus on the normal aspects of family living rather than on the atypical, abnormal forms more often reported
4. To test objectively what "everybody knows"—which may be untrue
5. To recognize the family as the hub of society around which all other institutions and groups have revolved in every culture known to man throughout all of history
6. To learn more about the contribution of family life to human development
7. To keep up with the changes in families resulting from their adaptation to changing social conditions
8. To foresee predictable problems and potentials in families as they change in form and function over the years
9. To establish reliable bases for making individual and family decisions about matters that occur and recur throughout the life span
10. To adopt valid plans and policies for future family situations in a given home, community, or nation

Behavioral science family studies

Families can be studied from many points of view, each providing a different aspect of the reality to be found in family contexts. Since families are the laboratories of life as most people live it, they are important testing grounds for all kinds of theories, programs, and evaluative studies recommended by the various professional disciplines. The helping agents of the society must have an understanding of families in order to gain access to them.

Family study, as presented in this book, is an ongoing activity of the several behavioral sciences and disciplines. Table 6–1 lists a series of 15 of the social sciences and disciplines conducting research on one or more aspects of family life. The illustrative studies listed are a representative sample of the kinds of studies that have been undertaken in any given discipline. The listing of representative researchers is only that and no more, and necessarily omits many productive scholars whose work is acknowledged elsewhere. The table serves to give an overview of the types of family research students of the different disciplines may encounter in their study of families and their members.

Interdisciplinary family research

Interdisciplinary research is productive because it makes more than one vantage point available at a time. The specialized concepts of the different disciplines provide, as it were, a variety of lenses, which, as they are combined, add depth to the field. Each of the behavioral sciences has its own basic assumptions, concepts, and methods of study. A particular group of related concepts, or conceptual framework, focuses attention on a particular facet of family life. A multifaceted view is possible with an interdisciplinary approach. There are five main approaches to interdisciplinary family research

1. The *institutional-historical* approach combines history and sociology. It sees families as institutions acting upon and reacting to other social, material, and cultural components within a society. As a conceptual framework it is most useful in tracing family change over long periods of time. It does not attempt to deal with interpersonal interaction or with the behavior of families and their members.

2. The *structure-function* approach comes from anthropology and sociology. It views the family as a social system within society interacting with other social systems, like the school, or functioning in small groups, such as the husband-wife dyad. This approach copes well with the concept of the interaction of the family with other institutions, but it does not deal with change.

3. The *interactional* approach has developed from sociology and social psychology. It sees the family as a relatively closed system of interaction.

Table 6-1
Behavioral Sciences and Disciplines Involved in Family Study

Disciplines	Illustrative studies	Representative researchers*
Anthropology Cultural anthropology Social anthropology Ethnology	Cultural and subcultural family forms and functions Ethnic, racial, and social status family differences Families in primitive, developing, and industrial societies	Clyde Kluckhohn Oscar Lewis Helen and Robert Lynd Margaret Mead George Murdock
Counseling Counseling theory Clinical practice Evaluation	Dynamics of interpersonal relationships in marriage and family Methods and results of individual, marriage, and family counseling	Rollo May Emily Hartshorne Mudd James K. Peterson Carl Rogers
Demography	Census and vital statistics on many facets of family life Cross-sectional, longitudinal, and record-linkage surveys Differential birth rates Family planning and population control	Hugh Carter Harold Christensen Paul Glick Philip Hauser P.K. Whelpton
Economics	Consumer behavior, marketing, and motivation research Insurance, pensions, and welfare needs Standards of living, wage scales, socioeconomic status	Howard Bigelow John Kenneth Galbraith John Morgan Margaret Reid
Education Early childhood Early elementary Secondary College Parent Professional	Child-rearing methods Developmental patterns Family life education Motivation and learning Preparation for marriage Sex education	Orville Brim Catherine Chilman Harold Lief Nevitt Sanford Ralph Tyler James Walters

(Continued)

Table 6-1 continued

Disciplines	Illustrative studies	Representative researchers*
History	Origins of family patterns	Arthur Calhoun
	Predictions of the future of families	Franklin Frazier
	Social influences on the family	Edward Westermarck
	Social trends and adaptations	Carle Zimmerman
Home economics	Evaluation of family practices	Muriel Brown
Family relationships	Family food habits and nutrition	Irma Gross
Home economics education	Home management practices	Evelyn Spindler
Home management	Relationships between family members	Alice Thorpe
Nutrition		
Human development	Child growth and development	Urie Bronfenbrenner
Child development	Developmental norms and differences	Erik Erikson
Adolescent development	Nature of cognitive learning	Robert Havighurst
Middle age and aging	Cross-cultural variations	Lois Barclay Murphy
	Personality development	Bernice Neugarten
	Social roles of aging	Jean Piaget
Law	Adoption and child protection	Paul Alexander
	Child care and welfare	John Bradway
	Marriage and family law	Marie Kargman
	Divorce and marital dissolution	Harriet Pilpel
	Sexual controls and behavior	Max Rheinstein
	Parental rights and responsibilities	Lenore Weitzman
Psychoanalysis	Abnormal and normal behavior	Nathan Ackerman
	Clinical diagnosis and therapy	Erik Erikson
	Foundations of personality	John Flugel
	Stages of development	Irene Josselyn
	Treatment of mental illness	Harry Stack Sullivan

(Continued)

128

Discipline	Topics	Research workers[*]
Psychology Clinical Developmental Social	Aspirations and self-concepts Drives, needs, and hungers Dynamics of interpersonal interaction Learning theory Mental health Therapeutic intervention	Rosalind Dymond Gerald Gurin Robert Hess Eleanore Luckey Frederick Stodtbeck John Whiting
Public health	Epidemiology and immunization Family health and preventive medicine Maternal and infant health Pediatric health education Venereal disease	Cecelia Deschin Nicholson Eastman Earl L. Koos Niles Newton Clark Vincent
Religion	Church policies on marriage and family Families of various religions Interfaith marriage Love, sex, marriage, divorce, and family in religious contexts	Stanley Brav Roy Fairchild Seward Hiltner John L. Thomas John C. Wynn
Social work Family casework Group work Social welfare	Appraising family need Devising constructive programs for family assistance Measuring family functioning	Dorothy F. Beck L.L. Geismar James Hardy Charlotte Towle
Sociology	Courtship and mate selection Family formation and functioning Effects of social change on families Family crises and dissolution Prediction of family success Social class influence on families	Ernest W. Burgess Ruth S. Cavan Harold Christensen Reuben Hill Judson Landis Marvin Sussman

*Illustrative of those research workers whose published findings may be available to students of the family in various disciplines; not an all-inclusive listing.

It is especially fruitful when applied to studying processes of communication, conflict, decision-making, problem-solving and reaction to crisis. It focuses on family members in given groups of families rather than on cultural patterns or institutional aspects of family life.

4. The *situational* approach has roots in both psychology and sociology. It is helpful in exploring the related elements in a given situation within a family. Its strength is its ability to capture the interplay of family members with each other and with the family as a whole. Since it relies on observation and interviewing, it makes little attempt to record changes in families over long periods of time, or to study the ways in which families interact with other groups in society.

5. The *family development* approach combines the concepts, insights, and methods of a number of disciplines. From rural sociology comes the generational sweep of the family life cycle (Chapter 7). From human development study come awareness of developmental tasks (Chapter 8), of critical periods of development, and of the best time for teaching these concepts. From sociology come the ideas of social change (Chapters 2, 3, and 4), of social class (Chapter 5), and of the cultural influences that shape and are shaped by families. From psychology are borrowed the contributions of learning theory and interaction processes. From home economics are taken the themes of child development and family relationships, home management, housing, and family practices. Family development is an intricate complex that offers much to family study (Kirkpatrick 1967; Broderick 1967).

Qualities of family development study

Family development follows the orderly sequential changes in growth, development, and dissolution or decline throughout the entire family life cycle. Recognizing the unbroken flow from generation to generation, family development sees family life cycles overlapping one another in intergenerational interaction in predictable ways throughout the full life span. Simply summarized, family development study:

1. Keeps the family in focus throughout its history
2. Sees each family member in interaction with all other members
3. Watches the ways in which individuals and the family unit influence one another
4. Recognizes what a given family is going through at any particular time
5. Highlights critical periods of personal and family growth and development
6. Views both the universals and the variations among families
7. Beams in on the ways in which the culture and families influence each other
8. Provides a basis for forecasting what a given family will be going through at any period in its life span

Table 6-2
Properties of the Developmental Approach

Social time:
Copes well with action and interaction, as well as with change and process over time. The time span is the life cycle of the nuclear family, the basic time units are stages demarcated by spurts of growth and development.

Social space:
1. Area: Emphasizes changing internal structure and development of family. May cope with family systems and collateral systems and with the personality system of members.
2. Environment: Cultural imperatives and demands.
3. Peripheral: Agencies outside the family; members' outside activities, physical elements.
4. Residual: Not determinable. Potentially can cope with full array of social and cultural elements with which the family has contact, including the social system (in structure-function terms).

Structure:
1. Units of study: Family group (basic); interacting individuals, individual.
2. Configuration: Basically life cycle and stages, family tempos and rhythms.
3. Cohesion: Basically developmental tasks (interrelating stages with one another) and roles and functions (interrelating individuals within stages).

Bridges:
1. Conditions: Basically teachable moment (physical maturation, cultural prerequisites, communication) and psychological elements such as perception, identity formation, and motivation.
2. Mechanisms: Little development apparent. Can probably borrow heavily from interactional and micro-functional approaches.

Overt behavior:
1. Transactional: Treatment of transactional behavior only now beginning; only limited development shown.
2. Interactional: Strong development likely. Can cope with individual interacts as well as process within a stage; stages and development allow treatment of long-range changes and process over time.
3. Actional: Little added development to date but leans on psychology of child development for identification of stages of individual growth and development.

Source: Reuben Hill and Donald A. Hansen, "The Identification of Conceptual Frameworks Utilized in Family Study," *Marriage and Family Living 22*, no. 4 (November 1960): 308, used with permission.

Ways of anticipating what to expect are inherent in family development. Knock on any door, and what will you find within? No one can tell you exactly, because each family differs in many ways from any other. But, generally, you can predict somewhat reliably the overall pattern of a family's activities if you know these three things: (1) where the family is in time (in history, year, season, day, and hour) and in its life cycle; (2) the number, age, and relatedness of the family members in the household; (3) how the family rates in the community, as seen in its ethnic, religious, and social class status. When you know these three things before you meet a given family, you know what significant elements to look for and what forces you may expect to find in action within the family and its members (Table 6-2).

Longitudinal family research differs from horizontal studies that explore aspects of a population at any given time. Longitudinal research is especially fruitful in that it:

1. Keeps each participant in focus, so that developmental patterns and individual differences can be seen
2. Provides a time dimension for studying individuals, families, interrelationships, recurrent crises, and growth plateaus
3. Gives a basis for comparing different patterns of development among individuals and families
4. Makes it possible to describe the tendencies and trends that appear to be general within a population. For instance, from such norms and general patterns, early-developers and late-maturers at puberty can be spotted. Longitudinal studies in human development parallel longitudinal family studies throughout the twentieth century.

Growing edges of family development

Family development study has not yet achieved a fully developed theoretical base thoroughly tested by research. Functioning best in longitudinal research, it encounters a number of problems that smaller, shorter-term, horizontally designed studies do not have. Data from families over their entire life spans are hard to gather, largely because families outlive the research team, as well as its commitment, its financing, and its authority to continue. Keeping in touch with the same families over many months and years is made difficult by changes in their residence, configurations, and interest in the project over a considerable period of time. Ingenious ways to circumvent these research problems are being devised as the family development approach is explored. Still lacking to date, however, are adequate cross-cultural and subcultural studies in family development.

There are of course some limitations in the family development approach. While studying normal, intact families, it may lose track of deviant families with problems such as premature dissolution, divorce, remarriage, single parenthood, stepparents, and the many combinations of "his children, her children, and their children."

No one knows better than those who use the family development approach the many problems it presents. Nevertheless, interest in this way of seeing and studying families has been growing ever since it was first designed in preparation for the first National Conference on Family Life in Washington, D.C., in 1948. Year by year its scope and content are increased through accretions of longitudinal research data coming out of child development centers, human development programs, and most recently family study centers in major universities across the United States.

Data available from longitudinal family studies and official government census figures and projections, as well as other research findings from many sources, have all served to add form and substance to the conceptual framework of *Marriage and Family Development* in the chapters that follow.

development over the
life cycle

part three

To everything there is a season, and a time to every purpose under the heaven:

A time to be born, and a time to die; a time to plant, and a time to pluck up that which is planted. . .

A time to weep, and a time to laugh; a time to mourn, and a time to dance. . .

A time to get, and a time to lose; a time to keep, and a time to cast away. . . .

Ecclesiastes 3:1–6

The family life cycle

chapter seven

If you know three things about a family, you can predict somewhat reliably what is going on within it. These indicators include first of all the family's composition; secondly, the family's ethnic, racial, and social status (Chapter 5), and finally, the family's placement in time—in its particular life cycle, within an era of rapid social change (Chapter 3), in a given season, on a certain day, and at a specific hour.

Family tempos and rhythms

Families have a developmental history marked by periods of dynamic action and spelled by intervals of relative calm. This is true even within the space of a day, a week, a season. Typically, the family day begins with

137

the bustle of arising, washing, dressing, collecting the day's equipment, and getting into the day's activity. This first spurt of energy is followed in many homes by the midday pause when no one is home but mom and the dog. By late afternoon the rush of homecoming begins. This is the time for reporting on the day, fixing equipment, cleaning up, and preparing the evening meal. Many families customarily eat together, sharing not only the evening meal but their attention and mutual interests. Outside pressures then are suspended temporarily, and a high degree of family interaction is possible. Between the evening meal and bedtime, activities vary according to the age and interests of the family members, the stage of the family life cycle, and its orientation.

The family may spend a quiet evening at home, with the peace broken at intervals by conflict over the choice of television programs, the use of the telephone, or by the contending pressures of privacy and group demands. There may be guests who are entertained by the whole family, by the adults only, or by the children. Retiring tends to be serially routinized, with the youngest going to bed first, and the others according to age and interest.

Weekly rhythms are fairly predictable in most families. Monday through Friday routines are built on work and school schedules. Saturday and Sunday are the weekend intervals filled with shopping and food storage, cleaning and making ready for the coming week, individual and whole-family recreation (travel, trips, picnics, hobbies, movies, entertaining, and "just being lazy") and religious services for the various family members.

In most parts of the country seasonal variations follow a predictable pattern. Spring is associated with housecleaning, gardening, and storage of winter clothing and equipment; summer, with more out-of-doors living, sports, and vacation activities; autumn, with the busyness of organizational, educational, and vocational life, and readying the home for fall and winter activities in the community. Late in the fall, there is the flurry of "getting ready for the holidays" in home, school, and community, followed by the bustle of seasonal entertaining and festivities in various settings. By midwinter, families settle down to indoor activities and to routines established for getting things done before spring rolls around again.

Family members' life spans

The stages through which a family may be expected to pass can be generalized from statistical profiles of family experience in much the same way that life expectancy can be predicted from the actuarial tables compiled by life insurance companies. Data for an individual family member may deviate from the schema at any point without invalidating the predictions, which hold true at a given time for the population as a whole.

Woman's life today

Using official figures from the United States Bureau of the Census and the National Center for Health Statistics, the life of a woman living in the United States today may be outlined as follows. She comes into her family of orientation at birth; she goes to kindergarten at five, starts school at six, enters her teens at thirteen, and marries when she is 21, more or less. At this point she leaves her family of orientation and enters her family of procreation. Her first child is born about two years later, and her last child arrives before she is 30. By the time she is 28, her first child is in kindergarten, and a year later will go to school. He becomes a teenager when she is about 35, and he marries when she is in her early forties. Her last child marries before she is 50 (earlier for daughers, later for sons). She shares her middle age in the empty nest with her husband until his death, which comes when she is in her late sixties. Then she has a decade, more or less, of widowhood until her own death (Table 7-1).

The college-educated woman marries later than her less-well-educated sister, she has her first baby at a later age, and enters the next stages of the family life cycle somewhat later. However, the smaller number of children borne by college-educated women offsets their later age at marriage to some extent. Thus the life cycle profiles for the college woman and the typical American woman in the United States tend to parallel each other in the latter half of life, from the launching stage onward.

The typical American woman spends the first two decades of her life growing up and getting ready to have children, the next 25 to 30 years bearing and rearing children, and the last 25 to 30 years alone or with her husband after their children have grown and gone. More than half of her married life remains after her children have left home.

Such a view of life through the years raises many questions about the kind of education a girl needs, not only for the immediate future, but also for the years ahead. What will a woman need to prepare herself for the long middle years after her parental role is over? The successive roles of a woman are played out not only in the quick-moving years of young womanhood, but through the ever-changing tempos of the entire family life cycle.

Modern man's life

The profile of the life of the man in the American family (plotted using medians and norms from the United States Bureau of the Census and data from the National Center for Health Statistics) differs slightly from that of the American woman. Like her, the male enters his family

Table 7–1
Life Span of a Modern American Wife and Mother

76		Death	76±
72			
68	Widow	Death of husband	69±
64			
60			
56			
52	Middle-aged and aging wife (empty nest)	Last child marries	52±
48			
44	Mother at launching stage	First child marries	46± / 44±
40			
36	Mother of teenagers	First child teenager	36±
32	Mother of school-age children	Last baby born	30±
28	Mother of preschool children	First child in school	29±
24	Childbearing mother	First baby born	23±
20	Young wife	Marries	21±
16			
12		Enters teens	13
8			
4		Goes to school	6±
0		Born	0

Family
of
Procreation

Family
of
Orientation

Source: Based upon current data from the U.S. Bureau of the Census and the National Center for Health Statistics, Washington, D.C.

of orientation at birth, starts kindergarten at five, goes to school at six, and becomes a teenager at 13. He marries two years later than the woman, when he typically is 23 years of age, more or less. At this point he becomes part of his family of procreation. His first child is born a little more than two years after his marriage, when he is about 25. His last child is born when he is in his early 30s and he becomes a father of teenagers when he is about 38 years of age. When he reaches his mid-40s he becomes the father of the bride (or groom) when his first child marries. Soon after he reaches 50 his last child is married; by this time he probably is a grandfather. From now on he and his wife live in an empty nest, their parenting roles over. The chances are that he retires in his mid-60s. Characteristically, he is the first spouse to die, but if he survives beyond the average, he may or may not be widowed through his final years.

Each man attains the successive stages in his life cycle at his own particular pace. On the average, however, he can anticipate spending most of his adult life as a husband and father. He and his wife will spend the first two years or so as a couple before their first child arrives. Then, after his last child has married and left home, he may expect to spend another 14 years (plus or minus) as a member of a couple again. His second decade of life will be spent in becoming a young man, his third in becoming a father. His 40s will be characterized by the launching of children, teenagers and young adults into lives of their own. His 50s and 60s, after the peak of child-rearing responsibilities is passed, will be relatively quiet. A twosome once again, he and his wife will share the experience of grandparenthood. The chances are that he will leave his wife a widow, so that life insurance, retirement plans, housing requirements and related concerns must be considered as they plan for their later years (Table 7-2).

Stages in the family life cycle

There is a predictability about family development that helps us know what to expect of any given family at any given stage. Much as each individual who grows, develops, matures, and ages undergoes the same successive changes and readjustments from conception to senescence as every other individual, the life cycles of individual families follow a universal sequence of family development.

The family life cycle, used as a frame of reference, affords a longitudinal view of family life. It is based on the recognition of successive phases and patterns as they occur within the continuity of family living over the years. It opens the way for study of the particular problems and potentials, rewards and hazards, vulnerabilities and strengths of each phase of family experience from beginning to end.

Families mature as their children grow up through childhood into adolescence and finally into lives and homes of their own. Families that once expanded to accommodate the requirements of growing children must later contract as they release these same children as young adults. The bustling years when family life runs at a hectic pace eventually give way to the long, slow-moving years of the empty nest period when the middle-aged and aging parents face the latter half of their marriage together as a pair. With the prolongation of life, these later years present new opportunities and problems.

Families, like individual persons, progress from birth to death in the steps and patterns inherent in the human condition. And, like their

Table 7-2
Life Span of a Modern American Husband and Father

76		Death of other spouse	76±	
72				
68	Widower(?)	Death of one spouse	68±	
64				
60				
56	Middle-aged and aging	Last child marries	54±	Family
52	husband (empty nest)			of
	Father at			Procreation
48	launching stage	First child marries	48±	
			46±	
44				
40				
	Father of teenagers	First child teenager	38±	
36				
	Father of	Last baby born		
32	school-age children	First child in school	32±	
28	Father of		31±	
	preschool children	First baby born	25±	
24	Childbearing father	Marries	23±	
	Beginning family			
20				
16				
		Enters teens	13	Family
12				of
8				Orientation
		Goes to school	6±	
4				
0		Born	0	

Source: Based upon current data from the U.S. Bureau of the Census and the National Center for Health Statistics, Washington, D.C.

separate members, families express their individuality in the distinctive ways in which they proceed through the universal life cycle. Each family history has its own unique design.

Family life cycle division

The family life cycle may be divided into few or many stages on the basis of several factors. It is possible to think of a two-stage family life cycle: (1) *the expanding family stage*, taking the family from its inception to the time when its children are grown, and (2) *the contracting family stage*, in which children are being launched by the family into lives of their own, and in which the family continues to contract through the later years until only one or both of the original pair still remain at home. Such a two-stage cycle delineation is usually too gross for definitive study, but the factor of shifting plurality patterns in the family was one of the first used to identify stages in the family life cycle.

Years ago, Sorokin and others (1931) discussed a four-stage family life cycle based on the changing family member constellation within the family: (1) married couples just starting their independent economic existence, (2) couples with one or more children, (3) couples with one or more adult self-supporting children, and (4) couples growing old.

E.L. Kirkpatrick and others (1934) saw the stages of the family life cycle in terms of the place of the children in the educational system in a four-stage cycle: (1) preschool family, (2) grade school family, (3) high school family, and (4) all adult family.

In plotting the changing financial income and outgo patterns throughout the family life cycle, Howard Bigelow (1942) elaborated on the school placement factor in a cycle he demarked into seven periods: (1) establishment, (2) childbearing and preschool period, (3) elementary school period, (4) high school period, (5) college, (6) period of recovery, and (7) period of retirement.

The most complex breakdown of the family life cycle into stages to date elaborates the eight-stage cycle of this text into a 24-stage cycle (Rodgers 1960). Following not only the predictable development of a family as the oldest child grows, this proposal also keeps the youngest child in focus. Such a delineation calls for two preschool family stages, three school-age, four teenage, five young adult, and five launching stages. The first of these is the beginning family stage. The next 20 make provision in each family life cycle stage for a possible youngest child who theoretically plunges the family back into an earlier age group interest as younger children arrive. Dr. Rodgers explains, ". . . the solution follows Duvall quite closely. Birth, entry into school, departure from the family system, retirement, and dissolution of the system are easily identifiable. We can do this, however, for the additional position of last child, as well as first-born, which is a modification of the Duvall approach" (Rodgers 1962:62).

The 24-stage family life cycle proposed by Rodgers has not been used much in research, and there is little evidence that the youngest child's age and school placement critically affect a family's development (Aldous 1974:101). Furthermore, the elaboration is too detailed for ordinary use. Therefore, we continue to depict the family life cycle as consisting of eight stages (Table 7–3; see also Figure 7–1).

Table 7-3
Duvall's Eight-Stage Family Life Cycle

Designation and descriptive interval qualities

Stage
I	Married couples (without children)
II	Childbearing families (oldest child birth–30 months)
III	Families with preschool children (oldest child 2½–6 years)
IV	Families with school children (oldest child 6–13 years)
V	Families with teenagers (oldest child 13–20 years)
VI	Families launching young adults (first child gone to last child's leaving home)
VII	Middle-aged parents (empty nest to retirement)
VIII	Aging family members (retirement to death of both spouses)

Source: A modification of Duvall and Hill, 1948 formulation.

Figure 7-1
Percentage at Each Age of Married and Widowed Men and Women, by Stage of the Family Life Cycle (The divorced are not shown since the percentage never rises above 4.9.)

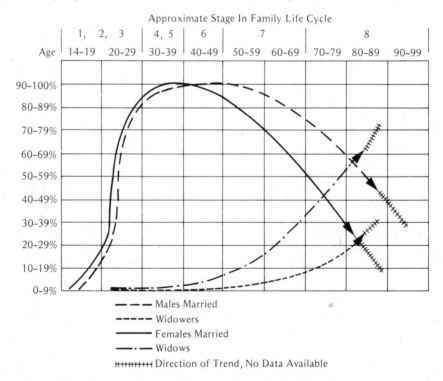

Source: Ruth Shonle Cavan, *The American Family*, 4th ed. (New York: Thomas Y. Crowell Company, 1969), p. 232; with data from U.S. Bureau of the Census, *Statistical Abstract of the United States, 1967* (Washington, D.C.: U.S. Government Printing Office, 1967), p. 33.

The eight-stage family life cycle

"The Duvall Eight-Stage Family Life Cycle" cited is a refinement of the 7-stage formulation developed for the first National Conference on Family Life (Duvall and Hill 1948). It represents a combination of four factors used in determining family life cycle stages: (1) plurality patterns, (2) age of the oldest child, (3) school placement of the oldest child, and (4) functions and statuses of families before children come and after they leave. This combination has proved to be workable in the study of American families, as well as of those in other countries. It parallels reliable data available from official government sources and from basic longitudinal family studies.

The age and school placement of the oldest child are used as criteria of family life cycle stage intervals from the arrival of the first child in the family to the launching-center stage, when the focus shifts to those remaining in the original family. Stage 6 (families as launching centers), begins with the first child's leaving home and concludes with the departure of the last child into a life of his or her own.

Overlap of family life cycle stages

A clear-cut sequence of stages in the family life cycle occurs only in a family with one child. In families with more than one child, there are several years of overlap at various stages. Our thesis is that families grow and develop as their children do. Our answer to the question of overlapping of stages is that a family grows through a given stage with its oldest child and in a sense "repeats," as subsequent children come along. We see a family being pushed into coping with new unknowns as its oldest child becomes a preschooler, goes to school, enters the teens, and finally leaves home for a life of his or her own.

As younger children come along, they arrive in a family already familiar with the normal sequence of children's growth because of their experience with the eldest. Thus, a younger sibling that is born at the time when a family is seeing its firstborn into preschool, arrives in a preschool family rather than in a childbearing family, because of the family's involvement with the oldest child.

The oldest child is always taking his family with him or with her out into the growing edges of family experience. Younger children necessarily arrive in a different family than that into which the firstborn came—a significant difference being the degree of the family's experience with children of various ages.

Variations in the typical family life cycle

Some individuals do not fit into the family life cycle typology. Those who never marry remain theoretically in their family of orientation

(Tables 7-1, 7-2), even though they may have left it. Couples who never bear, adopt, or rear children are, technically, married couples rather than families. Such alternatives as homosexual pairs, group marriages, communes, and other family-like households (Chapter 6) tend to remain outside the typical family life cycle.

Some married couples do not fit neatly into the family life cycle timetable. They marry earlier or later than the national norms. They bear their children earlier, later, or over a longer period of years than is typical. They, or their children, have exceptional abilities or disabilities that markedly affect their family life. One or more of their family members are away in institutions, or on government or corporate business, thereby altering the usual family expectations and experience. The problems of delineating family life cycle stages that hold for all families are many because families themselves are so varied.

Especially difficult to take into account are the many forms of broken and rebuilt families—with all that is involved in divorce, remarriage, and the establishment of families in which "your children," "my children," and "our children" are all part of the same family. Now, when divorce breaks so many families, there are more parents without partners and more remarriages, each with its own life cycle to complete in its own way (Chapter 18). Should increasing rates of divorce, delayed marriage, or alternatives to marriage become long-term trends, a decline in the proportion of adults experiencing typical family life cycles may be expected (Norton 1974:170).

Throughout the twentieth century to date, there has been increasing uniformity in the family life cycle, because of three trends: (1) increasing percentages of persons marrying, (2) decreasing childlessness, and (3) longer life spans of both males and females (in the past more families were broken earlier by death). One computation using birth cohorts of women born between 1890 and 1934 shows a steady increase in the proportion of women who have had a typical family life cycle, or one modified by a stable remarriage (Table 7-4).

Thus a woman born in the early 1930s, who would be in her 40s in the 1970s, is more likely to have had a typical family life cycle than her mother 20 years before, or her grandmother 40 years earlier.

Married couples as "families"

Three stages of the family life cycle, as we define it, deal with the husband and wife as a couple: stage 1 as a married couple before children come, and stages 7 and 8 as a married couple after their children have grown and gone. It can be argued that a couple without children is not a family, but more accurately a married couple.

However, when the whole family is viewed in perspective over the

Table 7-4
Increasing Incidence of Family Life Cycle Experience

Birth cohort	Number out of 1,000 women with typical or modified family life cycle experience
1890–1894	575
1900–1904	635
1910–1914	670
1920–1924	740
1930–1934	780

Source: Uhlenberg (1974:288).

years, the newly married couple appear as the "beginning family," which develops very quickly in the majority of cases into the childbearing family. The norm is for the young married couple to be a family-in-the-making not only because their children eventually make a family of them, but because they think of themselves as potential parents long before children actually arrive. In terms of the time factor alone, many couples spend as much time (or more) in their early married stage as expectant parents as they do as bride and groom.

The middle-aged or aging couple who have already been through the childbearing, rearing, and launching stages of the family cycle are still a couple, true. But they are parents of grown children, too. They quite probably have grandchildren. More often than not, they keep up the home base. They make a home for varying lengths of time for their married children and grandchildren and in some cases for their own aging parents and other older relatives. They continue to think of themselves as "family" and to function as family members long after their own children are grown and off in homes of their own. Therefore, we describe them as being in the later stages of the family life cycle.

Duration of family life cycle stages

Remembering that few families move through the family life cycle in ways that are "typical," it is possible nevertheless to plot the time usually taken by American families to progress through each of the eight stages of the cycle. This is done by utilizing census data that provide profiles of families as well as of individuals according to designated milestones in their life histories.

Americans usually think of a family as a unit consisting of a father, a mother, and two or three young children. Advertisements project just such a picture of family life. Church and school materials often portray this stage of the family life cycle as though it were the only one that mattered. Commercial word pictures commonly assume that the family with young children is *the* family. Holiday sentiments and everyday assumptions put this stage of the family life cycle so much in the foreground that no other seems to exist. Such a stereotype is understandable. Certainly the child-rearing and childbearing stages are highly important in family relationships, in the family's contact with school, church, and community, in the development of the personalities of the children, and for the family as a consumer, with its bulging appetites for more and ever more goods. Yet this period in the family life cycle is but a small fraction of the whole. It represents only a few years, an average of a dozen or so, out of the total of 50 to 60 years of the average family life span.

Figure 7-2
The Family Life Cycle by Length of Time in Each of Eight Stages

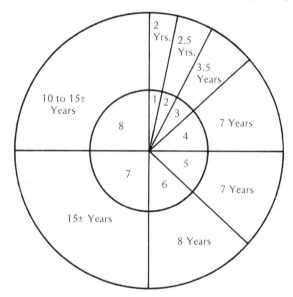

1. Married Couples (without children).

2. Childbearing Families
   (Oldest child, birth–30 months).

3. Families with Preschool Children
   (Oldest child 30 months–6 years).

4. Families with Schoolchildren
   (Oldest child 6–13 years).

5. Families with Teenagers
   (Oldest child 13–20 years).

6. Families Launching Young Adults (First child gone to last child leaving home).

7. Middle-aged Parents
   (Empty nest to retirement).

8. Aging Family Members
   (Retirement to death of both spouses).

Source: Based upon data from the U.S. Bureau of the Census and from the National Center for Health Statistics, Washington, D.C.

In marriage and family life courses in schools and colleges, it is usual to spend the greater part of the time on the processes leading to marriage, the adjustments of the newly married pair, and their functions as expectant and actual parents. This, of course, is justifiable in that it reflects the readiness of the student, as well as the significance of the husband-wife relationship, for the stability of the family. Yet such an emphasis gives an inaccurate portrayal of the time the married pair will spend together as a couple in the family they have established. Young adults about to finish their education, establish themselves vocationally, and get married can better make the decisions necessary for these immediate goals by keeping their probable entire family life cycle in mind.

If the man and woman contemplating marriage are of the average ages reported by the United States Bureau of the Census as typical at first marriage, birth of children, marriage of last child, and death of spouse, then the family cycle they may envisage for themselves is largely ignored in courses that focus solely on the young married couple. As is seen in Figure 7-2, one-half of the marriage typically is spent as a couple after the children have grown and gone.

The significance of the duration of the various stages—for education, budgeting, housing, health, recreation, home management, and a host of other family resources and services—excites the imagination and will be dealt with in part in the subsequent chapters devoted to each of the stages of the family life cycle.

Twentieth century changes in the family life cycle

Today, more children survive the early years of life; more mothers come through childbearing safely; and a larger percentage of men and women live out the full life span than in the past. Both husband and wife can now anticipate more years of marriage and family living than was typical at the beginning of this century.

Trends over three generations

Research into family development through studies of three generations of living American families shows that changes in the timing of family life cycle stages have taken place in this century, as shown in Table 7-5.

The grandparent generation, marrying in the first decade of the twentieth century, married at a later age, bore children at closer intervals, and continued childbearing for a longer period, producing more children than recent generations. The parent generation married in the depression era and delayed having children longer than did the grandparent or the married children generations. The grandparent generation spent more

Table 7-5
Years Married at Critical Points in Family Life Cycle
Stages in Three Generations

Critical point in family life cycle	Number of years married		
	Grand-parents married 1907	Parents married 1931	Married children married 1953
First child born	1.67	1.69	1.66
Second child born	4.45	5.27	4.59
Third child born	6.58	9.8	6.83
Last child born	14.6	10.4	*
First child launched	22.4	20.7	*
Last child launched	33.8	25.0	*

Source: Reuben Hill, *Family Development in Three Generations* (Cambridge, Mass.: Schenkman Publishing Company, 1970), Chap. 4, derived from Chart 4.01.
*Married children's family life cycle not completed at the time of the study.

years bearing, rearing, and releasing its children than did the two more recent generations. Trends in family life cycle changes over three generations are noted in 12 significant differences, summarized below (Hill 1970: 187–202).

1. Marriage occurs at earlier ages now than in former generations.
2. Fewer children are now born into families than in earlier generations.
3. Voluntary child-spacing is more probable now than in earlier generations.
4. Children are spaced more closely than in parents' generation (during the depression).
5. Grown children are launched earlier now than in previous generations.
6. Launching stage is shorter than in earlier generations.
7. Periods of childbearing, child-rearing, and releasing grown children are shorter now.
8. The empty nest stage occurs sooner for middle-aged couples now than formerly.
9. Middle-aged couples have a longer time together after their children are grown and gone.
10. There is a possibility of more years together after retirement now than formerly.
11. There is a likelihood of longer life for individuals now than in earlier generations.
12. Each family member has a larger number of older living relatives than formerly.

Twentieth century changes in the number and spacing of children and in the life expectancy of men and women have affected the life cycle of the typical American family in ways shown in Figure 7-3. Mothers who have married in the 1970s are younger by several years at the time of their last child's birth than were mothers who married in earlier decades of this century. Today's mothers are younger when their last child marries and thus have more years with their husbands after their children have grown and gone than earlier generations had. For "those couples who survive jointly until their last child marries, the resulting estimate of the length of the empty nest period is increased to 16.3 years (median age at death of one spouse, 68.6 years, minus median age at marriage of last child, 52.3

Figure 7-3
Life Span of Mothers in the U.S.A., Married 1900s–1970s

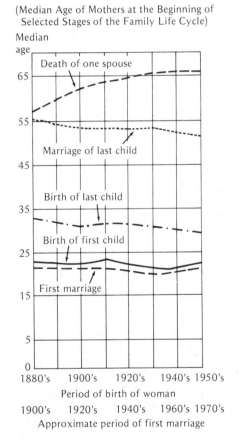

(Median Age of Mothers at the Beginning of Selected Stages of the Family Life Cycle)

Source: Paul C. Glick, "Updating the Life Cycle of the Family," paper presented at the annual meeting of the Population Association of America, Montreal, Canada, April 30, 1976.

years), for the young adults who are embarking on their first marriage during the 1970's" (Glick 1976:6).

Family life cycle changes
to come

Any forecasting of changes in the American family life cycle for the years ahead must rest on the assumptions that trends already underway will continue; that no great catastrophic upheavals in the form of external threats or internal disintegration will occur; and that the dominant values of the nation will endure. The children and young people of today will be attaining marriageable ages between now and the year 2,000. Adults will continue to marry, probably at later ages than in recent decades. Both sexes and members of minority families will attain higher levels of education than did their parents. Husbands and wives will be closer in age and interests than formerly. More wives will work for more years of their lives, and at better paying jobs than was possible before. As (if) economic conditions improve, more minority familes will have higher incomes, more prestigious occupations, wide social acceptance, and smaller families. Most married couples will keep house by themselves, as practically all of them do now. Divorce and remarriage will continue as an acceptable response to unsatisfactory marriage. Average life expectancy at birth will increase "from 67.9 for males and 75.7 for females in 1972 to 69.9 for males and 78.0 for females in 2020" (Census Bureau 1975:5; also Parke and Glick 1967:256).

From generation to generation

Before one family unit has completed its cycle, its grown children have embarked on theirs. Most twentieth-century American family members see a second, third, and perhaps even a fourth family life cycle spun off, as children marry and rear their children—who grow up, marry, and have children—who in turn marry and repeat the family life cycle pattern while older members of the family are still living.

A young couple know not only their own newly established family, but that of their parents, grandparents, and possibly their great-grand-parents as well. They can look forward to seeing their children and grand-children and possibly their great-grandchildren launched and married. As they relate intimately to the two or three older generations, and the two or three younger generations, they go around the family life cycle again and again and again with these other close kinfolk. Thus the term "cycle" is appropriate according to its dictionary definition, "any complete round or series of occurrences that repeats or is repeated." Such other terms as "lifetime family career," and "lineage family cycle" (Rodgers 1973;

Feldman and Feldman 1975) are interesting alternatives for the more common usage of "family life cycle."

The continuous spinning off of grown children's, grandchildren's and future generation's family life cycles we view as *the generation spiral*. As older family members die, their emotional, intellectual, cultural, biological, material, and personal legacies continue on through the generation spiral of which they have been a part. Ongoing participation and interaction flows between the generations in the typical family.

Reuben Hill (1970) sees parents of married children forming *the lineage bridge* between the elder and younger generations in the same family. Three-generational sharing of activities, visiting, and help exchanges are common. Each generation turns to relatives for help from time to time—the grandparents for help in illness and with household management, the parents for emotional gratification, and the married children for material assistance and child care.

In times of trouble, family members in older and younger generations most often step in to help. Outsiders from churches, social agencies, and health and welfare departments are least often credited as sources of aid (Figure 7-4). In one given year, a vast network of interaction between the generations was reported—3,781 specific instances of help given and received in illness, financial binds, child care, household problems, and emotional stress. As a result of this mutual interdependence, members of each generation reported that, by significant percentages, more was received from than given to their relatives (Figures 7-4 and 7-5).

The many ways in which families rely on one another within the generation spiral have been noted in studies through the years (Duvall 1954; Sussman and Burchinal 1962; and others). The popular notion of the modern family as a vulnerable little nuclear unit of husband, wife, and their children, unsupported by other caring relatives, is not borne out by research. Empirical evidence points rather to a modified extended family within a rich network of generational interaction (Litwak 1960; Sussman 1965; Hill 1970, etc.).

Interpersonal relationships increase as families grow

The size of the family increases by arithmetical progression—starting with two persons, as husband and wife marry and settle down to establish a family. Then the first baby arrives, followed by the second, and so on as long as the family grows in size.

According to the law of family interaction, with the addition of each new person to a family the number of persons increases in the simplest arithmetical progression in whole numbers, while the number of personal interrelationships within the group increases in the order of triangular numbers (Bossard 1945:292)

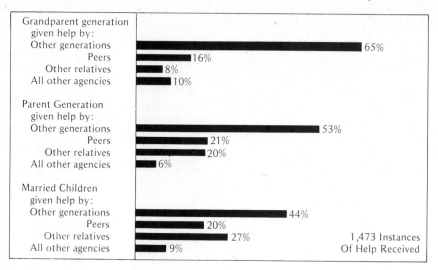

Figure 7–4

Sources of Help Received by Three Generations, over a Year's Time, by Percentages of Instances

Grandparent generation
  given help by:
  Other generations — 65%
  Peers — 16%
  Other relatives — 8%
  All other agencies — 10%

Parent Generation
  given help by:
  Other generations — 53%
  Peers — 21%
  Other relatives — 20%
  All other agencies — 6%

Married Children
  given help by:
  Other generations — 44%
  Peers — 20%
  Other relatives — 27%
  All other agencies — 9%

1,473 Instances
Of Help Received

Source: Reuben Hill, *Family Development in Three Generations* (Cambridge, Mass.: Schenkman Publishing Company, 1970), Chap. 3, "Interdependence among the Generations."

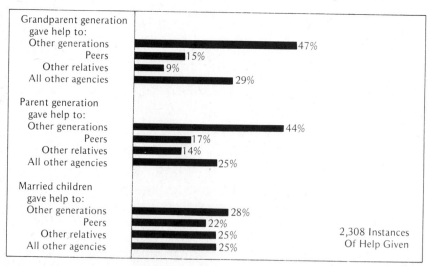

Figure 7–5

Help Given by Three Generations, over a Year's Time, by Percentages of Instances

Grandparent generation
  gave help to:
  Other generations — 47%
  Peers — 15%
  Other relatives — 9%
  All other agencies — 29%

Parent generation
  gave help to:
  Other generations — 44%
  Peers — 17%
  Other relatives — 14%
  All other agencies — 25%

Married children
  gave help to:
  Other generations — 28%
  Peers — 22%
  Other relatives — 25%
  All other agencies — 25%

2,308 Instances
Of Help Given

Source: Reuben Hill, *Family Development in Three Generations* (Cambridge, Mass.: Schenkman Publishing Company, 1970), Chap. 3, "Interdependence among the Generations."

To find the number of interpersonal relationships within a family, the following formula is used, in which x equals the number of interpersonal relationships, and y equals the number of persons:

$$x = \frac{y^2 - y}{2}$$

Applying this formula to a specific family, the following series emerges: number of persons in the family—2 3 4 5 6 7 8 9 and so forth; number of relationships in the family—1 3 6 10 15 21 28 36 and so forth.

Thus we see that a family consisting of a mother, father, and three children has a total of five individuals with a total of ten interpersonal relationships: father with mother, father with first child, father with second child, father with third child; mother with first child, mother with second child, mother with third child; first child with second child, first child with third child; second child with third child.

Assuming that all four grandparents are living, the family with three children consists of nine persons within the generation spiral (four grand-parents, two parents, and three children), within which a total of 36 interpersonal relationships is possible. As the three children marry, their three spouses swell the number of family members to 12 and their inter-relationships to 66, not counting any of the new in-laws. When each of the married children's families has its second child, there now is a prob-able number of interpersonal relationships totaling 153. As the great-grandparents die, they are replaced by new births in the youngest genera-tion. The last remaining great-grandparent in the final stage of his or her life cycle quite possibly is part of an eighteen-person family, with more than 150 interpersonal relationships in its generation spiral. Figure 7-6 shows graphically how rapidly family relationships increase through the family life cycle, merely within the generation spiral, and not counting any of the relatives by marriage, or the aunts, uncles, cousins and other kin who are considered part of the family.

Uses of the family life cycle concept

The Thirteenth International Seminar on Family Research brought together 70 social scientists from eastern and western Europe, Japan, and North America to review the relevance of the family life cycle concept in the study of family life. A variety of approaches to the use of the family life cycle were reported. Among these were (1) a descriptive use that follows life from the cradle to the grave; (2) a dynamic aspect that links functional relationships at one point in time with phenomena at another time; and (3) causal analysis that anticipates from earlier stages

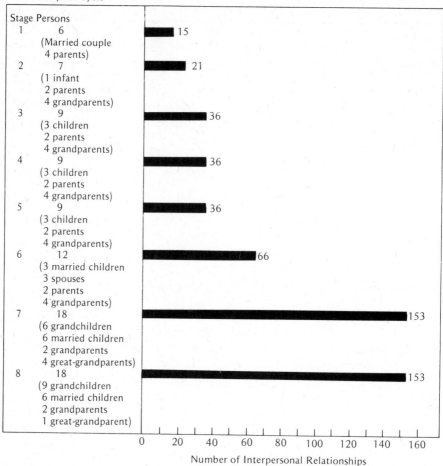

Figure 7-6
Possible Number of Interpersonal Relationships in a Three-child Family, by Stage in the Family
Life Cycle

Number of family
members at each stage of
the family life cycle

Stage	Persons	
1	6 (Married couple 4 parents)	15
2	7 (1 infant 2 parents 4 grandparents)	21
3	9 (3 children 2 parents 4 grandparents)	36
4	9 (3 children 2 parents 4 grandparents)	36
5	9 (3 children 2 parents 4 grandparents)	36
6	12 (3 married children 3 spouses 2 parents 4 grandparents)	66
7	18 (6 grandchildren 6 married children 2 grandparents 4 great-grandparents)	153
8	18 (9 grandchildren 6 married children 2 grandparents 1 great-grandparent)	153

Number of Interpersonal Relationships

what will happen at later stages in family life (Segalen 1974:817).
Professor William Goode concludes that, "we are once more able to understand how potentially fruitful a family cycle approach might be, even if
we cannot neatly put all families into a precise, concrete typology or
taxonomy of family cycles" (Goode, in Sussman 1974:60).

The family life cycle is a most apt tool for the training of paraprofessionals (Ogren 1971); for the use of doctors, nurses, home economists,
teachers, social workers, and other professionals who work with families;

and also for family members (present and future) for whom life cycle management is relevant (Duvall 1972). Knowing where a family is in its life cycle makes it possible to anticipate a number of vital factors—its relative income level, its consumer practices, whether the wife works, the couple's probable marital satisfaction, areas of possible family conflict, and the nature of its parent-child relationships for example. "Thus, the family life cycle stage concept has proven to have systemic qualities, because the families its stages group together share a number of other important properties" (Aldous 1974:115).

Whatever schema for defining family life cycle stages is used, it is merely a convenient division for the study of something that in real life flows from one stage to another without pause or break. The genius of the concept is its explicit awareness that each stage has its beginnings in stages past and its fruition in those yet to come. Being cyclical by definition, the family life cycle has no beginning and no end. No matter where you start to study a family by means of its family life cycle, there are always relevant roots in the near and distant past to be considered. Wherever you are at the moment, you have grown out of the stage just before and are heading into the stage ahead.

The concept provides a vantage point basic to family development study. It is the long view, penetrating longitudinally through the life history of a family, that keeps in perspective each of its members in relation to all of the others—past, present, and future. This may be why the family life cycle has proved to be superior to other variables in anticipating many facets of family behavior (Lansing and Kish 1957; Blood and Wolfe 1960; Feldman 1965; Hill 1970; Aldous 1974, and others noted in References).

Growth is the only evidence of life.
John Henry, Cardinal Newman

Developmental tasks: individual and family

chapter eight

Human development proceeds according to known principles that hold for everyone. Each individual grows in his own way and at his own rate, yet in conformity with the developmental program followed by every human being. Knowledge of the universal patterns and principles of human development is basic to an understanding of the ways in which families and their members undertake their developmental tasks.

The study of human development

Studies of childhood; of adolescence; and of young, middle-aged, and aging adults have recorded and outlined the process of human development throughout the life span. Professional observation and statistical evidence provide a remarkably consistent profile of human development from conception to the end of life.

Freud's schema of development

Sigmund Freud identified the first six stages of human development as: (1) *oral stage*, dominant during the first year, when the infant depends on feeding for his physical survival and emotional well-being; (2) *anal stage*, during which the toddler is expected to conform to adult expectations that center in his bowel and bladder training; (3) *phallic stage*, when the preschooler becomes impressed with his body and with his growing sense of power as an individual; (4) *oedipal stage*, when, during the early school years, the boy renounces his earlier tie to his mother and identifies with his father, while the girl becomes more feminine through her identification with her mother; (5) *latency stage*, during which reality orientation is in progress (following resolution of the oedipal conflict); and (6) *adolescence*, the period beginning with genital maturation and ending when heterosexual maturity and the ability to give and to receive love are attained.

Erikson's eight stages in the life cycle of man (Close 1960; Erikson 1950).

Erik Erikson has identified eight stages of life as critical in human psychosocial development. He points to the struggle between the negatives and positives in each crisis that must be resolved if the next developmental stage is to be reached. He emphasizes that no victory is completely or forever won as an individual goes from stage to stage in his psychosocial development.

1. *Infancy: trust versus mistrust.* The first "task" of the infant is to develop the "cornerstone of a healthy personality," a basic sense of trust—in himself and in his environment. This comes from a feeling of inner goodness derived from "the mutual regulation of his receptive capacities with the maternal techniques of provision"—a quality of care that transmits a sense of trustworthiness and meaning. The danger, most acute in the second half of the first year, is that discontinuities in care may cause the child's natural sense of loss (as he gradually recognizes his separateness from his mother), to grow into a basic sense of mistrust that may last through life.

2. *Early childhood: autonomy versus shame and doubt.* With muscular maturation the child experiments with holding on and letter go and begins to attach enormous value to his autonomous will. The danger here is that the child may acquire a deep sense of shame and doubt if he is deprived of the opportunity to develop his will while he is learning his "duty," and

therefore may come to expect defeat in any battle of wills with those who are bigger and stronger.

3. *Play age: initiative versus guilt.* In this stage the child's imagination is greatly expanded because of his increased ability to move around freely and to communicate. It is an age of intrusive activity, avid curiosity, and consuming fantasies that lead to feelings of guilt and anxiety. It is also the stage of the establishment of conscience. If the tendency to feel guilty is "overburdened by all-too-eager adults," the child may develop a deep-seated conviction that he is essentially bad, with a resultant stifling of initiative or a conversion of his moralism to vindictiveness.

4. *School age: industry versus inferiority.* The long period of sexual latency before puberty is the age when the child wants to learn how to do and make things with others. In the process of learning to accept instruction and to win recognition by producing "things," he is also developing the capacity to enjoy work. The danger in this period is the development of a sense of inadequacy and inferiority in a child who does not receive recognition for his efforts.

5. *Adolescence: identity versus identity diffusion.* The physiological revolution that comes with puberty—rapid body growth and sexual maturity—forces the young person to question "all sameness and continuities relied on earlier" and to "refight many of the earlier battles." The developmental task is to integrate childhood identifications "with the basic biological drives, native endowment, and the opportunities offered in social roles." The danger is that identity diffusion, temporarily unavoidable in this period of physical and psychological upheaval, may result in a permanent inability to "take hold," or, because of youth's tendency to total commitment, in the fixation in the young person of a negative identity, a devoted attempt to become what parents, class, or community do not want him to be.

6. *Young adulthood: intimacy versus isolation.* Only as a young person begins to feel more secure in his identity is he able to establish intimacy with himself (with his inner life) and with others, both in friendships and eventually in a love-based mutually satisfying sexual relationship with a member of the opposite sex. A person who cannot enter wholly into an intimate relationship because of the fear of losing his identity may develop a sense of isolation.

7. *Adulthood: generativity versus self-absorption.* Out of the intimacies of adulthood grows generativity—the mature person's interest in establishing and guiding the next generation. The lack of this results in self-absorption and frequently in a "pervading sense of stagnation and interpersonal impoverishment."

8. *Senescence: integrity versus disgust.* The person who has achieved a satisfying intimacy with other human beings and who has adapted to the

triumphs and disappointments of his generative activities as parent and co-worker reaches the end of life with a certain ego integrity—an acceptance of his own responsibility for what his life is and was and of its place in the flow of history. Without this "accrued ego integration" there is despair, usually marked by a display of displeasure and disgust.

Piaget's conception of cognition-development (Hunt 1961; White 1969; and Piaget and Inhelder 1969)

Piaget's work on the foundations of cognition during the first of life puts renewed emphasis on early human development and experience. He sees a definite order in which behavior and thought make their appearance as a result of a child's interaction with his environment. The infant is born with reflexes and built-in complexes of the senses, nerves, and muscles that he exercises and learns to use during his early sucking practice in the first month of life. Piaget sees this as "exercising ready-made sensormotor schemata." Sometime after the first month, the baby varies and combines his nursing behavior—looking while he sucks or turning his head toward moving objects in what Piaget calls "primary circular reactions." The infant's "secondary circular reactions," which come next, include initiating and anticipating the behavior of others and reaching out to them. This is close to what Erikson refers to as the basis of trust. Near the end of the first year the infant imitates, plays games, and becomes a social being who recognizes that what he does brings about some expected consequence, in what Piaget calls "coordination of secondary schemata." Between the first and second years of life, the toddler is curious, "into everything," craving more and more environmental stimulation in "tertiary circular reactions." Between 18 and 24 months vocabulary spirals, and the infant changes into a child who operates more by symbols, who remembers where things are and looks for them, and who delights in problem-solving. Piaget calls this stage the "internalization of sensormotor schemata."

Between 18 months and four years, during the child's "preconceptual phase," he accumulates images and forms "intuitions." By nine or ten a child is able to order objects serially by length, later by weight, and at 11 or 12 by volume, in "concrete operations." The third period, beginning at 11 or 12, is a landmark in that the individual can now deal with propositions as well as with concrete objects. This leads to the "formal operations" that provide the intellectual ability for the scientific method.

Bloom's review of longitudinal studies

Benjamin S. Bloom has analyzed 1,000 longitudinal studies of individuals who were repeatedly measured and observed at different points in their development. He found the results of many studies in close enough agreement to enable him to describe development quantitatively for 30 human characteristics. Thus he is able to predict the ages at which seven of these characteristics have reached a level of development representing 50 percent of their full potentiality (as expected at maturity). The seven (listed in Table 8-1) are: height by age two and one-half, general intelligence by four, aggressiveness in males by three, dependency in females by four, general school achievement by the third grade, and reading comprehension and vocabulary by age nine (Bloom 1964).

Thurstone's work (1955), reviewed by Bloom, found 80 percent of adult performance levels in children and adolescents in a number of characteristics: perceptual speed by age 12, space and reasoning factors by 14, number and memory factors by age 16, verbal comprehension by 18, and word fluency that reaches the 80 percent level by 20. Longitudinal studies of college students show ego development reaching 80 percent levels by age 18 and flattening out in a plateau by 25 (Sanford 1962).

Critical periods in human development

Critical periods in human development occur at the times when specific organs or other aspects of an individual's growth are undergoing most rapid change. It is during a period of accelerated growth that a given characteristic is most vulnerable to environmental factors. For instance, pregnant women who took thalidomide or who contracted German measles during the first three months of pregnancy bore infants whose defects (if observable) were in those parts of the body developing most rapidly at the time when the drug was ingested or the viral attack occurred.

Physical organs of the embryo emerge according to a precise schedule that is important for their full normal development and for their articulation into the rest of the organism. In this sequence of development each organ has its time of origin. The time factor is as important as the place of origin. If the eye, for example, does not arise at the appointed time, "it will never be able to express itself fully, since the moment for the rapid outgrowth of some other part will have arrived, and this will tend to dominate the less active region and suppress the belated tendency for eye expression. . . ."

The organ that misses its time of ascendancy is not only doomed as an entity; it endangers at the same time the whole hierarchy of organs. "Not only does the arrest of a rapidly budding part, therefore, tend to suppress its development temporarily, but the premature loss of supremacy to some other organ renders it impossible for the suppressed part to come again into dominance so that it is permanently modified. . . ." The result of normal development is proper relationship of size and function among the body organs—the liver adjusted in size to the stomach and intestine, the heart and lungs properly balanced, and the capacity of the vascular system accurately proportioned to the body as a whole. Through develop-

Developmental tasks: individual and family   163

Table 8-1
Critical Periods in Human Development (Theory and Research)

Age	Period	Freud	Erikson	Piaget	Bloom	Thurstone and others
23	Parenthood		Generativity			
22	Marriage					
21	Adulthood		Intimacy			
20						Word fluency
19						
18						Verbal comprehension Ego development
17						
16						Number and memory factors
15	Adolescence		Identity	Formal operations		
14						Space and reasoning factors
13	Teenage					

Age	Period	Freud	Erikson	Piaget		
12					Perceptual speed	
11						
10						
9						Reading comprehension / Vocabulary
8			Industry	Concrete operations	Intelligence	General school achievement
7		Latency				
6	School-age	Oedipal				
5		Phallic	Initiative	Preoperational: Intuitive		
4			Imagination	Preconceptual		Dependency / General intelligence
3	Preschool	Anal		Sensorimotor / Means—end behavior / Internalization		Aggression in boys
2			Autonomy			Height
1	Infancy	Oral	Trust	Circular reactions		
0	Birth			Reflexes		

Sources with approximate ages from Freud, Erikson, Piaget, Bloom, Thurstone, Sanford, works cited in *References*.

mental arrest one or more organs may become disproportionately small; this upsets functional harmony and produces a defective person (Erikson 1950).

Hypotheses and research findings concerning many facets of human development identify critical periods at which a given characteristic or ability emerges. New development arises out of foundations already present. Growth is sequential, each new aspect of development proceeding from previously established structure or skills.

Research findings underline the Freudian and Eriksonian statements on the crucial importance of the earliest months of life as the infant learns to nurse and develops a sense of trust—in himself, in his mother, and in his world. Piaget points to the critical significance of the first weeks and months in the development of intelligence and the ability to learn. Hundreds of studies tracing the development of many human characteristics have pinpointed the timing and significance of critical periods for the successful emergence of physical, intellectual, and personality factors. Some of these are indicated in Table 8–1, at ages approximated by Freud, Erikson, Piaget, Bloom, Thurstone, and others.

Patterns and principles of development

Human growth, development, and decline involve a number of types of change, 12 of which are listed in Table 8–2.

Each individual is unique in terms of both inherited and environmen-

Table 8-2
Twelve Types of Change in Human Growth, Development, and Decline

1. Changes in specificity (embryonic growth and development proceeds from simple cells to specific, functioning organ systems)

2. Changes in efficiency (digestive system is more efficient in childhood than in either infancy or aging)

3. Changes in kind (adult hair differs from baby down and also from thin, drying, aging hair)

4. Changes in color (skin and hair darkens through childhood; hair loses color, and skin darkens in later years)

5. Changes in number (teeth change from none visible at birth to fifty, more or less, in the preschooler; then school child gets permanent teeth, which may be lost over the years)

6. Changes in size (organs and stature become larger through the first twenty years; some shrinking of body size is to be expected in later years)

7. Changes in shape (profile of the body differs in infancy, childhood, adolescence, and adulthood in ways that are predictable)

8. Changes in texture (bones are soft in infancy; harden in childhood; and become brittle in aging)

9. Changes in flexibility (infant and child's body is elastic and flexible; adult muscles and joints stiffen through the years)

10. Changes in control (infant has little control; adult enjoys full control; aged lose some ability to control physical processes)

11. Changes in teachability (child learns many skills readily, adults with more difficulty)

12. Changes in physical satisfaction (infant, child, and adolescent enjoy physical activities; older adult finds less satisfaction in declining powers)

Model freely adapted and expanded from Boyd R. McCandless, *Children: Behavior and Development* (New York: Holt, Rinehart and Winston, 1967), p. 412.

Table 8-3
Principles Inherent in Development

1. Development results from both biological maturation and individual learning.
2. Development of human characteristics tends to be orderly, regular, and predictable.
3. Growth rates vary within the different stages of individual development.
4. Each individual grows at a pace appropriate for him, at his stage of development, in his environment.
5. Development tends to be sequential, with each added increment built on earlier ones.
6. Development of specific characteristics is based on previous progress in similar or associated forms.
7. Growth and development are most rapid during the early stages of life.
8. The first months and years are crucial foundations for later development.
9. Early verbal learning is essential for the development of later complex human skills.
10. Socially prescribed expectations order the major events of a lifetime in a given society.
11. Norms for given ages and stages function as social prods or brakes on behavior.
12. Development proceeds in a specific direction, from a known beginning to an expected end.
13. Anticipated end points in development serve as personal goals for individuals.
14. Personal goals are both individually and socially determined.
15. Attainment of personal goals brings a sense of fulfillment and success.
16. Developing individuals face certain responsibilities for maturing and achieving at every stage of life.
17. Individuals may be expected to be at work on developmental tasks appropriate to their stage of development.
18. Developmental tasks successfully accomplished lead to further developmental levels.
19. No one else can accomplish the developmental tasks an individual faces.
20. Few developmental tasks are completed in isolation; most depend on social interaction.
21. Helping persons (parents, teachers, etc.) can be of great help to a child at work on one or more of his developmental tasks.
22. Modification of environment has least effect on characteristics at their periods of least development.
23. Rates of growth and development may be modified most at times of most rapid change.
24. Assistance in development is most effective at times of fastest growth and readiness.

tally learned aspects, but there is a universally recognizable pattern of development throughout the life span. Human growth and development progress according to a number of principles, listed in Table 8-3.

Developmental tasks of individuals

Developmental tasks are defined as tasks that arise at or near a certain time in the life of an individual, the successful achievement of which leads to his happiness and to his success with later tasks—whereas failure leads to unhappiness in the individual, disapproval by society, and difficulty with later tasks (Havighurst 1972:2). These growth responsibilities are jobs to be done by an individual as he develops. As his physical growth proceeds from one stage of development to the next, the individual must learn to use his newfound powers; i.e., the infant learns progressively to suck, to drink, to swallow soft foods, to chew, and eventually to eat at the family table. Teething occurs automatically in time; learning to eat solid foods and to hold a spoon are developmental tasks of early childhood.

Developmental tasks arise at critical periods in an individual's growth, when others expect specific performance of him. A child is expected to learn to read when he goes to school; when he does, he and others (teachers, parents, and other kinfolk) are happy about his progress, and he goes on to more complex accomplishments in school and elsewhere. Should he find reading difficult to the point of failure, for any of a number of reasons, his school progress is slowed, he is unhappy about himself, and he faces the disapproval of others.

Origins of developmental tasks

Developmental tasks have two primary origins: (1) physical maturation, and (2) cultural pressures and privileges. A secondary origin derived from the first two is found in the aspirations and values of the individual.

As the individual grows, he matures. Growth represents much more than added stature and bulk. It involves the elaboration and maturation of the muscle, organ, bone, and neural systems of the organism according to a predictable sequence. Certain developmental tasks come primarily from the maturation of one or more aspects of the organism. Examples are many. As the infant's leg and back muscles develop strength enough, and as the neural connections mature to the point where the child has conscious control over movement, he faces the developmental task of learning to walk. When the adolescent girl's body develops into one resembling that of a woman, and as she begins to menstruate, she must come to terms with her femaleness and develop a wholesome acceptance of herself as a woman. Later, when she reaches middle age, menopause represents yet another developmental task—that of accepting the termination of her reproductive life and facing the challenge of aging. Many comparable developmental tasks present themselves throughout the lives of both men and women.

Cultural pressures may be recognized in the many rewards and penalties the individual receives (and anticipates) for his various behaviors. Society (in the form of peers, associates, parents, teachers, and all "the significant others" in his life) expects and often exerts pressure on the person to conform to the prescribed ways of behaving within a given culture. These expectations and pressures emerge at the times believed appropriate in the culture for the individual to function in the roles and statuses assigned to him. Unfortunately they may be too soon or too late for an individual.

By the time a child reaches a certain age, he is expected to eat solid foods, at another age to be toilet trained, at another to walk, at another age to talk, at another to respect property rights, at another to mingle socially with members of the other sex, at another to marry and "settle down," and so on through his entire life span. Regardless of what they are and when they come into effect, these expectancies impel the individuals of the culture to behave in certain ways and are thus an important origin of their developmental tasks. Examples in our society are: learning to read, learning to handle money responsibly, learning how to gain a place for oneself with one's age-mates, and establishing oneself as an acceptable member of a dating crowd as a teenager and among the young married set as a husband or wife.

Developmental tasks differ from culture to culture. Each cultural group has its own developmental definitions and expectations. The fact that these tasks also vary from region to region in our country—even from class to class in the same area—accounts for many persistent problems among children of different ethnic and cultural backgrounds.

Encouragement and support by family and friends are often essential in achieving developmental tasks that the individual alone might find too difficult. As cultural pressures work upon the maturing organism, the emergent personality is formed, with all of its idiosyncratic values and aspirations. These in turn significantly influence the direction and form of future developmental tasks. Two examples of developmental tasks derived primarily from the personal aspirations and values of the individual are choosing a vocation and achieving a personal philosophy of life, both of which always reflect the life around the person.

Basically, a developmental task is a thrust from within the individual to develop in such a way (by modifying present behavior) as to attain a desired goal. The push to change usually comes from within the person but may be evoked by the demands and expectations of others. It receives its direction from the cultural definition of what is expected of such an individual at his stage of development. A developmental task, although culturally defined, is neither a chore nor a duty, in the sense that it is externally imposed. It is rather a growth responsibility that the individual assumes for his own development as he adapts himself to his life situation.

The individual's assumption of a given developmental task consists of at least four interrelated operations: (1) perceiving new possibilities for his behavior in what is expected of him or in what he sees others, more mature than he, accomplishing, (2) forming new conceptions of himself (identity formation), (3) coping effectively with conflicting demands upon him, and (4) wanting to achieve the next step in his development enough to work toward it (motivation). To illustrate: a small boy sees somewhat bigger boys riding their bicycles (operation 1—perception); he conceives of himself as a potential bicycle rider (operation 2—identity formation); he resolves the conflicts between his mother's protests that he might get hurt and his own fears of failure with the expectancies of his peers and the demands of his father that he become a "big boy" (operation 3—coping with conflicting demands); and finally, he wants to learn to ride a bike enough to practice what it takes to become proficient in it (operation 4—motivation).

Most of the growth responsibilities the individual confronts result from the combined impact of his biologic maturing, the environmental forces that work upon him, and his own personal drives, ambitions, and value orientation. Thus the task of being weaned results from the baby's physiological maturation (teething, etc.), as well as from cultural pressures in the form of maternal insistence that he take solid foods, and his own desire to be a "big boy" and eat as the others in the family do. Teenage dating emerges partly from the biologic maturing of puberty, partly from the cultural pressures of friends and family to have a girl or boyfriend and go out to young people's activities in the community, and partly from the person's own aspiration to belong, to be accepted, to be a recognized member of the younger set in the neighborhood.

The teachable moment

When the time comes that the body is ripe for, culture is pressing for, and the individual is striving for some achievement, the teachable moment has arrived. It is at this very moment—at the convergence of its several origins—that the accomplishment of the developmental task is most highly motivated; at that time the individual is most truly *ready* for the next step in his development. Before that the person is not mature enough for the desired outcome, so that efforts to push him through a premature accomplishment may be largely wasted. Readiness also implies that the person has lived fully at his present stage and thus is not being hurried into the next stage.

An illustration is found in the early efforts to toilet train an infant. In the 1920s and 1930s, this training was often attempted while the baby was only a few weeks old. At that age, his sphincters were not ready for such control; his neural connections had not matured enough to make possible his cooperation; and his own aspirations were in quite another direction. It is not surprising to find that the precocious demands of the parent upon the child met with failure and often created persistent conflict. Knowledge of child development has modified these expectancies, and today good practice is to wait for signs that the baby is ready for toilet training before assisting him to achieve the task. This concept of readiness is well established in the field of human development.

The concept of the teachable moment goes a bit deeper, since it indicates specifically the three dimensions in which readiness emerges—in the physical organism, in the social pressures, and in the personal values of the individual. It is a useful guide for anyone responsible for the growth, development, and guidance of others: teachers, supervisors, parents, indeed anyone who works with, or cares about, other people. For it provides a gauge of what may be expected of given persons and an approximate timetable for anticipating change. This ability to predict what persons at various stages of development are, or soon will be, ready for is of paramount importance to curriculum formulators and educators in general. If we assume that the general purpose of both family life and education is to assist the individual to grow up to his own best potential, we see that some knowledge of developmental tasks—and especially of the teachable moments at which these tasks arise—is highly relevant.

> There is a tide in the affairs of men,
> Which, taken at the flood, leads on to
>   fortune;
> Omitted, all the voyage of their life
> Is bound in shallows and in miseries.
>
>> Shakespeare,
>> *Julius Caesar*, IV, 3

Developmental tasks of the individual through life

The developmental tasks faced by an individual as he or she progresses through the years from birth to death are innumerable. It would be impossible to list completely all of the growth responsibilities to be achieved by any one person. Yet, there are certain general categories of tasks that allow us to catalog the more common developmental tasks within our culture. A formulation of this type is found in Table 8-4.

Such a listing of the individual's developmental tasks is not all-inclusive, nor is it universally applicable. Different cultures and subcultures make different demands on their members. In most of the cultures of the world today, the general expectancies change from time to time, so that the developmental tasks of one generation differ somewhat from those of the preceding or of the succeeding one.

Whatever the society in which the individual grows up, he faces the developmental tasks peculiar to it at every stage of his life span. The successful achievement of his developmental tasks brings the individual from a state of helpless dependence as an infant, through varying dimensions of independence as an adolescent, to a mature level of interdependence with his fellowman that lasts through the greater part of adulthood.

Interacting developmental tasks of family members

At any given moment, children are striving to meet their growth needs, parents to reconcile conflicting demands, and each individual to find himself in the midst of the security and threats of his particular world.

Table 8-4
Developmental Tasks in Ten Categories of Behavior of the Individual from Birth to Death

	Infancy (birth to 1 or 2)	Early childhood (2-3 to 5-6-7)	Late childhood (5-6-7 to pubescence)
I Achieving an appropriate dependence-independence pattern	1. Establishing oneself as a very dependent being 2. Beginning the establishment of self-awareness	1. Adjusting to less private attention; becoming independent physically (while remaining strongly dependent emotionally)	1. Freeing oneself from primary identification with adults
II Achieving an appropriate giving-receiving pattern of affection	1. Developing a feeling for affection	1. Developing the ability to give affection 2. Learning to share affection	1. Learning to give as much love as one receives; forming friendships with peer
III Relating to changing social groups	1. Becoming aware of the alive as against the inanimate, and the familiar as against the unfamiliar 2. Developing rudimentary social interaction	1. Beginning to develop the ability to interact with age-mates 2. Adjusting in the family to expectations it has for the child as a member of the social unit	1. Clarifying the adult world as over against the child's world 2. Establishing peer groupness and learning to belong
IV Developing a conscience	1. Beginning to adjust to the expectations of others	1. Developing the ability to take directions and to be obedient in the presence of authority 2. Developing the ability to be obedient in the absence of authority where conscience substitutes for authority	1. Learning more rules and developing true morality
V Learning one's psycho-socio-biological sex role		1. Learning to identify with male adult and female adult roles	1. Beginning to identify with one's social contemporaries of the same sex

Early adolescence (pubescence to puberty)	Late adolescence (puberty to early maturity)	Maturity (early to late active adulthood)	Aging (beyond full powers of adulthood through senility)
Establishing one's independence from adults in all areas of behavior	1. Establishing oneself as an independent individual in an adult manner	1. Learning to be interdependent—now leaning, now succoring others, as need arises 2. Assisting one's children to become gradually independent and autonomous beings	1. Accepting graciously and comfortably the help needed from others as powers fail and dependence becomes necessary
Accepting oneself as a worthwhile person really worthy of love	1. Building a strong mutual affectional bond with a (possible) marriage partner	1. Building and maintaining a strong and mutually satisfying marriage relationship 2. Establishing wholesome affectional bonds with one's children and grandchildren 3. Meeting wisely the new needs for affection of one's own aging parents 4. Cultivating meaningfully warm friendships with members of one's own generation	1. Facing loss of one's spouse, and finding some satisfactory sources of affection previously received from mate 2. Learning new affectional roles with own children, now mature adults 3. Establishing ongoing, satisfying affectional patterns with grandchildren and other members of the extended family 4. Finding and preserving mutually satisfying friendships outside the family circle
Behaving according to a shifting peer code	1. Adopting an adult-patterned set of social values by learning a new peer code	1. Keeping in reasonable balance activities in the various social, service, political, and community groups and causes that make demands on adults 2. Establishing and maintaining mutually satisfactory relationships with the in-law families of spouse and married children	1. Choosing and maintaining ongoing social activities and functions appropriate to health, energy, and interests
	1. Learning to verbalize contradictions in moral codes, as well as discrepancies between principle and practice, and resolving these problems in a responsible manner	1. Coming to terms with the violations of moral codes in the larger as well as in the more intimate social scene, and developing some constructive philosophy and method of operation. 2. Helping children to adjust to the expectations of others and to conform to the moral demands of the culture	1. Maintaining a sense of moral integrity in the face of disappointments and disillusionments in life's hopes and dreams
Strong identification with one's own sex mates Learning one's role in heterosexual relationships	1. Exploring possibilities for a future mate and acquiring "desirability" 2. Choosing an occupation 3. Preparing to accept one's future role in manhood or womanhood as a responsible citizen of the larger community	1. Learning to be a competent husband or wife, and building a good marriage 2. Carrying a socially adequate role as citizen and worker in the community 3. Becoming a good parent and grandparent as children arrive and develop	1. Learning to live on a retirement income 2. Being a good companion to an aging spouse 3. Meeting bereavement of spouse adequately

(Continued)

Table 8-4 (Cont'd.)

	Infancy (birth to 1 or 2)	Early childhood (2-3 to 5-6-7)	Late childhood (5-6-7 to pubescence)
VI Accepting and adjusting to a changing body	1. Adjusting to adult feeding demands 2. Adjusting to adult cleanliness demands 3. Adjusting to adult attitudes toward genital manipulation	1. Adjusting to expectations resulting from one's improving muscular abilities 2. Developing sex modesty	
VII Managing a changing body and learning new motor patterns	1. Developing physiological equilibrium 2. Developing eye-hand coordination 3. Establishing satisfactory rhythms of rest and activity	1. Developing large muscle control 2. Learning to coordinate large muscles and small muscles	1. Refining and elaborating skill in the use of small muscles
VIII Learning to understand and control the physical world	1. Exploring the physical world	1. Meeting adult expectations for restrictive exploration and manipulation of an expanding environment	1. Learning more realistic ways of studying and controlling the physical world
IX Developing an appropriate symbol system and conceptual abilities	1. Developing preverbal communication 2. Developing verbal communication 3. Rudimentary concept formation	1. Improving one's use of the symbol system 2. Enormous elaboration of the concept pattern	1. Learning to use language actually to exchange ideas or to influence one's hearers 2. Beginning understanding of real causal relations 3. Making finer conceptual distinctions and thinking reflectively
X Relating oneself to the cosmos		1. Developing a genuine, though uncritical, notion about one's place in the cosmos	1. Developing a scientific approach

Early adolescence (pubescence to puberty)	Late adolescence (puberty to early maturity)	Maturity (early to late active adulthood)	Aging (beyond full powers of adulthood through senility)
Reorganizing one's thoughts and feelings about oneself in the face of significant bodily changes and their concomitants Accepting the reality of one's appearance	1. Learning appropriate outlets for sexual drives	1. Making a good sex adjustment within marriage 2. Establishing healthful routines of eating, resting, working, playing within the pressures of the adult world	1. Making a good adjustment to failing powers as aging diminishes strengths and abilities
Controlling and using a "new" body		1. Learning the new motor skills involved in housekeeping, gardening, sports, and other activities expected of adults in the community	1. Adapting interests and activities to reserves of vitality and energy of the aging body
		1. Gaining intelligent understanding of new horizons of medicine and science sufficient for personal well-being and social competence	1. Mastering new awareness and methods of dealing with physical surroundings as an individual with occasional or permanent disabilities
Using language to express and to clarify more complex concepts Moving from the concrete to the abstract and applying general principles to the particular	1. Achieving the level of reasoning of which one is capable	1. Mastering technical symbol systems involved in income tax, social security, complex financial dealings, and other contexts familiar to Western man	1. Keeping mentally alert and effective as long as is possible through the later years
	1. Formulating a workable belief and value system	1. Formulating and implementing a rational philosophy of life on the basis of adult experience 2. Cultivating a satisfactory religious climate in the home as the spiritual soil for development of family members	1. Preparing for eventual and inevitable cessation of life by building a set of beliefs that one can live and die with in peace

Source: An elaboration of Caroline Tryon and Jesse W. Lilienthal III, "Guideposts in Child Growth and Development," *NEA Journal* (March 1950): 189.

There are times when members of a family find it easy to mutually support and sustain one another. This happens when the various developmental tasks of family members call for the channeling of energies in the same general direction. At such times the family moves as a unit to meet the developmental requirements of each member. Just as "naturally," on occasion, the goals, needs, striving, and developmental tasks of family members are in conflict. If we hold the entire family in focus, we see that much of the normal friction between members during the family's life cycle is due to incompatibility of the diverse developmental strivings of family members at critical points of growth.

From time to time the developmental tasks of the husband may conflict with those of his wife. A simple illustration is found in the young husband's developmental task of developing competency in household maintenance. His do-it-yourself projects clutter up the house at the time when his wife is trying to maintain a pleasant, attractive home amid the already heavy demands of infants and small children.

Developmental tasks of children conflict with those of their parents at several stages in the family life cycle. In adolescence the young person is struggling to emancipate himself or herself from the authority of the parents, whose own developmental tasks as parents call for sustained guidance and supervision of the not-yet-adult child. At such a time, storms brew and break within the family as normally as they do in the weather, when two or more energy systems moving in opposite directions collide.

Now unified, now atomized, each family lives out its own unique history in pulsing, throbbing rhythms and ever-changing tempos. Each family is an arena where interacting personalities try to achieve their own developmental tasks within the pattern of family life—which in turn is evolving in interaction with the larger society of which it is a part.

Basic family tasks

A family must perform certain basic tasks that are essential for its survival and continuity. Basic tasks of American families are:

1. providing shelter, food, clothing, health care, etc. for its members
2. meeting family costs and allocating such resources as time, space, facilities, etc. according to each member's needs
3. determining who does what in the support, management, and care of the home and its members
4. assuring each member's socialization through the internalization of increasingly mature roles in the family and beyond
5. establishing ways of interacting, communicating, expressing affection, aggression, sexuality, etc. within limits acceptable to society
6. bearing (or adopting) and rearing children; incorporating and releasing family members appropriately

7. relating to school, church, work, community life; establishing policies for including in-laws, relatives, guests, friends, mass media, etc.
8. maintaining morale and motivation, rewarding achievement, meeting personal and family crises, setting attainable goals, and developing family loyalties and values

All families have these basic tasks as long as they live. Each family performs its essential functions in its own ways, which may differ from those of others. Families in various ethnic, racial, and social class groupings operate within the freedoms and constraints of their subcultures as well as of those of the larger society. As long as families function adequately, their right to live as they wish is not challenged. However, when its norms are not met, society intervenes to protect its members. Welfare, police, fire, education, health departments, and other agency representatives, relatives, and friends invade the family's privacy to monitor, correct, supplement, or take over the basic tasks not being discharged at least minimally within that family. Basic family tasks are so essential that if the family does not perform them, others will.

Family developmental tasks

Family developmental tasks are those basic family tasks that are specific to a given stage of development in the family life cycle. Family developmental tasks are directed toward meeting the requisites for family well-being and continuation at any particular period in the life of the family. Family developmental tasks may be seen as those growth responsibilities that must be accomplished by a family at a given stage of its development in a way that satisfies (1) its biological requirements, (2) its cultural imperatives, and (3) its own aspirations and values—if the family is to continue as a unit. In much the same way that individual developmental tasks change over the years, so family developmental tasks shift with each stage of the family life cycle.

Family developmental tasks parallel the developmental tasks of individual family members and can be similarly defined. Thus—a family developmental task is a growth responsibility that arises at a certain stage in the life of a family, the successful achievement of which leads to present satisfaction, approval, and success with later tasks—whereas failure leads to unhappiness in the family, disapproval by society, and difficulty with later family developmental tasks.

Sources of a family developmental task

A family developmental task arises at any point in a family's life when the needs of one or more family members converge with the expectations of society in terms of family performance. As individuals develop, and as they respond to their associates' expectations with new aspirations, they make demands on their families to support their new individual developmental tasks. Such demands exert internal pressure on the family to change. Simultaneously, pressures constraining the family to conform to society's standards of conduct at that time are applied from outside the family. These community pressures vary according to the family's social status, age, and sex composition. The family's sense of identity, its reputation in the community, and its own aspirations are mobilized to meet the new challenges as a family unit, and the new family developmental task is undertaken (Aldous 1974:123).

Stage-critical family developmental tasks

Stage-critical family developmental tasks occur as the family enters each new stage of its development. Critical events such as being married, bearing children, releasing them as teenagers and young adults, and continuing as a couple through the empty nest and aging years (Table 8-5) propel a family into and through each new stage in its history. Each new developmental crisis necessitates new adaptations and imposes new responsibilities at the same time that it opens up new opportunities and poses new challenges. For instance, as the members of the newly married couple leave their parents' homes, their families are engaged in the family developmental tasks of the launching-center phase. The young couple enter their own marriage at its establishment phase and must deal with all the critical changes and developmental tasks involved in building a marriage and establishing a family.

Family aspirations and goals

Family aspirations are the short-term tension-reducing objectives that a family views as important at the moment. One family is building a new home; another is saving up for a vacation; a third is trying to get out of debt; while another is attempting to get its eldest child into college, to nurse an ill member back to health, or to release a young adult into marriage.

Family aspirations are specific to the individual family in its social group at a particular time. Such immediate objectives tend to shift as soon as one step has been reached. Thus, once the home has been built, other goals appear—for example, the new house must be furnished in the style to which the family is aspiring.

Beyond the specific, temporary, and individual aspirations of a given family are the objectives that society as a whole has for its families. National goals are concerned with family health, safety, stability, standards of living, and levels of education, and with the competence of families to develop citizens capable of functioning effectively in a free society. Some national goals for families are designed to protect the country as a whole. When atomic bombing was thought to be a real threat, families were di-

Table 8-5

Stage-critical Family Developmental Tasks through the Family Life Cycle

Stage of the family life cycle	Positions in the family	Stage-critical family developmental tasks
1. Married couple	Wife Husband	Establishing a mutually satisfying marriage Adjusting to pregnancy and the promise of parenthood Fitting into the kin network
2. Childbearing	Wife-mother Husband-father Infant daughter or son or both	Having, adjusting to, and encouraging the development of infants Establishing a satisfying home for both parents and infant(s)
3. Preschool-age	Wife-mother Husband-father Daughter-sister Son-brother	Adapting to the critical needs and interests of preschool children in stimulating, growth-promoting ways Coping with energy depletion and lack of privacy as parents
4. School-age	Wife-mother Husband-father Daughter-sister Son-brother	Fitting into the community of school-age families in constructive ways Encouraging children's educational achievement
5. Teenage	Wife-mother Husband-father Daughter-sister Son-brother	Balancing freedom with responsibility as teenagers mature and emancipate themselves Establishing postparental interests and careers as growing parents
6. Launching center	Wife-mother-grandmother Husband-father-grandfather Daughter-sister-aunt Son-brother-uncle	Releasing young adults into work, military service, college, marriage, etc., with appropriate rituals and assistance Maintaining a supportive home base
7. Middle-aged parents	Wife-mother-grandmother Husband-father-grandfather	Rebuilding the marriage relationship Maintaining kin ties with older and younger generations
8. Aging family members	Widow/widower Wife-mother-grandmother Husband-father-grandfather	Coping with bereavement and living alone Closing the family home or adapting it to aging Adjusting to retirement

rected to provide bomb shelters and conduct drills. In times of national emergency, such as war, families are expected to do their part for the war effort both on the home front and by sending eligible members into service. During the continuing energy crisis, it is important for families to cooperate in conserving the various forms of energy; so too when other shortages appear, families are urged to conserve, recycle, and make do in order that the nation as a whole not suffer severe deprivation. Many government programs that enlist family support have as their ultimate goal the common weal.

Family goals can be seen as falling between the short-term aspirations of a given family at a particular time and the long-term national goals for all families in the society. Ideally, a family's goals will have a positive effect on the lives of family members—motivating and supporting them at every step in their psychosocial development (Table 8-5). The modes and course of action followed by a family as it carries out its developmental tasks at any stage in its life cycle reflect the family's goals. Thus, family goals at the establishment phase of family life center on adjusting to living as a married couple. When children come, family goals involve providing for their care, nurture, and development. As children mature, family goals are focused on loosening family ties and releasing young adults into homes of their own. Family goals profoundly influence family functioning and developmental tasks at every stage of the family life cycle.

Families, as families, are seen to have responsibilities, goals, and developmental tasks that are specifically related to the development of their members. All of these developmental tasks—those of family members and of the family as a unit—shift as the family grows and changes, and are constantly being modified by the interplay of forces both within and outside of the family in every society, in every age.

We are marching along the endless pathway of unrealized possibilities of human growth.

Francis W. Parker

developing familes

part four

Marriage is a thing you've got to give your whole mind to.

Henrik Ibsen

Married couples

chapter nine

Marriage is a critical role transition point for couples marrying for the first time. It involves moving on from their families—and from the orientation phase of their development—to the unfamiliar husband-wife relationship. At this stage husband and wife concentrate their attention on their interpersonal relationship within the marriage and on their major goal of adjustment to life as a married pair. Typically, the couple have a year or two in which to establish their marriage before their first child arrives. Husbands and wives who neither bear, adopt, nor rear children continue throughout the marriage as married couples. For the remarried, the critical transition is the passage from earlier conjugal relationships broken by death or divorce to those now to be forged with the new mate in a new marriage.

Readiness for marriage

The majority of Americans eventually marry, usually while they are in their twenties. By then, they have been through two or more decades of personal development and are more or less ready for the privileges and responsibilities of marriage. Their friends and families expect them to marry at this time, reflecting the norms and expectations that serve as prods to behavior. From their awareness of the "social clocks" that tell them when they are early, late, or on time, people generally know the "right" time to get married and start a family (Neugarten 1968; Elder 1972).

Single white women tend to marry before they are twenty-four, after which age the marriage rate drops sharply. Black women marry at about the same rate throughout their twenties (U.S. Bureau of the Census 1971:2). Men tend to marry by their mid-twenties, if their income permits. The higher their income, the more likely young men are to marry (Cutright 1970). Family situations, educational attainment (or failure), individual differences, and changing economic conditions are responsible for wide variations in the timing of marriage. Marriages of the very young, the subject of so much concern between 1946 and 1956, have received less attention in recent years, even though they still present serious problems.

Young marriages

Teenage marriages in the United States have declined since 1956 (U.S. Bureau of the Census October 1974:67). Numerous studies have found that young marriages are predominantly between teenage girls and somewhat older males. Schoolgirl marriages are less stable than those of young adults (Burchinal and Chancellor 1963, and more recent census reports). Some characteristics of girls who marry before they are out of high school are summarized in Table 9–1.

Married college students have financial problems at all social class levels (Eshleman and Hunt 1967). Many student couples work up to 40 hours a week in addition to their homemaking and college work. Marrying while in college often puts an end to the wife's education, at least for a while. The college enrollment rate of women in their twenties more than doubled between 1960 and 1972 (Glick 1975:17), a reflection of American women's increasing interest in developing their talents and establishing their identities before and after they marry.

In recent years, more students have completed four full years of college (Figure 3–1), and more coeds postpone marriage until they have established themselves. This process may involve one or more jobs, as well as love and possibly sex experience before marriage (Chapter 2). Generally, the higher the income and educational level of the pair, the greater the likelihood of

Table 9-1
Schoolgirls Who Marry (Data Keyed by Number to Supporting Research References)

Factors related to early marriage	Girls who marry young tend to have:
Early heterosexual involvement	Started dating early (2, 3, 7, 9) Started going steady early (3, 7, 9) Gone steady more often (3) More often felt they were in love (3) Dated older fellow (3, 9) Become premaritally pregnant (1, 3, 7, 8, 9)
Personal inadequacies	Poor social adjustment (6, 9) Emotionally less stable (9) Lower intelligence test scores (5, 6) Poor school records (6)
Limited interest in education	Little interest in further education (9) Low level of aspiration (9) Parents with little interest in college education (9)
Unsatisfactory family situation	More disagreements with parents (7, 9) More brothers and sisters (5) Less stable, intact homes (6) Less attachment to father (7) Mothers who married in their teens (3)
Social disadvantage	Lower socioeconomic status (2, 3, 6) Rural or small-community background (1, 5) Little church contact (6)
High expectations of marriage	More close friends who married while in school (3) Expectations of being happier in marriage than before (8)

Keyed References:

1. Anderson, Wayne J., and Sander M. Latts, "High School Marriages and School Policies in Minnesota," *Journal of Marriage and the Family* 27, no. 2 (May 1965): 266–270.
2. Bayer, Alan E., "Early Dating and Early Marriage," *Journal of Marriage and the Family* 30, no. 4 (November 1968): 628–632.
3. Burchinal, Lee, "Adolescent Role Deprivation and High School Age Marriage," *Marriage and Family Living* 21, no. 4 (November 1959): 378–384.
4. Burchinal, Lee G., "How Successful Are High School Marriages?" *Iowa Farm Science* 13 (March 1959): 7–10.
5. De Lissovoy, Vladimir, and Mary Ellen Hitchcock, "High School Marriages in Pennsylvania," *Journal of Marriage and the Family* 27, no. 2 (May 1965): 263–265.
6. Havighurst, Robert J., Paul Hoover Bowman, Gordon P. Liddle, Charles V. Matthews, and James V. Pierce, *Growing Up in River City* (New York: John Wiley and Sons, 1962), chap. 9, "Marriage."
7. Inselberg, Rachel M., "Social and Psychological Factors Associated with High School Marriages," *Journal of Home Economics* 53, no. 9 (November 1961): 766–772.
8. Ivins, Wilson, "Student Marriages in New Mexico Secondary Schools," *Marriage and Family Living* 22, no. 1 (February 1960): 71–74.
9. Moss, J. Joel, and Ruby Gingles, "The Relationship of Personality to the Incidence of Early Marriage," *Marriage and Family Living* 21, no. 4 (November 1959): 373–377.

their having a stable marriage (U.S. Bureau of the Census 1972). Some of the factors related to marital competence are presented in Table 9-2.

Tests of marital readiness

An individual may be said to be ready for the new role of husband or of wife when he or she clearly shows signs of:

1. being willing to be an exclusive sexual partner
2. being able to enter freely into an intimate sexual relationship
3. having tenderness and affection for the other

Table 9-2
Forecast of Marital Competence and Satisfaction

Factor	Poor chance	Good chance
Personality	Immature, few interests, poor personal and social adjustment, limited interpersonal skills	Mature, flexible, well adjusted, and generally competent in interpersonal relationships
Education	Dropouts	At least high school graduation and some further education for both
Dating history	Started to date early; went steady early; sexual involvement early	General social skills with members of both sexes developed in dating; gradual love development
Courtship	Hurried; less than six months' acquaintance; no engagement period	Several years' courtship relationship; at least six months' engagement
Reason for marriage	Impulse, "on a dare," premarital pregnancy, to escape boredom or failure, because everyone else is	Desire for home and family; to establish a deep, meaningful relationship with beloved
Pregnancy	Premarital conception	Pregnancy delayed until full year following marriage
Social status	Lower	Middle or better
Parental attitudes	Oppose the marriage, rejecting the mate, grudging assistance	Supportive; provide assistance with respect for young couple's autonomy; consult young pair upon occasion
Wedding	Elopement and civil ceremony	Conventional, hometown, church-sanctioned; family and friends present
Economic basis	Uncertain income, poor-paying jobs, little security of employment, help from relatives urgently needed	Realistic planning on known income, both with salable skills and willingness to work, reasonable expectations of present and immediate future, mature responsibility

Source: Freely adapted from Lee G. Burchinal, "Trends and Prospects for Young Marriages in the United States," *Journal of Marriage and the Family* 27, no. 2 (May 1965): 251, based upon research results from numerous sources and inferences to be further tested.

4. showing interest in the other's emotional life and development
5. sharing intimacies with the other
6. merging personal plans with those of the other
7. having a realistic understanding of the other's personal characteristics
8. being realistic about the economic problems that marriage entails
9. being realistic about his or her capacity to contribute to the marriage
10. being ready to become a husband or a wife (Rapoport 1963:78).

These ten tests can be summarized as three tasks in personal preparation for marriage: (1) making oneself ready to take on the roles of husband or of wife; (2) disengaging oneself from especially close relationships that compete with commitment to the new marriage relationship; and (3) accommodating the patterns of gratification of premarital life to those of the new marriage (Rapoport 1963:74).

Unfinished earlier developmental tasks

Few young adults can pass all of the above marital readiness tests because they still have to complete one or more developmental tasks left unfinished in an earlier period of their lives. Research data show that people who had problems with their families as children or as adolescents are among those who report unhappiness, doubt, and conflict in their early marriages (Goodrich, Ryder, and Raush 1968:387). A girl who is still rebelling against her father's domination may carry this resistance over to her mate—much as mother-dominated men often continue to protect themselves from any female's too-possessive concern. Previously promiscuous individuals may have trouble becoming exclusive sexual partners after marriage. Financially irresponsible persons find it hard to be realistic about the economic problems marriage entails. Marriage does not magically complete the maturing process; it does test it severely.

Many a marriage is handicapped by the inability of one or both of the partners to do such simple things as balance a checkbook, plan a nutritious meal, or keep a responsible job. According to a nationwide study, 49 percent of Americans between 18 and 29 are proficient, 35 percent just get by, and 16 percent are functionally incompetent (U.S. Office of Education release 1975). Coping competence in everyday tasks varies widely according to sex, to race and nationality, and to areas of proficiency (Table 9-3). Modern couples find that they fare best when they assign roles corresponding to the skills and interests of each partner, rather than along more rigid traditional lines (Chapter 4).

As married couples become increasingly secure with one another, they may each develop proficiency, work through their personal hang-ups, and help one another with their individual developmental tasks—past, present, and future. Most husbands and wives continue to progress in their devel-

Table 9-3
Coping with Everyday Chores

Proficiency areas	Percentage of the United States population		
	Functionally incompetent	Just gets by	Is proficient
Getting and keeping a satisfactory job	19.1%	31.9%	49.0%
Managing a family budget	29.4	33.0	37.6
Ability to maintain good health	21.3	30.3	48.3
Ability to use community resources	22.6	26.0	51.4
Reading	21.7	32.2	46.1
Writing	16.4	25.5	58.1
Computation	32.9	26.3	40.8
Problem-solving	28.0	23.4	48.5
Over-all Competence	19.7	33.9	46.3

Source: Government-financed study by the University of Texas, reported by U.S. Office of Education, Washington, D.C., October 29, 1975.

opmental task accomplishment from their engagement on through the marriage.

Engagement progress toward marriage

The engagement period serves as a transition bridge between single and married life. Its purpose is to accustom friends and relatives to thinking of the betrothed as a pair, and to ready the couple for marriage. Each of the engaged pair is expected to develop the capacity to accept the responsibilities of marriage—materially, expressively, and functionally. Together they tackle such engagement tasks as developing mutually satisfactory patterns of relating to friends and relatives; working; playing; planning details of the wedding, the honeymoon, and the newlywed period; establishing a sense of unity as a couple ("we" and "us" rather than "I"); and building up the emotional momentum they will need to carry them through the establishment of their marriage.

Preoccupation with bridal showers, caterers for the wedding breakfast, and such pleasant details as what they will wear at the ceremony may divert the attention of an engaged couple from the responsibility of readying themselves for the realities of marriage. The two are wise to reach an agreement before they marry on such matters as the number and timing of their children (including family planning procedures acceptable to them both) and their choice of marital role options (Chapter 4). This involves discussion of such questions as the wife's employment, the husband's responsibilities in the home, and an acceptable balance of individual and joint social activities inside and outside their home.

Developmental tasks of the married couple

The excitement of the wedding passes quickly, and the newlyweds find themselves at last alone. The time has come for each of the pair to feel really married, and to begin to assume the roles of a married person. Typically this process consists of three stages: (1) the honeymoon, (2) the newlywed phase, and (3) the established marriage before the first child arrives (if ever).

Honeymoon functions

The honeymoon may be a weekend camping trip or a cruise to a far-off island. No matter what it costs, or how long it lasts, its purpose is to meld the newlyweds into a married unit. Each must develop competence as an intimate sexual partner if both are to enjoy a satisfying sexual relationship. The virgin at marriage may experience "honeymoon cystitis" for a while until her genitals become accustomed to coitus. The sexually inexperienced bridegroom may find it hard to maintain his erection in his eagerness to prove himself. The sexually experienced may have inappropriate responses and attitudes to unlearn. Each is becoming comfortable with his or her own body as well as with the partner's. Each is learning more about the personal habits and idiosyncrasies of the other. Both are getting accustomed to joint use of facilities that previously were not shared. Studies show that while the aspirations of newlyweds are high, their disappointments are keen when things do not go as smoothly as had been anticipated. "The difficulties about intimacy are seen during the honeymoon, if not before, where many couples go to great lengths to avoid being too much alone with each other" (Rapoport 1965:49).

The honeymoon is designed to give the newly married pair privacy in which to discover one another and the joys of being married. It gives the couple a change of pace in a pleasant setting. While enjoying themselves, they each practice such marital competencies as considering the other in making plans, resolving differences, accepting feelings, and respecting personal preferences. Meanwhile, they are both storing up memories of the delights of the honeymoon that will lift morale later on when the going gets rough.

Bride and groom "at home"

Once home from the honeymoon, the bride and groom have individual developmental tasks to perform as married adults. Some of these are: (1) realigning loyalties so that the spouse comes first; (2) participating in all that is involved in establishing the new home; (3) assuming his or her share of the responsibilities of being married; (4) becoming a more satisfied and satisfying sexual partner; (5) acquiring a self-image as a wife or husband and learning to interpret the appropriate conjugal roles in action; (6) relating to parents as a married son or daughter; and (7) outgrowing earlier dependencies for more mature and appropriate interdependence within the marriage.

Family and friends help by allowing the couple to get settled without unnecessary intrusion. They await the newlyweds' announcement of being "at home" before going uninvited to visit the new couple. They delay giving advice until asked, to avoid unwelcome interference. They telephone before coming by so that they will not drop in at inappropriate times. Most important of all, they do not take sides in differences that surface between the new husband and wife, so that the couple may make their own marital adjustments in their own way.

Origins of newlyweds' developmental tasks

The developmental tasks of the newly married couple spring from three sources. The physiological maturation process that husband and wife are undergoing gives rise to their first task—the coordination of their adult drives for growing sexual fulfillment. The second origin of the developmental tasks of the newly married couple is found in the cultural expectations and pressures that impel the pair to settle down and behave as married couples are supposed to in a given community. Thirdly, the man and woman are moved by their own personal aspirations to establish their marriage according to the dreams they both have built up over the years.

The multiple nature of the origins of the developmental tasks at this stage makes for some difficulties. What the culture expects and the young couple want do not always coincide. What the realities of the situation are and what the married pair dream of as right for them are rarely identical. The goals of the wife and husband may mesh in many respects, but may be a poor fit in others. Being married involves coming to terms with what is expected—by one's culture, by one's mate, by oneself, and as a couple.

Developmental tasks of the new husband

A new husband has all the tasks of an adult male of his age and status, as well as those associated with his new marital roles. He must develop the attitudes and behavior required of him as a married man, both with his wife and with former friends of both sexes. He is expected to get and hold a job and to carry his share of the couple's financial obligations. He has roles to play in his new home as a man, as a husband, and as a mate. His wife usually wants to tell him about her day, and to hear about his. She expects him to tell her that he loves her as often as she needs to hear it. His competence in two-way communication with his wife underlies many of the other tasks he faces, both now and in later stages of his marriage.

Each new husband develops his marital competencies in his own way. As long as his performance satisfies his wife, he is free to do whatever is comfortable for him. His roles in the neighborhood, in the larger community, and at his place of work are subject to the norms of these groups. Within his home he is his own man, with only himself and his wife to please.

A new wife's developmental tasks

The new wife has developmental tasks as an adult woman and wife that parallel those of her husband sexually, financially, maritally, and emotionally. In addition, she is expected in most communities to take the lead in homemaking and in the social life of the new couple, in consultation with her husband. She may or may not be gainfully employed, but in either case, her home is expected to be presentable, and to be organized to meet the needs of the couple in such elemental matters as adequate sleep, privacy, nutrition, clothing, and recreation.

Whether she married for the first time in her early twenties, as most brides do, or in her forties, fifties, or later, the new wife has the developmental tasks of all women of her age in her group. In addition, she has those individual tasks that are involved in being the wife of her particular husband at this specific time. These tasks revolve around his work, his family, his status, and his expectations as a person. Her husband, or she herself, may be marrying again after a former marriage has been broken by death or divorce. Latent jealousies and unfavorable comparisons with a former spouse are hazards to be avoided. The bride must also meet the challenge of relating to her new mother-in-law in such a way that she neither avoids her husband's mother, nor invites her intrusion (Duvall 1954).

Conflicting and complementary developmental tasks

At times the developmental tasks of husband and wife complement each other. At other times, the efforts of one conflict with those of the other (Table 9-4). When the two mutually support each other's efforts to achieve their developmental tasks, those tasks are complementary. When the working through of their tasks as husband and wife pull the members of the pair in opposite directions, the tasks are conflicting (Figure 9-1).

It takes conscientious effort and a great deal of interpersonal competence on the part of both partners to become aware of one another as distinct individuals with firmly rooted preferences, interests, values, predispositions, and expectations. Differences naturally arise from time to time and must be recognized and evaluated. Minor idiosyncrasies can be modified for the good of the marriage. Other issues are so important that ways must be found for coping with the conflicting forces within the partnership.

Marriage launches the new husband and his bride on a new and unfamiliar way of life. Somehow they must develop patterns of daily living

Table 9-4
Complementary and Conflicting Developmental Tasks of Husbands and Wives

Developmental tasks of the young husband	Developmental tasks of the young wife	Complementary and conflicting possibilities

Becoming established in an occupation
  Getting specialized training
  Assuming responsibility for getting and holding a job
  Working toward security and advancement in his work
	Making a home and managing the household
	  Getting settled in her home
	  Establishing and maintaining household routines
	  Learning the many skills of homemaking and housework
		Complementary: Shared responsibility in homemaking
		
		Conflicting: Husband engrossed in work away from home, while wife tries to elicit his active cooperation in homemaking

Assuming responsibility for the support of the family
  Earning the family income
  Planning for the long pull of family support through the years
	Becoming a financial helpmate in establishing the home
	  Working until her husband is established
	  Seeing her work as secondary and possibily intermittent
		Complementary: Both are economic partners through establishment phase
		Conflicting: Her work threatens his status as breadwinner

Establishing mutually satisfying sex relationships
  Awakening his wife sexually
  Developing competency as a husband
	Becoming a satisfactory sex partner
	  Learning her sex role as wife
	  Responding effectively and participating in their mutual fulfillment
		Complementary: Each has the task of communicating intimately with the other

Becoming "domesticated" as a married man
  Sharing leisure time with his wife
  Developing mutual interests
  Cultivating joint activities
  Getting into the young married set
	Assuming hostess and companionship roles as a married woman
	  Planning for recreational activities as a couple
	  Accepting and refusing social invitations
	  Entertaining their friends, associates, and families
		Complementary: Both husband and wife are learning to move in tandem in their social life as a couple

Figure 9-1
Conflicting and Complementary Developmental Tasks

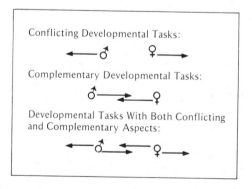

that express and satisfy them both. Each day brings decisions to make, problems to solve, and plans to outline for the ongoing development of the marriage they are establishing. Many of these interdependencies, which are vital to the continuity of the union, are mutually satisfying. Others are burdensome for one or both members of the pair. Fortunately, most couples find being newly married a happy state of affairs. "The best of all possible worlds, for most Americans, is to be newly married and not have children" (Campbell 1975:38).

In a smoothly functioning marriage, the couple strike a happy balance between individual autonomy and interdependence. They establish mutually satisfying modes of communication and attempt to meet one another's needs. They develop ways of resolving conflicts and making decisions that are acceptable to them both. Each of these achievements is made possible by the application of such qualities as empathy, supportiveness, understanding and intimate communication (Raush, Goodrich, and Campbell 1963:371).

Each pair approach their husband-wife-couple developmental tasks with varying degrees of readiness and flexibility. At first this may be done in a spirit of playing at being married. In time the couple begin to feel that theirs is a promising marriage—or that they had better part—depending on how well they accomplish their family developmental tasks as a married couple.

Family developmental tasks of the married couple

A couple must establish their marriage as a functioning unit of society, if they are to continue as a married pair. This means that they must accomplish their basic family tasks (Chapter 8). The stage-specific basic family tasks in the establishment phase of marriage are the family developmental tasks of the married couple and consist in:

1. finding, furnishing, and maintaining their first home
2. establishing mutually satisfactory ways of supporting themselves
3. allocating responsibilities that each partner is able and willing to assume
4. establishing mutually acceptable personal, emotional, and sexual roles
5. interacting with in-laws, relatives, and the community
6. planning for possible children
7. maintaining couple motivation and morale

What is expected of any given marriage depends largely on the couple's social status, ethnic and racial group, and family background (Chapter 5). Some families and communities have rigid expectations to which a couple must conform if they are not to risk ostracism. In the United States today, a couple are relatively free to live as they wish, within a minimum framework of societal demands. Both husband and wife interpret these norms and measure up to them in ways that seem appropriate, as best they can. Typically, the husband assumes the responsibility for any of the couple's activities that are related to his work; the wife takes the initiative in their social, religious, and family involvements; and both spouses share in the upkeep of their home.

Each couple enters marriage with their particular potentialities and problems. Each pair cope with the tasks of being married and of making the transition from previous roles and statuses with varying degrees of competence, creativity, and courage. The couple's success is dependent on their skill in accomplishing their developmental tasks both as individuals and as a married couple (Rapoport and Rapoport 1965).

Finding, furnishing, and maintaining their home

Finding and furnishing a suitable home to call their own (one that is within their means) is an exciting but difficult task for many a first-married couple. Their income is lower now than it will be later in the family life cycle. Their desires and dreams are often beyond their resources. Their unrealistic expectations of what comes with marriage have been built up over the years by personal fantasies, romantic myths, and hard-sell advertising.

Even before the inflationary spiral had peaked, the average American bride spent $183 on flatware and holloware, $179 on dinnerware and glasses, $119 on household linens, $118 on portable appliances, and $152 on cookware before the first year of her marriage (Porter 1972). The young couple may risk spending more than they earn, buying too much on credit, and getting into debt with multiple monthly payments for things they bought on the installment plan. Before they realize how much their regular costs will be for food, rent, utilities, fuel, car expenses, and all the rest, they are over-committed. Their families help out (Hill 1970); many couples rely on clothing bought before their marriage; and they struggle to meet the high cost of living with resources more modest than either of them had as single persons.

Two out of three young couples move early in their marriage. Men and women in their twenties move more often than any other group in the population as they marry, establish new households, and enter the labor force (U.S. Bureau of the Census December 1974:2). Young married couples move to improve their living conditions, to be nearer one or both of their jobs, or to provide a more suitable place for anticipated children.

Unless the problems that go with establishing and maintaining their first home are solved in ways that make sense to both spouses, their marriage will fail. The establishment phase is a critical period in the family life cycle, one marked by more instances of annulment, separation, and divorce than any future stage. The chances of failure are especially great for those who marry young, whose incomes are low, and who have children soon after they marry (U.S. Bureau of the Census 1972:3).

Supporting themselves and their household

In most marriages, both husband and wife work, at least until the first baby comes. Some husbands prefer full-time homemaker wives, but most young men find that the household can be supported with less strain when there are two paychecks in the family. Their wives concur, especially now when a number of conditions favor their employment. For example, (1) women marry at somewhat later ages; (2) they have more education and salable skills; (3) they can get better jobs now that equal employment legislation is in effect; and (4) wives command higher salaries now that the working married woman is no longer an issue (Chapters 3 and 4).

Decisions about spending the family income are more cooperative and democratic when both of the pair work. Husband and wife together make their financial plans, shop together for what they agree they need, read labels, inquire about warranties, and are increasingly aware of the quality of the goods they buy. Not all of them make and keep to a budget, but they are wiser in their planning than earlier generations were (Hill 1970).

Allocating responsibilities

Some husbands have little interest in housework, and their wives do not expect to work outside their homes (Goodrich, Ryder, and Raush 1968:388). Increasingly, young married couples allocate their responsibilities on the basis of their interest and competence (Chapter 4)—by improvising and learning from experience what division of labor works best for them. Educated married partners tend to believe in equalitarian relationships, but in actual practice the husbands have the greater voice in family decisions (Blood and Wolfe 1960; Centers, Ravan, and Rodrigues 1971). Working-class couples say the husband should be the dominant one, but their working wives have a relatively powerful say in household and financial decisions (Aldous 1974:70).

New consumer goods make housekeeping more interesting for both men and women than it once was (Lopata 1971:149). Husbands as well as wives today are adept at meal preparation with the help of convenience foods, packaged products, modern kitchen equipment, and outdoor grills. Merchandising appeals directly to the man of the house, reinforcing the trend toward the bisexual use of the kitchen. Some husbands pride themselves on their home-baked bread, gourmet meals, and new recipes using natural foodstuffs.

Laundry too has become familiar ground for both husband and wife. With the coming of the neighborhood laundromat, automatic washers and driers, and new fabrics requiring little or no ironing, what used to take Grandma all day to do is now a pleasant hour's activity for husband and/or wife. Boys taught by working mothers to care for their clothes will keep their homes neat without a full-time homemaker to pick up after them. Housekeeping no longer requires the full attention of any one person, except when there are small children in the home, or when other special demands exist—such as social and community use of the homes of ministers and civic leaders.

Becoming one—emotionally and sexually

Becoming married means working out comfortably interacting roles as husband and wife. It involves getting through to one another as fully and as freely as possible in the many dimensions of their relationship. It includes establishing the continuity of the mutually satisfying sexual relationships that cement the pair-bond and give a sense of unity to the marriage.

The enigmatic quality of marriage is due in part to the fact that Americans have not yet reached agreement on basic codes concerning the eternally troublesome questions of sex and love. Being in love is presumed by most young people to be sufficient grounds for marriage. Their elders, generally speaking, think that love is not enough to marry on, and they make a good case for their point of view. But to Joe and Jane in their teens or early twenties, the principal fact that impels them to marry, and to marry each other, is the unanswerable imperative, "It *is* love. We *must* marry."

Sex is, at its best, one of life's great fulfillments, but this blessing is unequally distributed among married couples, and frustration is experienced by many in their search for fulfillment. Sexual maladjustments of one sort or another are confusing and irksome to many couples, especially during the first few years of marriage. Generally speaking, many of their difficulties stem from the couple's inaccurate knowledge of the subtleties of the "facts of life." Ignorance and misinformation lead to unrealistic expectations, and disappointment results. The problem is not, of course, wholly a matter of knowledge and intent. It is greatly complicated by the fact that husbands and wives both bring to marriage numerous and significant unconscious needs and wants (Levy and Munroe, 1962).

Individual needs growing out of different hereditary makeup, different background of experience, and differing conceptions of the purpose of sex create barriers to mutual gratification. Intimate personal acts that enhance the sexual experience for one mate may offend the fastidiousness of the other. Guilt, shame, indecision, and, many times, deep and abiding hostility can become ingrained in the very fabric of sex in marriage. Hostilities may, over a long time, grow and fester, eventually impairing the whole marital structure.

There are often painful discoveries such as lack of sexual response of the wife, the "insatiability" of the husband, jealousies with or without foundation in fact, or inability to forgive past indiscretions. A spouse may have confessed some misdeed in an attempt to relieve guilt feelings, only to find the marriage bond threatened by candor. There is other evidence as well that previous sex experience is not necessarily conducive to good sex adjustment in marriage (Shope and Broderick 1967).

In time, sexual difficulties, like other conflicts and disappointments, are resolved in a number of greatly varying ways. Failure is seen in such solutions as resignation to one's fate, concealed (or ill-concealed) chronic frustration, overt hostility to the mate, generalized irritability, or adultery.

Four out of five wives married less than a year (82 percent) describe the sexual aspect of their marriage as good/very good. An even larger percentage (88 percent) of those who feel able to tell their husbands freely about their sexual feelings and desires report high satisfaction with marital sex during their first year of marriage (Levin and Levin 1975). These findings support Reiss's generalization that "the human sexual relationship is becoming less one of male satisfaction of body-centered sexuality supported by masculine peer groups. It is becoming much more a part of an equalitarian relationship that involves more than just physical attraction" (Reiss 1973:26).

Two people do not need to be identical to fit together well in action. Apparent differences may in fact be complementary qualities. Husband and wife achieve a good fit when they harmonize their needs and values, whether these are alike or not (Rapoport 1963). The development of patterns for resolving conflicts is related to the pair's growing empathy, mutual supportiveness, understanding, and genuine communication as a married couple (Raush, Goodrich, and Campbell 1963).

There is some evidence that married people are about as responsive to strangers as they are to their spouses, and that strangers tend to be nicer to them—which is seen as a built-in source of marital instability and disunity. On the other hand, the same researchers at the National Institute of Mental Health found that when spouses are faced with apparent discrepancies in their responses, they tend to reinterpret their replies so that they seem to be in agreement, thus attempting to maintain couple unity at all costs (Ryder and Goodrich 1966; Ryder 1968).

The unity of the couple is secured by a network of bonds that weave the two into two-in-one. The bonds are open systems of communication through which each reaches across to the other for the comfort, the love, the understanding, the sympathy, the loyalty, and the sense of purpose a man and woman need to feel truly married. Without such communication a person may ache with loneliness even while beside the mate. With a well-established communication system, the husband and wife feel united even though they may be separated by many months and miles.

When the spouses approach a conflict situation with mutual respect (rather than with an eye to bargaining or exerting leverage—Jackson and

Table 9-5
A Pattern for Problem-solving

Steps	Key questions	Purpose
1. Face the problem	What is the matter? Why do I/we think it is a problem?	To get problem into words. To uncover the fear involved.
2. Look at the causes	What has been happening? What has made it a problem now?	To get the buildup of the problem. To get a clear statement of what is bringing it to a head.
3. Set some goals	What do I want to accomplish for myself? For the other person? What do we/I want the situation to be?	To be sure of desires for self. To be sure that decisions will benefit others as well as self. To set a definite change to work toward.
4. Get more knowledge and understanding	What knowledge from the biological, psychological, and social sciences is applicable? Have I found all the available material in technical and popular literature? What has been the experience of other people in similar situations?	To increase understanding. To gain insight.
5. Be the other person (Try to be each of the other persons or groups of persons involved in the problem)	Just how would I, as this other person, think about it? And, as this other person, what would I feel?	To get the other person's point of view and emotional slant. To allow thinking and feelings of others to be a framework for the next step.
6. Consider what to do	What could we/I do about it? Will that bring me to my goals? Will it fit the thoughts and feelings of the other person?	To get a list of possible actions. To be sure they lead to the goals. To be sure they will be acceptable to the other person.
7. Make a plan of action	Just how can this be done? Who will do each part. How will I do it? Who will help me?	To plan how to do it. To develop a one-two-three plan. To select the person to help at each point if needed.
8. Check the plan with the goals	Will this plan lead you to your goals? Does it provide for each goal?	To be sure the plan is really directed at the desired solution. To be sure it covers all the goals set.
9. Plan the follow-up	What shall I/we watch for to be sure the plan is working?	To encourage watchfulness in using the plan. To encourage abandonment if it seems to be failing.

Source: An adaption of "A Pattern for Counseling," by L.A. Lynde, extension specialist in parent education, January 30, 1947.

Lederer 1969), their consciousness that they matter to one another is reinforced and they do not feel the need to fight for what they want. They are then free to develop the skills needed for solving their problems step by step as they arise (Table 9–5).

Interacting with in-laws and relatives

As they move from their parental homes to their own home-in-the-making, a man and woman marrying for the first time undergo a basic role shift. Simultaneously, they find themselves in three families—the wife's family of orientation, the husband's family of orientation, and the family they are establishing as their family of procreation. (See Tables 7–1 and 7–2.) Each of the couple's relatives on both sides of the family are now part of their larger kin network, to be remembered on special occasions and relied on from time to time throughout the marriage.

In-law relationships may be dreaded before marriage and avoided thereafter, in the stereotyped fear of intrusion that is the basis of the universal mother-in-law joke and of general mother-in-law avoidance (Duvall 1954). But more often kinfolk are counted on as friendly allies by young couples today—quite as much as by their parents and grandparents. In fact, the youngest generation is least likely to say that each generation should go its own way (Table 9–6).

By the time a couple has been married a year or more, their parents begin to hint that they look forward to becoming grandparents. Other relatives and friends of the pair also voice their encouragement of the potential parents. Typically, the first baby is now on the way (Chapter 7),

Table 9–6
Maintaining Intergenerational Relationships—Opinions by Generations

Opinion		Grandparents	Parents	Married children
A young couple and their parents-in-law should go their separate ways and see each other only occasionally	Agree	60%	42%	36%
	Disagree	29	46	42
	Undecided	11	12	22
Children who move up in the world tend to neglect their parents	Agree	22	20	9
	Disagree	64	69	74
	Undecided	14	11	17
A young couple has a real responsibility for keeping in touch with parents-in-law	Agree	65	65	74
	Disagree	13	21	14
	Undecided	22	14	12

Source: Reuben Hill, *Family Development in Three Generations* (Cambridge, Mass.: Schenkman Publishing Company, 1970): Chap. 3, "Interdependence among the Generations."

although some married couples prefer to remain childless, or to postpone their childbearing.

Choosing parenthood

Once, children came as a matter of course. Now, modern contraceptives make possible a conscious choice of parenthood and the timing of the child's arrival. A husband and wife may postpone having children for such reasons as: (1) awaiting their readiness for the responsibilities of parenthood; (2) advancing their careers (including the education and training needed for them); (3) avoiding the tragedy of unwanted children; and (4) helping to curb the world's spiraling population growth that threatens the quality of life of all mankind (Figure 9-2). The president of the National Academy of Sciences has warned, "The greatest threat to the human race is man's procreation. Hunger; pollution; crime; overlarge, dirty cities—even the seething unrest that leads to international conflict and war—all derive from the unbridled growth of human populations" (Handler 1969:14-15).

Figure 9-2
World Population Increase, 1750-2000

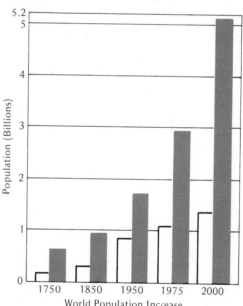

World Population Increase

Increase since 1750 is charted for developed countries (*white*) and underdeveloped countries (*black*). Classification as developed or underdeveloped is according to economic and demographic differences now prevailing. Data for the year 2000 are based on a United Nations projection that assumes slowly ebbing growth rates.

Source: The Rockefeller Foundation, *RF*, vol. 2, no. 2, p. 1, March 1975.

Table 9-7
Estimates and Projections of Total U.S. Population, 1970–2025
(Numbers in thousands)

Year	Series I	Series II	Series III
ESTIMATES			
1970		204,875	
1974		211,909	
PROJECTIONS			
1975	213,641	213,450	213,323
1980	225,705	222,769	220,356
1985	241,274	234,068	228,355
1990	257,663	245,075	235,581
1995	272,685	254,495	241,198
2000	287,007	262,494	245,098
2005	303,144	270,377	247,926
2010	322,049	278,754	250,193
2015	342,340	286,960	251,693
2020	362,348	294,046	251,884
2025	382,011	299,713	250,421

Source: U.S. Bureau of the Census, "Projections of the Population of the United States, by Age and Sex, 1975 to 2000, with Extensions of Total population to 2025 (Advance Report)," *Current Population Reports*, Series P-25, No. 541 (Washington, D.C.: U.S. Government Printing Office, February 1975), p. 1.

Official estimates of America's growing population with projections to the year 2025 appear in Table 9–7. Series I assumes 2.7 births per woman; Series II, 2.1 (replacement level); and Series III, 1.7 ultimate completed births per woman. Broadly interpreted, this means that if couples barely replace themselves in the years ahead, by the year 2000 the population will have grown to 262,494,000; and if they have an average of 2.17 children, by the year 2025 the total population will have swollen to 382,011,000.

Family planning

Preventing conception is the most widely approved method of family planning in the United States. Ninety-one percent of American adults think children should be planned (*Better Homes and Gardens* 1972:82). While the search continues for the perfect contraceptive (safe, effective, available, acceptable, inexpensive, and easy to use), millions of couples regularly use one or more of the various oral contraceptives, intrauterine devices, or other methods of controlling fertility. A woman faces less risk of losing her life using some method of birth control than she does using none, until the age of 40, when oral contraceptives may be hazardous (Tietze, Bongartz, and Schearer 1976). Voluntary sterilization, a safe procedure already legal in most states, is indicated for those couples for whom future childbearing would be unfortunate.

Table 9–8
Maternal Mortality in the United States Since 1950
(Mothers' Deaths per 100,000 Live Births)

1974 (est.)	20.8	1966	29.1
1973	15.2	1965	31.6
1972	18.8	1964	33.3
1971	18.8	1963	35.8
1970	21.5	1962	35.2
1969	22.2	1961	36.9
1968	24.5	1960	37.1
1967	28.0	1950	83.3

Source: U.S. Department of Health, Education, and Welfare, "Births, Deaths, Marriages, and Divorces, Annual Summary for the United States, 1974," *Monthly Vital Statistics Report*, Vol. 23, No. 13 (Rockville, Md.: National Center for Health Statistics, May 30, 1975), p. 4.

Improved maternal health and services have succeeded in reducing the numbers of mothers' deaths in pregnancy, childbirth, and the puerperium (Table 9–8).

The infant mortality rate for July 1975 was 15.2 per 1,000 live births, the lowest rate ever recorded in the United States (U.S. Department of Health, Education, and Welfare September 1975:3). If for some reason a couple should lose their baby, they need one another more than ever.

Abortion

When a married woman finds herself unwillingly pregnant, she and her husband may decide to terminate the pregnancy. The legalization of abortion has greatly reduced the dangers of the procedure. Although it is no substitute for effective birth control, abortion provides an additional choice after contraceptive failure. Blacks and other minorities seek a third more abortions per capita than whites. Married women have a fourth of the reported abortions (Gribbin 1975:10).

Attitudes toward abortion are mixed. Pope Paul's *Humanae Vitae* (1968) said that "direct interruption of the generative process already begun, above all directly willed and procured abortion, even if for therapeutic reasons, are to be absolutely excluded as licit means of regulating birth." Most non-Catholics prefer abortion to irresponsible parenthood. Four out of ten American adults think that family planning should include legal abortion as an alternative (*Better Homes and Gardens* 1972:83). Married women favor abortion if the mother's health is threatened, and most physicians approve of more liberal abortion laws (Westoff, Moore, and Ryder 1969).

Childlessness

There has been a remarkable decline in childlessness in recent decades— from 21 to 26 percent early in this century to a range of 9 to 14 percent in the past four decades (Glick 1976:7). Inability to conceive a child is a problem for less than 10 percent of American marriages today, thanks to medical advances in treating infertility. Although between 400,000 and 600,000 women spontaneously abort a conceptus, most of these women bear full-term babies thereafter. A few become discouraged after numerous attempts to have a child, and either remain childless or adopt one or more children to bring up as their own. Adopted children place their families within the family life cycle by age, as do children born to the couple.

Stepchildren

Stepchildren leapfrog their remarrying parents over the married couple stage and into a later stage of the family life cycle, according to the age of the eldest child. Couples who adopt children usually have time to plan for their coming, and they start together as parents. Stepchildren come with their natural parent into the new marriage, in which an unfamiliar adult now shares responsibility for them. It may be difficult for a stepchild to accept a new stepparent, or vice versa. Many of the half million adults who become stepparents each year learn eventually to love and to be loved by their "instant families," but it takes some doing (Stilley 1975).

The first pregnancy

The old folk-phrase "in the family way" expresses well the shift from marital to family roles that occurs during the expectant phase of the married couple stage of the family life cycle. The circle of intimacy now enlarges to include the expected baby. One young father-to-be says, "We're pregnant at our house," as he paints a crib for which his wife is knitting a coverlet. Many couples role-play being parents long before their first baby arrives. They develop new ways of caring for one another that prepare them for their roles as mother and father, acquiring in the process habits of tenderness and nurturance that the helpless infant will need. The responses of husbands and wives to pregnancy are mixed, as is seen in Table 9-9.

The developmental tasks of the expectant father and mother may be either conflicting or complementary or both. The more the two parents-to-be work together in preparing for their first baby, the greater will be their success in finding fulfillment in the generative process and in uniting to welcome their firstborn (Table 9-10).

Arranging for the baby

Birds build their nests by instinct. Human parents are free to improvise, plan, and learn their own nest-building methods throughout the expectant phase of the family life cycle. Some husbands and wives take the coming of their first baby casually and do very little about providing a place for it before its arrival. The story is told of the young parents who simply

Table 9-9
Effects of First Pregnancy on Some Husbands and Wives

Phase of pregnancy	Some husbands' responses	Some wives' responses
First trimester	Fear of losing wife and/or child (2, 3) Self-doubt as a future father (4)	Loss of interest in coitus (1) Less sexual effectiveness (1) Sleepiness and chronic fatigue (1) Nausea (1) Increased dependence (2, 3)
Second trimester	Increased respect, awe as quickening comes (3) Name for fetus coined (3)	Solemnity, hilarity, playfulness about fetal movements (3) Talk about and with fetus, i.e., "We're going shopping" (3) Increased eroticism (1)
Third trimester	Fear of coitus harming fetus (1) Abstinence difficult (1) Envy and/or pride at wife's creativity (2, 3) Worry over birth (2, 3) Keen awareness of male/female differences (2, 3)	Lessened sexual activity (1) Continence (often recommended by physician (1) Sleepiness (1) Backache (1) Abdominal discomfort (1) Sexual isolation (2, 3) Heightened sense of femininity (2, 3)
Postpartum	Eagerness to resume marital relations (1) Concern over endangering wife's recovery (1) Sense of triumph in becoming a father (3) Tenderness toward mother and baby (3)	Pain and fear of harm from too early coital resumption (1) Low eroticism (1) Concern about husband's continued abstinence, often suggested by physician for six weeks after baby's birth (1) Sense of completion as a mother (3)
Pregnancy as a whole	Increased romanticism (4) Increased nurturance (4) Increased participation in family life (4) Anxiety about costs (4) Concern about lack of skills in baby care (4)	Increased romanticism (4) Increased optimism (4) Family roles replacing marital emphases (2, 3) Fear of miscarriage, malformations, and/or death of baby (5) Pride in accomplishment (5)

[1] William H. Masters and Virginia E. Johnson, *Human Sexual Response* (Boston, Mass.: Little, Brown & Co., 1966).
[2] Arthur Colman and Libby Colman, *Pregnancy: The Psychological Experience* (New York: Herder & Herder, 1972).
[3] Max Deutscher, unpublished study of dreams and fantasies of first pregnancy; reported in "Pregnancy: The Three Phases," *Time*, 20 December 1971.
[4] Harold Feldman, "The Effects of Children on the Family, " in Andree Michel, ed., *Family Issues of Employed Women in Europe and America* (Leyden, Netherlands: E.J. Brill, 1971).
[5] Robert J. Havighurst, *Developmental Tasks and Education* (New York: David McKay Co., 1972), p. 87.

Table 9-10
Complementary and Conflicting Developmental Tasks during Pregnancy

Developmental tasks of the expectant father	Developmental tasks of the expectant mother	Complementary and conflicting possibilities
As the young couple go through the first pregnancy, there are times when their individual tasks complement each other in shared accomplishment as parents-to-be. Just as naturally, there are times when their individual developmental tasks conflict, and husband and wife are pulled in opposite directions. Illustrative instances are:		

Starting a family
  Planning the first child's arrival
  Learning what it means to become a father
  Giving his wife his support throughout her pregnancy and childbirth
	Starting a family
	  Planning the first child's arrival
	  Learning what it means to be a mother
	  Proceeding successfuly through the pregnancy and childbirth experience
		Complementary: both work together in the common tasks of becoming parents for the first time

Becoming a man in a man's world
  Finding himself among his fellow workers and male colleagues
  Taking jeers and taunts of other men good naturedly as his wife's condition becomes apparent
  Continuing some activities with "the boys" that do not include their wives necessarily
	Becoming a woman in a woman's world
	  Identifying with her women friends and neighbors in personal female ways
	  Participating in baby showers and other "women only" affairs
	  Borrowing and lending, sharing and being shared within the feminine fellowship of her relationship with "the girls"
		Conflicting: the husband is pulled into male circles, and his wife is being absorbed in feminine interests and functions

Being responsible as the main support of the family
  Getting to work on time
  Carrying a full load as breadwinner
	Seeing her chief jobs as mother-to-be- as well as wife
	  Letting up on her outside interests as the pregnancy advances
	  Becoming content to be wife and mother primarily
		Complementary: common task of nest-building
		
		Conflicting: he is pulled outward, and she is pulled inward in her childbearing

dumped the contents of a dresser drawer in a box and plopped the new baby in the drawer, which then served as a bed until the infant was big enough to sleep with his brothers. A maternity hospital reports that occasionally a baby arrives with no clothes to wear, no blankets, and no home to go to, but this is not the usual story, especially for the first baby. Later siblings may "make do" with provisions dating back to the arrival of their elder brothers and sisters, but some special provision is usually made for the first baby.

Some young couples must make drastic changes in their housing in order to make way for the expected first baby. Some modern apartment houses have rules that exclude children. A married couple whose first home has been in such a building must search out a more hospitable home base before their baby arrives. The husband and wife who have been floating from place to place in a series of rented rooms now want to settle down in something more permanent. The couple living with one set of parents quite likely now want a place of their own. There are couples who must find something less expensive than they have been enjoying in housing as soon as a baby is expected. Even more numerous are the young families-in-the-making who move to more desirable neighborhoods, sensing the importance of suitable neighbors, congenial companions, adequate play space, and good schools.

The husband and wife who stay on where they have been living make some rearrangements in their living space when a baby is expected. Room is provided and readied for the baby's sleeping, eating, bathing, and playing. This place may be a separate nursery complete with new baby furniture and sundry equipment, or it may be a corner that is equipped for baby care, out of the main household traffic. The differences in spatial arrangements are not important as long as husband and wife see eye to eye on them. Trouble comes when husband and wife hold fundamentally different views about the demands of expectant parenthood.

A problem that arises frequently as the household is being reorganized for the first baby is that the preparations and rearrangements envisioned by the wife are more elaborate and expensive than the husband deems necessary. As the principal breadwinner, he is aware of the new responsibilities that will fall on him as father and thus is reluctant to undertake any unnecessary expenditures. How the two resolve their dilemma depends in part on how well they achieve the other developmental tasks they face as expectant parents.

Meeting the costs of having a baby

Most wives work during most of their first pregnancy in anticipation of the high cost of having a baby. If the wife plans to quit her job while her children are young, her income will stop at a time when family expenses are high.

Some married couples save the wife's first earnings against the time when they will need money for the costs of having children, buying and equipping their home, and establishing the financial security needed by the parents of young children during the childbearing and child-rearing stages that lie ahead. Other newlyweds, who have been spending their joint income, are reduced to living on the husband's earnings alone at a critical time, since costs increase sharply with the arrival of the first baby.

The cost of having a baby was relatively low in the days when children were born in their parents' bed with only the family doctor, midwife, or neighbor in attendance. Today most babies are born in hospitals, where the costs are necessarily higher. Recent estimates of the costs of having a baby and raising it through its first year in the United States appear in Table 9-11.

Depending on their orientation, resources, and values, the young family may choose from a variety of solutions to their financial problems. The young family may float a loan, or dip into savings, or look to their parents for help, or go into debt or into an orgy of installment buying. But whatever they do, the decision is there to be made.

Costs of having a baby vary widely by region, size of community, and individual circumstance. Costs can be kept down by: (1) comparing prices charged by nearby hospitals, obstetricians, and family physicians; (2) exploring maternity benefits provided by various health insurance plans (well before the pregnancy); (3) going home as soon as medically feasible, with a practical nurse for a few days' home care; (4) encouraging family and friends to give practical shower and baby gifts; (5) accepting and refurbishing used baby furniture, equipment, infant clothing, maternity clothes, etc.; (6) keeping "frills" such as bathing tables, fancy baby toys, lamps and bottle-warmers to a minimum; (7) nursing rather than bottle-feeding the baby; (8) preparing infant food at home from family fare with blender, strainer, etc.; (9) doing baby's laundry at home; (10) keeping baby's wardrobe to a minimum; (11) simplifying recreational activities to include the baby at times; (12) exchanging sitter services with other young parents; (13) sharing baby's care with nearby relatives on occasion; (14) participating as a couple in the newborn's daily life, as much as possible.

Low-cost public and private clinics in many communities give prenatal, postpartum and infant care. Trained midwives (who routinely call on medical specialists for help, when needed) are available in some areas. Couples

Table 9-11
Cost of Having a Baby (Estimates, 1975)

Item	Cost
Hospital: 4 days at $100, delivery room, nursery, and extras	$ 500.00±
Medical services: obstetrician ($300–$500±), pediatrician, lab fees	600.00±
Baby furniture, equipment, at national mail order prices	300.00±
Infant clothing for first year at national mail order prices	200.00±
Maternity wardrobe (varies widely)	150.00±
Baby food, government estimates for non-nursing infant's first year	200.00±
Diapers and laundering, median costs for first year	200.00±
Baby-sitters and mother's helpers, baby's first year	100.00±
Prescriptions and drug supplies (baby lotions, shampoo, soap, etc.)	50.00±
Total	$2300.00±

Sources: Health Insurance Institutes estimates, 1974; Claire Williams, "How Much Does a Baby Cost?" *Redbook*, April 1976, p. 96; and Sylvia Porter, *Sylvia Porter's Money Book* (Garden City, N.Y.: Doubleday & Co., 1975), pp. 697–698.

who want to have their babies in a normal family atmosphere find the idea of midwives attractive and also appreciate the lower fees charged. Some couples, wanting to splurge on the first baby, run up their financial outlay well beyond customary amounts. This is an understandable celebration of becoming parents that may be worth the price to these young couples.

Maintaining morale as a married pair

A charming story about Elizabeth II describes an occasion when the Queen, appearing before the student body of a school for the deaf, was so weary that she could barely smile a greeting. The children, reading lips, broke into laughter when Prince Philip leaned over toward his wife and whispered, "Buck up, Little Cabbage." In most marriages, there are times when one or both members of the pair feel too tired or depressed to carry on. Ways of buoying up lagging spirits must be found if the couple are to keep going. The working man drops by the corner tavern for a beer where he tells the "boys" his troubles (Komarovsky 1964). The white-collar husband is more apt to bring his problems home to his wife, who likes it that way. She too needs a broad shoulder when the going gets rough, and looks forward to telling her husband about her day.

Daily living is filled with tedious chores that are seldom enjoyable and always unavoidable. As husband and wife sense one another's support, they find it easier to cope with tasks that might otherwise seem onerous. Humor, sensitive concern, expressions of sympathy and affection, and the offer of a helping hand when needed contribute to the morale of each partner and to the spirit of the marriage.

Goals and values jointly sought provide many young married couples with a continuing incentive and sense of direction. Couples living on incomes below the poverty level often lack the resources needed for escape from an exclusive preoccupation with making ends meet. The hopes of others, held in common, help to keep them working toward the realization of their dreams. As the excitement of early marriage subsides, the maintenance of morale becomes especially important for the continuing marriage.

You are the bows from which your children as living arrows are sent forth.

Kahlil Gibran

Childbearing families

chapter ten

The childbearing stage of the family life cycle begins with the birth of the first baby and continues until the firstborn is in preschool. During this period the husband and wife have their first experience as parents. They enter the stage as a married couple and leave it as established parents with one or more children. During this segment of the cycle, family life proceeds at a rapid pace through a series of overlapping phases. These involve the changing nature of the parents' roles; their tasks of settling down as parents; the child's developmental progress; and the appearance of family developmental tasks, some of which are fulfilled, some are left incomplete, and all are swiftly replaced by urgent new demands on the attention of the young family.

213

The first child's coming

Millions of children are born every year, and for most of their families childbirth is a normal experience. Most American babies are born in hospitals, where mother and child receive modern medical care. Some physicians advocate great gentleness in the handling of newborns; they recommend stroking the infant, keeping light and noise levels low, and postponing cutting the cord until breathing is well established (Leboyer 1975). Women are questioning routine hospital practices that make birth unpleasant for mother and baby. Among these practices are artificial stimulation of labor, routine episiotomy and use of forceps for delivery, delaying of first breast-feeding, and separation of the mother from her family during labor and birth (Arms 1975; Haire 1975). Increasing numbers of doctors, nurses, midwives, and hospitals are responsive to the feelings of mothers, and many now give psychologically sensitive delivery care with minimal environmental disturbance (Newton 1975; Flaste 1975).

Although adopting a child imposes no physiological burdens, it can involve another form of stress—a waiting period often longer than that of pregnancy. Liberalized abortion, access to contraception, and acceptance of illegitimacy and of a mother's rights to her child have reduced the numbers of babies available for adoption (Associated Press 1971; Brozan 1971). Americans are adopting Korean and Vietnamese orphans, as well as orphans of other racial, national, and ethnic groups. Jan de Hartog (1969) lists some of the objections he and his wife heard when they adopted two Korean girls: Why not a child from your own country? They will never be really yours; and you will never love them the way you love your own children. Mature adults can and do love their adopted children quite as much as any they might bear. Adoptive parents feel that it is the nurturing process rather than the birth itself that makes a child one's own. Although most children are older at the time of their adoption, some are newborn. These infants enter the childbearing stage of the family life cycle with their new parents, much as a firstborn does.

Settling down as a family

The first phase of the childbearing family stage is one of rejoicing. The man has come through the crisis of the birth of his first child with a sense of relief and satisfaction. He throws out his chest as he passes out cigars and announces the coming of his firstborn. The woman emerges from the first fatigue of childbirth with a feeling of accomplishment, a sensation of being part of the process of creation itself. She puts a ribbon in her hair and relaxes in the luxury of bed care and postpartum attention, replete with telephone calls from well-wishers, congratulations from her friends, and the beaming pride of her parents and of her husband's family. There is a new tenderness from her mate. There are flowers, gifts for the baby, and a general spirit of celebration.

By the third day mother and baby have made their first efforts to learn to live together. The mother has already taken the step that leads her into, or away from, active nursing of her baby. The baby has made his first adjustment to nursing and is either succeeding well or having trouble at his mother's breast. The new father's visits to the hospital are taken up with detailed accounts of what the baby is doing—how the nurses love him, how much handsomer, or brighter, or bigger, or quieter he is than the others in the nursery—and speculations as to which relative he resembles most closely.

With the homecoming of mother and baby from the hospital comes the end of the first flush of elation and the realization that parenthood is a strenuous responsibility. Now the care of the newborn is no longer in the capable hands of the nursing staff, but becomes a round-the-clock task of the young family. Baby's feeding schedule has to be worked out in ways that satisfy him and make sense in terms of the household. His bath time at first is marked by the nervous fumbles of the new mother, who has had only limited experience in handling a tiny baby.

Keeping the baby clean and dry seems to be an ever-present challenge at first, and the diaper pail fills up at an alarming rate, or so it seems to the young mother who assumes as one of her responsibilities the daily laundry connected with infant care. Discouragement is so common at this time that it is generally known popularly as "postpartum blues." Even in her weakened condition, the mother might manage all this if only she could get a good night's sleep. But adjustment to day and night schedules at home takes time, and the newborn's howls between 2:00 and 4:00 A.M. not only rob his parents of sleep, but also increase their insecurity about their competence in caring for him.

The coming of the first child is a crisis, in that it calls for reorganization of the family. Roles must be reassigned, new needs must be met in new ways, and family values must be reoriented. The parents may want babies, but may be dismayed to discover what they are like. Hundreds of couples studied over the years concur that parenthood is a critical experience, and that marital satisfaction drops sharply with the coming of the first baby (LeMasters 1957; Dyer 1963; Feldman and Rogoff 1968; Feldman 1969). One interpretation is that their first child forces the young parents to take the last major step into the adult world, as they encounter the developmental tasks that go with being responsible for another human being. Thus parenthood, even more than marriage, demands maturity in both husband and wife.

There may be a nurse for the baby in the upper-class family. In middle- and lower-class homes some female relative—usually one of the baby's grandmothers—comes in for a while and does the housework and the baby's laundry, gets the meals, and tries to keep things together until the mother regains her strength and has made some progress in caring for her baby.

Lacking such a willing relative, the young husband may bear the brunt of the new burden, hurrying home from work to pitch in and help his wife with all she was unable to accomplish around the edges of baby care through the day. The strain of double duty for both parents on a day and night basis may take its toll in frayed nerves and a kind of chronic fatigue that is characteristic of the period in many young families.

After a while, the baby becomes stabilized around a predictable schedule and sleeps through the night most of the time. The mother's strength returns, and she becomes more skilled in caring for the baby as a normal part of her day's work. Now bath time is fun for both. The daily outing becomes a lark, and shopping an outing. The outsiders who have helped out during the baby's first days at home have left, and father, mother, and baby settle down as a family. Thus begins the long pull of parenthood, with its alternating phases of pride, pressure, and enjoyment.

Infant development

Babies normally grow rapidly during the first months of their lives—faster than they ever will again. In fact, development slows down from the moment of conception on, so that each period of growth is faster than any that will succeed it. If an individual continued to treble his weight every six to twelve months, as he does his first year, he would become a multi-ton monster in time.

Human development is sequential—each new step in growth derives from what has gone before. Infant development provides the base for future growth—for what a person is to become. It is, therefore, the most important period for all facets of development—physical, intellectual, emotional, and social (Table 10-1).

Physical development advances most rapidly anteriorly during prenatal life and infancy. Thus, the neonate has a large head, but a small abdomen and legs. Within a week after birth the baby is capable of seeing, hearing, tasting, smelling, feeling, and responding to stimuli around him. These sensory capacities provide the channels for his intellectual development.

Intellectual development occurs progressively as an infant learns. During the first month he uses the abilities he was born with as he waves his arms and legs, cries, sucks, burps, and hiccoughs. The more he does these things, the better he does them, and the more sure of himself he becomes. Between the first and fifth months, the baby combines his skills as he looks or clutches while he sucks, sucks anything he can grasp, turns his head to watch moving objects, and begins to need active stimulation. Between the fifth and ninth months, the baby learns to initiate behavior, to look for lost objects, and to anticipate attention as a familiar person approaches.

By the end of his first year, the infant normally works hard to get something he wants; he imitates others, plays games, and enjoys socializing; he probably has mastered pulling himself upright, and possibly has begun to walk. Through the latter half of his second year, the baby is into everything, exploring his world. The more stimulation he gets, the better he likes it. The closer he gets to age two, the better he is at problem-solving, talking, remembering where things are, and finding them. He operates increasingly by symbols as he moves out of infancy and into early childhood (Piaget 1966; McCandless 1967:48-54).

Stimulation encourages an infant's intellectual development, according to studies of a number of tutoring projects for infants and their mothers in underprivileged areas. Tutoring consists of trips to stores, the fire station, zoo, and library; the use of story books, records, puzzles, blocks, drawing and craft materials; and conversation with the infant as well as encouraging support for the mother in her efforts to enrich her baby's life. Workers suggest that the ultimate intellectual level of a child could be established at the age of 21 months, much earlier than had previously been thought possible (Chilman 1966:81-87; Gordon 1969:57-59; and Leo 1968).

The ways in which parents relate to their babies significantly affect the children's development. Studies show that parents behave differently with their infant sons and daughters, thus reinforcing sex-appropriate behavior in the first year of life (Goldberg and Lewis 1969:21-31; Moss 1967:19-36). The relationships a woman reports having had with her own mother influence the ways in which she, in turn, relates to her infant (Moss, Ryder, and Robson 1967). Direct observation of mother-infant pairs shows that infants shape their mothers' behavior in noticeable ways (Moss 1965:482-486; Bell 1966).

Learning disorders, disturbed behavior, and difficulty in dealing with problems may result from early deprivation and frustration. The evidence is that it is impossible to "spoil" a baby. Parents are wise to meet babies' needs with a minimum of frustration. When an infant is left to cry out his discomfort and distress, he learns that no one comes to answer his cries. As a result, he either turns inward and away from others or toward them with anger.

Research and clinical evidence indicate that early child care fostering good physical, mental, emotional, social, and cognitive development has seven basic elements (Table 10-2, p. 220).

Table 10-1
Physical Development—Newborn to Two Years

Developmental dimension	Newborn
Height	Eighteen to twenty-two inches
Weight	Six to eight pounds
Proportions	Head large (one-quarter of total height); chest large; abdomen small; legs short
Bones	Cartilage present in ankles, wrists, soft spots in skull
Muscles	Heart and smooth muscles developed; skeletal muscles uncoordinated; sphincters weak
Sense organs	Sees, distinguishing light from dark; tastes; smells; and feels with little discrimination
Posture	Prone (on stomach) or supine (on back)
Manual skills	Random movements of hands; lashing when angry and with crying
Hair	Varies widely: none to much; often not typical of later hair; is generally lost
Teeth	None usually
Digestion	Stomach empties every three to four hours; liquids only
Urination	Kidneys functioning; no bladder control; voiding about twenty times daily
Respiration	Some wheezing; low susceptibility to infection; rapid breathing: thirty-four to forty-five inhalations a minute
Vocalization	Cries, hiccups, sneezes
Heartbeat	One hundred and thirty per minute at rest
Blood pressure	Low: about forty millimeters

For further detail, see Mollie S. Smart and Russell C. Smart, *Children: Development and Relationships* (New York: Macmillan Company, 1967), chaps. 3-4; Elizabeth Lee Vincent and Phyllis C. Martin, *Human Psychological Development* (New York: Ronald Press Company, 1961), pp. 127-140.

Infant (0–2 years)

Twenty-six to thirty-five inches

Birth weight triples in first year; by two years about thirty pounds

Face grows rapidly; trunk, legs, and arms lengthen

Soft spots in skull closed at one year; leg and arm bones elongated

Coordination improving; sphincters strengthening; back, leg, and arm muscles developing rapidly

One week, hears; three months, coordinates eyes; all senses developing; equilibrium weak

Three months, raises head and shoulders from prone position; four months, sits erect when held by hands; eight months, sits alone; nine months, creeps, crawls, stands by chair; twelve months, stands alone, soon walks

Four to five months, scoops up block with hand; eight months, picks up blocks in both hands, nine months, thumb and finger opposed in pincer grasp of tiny objects; two years, prefers one hand to the other

Typical color and texture established by second year

Second year, sixteen temporary teeth in order: four to fifteen months, eight incisors; twelve to eighteen months, four molars, eighteen to twenty-four months, four canines

First solids two to six months; three meals a day in first year; eats family foods by second year

Bladder grows slowly; voiding every two hours; may be dry by two years (varies widely)

Regular breathing established; steadies to twenty-five to thirty-five inhalations a minute; increased susceptibility to infection

Range rapidly increases to grunts, gurgles, babbling, imitating sounds, single words, phrases, short sentences

Decreases to one hundred and twenty-five to ninety per minute by two years

About eighty millimeters

Table 10-2
Stimulating Optimum Infant Development

1. Providing adequate nutrition—proteins, vitamins, minerals, and other necessary nutrients
2. Dealing with a baby in distress—colic, diarrhea, infection, etc.
3. Stimulating in accordance with an infant's needs, tolerance level, and capacity for enjoyment
4. Communicating with the baby—tactile and conversational contacts especially important
5. Giving opportunities for the exercise of emerging sensory-motor functions—feeling, touching, banging, throwing, and combining things; relating supportively with other children and adults
6. Encouraging the infant's efforts to develop new skills, to cope with problems, and to amuse, comfort, feed, and progressively care for himself
7. Continuing warm relationships—mother, father, siblings, and other relatives and friends

Source: Lois Barclay Murphy, "Children under Three . . . Finding Ways to Stimulate Development." *Children* 16, no. 2 (March–April 1969): 48–49.

Developmental tasks of infancy and early childhood

This first period of life takes the infant from birth, when he emerges as a helpless bundle of potentials, to the place where he is somewhat independent of others. At the end of this stage, the child has acquired a measure of autonomy, is taking solid foods, has achieved independent locomotion, and has mastered the first steps in a complex system of communication. Each of these accomplishments represents many hours of practice and real effort on the part of the child to achieve the developmental tasks involved. These developmental tasks can be summarized as follows:

1. Achieving physiological equilibrium following birth:

Learning to sleep at appropriate times
Maintaining a healthful balance of rest and activity

2. Learning to take food satisfactorily:

Developing ability to nurse—to suck, swallow, and adjust to nipple comfortably
Learning to take solid foods, to enjoy new textures, tastes, and temperatures, to use cup, spoon, and dishes competently in ways appropriate to his age

3. Learning the know-how and the where-when of elimination:

Finding satisfaction in early eliminative processes
Wanting to adapt to expectations of time and place of functioning as developmental readiness and parental pressures indicate
Participating cooperatively and effectively (depending on readiness) in the training program

4. Learning to manage his body effectively:

Developing coordination (eye-hand, hand-mouth, reach, grasp, handle, manipulate, put-and-take)

Acquiring skills in locomotion through kicking, creeping, walking, and running

Gaining assurance and competence in handling himself in a variety of situations

5. Learning to adjust to other people:

Responding discriminatingly to others' expectations
Recognizing parental authority and controls
Learning the do's and the don'ts of his world
Reacting positively to both familiar and strange persons within his orbit

6. Learning to love and be loved:

Responding affectionally to others through cuddling, smiling, loving
Meeting emotional needs through widening spheres and varieties of contact
Beginning to give self spontaneously and trustfully to others

7. Developing systems of communication:

Learning patterns of recognition and response
Establishing nonverbal, preverbal, and verbal communicative systems
Acquiring basic concepts (*yes*, *no*, *up*, *down*, *come*, *go*, *hot*, etc.)
Mastering basic language fundamentals in interaction with others

8. Learning to express and control feelings:

Managing feelings of fear and anxiety in healthful ways
Developing a sense of trust and confidence in his world
Handling feelings of frustration, disappointment, and anger effectively, in accordance with his development
Moderating demanding attitudes as time goes on

9. Laying foundations for self-awareness:

Seeing himself as a separate entity
Exploring rights and privileges of being a person
Finding personal fulfillment with and without others

Thus A Child Learns

Thus a child learns: by wiggling skills through his fingers and toes into himself, by soaking up habits and attitudes of those around him, by pushing and pulling his own world.

Thus a child learns: more through trial than error, more through pleasure than pain, more through experience than suggestion, more through suggestion than direction.

Thus a child learns: through affection, through love, through patience, through understanding, through belonging, through doing, through being.

Day by day the child comes to know a little bit of what

you know, to think a little bit of what you think, to understand your understanding. That which you dream and believe and are, in truth, becomes the child.

As you perceive clearly or dully, as you think fuzzily or sharply, as you believe foolishly or wisely, as you dream drably or goldenly, as you are unworthy or sincere—thus a child learns.

Frederick J. Moffitt
Associate Commissioner for
Elementary, Secondary, and Adult Education
New York State Education Department

Protecting baby's life and health

The first year of life is perilous. Currently, 1,800 out of every 100,000 infants die before their first birthday. Many of these infant deaths are unavoidable (due to congenital abnormalities, pneumonia, and immaturity, about which parents can do little). The opposite is true of preventable accidents. More babies die needlessly in accidents during their first year than in any single year of the preschool and school-age period—the time when accidents are the leading cause of death. The six leading types of accidents fatal to infants under one year of age are listed in Table 10-3.

The life and health of many thousands of other infants and young children are endangered by preventable diseases. The Government Center for Disease Control recommends the active and ongoing immunization of normal infants and children (and follow-up for adults), according to the schedule in Table 10-4. In addition, individual physicians and clinics vac-

Table 10-3
Fatal Accidents to Infants Under One Year of Age

Type of accident	Average annual death rate per 100,000 live births		
	Both sexes	Males	Females
All accidents	54.3	61.7	46.5
Inhalation and ingestion of food and other objects	16.1	19.2	12.7
Mechanical suffocation	11.6	13.3	9.8
Motor vehicle	9.8	10.0	9.5
Fires and flames	4.8	4.8	4.7
Falls	3.3	4.2	2.2
Drowning*	2.1	2.5	1.8
All other	6.6	7.7	5.8

*Exclusive of deaths in water transportation.
Source of basic data: Reports of the Division of Vital Statistics, National Center for Health Statistics.
Source: "Accident Mortality among Infants," *Statistical Bulletin*, vol. 56 (July 1975): 10.

Table 10-4
Protecting Children Against Preventable Diseases

Age	Type of immunization
2 months	Diphtheria-Tetanus-Pertussis (D-T-P) Vaccine
	Oral Polio Vaccine
4 months	D-T-P
	Oral Polio Vaccine
6 months	D-T-P
	Oral Polio Vaccine
1 year	Measles Vaccine
	Mumps Vaccine
	Rubella Vaccine
18 months	D-T-P
	Oral Polio Vaccine
4 to 6 years	D-T-P
	Oral Polio Vaccine
14 to 16 years	D-T Only
Every 10 years after	D-T Only

Source: Government Center for Disease Control, Atlanta, Georgia, 1975.

cinate against smallpox and certain types of influenza routinely, or when indicated.

Developmental tasks of the mother of the infant and young child

The first baby arrives in most families when the husband and wife are still working to establish their relationship as a married couple. Therefore, there is an inevitable overlapping of the developmental tasks of the young wife with those of the young mother during the baby's infancy. The young woman carries concurrently the unfinished business of being a competent and happy wife and that of becoming an effective and fulfilled mother. She masters many new skills during the infancy of her firstborn.

Breast-feeding pro and con

One of the first questions the new mother must answer is how her baby will be fed. Western cultures do not encourage a mother to nurse her baby. Feelings of false modesty, uncertainty about lactation, modern dress styles, community involvement beyond the home, busy medical and nursing personnel, and her husband's reluctance may deter a young mother. If she decides that it will not be possible or convenient for her to breast-feed her baby, she must learn to prepare, sterilize, refrigerate, and warm a formula for bottle-feedings. She may prefer to breast-feed for the baby's sake or for her own. Benefits to the baby include fewer infections; less diarrhea, colic, and diaper rash; higher levels of arousal and alertness; and the emotional benefits of frequent fondling and being held in his mother's arms. Some advantages available to the mother are speedier contraction of the uterus from hormonal stimulation of lactation, lower incidence of breast cancer, the convenience of sterile, warm, ever-ready milk, and the satisfactions of suckling (Bell 1966: 177–180; *Time* 1968:53–54).

At the close of the childbearing stage, the young mother has, it is hoped, learned to know and to love her baby and to have confidence in herself as a wife, a mother, and a person. These attitudes and values come as she achieves the developmental tasks of this stage of her development, which, in summary form, include:

1. Reconciling conflicting conceptions of roles:

Clarifying her role as a wife-mother-person
Reconciling differences in conceptions of these roles held by herself, her husband, and various relatives, friends, and significant others
Developing a sound, workable conception of what she expects of her child
Coming to a comfortable understanding of her husband's role as a young father

2. Accepting and adjusting to the strains and pressures of young motherhood:

Gearing activity to lessened physical vigor in the period of involution and lactation
Cooperating in the processes involved in effective infant feeding
Balancing the demands of the child, the expectations of the husband, and her commitments as a person with the limits of her abilities

3. Learning how to care for her infant with competence and assurance:

Assuming responsibility for the care of the child
Mastering the skills of feeding, bathing, protecting, and maintaining a healthy, happy baby
Learning how to anticipate and to recognize the needs of the baby
Becoming increasingly able to enjoy caring for the young child

4. Establishing and maintaining healthful routines for the young family:

Learning how to choose, prepare, and serve nutritious foods for both adult and infant needs
Reorganizing family routines to meet the changing needs of the growing child within the family context
Assuring a sufficiency of rest, relaxation, and sleep for the baby, the young husband, and herself
Readjusting time schedules to make way for the necessities and for some purely pleasurable activities within the young family

5. Providing full opportunities for the child's development:

Enriching the physical situation within the limits of family resources

Providing a plentiful variety of experiences in exploring, manipulating, and learning for the infant and small child

Protecting the furnishings and equipment in ways that keep to a minimum the physical restrictions imposed on the growing child (child-proofing the home)

Learning to enjoy and to wholeheartedly encourage the child's development and progress

Accepting the child as himself without undue pressure, disappointment, or comparison

6. Sharing the responsibilities of parenthood with her husband:

Recognizing the importance of the father-child relationship from the beginning. Encouraging the participation of the young father in the care of the baby and small child in appropriate ways

Bringing the young father into the planning, decision-making, and evaluating processes that make him feel that his wishes and values are being respected and appreciated

Establishing the habit of thinking of the child as "ours" rather than "mine"

7. Maintaining a satisfying relationship with her husband:

Protecting her husband's values as a person in the midst of the demanding pressures of young parenthood

Reestablishing ways of being a couple and preserving the unique values of husband-wife companionship throughout the infancy of the first child

Maintaining the joys of being a wife in the sexual, recreational, emotional, intellectual, and spiritual aspects of married living

8. Making satisfactory adjustments to the practical realities of life:

Assisting her husband in the financial and housing planning for the family

Adapting happily to the limitations of space and resources of the family

Enriching the family experience by innovative use of available facilities and resources

Supplementing the family income when it seems wise or necessary in ways that safeguard the well-being of all members of the family

9. Keeping alive some sense of personal autonomy through young motherhood:

Retaining some satisfying contacts with personal interests and stimuli

Continuing some aspect of personal development that is especially meaningful within the realities of the present family situation

Utilizing the unique experiences of young motherhood to attain the fulfillment inherent within it

Following her child's growth experiences out into new horizons of personal insight and growth

10. Exploring and developing the satisfying sense of being a family:

Initiating family recreation in which the whole family may participate with pleasure—picnics, trips to zoo and beach, music, automobile trips, etc.

Participating with other young families in community functions

Joining with other young wives and mothers in cooperative endeavors

Providing for whole-family participation in church, neighborhood, and community activities suitable to this stage in family development

Maintaining mutually supportive contacts with parental families

This is quite an assignment for the young wife and mother. No wonder so many young women feel overwhelmed during this phase of their lives. In the big, old-fashioned family (in which the young couple lived near, or sometimes with, their parental families), there was a sharing of the functions and responsibilities of childbearing and child-rearing. The support of other members of the extended family lessened the burden on the young mother. In the simple folk society, infants and young children are cared for cooperatively by any conveniently located adult.

Young families today are usually removed from the extended family and from the day-to-day supportive relationships it formerly provided. The inexperienced mother is alone with her baby for most of the waking day, and shares with her mate the child's care around the clock and calendar. In addition to caring for the baby and providing opportunities for his development, the young mother does the shopping, prepares food for the family, washes the dishes, cleans the house, washes, irons, and puts away the clothes, assumes responsibility for the family's social life, tries to be a good wife for her husband, and picks up the ever-present litter that goes with infancy.

A Cornell University study of 1,296 mothers found that those with infants under one year of age spent 50 percent more time doing housework than mothers whose youngest child is a teenager (9.3 versus 6 hours a day) (Walker 1969:5–6). Fatigue is a problem for mothers of infant-toddlers—significantly more so than for mothers of older children (Wiegand and Gross 1958).

The developmental tasks of the young mother are demanding. She succeeds in them as she gains confidence and acquires competence in her multiple roles. A family-affirming society might provide a variety of services and resources for childbearing families. At the present time, most young mothers do what they can with the help of their husbands.

Developmental tasks of the father of the infant and young child

The young father is not as directly responsible for his baby as is his wife, yet he faces certain inevitable developmental tasks arising directly out of his new status as father. The very fact that it is his wife rather than he who is most intimately related to the child's birth, nursing, and early care gives rise to some unique developmental tasks. Of course, it is humanly possible, as it is among other species, for the father to escape entirely the experiences of living intimately with his own young offspring. There are men, especially among the lower classes, who take little or no responsibility for the bearing and rearing of the child. In earlier times, a man left the care of the young child to the women of the household almost entirely. A father began his active role when his youngster could handle himself well enough to go along on hunting and fishing expeditions, or on short treks near home. Until then, or at least until the child was "housebroken," father's life was relatively undisturbed by baby.

Nowadays, a man improvises along with his wife as both of them attempt to find ways of living with the disturbing little newcomer that will be mutually pleasant and satisfying. Now, as always, a man is expected to be the primary breadwinner and to set up his little family in the style to which he wants them to become accustomed. But here too there are puzzling variations from the older norms. All in all, the young husband-father has quite a surprising number of developmental tasks to accomplish during the childbearing stage of the family life cycle, as we see in a summary of them:

1. Reconciling conflicting conceptions of role:

Settling on a satisfactory role for himself as father out of the many possible, conflicting conceptions held by himself, his wife, both families, friends, and others of influence

Coming to terms with what he expects of his wife, now mother of his child, with the conflicting expectations that each of them has, and with their other significant responsibilities—all of which must be kept in balance

Reconciling conflicting theories about childhood and arriving at a realistic set of expectations for his own child

2. Making way for the new pressures made upon him as a young father:

Accepting a reasonable share of responsibility for the care of the child, compatible with the realities of the situation at home and on his job

Being willing to accept without undue stress or complaint his wife's increased emotional and physical need of him during the time when she is not yet functioning at peak effectiveness

Assuming his share of responsibilities in representing the new family in the community in appropriate ways

3. Learning the essentials of baby and child care:

Acquiring enough knowledge about and skill in early child care to be able to function effectively in the baby's personal life

Practicing the fundamentals required in caring for a tiny baby and small child, both alone and with the mother present

Learning enough about early child development to know what to expect and to understand what is relatively normal at a given stage of development

Becoming increasingly able to enjoy intimate personal interaction with the baby

4. Conforming to the new regimens designed as most healthful for the young family:

Adapting his eating habits to conform to the new food intake patterns of mother, baby, and young family as a whole

Working out ways of getting enough sleep and rest around the edges of the young child's needs and disturbances

Designing new approaches to recreation that will fit in with the needs and limitations now operating in the family

Being willing to experiment with any promising possibilities that seem worth trying, rather than insisting that "life go on as usual"

5. Encouraging the child's full development:

Investing in the equipment and resources that will be most helpful and useful

Cooperating in child-proofing the home for the period of young childhood

Planning with his wife for the enriching experiences that will provide opportunities for the child's well-rounded development

Accepting the child as he is and encouraging him to be himself, rather than viewing him as a "chip off the old block" or a vessel for unfulfilled personal ambitions and dreams

6. Maintaining a mutually satisfying companionship with his wife:

Wooing her back into tender sweetheart and intense lover roles as she recovers from childbirth and the arduousness of the first mothering responsibilities

Seeing to it that the husband-wife relationship is neither chronically nor critically submerged beneath new parental responsibilities

Taking the initiative, when necessary, in renewing satisfying activities as a couple that may have been suspended during the pregnancy, childbirth, and lying-in periods

7. Assuming the major responsibility for earning the family income:

Carrying breadwinner responsibilities willingly

Augmenting the family income in ways that are appropriate as may become necessary

Being willing to accept assistance, as it may be required, from either set of parents, from the wife's supplemental earnings, from savings, or from loans or other mortgages on the future, at this time of relatively high needs and low income

Assisting in financial planning that will keep expenditures within available resources

8. Maintaining a satisfying sense of self as a man:

Continuing personal interests and pursuits compatible with childbearing responsibilities and limitations

Finding new levels of fulfillment in the new experiences of fatherhood

Growing as a person through the maturing experiences of sharing fully in the development of his baby and of enjoying the full bloom of womanhood in his wife

Mastering the infantile, jealousy-provoking impulses that might alienate him from his little family at the very times when they need each other most

9. Representing the family within the wider community:

Serving as chief representative of his family in the workaday world

Recognizing that he is the one to whom his wife looks for adult stimulus, interest, and activities while she is confined with baby care

Bringing home the ideas, the people, the projects that will keep the young family in touch with the larger community during childbearing days

Carrying on the amount of community participation compatible with the pressures at home and on the job

10. Becoming a family man in the fullest sense of the term:

Finding satisfactions in whole-family activities

Cooperating with his wife and baby in the new pursuits that appeal to them

Initiating experiences for the whole family that will broaden horizons and enrich their life together as a family unit

Enjoying the new dimensions of associations with other relatives, now viewed in their new roles as aunts, uncles, cousins, and grandparents of the new baby

Needless to say, all this is more than the average man bargained for when he fell in love and got married. As Frederick Lewis Allen used to say, "Everything is easier to get into than out of." Parenthood is surely a good example. It is so easy for most people to conceive, and so hard to deliver; so easy to dream of settling down and having a family, and so hard to meet the realities of family life when they flood in upon one.

Few men have been adequately prepared for what to expect when children come. They only rarely go through schools where boys as well as girls receive an educational program in preparation for marriage and family life. They grow up in homes where little has been expected of them in terms of direct child care. Until a man's first child appears, he usually has had very little first-hand experience with a baby. He doesn't know what to expect. He finds that his fingers are all thumbs in his first attempts to change or bathe or dress a baby.

Most difficult of all may be the intimate sharing of his wife with the intrusive little rival that now claims so much of her attention. The husband has had his wife all to himself during their courting and honeymoon days and has learned to take her for granted as his partner and companion during the establishment phase of marriage. He must now see her time, energy, and love directed to the demanding baby in ways that may fill him with intense feelings of being left out and neglected. It is a mature husband indeed, that soon after becoming a father can be so centrally involved in the new relationships that he feels a deep sense of belonging—and thus of security as a husband and father. One of the hazards to be expected in this stage of the family life cycle is that the mother may devote herself disproportionately to the new baby, and that the young father may retreat emotionally to a doghouse of his own making. Until he can share his wife maturely and participate with her in the experiences of parenthood, he may feel like little more than a fifth wheel around the place.

How well the young husband juggles the conflicting loyalties and expectations and manages the multiplicity of roles opening up to him depends in large measure on how ready he is for fatherhood and how successful he is in accomplishing the developmental tasks inherent in the childbearing stage of family life. As he succeeds in achieving his personal developmental tasks, he will be able to participate effectively in carrying out the family developmental tasks necessary for the survival, continuation, and growth of the family as a unit.

Developmental tasks of the childbearing family

With the coming of the first baby, the couple now becomes a family of three persons—mother, father, and child. The interrelationships within the family have jumped from one (husband-wife) to three (husband-wife, father-child, and mother-child). Husband and wife are typically in their mid-twenties as this stage begins, and nearly 30 when it ends—two and a half years after the baby's birth (Chapter 7).

The developmental tasks of the family in the childbearing stage are basically concerned with establishing the young family as a stable unit, reconciling conflicting developmental tasks of the various members, and mutually supporting the developmental needs of mother, father, and baby in ways that strengthen each one and the family as a whole.

With the coming of the first baby, there appear for the first time a new mother (in the sense that this woman has never been a mother before), a new father (who must learn what it means to function as a father), and a new family (that must find its own way of being a family). While the baby is learning what it means to become a human being by growing, developing, and achieving his developmental tasks, his mother is learning how to be a mother; his father is practicing what it means to be a father, and the new family is settling itself into family patterns for the first time in its history. This involves the simultaneous working out of the developmental tasks of the baby, the mother, the father, and the family as a whole. The basic developmental tasks of the childbearing family are discussed briefly in the sections that follow.

Adapting housing arrangements to the little child

In millions of families around the world, no special provisions are made for the infant and little child. He or she is carried about by the mother or an older sibling, either in someone's arms, in some kind of shawl or sling, or even wrapped tightly on a board. The baby sleeps with the parents until he is old enough to fend for himself with the other children of the household. There are many homes in the United States where a child never knows a bed of his own, where everything is "share and share alike" within the home from the baby's first appearance until he is grown and leaves for a home of his own.

As the standard of living improves among American families, giving the baby a special place of his own and adapting the family housing to the comfort and convenience of the little child has become the norm. Families with infants and small children are more likely to move than families at other stages of the life cycle (U.S. Bureau of the Census December 1974:2).

Interviews with members of three-generation families show that most couples stay put during the first year of their marriage, and then move to more appropriate housing soon after the arrival of their first baby (Hill 1970).

Many parents accept the fact that a little child is born with ten hungry fingers that must "get into things." They know that the rough and tumble of the baby's early exploration, soiling, and fumbling must be allowed for in the home they share with him. Rather than cooping him up indefinitely or forbidding him access to their living quarters, they so arrange the household that he may enjoy it with them with a minimum of restraint. To avoid the continual "No!" and to protect their belongings as well as their child, they child-proof the home (Table 10–5).

Meeting present and future costs of childbearing

The costs of the family at the childbearing stage tend to balloon because it is then that the past, present, and future needs of the family are simultaneously part of the family budget. The first baby comes on the heels of the establishment stage of the family, when payments for furniture, equipment, house, car, and other high-cost items are still being made. The first child represents current costs in terms of doctor and hospital bills, baby furnishings, layette, special foods and medicines, baby-sitter fees, and at least some new clothing for the mother after nine months of pregnancy.

Beyond the current costs are anticipated future outlays for each child in the family. Headlines quote the costs of raising a child to maturity at $70,000± (Berry 1975). Table 10–6 (p. 236) indicates the percentage of the total childrearing costs for such essentials as the child's share of the family food, shelter, transportation, clothing, etc.

The costs of rearing a child vary greatly according to type of community and region of the country, age of the child, and family income. Annual costs of rearing one child amount to 15 to 20 percent of the family income. Food and clothing costs rise at a faster rate than other items in a growing child's support. An 18-year-old costs from 30 to 50 percent more to maintain than does a one-year-old. College costs (Chapter 3), depending on where the student is enrolled, can add another $25,000± to the family's tab for each son or daughter it supports through to graduation.

It is not unrealistic to add the income a mother gives up to stay home during the childbearing and child-rearing years. Conservative estimates indicate a loss of approximately $100,000 for the college-educated mother who does not reenter the labor force until her child becomes a teenager (Porter 1975:705). Insurance safeguards the family while they are raising

Table 10-5

Child-proofing the Home During the Childbearing Stage

(Outlined Suggestions for Keeping Little Children from Getting Hurt or Destroying Property)

Item	Danger	Child-proofing suggestions
Furniture	Tipping over on child	Select big-bottomed, heavy, plain pieces (especially lamps and tables)
	Painful bumps	Rounded corners better than sharp
	Drawers dumped	Safety catch on all drawers (catch pegs at back hold them)
	Breaking treasured items	Pack away breakables or put in inaccessible places; use wall or hanging lamps instead of table and floor lamps wherever possible
	Soiling upholstery	Choose expendable items, or slipcover with washable fabrics, or upholster in durable, easily cleaned, figured patterns that can take it (feet, sticky fingers, moist surfaces, etc.)
Floors and floor coverings	Chilling in drafts and cold surfaces	Weatherstrip under outside doors in cold weather; supplement heating at floor level; cover with rugs
	Slipping and falling	Avoid hazardous waxing; discard throw rugs; keep traffic lanes as clear as possible
	Soiled rugs	Choose colors that do not show dirt, in patterns rather than plain; select washable or reversible rugs; plan to discard after childbearing stage is over
	Marring floors	Cover with relatively indestructible surface; plan to refinish after heavy-duty phases of family living pass
Walls	Marking and scratching	Choose washable papers or paints, or spray with washable plastic; convert a sizable section into blackboard (paint or large strips of paper), where child may mark; supply child with washable crayons; plan to redecorate when children are older
Table tops	Scarring and staining	Cover with formica, linoleum, terrazzo, marble, or other surface not harmed by wetting, soiling, and pounding; use secondhand items at first

(Continued)

Table 10-5, continued

Item	Danger	Child-proofing suggestions
Toys	Littered	Provide low shelves and accessible storage places
	Harmful paints and surfaces	Select things child can suck and chew without harm
	Sharp edges and corners	Choose toys that will not hurt child in bangs and bumps
	Swallowing	Nothing smaller than a plum for baby
	Breaking	Give child sturdy things he cannot easily break (frustrating him, and you)
Bathroom fixtures	Falling baby	Provide convenient bathing, changing, and toileting facilities for care of baby and little child
	Clinging child	Encourage child's independence as he becomes ready, by low steps by wash-bowl, low hooks for his towel, washcloth, and cup
	Training problems	Supply equipment he can manage himself when he is ready to care for his needs
	Running water	Allow for child's joy in water play by providing time and place for it with some supervision
Locked cupboards	Breaking treasures	Hang key high for door of good dish cabinet, etc.
	Swallowing poisons	Lock up paints, varnish, cleaning compounds, ammonia, lye, medicines, insecticides
	Inflicting wounds	Keep tools, guns, knives, and all other such objects locked away
Stairs and windows	Falling	Put gates at top and bottom of all stairways; give time to child as he learns to go up and down stairs; bar or tightly screen windows

Electric outlets	Shocking child	Cap low outlets; protect cords and keep to reasonable lengths; fence off with heavy furniture so child cannot introduce his finger, tongue, or object into outlet
Entranceways	Cluttering	Provide shelves for rubbers, mittens, and other small objects; make room for baby buggy, sled, stroller, etc.
	Soiling	Supply washable mats at outside doors to keep dirt from being tracked in; keep rubbers, boots, and wheeled objects near door
	Falling	Keep doorway gated or door closed or screen locked when baby begins to get around
Kitchen	Burning	Provide play space near but not at the stove; keep handles of pans turned in rather than out
	Lighting gas	Make burner knobs one of the "no-nos" that baby may not touch
	Lighting matches	Keep matches on high shelves; establish firm "no-no" policy on them
	Tripping workers	Fence off child's play area from main traffic lanes in kitchen, or provide high-chair play during meal preparation
	Cutting	Hang knives high on wall
General	Hurting baby	Minor cuts, bruises, bangs, burns, etc., are taken in stride; major ones are turned over immediately to medical attention (keep doctor's number and other resources on telephone pad)
	Damaging the house	Keep perspective of child being more important than things; use temporary, expendable things while children are small; plan to redo the place as youngsters near the teen years (they'll push for that anyway)

Table 10-6
Where childrearing dollars go

Item	Percent of total childrearing cost
Child's share of cost of the home	31.1%
Food	20.7
Transportation	17.2
Clothing	11.6
Medical care	5.1
Education (up to college)	1.9
All other costs	12.4
Total childrearing dollars	100.0%

Source: U.S. Department of Agriculture survey in Sylvia Porter, *Sylvia Porter's Money Book* (Garden City, N.Y.: Doubleday & Co., 1975), p. 704; see also: Jean L. Pennock, "Cost of Raising a Child," *Family Economics Review* (March 1970):15–17; and "Raising a Child Costs Plenty," *Family Financial Planning*, 15 July 1970, p. 1.

children, providing protection against accidents, lay-offs, and other family crises, as well as building up reserves for education and other advantages.

This meeting of past, present, and future financial needs in the child-bearing family stage causes expenses to spiral at a time when family income is relatively low and when the wife is likely to be no longer gainfully employed. Therefore, the pinch is on, and making ends meet is a real challenge to the young family. Families—each with their own problems and possibilities—meet this developmental task in many ways.

The young father may get an additional part-time job in an effort to make ends meet. This will supply more income, but at considerable cost—in time spent with his family, and possibly in fatigue, irritability, and strain. The young mother may go back to full-time employment soon after the baby is born. This will maintain the family income at the previous level, but it sacrifices the mother's full-time care of the child, their early hour-by-hour companionship, with its satisfactions for both baby and mother. Actually, if the mother has to replace herself in the home with a paid household helper, her work may not net the family much. If one of the grandmothers is available for the early child care and housework, the employment of the young mother may make financial sense, as it does in many lower-class homes.

Some young mothers have the kinds of salable skills that continue to supplement the family income even with a small child in the home. The young woman who is proficient in typing, tutoring, sewing, baking, cooking, or other moneymaking projects can often continue to earn some money even during the active childbearing and rearing stages. Some young women can do such things easily and well. Others find extra activities beyond those of caring for the children and the household an added strain that cannot be comfortably handled.

The couple may borrow money for some high-cost purchases—mortgaging their future by that much, but having the equipment when they need it most. Installment buying comes under this heading, since payments can be extended over a period of years for such things as a car, refrigerator, washing machine, and other items that mean much when children are small. The danger lies in taking on more installment purchases (with their interest charges) than the family will be able to pay off comfortably over the months and years to come. Borrowing is feasible only if the family can see enough income in the foreseeable future to take care of the payment of the loan, with its accumulated interest charges, within a reasonable length of time. Borrowing in a period of financial strain may be unwise, for it adds interest charges to the already too heavy expenditures.

Savings laid away earlier may be used for such items as the automobile, the first baby, or the furniture. The grandparents may pitch in with gifts that assure the young family of what they need as they need it. Some families can do these things well. Where there are tendencies to jealousy or rivalry between the two in-law families, or emotional immaturity and dependency on the part of one or both of the young parents, expensive gifts from grandparents may be hazardous.

"Making do" is one way of balancing the budget during this stage in the family life cycle. Many young families recognize that the household can be kept simple and inexpensive while the children are coming and growing. They choose furnishings that are expendable and place little importance on appearance. Later, when the children are old enough to appreciate nice things and to share in their care, the old, inexpensive, worn-out things may be replaced.

Which course the young family follows in accomplishing the developmental task of meeting the costs of the family at the childbearing stage depends on how they are approaching and meeting a number of their concurrent developmental tasks—especially those having to do with the allocation of responsibility, developing systems of communication, adapting relationships with relatives and friends, and working out a philosophy of life.

Assuming mutual responsibility

The first child brings new responsibilities in terms of round-the-clock care, including the intricacies of feeding, bathing, soothing, and diagnosing distress signals. Daily laundry of baby clothing is a new responsibility. Making formula for the bottle-fed baby is a daily job. Cleaning up the house now involves coping with the new activities and equipment incident to child care—an ever-present chore. At the same time the usual responsibilities of earning the family income, shopping, cooking, dishwashing, housecleaning, mopping, bed-making, and all the rest continue as before.

There are some responsibilities that will be automatically allocated to one or the other of the parents. The father assumes the role of primary breadwinner, and the mother of nursing the baby. Everything else that must be done in the young family may become the responsibility of either partner on either a short-term or a long-term basis. The usual pattern in the American family is for the wife to assume responsibility for child care, housework, laundry, and food preparation for both the baby and the adults, with the assistance of the husband in those chores that he is particularly inclined and able to do. For instance, now that the young mother is confined with the care of the baby, the husband may assume more responsibility for marketing and for other errands that he can take care of on his way home from work.

Facilitating members' role-learning

As both parents increasingly share the responsibilities for the family's welfare, certain roles are undertaken by the husband and others by the wife on the basis of strength. For instance, a number of young husbands take over some of the heavy cleaning and carrying jobs until the young mother has regained her strength and has the time and energy to do all the housework again. There are many possible ways of coping. In some beginning families the shopping is done by both members of the pair in weekly marketing excursions. With the coming of the first baby, the wife enjoys getting out of the house and taking the baby for a daily airing, and now shops more often while she is out with the baby.

Discussing common concerns is part of the process of sharing responsibility. The wife, who is home with the baby most of the time, looks forward to telling her husband about the events of their day. She brings up for her husband's approval purchases made or contemplated and mentions decisions that must be made in the immediate and distant future. The husband in turn keeps his wife informed about progress and problems on the job and discusses with her any possible alternatives for improving their financial or vocational position.

As the baby grows, he becomes accountable to his parents for his behavior—within reasonable expectations. This process is launched well before the 30-month age by which time the child has learned a set of expectancies of what to do and when and how. What constitutes good behavior and what is considered "being bad" varies enormously according to families, cultural groups, and developmental-traditional orientation. But in every home the child soon learns that he must assume certain responsibilities for himself and for his conduct, and that he is accountable to his parents for what he is and does. These responsibilities grow as the child develops; they are slightest when he is a tiny infant and increase as he approaches the "age of responsibility."

Long before the child is two years old, he has learned the basic response patterns appropriate for his little world. He has learned a degree of trust and confidence in his parents. He has learned how to express his annoyance and impatience with those around him. He has laid down the foundation of his emotional being in the loves and hates, fears and anxieties, joys and satisfactions that he has experienced and expressed during his early life with his family. His basic security as a personality rests on the faith in his world that he develops early in life through his trust in his parents—a trust based on his feeling that he is able to communicate, to be understood, and to have his needs met as they arise. By the time the family leaves the childbearing stage of the family cycle, the baby has learned the fundamentals of language and is talking in ways that may be understood not only by his parents, but also by others outside the family. He uses a growing number of concepts accurately and is fast becoming a fully communicating member of his family.

Communicating with one another in the family

Something new is added to family intercommunication when a baby comes into the household. The newborn makes his needs known through a series of signals and distress calls that have to be "received" by his parents with appropriate responses if he and they are to be comfortable. As he is able to communicate his wishes and feelings, and as his parents become increasingly skillful in understanding his communicative efforts, both baby and parents get a feeling of satisfaction in their interrelationship. When this developmental task is difficult, the baby and the parents find each other unsatisfying, even to the point of mutual frustration.

As the mother and father cuddle and fondle the baby, expressing their love for him in close person-to-person contacts, the baby learns to respond. He smiles when his mother or father comes near. He gurgles when they pick him up. He pats them when they care for him. He soon learns to hug, nestle, kiss, snuggle, and to express in the ways of his particular family the love he feels in response to those who love him.

Husband and wife must reestablish effective communication as they become parents. They have new feelings to share in the pride, joys, anxieties, annoyances, and insecurities of early parenthood. The danger is that their marriage may be eclipsed by their new family roles. Feldman (1961) observes that parents of infants talk less with each other, especially about personal things, than they did before their babies came. They tend to have fewer gay times, to laugh less, to have fewer stimulating exchanges of ideas, and to feel resentful more often. In general, the coming of the first baby has a sobering effect on the parents and a depressing effect on the marriage. Team research finds that with the coming of the first child, there is a shift from "we" to "I" in conversations between husband and wife. (Raush, Marshall, and Featherman pp. 11, 20). The advent of children is found by others to cause husband and wife to do less together and to grow apart from each other (Blood and Wolfe 1960:156, 174).

Sharing one's mate with the newcomer involves the establishment of especially sensitive and responsive communication systems. There is a need for mutual recognition of the multiple involvements of both the man and the woman as mates, as parents, and as persons. With the coming of their first baby, the young father must recognize his wife as also "mother." The wife must become accustomed to seeing her husband as also "father." Sometimes these terms are actually employed and continue to be used throughout the life of the family. In other families, these designations are used only occasionally in jest, but they serve the purpose of assisting the partners to accept, express, and internalize their new roles as parents.

It is usual for the sex life of the couple to decrease during the pregnancy, childbirth, and neonatal periods. By six weeks after the birth of the baby, the woman's pelvis is back to normal; the postnatal discharge has ceased; involution is complete; and normally she is physically able to enjoy an active sex life again. The reestablishment of the couple's sex relations is not a simple physiological problem; it has many intricate psychological aspects for both the wife and her mate. Research finds that having a baby is hard on a marriage in the sense that more sex difficulties arise—problems in which the wife is more concerned and the husband more dissatisfied (Feldman 1969).

Many a young mother experiencing for the first time the challenges of motherhood becomes so absorbed in its responsibilities and satisfactions that the husband is in danger of being pushed into the background, unless one of the pair takes the initiative in keeping their mate-love central in the family. It may be the man of the house who reestablishes some of the wooing and courtship processes that will get them both occasionally out of the house with its constant reminders of the baby. The renewal of sweetheart roles will often rekindle the banked fires of desire in both. It may be the wife who takes the initiative in reestablishing full marital relationships as soon as she is ready. One of the first steps the wife takes in this direction is that of making herself attractive for her man again.

Throughout the pregnancy she may have felt the loss of her sexual attractiveness, as her body became swollen with child and the maternal functions gained ascendancy. Now that the baby has safely arrived and is well on the way to healthy infancy, the young mother is free to take an interest in becoming attractive to her husband again. She may get some stylish new clothes to fit her now-slim silhouette. She may get a new hairdo and pay more attention to her figure and skin care. Quite likely she will watch her diet to keep her weight in line during lactation at the same time that she assures her baby of sufficient milk.

Medically and emotionally there may be some specific problems. It is usual in most hospitals to perform an episiotomy (cutting the perineum enough to let the baby through without the danger of tearing maternal tissue). Normally the perineum heals in a few days, but the itching of the healing tissues continues for a while. For some time afterwards, the memory of the pain in the sensitive area may make the reestablishment of sexual relations difficult. A young mother may complain that "the doctor sewed me up too tight," when the main trouble is the tightening of the tissues as she involuntarily tenses during stimulation of the area. Patient thoughtfulness on the husband's part and the active cooperation of the wife are usually all that is necessary for those who have previously known a good sex adjustment.

For couples whose early sex life has been frustratingly inadequate, the nursing period may be used as a protective device by the young mother. In some societies, and in some families here and now, the mother has been known to prolong the nursing of the infant as a way of protecting herself from the sexual advances of her husband. In still others, the young mother may complain of fatigue, ill health, or pain as a way of avoiding the reestablishment of active sex life as long as possible.

Happy families soon find their way through the emotional and physical problems involved. The best of them find that the infant's call for attention may interrupt the most tender embrace from time to time. It is at such times that the couple's communication systems and philosophy of life stand them in good stead as they meet the baby's need and return to each other in good humor without the overtones of frustrated, disgruntled impulses spoiling their relationship with one another.

The young family that manages to accomplish the several-faceted developmental task of refining its communication systems to accommodate its new constellation of emotional interactions will emerge from the childbearing stage with the sense of being a well-knit family. When difficulties in achieving the task are unresolved, the family may emerge from this stage with problems of poor integration that carry over to complicate further phases of its development.

Planning for future children

It is possible to conceive again as soon as marital relations are resumed after the birth of the first child. Some women, believing that lactation prevents pregnancy, continue to nurse the first baby as long as possible in an effort to delay the coming of a second child. Others refuse to resume sexual contact with their husbands until they are ready to accept the responsibility of the possibility of another pregnancy. More effective today is the medical assistance given the couple that allows them marital access at the same time that they are relieved of further parenting responsibilities until they are ready for their next child.

The procedure is a simple one. When the woman goes for her checkup six weeks after the birth of her child, her physician advises her on the practice that will best meet her situation. The method is important, but even more important for the well-being of the family is the philosophy underlying whatever is done.

The question of future children comes soon if something happens to the firstborn. The baby may be born with a congenital abnormality. Mongoloidism, hydrocephalus, and spina bifida are three such conditions apparent at birth. Or the baby may die, as some do each year, even as infant mortality rates decline sharply (Figure 10-1).

Some infants die suddenly for no apparent reason, making it important that parents be reassured that: (1) sudden death syndrome (SDS) is neither predictable nor preventable; (2) its victims do not suffocate or suffer; (3) it is not hereditary or infectious; (4) the disease is as old as biblical times; (5) it occurs all over the world; and (6) SDS kills one in every five hundred infants born in the United States (Pomeroy 1969).

After the first shock and disbelief at losing their firstborn, a couple may postpone their next baby out of fear of a second disappointment, or they may make plans for their next child as soon as possible, in an attempt to take their loss philosophically.

Relating to relatives and others

With the coming of the first baby, grandmother comes into her own in many families. She is welcomed as the one who holds things together during the baby's first days at home—the time when the mother is fully absorbed in the baby's care and in regaining her strength. As the young mother is increasingly able to take over full responsibility for her household with the assistance of the baby's father, the grandmother's role recedes in importance. About that time, other relatives begin to come by to see the new baby, to call on the new mother, and to bring gifts, advice, and warnings that have to be absorbed and dealt with one way or another.

In-law jealousies and juggling for power not infrequently emerge with the coming of the first baby. One parental family gives more, does more, demands more, or expects more of the little new family than does the other. If one or both of the parents are immature or on the defensive, the imbalance of grandparental interest may fan the flames of envy, jealousy, and insecurity to a white heat of passionate resistance.

In the mixed marriage, the interest of the grandparents in seeing that the new baby is baptized in the church of their faith rather than that of the other mate may become a battle royal—both grandparental families taking the attitude that "anything is fair in love and war." Earlier studies of many cases, in which both sides of the in-law relationship were analyzed, showed that battle tactics may range from covert hints and maneuvers to open aggression and abuse (Duvall 1954).

Even if the couple share the same faith, the coming of the first baby

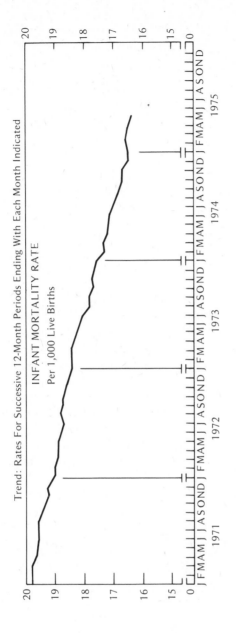

Figure 10-1

Decline in Infant Deaths, United States

Source: U.S. Department of Health, Education, and Welfare, National Center for Health Statistics, *Monthly Vital Statistics Reports* 24, no. 5 (July 24, 1975): 3.

may precipitate interference in religious practices, financial plans, household routines, social activities, and the like until the young family is able to establish its autonomy as a family unit.

The childbearing family is now a unit in the larger family circle—with all the problems and promises appertaining thereto. As the young family establishes itself as a comfortably interdependent unit within the larger whole, giving and receiving in ways that are mutually satisfying, it is ready for the years of interlocking family relationships that lie ahead. No man can live to himself alone. Few families, even today in our age of individualism, are entirely independent. Most of us benefit from serving and being served by our own flesh and blood—the brothers and sisters, parents, uncles, aunts, and cousins that make up our larger families.

Families tend to keep to themselves during the nesting time. This is a period when young families are apt to be highly mobile, since the young husband may move or be transferred from place to place as he establishes himself vocationally. Community contacts in any one location tend to be temporary at best. Old friends and family are left behind. Old interests and group ties may be weakened. After a man and his wife have become parents, they have little in common with their childless friends. They are not as available for gadding about as they were before the baby came. Since the cost of a baby-sitter must be considered every time the couple is invited to some social affair, they think twice before accepting the invitation.

Young parents today have developed some ingenious ways of working through this developmental task. In some neighborhoods, parents take turns minding each other's children, thus freeing each other for more social life. Some parents form sitter-pools, signing up for the times when they are available for the care of their neighbors' children—in exchange for like service in return. The sitters are experienced young parents themselves. They report finding satisfaction in serving in each other's families, in enjoying the resources of each other's homes, and in realizing through practical experience that one's own child is no worse than his age-mates in similar homes. A disadvantage is that the parent who is on duty as a sitter for another family must necessarily leave his or her spouse at home alone with their own children. Since this is usually during the quiet hours of the family day, when the children are asleep and the adults are free for their life as a couple, there may be something of a problem.

Another way of coping is the old-world custom of bundling up the baby and taking him along to any of the community or church affairs that continue to interest the mother of the family. This alternative is more widely used among lower-class families that rarely participate actively in a wide variety of community activities. Thus, family participation as such does not increase during the childbearing stage.

Upper-class families frequently have a nurse whose responsibility it is to care for the baby from the time it comes home from the hospital until he or she is old enough to be sent away to school. The nurse frees the mother and father from day-by-day responsibilities (except in times of emergency, such as the child's serious illness).

Maintaining motivation and morale

There is a fivefold crisis in family living at the childbearing stage:

1. Seeing beyond the drudgeries to the fundamental satisfactions of parenthood.
2. Valuing persons above things.
3. Resolving the conflicts inherent in the contradictory developmental tasks of parents and young children, and of fathers and mothers.
4. Establishing healthy independence as a married couple.
5. Accepting help in a spirit of appreciation and growth.

Faced with the daily round of diapers, dishes, and distractions, a young mother may feel weighed down with drudgeries to the point where she loses her sense of perspective. The young father, burdened with his new responsibilities and with the pressures of making ends meet, may feel harassed and may suffer from chronic stress. The young couple who sense beyond their daily duties the profound satisfactions involved in having their own child to care for find ways to shrug off needless worries and to adopt a lighthearted approach to their family life and to each other. They find joy in little everyday happenings. They delight in their youngster's development, as well as in his emerging skills and cute doings and sayings. They discover the spiritual meanings of their family life as they free themselves for the fulfillments of parenthood.

Things are in the saddle in many families at the childbearing stage. The parents have invested a great deal of themselves and of their resources in the effort of equipping a home they can be proud of. Along comes junior with none of the adult values of neatness and cleanliness in his makeup. On the contrary, he is bent on active exploration of as much of his world as he can get into his mouth, pound to a pulp, sit on, wet, or soil. The family soon has its back to the wall in a struggle of values. Which comes first—people or things, parents or children? Ideally, each learns from the others in time. The baby learns that there are certain things that must not be touched and certain values that are too precious to his parents to be ignored. While the parents are socializing their lusty little human, the infant, in turn, is changing a new mother and father into a set of experienced parents who are able to relax and take the daily issues in stride.

At this stage the family must work out the dynamics of its primary and secondary orbits. The basic conflict is between the mother-child and the wife-husband relationship. Arriving at the full realization that the husband-wife relationship must be kept primary can involve an agonizing struggle. Conflicting pressures can produce some tears, not a few tense moments, and a young mother torn by competing loyalties within herself. A philosophy of family life that views the husband-wife relationship as central to the stability and well-being of the entire family is the key to resolving this fundamental conflict.

The willingness to accept help—in the form of assistance and gifts from relatives; or professional guidance of physicians, marriage counselors, child-guidance experts, or others—depends in large measure on the family's philosophy. If the young family is developing a philosophy of humility, based on recognition of the interdependence of all humans, then they as family members can accept help with appreciation and without loss of self-esteem. Maturing families, as well as persons, grow from serving and being served by those in whom they have confidence. In this stage especially, the young father and mother can learn a great deal from parent-education experiences, as well as from family counseling programs that

Table 10-7
Childbearing Family Rituals

Times and occasions	Rituals, routines, and ceremonies
Morning awakening	Little child climbs into parents' bed Ritualized games and language play
Breakfast	Child eats from special dishes Baby's names for food and functions used by parents Routines for cleaning food spills and messes
Naptime	Ritualized procedures by mother and child Special blankets and toys Customary routines
Daily outings	Dressing child for going out Special possessions chosen for the trip Child allowed certain privileges
Father's homecoming	Child watches for father at window or door Mother and child welcome returning father Father brings surprises
Baby's bathtime	Special toys and procedures Father-mother-child play Drying, wrapping, cuddling routines
Bedtime for child	Stories, songs, prayers Tuck-in rituals and goodnight kiss "Drink a water" requests for attention Special light and cuddly toy for comfort
Special holidays	Birthday celebrations ritualized Visits to relatives Trips and vacations with baby Photographing baby in holiday settings Sitter routines as parents celebrate as a couple

provide opportunities to talk over their problems, evaluate their progress, and plan for their future as a family.

Family rituals and routines

If each new day in the life of the childbearing family started out without reference to those that had preceded it, life might be hectic indeed. Each new situation would be faced without the benefit of precedents and established procedures. Each person would be confronted with a multitude of possibilities that could be frighteningly confusing. The full weight of each new developmental task of individual or family would fall on the persons involved. Fortunately the tasks of family life do not weigh that heavily on anyone, partly because of the early establishment of family rituals. These help to reduce to familiar, comforting patterns many of the aspects of living together around the clock and calendar. Rituals that are commonly part of the childbearing stage of the family life cycle are listed in Table 10-7.

Rituals add a great deal to the life of the childbearing family. They provide the workable routines that ease the parents' days and nights. They give the little child reliable, secure expectations of what comes next, and they provide the simple, sweet sources of satisfaction that come to mean most in family living.

The child is father of the man.
Wordsworth

F amilies with preschool children

chapter eleven

While the first child is between two-and-one-half and five years of age, the preschool family typically has a second and possibly a third child, making a total of three to five persons, with the possibility of from three to ten interpersonal relationships. The possible positions in the family are husband-father, wife-mother, son-brother, and daughter-sister—each with its own developmental tasks. While the adults struggle with their child-rearing and personal tasks, the preschool child faces the crisis of initiative (expanding imagination) versus guilt (developing conscience), while younger siblings retrace, each in his or her own way, the developmental stages the eldest has completed.

Preschool children's development

Preschool children develop according to predictable principles of human development (Table 8–3). They are attaining some autonomy and

249

have made notable advances in terms of imagination, initiative, and independence. They are toilet-trained (most of the time), and are greatly impressed with a sense of their own bodies. They get about easily and communicate freely with words and symbols. Children of this age have already attained half their adult height and intelligence (Bloom 1964). They like to know how to do things, such as solving a problem or riding a tricycle. Their new abilities arise from three types of stimuli: (1) physical growth and development—necessary for such skills as hopping, skipping, jumping, and running; (2) availability of a variety of objects such as scissors, crayons, blocks, and toys; and (3) interaction with adults and children—through which they gain social experience (Bijou 1975:833).

Once past the preoccupation with self that characterizes babyhood, the preschool child begins to emerge as a social being—one who can share with others and participate as a member of his family. His pace of physical growth is slowing down, and many of his body activities are becoming routine. Progress in his emotional and intellectual development is increasingly apparent in his growing ability to express himself in speech and in his greatly expanded acquaintance with his environment.

Preschoolers can choose between two alternatives (orange or tomato juice), describe recent experiences (trip to the zoo), tell how to do things (play a game or hammer a nail); and they have begun to use categories (they can select one color, shape, or type from an assortment of mixed objects). The preschool years are the time in a child's life when a foundation is being laid for the "complex psychological structures that will be built in a child's lifetime. It is this period, more than any other, that makes each child a unique personality" (Bijou 1975:836).

Individual differences

Each child is unique. He grows at his own pace and is unlike any other human being in all respects. Normative listings, like that in Table 11–1, merely indicate the levels of development that *most* children of a given age have attained in terms of various characteristics. Many facets of a child's development cannot, of course, be included in such gross categories as height, weight, vocabulary, and mental, emotional, or social life. Within any of these broad groupings of characteristics there are tremendous differences (in literally thousands of qualities) and wide variations in patterns of growth and status of development among children of any age. Some children mature rapidly, others slowly. However, most grow at a pace that falls within the ranges indicated in general patterns of child development derived from study of many children over the years. No individual child is a statistic, but a living, growing human being. Although it is best to understand him as an individual, it is sometimes helpful to

Table 11-1
Development of the Preschool Child

Characteristic	Two and one-half to four years of age	Four to six years of age
Height	Thirty-three to forty-four inches (range)	Thirty-eight to forty-eight inches (range)
Weight	Twenty-three to forty-eight pounds (range)	Thirty to fifty-six pounds (range)
Bones	All seven ankle bones begun; bridge of nose forming; fusions occurring in skull;	spinal curvature beginning
Muscles	Steady growth and development; coordination increasing;	sphincters maturing and becoming controllable
Sense organs	Equilibrium improving	Farsighted by six years
Locomotion	Walks up and down stairs; runs well; jumps; tiptoes; hops with both feet; rides tricycle	Skips; gallops; hops on one foot; alternates feet in descending stairs; walks straight line
Manual skills	Small muscle skills developing in drawing, building, etc.	
Eye-hand coordination	Uses spoon; pours; puts shoes on; copies circle; draws straight line; catches ball; builds with blocks	Dresses self; cuts with scissors; copies square; designs and letters; throws and catches ball
Teeth	Four molars appear; twenty temporary teeth by three years	Loss of baby teeth begins
Digestion	General diet	Appetite slackens; less interest in food
Urination	Sense of bladder fullness developing	Complete control by six years usually
Respiration	Twenty to thirty inhalations per minute	Increased susceptibility to infection
Vocabulary	896 words by three years; 1,540 words by four years; simple sentences; "what" and "where" questions predominate	2,072 words by five years; 2,562 words by six years; more complex sentences of six to eight words; "how," "when," and "why" questioning
Thinking	Increasingly flexible through preschool years; concepts first acquired through concrete experience become abstract with experience in grouping objects, dealing with time, space, numbers, and processes; varies widely with intelligence and interaction with others	
Character	Increasing knowledge of rules; growing ability to judge right from wrong, to control himself, to internalize standards, and to make explicit demands upon himself	
Dominant emotions	Anger, temper tantrums, and negativism	Fears peak; fighting especially among boys; sympathy, empathy in simple forms evident
Social life	Parallel play; imaginary playmates; dramatizations	Social adjustment under way; varies according to playmates available

For further detail see Mollie S. Smart and Russell C. Smart, *Children: Development and Relationships* (New York: Macmillan Company, 1967), chaps. 6–9; Elizabeth Lee Vincent and Phyllis C. Martin, *Human Psychological Development* (New York: Ronald Press Company, 1961), pp. 127–140; Character Research Project, *The Growth and Development of Christian Personality*, 4th ed. (Schenectady, N.Y.: Union College, n.d.).

consider him in relation to other children of about his age and stage of development.

Physically, children range from broad and stocky to tall and thin, from large- to small-boned, from robust to weak, from obese to underweight, according to the norms. These differences, plotted on the Wetzel grids, can help the doctor to evaluate a given child's progress in his own growth track.

Mentally, children range from slow to quick within the "normal" IQ of 90 to 110, more or less. IQs below this range represent various levels of retardation. Higher scores indicate very bright children, some of whom test out as geniuses. Musical ability, rhythm, creativity, imagination, language sense, and other special talents or handicaps manifest themselves in some children quite early, and in others more slowly or not at all.

Emotionally, some children are fearful, anxious, or easily upset, whereas others seem to fear little or nothing. Some children are loving cuddlers, others seemingly less affectionate "by nature." Some children anger easily, lose their tempers, and fight their way through situations, while others just as "naturally" cope more rationally with their problems. Some children tend to be outgoing and friendly, some are shy and retiring, and still others can react either way depending on how they feel about the situation and about the people involved.

Individual differences arise from a complex of sources. Genetic programming is a factor. Some differences (present and to come) are determined by inherited genetic factors present in the DNA and RNA molecules found in the cells of their bodies (coloring, body type, handedness, for instance). Other differences among children are congenital, arising in the developing embryo or fetus before birth (due to thalidomide or Rh problems, congenital syphilis or rubella, for instance).

A host of acquired characteristics arise after birth. These come from the way a child is nurtured and the way he responds to the signals he receives from others (or from within himself). There is a tremendous difference (in end results) between the TLC (tender, loving care) a child receives from two parents who love and rear him in a happy home and the neglect a child knows at the hands of an unloved and unloving mother. At the far end of the spectrum is the "battered baby" syndrome, seen in young children who have been beaten by one or both of their parents. Wide variations are found between privileged and underprivileged children not only in their nutrition and general health, but also in their interest in learning, their response to others, and their basic stance toward life.

Children who are mentally alert and emotionally healthy tend also to be physically well developed (Abernethy 1936; Jones and Mussen 1958: 492-501; Ketcham 1960: 171-177; Mussen and Jones 1958:61-67; and Tanner 1963:817-847). Psychological states affect biological processes (and vice versa) in children as well as in adults, according to clinical evidence from psychosomatic medicine. Even within this broad generalization there are many exceptions, depending on the repertoire of responses an individual has for his many life situations. Much depends on the ways in which children accomplish their developmental tasks step by step through their growing years. In no other period of his life does a person face quite the same dramatic complex of roles and developmental tasks as that which confronts the preschool child when he begins to see himself and to be seen by others as no longer a baby, but as a person in his own right.

Developmental tasks of preschool children

1. Settling into healthy daily routines of rest and activity:

Going to bed and getting his needed rest without a struggle
Taking his nap or rest, and learning to relax when he is weary
Enjoying active play in a variety of situations and places
Becoming increasingly flexible and able to accept changes

2. Mastering good eating habits:

Becoming adequate in the use of the customary utensils for eating
Accepting new flavors and textures in foods with interest
Enjoying his food with lessening incidents of spilling, messing, and toying
Learning the social as well as the sensual pleasures of eating

3. Mastering the basics of toilet training:

Growing in his ability to indicate his needs for elimination
Cooperating comfortably in the toilet training program
Finding satisfaction in behaving appropriately as to time, place, and ways of toileting expected of boys/girls of his age
Becoming flexible in his ability to use the variety of resources, places, and personnel available to him

4. Developing the physical skills appropriate to his stage of motor development:

Learning to climb, balance, run, skip, push, pull, throw, and catch in whole-body use of large muscle systems
Developing manual skills for buttoning, zipping, cutting, drawing, coloring, modeling, and manipulating small objects deftly
Becoming increasingly independent in his ability to handle himself effectively in a variety of physical situations

5. Becoming a participating member of his family:

Assuming responsibilities within the family happily and effectively
Learning to give and receive affection and gifts freely within the family
Identifying with parent of the same sex
Developing ability to share his parents with another child and with others
generally
Recognizing his family's ways as compared with those of his friends and
neighbors

6. Beginning to master his impulses and to conform to others' expectations:

Outgrowing the impulsive, urgent outbursts of infancy
Learning to share, take turns, hold his own, and enjoy the companionship
of other children—and at times to play happily alone
Developing the sympathetic, cooperative ways with others that ensure
his inclusion in groups
Learning appropriate behavior for situations in which he finds himself
(times and places for noise, quiet, messing, nudity, etc.)

7. Developing healthy emotional expressions for a wide variety of
experiences:

Learning to play out his feelings, frustrations, needs, and experiences
Learning to postpone and to wait for satisfactions
Expressing momentary hostility and making up readily afterwards
Refining generalized joy or pain into discriminating expressions of pleasure, eagerness, tenderness, affection, sympathy, fear, anxiety, remorse, sorrow, etc.

8. Learning to communicate effectively with an increasing number of
others:

Developing the vocabulary and ability to talk about a rapidly growing
number of things, feelings, experiences, impressions, and curiosities
Learning to listen, take in, follow directions, increase his attention span,
and respond intellectually to situations and to others
Acquiring the social skills needed to get over feelings of shyness, self-
consciousness, and awkwardness, and to participate with other people
comfortably

9. Developing the ability to handle potentially dangerous situations:

Learning to respect the dangers in fire, traffic, high places, bathing areas,
poisons, animals, and many other potential hazards
Learning to handle himself effectively without undue fear in situations
calling for caution and safety precautions (crossing streets, greeting
strange dogs, responding to a stranger's offer of a ride, etc.)

Becoming willing to accept help in situations that are beyond him without undue dependence or too impulsive independence

10. Learning to be an autonomous person with initiative and a conscience of his own:

Becoming increasingly responsible for making decisions in ways appropriate to his readiness
Taking initiative for projecting himself into situations with innovations, experiments, trials, and original achievements
Internalizing the expectations and demands of his family and culture groups in his developing conscience
Becoming reasonably self-sufficient in a variety of situations—in accordance with his own makeup and stage of development

11. Laying foundations for understanding the meanings of life:

Beginning to understand the origins of life and how the two sexes differ; and to be aware of his or her gender
Trying to understand the nature of the physical world—what things are, how they work and why, and what they mean to him
Accepting the religious faith of his parents and learning about the nature of God and about the spiritual nature of life

The preschool boy or girl must achieve enough independence to be comfortable without his parents in a variety of situations. He or she must become reasonably self-sufficient both in the home and in outside settings, in keeping with his or her particular stage of development. The child who has had preliminary practice in crossing streets, managing his outside garments, going to the toilet alone, washing his own hands, using his handkerchief, and in handling everyday routines, accidents, and minor crises will be ready to enter school feeling self-confident enough to be ready for its challenges. If his parents have introduced stories, songs, pictures, conversations, excursions, and creative play materials into his life, he will be able to enter school as a contributor as well as a recipient. When the preschool child has successfully accomplished the developmental tasks of this stage, he is ready to go to school. The check test on readiness for kindergarten details some of the specific learnings derived from the preschooler's developmental tasks (Table 11–2).

Value of preschooling

Many of a child's developmental tasks are made easier when he is exposed to the social interaction, physical environment, and competent direction provided by a good preschool. Experience in nursery school, kindergarten, Project Head Start, day care center, or any of the other recently developed programs designed to encourage the young child's development has been shown to have measurable value. One project

Table 11-2
Child's Readiness for Kindergarten: A Check Test

	Always	Usually	Sometimes	Rarely
1. The child knows his name, address, and father's name.				
2. He is free from those physical defects which can be corrected.				
3. He knows the way to school and can find his way home again.				
4. He has been taught how to cross streets.				
5. He recognizes policemen, is not afraid of them, and will follow their directions.				
6. He can go to the toilet, manage his clothing by himself, and conform to expected modesty patterns.				
7. He can hang up his coat, put on his outdoor clothing, and recognize his own belongings.				
8. He is content to stay with adults other than those he knows well.				
9. He has had opportunities to play with children his own age and gets along well with them.				
10. He is familiar with some of the places in the neighborhood that are of interest to children his age (post office, grocery store, firehouse, a building under construction, etc.).				
11. He can entertain himself with constructive tasks for short periods of time.				
12. He is interested in books and will spend some time looking at them quietly.				
13. He attacks a new job willingly and welcomes new situations without fear.				
14. He is in the habit of sharing certain household tasks with other members of the family.				
15. He is patient about waiting his turn and respecting property rights of others.				
16. He can keep his temper, his tears, and his other emotional outbursts under reasonably good control.				
17. He is curious about many things and, with a little help from an adult, can follow up his interests.				

Source: Adapted freely from Fay Moeller, "Understanding Our Children," mimeographed (Storrs, Conn.: University of Connecticut Extension Service, 1954).

involving children from inner-city, low-income familes (tested before and after two years' nursery schooling) showed an average IQ gain of 14.7 points on the Stanford Binet scale (Kraft, Fuschillo, and Herzog 1968).

The major objectives of nursery schools for culturally deprived children are embodied in programs that (1) stimulate children to perceive aspects of the world around them and to fix these aspects by their use of language; (2) develop more extended and accurate apeech; (3) develop a sense of mastery over facets of the immediate environment and an enthusiasm for learning; (4) develop the ability to make new discoveries, to think, and to reason; (5) develop purposive learning activity and the ability to attend and to concentrate on an activity for longer periods of time (Bloom 1965:23–24).

The percentages of three-, four-, and five-year-olds in nursery schools and kindergartens have increased markedly in recent decades (Figure 11-1). Most black nursery school children (69 percent) are in public programs; the majority of white nursery school students (78 percent)

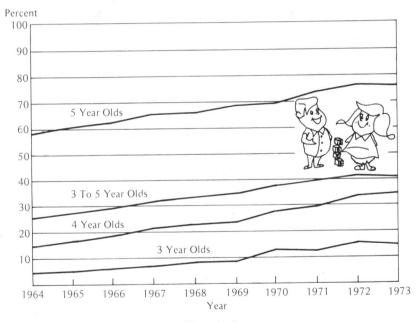

Figure 11-1

Percent of 3 to 5 year old children enrolled in nursery school and kindergarten: October 1964 to October 1973

Source: U.S. Bureau of the Census, "Nursery School and Kindergarten Enrollment: October 1973," *Current Population Reports*, Series P-20, no. 268 (Washington, D.C.: U.S. Government Printing Office, August 1974): Cover.

participate in private programs (U.S. Bureau of the Census August 1974: 1).

Developmental tasks of parents at the preschool stage

One fascinating facet of family life is that it is forever changing. No sooner has a fence been built to keep a two-year old out of the street than he is a three-year-old, capable of understanding why he must keep to the sidewalk. The period of teaching the youngster to keep dry is succeeded by one of helping him to get used to sharing his parents with a new baby. Just as a child has reached a stage when his mental growth has made him an increasingly interesting companion, he is away at nursery school or kindergarten.

Parenting without a partner

Millions of children grow up in one-parent homes, and the numbers increase each year. The sobering fact is that the proportion of children living with only one parent (usually the mother) has almost doubled since 1960. In 1960, 6.7 percent of all children under the age of six were living with their mothers only; by 1974 the percentage of preschoolers with mother only had risen to 13.2 percent (Glick 1975:1–2). More than one-third (35.2 percent) of all black children under three were living with their mothers only in 1974; the comparable figure for white children under three that year was 8.0 percent (Glick 1975: Table 3).

A mother raising a little child alone often assumes the responsibility of earning the family income in addition to that of caring for her home and youngster. Her child is still young, still dependent, and still in need of regular supervision and guidance, even though she must go out to work. A high-salaried woman can employ a competent housekeeper if she can find one. More often her mother or some other woman attempts to replace her in the home. A nearby day care center that can care for her child while she is away from home during the day is a blessing, especially if it provides more than minimal supervision, food, rest, and play materials—all so important at this stage of development.

Even so, when the working mother picks up her little one on the way home from work, she is tired and hungry—and very much on her own as she prepares the evening meal. Once she has fed her preschooler and tucked him into bed, she faces the lonely hours ahead in an empty house, with no mate to tell her troubles to, or to give her the solace and loving support she needs. Fathers raising their children alone face most of the same problems, for much the same reasons. It is no wonder that so many one-parent and other families with preschoolers rely so heavily on television to occupy the child's time while the adults are busy.

Relying on television—
a mixed bag

Preschool children are fascinated with television programs of all kinds. A Nielson study finds that many evening shows are watched by a larger number of two- to five-year-olds than are any of the daytime shows. The effects are particularly unfortunate for low-income children, who are found to watch television up to five to seven hours each weekday. The National Commission on the Causes and Prevention of Violence concludes that television has been so filled with violence that it is teaching American children moral and social values "inconsistent with a civilized society" ("TV Violence 'Appalling,'" *U.S. News and World Report* 1969: 55; see also, Daley 1969:99; and Cater and Strickland 1975).

Television has a potent influence on children—shaping their attitudes toward and expectations of themselves and others long before they can read and write. Used constructively, television can enlarge a child's world and bring him face to face with persons, places, ideas, and ideals. There are many ways in which parents can guide their children's television viewing. They can, for instance—

1. Become aware of what children are watching, rather than consistently using the TV set as a baby-sitter
2. Turn off undesirable programs and interpret their reason for doing so to their child—"Our family does not like such behavior."
3. Prepare a television guide for young children, using pictures of the clock, channel numbers, and television characters for children not old enough to read
4. Help little children to see TV commercials as ways people try to sell things—things that may be chosen or not by those who do the buying
5. Tell local television stations and the networks their choices, their objections, and their preferences
6. Request that the recommendations of the violence commission be implemented:
   a. an overall reduction in programs that require or contain violence
   b. elimination of violence from children's cartoon programs
   c. adoption of the British practice of scheduling crime, Western, and adventure stories containing significant violence only after children's bedtime
   d. permanent federal financing for the Public Broadcast Corporation to enable it to offer high-quality alternatives to violent programs for children
   e. intensified research by the networks into the impact of television violence (Tobin 1969; Bronfenbrenner 1967; and Kiester 1975).

A nationwide poll commissioned by *TV Guide Magazine* in late 1975 found that 86 percent of parents with children under six years of age favored a family viewing time in which the early evening hours would be restricted to television programs suitable for parents to watch with their children (Hickey 1975).

Programs designed especially for children of preschool age are shown on many channels at times convenient for both parents and their little boys and girls. Such programs as *Sesame Street*, professionally developed to offer preschoolers the basic knowledges and attitudes they need to develop well, make a real contribution to the life of the family with preschool children. That so many preschoolers are interested in them is a tribute both to the youngsters and to the programs.

Accepting each other in the family

A little child has a special need for the comfort of being loved, appreciated, and enjoyed for himself. Both parents may need to check possible tendencies toward trying to make the child over—tweaking and pulling at him with little criticisms rather than giving encouraging and appreciative little pats. They must recognize that it is their job to help the child develop the capacities he has rather than to try to build up their self-esteem by pushing him beyond what he can do. Avoiding the harmful practice of visiting "the curse of the norm" on any child and enjoying the unique individuality of each child are paired developmental tasks of prime importance.

Somehow parents have to learn to take their unavoidable failures, mistakes, and blunders in stride, without piling up feelings of guilt, blame, and recrimination. There is a need to accept each other's human failings as parents with understanding and sympathy, rather than with blame. In a day when so much emphasis is placed on parent-child relations—while at the same time so little is known about how to keep from foisting one's own frustrations and insecurities on one's children—parents need each other's help in striking a balance between worry and nonchalance, between self-recrimination and indifference. We all make mistakes, but if our basic attitudes are wholesome, loving, and friendly, the mistakes are going to be more than offset by good feelings.

Studies show that wives and husbands at the preschool family stage have less emotionally-charged interaction with each other than they had earlier in their marriages (Feldman 1961). During this period they have fewer arguments, feel resentful or misunderstood less often, and tend less often to refuse to talk because they are angry with each other than at any other time since they married.

At the same time, the marriage has fewer positive supports at the preschool stage than it formerly did. Husband and wife have fewer jaunts away from home and less often laugh together, work together on a stimulating project, or calmly discuss something with each other than formerly.

By now the parents seem to have settled into the business of child-rearing with fewer negative feelings and less fun as a married pair than they had earlier.

At this stage the parents may need to strengthen their creative partnership and to express their affection in ways that will keep their relationship from falling to a humdrum level. The expression of affection for each other may seem like an odd "task" to set up, but lack of such expression ranks high among the grievances husbands and wives list when trying to analyze their sources of unhappiness (Terman et al. 1938: Chap. 5). Apparently it is easy to fall into the habit of assuming that the other partner will take for granted the love that each really wants and needs.

Continuing to develop as married adults

The many demands and pressures on each parent may tend to leave little time for them to enjoy each other's company and the hobbies or pursuits that may have been initially responsible for drawing them together. The mother may be so concerned with the demands of child care and homemaking that she gives little thought to her need for continuing to develop as a person. The father may be so taken up with his work that he no longer takes time for just enjoying life with his wife.

Yet this is a time when husband and wife must learn to keep their marriage alive and growing. If their relationship is to be enduring and satisfying, it must meet their needs as persons and as a couple. Couples who succeed in this developmental task encourage those individual and joint tastes, interests, and friendships that strengthen their confidence in themselves and in each other.

Family developmental tasks at the preschool stage

While the preschool child is achieving his developmental tasks, and the adults are attempting to accomplish theirs as parents and as husband and wife, the family as a whole is concurrently facing the family developmental tasks of the preschool stage:

1. Supplying adequate space, facilities, and equipment for the expanding family
2. Meeting predictable and unexpected costs of family life with small children
3. Assuming more mature roles within the expanding family
4. Maintaining mutually satisfying intimate communication in the family
5. Rearing and planning for children

6. Relating to relatives
7. Tapping resources outside the family
8. Motivating family members

Supplying adequate space, facilities, and equipment for the expanding family

Housing now should promote the growth of the preschooler, afford a good start for his younger sibling, and allow some privacy and comfort for the parents. Nothing can be a greater challenge to good family growth than the lack of enough space to accommodate the interlocking needs and problems of group and individual maturation. Fathers with preschool children spend significantly more time out of the home than men whose children have grown. Among the reasons for fathers' absenting themselves from their young families is their need for privacy and a chance to concentrate on their own projects (Smith, Downer, and Lynch 1969).

Inefficient houses and inadequate household equipment complicate the mother's already onerous task of dividing her time between the needs of her children and the demands of the household. Facilities adequate for the varying sleep and rest requirements of the several members of the family are a real asset. Parents now especially need privacy for their more intimate moments together—free from the ever-present interest of the inquiring preschooler and his "Watcha doing?" The child-proofing of the house mentioned earlier carries over into this stage. These safeguards are especially necessary now, when protecting the new baby without unduly restraining the preschool child becomes an additional factor of importance.

This is the stage when climbing, pulling, and hauling equipment give the preschooler the large-muscle exercise and skill-development opportunities he needs. At the same time, it takes him out from under foot, assuring both his parents and his new sibling of some relief from his boisterous activity. When the entire neighborhood seems compressed and hemmed in because of social barriers, the problem of full expression of the individual and the family is compounded. Readily accessible play facilities, recreational areas, and parks are needed to provide an outlet for family tensions.

Meeting the costs of families with small children

More than a third of American mothers of preschool children work. Some have part-time jobs, but the majority (69 percent) work full time. Among mothers with toddlers under three years of age, blacks are twice as likely as whites (36 compared with 17 percent) to hold full-time jobs as working mothers throughout the year (Waldman 1975:64–65). Most of these mothers of preschoolers work because they must, either to supplement what their husbands earn, or because theirs is the only paycheck in the family. The majority of mothers of preschool children see themselves primarily as homemakers, even when the family's expenses are great. So, they and their families tighten their belts and make ends meet as best they can.

If the family income is fairly steady, it is possible to budget carefully for the normal expenditures of the growing family—so much for food, clothing, sitter fees, recreation, utilities, rent or house payments, and the rest. When the income fluctuates, as it does in times of unemployment or of sickness or accident, major adjustments may be required.

The preschool stage is notorious for its unpredictability. The family may be getting along fine, with income matching outgo, when suddenly something happens that throws the whole financial picture out of focus. In early childhood there is a multiplicity of minor illnesses, any one of which can upset the family budget temporarily. As the older child ranges further afield in the neighborhood, to nursery school, kindergarten, play lot, park, and beach, he comes in contact with many more children than he met as long as he was content in the house and yard. These increased contacts multiply exposure to infections so that childhood diseases are common for the preschooler and quite often for the baby sister or brother as well.

Accidents, falls, burns, and cuts are even more upsetting because the factor of suddenness is added to the distress of disablement. Another significant aspect of children's accidents is the amount of guilt they arouse in the parents. When a long-continuing illness or an abrupt accident results in a deforming handicap or a crippling condition, critical shifts in the economic arrangements as well as in the emotional relationships of the family may become necessary. Intelligent medical and social management are often required to keep the bodily ailment from producing emotional maladjustment in its wake.

The high cost of medical care, continuing insurance drains, installment buying, debts, and mortgages complicate even well-planned family economies and are disastrous to those less carefully organized. In recent years, a growing awareness of the financial hazards facing young families has led to the development of such cushioning resources as group hospitalization and medical service plans, well-baby clinics, cooperative nurseries, child guidance clinics, mental hygiene services, family service facilities, parent education agencies, adult and child recreational programs, and special facilities for the care and education of all types of exceptional children. That such helpful resources are not yet generally available—or even known—to the rank and file of families who need them is all too true in most communities.

*Assuming more mature roles
in the family*

Daily round-the-clock child care (involving "chasing the children" as they play in yard and neighborhood, to properly supervise their play and protect them from danger), as well as attending to the needs of the infant and doing the housework (marketing, cooking, baking, cleaning, dishwashing, sewing, washing, ironing), is generally assigned the young wife and mother in our society. In former days these many responsibilities were divided among other grown and growing members of the family.

Nowadays, many a young father returns home from work to find his wife busy with her end-of-the-day chores, the children irritably clinging to her while she tries to get the evening meal. He steps in and volunteers to take the children off her hands or to do some of the chores that she has not been able to finish through the hectic pace of the day. He may be tired, but he comes in fresh from the outside without the accumulation of mutual annoyance and frustration that so often marks the young mother's hour-by-hour life with active young children. The father can whisk them off for a frolic or give them their baths or take over their feeding with a light touch just because he has been out of the house all day.

An exploratory study of the percentage of time married men spend in various activities finds that fathers of preschool children are more involved in household responsibilities than are husbands at any other stage of the family life cycle. Fathers of young children spend more time in child care than in all other household tasks combined (Table 11–3).

Table 11–3
What Husbands Do in the Home,
by Percentage of Time Spent and Stage of the Family Life Cycle

Activities in/out of the home	Preschool	School-age	Empty nest	Post-retirement
In the house:				
Household tasks	12.6	3.9	4.6	9.0
Food operations	2.9	2.7	2.2	4.6
House care	2.1	1.4	2.2	3.9
Laundry	.3	.5	.2	.5
Care of children	7.3	—	—	—
Business	.1	.2	8.1	.3
Conversation	3.6	4.9	4.7	5.0
Personal Care	4.5	3.2	9.3	8.5
Eating	5.2	3.9	6.2	5.3
Leisure	9.9	14.8	18.3	29.6
Out of the house	64.5	66.1	48.8	42.1

Source: Ruth H. Smith, Donna Beth Downer, and Mildred T. Lynch, "The Man in the House," *Family Coordinator* 18, no. 2 (April 1969): 109.

Father's presence in a child's life is important for his or her full development. A little girl gets a sense of being a desirable, capable feminine person both through identifying with her mother and by attracting the interest of her father—the first important man in her life. Association with a strong, limit-setting, affectionate father is critical in the establishment of a boy's masculinity in the first five years of life (Biller 1967; Mitscherlich 1969; Popenoe 1968; and Walters 1976).

The man of the house often undertakes such heavy household tasks as window-cleaning, wall and floor washing, and trash dumping when his wife's time and strength are barely adequate for the many other demands on them.

The young husband, too, may be sorely pressed for time and energy at this stage of his life. This is the time when the man of the house is trying to get ahead on his job. He possibly is taking an evening course or two with an eye to advancement. He may be doing what overtime he can get to help make ends meet. Even if he is willing to help out at home, there is a limit to what any one person can do comfortably and well.

The preschool child is old enough to assume some real responsibilities. He gradually takes over more and more of his own care in toileting, washing his face and hands, dressing and undressing, and picking up his toys, with help or supervision as needed. As the child enters the preschool period, he or she has begun to take a real interest in what is going on in the household and wants to participate. The little girl of two and a half or three begs to help make beds, to sweep the floor, and to wash dishes when her mother is occupied with these tasks. The child identifies with the parent of the same sex and likes nothing better than acting out the sex role. Parents are wise not to discourage these efforts on the part of the small child "to help." They share with the child the jobs he or she can join in, not so much in the interest of the child's labor, but especially because helping makes the youngster a participating member of the family. The child learns thus to internalize his or her sex role.

Many young families sail smoothly through the preschool family stage in these days. Modern equipment in the kitchen and laundry eases the load that the young mother must carry. Miracle fabrics are easy to keep clean and need practically no ironing. Prepared baby foods and frozen products that can be readied for use in a few moments are a godsend. The modern young mother's ability to plan her work—putting the essential tasks on the agenda and letting the relatively unimportant things slide—removes much of the strain from daily routines. Spacing the arrival of the children so that each is assured the care it needs without unduly taxing the mother's strength does much to keep the young family on an even keel during the preschool stage, when life can easily become quite hectic.

Success in achieving this developmental task is not just a matter of how much or how little there is to be done, but rather of how decisions are made, how roles are assigned, and how the several family members feel about their responsibilities. If each family member feels pride and pleasure in doing his tasks, if each is accountable to the others for common concerns, if each feels needed and appreciated, the family is finding happiness and achieving integration as a working unit.

Maintaining mutually satisfying intimate communication

By the time the first child is a preschooler, his parents have been through the full process of conception, pregnancy, childbirth, and establishment as a full-fledged family at least once. Learning theory would suggest that the experienced couple should find it easier to take further pregnancies and children in stride now than when their first baby came. However, the second child has an even more negative effect on a couple's marital happiness and satisfaction than did their firstborn. Several observable factors indicate that parental roles are hard on the marriage. Among these are: "lowered satisfaction in marriage, perceived negative personality change in both partners, less satisfaction with the home, more instrumental conversation, more child-centered concern and more warmth toward the child, and a curvilinear effect for sexual satisfaction although ending lower" (Feldman 1969).

Couples with only one child expected that their situation would get better as the child got older. They looked foward to their child's interfering less with their marriage, to having the house look better, to being less tired, nervous, blue, and tied down; and to having more and better sexual relations as their child became more mature (Feldman 1969:17).

Finding the time, privacy, and energy for tender, close relationships as a married couple may be difficult when children are young. Sharing bed or room with a child old enough to be aware of what is going on robs a husband and wife of much-needed privacy. Days and nights of nursing a sick youngster rob even the most loving husband and wife of their ardor for each other. Just getting through the day's work may bring the couple to bed too tired for anything but sleep. Knowing from experience the power of their fertility tends to make the woman wary of her husband's approaches unless she has confidence in the family planning procedures. What once was entered into with joyous abandon now may become a marital duty unless the couple provides for their sex life together amid the welter of other demands.

The expanding stage of the family life cycle is so explosive and so full of new experiences, feelings, decisions, and needs to evaluate that communication systems become extremely important at the very time that they are most difficult to keep open and in good working order. But few things are more important to happy family life.

Rearing and planning for children

Childrearing during the preschool stage is one of the family's most urgent developmental tasks. This is the time in children's lives when they are forming basic attitudes toward themselves, their family, and their world. Lacking sound knowledge and wholesome attitudes, children have dangerously shaky foundations for their further development. Parents sense in their children's identification with them that they serve as all-important models of how to live. Problems in childrearing surface daily that tax parents' ingenuity and force them to examine the true nature of the values they profess to hold. Two of the more difficult aspects of childrearing today are (1) helping a child to develop a positive self-concept, and (2) handling aggression. These tasks are at once more crucial and more demanding for parents belonging to minority races and ethnic groups.

Black children who encounter racial insults outside their homes need to know that racist attacks are more demeaning to those who denigrate than to those who are insulted. They can be shown that fighting injustice is praiseworthy, but that inner controls and discipline are indispensable. This is especially relevant for blacks because hostility is so prevalent in their environment (Comer and Poussaint 1975).

Rearing children at the preschool stage of family life is a noisy undertaking. The baby babbles and gurgles and sputters and fusses and "practices" his vowels. The preschool child's language development is more rapid than it will ever be again. Research finds that typically the preschool child learns to use hundreds of new words each year, and that his use of complete sentences is established by the time he is three (McCarthy 1954). Speech and learning are so closely associated that in a real sense a little child learns as he talks and talks as he learns—in increasingly effective ways.

With the coming of the new baby, the emotional constellations of the family shift, as the firstborn accepts his displacement as well as he can, and as the parents find a place in their home for the little newcomer at the same time that they safeguard the security of the older child. There may be a tendency for parents to be emotionally warmer with the second baby than they were with their first (Lasko 1954). This does not mean that they love the second baby more, but rather that they have become more familiar with their roles, and so are able to relax and enjoy the new baby more fully than they could in their first experience as parents.

Understandable as the parents' feelings and emotional expressions are, it may be hard for the firstborn to accept their open display of affection for the little new rival. Therefore, the mother and father create new ways of handling the older child that give him the assurance that he is loved, needed, and wanted for himself. Wise parents provide some special time with their firstborn when the new baby does not intrude. It sometimes helps to let the firstborn know that just because he is older, he occupies a special place in their lives that no younger sibling can ever fill. Some increase in responsibility for the firstborn may be reassuring to him if it is not overdone.

The older child sometimes lets his parents know of his need for being babied too, in regressive acts: wetting himself when he has long since learned to be dry, wanting to take milk from a bottle when he has already established more mature eating and drinking habits, wanting to be cuddled and fussed over as the baby is, even trying to put himself in the baby's place—literally in the buggy or the crib. These are signals a sensitive parent sees as indications that the older child needs more close, demonstrable affection and attention than he has been getting. Ridiculing, belittling, ignoring, or denying a child's effort to communicate his emotional needs cripples the communication systems, and causes explosive feelings to be bottled up—with unfortunate results to the youngster, the younger sibling, and the family as a whole.

The child who is prepared for the coming of his new baby sister or brother can handle with less distress the jealousy and rivalry he feels at the time of his displacement by the new rival. Before the baby comes, the older child needs his parents to help him understand what is happening and to assure him that this is to be *his* baby as well as theirs, and that they will continue to love him after the baby comes, as they have before.

Sex education is already underway in the way parents bathe and diaper the baby, avoid or answer children's questions, teach correct names for body parts and functions, handle sex play, and express their love for one another. Experts advise parents to be free and comfortable about sex without being either aggressive or entirely uninhibited about it (Masters and Johnson 1975:68). Wholesome materials, helpful in the early sex education of children, can be found in libraries, book racks, and community agencies.

By the time the second baby has arrived, plans are usually made to avoid further pregnancies, since most Americans barely replace themselves in the population (Chapter 3). Few husbands and wives want large families; only 8 percent of wives between 18 and 24 years of age expect four or more children (*U.S. News & World Report* 1975:32); and later children are usually spaced at greater intervals (Leslie, Christensen, and Pearman 1955). These longer intervals can be seen as "breathing spaces" in which a family reestablishes itself and mobilizes its resources after the birth of one child before attempting the next.

Relating to relatives

At few stages in the family life cycle do relatives play as important a role as they do during the preschool period. Grandparents can do much to ease the pressures on the parents while children are young. A loving relative who is on hand while the new baby is coming and through the illnesses and accidents that occasionally hit the young family, cushions these crises in many a home. An aunt and uncle may get valuable experience at the same time that they relieve the young parents of their child care responsibilities. They may take over for a long evening, for a weekend or even for a week or two while father and mother slip off to regain their perspective as a couple on a brief vacation, on a business trip, or for a quick visit to old friends.

Problems come up, of course, when the substitute parents do not agree with the child guidance procedures or philosophy that the parents are trying to practice. A grandmother can "spoil" her young charges so that it may take weeks to rehabilitate them, if she is not aware of the parents' goals for their children. Or a too-rigid program of discipline suddenly imposed by some well-meaning aunt or uncle may boomerang in any number of ways. These things are being openly discussed in many families today. Thus the parents can give an explicit briefing to any child-serving relative on what is the usual practice, and why; what the child is and is not customarily allowed to do, and why; what routines are followed most conscientiously; and which of these can be allowed to slide when the situation warrants.

Children are remarkably resilient creatures and can take a great deal of inconsistency from the various adults that attend them, as long as they feel basically secure. Few children can be severely damaged by occasional lapses or changes of pace. Extremists who insist that grandparents are bad for children fail to see how much a child can learn from being handled differently by different persons; or how much a youngster benefits from the sense of ongoing family relations he gets as he clamors for tales of when his mother or father was young. One nine-year-old puts both values neatly when he says solemnly, "I like to go to Grandma's house, because she scolds so soft, and she tells me all about the olden days when Daddy was a little boy just like me."

Tapping resources outside the family

One hazard faced by the family with little children is preoccupation with itself. The young father puts in a full day on his job, rushing to night school or union meeting to better his chances for advancement, and helping out at home in the many roles he feels are his in the family. The young mother is tied down with little children so much day after day that she may long for adult companionship, stimulation, and contact.

The little child leads the family out into wider horizons if he is allowed to range further afield. He goes to nursery school and then to kindergarten, bringing home with him new problems and experiences and later taking his parents out to parents' meetings, neighborhood projects, and community affairs. The preschooler is big enough now to go to Sunday school, and often starts his family in church activities that carry through the years. Periodic trips to the pediatrician or family doctor for preventive shots and checkups, as well as treatment for the various illnesses that befall him, bring both the child and his parents into relationship with the health facilities of the community. His enjoyment of the park, the zoo, the playground, the fire department, and the bakery frequently gets his whole family out for jaunts into activities and facilities never before explored.

Motivation for life's dilemmas

By the time the oldest child is four or five and the next baby already on the scene, the family is face to face with a number of dilemmas that challenge its way of life. Kirkpatrick mentions several that are particularly relevant at this stage of the family life cycle: (1) freedom versus order and efficiency, (2) free expression of personal potentialities versus stable goal expectations, (3) personal self-expression versus child-rearing, (4) work achievement versus love-reproduction functions, (5) flexible training versus rigid child-rearing, (6) high aspiration levels for children versus realistic expectations, (7) family loyalty versus community loyalty, and (8) extensive casual association versus restrictive intensive association (Kirkpatrick 1963:90–95).

Each horn of each dilemma has its values and its price. Freedom is greatly to be desired, but its price is conflict and confusion in the family. On the other hand, order and efficiency are worthwhile values, but their cost is reckoned in terms of personal frustration and submission to authority. And so it goes. Every family must work out, in ways that make sense to its members and to itself as a unit, those answers to the eternal questions of life that suit them in their situations. The family's conceptions of their common life are constantly undergoing change. Some factors contributing to this process are (1) the addition of each new member; (2) the stimuli of other ways of life seen in the community and among their associates; (3) the new ideas and insights any of the family members get (in association with others, in reading, in educational, social, religious, and other contexts); (4) the old and new tastes of joys and satisfactions that ought to be safeguarded; and (5) the various stresses, strains, and challenges that back them to the wall and force them to take another look at life as they are living it.

The young father, driven through his twenties and thirties by efforts to get himself established vocationally and to keep his little family afloat financially, may push himself so hard that he has little time for continuing his interests as a person or for enjoying his family along the way. This is especially true in some middle-class families where mobility drives keep a man lashed by hopes for advancement and chained to his job and its demands. Upper-class fathers find it easier to keep up their club memberships (for business and professional reasons, it's true), and to maintain regular programs of recreation with other men, as well as in the young married couple set. Lower-class families make the poorest articulations with the wider community in the health, recreational, educational, vocational, and social aspects of life, as studies previously quoted (Chapter 5) so emphatically indicate.

The young mother finds meanings in life as a person outside the family during intervals that she manages to fit in around her homemaking and child care responsibilities. It may be in some parents' group, community service project, church circle, political campaign, course of study in the evening, or Saturday afternoon employment that she finds her identity as a woman and brings home, after a few hours of wider horizons, the perspective and point of view that enrich the family as a whole. A major longing of college-educated mothers of young children is for periods of adult association, mature stimulation, and challenging activities with persons their own age. This is one of the prime motivators behind the young mother's desire for a job. When openly recognized by the family, many opportunities besides gainful employment may appear quite as satisfying, unless the financial needs of the family require it.

Busy young parents find their time and energy well-spent when they give themselves to their marriage and to each other in ways that build morale—so vital at this stage.

*Children begin by loving their parents;
as they grow older they judge them;
sometimes they forgive them.*

Oscar Wilde
The Picture of Dorian Gray

Families with schoolchildren

chapter twelve

When the first child goes to school, at about six years of age, the family enters a new stage of its life cycle. This stage, which is characterized by the presence of school-age children, continues until the child becomes a teenager, at 13. Before the end of this period, it is likely that the family will have seen the birth of younger siblings and that it will have reached its maximum size in number of members and of interrelationships. Typically the American family at this stage consists of four to six persons, who maintain from six to 15 interpersonal relationships. The possible range in age is from infancy (youngest child) through plus or minus 40 (father). The eldest child is a school-ager. The parents' crisis continues to be that of self-absorption versus finding fulfillment in rearing the next generation. The school-age child's developmental crisis is risking a sense of inferiority as he develops the capacity of work enjoyment (industry). The family developmental tasks revolve around the major goal of reorganization to make way for the expanding world of school-agers.

These are busy, full years of family living. Children are running in and out of the house; many projects are under way; and the adults are busy keeping the household in good running order and following their youngsters out into wider contacts in the larger community. Concurrently, the school-ager, his younger siblings, his parents, and his entire family work at their developmental tasks, sometimes in harmony, sometimes in discord, but always with the urgency that accompanies growth.

Development of school-age children

Elementary schoolchildren differ considerably within a wide range of normal physical, mental, and social development. They enter school as little children and emerge seven years later at various stages of puberty. Growth in height is steady until the years between nine and twelve, when early-developing youngsters, especially girls, grow taller due to the pubertal growth spurt. Weight increases gradually, and more mature distribution of fat occurs in most children. Appetite varies from poor to ravenous, and digestion is generally good. Bladder control is established, with only infrequent lapses. Bone replaces cartilage in the skeleton, and permanent teeth come in as baby teeth are lost. Muscular strength and skills increase, bringing a sense of mastery to many children. The school years are a vigorous, healthy period for most children.

Intellectually, schoolchildren are involved in what Piaget has called "concrete operations." Children develop concepts (mental tools making sense of a multitude of particulars) through ordering and classifying objects and ideas. This includes collecting and arranging things, learning to read, playing with words and their meanings, and enjoying riddles, jokes, and jingles. They begin to see order in the universe through their study of mathematics and science, to know where places are through geography, and to understand the sequence of events through history. Everything they learn later in school is largely determined by what has been learned by the end of the third grade, and by the time they reach the eighth grade, they will have completed 75 percent of their development of general learning (Bloom 1964:110).

Children rapidly learn appropriate gender roles in the early grade school years (Baldigo 1975:38). They know what activities are all right for boys (playing with trucks, bat and ball, etc.); for girls (playing with dolls); and that either sex may play with sand or slides (Hartley and Hardesty 1964:48). When eight- to eleven-year-old boys are asked, "What is expected of boys?" they reply that adults expect them to be noisy, to get dirty, to mess up the house, to be naughty, not to be crybabies or softies, and to get into more trouble than girls. Furthermore, they feel that boys cannot do many of the things that girls do, but that girls may do many of the things boys do (Hartley 1959). Most fifth graders believe that either sex may work as doctors, lawyers, or college professors, but not as nurses. Nursing is assigned by 54 percent of the children to women only (Hammel 1975). Children of working mothers have more flexible sex roles than do children of full-time housewives (Etaugh 1974). In general, older children have less flexible sex roles than do younger ones (Baldigo 1975:38).

Peers become increasingly important to children throughout the school years (Harris and Tseng 1957) both as a source of approval (Havighurst 1972:22), and as playmates. Boys and girls have friends of both sexes, and most of them acknowledge having sweethearts while in elementary school (Lewis 1960; Broderick and Fowler 1961). Throughout the school years the child must move forward in many areas of his life—a fact that is reflected in his age-specific developmental tasks for this highly important period.

Developmental tasks of the school-age child

1. Learning the basic skills required of schoolchildren:

Mastering the fundamentals of reading, writing, calculating, and the scientific, rational approach to solving problems
Extending understanding of cause-and-effect relationships
Developing concepts essential for everyday living
Continuing to develop the ability to reason and to do reflective thinking

2. Mastering the physical skills appropriate to his development:

Learning the games, the sports, and the various roles in activities pursued by children of his age and sex in his community (ride a bike, swim, skate, play ball, row a boat, climb a tree, etc.)
Developing abilities needed in personal and family living (bathe and dress himself, care for his clothing, make his bed, cook and serve food, clean up after activities, maintain and repair simple household equipment, etc.)

3. Developing a practical understanding of the use of money:

Finding socially acceptable ways of getting money for what he wants to buy
Learning how to buy wisely the things he most wants with what he has, and to stay within his available resources

Learning the value of saving for postponed satisfactions

Reconciling differences between his wants and his resources, and accepting the fact that others may be poorer or richer than he

Acquiring a basic grasp of the nature and function of money in everyday life in the family and in the larger community

4. Becoming an active, cooperative member of his family:

Gaining skill in participating in family discussions and decision-making

Assuming responsibilities within the household and finding satisfaction in accomplishment and belonging

Becoming more mature in giving and receiving affection and gifts—between himself and his parents, his siblings, and his relatives within the extended family

Learning to enjoy the full resources and facilities available within the family, and to take the initiative in enriching them as he becomes able

5. Extending his abilities to relate effectively to others, both peers and adults:

Making progress in his ability to adjust to others

Learning to stand up for his rights

Improving his abilities both to lead and to follow others

Meeting basic social expectations—learning simple conventions, rules, customs, courtesies, and standards of his family and groups

Learning genuinely cooperative roles with others in many situations

Making and keeping close friends

6. Continuing the learning involved in handling his feelings and impulses:

Growing in his ability to cope with simple frustrations

Exploring socially acceptable ways of releasing negative emotions effectively

Becoming more mature in expressing feelings in ways and at times and places appropriate within his culture

Gaining skill in sharing his feelings with those who can help (parents, teachers, close friends, scout leaders, etc.)

7. Coming to terms with his or her own sex role, both now and as it will become:

Learning what is expected as appropriate behavior for boys, for girls, for men, for women, for married people, for parents, and for other adults

Clarifying knowledge about the nature of sex and reproduction

Adjusting to a changing body in the pubertal growth spurt as teen years
approach (accepting the new size and form, function and potentials
of pubertal growth)
Thinking ahead wholesomely to what it will be like to be grown up as a
man or woman

8. Continuing to find himself as a worthy person :

Identifying with his own age and sex in appropriate ways
Discovering many ways of becoming acceptable as a person; gaining
status
Growing in self-confidence, self-respect, self-control, and self-realization
Extending the process of establishing his own individuality

9. Developing a conscience with inner moral controls:

Distinguishing right from wrong in a variety of situations
Learning that rules are necessary in any social enterprise
Developing the ego strength for principled moral behavior
Trying to live according to appropriate social and moral values (Havig-
hurst 1972:29–30)

Success depends on the opportunities available for development in
the home, in the school, and in community life. It depends in large
measure on how skilled parents and teachers are in anticipating and
recognizing the child's developmental tasks as they come along and in
providing growth opportunities at crucial times. But children differ
widely, as do parents. And, while children are struggling through their
growth stages, the parents too are hard at work on their developmental
tasks.

Developmental tasks of
schoolchildren's parents

Parents know full well that they are needed throughout the bustling
years of the school-age period. But on the whole, this is a less hectic time,
since household routines have become established, and the children are
growing at a less rapid rate than they did as infants or preschoolers.
School-age children generally are satisfied with their relationships with
their parents and are involved to a considerable degree in family activities
(Hawkes, Burchinal, and Gardner 1957).

School-age children describe the perfect parent as home-loving,
wakeful, ready to play, generous, slow to anger, open-minded, and quick
to forgive. Not that the youngsters want their parents to be perfect—that

would be too hard to live up to!—according to the more articulate of those interviewed (Blum 1969:98).

Providing for children's special growth needs

Modern parents are constantly being challenged to provide opportunities for the child to do those things for himself that are within his abilities. It is helpful to the accomplishment of the child's developmental tasks if he can share in family decisions, responsibilities, and opportunities. Family discussion and joint planning offer openings for school-agers to join with their parents, brothers, and sisters in establishing family policies. Everyone gains from such firsthand experience in democratic interaction and orderly ways of doing things.

School-age children can be expected from time to time to contract childhood illnesses involving special care and family accommodations for the incapacitated. Even more challenging are the various handicaps that come to light when children go to school. Numerically, eye conditions needing specialists' care lead all other children's handicaps, followed by emotional disturbances, speech problems, mental retardation, hearing impediments, and orthopedic conditions (Figure 12-1).

In terms of the risk of meeting accidental death, the school-ager statistically is more than twice as safe as his parents, nearly three times as safe as his grandparents, and more than eight times as safe as his retired great-grandparents. Schoolchildren who tend to have accidents more than others are found to have emotional problems and to have parents who are anxious, insecure, and nonassertive (Marcus et al. 1960:53–54).

Parents are under pressure from neighbors and other members of their social class to have their children measure up to the demands and expectancies of the culture. This tends to shape even the most developmental family into more traditional lines as soon as the children reach school age. "What will the neighbors think?" or "What will the teacher say?" exert powerful pressures to conform on the school-age family. When traditional striving for good manners collides with developmental conceptions of parent-child rapport, the traditional patterns win out in most homes studied (Duvall 1946:202).

Enjoying life with children

Parents who can relax and enjoy their children find life unfolding all around them, as they see it anew through children's eyes. Long-forgotten joys and pleasures are renewed when they are shared with children who delight in them. New vistas and fresh perspectives from different vantage points open up with a child companion. What might have been an ordinary business trip turns out to be an adventure when a ten-year-old goes along:

278   Developing families

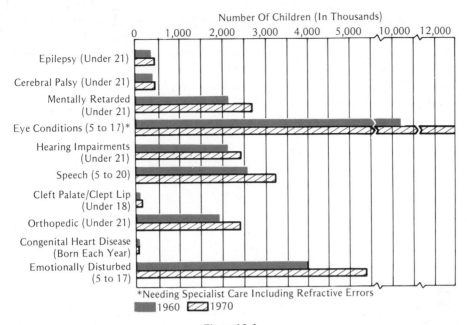

Number Of Children (In Thousands)

| | 0 | 1,000 | 2,000 | 3,000 | 4,000 | 5,000 | 10,000 | 12,000 |

Epilepsy (Under 21)
Cerebral Palsy (Under 21)
Mentally Retarded (Under 21)
Eye Conditions (5 to 17)*
Hearing Impairments (Under 21)
Speech (5 to 20)
Cleft Palate/Clept Lip (Under 18)
Orthopedic (Under 21)
Congenital Heart Disease (Born Each Year)
Emotionally Disturbed (5 to 17)

*Needing Specialist Care Including Refractive Errors

■ 1960 ▨ 1970

Figure 12-1
Millions of Children Have Handicaps

Source: Elizabeth Herzog and Catharine Richards, eds., *The Nation's Youth*, Children's Bureau Publication, no. 460 (Washington, D.C., 1968), Chart 38.

I was at the meetings in Omaha for three days; took Janice along, and we had a great time. As you would guess, I did many things I would not have done had I gone alone: climbing on foot to the top floor of the hotel and looking out over the city from the fire escape; climbing to the very top seat in Omaha's immense auditorium; walking all the way across the Missouri River bridge to Council Bluffs and standing midway on the bridge with one foot on the Iowa side of the line and the other foot on the Nebraska side; going to the top of the Woodman of the World Building. . . .

There was much other fun too: being proud of how sweet she looked; enjoying her ways of packing and unpacking; watching her select items at Bishops Cafeteria and her enjoyment of her favorites; appreciating the fact that she surprised me the second afternoon and did the wash for us in the bathroom sink . . . observing the things she enjoyed most . . . . People without children miss half the fun in the world! (Fulcomer)

Families with schoolchildren   279

Enjoying one's children means accepting them as persons in their own right. Parental acceptance presupposes unconditional love for one's children—seeing them as persons with the right to express their real feelings, valuing the unique personality of each of their children, and recognizing that children need to pull away from their parents as they become increasingly autonomous individuals (Porter 1954).

Encouraging children's growth

Encouraging a child's growth involves letting him go. As the school years progress, there are longer and longer absences from home. The child is away from home throughout the school hours, which often include the lunch period as well as morning and afternoon sessions. If he or she is getting normally involved in sports, clubs, and friendship groups, the after-school hours are increasingly given to these interests, so the youngster comes home tired and bedraggled just in time for the evening meal. There are frequent requests to spend the evening at someone else's home and occasions when spending the night with a close buddy is terribly important. Soon there are weekend trips with scouts or other youth groups, and then come the longer periods during summer vacation when children of school age are off to camp or visiting relatives for weeks at a time. All this is good for the child—developing independence, widening social experience, and generally contributing to personality growth.

As children become increasingly involved with friends their own age, their orientation tends increasingly toward their peers. Parents can encourage these associations, for research shows that children who are well-adjusted family members tend to retain family identifications, norms, and values even while associating with others (Bowerman and Kinch 1959). Mothers with emotionally satisfying friendships may find it easier to let their children go. Unfortunately, however, mothers old enough to have school-age children tend to have fewer close friends than do younger and older wives (Williams 1958).

School-agers often quote other adults as authority figures. A secure parent can take a child's, "But the teacher says so," as an indication that the youngster is venturing away from home intellectually as well as physically. He is finding new models, new attitudes, and new viewpoints to explore beyond the immediate family. Parents who can empathize with their children's interests and who can loosen the apron strings at this point have less difficulty untying them in another few years, when the youngsters become teenagers.

Parents who cultivate interests beyond their children probably have less difficulty letting them go than do those who devote their lives to their children. Research at Cornell finds that husbands and wives with school-age children work together on projects more often than do those at either the preschool or the teenage stage of the family life cycle (Feldman 1961). This is the time when building a boat, equipping a summer camp, and fixing up the house preoccupy father and mother. Now, too, entertaining others in the home and going as a family to company picnics and social affairs with the husband's work associates are at an all-time high (Blood and Wolfe 1960:158–159). Such activities shared with the children (as part of an overall parental stance of involvement in whole-family pursuits) may develop into continuing interests for the married pair as a couple.

Family developmental tasks at the school-age stage

By the time their eldest is in school, the husband and wife have been married seven years or more, have been parents for at least six years, and have settled into familiar ways with each other and with their children. The developmental routes traversed by the oldest child are gone over again by the younger children—each in his turn, each in his own way. Family developmental tasks at this stage include:

1. Providing for children's activity and parents' privacy
2. Keeping financially solvent
3. Furthering socialization of family members
4. Upgrading communication in the family
5. Establishing ties with life outside the family
6. Developing morally and building family morale.

Providing for children's activity and parents' privacy

Now that families live mostly in cities, towns, and suburbs, homes are smaller and space is more limited, both indoors and out, than it once was. Thanks to better nutrition and preventive medical care, today's children are bigger, stronger, and more vigorous, age for age, than was true a generation or two ago. No comparable change has occurred in the desire of parents for privacy and a little peace and quiet in their lives. Today's developmental family's house during the preschool and school-age periods is cluttered, toy-strewn, and noisy.

Providing outlets for the needed exploration and activity of vigorous, growing children within the limits of cramped housing, small yards, remote playgrounds, traffic-filled streets, and cranky neighbors is not an easy task. Parents in some crowded lower-class neighborhoods solve the problem by letting the children roam the streets and play in the alleys, thus risking life and limb. Social clubs and settlements set up programs that help in some of these congested areas, but the needs are still unfulfilled. Upper-class families usually have more space and, except for those urban cliff dwellers who live in crowded metropolitan apartment houses, have areas the children can call their own to play in, either on the home grounds or at their private schools. Many middle-class families, feeling pinched by living so closely with their children in common living quarters, work out elaborate rituals and routines aimed at making optimal use of available space.

Keeping financially solvent

The triple threat of keeping up payments, keeping up with the Joneses, and keeping out of debt is a real strain now. Costs will zoom even higher before there is any relief. But now, when the firstborn is in school and younger children are coming along, comes the bulging budget characteristic of expanding families. In low- and moderate-income families, where food, clothing, and medical costs are always a big part of the household expenses, these items take a big bite out of what money there is. Fixed costs such as car expenses, rent or house payments and maintenence, utilities, insurance, bus and lunch money, as well as all the expected items like dues, school collections, allowances, and recreation add to the financial burden. No wonder so many family men look a little frayed at times.

Older children get occasional jobs in the neighborhood and the mother may have found work that fits the demands of the growing family. In one recent year, more than half the mothers with school age children were employed, the majority full time (Waldman 1975:64).

Grandparents may give the children clothing and bicycles, take the family on vacation trips, loan money for big items like a new house or car, and provide sitter and nursing services on occasion (Sussman 1953; Duvall 1954: 89–99). Income tax exemptions for the children and unemployed wife are a help, but are never enough to cover the costs at this stage of the family cycle.

The middle-class father works overtime or ekes out his income with a part-time job now and then. For the lower-class family, the problem is frequently solved by the mother's employment. The children are then left under the casual supervision of whoever happens to be at home. The upper-class family's financial problems are less, for by definition the upper-class home is more affluent. Even so, the cost of keeping up appearances, sending the youngsters to the proper private schools, maintaining memberships in exclusive clubs, and participating in the right charities adds up faster than the money rolls in, in many a supposedly well-to-do family. Here the problems are compounded by pride. Measures that lower-status families can take without losing face are viewed as last resort solutions by the families "on the hill."

Furthering socialization of family members

New roles for new times are being learned by every member of the family with school-agers. A plethora of new tasks and expectations consumes the time and energy of families at this stage in the life cycle.

Higher standards of living put a heavier load of responsibility on the home than used to be expected. It is no longer enough to put food on the table. It must be a carefully balanced meal, supplying just the right number of calories for the individual family members; attractive in color and tasty, with the right combination of textures, flavors, and personal preferences; full of vitamins, body-building proteins, minerals, and even trace minerals. It isn't enough to keep a child neat, clean, and obedient—today we must be concerned for his growth as a personality. It isn't enough to keep a man's shirt buttons on—now a wife must be concerned with all that goes into mending a wounded ego and keeping her husband a growing, happy person. It isn't enough to keep house for the family—now a woman is expected to do her share of community housekeeping by working for a school bond issue, getting out to parent-teacher meetings, helping to run the block meeting, and dealing with whatever happens to be the pressing issue of the day.

Middle-class white families have been moving to the suburbs surrounding America's large cities so that their children may have space for play, and may attend schools that have higher academic standards and fewer students of other races than inner-city schools. When large numbers of white families with school-age children move to the suburbs, black and other minority children fill the big city schools. This effect was seen following the "white flight" from Atlanta during the years marked by vigorous desegregation efforts in the nation (Table 12-1).

The price that these white families pay for suburban living is real, both in monetary and psychic terms. The whole family misses the advantages of urban living, including proximity to groups of varied racial and ethnic backgrounds. The suburban family is organized around the mother, with father at home too infrequently to fill the roles he could if he lived nearer his work.

The irony is that just when a man is most needed around the house for all the repairs and refurbishing that are part of home-ownership, he is not as readily available as he was when they lived in the city, where services around the place were provided by others. The pressure is eased somewhat by the five-day week, which gives the father to his family on Saturdays and Sundays—unless the golf bug bites him first!

Table 12-1
Enrollment by Race in Atlanta's Public Schools, 1963–1974

September enrollment	Black children	White children
1963	53,147	53,608
1964	55,336	52,434
1965	60,832	49,020
1966	64,301	48,526
1967	67,148	46,270
1968	68,662	42,506
1969	70,296	39,229
1970	72,214	32,935
1971	72,351	27,688
1972	73,985	21,683
1973	71,786	15,997
1974	72,106	12,884

Source: John Dillin, "Racial Balance in U.S. Schools: Will 'Desegregation' Mean '90 Percent Black'?" *Christian Science Monitor*, 19 June 1975, p. 15.

Even with modern equipment, mothers of school-age children spend more time laundering than homemakers did years ago (Van Bortel 1956). The new fabrics take special care, and family members have more clothes and change them more often than did their ancestors.

Cooperative efforts in the family's meal preparation, serving, and cleaning up divide the daily responsibilities. When roles are assigned on the basis of interest, ability, and preference, children learn how to function in the household with their parents.

Children get satisfaction from working with adults. When eleven- to thirteen-year-old boys were asked, "What things do you do at home or in school that make you feel important and useful?" 40 percent mentioned some adult role around the house. The item next most frequently mentioned was use of skills (28 percent); and 18 percent said, "giving help" (Survey Research Center 1960:215).

School-age children are expected to read with comprehension, to write with clarity, to compute with accuracy, and to become familiar with the world in which they live. Studies find that children's educational achievement depends not only on the competence of the school staff, but also on the families from which the pupils come. Wide differences in children's school achievement are found to be significantly related to the home's influence on a child's language development and on his general ability to learn. School achievement depends on such family factors as: (1) *achievement pressure* (parents' aspirations for the child and their interest in, knowledge of, and standards of reward for the child's educational achievement); (2) *language models* (the quality of the parents' language and the standards they set for the child's speech); (3) *academic guidance* (the availability and quality of academic guidance and help provided in the home); (4) *activity in the home* (stimulation provided in the home to explore various aspects of the larger environment); (5) *intellectuality* (intellectual interests and activities in the home); and (6) *work habits* (household routines and emphasis on regularity in the use of time and space) (Bloom 1965:23).

Nationwide responses of mothers of first-graders indicate that parents of high-achieving compared to low-achieving children read more aloud to their children, talk longer with their children about school and other things of interest to the youngsters, permit less use of television, play more mentally stimulating games in the family, and see college as essential for their sons and daughters (Gallup International 1969:49–50).

Moreover, there is evidence that achievement strivings during the first four years of school are predictive of future achievement in adolescence and adulthood (Moss and Kagan). A study of third- to sixth-grade boys finds that those children whose parents were both coercive and autonomy-granting were successfully assertive in the academic setting as well as in the spheres of social influence and friendship (Hoffman, Rosen, and Lippitt 1960). Such data suggest strongly that school-agers need firm controls from their parents, as well as a chance to prove themselves autonomously. Other significant adults—teachers, scout leaders, relatives, and friends of the family—further reinforce family values for a child (Zimmerman and Cervantes 1960).

Dr. Catherine S. Chilman summarizes the findings of more than a score of studies comparing child-rearing patterns used in raising children who are achieving well educationally with practices and patterns more often found in very poor families (Table 12–2).

Ultimately, each child must do his or her own learning, and must acquire the willingness and the discipline to do the work expected of him both at school and at home. Thus he and his family continue their socialization throughout the school years.

Upgrading communication in the family

Marital satisfaction is found to be at a low ebb during the school-age stage of the family life cycle. This conclusion is stated in two widely separate studies published simultaneously. One investigation of marital interaction throughout the years of marriage showed that 147 husbands and wives found that levels of satisfaction with finances, task performance, companionship, sex, and relationships with children were at their lowest while there were schoolchildren in the home (Burr 1970).

A Cornell University study of the marital satisfaction of 1,598 couples over the family life cycle found that fewer husbands and wives reported satisfaction in their marriage "all the time" during the school-age stage than at any other time in their lives together. Furthermore, significantly

Table 12-2
Family Factors Conducive to and Limiting of Children's School Achievement

Conducive	Limiting (more typical of low-income families)
1. Infant and child given freedom within consistent limits to explore and experiment	Limited freedom for exploration (partly imposed by crowded and dangerous aspects of environment)
2. Wide range of parent-guided experiences, offering visual, auditory, kinesthetic, and tactile stimulation from early infancy	Constricted lives led by parents; fear and distrust of the unknown
3. Goal-commitment and belief in long-range success potential	Fatalistic, apathetic attitudes
4. Gradual training for and value placed upon independence	Tendency for abrupt transition to independence: parents tend to "lose control" of children at an early age
5. Parents serve as model of educational-occupational success and continuing development; high achievement needs in parents	Tendency to educational-occupational failure; reliance on personal versus skill attributes of vocational success
6. Reliance on objective evidence	Magical, rigid thinking
7. Much verbal communication with a flexible, conceptual style and emphasis on both speaking and listening	Little verbal communication, especially of an interactive, conceptual, flexible kind
8. High value placed on academic success	Academic achievement not highly valued
9. Democratic child-rearing attitudes	Authoritarian child-rearing attitudes
10. Collaborative attitudes toward the school system	Fear and distrust of the school system
11. Value placed on abstractions	Pragmatic, concrete values

Source: Catherine S. Chilman, *Growing Up Poor*, Welfare Administration Publication, no. 13 (Washington, D.C., 1966), p. 43.

more wives reported having such negative emotions as feeling resentful, misunderstood, or not needed more often while dependent children were in the home than at any other time in their marriages (Rollins and Feldman 1970).

It may be that this decline in the mates' satisfaction with each other results from the eclipse of the husband-wife relationship by the responsibilities of parenthood. The school-age family is a network of communication ties. There are 15 possible interpersonal relationships in the four-child family. The children now are full of experiences to relate, questions to ask, and sheer exuberance to express. Each is uniquely at work on his developmental tasks within his position in the family. Boy or girl, first-born or younger child, each struggles to establish his identity as a separate person within the family—one who is and must be different from his siblings (Koch 1960). Longitudinal studies indicate that earlier problems such as destructiveness, temper tantrums, and overactivity decline rapidly throughout the school years (Macfarlane, Allen, and Honzik 1954). However, firstborn children, more than their younger siblings, present special problems—excessive demands for attention, restlessness in sleep, and physical timidity—between ages six and twelve. Firstborn girls especially have problems indicating tension and withdrawal at the age of six and again at eleven. At this stage, withdrawing and internalizing patterns are seen more often in firstborn than in second-born boys, who tend to be more overt and aggressive.

Quarreling, jealousies, rivalry, and other confictive relationships between siblings reflect struggles for parental attention and also the different stances adopted by firstborn, second-born, and later children as individuals. Research finds that ordinal position influences personality development. Each child enters the family at a different moment in its history and establishes his own role patterns and relationships with the others accordingly. (Bossard and Boll 1956; Toman 1961; and Packard 1969).

Except for twins, the ages of siblings differ so widely that their interests—as children of school age, preschool stage, and infancy—are worlds apart. Yet they all compete for the resources of the family (the use of the television set is a good example), for status and affection, and for special recognition. Each child needs and strives to have his own intimate association with the parents.

The school-age youngster comes home from his rigorous day in classroom and playground full of pent-up emotions that could not be fully expressed in front of teachers and classmates. He brings his frustrations, disappointments, and unexpressed hostilities home, where he very likely takes them out on the first available family member. This is not to be condemned. One of the chief functions of the home is to serve as an emotional reconditioning center for its members. This does not make for peace and quiet. On the contrary, feelings explode all over the place, and the children get into squabbles seemingly without provocation.

When communication systems are open within a family, love can flow through, counteracting the destructive emotions produced by everyday living and renewing the spirit of every member. Love implies a two-way flow between each person and the next—an exchange that removes hates and angers and restores the warmth of belonging and the joy of living in a family. Like a river that purifies itself so long as it runs free, the stream of human emotions within a family renews and refreshes the human spirit so long as communication systems allow it free passage.

Establishing ties with life beyond the immediate family

American families enjoy vacation trips and leisure activities together. Fully 70 percent of some 356 recreational pursuits are engaged in with other family members (Kelly 1975). Families do less arguing and feel less anger and tension on vacation than they do at home (Rosenblatt and Russell 1975). Once they get away from the stress of their usual roles at home, school, and work, they find interests beyond themselves and their daily routines.

A feeling of closeness to the relatives of the family is achieved over the years by letter-writing, visiting, holiday observances, vacation-sharing, gift-giving, services rendered and received, and by any means that helps the members of the family to maintain contact with each other. The process is furthered by the family loyalties that bind the family together, regardless of what any member may or may not do.

A school-age boy or girl is old enough to visit relatives for a week or more, or even for a whole summer vacation without becoming homesick or too dependent on a hospitable household. Going to the grandparents' home for special holidays is a thrill now, when the children are old enough to appreciate such treats, and to take care of their own needs and interests in new settings with only casual supervision.

Even more important than what the relatives *do* for the school-age boy or girl is what they *are*. In even the most homogeneous family, many differences in personality strengths and weaknesses, behavior patterns, and value systems are represented by the members of the extended family group. These variations are fascinating and instructive to all.

Left to themselves, children make friends with all kinds of people. When they are allowed to relate to many different types of children, they learn ways of coping with life situations that will help them now and in the future. "Undesirable friends" from the parents' viewpoint can be discouraged when: (1) the children engage in disturbing or compulsive sex play, (2) the other child tends to violence, and (3) the friends engage in lawless behavior when they are together (Brenton 1975:21). Otherwise, children from different ethnic, racial, and social class backgrounds expand one another's experience of the real world. Thus the child who is allowed to associate only with "our kind of people" is deprived of a valuable component of education for life in the community.

"Little sweethearts" are important to boys and girls. Understanding that they are a normal part of growing up, are usually outgrown in time, and can be safely accepted within the family as "best friends" at the moment, helps parents to keep the perspective they—and their children— need.

Family involvement in the community is intensified when parents believe that their children will benefit directly from their efforts. Getting pledges for a special neighborhood project, a new school addition, or playground equipment now takes on special meaning. Ridding the community of harmful influences on children now becomes urgent family business.

Schoolchildren take their families with them into the larger community and its interests. Parents are pressured to become active in parent-teacher associations, youth-serving agencies, church programs, and athletic and cultural functions in which their children are taking part. They are urged to visit the school for special programs, to participate in parents' study groups, and to become active in community life as soon as their children are in school. Widening involvements help to mature the family and its individual members, as they carry out this developmental task together.

Developing morally and building family morale

Moral development is a long process—one that is not fully accomplished in the school years. It proceeds throughout the first three decades or more of life, as the developing person becomes increasingly capable of abstract thinking and moral judgment. Parents become especially concerned about the moral development of their children when they are exposed, as school children, to wide variations in the conduct of people outside the family. Attempts to teach "character traits" over the years have failed to bring the success expected. In recent years, Piaget's work in the development of cognitive thinking (Chapter 8) has led to recognition of the idea that moral thinking progresses sequentially from one stage to the next and is marked by ever-increasing differentiation and integration. Each stage in moral development is characterized by better cognitive organization than the one before it, since it includes everything from the earlier stages, but makes new distinctions and organizes them more comprehensively (Table 12–3).

The stages come one at a time and always in the same order in an invariant developmental sequence. Children and adolescents comprehend all stages up to the one they are in, but not those beyond their own. Significantly, they prefer the next stage beyond the one of their present moral thinking. Kohlberg's research finds that the sequence of stages is not affected by one's cultural or religious orientation. The only difference is in the *rate* at which individuals progress toward more mature moral thinking. Children of middle-class families move faster and farther in their moral thinking than do lower-class children (Kohlberg 1968:30). One factor may be the conscientious efforts middle-class parents make to uphold standards of conduct for themselves and for their children. Youngsters who resist temptation may be rewarded by their parents for the self-control they demonstrate by postponing satisfactions, and may therefore move more rapidly through this developmental sequence than do boys and girls whose families model different life-styles and values.

The morale of families with school children appears to be related to how effectively they are able to cope with community pressures and to give clear interpretations of their own values to their children. As soon as the child is old enough to go to school, he comes face-to-face with ways

Table 12-3
Sequential Development of Moral Thinking

Moral levels	Moral stages	Moral reasons	Human life valued
Preconventional (Ages 4–10)	1. Unquestioning deference to authority figures; good and bad behavior depend on physical consequences	Obey rules to avoid punishment	Value of human life confused with value of things
	2. Reciprocity, fairness, and equal sharing seen pragmatically	Return favors and conform for rewards	Human life satisfying to self and others
Conventional (Varies widely)	3. Conforming to, maintaining, supporting, and justifying the rules of one's family, group, and nation	Conform to escape disapproval	Value of human life based on love and empathy
	4. Doing one's duty, respecting authority, and maintaining the social order for its own sake	Conform to avoid blame and guilt	Life is sacred
Postconventional (Attained by exceptional adults)	5. Right action defined in terms of rights and standards of whole society; legalistic, official morality of American government	Conform to gain respect of those concerned with community well-being	Life is a universal human right
	6. Self-chosen ethical principles, such as justice, equality of human rights, and respect for individual dignity	Conform to avoid self-condemnation	Belief in the sacredness of human life as a universal respect for the individual

Source: Adapted from Lawrence Kohlberg, "The Child as a Moral Philosopher," *Psychology Today* 2, no. 4 (September 1968): 25–30.

of life that are different from those of his family. Some of these variations on the theme of life look good to him, and he brings them home in the form of questions about and demands for a new order of things. The family must then test its way of life in terms of child-introduced community pressures. Something has got to give. Either the family gives way to the child's pleas that "all the other kids are doing it," or the youngster faces up to the finality that "this is the way we do it in *our* family." Either outcome is the result of some testing and review of the merits and penalties of a certain stand or value.

By the time the boy or girl reaches the third or fourth grade in school, these culture conflicts may take the form of episodes of open rebellion. The preadolescent finds adults generally trying. Both boys and girls are skeptical of the other sex and band together in tight little groups of the same age and sex. Boys now reject such adult-imposed "sissy stuff" as cleanliness, obedience, and politeness, and often become antagonistic, rebellious, uncooperative, restless, and very noisy. Dr. Luton D. Ackerson, studying 5,000 nondelinquent boys and girls at the Illinois Institute for Juvenile Research, found that behavior problems are more frequent among nine- to thirteen-year-olds than among any other age group. There is more fighting, rudeness, and disobedience among preadolescent children than among either the younger or older age groups (Ackerson 1952).

Actively interpreting why some things are wrong and others right, why some actions are good and others bad are aspects of this developmental task that families face all through the school-age stage. Such teaching is not easy, especially in this day and age when family values are changing. But nothing is more important to a family's basic integrity, or to a youngster's sense of what he and his family stand for in a world where individuals have to stand for something, lest they fall for anything (Miller and Swanson 1958).

Dovetailing the many developmental tasks of all members of the school-age family in harmonious, satisfying ways is a challenging job. It has its reward in the sense of accomplishment that comes from individual and group achievements, as well as in the family solidarity that is peculiarly meaningful at this stage.

Each youth sustains within his breast
A vague and infinite unrest.
He goes about in still alarm,
With shrouded future at his arm,
With longings that can find no tongue.
I see him thus, for I am young.

By an Oklahoma High School Boy

Families with teenagers

chapter thirteen

A family enters the teenage stage of the family life cycle when the oldest child becomes 13 and leaves it when the first child departs for marriage, for work, or for military service, as a young adult. Typically, the teenage stage lasts six or seven years, but it may be as short as three or four years— if, for instance, the oldest child marries or drops out of school and goes to work at 16. The stage is prolonged when the first child to be launched delays his leaving home until later.

The father at the teenage stage is usually close to or in his forties. His wife is typically about two years younger, entering the stage in her mid-thirties and leaving it in her mid-forties. By this time she is in her menopause and possibly has a "change of life baby," as the late-arriving infant is sometimes called. The other children by this time are most likely school-agers.

A family with four sons and daughters is made up of six persons holding a maximum of four positions: husband-father, wife-mother, son-brother, and daughter-sister. Each has developmental tasks as parent, teenager, school-ager, or younger child. Father and mother cope with guiding the next generation and face the possible risk of interpersonal impoverishment. The overall family goal at the teenage stage is that of loosening family ties to allow greater responsibility and freedom, preparatory to releasing young adults-in-the-making.

Between twelve and twenty

Boys and girls enter the teen years as children and leave as adults. It is during the teen years that young people mature and begin to live their own lives as autonomous persons. The major thrust of the second decade of life is physical maturation. Boys become men and girls attain womanhood during pubescence, the period marked by the maturing of the sex glands in both boys and girls.

Early puberty, prolonged adolescence

Childhood ends sooner now than it did in earlier generations. The trend is for pubescence (or puberty) to begin some four months earlier every ten years (Blos 1971:969). It is not unusual for some fourth and fifth grade girls to show signs of early maturing, and to be well into adolescence when they reach their teens. Boys also mature earlier than they once did, but generally their puberty comes later than that of girls, as it always has. The bodily changes that come with maturation (Chapter 1) are so striking that they tend to give the pubescent child an unwarranted sense of being quite grown up. But the young adolescent of 13 is still a child, psychologically, no matter how physically mature she or he may be (Blos 1971:970). Early-adolescent boys are no match for girls their age, who tend to be larger physically and more socially mature than are the boys in their class in school. Efforts to push early adolescents into early dating, therefore, tend to be counterproductive.

Some authorities suggest that it is wise to separate the sexes during early adolescence for both psychological and biological reasons. Because of the discrepancies in male and female puberal development (physically, intellectually, socially, and psychologically) boys and girls are not comfortable as companions in work or play during the junior high school years. Young adolescent boys who associate primarily with their male peers tend to establish their male identity more firmly and lastingly (Blos 1971:971).

Adolescence lasts longer today than it once did. At the turn of the century, when most Americans lived on farms, a boy could do a man's work by his midteens. Great-grandfather typically left school at age 14 and went to work at any of the many jobs then available to a young man willing to learn as he earned. This is no longer possible. Today's vocations require levels of prior education and training that are usually not attained until the early twenties, or even later. Thus, with early puberty and later adulthood, adolescence seems to stretch ahead like "Route 66 that goes on and on," as one 18-year-old puts it.

By the middle and later teens, many boys are as interested in girls as most girls have been in boys for some time. The sexes now enjoy one another, seek each other's company, pursue common interests (music, drama, sports), and are learning to be attractive to persons of the other sex. Emotional and social development now comes to the fore, giving way to concern for academic progress only when career plans and getting into college become personally pertinent (Havighurst 1972:43).

One statewide survey of five thousand students found that the dominant concerns of seventh through eleventh graders were in the areas of peer relationships, mental health (including self-understanding), and sex education (Byler, Lewis, and Totman 1969). Many schools are attempting to meet these urgent needs of teenagers with carefully designed curricula in family living and sex education.

Schooling in the teen years

High school graduation is so commonplace today that those students who do not finish are called "drop-outs." Cultural and economic pressures abound. Parental aspirations, the glutted labor force, and the effects of the implementation of equality of opportunity requirements impel today's teenager to get as much education as possible. Public community colleges, student loan programs, scholarships, work-study possibilities, and special inducements for minority students have brought college within the range of many young people who are the first in their families to go to college. In the 1930s colleges were made up largely of upper-middle-class students. In 1974, 60.7 percent of all entering freshmen came from families with incomes under $20,000, so that large numbers of students were getting supplemental help in addition to their parents' support (Table 13-1).

The "baby boom" that occurred between 1957 and 1965, when there were more than four million births each year, provides the basis for modestly reliable estimates of swelling college enrollments through 1980 (Table 13-2).

Whether or not a young person will attend college is related to his parents' education, their occupations, and the family income, according to census reports over the years. Now that minority students and faculty are being actively sought by colleges and universities, more potentially able students may try to go to college than would have considered the possibility before. That not all of them are well prepared for college is evident from the College Entrance Examination Board's Scholastic Apti-

Table 13-1
Sources of Financial Help Supplementing Family Support
of Entering Freshmen, Fall 1974

Financial help	Percentage of entering freshmen
Basic Educational Opportunity Grant	18.7%
Supplemental Educational Opportunity Grant	5.3
College Work-Study Grant	9.9
State Scholarship or Grant	18.0
Local or Private Scholarship or Grant	22.3
Federal Guaranteed Student Loan	10.5
National Direct Student Loan or Other Loans	19.1
Full-time Employment	9.3
Part-time Employment	73.2

Source: Cooperative Institutional Research Program, *The American Freshman: National Norms for Fall 1974* (American Council on Education and the University of California, Los Angeles, 1975), pp. 133–134.

Table 13-2
College Enrollments in the United States, 1960–1980

Year	Number of college students enrolled
1960	3,570,000
1965	5,526,000
1966	6,085,000
1967	6,401,000
1968	6,801,000
1969	7,435,000
1970	7,413,000
1971	8,087,000
1972	8,313,000
1973	8,600,000
1975	9,147,000*
1980	10,284,000*

*U.S. Bureau of the Census projections
Source: U.S. Department of Health, Education and Welfare data for various years; see also: Ben J. Wattenberg, *The Real America* (Garden City, N.Y.: Doubleday & Co., 1974), p. 80.

tude Test scores (SAT) of one million high school seniors who scored lower in 1975 than had seniors in previous years. Between 1963 and 1975, the average verbal ability score dropped from 478 to 434, and the average mathematical ability score declined from 502 to 472 on nationwide college entrance examinations. Scientific knowledge and writing skills similarly were at lower levels in 1975 than in earlier years (National Assessment of Educational Progress 1975).

Many teenagers are unable to write a simple expository paragraph in intelligible English. They tend to use sentence fragments rather than correct sentence structure—writing as they would talk on the telephone, in the idiom of the mass media. Their writing style reflects the many hours they have spent in front of the television screen rather than the efforts of their English teachers over the years (Fiske 1975:42 and Sheils 1975: 58-65). Seventeen-year-old girls do better than boys their age in reading, writing, literature, and music, but less well in mathematics, science, social studies and citizenship ("Girls Lag on Tests" 1975:54). Test results in these fields suggest that members of both sexes are still responding to traditional gender role expectations during the teen years; and that schools and families may be steering girls into the humanities and boys into science and mathematics.

Seven out of ten students of both sexes rate themselves high in such qualities as academic ability and drive to achieve. The majority (76.3 percent of the girls and 73.8 percent of the boys) who enter college expect to get bachelor's degrees; and more than half see their chances as good that they will find jobs in the field of their choice (Cooperative Institutional Research Program 1975:131).

Most teenagers today enjoy going to school. The Purdue Opinion Panel poll of representative high school students, conducted between 1953 and 1967, found that three out of four teenagers stated that they liked school (Table 13-3). The small percentage of students expressing negative sentiments has been constant over the years. Teenagers' positive feelings about school have shifted from the unqualified, "I like it very much," to the more moderate, "I like it most of the time," suggesting that teenagers today tend to be more perceptive, more critical, and more outspoken than young people their age were even a dozen or more years ago.

Achievement drive in a teenager appears to be closely related to his family relationships. Those with low drives for achievement tend to come from families where there is (1) a close mother-son relationship marked by dependence, (2) low standards, of the "not caring" sort, and/or (3) too high and too early expectations that are beyond the child's readiness and ability (McClelland 1961).

Money is not the primary objective of contemporary youth. Many

Table 13-3
How American High School Students Feel about School

Student responses	1953	1958	1965	1967
I like it very much.	32%	27%	21%	16%
I like it most of the time.	43	46	51	57
I don't like it very much.	23	24	24	25
I dislike it.	2	3	2	2

Source: Thomas R. Leidy and Allan R. Starry, "Contemporary Youth Culture," *NEA Journal* 56 (October 1967): 8, from Purdue Opinion Panel polls between 1953 and 1967.

of them are influenced more by the challenge and stimulation of a future career, by the opportunity to make a meaningful contribution, and by the ability to express themselves, than by the money that can be earned in a given line of work (Fortune-Yankelovich Survey 1969:70-71; 179-181). A study of adolescents' vocational aspirations found that high aspirers more frequently report (1) feelings of parental rejection, (2) favoritism shown toward another child in the family, (3) less attachment to parents, (4) less childhood happiness, and (5) other indications of unsatisfactory interpersonal relationships in the family—so that climbing the occupational ladder may be seen as an escape (Dynes, Clarke, and Dinitz 1956:212-215).

A University of Chicago team found that the high-IQ adolescent appears to prefer safety, whereas the adolescent with high creativity chooses the anxieties and delights of growth. Parents of high-IQ students tend to recall more financial difficulties in their childhood, and thus may have felt more insecurity than did the parents of students with high creativity, who tend to take risks, to permit divergence, and to promote their children's openness to experience, values, interests, and enthusiasms (Getzels and Jackson 1961:351-359).

Leaders now are aware of the plight of all minorities, including youth, for whom the path to fulfillment is rigorous. Researchers estimate that 30 percent of the teenage boys and 20 percent of the girls find the pathway to adulthood blocked, so that it is extremely difficult for them to grow into responsible adults. These are the youngsters who drop out of school at 15 or 16 with a history of failure, frustration, and maladjustment in school, home, and community (Havighurst 1960:52-62).

Evidence that some adolescents are more vulnerable to delinquency than others is generally accepted. Research projects concur that most teenagers who violate the laws are disadvantaged lower-class youngsters. Young offenders from the other social classes are more apt to be emotionally disturbed, as is clear from Dr. Miller's estimations of delinquency distribution (Table 13-4). Acceptance of the fact that the vast majority of teenage boys and girls are responsible, law-abiding young people has tended to discourage the practice of stereotyping of anyone between 12 and 20 as a potential troublemaker or an out-and-out delinquent (Kvaraceus, et al. 1959:24-31).

Rearing teenagers is a challenge

Parents find it hard to guide teenagers today. Television, the movies, and other mass media regularly promote values inherent in materialism and hedonism. Self-indulgence, immaturity, overt sexuality, sadism, and violence are exploited as part of the multimillion dollar business of attracting young consumers. Widely publicized increases in drinking and

Table 13–4
Distribution of "Delinquent" Individuals

Social class status	Demonstrable emotional disturbance	Little or no serious emotional disturbance	Percentage of all delinquents
Lower class	15%	70%	85%
Non-lower class	10	5	15
Total	25%	75%	100%
	Degree of emotional disturbance		

Source: William C. Kvaraceus and Walter B. Miller, with the collaboration of Milton L. Barron, Edward M. Daniels, Preston A. McLendon, and Benjamin A. Thompson, *Delinquent Behavior* (Washington, D.C.: National Education Association, 1959), vol. 1, p. 54.

drug-usage, venereal disease, and premarital pregnancy among the young suggest to many anxious parents that their teenagers are espousing values alien to those of the family. Parents tend to value consideration above violence, sexual fidelity above promiscuity, and planning for future goals above irresponsible self-indulgence (LeMasters 1969:176–191).

Drugs and drinking among adolescents

One out of five 14 to 15-year-olds smokes pot, and the use of marijuana in this age group more than doubled between 1972 and 1974 (National Institute on Drug Abuse 1975). Millions of teenagers have experimented with illicit drugs, and millions are regular users today. "High-school drug users are more likely to have regular highs from psychedelics (LSD), barbiturates, cocaine, and even heroin, as well as marijuana, several times a month at least. Further, young people do not try drugs *instead* of alcohol, but in addition to it. Alcohol, in fact, continues to be used far more generally than drugs—58 percent in high school," according to a national survey of representative high school and college students made for the Drug Abuse Council (Yankelovich 1975:39–42).

Some 28 percent of 13,000 teenagers in 450 schools around the country reported that they had been drunk at least four times in the last year, and that this had got them into trouble with their peers or superiors at least twice during the year. Sons and daughters of drinking parents drink more frequently, and boys drink more often and more heavily than do girls (National Institute of Alcohol Abuse and Alcoholism 1975).

Some adolescents use drugs (including alcohol) for psychological reasons—to overcome depression or as a way of modifying their inner feelings and emotional states, much as they do when they listen to folk-rock and the blues (Kohlberg and Gilligan 1971:1060). Teenagers are inventing new social controls to limit the dangers of drug abuse, such as self-education about the effects of drugs and about the conditions under which the dangers of using drugs are minimized. Thirty-five percent of all students refuse to use drugs on moral grounds. Another 23 percent of all students have been dubbed by the researchers as "Conscious Non-users." These are young people who reject authority, who seek excitement and novelty, and who represent a new value system that pervades all phases of life: (1) new moral norms in personal and public morality; (2) changing attitudes toward work and money as measures of success; and (3) concern with self-fulfillment and gratification (Yankelovich 1975: 41–42).

Sexual activity of teenagers

As he gains increasing cognitive competence in adolescence, many a teenager is puzzled by the inconsistencies he comes to see in what he has been told about sexual activity:

1. Sexual activity—self-administered or otherwise experienced—is bad.
2. Sexuality provides pleasure.
3. If sex is pleasant, it should not be bad (Kagan 1971:1002).

Adolescents have to deal very early with the temptations of masturbation, petting, intercourse, and homosexuality. They have matured biologically and emotionally at a time when widespread sensuality is lauded within the culture. Peer-pressures combined with sexual urges become increasingly hard to resist. Many young people question older beliefs and look for a new set of premises. "In our society, standards surrounding family, religion, sexuality, drugs, and school are among the major ideological dragons to be tamed" (Kagan 1971:1003).

Schoolgirls with sexual experience worry about becoming pregnant (Table 13–5; see also text and references in Chapter 2).

School-age girls and boys who are experimenting with sex are not ready to start families. But many do not know where to turn for help in avoiding pregnancy. Doctors, social workers, and teachers in some communities are able to identify potential school-age mothers before the fact of pregnancy, and to provide the help that is needed while there is yet time. "The cost of unwanted pregnancy for prenatal, postnatal, and pediatric care exceeds drastically the cost of [health] service to the never-pregnant teenager" (Dickens, Mudd, and Huggins 1975: 181; see also Zelnik and Kantner references in Chapter 2).

Anxious, threatened, and insecure parents fail to give their teenagers the firm guidance they need, and they sometimes alienate their children. Often overlooked is the possibility that parents and adolescents may retain their mutual respect and understanding even though they may differ in their values and behavior (Conger 1971:1120). Teenagers have to grow beyond their parents' life style, but they still need appropriate

Table 13-5
Adolescent Nonvirgins' Attitudes and Behavior Related to
Sexual Responsibility, by Age and Experience

| | | By age | | By coital experience | |
Attitude or behavior	All	13-15 years	16-19 years	With current intercourse	With no current intercourse
Sometimes worry about becoming pregnant	70%	61%	72%	71%	68%
Do not know where to get contraceptive	16	32	9		
Would have abortion if became pregnant	18	2	23	23	
Would get married if became pregnant	31			31	30
Have been pregnant	23	11	28	28	7

Source: Selected from R.C. Sorensen, *Adolescent Sexuality in Contemporary America, Personal Values and Sexual Behavior Ages 13-19* (New York: World Publishing Co., 1973).

parental models to build on, and they need their parents' love and concern more than they know (Lorenz 1970:333-377).

Adolescents need parents

Adolescence is a period of strain in most families. As teenagers strive to establish their identity and to emancipate themselves from their parents, the parents tend to feel that their children undervalue them—and the adolescents believe that adults generally depreciate teenagers. Separate studies find, however, that adolescents have a higher opinion of adults than do their parents, that both generations have favorable opinions of teenagers, and that adolescents rate parent-adolescent relationships more favorably than do their mothers or fathers (Hess and Goldblatt 1957: 459-468; Henderson, Connor, and Walters 1961).

Conforming teenagers, who less often break rules and regulations, tend more than others to have favorable images of their families and to rate their parents' discipline as fair and their family relationships as democratic and affectionate (Slocum and Stone 1959:245-250). There is also evidence that lower-class families value conformity and respectability more than do middle-class families. The latter tend more often to encourage their children to develop as persons in their own right (Tuma and Livson 1961; Duvall 1946; Kohn 1959; and references in Chapter 5).

Gradually throughout adolescence, teenagers shift their orientation from family to friends, as Table 13-6 indicates. During this transition period, teenagers tend to be parent-oriented when making important decisions about companions and about questions of right or wrong;

Table 13-6

Percentage of Students by Grade and by Orientation

Orientation toward	Grade in school						
	4th	5th	6th	7th	8th	9th	10th
Family	87.1%	80.5%	80.2%	66.7%	41.7%	44.7%	31.6%
Neutral	6.9	12.2	11.2	9.3	18.3	22.4	20.2
Peers	5.9	7.3	8.6	24.1	40.0	32.9	48.1
Number	101	82	116	108	115	85	79

Source: Charles E. Bowerman and John W. Kinch, "Changes in Family and Peer Orientation of Children between the Fourth and Tenth Grades," *Social Forces* 37, no. 3 (March 1959): 206–211.

they more often follow their peers in matters of taste in dress, movies, television, and music (Stinnett and Walters 1967; Brittain 1963). On questions of educational plans and future life goals, parents have a stronger influence than do peers. Furthermore, in critical areas, teenagers' interactions with one another tend to reflect their parents' views. (Kandel and Lesser 1972).

During the teen years young people gradually come to understand themselves as members of their own generation. They must explore and draw on the resources within and beyond their families for all they require to accomplish the developmental tasks that lead into effective adulthood.

Family dilemmas at the teenage stage

Modern families ride the horns of at least six dilemmas throughout the teen years (Duvall 1965): (1) firm family control versus freedom for the teenager; (2) responsibility vested in parents versus responsibility shared with teenagers; (3) emphasis on social activities versus academic success; (4) mobility versus stability for the family and for the teenager; (5) open communication with outspoken criticism versus respect with peace and quiet; and (6) dedicated lives versus an uncommitted stance toward life. Each dilemma involves the challenge of choices to be made and values to be held. Families grow strong by working through their dilemmas with today's teenagers. Young people mature as they explore the alternatives open to them and to their families in the modern world.

A family cannot allow itself to be buffeted about by every social wind that blows and still feel steady and strong within itself. Conversely, a family that does not bend with the pressures of the times will break under their stress. With no convictions and values, the family is a tumbleweed, without roots or stability. With a philosophy of life that is too rigid and narrow, a family risks the alienation of its teenagers and grown children and its own integrity as a unit.

Developmental tasks of teenagers

1. Accepting one's changing body and learning to use it effectively:

Coming to terms with the new size, shape, function, and potential of one's maturing body

Accepting differences between one's own physique and that of age-mates of the same and other sex as variations that are normal and to be expected

Understanding what pubertal changes mean and wholesomely anticipating maturity as a man or as a woman

Caring for one's body in ways that assure its health and optimum development

Learning to handle oneself skillfully in the variety of recreational, social, and family situations that require learned physical skills

2. Achieving a satisfying and socially accepted masculine or feminine role:

Learning what it means to be a boy or girl in one's culture

Anticipating realistically what will be involved in becoming a man or a woman

Setting one's personal course within the leeway of sex-role expectations and practice allowed by one's family and community

3. Finding oneself as a member of one's own generation by developing more mature relations with one's age-mates:

Becoming acceptable as a member of one or more groups of peers

Making and keeping friends of both sexes

Getting dates and becoming comfortable in dating situations

Getting experience in loving and being loved by one or more members of the opposite sex

Learning how to get along with a wide variety of age-mates in school, neighborhood, and community settings

Developing skills in inviting and refusing, solving problems and resolving conflicts, making decisions, and evaluating experiences with one's peers

4. Achieving emotional independence of parents and other adults:

Becoming free of childish dependence upon one's parents

Developing more mature affection for parents as persons

Learning how to be an autonomous person who is capable of making decisions and running his own life

Growing out of the dependence of childhood and the impulsive independence of adolescence and attaining a mature interdependence with others (parents, teachers, and all authority figures, especially)

Learning to be an adult among adults

5. Selecting and preparing for an occupation and economic independence:

Seeking counsel and getting specific knowledge about possible fields of work within the limits of real possibilities
Choosing an occupation in line with interests, abilities, and opportunities
Preparing oneself through schooling, specialized training, and personal responsibility to get and hold a position
Getting tryout or apprenticeship experiences wherever possible along the lines of future vocational interests

6. Preparing for marriage and family life:

Enjoying the responsibilities as well as the privileges of family membership
Developing a responsible attitude toward getting married and having a family
Acquiring knowledge about mate selection, marriage, homemaking, and child-rearing
Learning to distinguish between infatuation and more lasting forms of love
Developing mutually satisfying personal relationships through processes of dating, going steady, effective courtship, and becoming involved with a loved one
Making decisions about the timing of engagement, marriage, completion of one's education, fulfillment of military service requirements, and the multiple demands on young people of marriageable age

7. Developing the intellectual skills and social sensitivities necessary for civic competence:

Developing concepts of law, government, economics, politics, geography, human nature, and social organization that are relevant to the modern world
Gaining awareness of human needs and becoming motivated to help others attain their goals
Acquiring problem-solving methods for dealing effectively with modern problems
Gaining ability to communicate competently as a citizen in a democracy
Becoming involved in causes and projects outside oneself and becoming a socially responsible person

8. Establishing one's identity as a socially responsible person:

Attaining a mature set of values and ethical controls appropriate to one's culture

Developing a workable philosophy of life that makes sense in today's
world

Implementing worthy ideals and standards in one's life

Assuming social obligations and responsibilities that express one's feeling
of relatedness to others and to society at large

Learning to see oneself in relation to the universe and to the whole
human race

The developmental tasks of adolescents were originally formulated
from intensive longitudinal studies. Since then, young teenagers have been
able to identify their own developmental tasks, using Dales's scalogram
analysis (Dales 1955). Increasingly precise criteria for success or failure
and for early, expected, and late accomplishment of each of the developmental tasks of adolescence may in time give an even finer cutting edge
to this useful tool.

The ethnic, racial, and social class background from which adolescents
come influences the priorities they place on the several concurrent developmental tasks confronting them and the success they have in achieving
them. Lower- and lower-middle-class teenagers striving toward upward
mobility set tasks for themselves that are quite different from those of
their peers who are content to continue the patterns of their past. Conversely, middle- and upper-class young people unwilling to carry out the
aspirations of their parents, or unable to live up to the traditions of their
families, often rebel and become downward mobile—adopting lower-class
behavior and goals.

Middle- and upper-class adolescents are under strong family pressure
to associate with young people from families like their own, to cultivate a
variety of social, cultural, and athletic skills, to get wide social experience,
to complete their education, and to establish themselves vocationally
before getting married. Middle-class parents tend to be protective of their
children, especially their daughters, and to keep their adolescents financially dependent until their schooling is over. Upper-class adolescents are
often away at school, and then go into marriage as girls, or into the family
business or self-chosen careers as boys.

Minority-group adolescents and those from impoverished backgrounds
who drop out of school find it hard to get work when times are bad. The
boys tend to give primary loyalty to their peers from early adolescence
onward and before the teen years have ended may espouse delinquent patterns of behavior. Somewhat more than half of all working-class boys and
girls are upwardly mobile, succeeding in the developmental tasks that
make for success in middle-class life. Inner-city adolescents become more
sexually active in the early teens, so that in many cases illegitimacy and
early pregnancy cut short the education and upward mobility efforts of
girls. The majority of working-class people adopt one of three ideologies:

(1) a rather conservative economic-instrumental view of life; (2) a religious fundamentalist ideology: or (3) a simple "poverty-culture" ideology (Havighurst 1972:71–72). Success in the developmental tasks of adolescence is profoundly influenced by the ways in which parents perform their own developmental tasks at this stage.

When the parents accept themselves as they are, with all their weaknesses and strengths, and when they accept their several roles at this stage of development without undue conflict or sensitivity, they set the pattern for a similar sort of self-acceptance in their children. The adolescent girl then has, in her mother, a model for her role as a girl and as a woman; and the boy has a similar role model in his father. The early adolescent boy may be small in stature and a bit behind schedule in his physical development, but if he has worthy models to follow and understanding parents who help him live with himself, he can focus on the developmental tasks that he is able to achieve, so that his self-confidence is buttressed. Attempting tasks for which he is not yet ready invites failure, a sense of defeat, and the rage of frustration. A young person is more likely to accept himself or herself when there is a climate of acceptance within the family—an acceptance based on respect for each member as a person.

Developmental tasks of teenagers' parents

Parents of teenagers have as a major task standing firm against unreasonable testing of the limits allowed in the family—while at the same time gradually involving the adolescents in family decisions. Parents who have a solid relationship are fortunate, for this allows them to weigh their adolescent's proposals objectively and to join in encouraging him to pursue his goals—as many an adolescent would, if he dared. This involves the parental task of setting reasonable limits that expand as teenagers mature. As time goes on, the teenagers become more self-directed and depend less on their parents for discipline.

When he reaches the teenage stage of the family life cycle the father is carrying many responsibilities. He must perform a series of developmental tasks if he is to come through this period without faltering. He usually sees himself as the family's main source of support—his wife and older children contributing whatever they can at this expensive stage of family life. He gains their cooperation in keeping financially solvent by acquainting them with the family's economic status, and by sharing the control of money matters with them. He tries to be the kind of man his wife and children can be proud of, to be understanding of their problems, and to be accessible to them. Instead of playing a heavy authoritarian role with his teenage children, he works with them and with their mother, adopting policies that gradually release the adolescents from parental control. Meanwhile, he is gaining in self-understanding as he interacts with his growing young people. This is the time of life when a man needs to bolster his feeling of inadequacy, to broaden his interests, and to keep up-to-date on current thinking, social attitudes, and changing folkways so that he will not feel that life is passing him by. He does what he can to keep up his personal appearance and to give his wife the devoted attention that keeps their marriage from going stale.

A mother of teenagers often has to work at the task of trusting her adolescent children, believing in them, and delighting in their development, instead of feeling bereft when they no longer need her mothering as they did as little children. She may have to remind herself that her own health and grooming are quite as important for family well-being as her looking after her growing children. Now is the time of life when "the woman of the house" can encourage her teenagers to become active partners in running the household and in making decisions that affect the family. She takes professional pride in creating a family atmosphere that is relaxed, comfortable, friendly, and cooperative, one in which "everyone spoils everyone else." Whether she has an outside job or not, she thinks of herself as her husband's partner and companion as they guide their children and plan for their future together. She encourages her husband's development as a person, and looks to him to support her interests, as well as those they share as a couple. Her response as a marriage partner grows out of her need for her husband's love and out of her sensitivity to his need for her. Parents of teenagers find this stage of life satisfying when they do not expect too much of themselves, or of their children, but are content to enjoy one another and their lives as a family.

Family developmental tasks at the teenage stage

While mother, father, teenager, and possible younger siblings are working through their individual developmental tasks in the midst of social pressures that often thwart and hinder them, the family as a whole is busy at the essential family developmental tasks of the teenage stage:

1. Providing facilities for widely different needs within the family
2. Working out ever-changing financial problems
3. Sharing the responsibilities of family living
4. Keeping the marriage relationship in focus
5. Bridging the communication gap between the generations
6. Keeping in touch with relatives
7. Widening the horizons of teenagers and their parents
8. Maintaining the ethical and moral stance that is meaningful to them

*Providing facilities for widely
different needs*

At no other time in the family life cycle do family members feel as intensely about the house and its facilities as they do during the teenage family stage. Now the teenager's need for acceptance in larger social circles makes him (or, more often, her) push for nicer, better, bigger, more modern furnishings and equipment. The house that some years ago was child-proofed and stripped of all breakable elegance must now bloom in the styles of the period, since teenagers see the house as a reflection of themselves and of their family.

One of the first signs of adolescence noted by mothers is a critical attitude on the part of the youngster about the physical features of the home. Studies of the health and development of normal children find that with the onset of adolescence youngsters tend to compare their homes unfavorably with others in the community; they find it hard to accept the fact that they cannot use the telephone for hours on end, and they feel that they should have top priority in the use of the bathroom (Butler 1956).

The dating adolescent girl wants an attractive setting in which she can entertain her boy and girl friends. She needs some privacy in these facilities at least part of the time, away from the ever-watchful eyes and ears of younger siblings, parents, and other family members. The rest of the family needs to be somewhat protected from the noisy activities of teenagers—radios turned up full blast, the record player blaring out the same popular tune over and over again, the giggles, the chatter, the shrieks, and the endless telephone conversations that mean so much to teenagers and yet so often fray the nerves of adults. Now, when so much emphasis is placed on popularity and social life, middle-class families do what they can to provide facilities for it.

Individual differences among the children of a family call for a variety of facilities during the teen years. Some boys enjoy the superior social-emotional adjustment of early maturation; others, less far along in their physical, emotional, and social development, tend to be less poised and conforming and more active and adventuresome as teenagers (Jones 1965). The big, well-developed teenager tends, therefore, to be involved in sports, social activities, and community projects, while the late-maturing boy throws himself into music, applied science, a series of hobbies, or a variety of other interests for which physical size and social competence are not requisites.

The teenage boy does less of his dating and entertaining at home than does the girl, and so tends to demand less in refurbishing and "style." The pressures he puts on the home as a teenager are more apt to be for space for his hobbies and for his gang of buddies. As the fellows gather in the basement to fix a model plane, or in the yard to "soup up" the jalopy, or over the shortwave set in his room, there are bound to be some raids on the household's supplies of food and drink, rags and string, and all the other necessities that go into the completion of a project— and a man!

Teenagers tend to compete with their parents for the use of household equipment as they begin to adopt adult ways. One study finds that the sharing of equipment and space for the leisure activities of teenagers and other members of the family would be less of a problem if fewer and less diversified activities were carried on in the same room. Listing these activities as (1) quiet or private—reading, study, etc., (2) social—entertaining guests, music, records, television, etc., and (3) active—dancing, painting, carpentry, etc., the investigators recommend creating three distinct activity areas—private, social, and active—to be used interchangeably, depending on the demands of the various family members (Withrow and Trotter 1961:359–362).

While the teenager is crowding the house with his or her dating, recreational, and work interests, younger siblings are growing up, and their interests and needs must be taken into account. Younger brothers and sisters often resent teenage interests and activities that signal the end of familiar patterns formed during years of play together. At the same time, father and mother continue to be persons who need and have a right to a little peace and quiet in their lives. The family that tries to meet this multidimensional demand for adequate facilities during the teenage stage has some tall stepping to do. The adaptations and improvements involved more than likely cost money—plenty of it—as we see in the next section.

Working out ever-changing financial problems

The teenage family feels pressure for physical expansion and renewal of its facilities. The refrigerator is no longer large enough to stock with the variety of snacks and meals demanded by the family. It would be nice to have another bathroom, car, television set, deep freeze, rumpus room, or a den (where mother and father could take refuge when the teenagers are entertaining), or some new furnishings to replace "this old stuff" that is suddenly so hideous in adolescent eyes. Meanwhile, the father sees the costs of college, social life, and weddings ballooning up ahead of him.

Adolescents are very much concerned with money problems. A great many junior and senior high school students have difficulty keeping up with school expenses and feel embarrassed because of lack of funds (Bloom 1955).

This is the time when a teenager gets a part-time job that will not interfere too greatly with school work and yet will bring in some regular money of his or her own. When employment opportunities are good, a teenage boy can find work in a neighborhood shop, store, or garage, or on the golf links. The adolescent girl is in demand as baby-sitter, household helper, and in many places as saleswoman or clerk in a local store or office. These may be valuable experiences if they do not cut short the young person's educational program and if the income from self-employment is recognized in the family as of special interest to the adolescent.

Families differ greatly in money practices. Some appropriate the children's earnings as part of the family income, as once was traditional. Others consider the child's earnings as his/hers to do with as he/she pleases. Still others keep a supervisory eye on teenagers' earnings, and while they respect the young person's wishes, try to guide him to plan wisely for future needs. There are still some traditional homes in which either the father or the mother holds the purse strings and the young people have no voice in the family finances. A growing number of families are more democratically oriented. Family income and expenditures are discussed and money planning is done jointly, with all members of the family participating. In these homes, young people gain experience in handling money and in dealing with financial problems. This process also makes them aware that their wishes and rights are being considered in the family as they grow up.

The chances are that the mother will think about getting a job now, if she is not already working. Unless she gets a high-paying job, she could in effect lose up to half of her earnings because of the added expenses her labor-force participation would entail: income taxes, insurance, social security and other deductions, professional and/or union dues, transportation, lunches, extra clothing and grooming costs, household help, added family meals out (when she is too late or too tired to cook at times), and other unforeseen costs (Porter 1975: 475–476).

Harder to calculate and even more important are the possible benefits or psychic costs of her working—the satisfactions or frustrations of the job, the enrichment or strains affecting the husband-wife relationship, and the benefits or threats to mother-adolescent relationships. There is evidence that the adjustment between adolescents and their parents is better when the mother is employed part-time than when she is a full-time homemaker (Nye 1952; Jessen 1975). One interpretation is that it is easier for children entering adolescence to emancipate themselves when their mother is not entirely dependent on her children for her sense of being needed. If she has a part-time job, she not only helps out financially, but very likely widens her horizons and extends her role as wife, mother, and self-sufficient person.

Teenagers whose mothers are employed tend more than others to feel that the outside work does not threaten the marital relationship. Furthermore, both boys and girls usually accept their mother's employment, especially in those homes where the father participates in household tasks (King, McIntyre, and Axelson 1968:633–637).

Family situations differ widely, and many wives find it impossible or impractical to work outside the home. Because of the removal of traditional taboos about women working, a family has a choice about the matter today. That so many families in the teenage stage find economic and emotional pressures eased when the mother has some gainful employment is a trend worthy of note.

Sharing responsibilities of family living

By the time a girl becomes a teenager, she sometimes enjoys preparing a family meal or buying new curtains for her room out of her own money. The boy who does a better job than his father at making household or automobile repairs gets satisfaction from sharing these new responsibilities in the home. Teenagers are still accountable to their parents, but as they mature they progressively assume more and more responsibility for their behavior and for the family's well-being. The traditional family, with its father-head, is on the wane in twentieth-century America, and democratic practices are widely accepted in families with teenagers (Briggs and Schulz 1955).

Studies show that most household tasks are jointly undertaken by the various members of the family, with no one member assuming complete responsibility. Too frequently, however, teenagers seem to be restricted to a set of classic chores—for the girls, setting and clearing the table; and for the boys, removing the trash. The parents take on the more challenging activities of meal preparation and household repairs—jobs that could give teenagers and their younger brothers and sisters pride in achievement (Johannis 1958:61–62; Duvall 1966:191–200).

Mother and father clearly hold the balance of power in deciding who will participate in the various activities involving family members. Although most determinations are jointly made by two or more family members, significantly more parents than teenagers have a voice in decisions affecting the family's social activities. For example, four out of five fathers (83.8 percent) decide who uses the family car, a decision that reflects the wishes of about half of the mothers (51.9 percent), less than one out of four teenage sons (23.8 percent), and 13.4 percent of the teenage daughters. Twice as many parents as teenagers decide who will go on outings or summer vacations, and half again as many mothers as teenage daughters decide who will use the living room (Johannis and Rollins 1960:59–60).

Keeping the marriage in focus

By the time a father and mother have been married for 15 or more years, they may have become so preoccupied with their parental responsibilities that their marriage no longer holds a central place in their lives. The man of the house tends to be absorbed in his work roles and associations. His wife, carrying through the years the major responsibility for the home and children, may feel "bogged down," work-worn, and devoid of the glamour that her teenagers' magazines portray so fetchingly. Putting the marriage back in focus may be a major family developmental task at this stage.

At the teenage stage of the family life cycle, the middle-aged husband shows little of the ardor that his teenagers demonstrate in their love-making. The wife feels taken for granted. She must be constantly on tap to serve family needs, yet she experiences few of the fulfillments that are supposed to go with marriage. One function of communication in marriage is that of sharing with one's partner the pleasant and unpleasant events that have happened during the day while each has been at work at his or her own tasks. Yet few of the wives in the Detroit Area Study spontaneously mentioned interaction with their husbands after a bad day. During the honeymoon stage of the marriage 70 percent of the brides appear to have kept their problems to themselves. The percentage of silent wives increases as the marriage continues, until at the teenage stage 98 percent of the wives report neither positive nor negative interaction with their husbands at the end of a bad day (Blood and Wolfe 1960:188). It is safe to assume that the reason is not that mothers of adolescents have no bad days, but rather that their communication with their husbands has declined to the point where they no longer burden their mates with their problems.

Wives who are about the same age as their mates are more satisfied with marital love than wives older or younger by four or more years (Blood and Wolfe 1960:227). College-educated people find greater fulfillment in their marriages than do those with less education, possibly because their schooling involved deferred gratification in adolescence and the development of a richer repertoire of emotional and sexual expression.

As the family reaches the teenage stage, its children are more active socially than they were at younger ages. Boyfriends call for the adolescent daughter. Her excitement in getting ready for her dates is often contagious, causing her parents to relive some of their courtship experiences.

Couples with teenagers are able to enjoy happy and relaxed times away from home more often than they could when their oldest child was still a school-ager (Feldman 1965:41). Now that the oldest child is old enough to be left in charge of the home for short intervals, husband and wife are freer to get away for an occasional evening, or to take a weekend trip together from time to time as the husband's schedule allows. Letting the adolescents perk things up in the family as they want to is often fun for the parents as well as for the youngsters. When the mother gets a smart new outfit, she gets the feelings that go with it and once more attracts her husband's interest in her as a woman. When the father gets into the tweed jacket his son insists is right for him, he assumes the gay-blade air that seems appropriate; he throws back his shoulders, pulls in his tummy, and woos and charms his own wife as only he can. Keeping a marriage vigorously alive consists of much more than so-called marriage hygiene—it rests on the eagerness of the husband and wife to attract and to be attracted by each other. This desire can restore the life and the lilt that are found in a radiantly alive marriage.

Bridging the communication gap

Adolescents turn increasingly to their peers with their intimate confidences during the teen years. Parents who understand that young people must identify with their own generation if they are to emerge as full-fledged young adults refrain from prying pressures that alienate them even further from their teenagers. Wise parents guide their adolescents with a loose rein, letting them have their heads, knowing that they will not stray too far from the fold if they are not driven from it. Being available for companionable chats now and then is better than loosing a barrage of questions as soon as a teenager sets foot in the door. Adolescents need parents and go to them willingly in families where communication is good.

Communication bogs down between the generations in many families. A teenager may interpret his or her parents' interest as intrusion and parental suggestions as attempts to control. Many parents cannot talk with their adolescents about personal topics, partly because their concern is so great, and partly because of their own embarrassment. A teenager's sexual interests and activities are avoided or treated so gingerly in many families that neither generation is comfortable discussing them (Dubbe 1957; Bienvenu 1969; Hill 1973; Duvall 1976).

Two factors in the parents' ability to communicate with teenagers are: (1) their willingness to listen, and (2) ongoing acceptance and affection. When parents are attentive to what a teenager is trying to tell them, the youngster senses their interest and respect. Runaways are found characteristically to report that their parents did not listen (Blood and D'Angelo 1974:490), and runaway adolescent girls tend to feel unloved at home (Robey, Rosenwald, and Rosenwald 1964). Feelings of alienation predominate when affectional ties are weak (Allen and Sandhu, 1967). Parents are found to affect the lives of their sons and daughters in decidedly different ways. Mothers generally have greater influence than do fathers on their teenagers (Stinnett, Farris, and Walters 1974).

Parents of certain ethnic and racial groups who hold to the old ways in which they were reared find it hard to bridge the growing chasms between the generations. Middle- and upper-class families tend to be more democratic and to have fewer communication problems with their adolescents than do lower-class families (Benson 1955; Nye 1951; Maas 1951). Indeed, among certain groups, the generation gap is found to be a myth (Thurnher, Spence, and Lowenthal 1974).

Young people have a vested interest in accentuating differences between the generations, while parents have a stake in minimizing those differences (Bengtson 1971:89). Youth is more explorative, daring, and up to the minute than is maturity. Young people enjoy the contrast. They want to be out ahead. But it is also exceedingly important to the adolescent for dad and mom not to get *too* far behind. Teenagers take pride in their parents' progressive point of view and in their social and civic activities and interests. They are concerned about the way their parents look and behave in public. Young people not only are proud of parents who possess social poise and who enjoy cultural activities and events, but seem to find it easier to communicate with them.

Parents who have been considered perfect by their little children come in for criticism and faultfinding as these same children reach adolescence. The schoolboy brags about his father's prowess and boasts of his mother's beauty. The same young fellow as a teenager groans over his father's old-fashioned behavior and begs his mother not to appear at a parent-teacher meeting in "that old thing." Adolescent criticism of parents is evidence of the young person's struggle to free himself from his close emotional attachment to his parents and to develop a more mature relationship with them.

The teenager who achieves emancipation from his parents emerges as a young adult capable of mature affection for his mother and father as persons. He becomes an autonomous person, comfortable in his interdependent relationship with his parents, and capable of mature feelings of genuine love and appreciation for them. But in the meantime, throughout adolescence, relationships between the generations are frequently strained (Duvall 1976).

Parents need the love, confidence, and respect of their teenage children. They need it for the sense of success and accomplishment it gives them, for they have invested a great deal of themselves in the rearing of their sons and daughters. But they gain and maintain that love and respect only so long as they meet dependably, day by day, the developmental needs of their children. During adolescence those needs are as vital as at any other period of the child's development, and the understanding parent is just as necessary in the adequate meeting of those needs. Adolescents need parents, and they know it—most of the time.

Keeping in touch with relatives

The teenage stage of the family life cycle is a testing time for the immediate relatives. If they pass youth's rigorous standards of acceptability, they can contribute much to and gain much from association with the young relatives. If they remain rigidly rooted in "old-fashioned" ways and ideas, young people will eschew them heartily and will associate with them only under duress. An understanding grandparent can bridge the gap not only between the first and third generations but also between grandchild and parent. A sympathetic uncle, aunt, or cousin has a real role to play by offering a home away from home—as a parent once removed, a guide without the heavy hand of authority, or a wise counselor who is not too close to the teenage boy or girl. The narrow-minded "old maid," male or female, married or unmarried, is rarely a welcome guest in the teenage family, for he or she conveys too much implied criticism and personifies too clearly the frustrations that burden youth.

Broad-minded or narrow, generous or stingy, wise or foolish, relatives have to be taken in stride by most families. You dare not offend Aunt Amy no matter what you think of her. You cannot go and live with your sophisticated cousin however much you would love it. You should not imitate drifting Uncle Mike regardless of how much you envy his freedom. You go to family gatherings and size them all up, observing the courtesies that are expected and learning a great deal about your roots and your forebears as you see these kinfolk in action.

When graduation day arrives, and your relatives gather to do honor to you, you in turn can afford to be proud of your family and glad to be part of them. You want to be worthy of them and to measure up to their expectations of you. You recognize yourself as a member of the larger family group and feel sorry for the boy or girl in your class who has no family to call his own.

Younger cousins and other relatives may idolize the teenager and thus may contribute significantly to his or her development. Relatives have a real place in the family—a lesser one perhaps in the teenage family than before or after—but a place, nevertheless, that is real and important.

Widening horizons of teenagers and their parents

In its teenage stage the family ranges farther afield than it ever has before. The children are now old enough to enjoy a whole-family vacation to more distant points of interest than was feasible before. Trips to historic shrines and cultural areas now take on real meaning for the family. Horizons expand for individuals, too. The teenager goes off with his friends for a weekend or a summer. The father is away on business trips from time to time. The mother is sent as a delegate to the state or national convention of her favorite organization. The family is beginning to scatter, foreshadowing the individualization process characteristic of the empty nest stage just ahead.

Getting and keeping a job is important for a teenager's self-confidence, independence, and experience in productive work. Middle-class adolescents can usually find work in their home communities; upper-class teenagers often work part time in their father's office or on his staff; but lower-class youths too often roam the streets with nothing to do. Over the years, twice as many black and other minority young people have been unemployed as whites (Figure 13-1).

The social development of teenagers depends on friendships with members of both sexes and on the activities that go with dating, courtship, and becoming emotionally involved with others. Little change has been noted in dating among white high school students since 1964; however the dating behavior of black teenagers is becoming more like that of their white peers (Dickinson 1975). During the entire second decade of life, members of the peer group are especially important to the young person. It is in the face-to-face contacts with friends of one's own age that decisions are made, skills are developed, and values are weighed in everyday interaction.

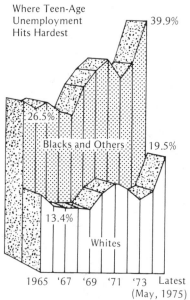

Where Teen-Age Unemployment Hits Hardest

39.9%

26.5%

Blacks and Others 19.5%

13.4%

Whites

1965 '67 '69 '71 '73 Latest
(May, 1975)

Note: Figures are seasonally adjusted.
Source: U.S. Dept. of Labor

Figure 13-1
Where Teen-age Unemployment Hits Hardest

Source: U.S. Department of Labor, in "A Half Billion Dollars to Put Restless Kids to Work," *U.S. News & World Report*, 30 June 1975, p. 67.
Reprinted from *U.S. News & World Report*. Copyright 1975 U.S. News & World Report, Inc.

Guidance, confidences, and counsel from beloved older friends (teacher, minister, youth leaders, etc.) may be more important to the teenager than one suspects. Such close ties outside the family may be perceived as a threat by the parent who is not prepared to release the teenage child. Accepting the teenager's intimate friends and the confidences that young people normally share makes it easier for parents to take adolescence in their stride. Otherwise, the teenager's task of reaching out to others may frighten the parents into resistance or retreat.

The teenager's early love experiences are a case in point. To those involved, the crushes and infatuations of early adolescence are important and especially precious. It is dangerous for one or both of the parents to ridicule these early involvements as "puppy love" or to ignore them as "kid stuff," for in so doing they alienate their own youngster—but only rarely weaken the outside ties. When the family can make this special friend welcome at home, treat him or her and the relationship with respect, and take it for what it is and nothing more, both the family and the adolescent are free to grow through the experience to new levels of maturity.

Group life is a magnet for the adolescent. Many teenagers want to belong to more organizations and to get into more activities than can comfortably be carried. They want to belong to the band or the glee club, to the drama group or the ball team, to social clubs and hobby groups. Life is opening up and everything must be tried and tested. Political organizations and social action groups quite distant from the family's orientation may be explored, as much to see what they are like as to stretch away from the family's affiliations into those peculiarly one's own.

Parents who can accept these adventures of their youngsters as a normal part of growing up, without feeling unnecessarily afraid or personally threatened, can argue the merits of this cause or that with their budding citizen without going off the deep end in repression or repudiation. Families who join their young people in exploring and evaluating new ways of looking at things acquire the flexibility that the modern age requires.

Maintaining sound ethical and moral standards

During their restless searching, teenagers need reliable points of reference. These are the years when parents must defend and adhere firmly to sound principles and standards of conduct. Their own genuine commitment is the most eloquent argument they can offer. Safeguarding adolescents from life's disasters is quite as important as giving them room to grow. Teenagers' families face real problems in this stage. They may find themselves grappling with delinquent tendencies, irresponsible conduct, truancy, questionable companions, confusions about love, sex, and marriage, and blocked pathways to adulthood as adolescents go through the teen years.

Moral development may undergo a major shift during the teenage stage. During preadolescence, stress is normally placed on accepting the rules of the family, group, and country as valid in their own right. In adolescence, conformity is no longer automatic, but is based increasingly on understanding. The social order is examined, justified, and finally preserved and supported. An occasional adolescent may adopt an autonomous moral stance that isolates him from former companions and from groups with which he was identified (Kohlberg and Gilligan 1971:1066–1067).

There is nothing new in adolescent rebellion—only in some of its current manifestations. Youth has always seen parents as "old fogeys" for accepting conventional norms. Young people of spirit have always resisted their parents' attempts to impose established standards on their generation. Today's adolescents are not the first to see adults as hypocritical and insensitive. This has been the rallying cry of the younger generation from time immemorial, as they have tried to bring about changes in life as they saw it. Questioning adolescents have always expected to remake the adult world along the lines of their youthful dreams, and every once in a while they have succeeded (Kohlberg and Gilligan 1971:1081).

Parents and teenagers learn from one another in a fast-changing society. Their value orientations mutually reinforce one another. In a pluralistic society, the family serves as the mediating link between adolescents and the groups—representing a multiplicity of views—to which they turn for value development (Bengtson 1975:369; Kandel and Lesser 1972). The anxieties parents have about the hazards confronting youth in the areas of drugs, drinking, sexual activities, and other risk-taking conduct are often muted when family discussions reveal their adolescent child's emerging values. "These new values are not simply a matter of adopting a freer and more casual life style. They symbolize a profound value transformation affecting every phase of life" (Yankelovich 1975:41).

Families teach their teenagers trust by trusting, values by valuing, and love by loving. Parents are the source of the first love their adolescents knew. They have served their sons and daughters through a dozen years and more as models of living with the triumphs and tragedies of everyday interaction. Now, with the coming of the teen years, the direct "teaching" so often interpreted by adolescents as "preaching" is no longer necessary.

The parents have already made their imprint on their children. Together the generations may examine the ideas and values and evaluate the policies and standards that they see in behavior all around them. Now the whole family is free at last to talk over the things they read and observe, as people with common interests and concerns.

This time, like all times, is a very good
one if we but know what to do with
it.

Emerson

F amilies launching young adults

chapter fourteen

The young of the family are ready to be launched in the latter teen years. This stage of the family life cycle is sharply marked by the young person's departure from home—to marry, to take a full-time job, to begin military service, to attend college. In each case, the young person leaves the parental home, never again to return as a child.

The stage begins with the first child leaving home as a young adult; it ends with the empty nest, as the last child leaves home for a life of his or her own. The launching stage may be extremely short, as is the case in the family with one child, a daughter, who marries the year she graduates from high school. Or the stage may extend over a considerable period of time, as happens occasionally when an unmarried son or daughter stays at home permanently or indefinitely as a dependent. In the United States today the stage typically lasts six to seven years (Chapter 7).

The processes of launching start during the earlier life cycle stages of the family, as the child or young person prepares for the decisions that shape his future. The process of cutting apron strings characterizes the teen years and sets the stage for the son's or daughter's emergence as an emancipated young adult. No matter how abrupt it may seem, the departure of the young person from his home is actually the culmination of a process that has been going on through the years.

From maximum size at the beginning of the stage, the nuclear family shrinks during the launching period to the original married pair. Before the stage is completed, the husband-father may also be a grandfather, and the wife-mother a grandmother, as the first-married son or daughter has children. The younger siblings now hold positions of son-brother-uncle and daughter-sister-aunt. Similarly, with the marriage of the first child, the mother becomes a mother-in-law, the father a father-in-law, and their children brothers- and sisters-in-law of the newly recruited members of the family by marriage.

Parents at this stage are breaking the patterns and habits of two decades as they let their children go. Never again will the relationship between them and their offspring be quite the same. Fathers and mothers who successfully launch their children into the world are usually those whose emotional lives do not revolve around the continuing dependence of their children.

The launching stage is marked by the simultaneous release of the family's children and the recruitment of new members (and their families) by marriage. Positional developmental tasks continue for the parents: as mother, homemaker, wife, person, and probably mother-in-law and grandmother; as father, provider, husband, person, and possibly father-in-law and grandfather. The children have their developmental tasks as young adults and younger children in the family of orientation, and when they marry, as husbands and wives in the establishment phase of their family of procreation. Family developmental tasks are critical while the family is shifting from a household with children to a husband-wife pair. The major family goal is the reorganization of the family into a continuing unity while releasing matured and maturing young people into lives of their own.

Life planning by young adults

It is not easy to find one's niche in the complex modern world. Some young people make few life plans because of discouragement and disillusionment. These so-called losers may turn to drugs to ease their pain. Psychologically, drug abusers feel alienated, left-out, lonely, like "black sheep" and second-class citizens. An eight-year national longitudinal study of 1600 young men found that drug usage peaks in the college and military years, and that by age 23, 62 percent had tried marijuana (one-third had used it weekly between the ages of 20 and 23), 32 percent amphetamines, 19 percent barbiturates, 22 percent psychedelics, and more than 6 percent heroin (Johnston, O'Malley and Eveland 1975). Although many students use drugs on occasion, few show such symptoms of drug abuse as preoccupation with drugs, exclusive association with other drug users, negative self-esteem, and inability to carry on a student's life. The research team distinguishes between drug abusers and drug users (who more closely resemble the nonusers); see Table 14-1 (Yankelovich 1975:41).

Some young people plan farther ahead than do others. In general, interest in life planning and the ability to plan one's life predictably are a function of social class level—the higher the level the greater the interest. A study including 2,700 public, private, and trade high school students and 349 Yale undergraduates explored the question, "How far ahead have you planned your life?" The percentage of high school students from higher class families who were planning five or more years ahead was double that of students from the lowest social class with similar plans (a ratio of approximately 20 to 40 percent). The researchers conclude that "length of life planning had a reliable positive correlation with both the occupational and educational status of the young respondents' fathers" (Brim and Forer 1956).

Upward mobile parents tend either to carry their children along with them or to encourage their young people to climb; young people from nonmobile families tend to remain static in the great majority of cases—85 percent in one study (McGuire 1952:113). Significantly more boys than girls tend to make extended life plans (Brim and Forer 1956:58),

Table 14-1
Drug Abuse Among the Discouraged

Student's self-reported behavior	Drug abusers	Drug users	Nonusers
"Unable to finish projects"	47%	26%	26%
"I never found a group where I belong"	34	8	8
"Things often seem hopeless"	43	17	19
"Every time I try to get ahead someone or something stops me"	47	21	18
"Feel angry and frustrated most of the time"	42	24	20
"Often find it hard to get through the day"	36	19	18
Have run away from home	66	37	
Have failed courses	36	16	
Have been expelled	70	41	
Have damaged property on purpose	62	43	
Buy drugs to keep on hand	89	41	
Sell drugs for profit	51	14	

Source: Daniel Yankelovich, "Drug Users Vs. Drug Abusers," *Psychology Today* (October 1975):41.

probably because many girls know that the future will be greatly influenced by marriage and by the plans of a husband. In both sexes there is more upward mobility drive among those whose family and interpersonal relations have been difficult than among those whose early interpersonal relations have been satisfying (Ellis 1952). High levels of aspiration of university students are related to (1) feelings of not being wanted by parents, (2) favoritism shown by parents, and (3) little attachment to parents (Table 14-2).

These findings support current psychoanalytic assumptions and general social theory that unsatisfactory interpersonal relationships in the family of orientation are significantly related to high aspirational levels. The hypothesis is that some young people, whose family life has been unhappy, struggle to better themselves as soon as they can cut loose from family ties. In some cases the high levels of aspiration are fantasies not related too closely to what is realizable. In others actual social mobility results from realistic efforts to improve.

Identification with some older person who serves as a model for the emerging young adult is a factor. The girl identifies with her teacher and wants to be just like her when she grows up. The boy greatly admires his coach or his leader at the YMCA and goes off like his hero for specialized training, possibly at the same college and professional school. In such cases, the young adult patterns himself after the much admired adult and so makes the decisions and follows the course that brings him closer to his ideal.

To summarize, factors influencing the young adult's life planning and specific decisions upon leaving his family of orientation tend to operate in the following directions:

1. The discouraged "loser" turns to drugs rather than to future plans.
2. The higher the parents' social class, the farther ahead the young person plans his life.
3. Young adults from upward mobile families tend to continue climbing.
4. More young men than young women plan ahead.
5. Young adults from unhappy homes tend to have higher levels of aspiration than do young people from satisfying family backgrounds.
6. Young people who identify with an admired adult tend to pattern themselves after that older person in their own life plans.

Developmental tasks of young adults

Throughout the first two decades of life as a child and as a teenager, a person lives within the expectancies of his age and grade. Now, as a young adult, he or she emerges from the norms of the age-grade system and steps out into a future of his or her own making. From now on

Table 14-2
Interpersonal Relationships in the Family and Aspirational Level of 350 University Students

Feelings of not being wanted by parents	Levels of aspiration	
	High	Low
Father	(N = 117)	(N = 223)
Some	41.9	24.7
None	58.1	75.3
Mother	(N = 122)	(N = 223)
Some	34.4	20.2
None	65.6	79.8

Favoritism shown by parents	Levels of aspiration	
	High	Low
Father	(N = 95)	(N = 188)
Yes	45.3	30.9
No	54.7	69.1
Mother	(N = 95)	(N = 188)
Yes	41.1	25.0
No	58.9	75.0

Degree of attachment to parents	Levels of aspiration	
	High	Low
Father	(N = 110)	(N = 222)
Much	33.6	50.9
Little	66.4	49.1
Mother	(N = 123)	(N = 223)
Much	52.8	66.8
Little	47.2	33.2

Source: Russell R. Dynes, Alfred C. Clarke, and Simon Dinitz, "Levels of Occupational Aspiration: Some Aspects of Family Experience as a Variable," American Sociological Review 21, no. 2 (April 1956): Tables 1, 2, and 3, pp. 212–215.

success or failure will depend largely on the choices he or she makes as a person. A young adult must make a career choice and get the education required for it. Each young person tries to establish autonomy either as a single person, or as a husband or wife. If marriage has high priority, a series of tasks is involved: appraising love feelings, becoming involved, making the choice of whom to marry, getting engaged, being married, and establishing a family (Chapter 9).

No other period of life has so many teachable moments cascading all at once upon a person. Face to face with the adult world, the young man or woman is eager to learn—in action. Few formal or theoretical opportunities for learning what is involved in any of the most crucial of life's decisions are available. Indeed, "early adulthood is the most individualistic period of life, and the loneliest one, in the sense that the individual, or at the most, two individuals, must proceed with a minimum of social attention and assistance to tackle the most important tasks of life" (Havighurst 1972:83).

That so many young adults accomplish these multiple tasks so well is a credit to their generation. It is understandable that many young men and women are baffled and bewildered by the multitude of major decisions they must make during this period of life. The impulsive may rush into premature "solutions" only to find themselves caught in one of the many traps for the unwary. The hesitant mark time for fear of making mistakes. They postpone committing themselves until they "find themselves," and for a year or more may travel about taking dead-end jobs and discussing with their fellows the problems of the world.

In the adult society prestige and power depend not so much on age as on skill, strength, wisdom, and family connections. Achieving one's life goals today is not nearly so much a matter of waiting until one grows up to them as it was in earlier times. There must be a strategy, based on an understanding of the new terrain, that can only be got by scouting around and learning the lay of the land for a few years. This is what young people do, and it often takes several years to learn how to get about efficiently and to go where one wants to go in the adult society in America (Havighurst 1972:84–85).

Choosing a vocation

In some cultures a young man is expected to follow in his father's footsteps and carry on the family business. In the United States this pattern tends to hold largely in upper-class families, where wealth and holdings necessitate grooming the sons of the family to carry on the family traditions. Young people today face many more vocational possibilities than were formerly available. In 1870 there were only 338 vocations, in contrast to tens of thousands by the late twentieth century—in electronics, atomic energy, radar, television, plastics, medical, chemical, biological, and behavioral science.

Most young people between 16 and 24 years of age are working (55 percent in 1974). Increasing numbers of young women see themselves as members of the working force. In some segments of the population in recent years, young women have been rejecting economic dependence and the unalleviated household responsibilities of the traditional wife-mother role. By the mid-1970s the majority of college women in one study believed that their careers were of equal importance to those of their husbands and that they should share equally in the financial support of their families. They expected to work all of their adult lives and to get substantial help from their husbands with household chores (Parelius 1975:151). Marriage still holds first place in the future plans of the great majority of American girls, but many of them think also in terms of developing vocational skills that will serve them through the years. As more fields open up for women, girls as well as boys face inevitable vocational choices.

There is much to learn about specific vocations and about one's individual aptitudes, interests, preferences, and preparation. Part-time jobs, summer employment, and apprenticelike opportunities are helpful to many young people. Vocational guidance is available in many schools. Testing and counseling programs are designed to help young people find themselves in occupational fields suited to their abilities.

Maturity, enthusiasm, poise, appearance, and the ability to work with people top the list of qualities sought by prospective employers when hiring college graduates. Company representatives advise liberal arts students to take business or technical courses and to have clear career goals when they apply for a job (Hacker 1976:4).

Parents who encourage their sons and daughters to explore various possibilities and to get the training needed for the chosen field greatly assist young people in accomplishing this developmental task.

Getting an education

College and professional school enrollments continue to climb, in the face of forecasts to the contrary. The National Center for Education Statistics reported increases in enrollment at all levels of advanced education in the autumn of 1975 (Table 14-3; see also Table 3-2). The all-time high in college attendance is expected to continue until the early 1980s, when a slow decline will begin. Women's colleges, coed institutions, black colleges—all are flourishing, in spite of the rising costs of education.

Basic costs of tuition, room, and board in both private and public colleges nearly doubled between 1965 and 1975 (Table 14-4).

Table 14-3
College and Professional School Enrollments, 1970 and 1975

Type of school	1970 enrollment	1975 enrollment (est.)	Percentage increase
Two-year colleges	1,630,000	2,335,000	43%
Four-year colleges	6,290,000	6,993,000	11
Graduate schools	1,031,000	1,232,000	19
Law schools	82,499	115,000	39
Medical schools	40,238	55,500	38

Source: National Center for Education Statistics, in "That Slack Year in Colleges—Why It Isn't Happening," *U.S. News and World Report,* 10 November 1975, p. 45.

Table 14-4
Average College Costs for an Academic Year, 1965 and 1975

Average cost	Public colleges		Percentage increase	Private colleges		Percentage increase
	1965	1975		1965	1975	
Tuition	$243	$482	98%	$1,008	$2,381	136%
Room	271	556	105	331	632	91
Board	436	675	55	488	731	50

Source: National Center for Education Statistics; American Association of University Professors, in "Zooming Prices on the Campus," *U.S. News & World Report,* 1 September 1975, p. 45.

A bright student from a poor family can get financial help as needed, especially if he or she is from a minority group. Some middle-income families cannot afford the full costs of college, especially if they have other young adults in school at the same time. Federally assisted student loans are available through colleges and universities to help needy students (Chapter 3; Porter 1975:393-397). Colleges determine the amount of aid they give a student (in scholarships, low-interest loans, and/or part-time jobs) on the basis of the family's assets, assured income, and such special circumstances as unusual medical expenses, support of other dependents, and unemployment of one or both parents.

Estimates of an American's lifetime worth increase with each additional level of education. The conservative estimate of a college graduate's total future earnings by the United States Bureau of the Census (1974) is close to $900,000, while a high school graduate's lifetime earnings are considerably less than $600,000 (Figure 14-1).

Even so, some experts are beginning to question the value of a college education. They point out that the difference between the incomes of high school and college graduates has been diminishing in recent years, because the kinds of jobs that used to enable college graduates to reach higher income brackets are no longer so numerous (Freeman 1976; see

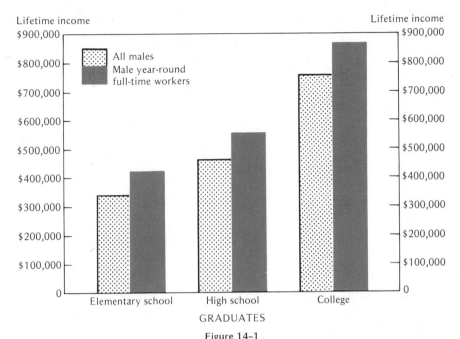

Figure 14-1

Estimated Lifetime Income in 1972 for all Males and Male Year-Round Full-Time Workers 18 Years Old and Over, by Educational Attainment

Source: U.S. Bureau of the Census, "Annual Mean Income, Lifetime Income, and Educational Attainment of Men in the United States, for Selected Years, 1956 to 1972, *Current Population Reports*, Series P-60, no. 92 (Washington, D.C.: U.S. Government Printing Office, March 1974).

also Chapter 3). Others point out that many students go to college because they do not know what else to do. Young adults are "warehoused" on campuses because society does not know what to do with them, says Caroline Bird (1975). When unemployment rates are high, labor unions do not want inexperienced young workers in the labor force, so young adults tend to remain in a holding pattern on campus, where they have the status of students whether or not they are getting anything of real value out of their college experience.

Student unrest can be seen in the shifting moods of students in recent decades. Postwar students in the 1950s were known as "the silent generation" who married young and went on to build suburban homes and raise a bumper crop of babies. During the turbulent Sixties, violent rebellions broke out on campuses across the country as students protested the Vietnam war, demanded more relevant education, especially for blacks, and expressed their anger at compulsory military service. With the end of the draft and the reality of rising unemployment due to the economic recession of the Seventies, students focused on personal academic progress in their efforts to survive within the system. Student attitudes fluctuate as they reflect the concerns of the larger population, since "students are imbued with the same idealism and infected with the same virus of corruption as are their elders" (Hechinger and Hechinger 1975:49). Because they are relatively free from societal responsibilities and are heavily concentrated on campuses, college students are easily accessible to journalists and social scientists. The resulting flow of reports and surveys appearing in popular and professional publications and relayed by the news media tend to magnify the significance of student concerns and behavior.

Establishing autonomy as a single person

Three out of five young adults between the ages of 18 and 24 are single (67.5 percent of the men and 50.4 percent of the women), according to the United States Bureau of the Census. The number of young adults living in "bachelor" quarters with no relatives present more than quadrupled between 1960 and 1974 (Glick 1975:8). The recent increase in the number of unmarried young adults appears to be due in some measure to their deliberate choice of singlehood. Many young men and women are postponing marriage in order to establish their autonomy and gain a sense of personal accomplishment and "freedom to be." Demographer Paul C. Glick suggests a number of interrelated factors that account for the delay in marriage: (1) the greater number of women going to college (three times as many in 1972 as in 1960); (2) an excess of women of marriageable age, resulting in a "marriage squeeze;" (3) the sharp increase in the employment of women and amazing decline in the birth rate; (4) expanding roles open to women outside the home; and (5) the revival of the women's movement (Glick 1975:3-4).

Some young men and women may fail to marry for any of the reasons that traditionally have prevailed; others appear to be avoiding the "marriage trap" as a negative response to social pressures to get married and follow traditional masculine and feminine roles (Table 14-5).

Twenty-year-old Martha expresses negative feelings about marriage when she says:

> I just don't do so good boy-girl-wise. Who knows where it comes from? Am I afraid of boys? Probably. My father drilled into me that boys will try to get as much as they can from a girl right from the first date. . . . Marriage has never been one of my priorities, and especially now; I'm really down on it. I enjoy being with girls a lot more. They won't hurt you like guys always do. . . . Why shouldn't I be afraid of marriage? I haven't seen many great marriages around. My parents have had really bad troubles, a lot of screaming and yelling. My mother walked out more than once. . . . (Wilkes 1975:86-87)

Table 14-5
Failure to Marry and Deliberate Choice of Singlehood

Why young adults fail to marry	Why young adults choose to remain single
Dependent relatives	Career opportunities
Hostility toward opposite sex	Independence
Disenchantment about marriage	Self-development
Homosexuality	Freedom to experiment
Inability to live intimately	Avoidance of "marrying down" as women
Poor health and/or disabilities	Preference for varied opportunities
Unattractiveness	Sexual availability
Unrealistic romantic expectations	Satisfying friendships
Social inadequacies	Travel and mobility
Insufficient income as men	Chance to establish personal autonomy
Inability to find a suitable mate	Opportunity to develop own life style
Isolation from potential mates	Ongoing supportive associations and close caring
Not being chosen	relationships as singles

Sources: Peter J. Stein, "Singlehood: An Alternative to Marriage," *The Family Coordinator* 24, no. 4: 489-503; Margaret Adams, "The Single Woman in Today's Society," *American Journal of Orthopsychiatry* 41 (1971): 776-786; Robert Bell, *Marriage and Family Interaction* (Homewood, Ill.: Dorsey Press, 1971); Manford H. Kuhn, "How Mates Are Sorted," chap. 8 in Howard Becker and Reuben Hill, *Family, Marriage, and Parenthood* (Boston, Mass.: D.C. Heath & Co., 1948), pp. 246-275; Jessie Bernard, "Note on Changing Life Styles, 1970-1974," *Journal of Marriage and the Family* 37, no. 3 (August 1975): 582-593; Elmer Spreitzer and Lawrence E. Riley, "Factors Associated with Singlehood," *Journal of Marriage and the Family* 36, no. 3 (August 1974): 533-542; and Peter Stein, *Single in America* (Englewood Cliffs, N.J.: Prentice-Hall, 1976).

Lilith speaks of the abundant opportunities she has had as a single when she says:

> There are so many things I want to do. Now that I've completed school and am making a good living, there is fun to be had. I've started a dance class, learned pottery, and joined a women's group. (Stein 1975:494)

Failure to marry used to be discussed in terms of "rejects" who were possibly poor marriage risks (Kuhn 1948:250). Spinsterhood, especially, was attributed to lack of sexual appeal, inability to commit oneself to another person, and lesbianism (Duberman 1974:116). Another contributing factor is that more single women than men are heads of families and are supporting dependent relatives (Bernard 1975:592).

Men with low incomes tend to remain single, as seen in Figure 14-2. A too-early marriage can trap a man. He is not able to find the time and leisure for intellectual growth amidst the constant pressures of earning a living to support a wife and family. When he has little time to write, to experiment, to explore and create, he feels cramped and harassed, as does a wife tied down too early to household responsibilities (Mueller 1955:1-2).

High levels of intelligence, education, and occupation are associated with singlehood among women (Spreitzer and Riley 1974). Far from

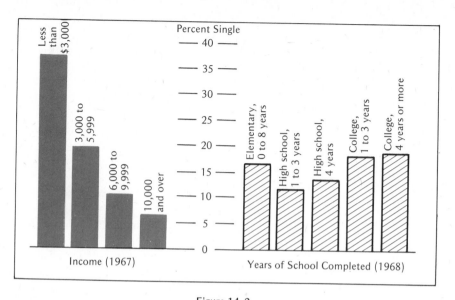

Figure 14-2
Percentage of Single Men Twenty-Five to Thirty-Four Years of Age, by Income and Education
Source: U.S. Bureau of the Census, "Marital Status and Family Status: March 1968," *Population Characteristics*, Current Population Reports, Series P-20, no. 187 (August 11, 1969), p. 2.

being "rejects", many of these bright young career women have chosen not to marry (Havens 1973:980), rather than to "marry down." For instance, 42 percent of women scientists and engineers have not married, in contrast to only 7 percent of their male counterparts (David 1973:82).

The number of unmarried men and women under 25 who are living together has increased rapidly since 1960. A significant minority of the 60,000 young adults living with members of the opposite sex are in college (Glick 1975:9). Half of the men (50.8 percent) and four out of ten women (39.8 percent) entering American universities in the fall of 1974 approved of living together before marriage, and similar percentages of both sexes thought that sex is all right if the people like each other (Cooperative Institutional Research Program 1975:132).

Students who live together on campus are found to be less apt to attend church, more likely to identify with a liberal life style, and to be drug users (Henze and Hudson 1974:722–735). One-third of the 1,100 cohabiting students on another state univeristy campus reported that they have lived with a member of the opposite sex at one time or other. These cohabiting students differed little from their noncohabiting counterparts in terms of family and community background or levels of intellectual and emotional functioning. In fact, cohabitation is interpreted by the authors of the research report as "a natural addition to these students' interpersonal experience" (Peterman, Ridley, and Anderson 1974:344). Studies in 1959 and 1973 of students in a liberal coeducational college found that the women's earlier conservative standards had changed and had become more like those of the men a dozen or more years later. In the 1973 questionnaires 66.7 percent of the students, in contrast to 19.2 percent of the 1959 sample, approved of premarital intercourse for women. Furthermore, those students with high self-esteem reported more coital partners than did those with low self-esteem (Perlman 1974:470–473). Coeds who seek contraceptive help are found, significantly, to be those who (1) endorse the right of the individual to choose his or her own sexual life style; (2) believe themselves to be attractive to men; and (3) are committed to their lovers as future marriage partners. The researchers conclude that "these three variables seem to be part of a general acceptance of one's own sexuality" (Reiss, Banwart, and Foreman 1975:628).

It is too early to tell whether today's single young adults will never marry, or whether they are merely postponing marriage until they feel personally ready for it. It could be that establishing his or her full autonomy as a person—educationally, occupationally, sexually, and emotionally—before undertaking the responsibilities of marriage, is the young modern's response to the too-early marriage so widely condemned as unstable.

Appraising love feelings

Love feelings are difficult to appraise during the young adult years when they are confused and intertwined with maturing sex drives. In a culture that allows freedom of access between the sexes from an early age and sees love as a basis for marriage, it becomes imperative to understand and to gauge love as best one can. By the late teens and twenties a young person has known many kinds of love, from intense, short-lived infatuations to longer lasting attachments that continue over the years. Twenty points of comparison between infatuation and love are summarized in Table 14–6.

One of the most important things a person learns within the family during the years of childhood and adolescence is to love.

> By the time boy meets girl, a great deal has happened to both of them to make them ready for their interest in each other. In fact, by that time they both are old hands at loving, in many ways. Each has grown up through the phases of emotional maturity to the place where he and she are capable of loving and being loved. In a real sense you *grow* into love, both individually and as couples. (Duvall 1963:47)

Love develops over time in a given relationship, too. Reiss (1960)

Table 14-6
Differences Between Infatuation and Love

Infatuation	Love
1. Is the term applied to past attachments, often	1. Is the term used to refer to a current attachment, usually
2. Focuses frequently on quite unsuitable persons	2. Object of affection is likely to be a suitable person
3. Parents often disapprove	3. Parents tend to approve
4. Feelings of guilt, insecurity, and frustration are frequent	4. Is associated with feelings of self-confidence, trust, and security
5. Tends to be self-centered and restricted	5. Kindlier feelings toward other people generally are associated
6. Narrowly focuses on only a few highly visible or fantasied traits	6. Broadly involves the whole personality
7. Most frequent among young adolescents and immature persons	7. Grows through the years with emotional maturity
8. Simultaneous attachments to two or more at the same time are possible	8. Loyalty centers in mutual commitment and involvement
9. Can reoccur soon after a previous affair is over	9. May slowly develop again after a previous lover has gone
10. Boredom is frequent when sexual excitement dies down	10. An ongoing sense of being alive when together precludes boredom
11. Partners depend on external amusement for fun	11. Joy is in many common interests and in each other
12. Little change in the relationship over time	12. Relationship changes and grows with ongoing association
13. Shallow sensations come and go	13. Deepening feelings provide steady warmth as more of life is shared
14. Problems and barriers are usually disregarded	14. Problems are tackled and worked out as they arise
15. Romantic illusions have little regard for reality	15. Faces reality with faith in growth and improvement
16. Tends to last only a short time	16. Tends to last over a long period of time
17. Little mutual exploration of personality values and aspirations	17. Shares hopes and dreams, feelings and meanings
18. May be stereotyped "romance for romance's sake"	18. Tends to be highly individual, unique, and person-centered
19. Can exploit the other as a person	19. Has a protective, nurturing, caring concern
20. A poor basis for marriage	20. Enough to build a marriage on, perhaps—if other things are right

Source: Evelyn Millis Duvall and Reuben Hill, *When You Marry*, rev. ed. (New York: Association Press; Boston: D.C. Heath and Company, 1967), pp. 40–41, quoted with permission.

has proposed the "wheel theory of the development of love" in which (1) the initial rapport between two people leads to their (2) revealing themselves to one another, whereupon they become (3) mutually dependent and thereby (4) fulfill their personality needs. These four processes turn one into the next and constantly reoccur in a circular pattern, carrying the two deeper into love. Or, the wheel slows as the relationship weakens; less rapport decreases self-revelation, mutual dependency, and need fulfillment.

Borland (1975) proposes a "clockspring alternative model" to the wheel theory of love development, with one's "real self" at the center of the spring. She defines the real self as "the total self as the individual perceives himself. This self concept includes not only his ideal self—what he thinks he should be—but also such elements as what he would like to be, how he believes others perceive him, his aspirations and regrets, his positive and negative attributes" (Borland 1975:291). The four processes (rapport, self-revelation, mutual dependency, and meeting of personality needs) wind the lovers into closer and more intimate understanding of each other's real inner selves. The more tightly the relationship winds around the person's real self, the more difficult it is to unwind. A love relationship can wind and unwind and then wind again like a clock spring—in constantly pulsating, demoralizing or revitalizing involvement (Figure 14-3).

Becoming involved as a pair

Occasionally one hears of a couple who "fell in love at first sight," married within a few days, and lived happily ever after. Usually the process of becoming a pair is neither that simple, nor so fast. Social scientists who have studied the progressive involvement of couples (see Chapter 9), are able to trace the process of pair formation through dating and courtship, in a series of steps that lead to marriage.

Lewis (1973) has brought together major findings about couple involvement in a premarital dyadic formation framework consisting of six sequential achievements:

1. The achievement of perceiving similarities (in each other's socio-cultural background, values, interests, and personality);

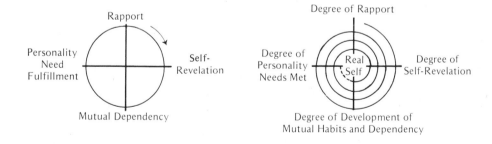

Reiss's Wheel Theory   Borland's Clockspring Model

Figure 14-3
The Wheel Theory and the Clockspring Models of Love Development

Source: Ira L. Reiss, "Toward a Sociology of the Heterosexual Love Relationship," *Journal of Marriage and the Family* 22, no. 2 (May 1960): 139-145 and Dolores M. Borland, "An Alternative Model of the Wheel Theory," *The Family Coordinator* 24, no. 3 (July 1975): 289-292.

2. The achievement of pair rapport (as seen in the couple's ease of communication, positive evaluations of each other, satisfaction with their relationship, and validation of themselves by one another);
3. The achievement of openness between partners through mutual self-disclosure;
4. The achievement of role-taking accuracy (competence in mutual empathy);
5. The achievement of interpersonal role-fit (as evidenced by the pair's observed similarity of personalities, role complementarity, and need complementarity);
6. The achievement of dyadic crystallization (as seen in the pair's progressive involvement, functioning as a dyad, boundary establishment, mutual commitment to one another, and identity as a couple).

Longitudinal studies of dating pairs on campus over a period of two years found substantial support for the six-step formulation in the experience of student couples' progressive involvement (or breakup). Figure 14-4 is a schematic presentation of the six dating pair processes and possible outcomes in terms of pair continuance or dissolution.

Friends and family members push promising pairs together when they invite the two, as a couple, to social events, family meals and trips; assume that the pair will come together; comment on what a nice pair the two make together; and tell them that they are "made for each other." The positive social reactions of significant others enhance the couple's commitment, their boundary maintenance, dyadic functioning, value consensus, and dating-courtship status. As the pair internalize the social acceptance of their relationship, they are launched into a still more permanent union (Lewis 1973).

Systematic study of communication among casual dating couples, seriously dating pairs, and marriage-bound couples shows that communication develops within the dating relationship, so that marriage-bound pairs are more able to discuss and manage possible conflict than are couples at earlier stages in the courtship process. The researcher suggests that couples at later stages of dating have not only gone through developmental processes successfully but that they have also survived what might be a filtering or selective process (Krain 1975).

Selecting a marriage partner

Couples may break up at any stage of their association (Figure 14-4). Those who continue on into marriage proceed through the dating and courtship process with some mutual feeling that they are "right for each other." Mate selection has been studied for many years. In repeated research only two significant factors have remained constant—homogamy and propinquity.

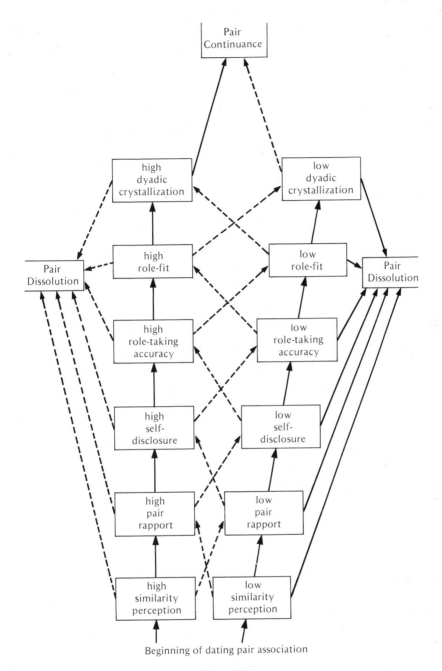

Figure 14–4

Game Tree Model of Couple Involvement or Dissolution

Source: Robert A. Lewis, "A Longitudinal Test of a Developmental Framework for Premarital Dyadic Formation," *Journal of Marriage and the Family* 35, no. 1 (February 1973): 19. Copyright 1973 by National Council on Family Relations. Reprinted by permission.

Folklore has it that opposites attract. Actually, marriage partners tend to be like one another in physical, psychological, and social characteristics. Homogamy, the tendency for marriage partners to have similar characteristics, has been found in hundreds of studies of many thousands of couples over several decades of the twentieth century. Hollingshead (1950) includes a bibliography of studies of homogamy up through the late 1940s. He suggests that racial mores divide possible marriage partners into two pools of one's own and other racial groups, the tendency being for an individual to fish for a mate only in his or her own racial pool. Religion divides each race into even smaller pools. In the United States, the overwhelming tendency is for Jews to marry Jews, Catholics to marry Catholics, and to a somewhat lesser degree Protestants to marry Protestants. Ethnic origins further limit an individual's marital choice. Social class and education decrease still further the size of the pools of eligibles from which a person is most likely to find a marriage partner. In most cases, a person eventually marries someone very similar to himself (Hollingshead 1950:627).

Studies and census reports over the past 25 years find that the tendency for like to marry like still holds in the majority of cases. In 1970 less than one percent of all marriages in the United States were interracial. This represented a slight increase over 1960 figures. At that time, four-tenths of one percent of couples had married across racial lines (U.S. Bureau of the Census 1970). Interracial marriages may continue to increase somewhat, as opportunities increase for members of minority races to get an education, earn a good income, and become acceptable in social circles where potential mates are found.

Interfaith marriages are hard to estimate because the 50 states do not require information about the religious affiliations of applicants for a marriage license. Cavan (1970) hypothetically suggests the probabilities of interfaith marriage by the nature of the in-groups involved. These may be hostile, indifferent, or friendly to each other. They may show a strong preference for marriage within their own group (endogamy); or they may endorse preferential endogamy or relatively permissive endogamy (Table 14–7).

Propinquity (living nearby) is a powerful factor in mate selection. Americans tend to marry their neighbors and associates at school and work. Over the years studies of both rural and urban populations in the several regions of the country show a continuing tendency for marrying couples to come from the same county, or from within 20 city blocks of one another (Bossard 1932–33; Davie and Reeves 1938–39; Kennedy, 1942–43; McClusky and Zander 1940; Mitchell 1941; Clarke 1952; Catton and Smircich 1964; and Clayton 1975). Mobile as Americans are, when they reach the point in their lives for serious courting and getting ready to marry, they choose someone nearby to be close to.

Table 14-7

Probable Intermarriage Among Hostile, Indifferent, and Friendly In-Groups

	In-Group A: hostile to other in-groups; strongly endogamous	In-Group B: indifferent to other in-groups; preferential endogamy	In-Group C: friendly to other in-groups; permissive endogamy
In Group D: Hostile to other in-groups; strongly endogamous	No intermarriages	Almost no intermarriages	Few intermarriages
In-Group E: Indifferent to other in-groups; preferential endogamy		Many intermarriages	Many intermarriages
In-Group F: Friendly to other in-groups; permissive endogamy			Almost no restrictions on intermarriage

Source: Ruth Shonle Cavan, "Concepts and Terminology in Interreligious Marriage," *Journal for the Scientific Study of Religion* 9, no. 4 (Winter 1970): 314.

Becoming engaged

Getting engaged may seem like a pleasant "task" to set up for young adults, but it is a many-faceted responsibility that is not easy for many a couple. In-depth studies of couples approaching marriage consider three crucial tasks: (1) making oneself ready to take over the role of husband or wife; (2) disengaging oneself from especially close relationships that compete or interfere with commitment to the new marriage; and (3) adapting the patterns of gratification of premarital life to patterns of the newly formed couple relationship. To prepare themselves for marriage there must be a shift from self-orientation to mutuality and the development of a couple identity by the end of the engagement period (Rapoport 1964).

That engagement success is predictive of marriage success, is evident in the actual scores of both men and women participating in a longitudinal study of 666 couples from engagement to marriage by Burgess and Wallin (Table 14-8).

Engagement rituals contribute to the success of the engagement period. Many engaged pairs share the rituals of their respective families as a way of giving a sense of belonging to both families, and also as a way of selecting those common rituals that both may enjoy and want to continue in their own family-to-be. Having Sunday dinner with his or her family, participating in family celebrations, going on family picnics, and attending church and community functions with one or the other family are illustrations of the way rituals in the engagement weave the couple into the larger family life.

Table 14-8
Relation Between Engagement Success and Marital Success for Men and Women
(Percentage Distribution for 666 Couples)

Engagement success scores	Men			Women		
	Marriage success score			Marriage success score		
	Low	Intermediate	High	Low	Intermediate	High
High (180 and over)	0.0	16.0	84.0	0.0	9.1	90.9
Median (150–159)	6.7	38.7	54.7	6.7	32.2	61.1
Low (100–109)	40.0	40.0	20.0	28.6	57.1	14.3

Source: Ernest W. Burgess and Paul Wallin, *Engagement and Marriage* (Chicago: J. B. Lippincott Company, 1953), excerpts from Table 81, p. 547.

Some engagement rituals are oriented toward the future—anticipating and preparing for the couple's marriage and family life. Ritualized house-hunting, Saturday afternoon window-shopping, contributing to the piggy bank for special funds, calling on recently married friends, having a series of premarital conferences, and attending courses for engaged couples, all are practices that tend to become future-oriented rituals during the engagement period.

A couple may move into marriage from a personal understanding that may have been tested in a period of living together, without the formality of an engagement. But by the time they marry they will have accomplished three important tasks. Specifically, they will have: (1) established themselves as a pair—in their own eyes and in the eyes of both families and of their mutual friends, (2) worked through intimate systems of communication that allow for exchange of confidences, an increasing degree of empathy, and the consequent ability to predict each other's responses, (3) planned specifically for the marriage that lies ahead, both in practical matters—deciding where and on what they will live; and in the realm of values—reaching a consensus on how the common life will be lived.

Being married

A bride and groom may be married barefoot at the edge of a beach, on a mountain ski slope, under a flowering tree, in a quick civil ceremony in the office of a justice of the peace, or in a conventional ceremony in the bride's church with some or all of the trappings of a church wedding: long white bridal gown and veil, bridesmaids and ushers, music, flowers, one or more officiating clergy, and members of both families and their friends present.

College-educated middle-class couples were the innovators who introduced the "new weddings" (Seligson 1973) that break with tradition and follow the idiosyncratic ideas of the young pair. The overwhelming majority of weddings in upper-class families have remained rigidly conventional throughout recent decades. Most marriages of people in the Social Register are solemnized in church weddings—only a small percentage in civil ceremonies (Blumberg and Paul 1975). Americans in all social classes spend billions of dollars annually on weddings and on the accompanying activities. It is estimated that the father of the bride spends an average of $1,666 for the expenses of the wedding day (Davidson 1966). A working man has been known to spend thousands of hard-earned dollars on an elaborate wedding for his only daughter with the idea that "nothing is too good for our little girl." Other families and their young adults prefer to use the money that might have gone into an expensive wedding for furnishing the couple's first home. One harassed father is said to have offered his daughter a check for five hundred dollars if she and her husband-to-be would elope.

Whatever the type of ceremony and its social accompaniments, the most important factors are the persons involved, rather than the things. A wedding that is planned to meet the needs of the situation as well as the preferences of the couple and their families is a multifaceted responsibility involving numerous specific decisions (Duvall and Hill 1960: 171–191). These choices are usually made by the couple and their families, the bride and her parents taking the major responsibility for the social aspects of the affair. The newly-married pair now enter the establishment phase of the family life cycle, facing all of the developmental tasks it holds for them—as individuals and as a pair (Chapter 9).

Development tasks of families
launching young adults

As they always have, most families today play active roles—over a considerable period of time—in getting their young people successfully launched into the world. While the first child is busy getting established as an autonomous young adult, there are probably one or more younger children still in the family, each with his or her own developmental tasks to accomplish. So, the family's tasks involve not only assisting the young adult to become successfully autonomous, but also maintaining a home base in which the other members of the family can thrive.

Family developmental tasks at the launching-center stage are:

1. Rearranging physical facilities and resources
2. Meeting the expenses of a launching-center family
3. Reallocating responsibilities among grown and growing children
4. Coming to terms with themselves as husband and wife

5. Maintaining open systems of communication within the family and between the family and others
6. Widening the family circle through release of young adult children and recruitment of new members by marriage
7. Reconciling conflicting loyalties and philosophies of life.

Rearranging physical facilities and resources

These are the accordion years of family life. The young adult's room lies empty through the college year, or while he is away for service, only to suddenly come alive during a holiday or a leave, when the young person and his or her friends swoop in for a few days and nights. The family goes along on an even keel for some weeks and then must mobilize itself and all of its resources for a wedding, or a graduation, or both, which in turn will keep the household humming and the house bulging at the seams.

The physical plant is sorely taxed at this stage. The family car that the father uses to get to work, and that is needed for the weekly shopping, is in constant demand by the young man or woman of the family whose engagements far and wide loom large in importance during the launching stage. Teenage siblings clamor for their share of the use of the car, the telephone, the television set, and the living room, until, as one harassed father described it, "This is the stage of life when a man is dispossessed in his own home." A mother comments somewhat ruefully that she doesn't mind the noise and the expense of young people in the home, but she will be glad to regain the use of her own living room when the courting couples have finally found homes of their own. Few families complain when facilities are sorely taxed at this stage of family living, but the fact remains that for many, the flexible rearrangement of available resources to meet the variety of functions within families at the launching-center stage is a task indeed.

Meeting the expenses of a launching-center family

With some exceptions, families at this stage are carrying their peak load of family expenses. These are the years when the young adult needs financial help to carry him or her through college or other educational programs, to get specialized training and experience, to get established during the "starvation period" of any of the professions, to pay union initiation fees and dues as workers, and to finance the wedding and the new home-in-the-making. Such costs are over and above the already established expenditures budgeted for the family. Many young people today help by earning what they can, as young adults always have, but few are in a position to contribute heavily to the family budget at the very time that they are establishing themselves independently.

Family expenditures are highest when the oldest child is about 19 in families of one, two, or three children. Costs mount until this period and rapidly decline as the children are launched. Only the family with no children escapes this peak load that comes typically 20 to 25 years after the parents' marriage (Figure 14–5).

A professional or business man is, fortunately, at the height of his earning power; but clerical, sales persons, operatives, and service workers now are earning less than they did at an earlier period (Oppenheimer 1974: 236). So, some supplementation may be necessary to carry the costs of launching-center functions.

The husband may work overtime as a laboring man, get a summer job as a teacher, or try to fit a part-time job in with his regular position. His wife now is possibly in the labor force. The young adult and other children in the family may have jobs of some kind on a part-time basis while in school and full-time after their education is completed. These sources of income may not be sufficient to meet such special costs as those involved in an expensive wedding or college tuition and fees. The family may float a loan, borrow on life insurance, increase the mortgage on the house, or tighten its belt wherever it can to meet the current emergencies. Providing for a family at the launching-center stage is a challenging task, as few will deny.

Reallocating responsibilities among grown and growing children in the family

Young adults and older teenagers thrive on coping with real responsibilities of their own. This is the stage when father and mother can sit back and let the children run their own affairs in many a situation. At this time the "smothering mom" is a liability, and a father who is too prone to "snoopervise" is a threat to the autonomy of the young adult. The happy family at the launching-center stage is one in which tasks and responsibilities are assumed by members of the family on the basis of interest, ability, and availability.

The successful accomplishment of this task depends on the flexibility of the roles of the two parents as well as on the growing ability of the young adult(s) and younger siblings to assume and carry through effectively the tasks of the household. As young adults begin to take on more real responsibility for their own and for the family's welfare, the parents play the complementary roles of letting go and standing by with encouragement, reassurance, and appreciation.

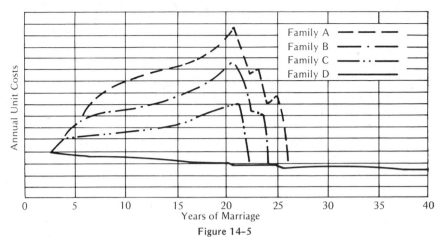

Figure 14-5

Hypothetical Annual Cost of Supporting Four Families for Forty Years

Source: Howard F. Bigelow, *Family Finance* (Chicago: J.B. Lippincott Company, 1953), p. 333.

Family A consists of a husband and wife who bring up three children, a boy born at the end of the second year, a girl born at the end of the fourth year, and a boy born at the end of the sixth year of their married life.

Family B consists of a husband and wife who bring up two children, a boy born at the end of the second year and a girl born at the end of the fourth year of their married life.

Family C consists of a husband and wife who bring up one child, a boy born at the end of the second year of their married life.

Family D has no children.

It is assumed in each case that the husband and wife were married when he was twenty-five and she was twenty-three, and that each family supports each of its children for nineteen years, providing them with a high school education. On the nineteenth birthday, each child leaves home and becomes self-supporting.

Rediscovering themselves as husband and wife

Parents often live vicariously through all the terrors and threats of emancipation that beset their young people, at the same time that they as people are living through the "crisis of the middle years."

Being middle-aged today is a far more complex business than it used to be in the day of Whistler's mother. Then, a woman in her forties was physically and psychologically ready to retire to her knitting. Today's middle-aged woman, thanks to better nutrition, medical services, lightened burdens at home, and shifting feminine roles, still has a "head of steam up," both physiologically and emotionally. She is apt to be vigorous, often feeling better than she has in her whole life. Even menopause, dreaded by women in earlier eras, now can be taken in stride (Chapter 15). The woman with nearly grown children has found her strengths and her weaknesses. She has tasted the sweetness of affection and learned to enjoy creative companionship with her husband and children. Husband and wife, now more often than they have in years, work together on projects and have stimulating exchanges of ideas.

Now, suddenly, before she has quite prepared herself for it, her children are no longer children; they are taking their confidences and their loves outside. Her husband, now at the peak of his business or career, is engrossed in his work. Her house is in order. Where does the middle-aged woman go from here? What loves can take the place of those so suddenly torn away? What tasks will absorb the energies and the skills that cry for channelling? If she clings to her children, she is a "mom." If her interest in her husband's career becomes too absorbing, she is a "meddler." If she spends her time in a dizzy round of matinees, bridge parties, and beauty parlors, she is a "parasite." If she devotes herself to a quest for her soul through various cults and sundry religions, she is suspect. Her salable skills are at least two decades old—largely unused and perhaps out of date since she left them to get married. As a modern, liberated woman her sexual demands on her husband may leave her frustrated and further threaten him with a sense of personal inadequacy (Chilman 1968). It may be partly for these reasons that by the age of 40, according to the Marriage Council of Philadelphia, 50 percent of the husbands and 26 percent of the wives have had at least one extramarital affair, and some 63 percent of women married for more than a decade claim that they are less happy than they were when they first married (Marriage Council Newsletter September 1969:1).

There is evidence to indicate that men also face a crisis in the middle years, for the basic problem is the same for men and women alike. Briefly it is this. Throughout their lusty twenties and pushy thirties most American men, driving to "get ahead," fasten their eyes on distant goals and dream hopefully of success, although few reach the top. Those who do often struggle to maintain and improve their position in the competitive scheme of things where others are always jockeying for more power and prestige. The glamour dies in the struggle, and for too many American men in their forties and fifties "success" is no more than ashes in the mouth.

The multitude of hardworking fathers who never reach the top must face the reality of their limitations and accept their lot for what it is, mediocre and bitter although it may be. "I am just a minor guy in a minor rut, living life in a minor key," says one man.

Men are further troubled by signs of diminished masculinity—an attribute highly prized by American males. The slowing up characteristic of the middle-aged father—seen in contrast with the youthful vigor of his growing sons and daughters—is personally threatening to many men. Lessened potency and sexual excitation are too frequently attributed to monogamous monotony. The "dangerous period" for men comes when a man feels he must prove his virility to himself, even, if need be, with more youthful partners. With the burden of guilt that this carries, is it any wonder that he is too easily upset by his son's girl troubles or his daughter's involvements? The time of launching, today, is unfortunate both for parents and for young adults. Two types of crises in collision mean trouble in many homes.

The question "How well have we done by our children?" is pertinent. Through many sleepless nights, parents grapple with the haunting fear that somehow, some way, they might have done a better job with those children who are now beyond their parental ministrations. Parents recognize that the family at the launching stage is being evaluated on its success through its products, the children. Yet the problems that go with achieving full adulthood maritally, vocationally, and intellectually are so many and the solutions so few!

Someday, perhaps, we will know more about these things. We will be prepared for the head-on collisions of children and their parents bent on urgent, not-to-be-denied tasks. Today we stumble along doing amazingly well, considering all the threats with which we live in the launching-center stage.

Maintaining communication within the family

Both happily and unhappily married men and women feel that communication contributes more to happiness in marriage than any other factor. Being in love with each other is ranked second in importance for marital happiness, and their emotional need for each other is rated third. By contrast, such things as possessions and good food are considered least important (Landis 1969).

Being able to get through to one another in the family is especially important during the launching stage. This is the time when the young adult is emerging from his family and is working through some of the most important and most complex tasks of his life. The young person who can freely bring his questions and his alternative solutions to his parents as sounding boards can get invaluable help from their perspective.

At the same time, the parents face the possibility that critical young adults will challenge their way of life. As Russell Baker wryly observes, "Now they are trapped between grandfather's wheezing and the homiletic tedium of two or three young fogies denouncing the shallowness of their goals" (Baker 1967).

Young adults and their parents often disagree on matters that affect them both. More young than older adults hold liberal attitudes about religion, abortion, premarital sex, and smoking marijuana (NBC National News Poll 1976). It is not unusual for parents to question their nearly-grown sons' and daughters' choice of vocation, intimate associates, marriage partners, their use of time and money, and many other decisions that young adults feel they have a right to make on their own. When one or both parents have difficulty freeing their young adult children to live their own lives, communication between the generations in the family is especially difficult.

Peer pressures on young people and their parents often pull in opposite directions, further complicating family interaction. So, this developmental task is difficult to achieve satisfactorily. It can be successfully accomplished if a solid foundation of good parent-child relationships has been established, and if now, at the "proving time," the young adults feel that whatever happens, their family is back of them—with faith in their ability to work things through and the willingness to look at any situation with loving concern.

Widening the family circle

With the first marriage of one of the children of the family comes the first experience of sudden expansion. The extended family now includes both the new family unit being established and also, with more or less interaction, the family of the son- or daughter-in-law. The family in its earlier expanding stages took upon itself one child at a time (except in multiple births), and that as a tiny infant. The widening of the family circle at the launching-center stage is dramatically different in two major respects: (1) the addition is multiple, consisting of the entire family of in-laws, and (2) the additional persons are at varying levels of maturity, with a preponderance of adults.

The situation is complicated by the fact that while the young adult of the one family is intimately known within his or her own family, he or she remains for a while an outsider to the young mate's family of orientation. If there is too close a bond between one young adult and his or her parents, it is difficult for the new unit to achieve equilibrium, as we see in the following analysis:

> Every married couple belongs to three families. They belong first of all to themselves. They are the *we* of the new family they are founding together. But, at the same time, they belong also to *his* family and to *hers*. If they are to establish a strong family unit of their own, they must inevitably realign their loyalties to the place where *our* family comes before either *yours* or *mine*.
>
> This is the elemental triangle of married living. Unless the cohesive force in the new family unit is stronger than that which ties either of the couple to the parental home, the founding family is threatened, as we see in the figures [Figure 14-6].

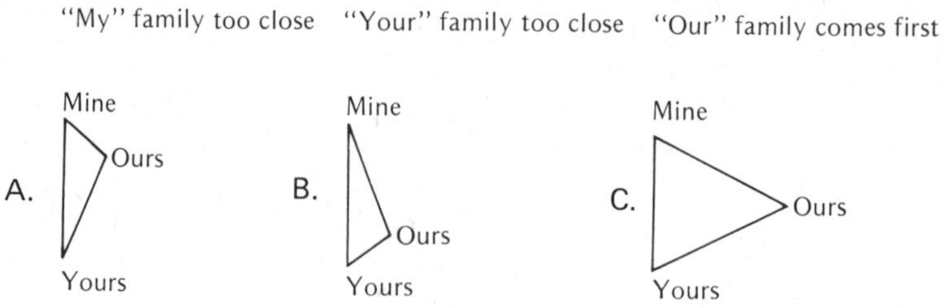

"My" family too close   "Your" family too close   "Our" family comes first

Figure 14-6
The Elemental Triangle of Married Living
Source: Evelyn Millis Duvall, *In-Laws: Pro and Con* (New York: Association Press, 1954), p. 279.

In Figure 14-A, *you* have in-law trouble because *my* family is too close. It may be because I am still immature and not ready to emancipate myself from my parental home. It may be that one or more members of my family are possessive and find it difficult to let me go. It may be that circumstances within my family require from me more loyalty and attention than I can comfortably give at the time that I am involved in building my own home and marriage. Whatever the reason, if the forces pulling me/us toward loyalties to *my* home are too strong, the development of *our* common sense of identity is delayed or weakened.

In Figure 14-B, *your* family is too close, and so *I* have in-law trouble. Because *you* are bound so tightly to *your* family, I am pulled away from mine, and *we* make little progress in establishing *ours*.

In Figure 14-C, *our* family unit comes first in our joint loyalties. We are threatened neither by the ties that bind us to *your* family, nor by the bonds that unite us to *mine*. We are able to make progress as a new family because the force of our common identification pulls us out and away together into a home of our own. Now we can share in the common heritage of both your family and mine because we are not threatened by the pull from either. Only thus are *we* free to enjoy being members of the entire extended family, without the stress of in-law strains. (Duvall 1954:278-279).

Reconciling conflicting value systems

During this period a young person is apt to try out conflicting ways of life, in an effort to test his background and to catch a glimpse of his potential future. At only one time within his life span—when he is being launched from his home base into a life of his own—is the young adult free to pull loose from old allegiances without basic threats and instabilities. The young man or woman critically reviews his life within his family of orientation and makes comments from time to time that may severely challenge his parents and their ways of dealing with him.

The two generations even see their differences differently. Members of the younger generation want to establish their own values in line with the changing world around them (Chapter 3), so they stress the differences between themselves and their elders. Their parents are concerned with having "social heirs," so they tend to minimize conflicting value systems that might jeopardize the cohesion of the family (Bengtson and Kuypers 1971).

However, evidence from a number of substantial studies points to a remarkable congruence of values and attitudes between the young adult and parental generations (*Center Magazine* 1969). Less than one-fourth of the most liberal students feel that the differences between their own values and those of their parents are very great. The majority of 18- to 24-year-old men and women in and out of college clearly identify more with their families than with their own generation, according to their own reports (Table 14-9).

Some young people get into trouble as they sample strange new ways. Queenie, in Noel Coward's *This Happy Breed*, runs off with a married man, is deserted, tries to make a go of running a tea shop in southern France, and finally is brought back home to a reconciliation by a loyal lover who grew up next door. Not all youthful mistakes are as critical. Not all turn out so well in the end. But in some way or other most young people blunder as they try their wings and attempt to fly off into life on

Table 14-9
Young Adults' Values and Identification with Their Families and Peers

	No college	Practical college*	Forerunner college†
Differences between parents' and your values:			
Very great	15%	11%	24%
Moderate	41	49	51
Slight	44	40	25
Identification and sense of solidarity with:			
Family	82%	78%	65%
Own generation	60	65	68

Source: *Fortune*-Yankelovich Survey, "What They Believe," *Fortune* (January 1969): 70–71, 179–181.
*Students in practical colleges have definite career plans (business, engineering, etc.).
†Students in forerunner colleges have intangible career plans (arts and humanities largely).

their own. Parents who are patient while these efforts are being made are of far more help than those who stand by clucking their fears as the fledgling leaves the nest. Families who stand by, offering assurance, encouragement, and help as needed, especially in any of life's firsts (first formal party, first job, first trip away from home, and the rest), give their young people the stable home base that is required for a successful launching.

While the young adults are gaining the strength to live independently and showing by their words and actions that their lives are not going to be exact copies of those of their parents, the younger children in the family may be torn by the obvious conflicts between their parents and their older siblings. It is normal for younger children in the family to value highly the attitudes and judgments of their older brothers and sisters.

Families that succeed in maintaining a secure home base for the younger members of the family during the launching-center stage are those that attempt to accept comfortably the way of life the young adult has chosen. They do not feel too threatened by it. They help a younger sibling to see that there are many good ways to live a life, and that when his time comes, he too will find his way for himself.

Age is not all decay; it is the ripening, the swelling of fresh life within, that withers and bursts the husks.

George Macdonald

the second half of marriage

part five

Sing a song of seasons!
Something bright in all!
Flowers in the summer,
Fires in the fall.

Robert Louis Stevenson.

Middle-aged parents in an empty nest

chapter fifteen

The family life cycle stage of the middle years starts with the departure of the last child from the home and continues to the retirement of the husband or the death of one of the spouses. This may be a period of only a few months or years, as in the case of the late launching of a son or daughter or of the early retirement of the man of the house. The stage may stop abruptly with the premature death of either husband or wife. It may be delayed indefinitely by a dependent child who stays on at home.

In this latter half of the twentieth century, the period of the couple's middle years typically lasts longer than any other stage in the family life cycle. Up to the turn of the century, the likelihood was that a woman would be widowed before her last child left home; or that the mother would have died before seeing the first of her children married. Now the married couple have an average of 16 to 18 years together between the departure of their last child and the death of the first spouse (Figures 7-1, 7-2, 7-3; Table 15-1).

The husband and wife are usually close to 50 when they enter the postparental middle years and somewhere near their mid-sixties when the man's retirement takes them into the final stage of the family life cycle. Throughout the middle years the married couple alone constitute the nuclear family, maintaining their husband-wife interaction as the central interpersonal relationship. At this time, each occupies several positions with multiple roles in the family: husband, father, father-in-law, and grandfather; and wife, mother, mother-in-law, and grandmother, as well as son and daughter of aging parents. Husband and wife in the middle years are the generation between, with both younger and older members of the family looking to them for strength and support from time to time.

The departure of grown children from the home to establish their independence is a turning point for the family. It is a crisis in the sense that each member, and the family as a whole, enters a period in which new patterns must be established and former habits abandoned as inappropriate. However, Neugarten (1970:87) observes that when the empty nest stage comes at the expected time it represents not so much a crisis as a matter of timing and adjustment—to a normal aspect of the sequence and rhythm of the life cycle.

That middle-aged parents are new in this century, statistically speaking, is clearly shown in the 1890 column of Table 15-1. The typical wife

Table 15-1
Ages of Husband and Wife at Critical Stages in the Family Life Cycle in the United States, 1890, 1940, 1950, 1960, 1980

Stage of the family life cycle	1890	1940	1950	1960 (averages)	1980 (projections)
Median age of wife at:					
First marriage	22.0	21.5	20.1	20.1	19–21
Birth of last child	31.9	27.1	26.1	25.9	26–28
Marriage of last child	55.3	50.0	47.6	47.1	47–49
Death of husband	53.3	60.9	61.4	63.5	65–67
Median age of husband at:					
First marriage	26.1	24.3	22.8	22.3	21–23
Birth of last child	36.0	29.9	28.8	28.0	28–30
Marriage of last child	59.4	52.8	50.3	49.1	50–52
Death of wife	57.4	63.6	64.1	65.5	68–70

Source: Paul C. Glick, "The Life Cycle of the Family," *Marriage and Family Living* 17, no. 1 (February 1955): 3–9; Paul C. Glick, *American Families* (New York: John Wiley and Sons, 1957); Paul C. Glick and Robert Parke, Jr., "New Approaches in Studying the Life Cycle of the Family," *Demography* 2 (1965): 187–202; averages for 1960 and projections for 1980 derived from Bureau of the Census data with methods similar to those used for earlier years; see also Robert Parke, Jr. and Paul C. Glick, "Prospective Changes in Marriage and the Family," *Journal of Marriage and the Family* 29, no. 2 (May 1967): 249–256.

and husband of that era did not survive the marriage of their last child. Today more adults live out their life span, and since they have fewer children and have them early in the marriage, spend more years as middle-aged and older adults in an empty nest.

Four-fifths of the population growth in the United States between now and the year 2000 will be among people aged 35 and older, (Table 15-2). This means that middle-aged and older people will be more numerous and more highly visible, and that the empty nest stage of the family life cycle will be seen as normal and to be expected by more and more parents.

Developmental tasks of the postparental woman

The developmental tasks of the middle-aged woman have a biological basis in the gradual aging of the menopausal and postmenopausal woman; a cultural basis in the social pressures on and expectations of her; and a personal origin in the individual life-style the woman has developed over the years. Her personal aspirations are by nature idiosyncratic. Social expectations tend to follow certain patterns within a given culture, and can thus be anticipated and discussed.

Encouraging young adult sons and daughters to be autonomous

For 20 or more years the middle-aged wife and mother gave top priority and most of her time and attention to the bearing and rearing of her children. The last child to leave home makes obsolete her central mothering tasks and necessitates her undertaking new roles for the years ahead. Up to this point she has invested a great deal of emotional energy in her children. Now that they are no longer at home, her first tendency may be to follow them with her continuing maternal concern in ways that delay their full autonomy as young adults. Her first task, then, is to

Table 15-2
United States Population Growth by Age Groups, 1975 to 2000

Population by age groups	1975	2000 (estimates)	Percentage increase
Children and teenagers	74,839,000	80,743,000	8%
Young adults 20–34	50,169,000	54,925,000	9
Younger middle-aged 35–49	34,655,000	60,855,000	76
Older middle-aged 50–64	31,746,000	39,065,000	23
People 65 and over	22,262,000	28,842,000	30

Source: U.S. Bureau of the Census, and estimates of the U.S. News & World Report Economic Unit, "A Look at Americans in Year 2000," *U.S. News & World Report*, 3 March 1975, p. 35.

set her children free at the same time that she frees herself from her emotional need to be needed by her children. She must convert the formerly dependent mother-child relationship into one of mature inter-dependence, in which she and her grown children mutually support and encourage one another without intruding into one anothers' lives. She must learn to stand by, offering assistance only as it is requested; and she must avoid hovering over her grown sons and daughters with too smothering attention.

This task is easier for the mother who has been releasing her children to make their own decisions all through the years. It is hard for the mother who clings, and who refuses to let her children go, now that they have become adult. In either case, a mother can encourage her children to become autonomous by seeking other outlets for her need to provide nurturance. She may throw herself into other projects, into her career, and/or into community service and concern for children and youth generally. Freed of a consuming need to be needed by her own children, she can accept young adult sons and daughters, their husbands, wives, and children as dear friends whose independence is respected and promoted.

Maintaining a healthy sense of well-being

Menopause takes place sometime in a woman's late forties and early fifties. Biologically, menopause signals the close of the reproductive cycle, the cessation of menses, and the slowing down of ovarian functioning. The latter upsets the endocrine balance and brings on one or more of the familiar signs of the woman's "change of life": hot and cold flashes, sweating, excitability, and other symptoms. How well a middle-aged woman weathers her menopause depends on her success in adapting to its inevitable physical changes and those that are to come—changes in skin, hair, eyes, energy level, body tone, and weight gain. Middle-age once was defined as "that time of life when one stops growing everywhere except in the middle."

Many a modern woman finds that the middle years have their own charm. With a healthful regimen of weight control, regular exercise, well-balanced diet high in proteins, fresh fruits and vegetables, adequate rest, and whatever else her doctor prescribes to keep her fit, she feels as good now as she ever did. She has time now to do the things she has always enjoyed, and to develop new interests that keep her vitally alive.

A woman's sense of well-being is expressed in her grooming and clothes. She finds her own style, avoiding both dowdiness and ridiculous extremes in fashion. She learns to dress comfortably, suitably, and attractively, to please herself and others. Her successful adjustment is assured when she is able to recognize and enjoy the special bloom and the more relaxed pace of maturity.

Enjoying career and creative accomplishment

More than half of America's middle-aged women are employed. Some have been working for many years; others are newcomers to the working force at the empty nest stage of family life. Postparental wives help their husbands to build up the financial resources depleted during childbearing and rearing. Also rewarding is the sense of being productive and of making progress in line with their mature wisdom and talents. Other satisfactions can be found in being of service, in being creative, and in being recognized as competent on the job. Success in her work depends on how well the middle-aged woman allots the time and energy she gives to her job, to homemaking, and to other responsibilities. A sensible balance prevents strain and chronic fatigue or pressure.

Stanford University's 50-year study of 700 gifted women, initiated by Lewis Terman in the 1920s, shows that career women are more satisfied with their lives than women who have been full-time housewives. Of these talented women, now in their 50s and 60s, 79 percent of those who followed careers and not quite 20 percent of the homemakers are now highly satisfied (Stanford 1975). Extension programs of universities and community colleges and adult education programs in many places help mature women to upgrade their skills, if and when they reenter the labor force.

Creative activity in the arts, music, literature, sports, writing, and volunteer work gives many women a sense of accomplishment that is not contingent on monetary reward. A wife can find personal satisfaction in working side by side with her husband as one or both of them run for public office, cooperate in a business or profession, or in community service. The woman left alone in her middle or later years welcomes the resurgence of strength that comes from taking part in the life around her in creative ways.

Relating to aging parents

Both middle-aged parents may have aging parents. In most American families, the wife assumes major responsibility for older relatives, her husband contributing whatever help he is inclined to give. Theoretically this is a family developmental task that both members of the middle-aged couple jointly assume. Actually, it is the wife who is generally expected to look after aging relatives as one of her social roles as wife. It is she who keeps in touch by telephone, letter, and visiting. It is she who remembers birthdays and other special occasions. It is she who serves as a buffer between the demands of the older and the younger generations in the family. It is she who, in consultation with other kinfolk, helps both sets of aging parents to find satisfactory supports for their failing powers.

The various social classes have different ways of viewing this task and of accomplishing it. In upper-class families the elders live well by themselves, they take an interest in but are not dependent on their grown sons and daughters. In middle-class families unresolved parent-child conflicts may surface and cause problems when the older and middle generations are thrown too close together. In lower-class families three generations often live together, the grandparents keeping house and looking after the children while the middle-aged support them all (Havighurst 1972:105).

The time comes in all families when failing health and eventually death overtake the aging members of the family. It is usually the midde-aged daughter or daughter-in-law who steps in to give supportive care during critical and chronic illnesses and at the time of bereavement and adjustment to widowhood. These critical tasks take precedence over others in the expectations of most middle-aged women and their families.

Keeping social life satisfying

The postparental wife is free at last to use her leisure time as she herself chooses. While she was rearing children, her social life was bounded on one side by her children's commitments (school, PTA, Little League, recitals, etc.), and on the other by the expectations and demands connected with her husband's work. Now that both children and job-related social activities are less demanding, a woman has the time and the resources with which to pursue her own interests, as soon as she discovers them.

She accomplishes this development task as she develops interests and skills that bring her special satisfaction, recognition, and a sense of fulfillment. She may throw herself entirely into some all-absorbing project, or she may balance active and passive, collective and solitary, service-motivated and self-indulgent pursuits. Many a middle-aged woman makes an art of friendship, keeping in touch with old friends, cultivating new ones among the refreshing personalities she meets, exchanging social invitations with people she enjoys, and becoming an increasingly friendly person who values her friends and enjoys being with them. Middle- and upper-class women make up the women's clubs that abound in American life. For the woman who enjoys structured activities, and who can handle the tensions, power groups, and personality problems that crop up from time to time in ongoing associations, this can be personally satisfying. As long as a woman keeps vitally alive and involved in something she finds rewarding, she is doing well.

Assuming civic and community responsibilities

Middle-aged women are often sought after as leaders in the community. Civic involvement fills the vacuum left by their recently departed grown sons and daughters, in many cases. At this stage of life a woman may take on responsibilities in church, social service organizations, or political groups for which she had little time before.

Civic involvement varies according to social class. Middle-class and upper-class women are generally more concerned with a wide variety of local, state, national and world affairs. Working-class women tend to have less interest in the social and civic life of the community except as it affects their husbands' work or their children's lives (Havighurst 1972: 99). With the spread of education, the upgrading of television programming, and the general increase of interest in social problems, more and more women of various social-class levels may be expected to play active roles as citizens.

Sooner or later every wife and mother faces her developmental tasks in her own way with the coming of her middle years. She is successful if she finds happiness and satisfaction at this stage of life. National surveys report that postparental women experience greater happiness and enjoyment of life than do women of similar age with one or more children still at home (Glenn 1975). For instance, when University of Michigan research teams asked, "Taken all together, how would you say things are these days—would you say that you are very happy, pretty happy, or not too happy?" more than four out of ten postparental wives and only three out of ten parental wives in the 50–59 year-old groups said they were "Very happy" (Table 15–3).

For the first time in her life a woman is now free to live on her own terms. For the first 20 or more years she did what her parents wanted her to do; for the next 20 years or so she did what her husband and children asked her to do. Now she and her husband are free to do what they want to do—if they can achieve the developmental tasks of this stage of life.

Developmental tasks of the middle-aged husband

A husband and father in the middle years finds some of his developmental tasks easier than the parallel tasks his wife has. It probably is easier for him than it is for her to encourage the autonomy of their chil-

Table 15-3
More Postparental than Parental Wives Say They Are 'Very Happy' in U.S. National Samples, 1972 and 1973.

Age groups	Parental	Postparental
40–49	42.5% (167)	48.2% (56)
50–59	29.4 (85)	41.9 (117)
40–59	38.1 (252)	43.9 (173)

Source: Combined data from the 1972 and 1973 General Social Surveys, conducted by the National Opinion Research Center, reported in Norval D. Glenn, "Psychological Well-being in the Postparental Stage: Some Evidence from National Surveys," *Journal of Marriage and the Family* 37, no. 1 (February 1975): 106.

dren, because the children have been her main responsibility through the years of their growing up. It usually is easier for a middle-aged man to find continuing satisfaction in his work than it is for his wife, whose employment may have been secondary to her homemaking responsibilities through the years.

Most men assign to their wives the social and familial aspects of their lives, expecting the woman of the house to give and respond to social invitations, to arrange for joint family functions, to look out for aging relatives, and to maintain contact with their friends and with their grown children's families. Increasing numbers of men are becoming involved in maintaining a pleasant home and in enriching their marriages (Chapter 4). In addition to these family developmental tasks, which they jointly assume with their wives, there are at least four personal developmental tasks that middle-aged husbands must achieve if they are to find happiness now and throughout the later years of life.

Keeping up his appearance
and health

There is no male menopause, since menopause is the cessation of menses. The middle-aged and older man, however, does experience a gradual diminution of gonadal functioning. A New York University Medical Center endocrinologist reports that about one-third (30–35 percent) of men experience a male climacteric between the ages of 58 and 68. This is a physiological condition that responds well to hormone therapy (Kupperman 1975:61). Twice as common in the middle-aged male is emotional and cultural anxiety about growing older. The man worries about his weight, his thinning hair, his waning virility. In the "frenzied fifties" he undergoes strains and frustrations that express themselves in ulcers and other illnesses, real or fantasied. He may nurse a continuing discontent with himself and undertake an unending search for self-esteem.

This is enough to give him a chronic feeling of fatigue, even when he is in fact not working unusually hard.

The middle-aged man who keeps up his appearance, upgrades his wardrobe, and pays attention to his grooming improves his self-image and feels better for it. Many a 50-year-old man goes in for regular exercise, periodic medical and dental checkups, and a well-balanced diet. Quite possibly his wife encourages these healthful practices and looks out for his well-being. As she expresses her pride in the way he looks and feels, he responds to her admiration and maintains an active interest in her and in their marriage. The middle years can be good ones, as soon as a man finds that he can enjoy maturity for all it has to offer.

Pursuing his job interests

By the time a man's children have grown and left home, he may be at the peak of his career as a business and professional man. He has learned what he can do and finds satisfaction in his competence. Or, he feels that he has gone as far as he can go in his present job, and may retool for a second career that offers more challenge and a greater future. Now that the family's expenses are not so great, he can take time off for the training he needs, with his wife's backing.

The crisis of the middle years lies in the discrepancy between a man's earlier dreams and his actual achievement. He may have to face the fact that he has gone as far as he will ever go and come to terms with reality without regret, recrimination, or discouragement. His satisfaction in his work is intensified when he feels needed and useful, when he is able to help younger men take over without feeling personally threatened, and as he lets established routines and experience replace his earlier over-zealous drive.

The blue-collar working man often finds his job monotonous after 20 or 30 years of the same operation. He may go after an advancement with some encouragement from his superiors, but his chances of employment elsewhere are not great in a time of general unemployment and of company reluctance to hire middle-aged and older men. A working man may give more of his time to his union and find some satisfaction in working with his fellow members to improve their situation.

Cultivating satisfying leisure-time activities

The middle-aged man probably has more leisure now than he has ever had. A shorter work week, less pressure to get ahead, and seniority built up over the years allow a man time for pleasure where he finds it. Now he has the resources to do some of the things he has always wanted to do. He may master some art or skill sufficiently well to gain recognition and a heightened sense of pride in his workmanship. He probably spends less time engaging in team sports and gets more pleasure from activities that he can carry on through the years—golf, tennis, fishing, boating, swimming, gardening, camping, travel, and the like.

It may be a temptation for some men to spend more time with a beer in front of the television set; to pass many an hour with "the boys" at the bar, or to try other passive ways of killing time—all of which bring less ongoing satisfaction than the more creative use of leisure time. A man is wise to balance active with sedentary leisure interests; to enjoy both solitary and social hours; to spend more time with his wife—doing together with her the things they both enjoy; and in general to use his leisure in ways that refresh and renew his own outlook on life.

Carrying community and
political responsibility

Middle-aged people carry the greater share of the obligations of citizenship. They have the greatest influence and tend to be sought after as leaders in a community's civic life (Havighurst 1972:98). Many a man enjoys keeping abreast of what is happening locally and on the wider scene. He sees much that should be done in government and may throw his own hat in the ring, or back some other person for a political office. He is at the age when his counsel is sought, so he may enjoy serving as a volunteer or as a board member in any of the many agencies that see to the needs of the community.

The man who is willing to keep alert and active during his middle years can reap the harvest of good living that he has sown in earlier years. He can relax now and enjoy the fruits of his labors, in the sense that "you can't take it with you." Now he can discover the richness of mature marriage, the satisfaction of fellowship with grown children, the warmth of friendships that have lasted over the years, the excitement of adventure and novel experience, and the rewards of productivity. None of these dividends "come due" in the middle years without some investment of himself. They are all satisfactions that grow out of successfully achieving the developmental tasks of this stage of life. When a man does a good job with these tasks, he finds that happiness is a by-product of his efforts. As long as there is life, there can be growth, and the middle years are no exception.

Family developmental tasks in
the middle years

The empty nest stage of the family life cycle has a full complement of family developmental tasks that are necessary for family continuity, survival, and growth. These family developmental tasks can be outlined briefly as:

1. Providing for comfortable, healthful well-being
2. Allocating resources for present and future needs
3. Developing patterns of complementarity
4. Undertaking appropriate social roles
5. Assuring marital satisfaction
6. Enlarging the family circle
7. Participating in life beyond the home
8. Affirming life's central values.

Providing for comfortable, healthful well-being

Most couples are home-owners by the time they have launched their children. Two out of three American families own their own homes, which they acquired while they were raising their children, in most cases. Now that the children have grown and gone, the chances are good that the middle-aged couple will stay on in their home for a number of reasons: (1) they feel that this is home for them; (2) they are near their work; (3) here they have familiar neighbors, friends, and ways of life established over the years; (4) their grown children return home for family celebrations and enjoy having a familiar home base; (5) the middle-aged couple provide continuity by maintaining the home site, keepsakes, traditions, memories, and customs that contribute much to family stability and enjoyment.

After 20 or 25 years or more of marriage a man and his wife should have learned what is important to them in a home. If they enjoy their yard with its garden, it should be part of their plans for the future, but if it has been primarily for the children and of little or no interest to either of the married pair, then this may be the time to move into an apartment or a less burdensome house. If they do move, they will need to look not only for present comfort and convenience, but also to the years ahead. Their task is to arrange for a home that reflects their interests, so that it becomes for both of them a satisfying place in which to live.

Remodeling the home after the children leave is a pleasant project for the middle-aged couple. Now that the place is theirs alone, it can be refurbished around their particular interests rather than in terms of what the children need. One of the upstairs bedrooms may become a cozy den or hobby center. The back porch may be closed in for intimate dining. They may decide to make a bedroom and bath on the first floor. Such an arrangement saves steps while they are alone and comes in handy when sickness strikes, or when aged relatives have to be given a home. The second floor may be rented out or closed off except for times when the grown children are home with their families. There is time and money now to remodel the kitchen with an eye to good management and efficient operation as well as to its function as living center of the home—with telephone at hand, a comfortable chair or two, and a pleasant place to eat. They may redecorate with an eye to entertaining freely, or to using home as a pleasant, comfortable haven from the world and its people. Whatever is done, it can express the needs, values, and interests of the husband and wife in their middle years and in the foreseeable future, when their own failing powers will call for convenient, safe housing facilities.

A man is more likely to develop a heart condition or cancer, or to have a stroke between the ages of 45 and 64 than ever before in his life (Figure 15-1). This means a long convalescence, unemployment—and a fresh awareness of the importance of good health habits, if he is lucky enough to get another chance. Let one of their friends or neighbors succumb to a heart attack or stroke and the couple is motivated as never before to protect their own health in every way they can by taking such measures as:

1. Getting regular daily exercise
2. Sharply reducing or stopping their smoking
3. Limiting their consumption of alcohol
4. Having physical checkups that include blood pressure, cholesterol and triglyceride levels
5. Regulating their diet to maintain optimum weight and health
6. Avoiding unnecessary strain and tension

Wives help their husbands to monitor their health, eat sensibly, get needed relaxation, and get the care they need when they are ill. Husbands concerned for their wives' mental and physical health plan enjoyable recreation for them both, and do what they can to encourage their wives to keep in good condition.

Allocating resources for present and future needs

In the middle years, the husband's income is still at or close to its peak, while costs have dropped sharply as the children have left home. Couples have fewer debts now than at any time since they were married (Lansing and Kish 1957:514). The scrimping days of trying to make ends meet are over for most couples. The house is furnished; the car and the last baby are paid for; and the couple can relax and enjoy their earnings in the breathing spell that is theirs now—before retirement and the costs of the later years are upon them. Two facets of this task call for special attention: (1) learning to spend money for personal gratification after

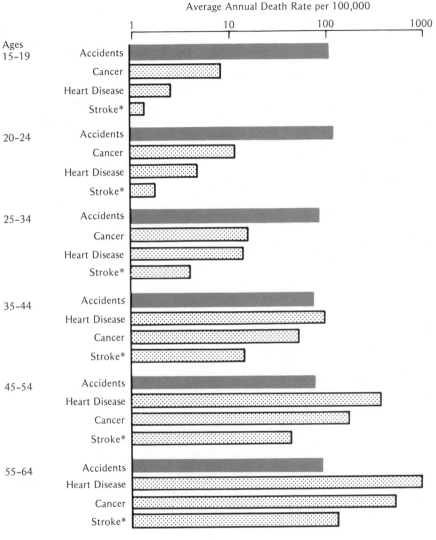

United States, 1972–73

Average Annual Death Rate per 100,000

*Cerebrovascular disease.
Source of basic data:
Reports of Division of Vital Statistics, National Center for Health Statistics.

Figure 15-1
Accidents and Other Major Causes of Death Among Men at the Working Ages
Source: *Statistical Bulletin*, (New York: Metropolitan Life, September 1975), p. 2.

years of self-sacrifice and of thinking first of the children and their needs, and (2) planning for a secure old age.

Planning financially for the later years is highly motivated during middle age. Few parents want to be beholden to their grown children for support during their own old age. They realize that neither Social Security nor Old Age Assistance will keep them on anything more than a subsistence level.

Realistically, most families can anticipate a sharp drop in income with the man's retirement (Figure 15-2). Thus they continue the pattern of putting their money away for a rainy day that has been established through their earlier years in the family. National analyses of saving by age groups indicate that middle-aged families tend to be the biggest savers and to place more emphasis on building up a reserve than any other age group (Brady and Froeder 1955).

Planning for old age should include recognition of the fact that the average age at which men die is lower than the average age at which women die. In the older age groups, there are many more widows than widowers. In fact, after age 70 there are more widows than wives. Men need to provide not only for their own support in old age, but for the support of their widows. This is more than a matter of stocks and bonds and life insurance. It means preparing the wife to fend for herself if and when she is left alone.

Several steps in preparing for widowhood are indicated: (1) Find

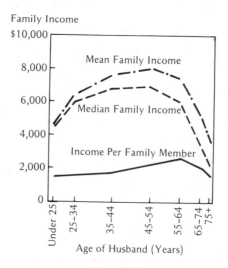

Figure 15-2

Family Income and Income per Family Member, for Husband-Wife Families (United States, 1960) Source: Paul C. Glick and Robert Parke, Jr., "New Approaches in Studying the Life Cycle of the Family," *Demography* 2 (1965): 199.

one or more close confidants besides the husband. A good woman friend will do. An understanding lawyer-friend, a sensitive pastor, or an old friend of the family may be tapped to serve as counsel and confidential ear when widowhood comes. (2) Make sure that both husband and wife know the full state of their financial affairs. The older pattern of the husband carrying the full responsibility for the money matters in the marriage meant that many mature women were like babes in the woods when their husbands died. They were easy prey for charlatans and sundry "widows' rackets." Today's couples more often share responsibility for financial planning through the years, a practice that leaves the widow better prepared to carry on when she is left in charge. (3) Encourage one or more absorbing interests in life that keep pulling toward the future. A crocheted afghan is a start, but it is not enough for most women. Active work in the community gives a woman something to grow on and into. A job outside the home may do it. Whatever it is, a woman in the middle years must have something to live *for* as well as to live *on*. If it can be both, she is doubly protected.

The chances of the wife's working are greater in the middle years than at any other time in the family life cycle (Figure 15-3). The middle-aged wife's income may be welcome for future security planning as well as for luxuries and pleasures. A combined income now may make it possible for the couple to buy a nice home, or fix up the old one, or take

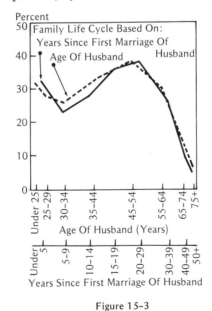

Figure 15-3
Percentage of Husband-Wife Families with Wife in Labor Force (United States, 1960)
Source: Paul C. Glick and Robert Parke, Jr., "New Approaches in Studying the Life Cycle of the Family," *Demography* 2 (1965): 197.

a long-dreamed-of trip abroad, spend a winter holiday in a southern clime, or budget more lavishly for their clothes and personal grooming than was possible before. Some husbands are secure enough as males not to be threatened by their wives' earning power; they are able to enjoy the economic partnership involved in team earning, shared planning, and joint spending.

Learning to "live it up" may be a more difficult task in the middle years than planning for the future. When two people have been future-oriented throughout their whole life together as a pair, it is not easy to suddenly shift into spending for present pleasures. Getting away for an occasional holiday while the children were growing up has prepared some couples for their freedom in the middle years. Spending something for immediate fun and pleasure through the years, even when the going has been rough, gives some basis for relaxing and enjoying life now. Even finding pleasure in freedom and in enjoying life has to be learned, as many a lonely middle-aged or older person discovers. This is the function of developmental tasks, which are built on the past and pointed toward the future at every stage of the life cycle.

Developing patterns of complementarity

Complementary roles have been defined as "interlocking systems in which each unit shapes and directs the other units in the system. This effect is reciprocal; changes in one role cannot be made without corresponding changes in other roles which are involved in it. For example, changes in the role of wife will be accompanied by changes in the role of husband; changes in the role of employer will involve changes in the role of employee. Changes in the role of mother will involve changes in the role of the father and in the role of the child" (Hartley and Hartley 1952).

Deutscher describes six different patterns of complementarity in the Kansas City middle-class panel of middle-aged adults that he interviewed:

1. *Reciprocal bolstering*—through appreciation, consideration, and standing by with encouragement through crises
2. *Mutual activities*—increased participation in recreational pursuits that both enjoy together
3. *Relaxing together*—as "joint idlers in a restful paradise of peace and quiet"
4. *Joint participation in husband's occupation*—in which the wife becomes absorbed in helping her husband in his work
5. *Constructive projects*—in which both members of the couple join forces to fix things up, in one project after another
6. *Separate interests*—as the husband remains absorbed in his work, and

the wife goes on with whatever special interests she has or can find (Deutscher 1954).

The self and other role-images of both men and women appear to change as they grow older, in two distinctly different patterns. Men, oriented primarily outside the family in their young adulthood, show a gradual decline in affective expressiveness and a withdrawal from emotional investments as they age. In contrast, as women move through the middle years, they become more self-confident, emotionally more expressive, more expansive, and in some ways even dominant over their husbands.

The young woman is a bland figure, lacking autonomy and symbolizing tenderness, intimacy, and sexuality. The more mature woman is the key figure in the family, struggling with problems of retaining and controlling the young, channeling her own needs for self-assertion, and possessing great depths of feeling sometimes accompanied by impulsive, egocentric qualities. Women stress the aggressive qualities of the older woman, whereas men see her either as benignly maternal or as domineering (Neugarten and Gutmann 1958).

Undertaking appropriate social roles

A social role is a pattern of learned behavior appropriate to a given social status. A social role is developed by an individual as his response to what is expected of him by others—modified by his own perceptions, values, and aspirations.

A man or woman in modern society is expected to fill such social roles as (1) parent, (2) spouse, (3) child of aging parent, (4) homemaker (male or female), (5) worker, (6) user of leisure time, (7) church member, (8) club or association member, (9) citizen, and (10) friend. The quality of a person's life is judged generally by the way he or she fills these roles. When performance approaches the ideal expectations of American society generally, it is rated "high"; when performance is average (4 to 5 on a 0-9 scale), it is rated "medium"; while failure is rated "low." Actual scores on performance in each of ten social roles for men and women in four social classes in the Kansas City study gives the multidimensional picture seen in Table 15-4.

Several observations are of interest in comparing the performance scores on the developmental tasks of middle age by social class, sex, and social role. In general we note that:

1. The higher the social class, the higher the performance score on developmental tasks for both men and women in all social roles.
2. Women tend to get higher scores than men in such roles as parent and

Table 15–4
Performance Scores of Kansas City Adults on the Developmental Tasks of Middle Age

Area	Men (age 40–70) Social class*				Women (age 40–70) Social class*			
	I	II	III	IV	I	II	III	IV
Parent	6.00	5.50	5.21	3.90	6.44	5.48	5.88	4.84
Spouse	6.00	5.57	4.87	4.13	6.17	5.94	5.46	3.62
Child of aging parent	5.89	6.06	5.89	5.00	5.75	5.90	5.94	5.75
Homemaker	5.64	5.70	5.55	4.38	5.93	4.86	5.40	3.68
Worker	7.31	5.67	5.36	3.54	6.25	5.97	4.50	3.61
Leisure participant	5.97	5.64	4.21	3.50	6.32	5.05	4.33	2.66
Church member	4.19	3.39	3.19	3.06	4.70	3.57	4.23	4.18
Club and association member	5.55	3.03	2.47	1.89	5.13	2.34	1.91	0.84
Citizen	5.21	4.11	3.64	3.44	4.57	4.01	3.06	3.91
Friend	5.27	4.38	4.02	3.75	6.32	4.59	3.85	2.52

Source: Robert J. Havighurst and Betty Orr, *Adult Education and Adult Needs: A Report* (Chicago: Center for the Study of Liberal Education for Adults, 1956), p. 32.
* I—upper-middle; II—lower-middle; III—upper-lower; IV—lower-lower (as defined by Warner and other writers on social class in America).

church member, but men do better than women as club and association members and as citizens, generally for all social class levels.

3. Scores ranged from .84 (lower-class women as club and association members) to 7.31 (upper middle-class men as workers). More than half (47 out of 80) got "medium" scores between 4 and 6; 24 out of 80 scored less than 4 ("low"); and 9 of the 80 scored over 6, or "high medium."

The lower-class man or woman views the years between 40 and 60 as a decline in which he or she is "slowing down," a "has-been." The middle-class man sees the middle years as the period of his greatest productivity and major rewards, the "prime of life." The upper-status woman feels the loss of her children from the home, but also a sense of mellowness and serenity. It is a time when "you enjoy life—you're comfortable with yourself and the world—you're no longer *adjusting* as you were before" (Neugarten and Peterson 1957:500).

One student of the roles played by middle-aged husbands and wives finds a direct relationship between the complementary of their roles during the postparental years and their satisfaction with the period. Three-fourths of the husbands and wives interviewed evaluated the postparental phase of the family life cycle as better than or as good as the preceding stages, and only three individuals reported the postparental stage as worse than earlier periods of the marriage. (Deutscher 1959:44).

*Assuring marital interaction
and satisfaction*

An important task of the middle years is finding each other as husband and wife again. Not since their honeymoon days have the two been thrown so closely together, with no children or responsibilities of child-rearing to divert them from each other. From a distance, one would expect such a state of affairs to be welcomed by both the man and the woman he chose to be his own. Yet, for many couples it is a real task to be worked on if they are to reach the point where life together once more has meaning, purpose, richness.

Studies find that the marriage relationship is important for personal life satisfaction. Postparental couples tend to turn to one another and to recultivate their relationship once their children are no longer dependent on them in the home (Petranek 1970, 1971). A good marriage is of increasing significance for life satisfaction as the years pass (Peterson 1968).

Pioneer studies of marital happiness reported less satisfaction in the middle than in the earlier years of marriage (Blood and Wolfe 1960; Bossard and Boll 1955; Feldman 1965; Gurin, Veroff, and Feld 1960; Pineo 1961). At that time it was thought that the later years were a time of "disenchantment" (Pineo 1961) and "disengagement" (Cumming, Dean, Newell, and McCaffrey 1960).

More recent research findings emphasize the possibilities for even greater marital happiness after a couple's children have left home. A study of 799 husbands and 799 wives found that the majority of the couples' satisfaction with their marriage increased postparentally to about the level of high satisfaction that they had had as young expectant parents (Rollins and Feldman 1970:24). Marital relations scores top all others in the perceptions middle-aged couples have of their current period of life and life satisfaction (Hayes and Stinnett 1971). See Figure 15-4, which compares life satisfaction scores of middle-aged husbands and wives in seven areas of life.

More couples in the middle years of marriage have high marital adjustment scores than do those whose children are yet to be launched (Johnson 1968:188); and many working-class and middle-class postparental couples see their middle years as the best yet (Saunders 1969:131). Companionship is seen as the most rewarding aspect of marriage by 62 percent of 360 middle-aged wives and husbands, most of whom were satisfied with their marital relationships (Hayes and Stinnett 1971:672). Dizard (1968) found that if mutual understanding continues, a couple does not need to grow apart in the middle years. Both empathy and communication appear to contribute to good marital adjustment in the middle years, especially when the two partners' communication is mutual and not overburdened

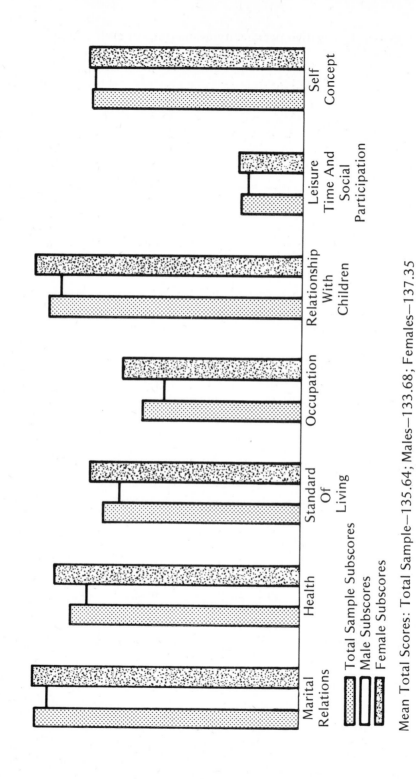

Figure 15-4

Middle Years Life Satisfaction Scores of 360 Husbands and Wives

Source: Maggie Parks Hayes and Nick Stinnett, "Life Satisfaction of Middle-Aged Husbands and Wives," *Journal of Home Economics* 63, no. 9 (December 1971): 672.

with unpleasantly negative personality evaluations of each other (Johnson 1968:219–220; Lowenthal and Chiriboga 1972:12; Saunders 1969:194). Professor Anderson speaks of "the abiding desire in each mate to maintain a relationship in which each feels accepted, valued, recognized, and loved as an attractive, stimulating, and dependable companion in a mutual quest to understand and fulfill the purpose of existence" (Anderson 1974:467–469).

Leisure activities (enjoying weekend recreation together, working together around the house and yard, attending plays and musical events) contribute to marital satisfaction in the middle years (Deutscher 1959:110). Leisure activities are especially critical in determining marital satisfaction before children come and again after they are launched—"when the marital relationship is reestablishing itself and a new dyadic adjustment becomes necessary" (Orthner 1975:101).

The sexual satisfaction of wives is closely related to both communication and happiness in marriage (Levin and Levin 1975:57). Of 100,000 women surveyed, more than two-thirds of the wives describe their sex lives as good or very good, regardless of how many years they have been married (Levin and Levin 1975:54). Neugarten (1970) found middle-class and working-class women between the ages of 43 and 53 developing renewed interest in their intimate marital relations. Kinsey and associates reported that middle-aged married women have as high or higher incidence of orgasm in their forties and fifties as they did in their twenties (Kinsey, Pomeroy, Martin, and Gebhard 1953:154). Masters and Johnson found that wives who have had happy, well-adjusted, stimulating marriages go through the middle years with little or no interruption in the frequency of, interest in, or enjoyment of sexual activity with their husbands, who normally continue active marital relations well into their seventies and eighties (Masters and Johnson 1968:271, 275).

Middle-aged husbands may experience a decline in sexual adequacy in the middle years because of such problems as: (1) boredom with the same sex partner; (2) preoccupation with their jobs; (3) mental or physical fatigue; (4) overindulgence in food or drink, or both; (5) infirmities in spouse or self; or (6) fear of poor sexual performance (Masters and Johnson 1966:264). The understanding cooperation of middle-aged husbands and wives in continuing their active sex life is important in safeguarding the vitality of their marriage.

Anxiety about declining virility and personal attractiveness may cause some middle-aged men to look for reassurance and variety in sexual encounters outside of marriage. Among postparental husbands, one-half expressed a desire for and one-fourth have been involved in extramarital affairs (Johnson 1968:141, 150). Poor marital adjustment and satisfaction are significantly related to husbands' (but not to wives') extramarital involvements (Johnson 1968:162, 164). About one-third of all wives in the *Redbook* study reported having had lovers outside of marriage. The longer a woman had been married, and the greater her opportunities for extramarital affairs, the more likely she was to have them (Levin 1975:40, 42). Some of the wives reporting extramarital experience said they were happily married and sexually satisfied with their husbands, but more of them than of the faithfully monogamous were dissatisfied with their marriage or their marital sex lives, or both (Levin 1975:42). The researcher concludes, "the satisfied experimental wives, who constitute a very small minority, are living in marriages in which sexual exclusiveness is not part of the commitment" (Levin 1975:44).

Dr. Leon Zussman and his wife Shirley, a psychologist, who conduct therapy programs for middle-aged people with sexual problems, are said to recommend intimate husband-wife talk as essential for maintaining understanding and interest in each other through the years (Irwin 1975: 25). When each partner understands what the other is going through (the wife's menopause, the husband's anxiety about his aging appearance and functioning, for instance), they are more likely to mutually support one another than to become alienated and disillusioned about their marriage.

When they have a mature appreciation of sex, and of each other, a middle-aged couple may become capable of a more prolonged mutual orgasm that is far more deeply satisfying to both partners than anything they were able to achieve in their earlier years together. Meeting each other's needs emotionally as well as sexually draws the mates together as a couple. At this time the middle-aged man and woman each need the reassurance, the appreciation, and the encouragement to be what they are that comes from feeling fully accepted and truly close to each other in marriage. Failure in this task brings the aching loneliness so frequent in later years. Success in intimate interaction brings immediate contentment and paves the way for smooth going through the rest of life together.

Enlarging the family circle

The empty nest is not as empty for some as it is for others. It can fill up with grandchildren. As one grandfather in his early fifties observes, "What's all this about the empty nest? The old nest here is bursting at the seams with five wonderful grandchildren and two sons-in-law extra— all besides the two daughters who used to roost with us!"

Becoming accepting and acceptable in-laws, welcomed and welcoming grandparents, in mutually satisfying intergenerational relationships, is a highly rewarding developmental task to accomplish during the years immediately following the marriage of the grown children of the family. Failure in this task causes the family to be fragmented, and brings loneliness and heartache to members of all three generations (parents, grown children, and their children). Success, (achieved by many families), allows the middle-aged pair to keep its warm sense of being a family. The grown children feel secure in their roots, knowing that, as the family's traditions and values are carried forward, its continuity is assured (Sussman 1959: 18).

An exploratory study of several thousand in-law relationships attempted to discover what causes difficulties and what is conducive to harmony between in-laws. More than 75 percent of the factors contributing to in-law harmony had to do with mutual acceptance and mutual respect (Duvall 1954:336). Problems arise when a middle-aged parent has difficulty letting a grown child go, or accepting the grown son's or daughter's choice of a mate. Mothers more than fathers have—and become—in-law problems, probably because their child-rearing responsibilities have been primary in their life interests through the years. The boy's parents more than the girl's are apt to find acceptance of the marriage and the marriage partner difficult, possibly because the girl's parents have had more of a hand in the mate choice, as Komarovsky suggests (Komarovsky 1950: 516).

The chances are that the mother-in-law who can wholeheartedly and enthusiastically welcome her children-in-law has been a good mother in the developmental sense all along, while the selfish, possessive mother finds it hard to be a good mother-in-law. An attitude of acceptance is needed:

> You (mother-in-law) have been "in training" for the full acceptance of your children-in-law for many years. As you accepted your children's friends and pals and playmates through the years of their childhood, you learned how to love others just because they were those your children loved. Adolescent crushes and love affairs you could take in your stride as further practice in letting children go and in accepting those they found lovable. So now, when the children marry, you can accept their mates, because you have learned to let your love for them swell to include their loved ones. (Duvall 1954:347–348)

Folklore has it that when grown children marry they become completely independent, neither asking for nor receiving assistance from their parents. Actually, a great deal of mutual support and help continues between the generations after grown children marry. Sussman's study of intergenerational help in middle-class families concludes that there are well-established patterns of giving and receiving between middle-aged parents and their children's families that are related to the continuity and success of intergenerational family relationships.

> Parents... wished to help their newly married children to become established on their own class level or even a higher one, and, in turn, wanted affectional response from them. They believed children to be more appreciative of their finan-

cial and service help after marriage. This was because they now faced the problems of establishing a new household and family. Many children realize, perhaps for the first time, the efforts their own parents had exerted in providing for them. However, most parents have no intention of subsidizing their children's families permanently, and many learned that help given in moderation was more prudent than unrestrained giving. When given in moderate amounts, it did not create conflict with the new family head. Parents also indicated that by mutual aid with married children in nursing care, house repairing, vacation planning, and similar activities, they enriched one another's lives, took pride in their achievements, and felt that each had some part in the other's success. (Sussman 1953:27-28)

A three-generation family study in the greater Minneapolis area shows that personal contact with younger and older family members is maintained through frequent visits by large percentages of both men and women in all age groups (Table 15-5).

With the coming of the middle years in the family, time and money are available and interest in cementing relationships in the family generally increases. When one's own children are grown and gone, there is often a desire to become reacquainted with nephews and nieces and to come closer to the other relatives in the larger family circle.

There are certain hazards to be avoided in relationships with brothers' and sisters' families. In an exploratory study of in-law relationships, the one role more difficult to play successfully than any other (except for that of mother-in-law), was that of sister-in-law. The findings indicate that some sisters-in-laws are possessive, meddling, and intrusive in much the same way that mothers-in-law are. In addition, a considerable amount

Table 15-5
Intergenerational Visiting by Men and Women

Frequency of visits	Parents—Grandparents		Married children—Parents		Married children—Grandparents	
	Male	Female	Male	Female	Male	Female
Daily or weekly	36%	54%	74%	69%	32%	41%
Monthly	52	39	23	25	16	15
Quarterly	9	6	—	6	36	33
Yearly	3	—	3	—	16	10
Total	100%	100%*	100%	100%	100%	100%*

Source: Reuben Hill, *Family Development in Three Generations* (Cambridge, Mass.: Schenkman Publishing Company, 1970). Chap. 3, Table 3.01.
*Due to rounding of figures, the columns may not total 100 percent.

of sibling rivalry (competitiveness, jealousy, envy, comparing, bickering, and belittling) seems to continue into adulthood. Sisters-in-law are especially susceptible to this problem in the larger family interrelationships (Duvall 1954:221–243).

More parents between 45 and 54 report satisfying relationships with their children than any other age group (Gurin, Veroff, and Feld 1960: 136–137).

Margaret Mead sees today's grandparents as experts in change, who have much to offer children by communicating to them a sense of wonder at man's achievements during their lifetime. They, who have seen the first airplane, talking movies, television, computers, and satellites can share with their grandchildren faith in a future in which almost anything can happen (Mead 1966:28, 30).

Grandparents contribute a sense of history and perspective to family discussions. They have more leisure to discuss problems with the young than have their busy parents, in many cases (Ligon 1973:5). Working-class grandmothers may take charge of their grown children's families, thus enabling their daughters to work outside the home (Havighurst 1975:8).

Middle-class grandparents are less likely to live with their married children. But the majority find pleasure in their grandparenting for any of several reasons: (1) biological continuity with the future; (2) emotional self-fulfillment; (3) feeling needed as contributing family members; (4) aspiring vicariously through the new generations. Middle-aged grandparents are more likely to have fun with their grandchildren than are the elderly, who tend to be more formal and remote as grandparents (Neugarten and Weinstein 1964).

To enjoy the fellowship of growing children, to be accepted by them as pleasant companions, to hear their confidences, and to share the mysteries of life with them—all are deep satisfactions. It is rewarding, too, to look back on a job well done, as grown children establish themselves in their families and carry on some of the family traditions and values. Grandparents who learn early to master the arts of intergenerational relationships build not only for the moment, but also for the years that lie ahead as their grandchildren grow up and become adolescents, are launched, and go on into their homes.

Problems between brothers' and sisters' families sometimes arise out of efforts to plan for the care of aging parents. When one's parents need financial support, or when one or both of them need a home in their later years, the problem may precipitate a crisis among the grown children in terms of whose responsibility it is and which one should do what to help carry the load. Old grudges may be dredged up and old resentments aired until feelings run so high that the whole family is unpleasantly involved. Bitterness in the family is of little comfort through the middle and later years. Better by far is the effort to work things out harmoniously with the others in the larger family.

Aging parents who are financially quite independent and whose health does not yet require special care still need the attention and loving interest of their grown children. There are strong social pressures for "being nice to" one's aging parents; everything from neighborhood gossip to newspaper headlines heaps criticism on the heads of men and women who woefully neglect their parents in their later years. Respect for elders is not as strong in the Western world as it is in the East, but even so, some filial devotion is expected in the form of occasional visits, letters, telephone calls, and gifts on special days. Many of the little rituals help aging parents to feel that they are loved and appreciated.

For many mature men and women, giving affection and attention to aging parents is an easy task. For others, whose earlier relationships with their parents have been uncongenial or full of conflict, there may be real problems. It is likely that keeping close to aging relatives is more difficult for the upward mobile man or woman than it is for the married couple whose ways of life are still quite similar to those of their parents. Being ashamed of the old-fashioned, old-world ways of parents of an ethnic group is a frequent impediment to the comfortable accomplishment of this task.

Cavan anticipates a decline of tension between middle-aged adults and aging parents as urbanization and acculturation increase. As older family members are fully accepted, they, their adult children, and the grandchildren benefit (Cavan 1956).

Participating in community life

When children have grown and gone and the middle-aged husband and wife are alone, with fully half of their adult lives together stretching ahead of them, it is time to get out and build a broad base for life as a pair. One middle-aged woman who keeps active in many projects outside her home says that she feels that these are the years when she is storing up sweetness for the rest of her life. Much as the honeybee fills up the many cells of the honeycomb for the winter months that lie ahead, so a middle-aged human stockpiles memories of activities enjoyed, projects completed, and friendships made as safeguards against loneliness in the later years when activities, of necessity, must be curtailed.

The man has his work, and many satisfied, active women have theirs too. Dr. Rose's study of life satisfaction among middle-aged, middle-class men and women reveals a larger proportion of satisfied than dissatisfied women among those gainfully employed outside the home. Working mothers were the most satisfied with their lot, especially if they found job status and satisfaction in their work. The middle-aged women who had married young (before learning the skills they would need as their central roles changed in middle life) were the most dissatisfied with their lives (Rose 1955:15–19).

Sussman's investigation of what middle-aged parents do when their grown children leave found that most couples increase their mutual undertakings both within and outside the home. Such shared activity patterns as listening to the radio, viewing television, playing games, conversing, entertaining friends, doing housework and making home repairs, dining out, attending clubs, movies, and concerts, taking long vacation trips, and acquiring a summer place all increased with the leave-taking of the children. These new activities were associated with the increased leisure and affluence that come as children cease to be dependent (Sussman 1955:338–341).

These are the years when a woman is free to take an active part in some community project in which she has become interested. While her children were small, she did well to get to the parent-teacher meetings in their school. Now she may attend state and national meetings; she may hold a responsible office; she may go to the state capital to plead for a worthy piece of legislation. At the same time the middle-aged man is taking on more responsible positions in his club, organization, or union.

The middle-aged of the working class tend to spend most of their leisure time around home or "with the boys" (lower-lower class), whereas the middle-aged people who are successfully active in the community are generally from the middle-class, according to findings of the Kansas City Study of Adult Life (Havighurst 1957:341; Havighurst and Feigenbaum 1959).

Intensive interviews with upper-middle-class college-educated women ranging in age from 47 to 65 found most of them adapting satisfactorily to middle age. They were in excellent health; their marital relationships were improving; some were working; others were active in volunteer and church work; in fact, great involvement with people was for them a primary aspect of the role change of the middle years (Davidoff and Markewich 1961).

Many women see the middle years as a period of greater freedom for self-expression. They now have the chance to expand their activities or to develop latent interests and talents. Their lives in the middle years are characterized by marked changes in activity and by major shifts in their self-image (Neugarten 1966).

Social participation is found to be associated with life satisfaction among both men and women (Rose 1955; Hayes and Stinnett 1971). Successful participation in community life in the middle years depends on the foundations laid for it in the earlier years of marriage. As the family has projects and purposes beyond its own immediate interests through the years, it prepares for wider participation and accomplishment in the middle and later years.

Affirming life's central values

A couple's central values are affirmed in everything they do toward the accomplishment of all the other developmental tasks of the middle years. They express their value systems as they create and maintain a pleasant and comfortable home; as they enjoy their financial peace of mind and plan for old age security; as they carry out their household responsibilities together; as they draw closer together as a couple; as they work out warm, mutually satisfying relationships with the families of their grown children, as they keep in touch with their brothers' and sisters' families, as well as with their aging parents; and as they participate within the larger community. In so doing they find themselves as persons, as a couple, as family members, as workers, as citizens, and in all the other roles that society expects of them and that their personal aspirations define for them.

It is seldom necessary to talk long and loud about one's concept of life or the values one lives by. Most men and women reveal their true attitudes most eloquently through their actions—by the stands they take on current issues; in the way they are willing to be counted in a controversy; by what they do about what they believe to be right and just and good and true. By the time a husband and wife reach their middle years together, they have worked out a life-style that makes sense to them as a couple.

Values are highly variable, since they reflect each individual's unique personal history and life-style (Bengtson 1975). Being middle-aged means living in the middle of things as a link in the continuing story of life (Janeway 1971:174). Mature adults both influence and are influenced by the young. Some middle-aged people, noting that the young seem to be finding life more fulfilling, humane, and pleasurable, may adopt their hang-loose attire and nontraditional sexual patterns—or perhaps merely take up yoga as dowagers (Bengtson, Furlong and Laufer 1974:25). Others remain work-oriented and (significantly more than young adults) believe that hard work and self-sacrifice lead to success. They say they like their jobs, and they feel proud of the work they do (*Better Homes and Gardens* 1972:116–123). Participation in religious activities remains surprisingly constant at 21 percent among American adults between the ages of 18 and 50 or more (Gallup 1976).

Married people are found to get significantly greater satisfaction from life than do single, separated, divorced, and widowed men and women (Neugarten, Havighurst, and Tobin 1961). These findings suggest that marriage contributes to satisfaction with life and that many married people succeed in their developmental tasks on through their middle years.

It's never too late to learn. In the reaffirmation of life's values, a couple can still make progress toward developing unity and integrity in the leisure of their middle years. Nothing can bring greater satisfaction than finding that, viewed from a mature vantage point, life all adds up; and that together the two know who they are and where they are headed in the business of living.

Grow old along with me!
The best is yet to be,
The last of life for which the first
was made. . . .

Robert Browning

Aging family members

chapter sixteen

The final stage of the family life cycle begins with the man's retirement, goes through the loss of the first spouse, and ends with the death of the second. Because women live longer than men and usually are younger than their husbands, they are more often widowed than are men (Chapter 17).

The aging family stage begins with two positions, husband and wife, and ends with one, the surviving spouse. Beginning with one interpersonal relationship, the nuclear family ends with none. The aging couple continue to be "family" to their grown children, grandchildren, and great-grandchildren. The pair face together the family developmental tasks of the final stage of the family life cycle. The challenge of senescence is the preservation of ego integrity—without which despair may mark the final years. The goal of this period is successful aging through continued activity and comfortable disengagement.

America's aging

The number of people over 65 years of age in America's population has increased steadily in the twentieth century (Table 16-1). By 1975 there were over 22 million people 65 years of age or older in the United States, with millions more about to retire in the decade to come. This represents a 30 percent increase in the numbers of persons 65 and over in the final quarter of the twentieth century.

By the mid-1970s, an American's expectation of life at birth had increased to an all-time high. The male newborn's expected lifetime in 1974 was 68.2 years and the female's 75.9 years, representing the largest annual predicted increases in longevity for both sexes in two decades (U.S. Bureau of the Census 1976). With continued improvement of medical care and health practices, a 65-year-old man in 1970 could expect to live to be 78, while men who reach 65 in the year 2000 may expect to live to age 83. For the 65-year-old woman, the corresponding ages are 81.5 and 86 (Neugarten 1975:22). Longevity has become so commonplace that families and society as a whole must come to terms with the rising tide of the aging.

The frail and failing elderly

Life becomes a burden for many of the frail elderly, whose critical or chronic illnesses drain them of their physical strength and financial

Table 16-1
Over-sixty-five Population of the United States, 1900–2000

Year	Population over 65
1900	3,100,000
1910	3,985,000
1920	4,929,000
1930	6,706,000
1940	9,031,000
1950	12,287,000
1960	16,658,000
1970	19,585,000
1980	23,063,000
1990	27,005,000
2000	28,842,000

Source: U.S. Bureau of the Census, "Projections of the Population of the United States, by Age, Sex, and Color to 1990, with Extensions of Population by Age and Sex to 2015," *Population Estimates,* Current Population Reports, Series P-25, no. 381 (December 18, 1967), series B and earlier data from the Bureau of the Census, released by the Population Reference Bureau, Information Service, June 4, 1969; and *U.S. News & World Report,* 3 March 1975, p. 35.

resources. The very old outlive their friends and families. They, and many others in failing health, are lonely, alone, and dependent on the resources of the community. The elderly often resent the insults of aging as they lose their strength, their eyesight, their hearing, their former sources of satisfaction, and the desire for life itself. The feeble old fill nursing homes and come to the attention of the public and members of the helping professions.

Social workers, physicians, psychiatrists, and other professionals who work with the aging see those whose needs are greatest. They emphasize the needs of the weak and helpless elderly for adequate food, living arrangements, health care, financial assistance, and supportive services of all kinds. Research findings show that some 40 percent of all Americans over 65 must limit their activities for health reasons (Neugarten 1975:7).

People over 65 are more susceptible to mental illness than any other age group. Psychiatric research finds that the incidence of suicide increases with age, especially among elderly white men, for several reasons: loss of status, the desire to protect their widows' financial security, and the wish to escape physical dependence and suffering (Butler 1975:893). Studies of the aging process find that the decline of intellectual abilities is caused by specific diseases rather than by senescence. The psychiatric disorders commonly found among the elderly are similar to those affecting the young (Butler 1975:899).

Old people are not revered for their wisdom and experience in a culture that values youth and change. Societal perceptions of the elderly put an added burden upon them:

> The old are poor in a society that values wealth. They are uneducated or miseducated in a society that values relevant education. Their years are numbered in a society that makes capital investment in human beings (e.g. education) with a view to future payoff. Our values thus put a burden on old people as a category. (Hochschild 1973:20)

Individual differences are especially great among the aging because people become more and more themselves as they grow older. Some are miserable; others are enjoying the best years of their lives. Some continue working into the seventies or longer; others retire in anticipation of "living it up" after a lifetime of hard work. Some older people are rigid and ineffectual in coping with change; others enjoy the continuing challenges of life. Some are depressed and self-pitying, others are optimistic and outgoing. The future may bring with it attitudes of greater tolerance and social permissiveness. Acceptance of a wider variety of life-styles would encourage people to be themselves—to develop and to seek fulfillment according to individual preferences. "We may come to diminish the importance of chronological age as a major distinguishing feature between individuals, and instead of speaking of social roles for *the aged*, come to speak of the social roles of *individuals* who happen to be young, middle-aged, or old, but more important, who happen to have different tastes, different goals, and different ways of enhancing the quality of their lives" (Neugarten 1970:23).

The rise of the "young-old"

Stereotypes about aging have it that the old are feeble, dependent, petulant, and impoverished, as indeed some of them are. But recognition of the great diversity among retirees is growing. Many remain active, vigorous, and in good health for years after they have retired. Since more people are living longer, some 15 percent of the population is between 55 and 75. Among these are the "young-old" who are comfortably well-off, in the prime of life, increasingly well-educated, politically active, and freer from family and work responsibilities than they, or their age group, have been in any era (Neugarten 1975:22–23). This is a new phenomenon in the history of mankind—the first generation of self-fulfilled, able people ready to serve their world with their time and talents.

Studies of a group of people during their young adulthood and of the same group 40 years later, show a conspicuous continuity in personal characteristics. These older people are adaptive, resourceful, and diverse in life-style and personality (Maas and Kuypers 1974). Biography is replete with vivid examples of creativity lasting well into the later decades. Agatha Christie wrote mysteries until her death in the 80s. Bernard Baruch at 76 became the United States representative on the Atomic Energy Commission of the United Nations and formulated the Baruch Proposals for international control of nuclear energy. Konrad Adenauer was Chancellor of West Germany from 73 to 87. Julia Ward Howe, author of "The Battle Hymn of the Republic," wrote her familiar "At Sunset" when she was 91. Charles Kettering was director of General Motors until he was 71. Helen Keller, deaf and blind from early childhood, was traveling all over the world at 77 when she said, "Joy in adventure, travel, and love of service to my fellowmen was stronger than physical handicaps" (Keller 1956:2).

Age is not measured by chronological age alone. Out of a group of typical old people, half of those between 65 and 69 answered the question "How old do you feel?" by replying "middle-aged" or even "young." Only those past 80 answered invariably that they felt "old" or "aged" (Havighurst and Albrecht 1953:9). In contrast, when undergraduates were asked, "How young or old do you feel?" a surprising number said that they felt old (Sarason, Sarason, and Cowden 1975:586; see also Maynard 1973). Both optimism and oppressive anxiety about one's present and future condition can occur at any age. There are at least three patterns of aging. These may be observed in: (1) creative and autonomous people like Toscanini, whose essential aliveness of spirit keeps the body alive; (2) adjusted people, such as the professional man who prides himself on being "well-preserved"; and (3) anomic people, who die soon after retirement or upon being widowed, in a metaphorical suttee; "such people live like cards, propped up by other cards" (Riesman 1954:383). A safe conclusion is that all older people must learn new roles appropriate to their stage of life. Some do well, and others fail.

Patterns of retirement

Compulsory retirement is a misfortune to many able workers whose sense of being alive depends on being needed. Psychologists see a person's relationship to his work as one of the important determinants of his sense of the passage of time, which in turn shapes and becomes his psychological sense of aging (Sarason, Sarason, and Cowden 1975:584).

A study by the Section on Mental Health of the Aging, of the National Institute of Mental Health, identifies four patterns of retirement: (1) *maintenance*—a common pattern in which the retiree tries, after retirement, to satisfy the same needs in the same way as before, making extraordinary efforts to continue working in one form or another; (2) *withdrawal*—an equally common pattern in which retirement is seen as a time to relax and to give up many former interests without adopting new ones; (3) *changed activities*—in which the individual attempts to satisfy the same needs by engaging in a different set of activities; and (4) *satisfying a new and different set of needs* after retirement than he or she did before. These are the people who see retirement as a chance to do things they have always wanted to do (Sheldon, McEwan, and Ryser 1975).

Today, more men are retiring at 65 or earlier than in the past. Only 22 percent of American men over 65 were still working in 1974, in contrast to 42 percent in 1940 who continued to work after they had reached 65. With more companies encouraging early retirement and more men opting to quit work at or before their 65th birthdays, more aging couples are confronted with the complex decisions of the postretirement years.

The former director of the National Institute of Mental Health lists ten decisions affecting the success of retirement for a man and his family:

1. Move to a new locality, or stay within a familiar circle of friends?
2. Continue in a variation of the old job, or go on to something new?
3. Live in a house, an apartment, or a retirees' community?
4. Find a climate conducive to maximum health?
5. Explore all available medical resources?
6. Compare cultural resources?
7. Devise a realistic budget for present and future needs?
8. Seek opportunities for satisfying volunteer activities?

9. Consider possible dependent-others in future planning?
10. Locate where family ties may be maintained—neither too far nor too close?

"Careful thought and honest answers to these questions will go far to make the later years full and enjoyable" (Felix 1975).

Developmental tasks of the aging couple

Family development continues through the final stage of the family life cycle in the interaction of the family members. As adult children achieve their "filial maturity" (Blenkner 1965), the older couple is accomplishing reciprocal parental maturity. An aging pair's developmental tasks are intertwined now that they face the rest of life together. Both seek mutually satisfactory answers to such questions as where they will live, and on what, and how they will relate to one another and to the other important people in their lives. Both husband and wife now face the common task of developing a life-style that will be meaningful to both. Each must adjust to his or her declining health and strength and to that of the other member of the pair.

In time, one spouse dies and leaves the other widowed, as we see in Chapter 17. In some cases, the original marriage breaks in divorce, as is discussed in Chapter 18. Most older couples continue on together for as long as they both live, carrying out during the final stage of the family life cycle their joint family developmental tasks:

1. Making satisfying living arrangements as aging progresses
2. Adjusting to retirement income
3. Establishing comfortable routines
4. Safeguarding physical and mental health
5. Maintaining love, sex, and marital relations
6. Remaining in touch with other family members
7. Keeping active and involved
8. Finding meaning in life

Making satisfying living arrangements

After retirement an aging couple may live where they please. They usually want to live independently as long as possible, in a place where they have privacy, safety, a sense of mastery over their environment, psychological stimulation, convenience, quiet, and congenial neighbors, at a price they can afford. Early in the retirement years their options include: (1) remaining in their own home; (2) moving into an apartment or mobile home; (3) going into a retirement community, and/or settling in a warmer climate. As health fails, it may become necessary to consider nursing homes, extended care facilities, or living with grown children (Havighurst 1972:114–115; Montgomery 1972:37–46).

Older people move less than any other age group. In one recent year, nearly four out of five (78.6 percent) Americans 65 years of age or older remained in the same house (in contrast to 24.5 percent of those aged 25–29) (U.S. Bureau of the Census 1974:12). In recent years a greater number of financially secure retirees have been moving to congenial communities where the weather is warm and life is geared to mature adult interests—but the percentage of old people who can afford such living arrangements is still small (Golant 1975). More unmarried older couples are living together, presumably for companionship without loss of survivor benefits through marriage. "Another 'variant family form' is the commune, a type of living arrangement that has not been adequately quantified on a nationwide basis, partly because many of the communes are not welcome in their neighborhood, and would rather not be identified in a census or survey" (Glick 1975:13).

Experts predict that more and more older persons will be living in metropolitan and suburban communities and that large numbers of low-income old people (especially nonwhites) will be living in inner-city public housing and other low-cost facilities and in planned retirement communities appealing to older people with varying life-styles (Golant 1975: 22–23).

Infirm older people with multiple disabilities may have no choice but to enter nursing homes. Nursing home care is seen as a last resort because it involves the loss of some personal dignity, privacy, freedom, and independence; because it imposes strict conformity to institutional routines and rules; and because of its high cost (Smith 1975:8). The recognition that one's disabilities are permanent, and that death is inevitable if not imminent, added to stories in the press about squalid conditions and inadequate care in many nursing homes, does little to brighten the picture in the minds of the nation's infirm aged. The United States Senate's Subcommittee on Long Term Care reports that there are more nursing home beds (1.2 million) than hospital beds (1 million) in the United States and that the number of patients in nursing homes is increasing rapidly (210 percent in the decade 1960 to 1970). The average age of nursing home patients is 82, and most of them will die in the nursing home (Whitworth 1975).

A declining percentage of the aged live with their grown children, even though both generations might benefit in some instances. "The task before us is to learn when this may be sound and when it may be disastrous, and the techniques that work in living together, so that we may equip our families to make sound choices" (Schorr 1960:18).

Hundreds of husbands and wives who have found ways of making a home for their aging parents that worked out happily for all concerned volunteer their recommendations for harmonious three-generational living along the following lines:

1. Develop together a clear understanding of financial, household, and other responsibilities so that each one may know just what is expected of him or her.
2. Be reasonable in your expectations of one another. No one is perfect. Everyone makes mistakes from time to time. Perfectionists are hard to live with in any family.
3. Make some provision for protecting the personal property of each member of the family. It may be little more than a closet or a bureau of his or her own, but everyone welcomes some place for his things that will be respected as his alone.
4. Respect each person's need for privacy. It is not only the great who need their "islands of solitude," as Adlai Stevenson suggested. The elderly, the adolescent, and all the rest of us from time to time desire undisturbed privacy. We have the right to open our own mail, answer our own phone calls, and make our own friends with some sense of privacy.
5. Encourage each member of the household to develop his own talents and to pursue his own interests in his own way. This means you, too.
6. Jointly plan for whole-family activities so that each may have a share in deciding what is to be done and what part he or she will play in the affair.
7. As disagreements arise, and they will from time to time, take the time to hear the other(s) out. Listen well enough to grasp what the situation means to those who differ from you. Respond to their feelings as well as to the "sense" of the situation.
8. Unify the larger family unit, sharing the household's hospitality by celebrations and rituals that bring the family closer together in its own most meaningful ways.
9. Take a positive attitude toward your joint living arrangement by being appreciative of the benefits derived from sharing the household, instead of merely bemoaning the sacrifices involved.
10. Gain some perspective by realizing that through the ages families have lived more often together than in the little separate family units more popular today (Duvall 1954:323–324).

Within the framework of good housing, some specific practices are suggested as sensible for aging persons' homes by the National Safety Council. Among these are putting a light near the bed, tacking down or removing throw rugs, lighting the bathroom upon entering, wearing glasses when opening the medicine cabinet, taking it easy on hot days, wearing a hat when working in the sun, carrying loads that are not too heavy, and holding the handrail when going downstairs. Since accidents occur much more often during the latter decades of life, such precautions are important for aging family members who want to remain active and independent as long as they can.

Whatever the situation, whatever the decisions that have to be made, the developmental tasks of the aging man and his wife must be accomplished as a team. Together they make their home where it suits them best, for as long as it meets their needs. As they accomplish this task successfully, they are content in their surroundings and happy in their physical setting. When they fail to work out the fundamental responsibilities of finding a satisfactory and satisfying home for their later years, they face the unhappiness that so often accompanies failure in any of the developmental tasks at any stage of the life cycle.

Adjusting to retirement income

In the United States, it is generally assumed that a man will retire at or near age 65. This is true particularly of men employed in industry and in some professions, such as teaching, where policies for retirement are fixed. In general, fewer men are employed now after age 65 than was true in earlier decades, as we see in Table 16-2.

There is nothing mandatory about retirement for many men. A good many self-employed people continue to work on through their later years. The doctor, lawyer, writer, farmer, artist, carpenter, or businessman who is not retired under company policy often continues to work long after retirement age, thus postponing the problems of retirement for himself and his family.

Table 16-2
Labor Force Participation Rates of Men over Sixty-five, 1900–1975

Year	Percentage of men over 65 employed
1900	63.2
1920	57.1
1930	55.5
1940	43.3
1950	45.0
1955	42.9
1960	41.2
1965	39.6
1970	38.0
1975	36.5

Source: Philip M. Hauser, "Changes in Labor-Force Participation of the Older Worker," *American Journal of Sociology* 59, no. 4 (January 1954): 315; data drawn from U.S. Bureau of the Census, "Projected Growth of the Labor Force in the United States under Conditions of High Employment: 1950 to 1975," *Labor Force*, Current Population Reports, Series P-50, no. 42 (December 10, 1952), and from John Durand, *The Labor Force in the United States, 1890–1960* (New York: Social Science Research Council, 1948), pp. 208 ff.

Sharp curtailment of family income is one of the immediate retirement adjustments. For instance, between 1961 and 1967, when incomes were rising for men of all educational levels, there was a sharp decline in family incomes as family heads neared retirement (Figure 16-1).

The financial pinch felt by aging family members is significantly greater than that affecting middle-aged parents or their married children, as is seen in the responses of the members of the three generations studied by Reuben Hill (Table 16-3).

Americans over 65 represent 10 percent of the population—but 20 percent of the poor. "Overall, one of every three elderly persons is in a state of severe economic deprivation" (Butler 1973). Retirees are boxed in; their earnings are sharply reduced and their savings are eroding because of rising costs and inflation (Chapter 3).

Some workers have to retire for health reasons and then find rising medical and hospital costs a severe economic problem. The Medicare legislation of 1965 alleviates some but not all of the financial burden of medical care for older Americans.

Medicare is a federally sponsored hospital and medical insurance

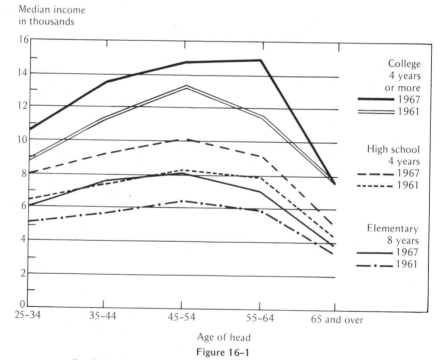

Figure 16-1

Family Income in the United States by Education and Age of Head

Source: U.S. Bureau of the Census, "Income in 1967 of Families in the United States," *Consumer Income*, Current Population Reports, series P-60, no. 59 (April 18, 1969).

Table 16-3
Adequacy of Family Income in Three Generations

	Grandparents	Parents	Married children
Do without many needed things	28.0%	4.7%	1.2%
Have the things we need but none of the extras	23.5	5.9	4.8
Have the things we need and a few of the extras	30.5	61.0	76.0
Have the things we need and any extras we want	3.5	14.2	16.8
Have the things we need and any extras we want, and still have money left over to invest	14.5	14.2	1.2
Total	100.0%	100.0%	100.0%
Number of families	85	85	83

Source: Reuben Hill, "Decision Making and the Family Life Cycle," in Ethel Shanas and Gordon F. Streib, eds., *Social Structure and the Family: Generational Relations* (Englewood Cliffs, N.J.: Prentice-Hall, 1965), p. 123.

program for people 65 or older. It provides basic protection against the costs of inpatient hospital care; posthospital extended care; posthospital home health care; supplemental protection against costs of physicians' services, medical services, and supplies; home health care services; outpatient hospital services and therapy; and other services. Medicare pays most, but not all, hospital and medical costs for people who are insured. It is available to people over 65 upon application through the local Social Security office.

Medicaid, an assistance program jointly financed by federal, state, and local taxes, pays medical bills for eligible needy and low-income persons: the aged, the blind, the disabled, members of families with dependent children, and some other children. Medicaid differs from state to state, since each state designs its own Medicaid program within federal guidelines. Medicaid pays for at least these services: inpatient hospital care; outpatient hospital services; laboratory and X-ray services; skilled nursing home service; physicians' services; and also, in many states, such services as dental care, prescribed drugs, home health care, eyeglasses, clinic services, and other diagnostic screening and preventive and rehabilitation service. Medicaid can pay for what Medicare does not cover for people who are eligible for both programs. Citizens may apply for Medicaid at their local welfare office (*Medicaid, Medicare: Which is Which?*). In addition, almost all Americans over 65 are covered by hospital insurance (Figure 16-2).

Upon reaching age 65 (or somewhat before), Americans must apply for Social Security and Medicare, neither of which come automatically. As retirement approaches it is wise for the couple to review their assets and to shift at least some of their holdings into high-income stocks and bonds that will give them an assured income. Profits can be taken after retirement when their income tax bracket is lower. This is the time to

Aging family members   395

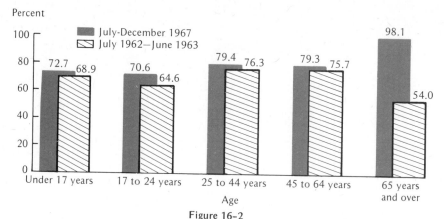

Figure 16-2

Percentage of Persons with Hospital Insurance Coverage, by Age

Source: U.S. Department of Health, Education, and Welfare, Public Health Service, *Monthly Vital Statistics Reports* 18, no. 3 (June 23, 1969): 1.

clear up long-term debts, avoid installment buying, speculation, and other high-risk ventures. Retirees are wise to establish a comfortable cushion fund, to live within a realistic budget, and to consider putting some of their assets into an annuity and/or a trust fund, to assure an adequate income for their remaining years, insofar as is possible.

Postponing retirement makes sense for many an able older worker and his family. Each year of employment after 65 increases the amount of retirement benefits. Working men and women are better off than the retired of the same age and occupational level, both economically and psychologically. Students of the problem lean toward a general recommendation of more flexible retirement ages, with more opportunities for creative activity for the man or woman who wants to continue active production than are now available.

Establishing comfortable routines

One of the most baffling tasks facing the aging couple involves adjusting to being at home together all day—a potential source of friction. Always before, except for brief periods of illness or layoffs, the husband has been away at work during the working day, leaving the home and its care in the hands of the wife. Now that both of the pair are at home all day, every day, the man may "rattle around like a pebble in a pail," as one older man puts it, with nothing to do except get in his wife's way and feel that he is a nuisance around the place.

The problem is quite different for the wife. She, in one sense, "retired" some years ago when the last child was launched and by now has made her adjustment to life. In another sense she never really "retires" as long as there are meals to prepare, beds to make, and household routines to see to. In her later years, she will taper off in the amount of heavy physical work she undertakes. She may get some additional equipment to carry some of the load that now is too burdensome for her failing strength. She may hire some of the heavy work done on a regular or on a seasonal basis, but fundamentally her job as housekeeper and homemaker continues.

Interviews with retired men and their wives find the women continuing such traditional responsibilities as laundry, ironing, dusting, and making beds; but with retirement such tasks as moving and fixing furniture, repairing a faucet, removing and burning trash, and paying household bills shift from the wife to the husband (Ballweg 1967).

Retired men spend much less time out of the house than they did at earlier stages of the family life cycle; and they are more than twice as active in household tasks as they have been at any time since their children were young (Table 11–3).

In many families today, patterns of working jointly as homemakers have been established through the years, so that now, in the postretirement period, the two continue on in the double harness to which they have become accustomed. Responsibilities are assumed on the basis of interest, ability, and strength, the husband routinely assuming some chores, the wife others, and both tackling together the jobs that they enjoy doing as a team. When illness strikes, or when one of the partners is out of the home for a time, the other can then take over, because he or she is already familiar with the processes involved. Decisions are jointly made; authority is assumed by the couple as a unit. Each is accountable to the other and to the realities of the situation, in the family that has already laid a foundation for joint homemaking responsibilities throughout the various stages of the family life cycle.

Protecting physical and mental health

The process of aging brings with it a variety of human needs that husband and wife can help each other to meet—as individuals and as a couple. Physical vitality declines. Eyes, ears, and teeth perhaps need mechanical assistance in the form of glasses, hearing aids, and dentures. In time, the couple find that they do not get around as much, as far, or as easily as they once did. All of these things are normal and to be expected in the later years.

Illnesses and accidents are more costly and critical, and ailments more apt to be chronic in old age than they are in earlier stages of the life cycle. Since women tend to live longer than men, on the average, it is usually the wife who nurses her husband through the illnesses that beset him in the later years. At first she may consider his condition to be temporary.

In time comes the realization that the husband cannot recover and that the disease will cause death, after a long period of disability. The wife's acceptance of the chronic nature of her husband's illness is made easier by the fact that many of the illnesses of the aging begin with mild disabilities and progress very slowly toward complete helplessness; so she adjusts slowly, taking each change as it comes. One by one she takes over responsibilities new to her. She may have to make decisions in which she has had little practice or previous experience, such as taking charge of the finances of the household. She may have to give physical care and at times even protect her husband from the results of his mental wanderings. Care of a chronically ill husband is one of the most difficult tasks that the older wife meets.

The husband faced with the illness of his wife may have an even more difficult task, in that much of what is now expected of him is unfamiliar to him as the man of the house. His wife, who has always provided for his needs, now helplessly depends on him to serve her. He must know how to cook an edible meal, care for a disabled patient, keep the house reasonably neat and clean, and function in what traditionally is the woman's sphere of the home.

Traditionally oriented men who have never learned to be at home in the house are apt to be uncomfortably awkward when the burden of homemaking falls on them. Men who define their roles as males more flexibly, who have always been at ease with the intimate, everyday routines of family living, find these tasks much easier and far more comfortable.

Husbands and wives who have maintained healthful routines through the years fare better in their nurturance of each other as an aging pair than those who have neglected their common health in the earlier stages of life together as a married couple. A good example is found in nutrition, so closely related to the well-being of the older person. The family that has existed for 30 or 40 or more years on a meat-and-potato-and-gravy diet may find it difficult to switch to the high-protein, fresh fruit and vegetable regimes recommended for the aging.

Figure 16-3 outlines the dietary needs of a man of 60 as contrasted with the standard diet at 30. We note that after age 60 the man or woman needs considerably less fat and carbohydrate and more of the protective foods: vitamins, minerals, and proteins. Reasons for nutritional differences between age 30 and 60 are (1) decreased physical activity after the active thirties, and the slowing down of body processes after 60; and (2) the greater need for body building blocks for fitness during the aging process than during the peak years of adulthood.

Malnutrition—"the tea and toast syndrome"—and alcoholism often bring on symptoms of senility that can be reversed with improved health

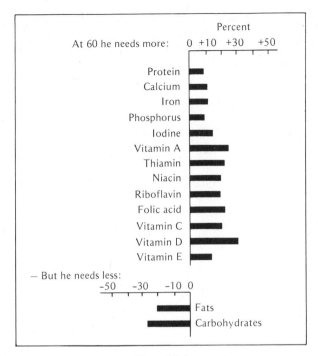

Figure 16-3
Dietary Needs of Normal Man of Sixty Compared to Standard Diet at Age Thirty
Source: C. Ward Crampton, *Live Long and Like It* (New York: Public Affairs Committee, 1948), p. 19.

habits (Butler 1975). Actual brain damage affects 5 percent of people over 65 and an estimated 87 percent of nursing home residents (Goldfarb 1972).

Most elderly mental patients are from the working-class. Middle-class old people are less likely to be consigned to custodial care. Emotionally-disturbed upper-class patients are more often treated with psychotherapy (Kahn 1975:28). "Reality orientation" is now being used successfully to help confused older patients to regain contact with reality and thus maintain their sense of identity (Folsom 1972). Geriatric medicine is increasingly concerned with putting more life into the later years, as well as with adding years to life.

Preventive regimens, such as a healthful balance of rest and activity; regular medical, dental, and eye checkups; sensible acceptance of whatever aids and supplements may be prescribed; a variety of absorbing interests; the avoidance of extreme stress; and good mental hygiene go a long way toward assuring both husband and wife of maximum well-being during their later years together.

Maintaining love, sex, and
marriage relationships

Studies of the aging agree that married people are happier and live longer than do those who are single, widowed, or divorced, No activity, no matter how engaging, contributes to good adjustment in aging unless it is accepted by both aging spouses (Peterson 1973:525). In a good marriage each partner receives the love and attention of someone who is needed and cherished. Both are able to relax and feel settled when things are going well, and to mutually support one another when life's problems come. Their marriage solves most of the needs for love and companionship of the aging pair (Lasswell 1973:518).

Some 408 older husbands and wives connected with senior centers say that companionship and the ability to express their true feelings are the most rewarding aspects of the present phase of their marriage, which they see as the happiest period of their lives together. They list respect, sharing common interests, and love as most important for success in marriage. The morale of these older people is positively related to their happiness in marriage, and to the feeling that their marriage is becoming better as time goes on (Stinnett, Carter, and Montgomery 1972).

Many older adults have been conditioned to believe that sexual capacity declines with age, that sexual activity is bad for their health, and that the continuing presence of sexual desire is abnormal. Sex research finds that although there is a slowing down of sexual capacity in both male and female in the later years, the pleasure in sexual activity continues and may actually increase (Lobsenz 1975). Ill-health can diminish the sex drive, but decreased sexual activity stems more from social prohibitions and emotional problems than from the process of aging itself (Young 1975).

Studies of 700 older people, by Clyde E. Martin (1974) of the national Gerontology Research Center, show that sexual performance persists at least into the 70s and 80s and that sexual activity is highly beneficial to health. Furthermore, many elderly couples perfect the art of lovemaking so that they reach new levels of satisfaction (Butler 1974). Education and high socioeconomic levels are associated with positive interest in sex at advanced ages (Feigenbaum, Lowenthal, and Trier 1966).

In a study of 799 predominantly white, educated, middle-class couples classified according to Duvall's eight stages of the family life cycle, aging couples in retirement were found to be happier in their marriages than they had ever been. Nine out of ten of the husbands (94 percent) and of the wives (88 percent) said that their marriages were going well most or all of the time. Few husbands (6 percent) and wives (10 percent) said that they had negative feelings about their marital relationship more often than once or twice a month. Positive daily companionship with each other was reported by one out of three husbands and wives. The overwhelming majority of the husbands (66 percent) and the wives (82 percent) found the present stage of the family life cycle "very satisfying" (Rollins and Feldman 1970).

Blacks and others with inadequate incomes, low education, and / or physical disabilities are most susceptible to marital dissatisfaction. But regardless of race or income level, couples whose children have grown up and left home are more satisfied with their marriages than are those still raising children (Renne 1970). Burr (1973:45) suggests that "the number of role discrepancies in the marital relationship influences marital satisfaction and this is in inverse, linear relationship." It may well be that role strain is least and marital satisfaction is greatest at both ends of the family life cycle (Rollins and Cannon 1974:281).

Less tangible but quite as important is the emotional building up that each spouse gives the other through their everyday life together. The embittered couple are bent on belittling and tearing each other down by assaults on ego and self. More productive is the support given to one another by husbands and wives who have built up patterns of mutual encouragement and appreciation on which they can lean as other faculties fail. The wife who can bolster her husband's sagging ego as he adjusts himself to diminished usefulness is often a key factor in his eagerness to start fresh in some other line, or to concentrate on some single facet of a former pursuit that can now pay off in fulfillment and satisfaction. The husband who can make his wife sense his devotion and appreciation for all she has done and all that she is helps her to feel desired and desirable— a feeling that is more important than ever in the sunset years. A heart-warming way of doing this was chosen by a man who, on his fifty-fifth wedding anniversary, inserted the following advertisement in his local paper:

> To my sweetheart, Sophie Hensel, I wish to thank you publicly for your love and devotion and for fifty-five years of wedded happiness made possible by your unmatched qualities as wife, mother, mother-in-law, grandmother, and great-grandmother. We all revere you. Your husband, Henry Hensel. (AP release 1953)

Maintaining contact with the family

Four out of five older Americans are members of families, and most of them are glad of it. A two-way, three-generational flow of emotional and financial support between older parents and their grown children's families is general. A study of low-income southern blacks concludes that these urban elderly people still depend, as they always have, on their families as their first line of support. "It thus appears that family functioning among blacks is still highly supportive, to the extent possible, for aged family members" (Jackson 1972:27). The poor generally look to their relatives for assistance, and the more affluent get and give help in gifts and legacies—a major theme in some recent research reports (Adams 1970; Aldous 1967; Hill 1970; Shanas and Streib 1965; Streib 1972; Sussman and Burchinal 1962). The process of disengagement involves reentry *into* the family; as the aging selectively retire from many active and time-consuming community roles, they characteristically enjoy more family interaction on through the later years (Cumming and Henry 1961; Havighurst, Munnicks, Joep, and Neugarten 1969; Maddox 1968).

Upwardly mobile family members may be expected to have less in common with their aging parents than do more conforming individuals. People who marry within their own group usually experience less conflict with their own parents than do those whose marriages have been less homogamous. Some family members love and revere their aging relatives and welcome a chance to serve them even in a culture that fosters individualism and the independence of family members. To other families, older parents are a burden that is assumed only reluctantly and as a last resort.

The problem is especially acute when the elderly person is blind, crippled, bedridden, or so senile that he or she needs protective supervision. If the family must provide the constant supervision that such care entails, it can become a severe mental and physical strain unless a companion or nurse is employed to share the load. In cases where institutionalization is indicated, the family must not only select carefully the most suitable resource and prepare the senile person for it, but must also cope effectively with the feelings of guilt and implied rejection that "putting a loved one away" has meant in our culture.

In a study of older people in a midwestern town with a population of about seven thousand, only 15 percent of the parents over 65 years of age were characterized as dependent and neglected, while 85 percent were seen as relatively independent, as we see in Table 16-4.

The Cornell Study of Occupational Retirement found that the great majority of the older parents in their sample of 2,300 maintain frequent contact with their children's families. Three out of four see their children often, and 70 percent see their grandchildren often. Other relatives are considerably less often in touch with these older persons. Only one-third see their brothers and sisters often; a fourth see their nieces and nephews often; and only 12 percent are in frequent touch with their cousins (Streib and Thompson 1960:476).

Most grandparents find significance in their grandparenting roles, along a number of lines (Table 16-5). Maintaining close and meaningful contact with married children and grandchildren can be a most rewarding task of the later years.

Keeping active and involved

Aging husbands and wives tend to become less active in community activities. Some are not physically able to get about as they used to do. Others lack transportation for getting places. Many have lost interest as time goes by, and spend more and more time by themselves at home.

Table 16-4
Relative Independence of Parents over Sixty-five Years of Age

Independence		Dependence and neglect	
Parents and children are mutually independent but maintain a close social and affectional relationship	27%	Parents share child's home but are somewhat burdensome	1%
Parents and children are considered as independent adults but may share home or advice with each other	44	Parents live alone but children come in regularly to give care	5
Parents are responsible for children full or part time	1	Children are distant and seldom see parents	8
Parents have some responsibility for children	5	Parents have no interest in the children	1
Parents share home of children and are a help to them	8	Parents are completely neglected by children	0
Total	85%	Total	15%

Source: Ruth Albrecht, "Relationships of Older Parents with Their Children," *Marriage and Family Living* 16, no. 1 (February 1954), excerpts from Table 1, p. 33.

Table 16-5
Multiple Meanings of the Grandparent Role

Meanings and significance of being grandparents	Grandmothers (N = 70)	Grandfathers (N = 70)
1. Biological renewal and/or continuity "It's carrying on the family line."	29	16
2. Emotional self-fulfillment "I was too busy with my own children."	13	19
3. Resource person to the child "I set aside money especially for him."	3	8
4. Vicarious achievement through the child "She'll grow up to be a beautiful woman."	3	3
5. Remote: little effect on the self "I don't even feel like a grandfather."	19	20
6. Insufficient data	3	4

Source: Bernice L. Neugarten and Karol K. Weinstein, "The Changing American Grandparent," *Journal of Marriage and the Family* 26, no. 2 (May 1964): 199–204; and also chapter 31 in Bernice L. Neugarten, ed., *Middle Age and Aging* (Chicago: University of Chicago Press, 1968), p. 282.

A study of men and women over 65 years of age in rural New York found that physical inability, lack of interest, and lack of transportation were the three reasons most frequently given by the aging for their reduced organizational participation, as we see in Table 16-6.

Interviews with 500 recent retirees found that high morale is significantly related to activities that involve helping others (Sheldon, McEwan and Ryser 1975:136). Concern for others takes many forms, such as sharing one's accumulated wisdom and experience by teaching, consulting, and working with others in community organizations. Even though physical limitations restrict mobility, increased emotional, intellectual, and spiritual sharing is still possible—even for wheelchair patients. Participation then takes the form of reaching out for friendships or associations that are mutually rewarding (Pfeiffer 1974). Friendships between men and women are meaningful at all ages. The older women most likely to have men friends are employed, active in voluntary associations, and married to men in white-collar jobs who initiate a large proportion of the couple's cross-sex friendships (Booth and Hess 1974:46).

The Kansas City Study of Adult Life finds that one-third of the old people in their population are mature, integrated, and functioning well—with strong egos, a sense of mastery and control, a feeling of self-worth and a willingness to take on new roles and responsibilities to replace those lost at retirement. The conclusion is that remaining active is good for older people's morale and sense of satisfaction with life (Havighurst, Munnicks, Joep, and Neugarten 1969; Neugarten 1968).

A study of the adjustment to retirement of men betweeen the ages of 70 and 75 in seven countries shows that those who gradually slow down their activity remain happy and busy during the years of lessening physical vigor. Some become creative in new leisure activities, others develop and expand their participation in the community in ways that continue to

Table 16-6
Reasons Given for Less Time Given to Organizations by
143 Men and Women over Sixty-five Years of Age in Rural New York

Reasons for less organizational participation	Number of times mentioned
Not physically able	51
Lack of interest	41
Lack of transportation	24
Not enough time	17
Can't afford it	14
Moved to a new neighborhood	7
Other	9

Source: Roland L. Warren, "Old Age in a Rural Township," *Age Is No Barrier* (Albany, N.Y.: New York State Joint Legislative Committee on Problems of the Aging, 1952), p. 156.

bring them satisfaction (Havighurst 1972:113). A seven-year study of 4,000 men and women, initiated one year before they retired and repeated a number of times after their retirement, found that retrenchment in one sphere does not imply retrenchment in others, and that retirees demonstrate impressive adaptability and tolerance for change (Streib and Schneider 1971).

Success in this developmental task lies in the ability to remain curious and concerned and to retain patience in the present and faith in the future. Those who find the aging years good are "self-educable, self-sufficient, and aware of all that is taking place about them. They smile and stand straight. They listen and they give of themselves to others of every vintage" (Perara 1974).

Finding meanings in life

It is well known that old people reminisce about their earlier life experiences. Reminiscing is not a sign of senile maladjustment, but of a search for the central meanings of life. This is essentially healthful, because it: (1) provides material for a life review; (2) makes it easier to adjust sensibly to difficult situations; and (3) contributes to a perspective in which life makes sense (Pincus 1970; Lewis 1971; and Moberg 1972).

Late in life many earlier activities are no longer possible, but religious faith and practice have no age limits (Beard 1969). However, many people drop out of church in the later years for reasons of failing health, reduced income, and feelings of being unappreciated or of being pushed out by younger generations (Moberg 1972:52). Life-history interviews with over 600 men ranging in social status from New York's skid row and urban lower-classes to the upper-middle class found widespread religious disaffiliation at all socioeconomic levels. With advancing age, church attendance becomes less important to rich and poor alike. An exception is found in skid row men, who, having dropped out of society, maintain ties with few organizations—save for the churches that have been established to serve them (Bahr 1970).

A Duke university study of people ranging in age from 60 to 94, conducted over a period of 20 years, concluded that the elderly do not become preoccupied with religion or religious activities. In fact, there is a general shift from more church attendance in childhood to less in old age. However, positive religious attitudes remain, despite a decline in religious activities. Religion was found to be an important factor in promoting a feeling of usefulness, happiness, and personal adjustment (AD 1976:39-40).

The closer individuals come to the end of life, the more they believe in life after death. Among the over-95 age group in one study, 100 percent of both men and women were certain of an afterlife (Cavan, Burgess, and

Goldhammer 1949:58). Chapter 17 explores what death means to the dying and to members of the dying person's family.

Many older people today want to live more, not just longer. They value a sense of dignity and worth as persons. An official government publication says in part, "To most older Americans, a high degree of independence is almost as valuable as life itself. It is the touchstone of self-respect and dignity. It is the measure they use to decide their importance to others. And, it is their source of strength for helping those around them" (*The Older American* 1963:7).

As one grows older, although the sight is dimmed, one perceives more acutely the glint of dew on the iris, the glory of a storm, the sweet peace of the woods at dusk—as one did as a child.

> The real bond between the generations is the insights they share, the appreciation they have in common, the moments of inner experience in which they meet. . . .
>
> Old men need a vision, not only recreation.
> Old men need a dream, not only a memory.
> It takes three things to attain a sense of significant being:
>   God
>   A Soul
>   And a Moment.
> And the three are always here.
> Just to be is a blessing. Just to live is holy. (Heschel 1961: 15-16)

The young may die, but the old must.

Henry Wadsworth Longfellow

Death in the family

chapter seventeen

Death is a family affair. When word comes that a family member has died, everyone rallies around, attends the funeral if at all possible, and does what is possible to comfort those most personally involved. Every family faces death sooner or later—each in its own time, each in its own way.

The dying in the population

More Americans live out their life span now than in the past. In 1974, people of both sexes over the ages of 65 had the "lowest estimated age-specific death rates ever recorded . . . in the United States" (U.S. Department of Health, Education and Welfare 1975:4). White people have consistently lower mortality rates than do nonwhites (Kitagawa 1972:95). Low-income groups have high mortality rates, which in turn are related to differences in educational level, so that "at age 25, white females with at least 1 year of college could expect to live almost 10 years longer, on the average, than those who completed less than 5 years of school" (Kitagawa 1972:93).

Women outnumber men in the later decades of life—in keeping with their more favorable survival record throughout the life cycle. In 1974 there were more than 12.8 million women aged 65 and over, compared to some 9 million men over 65 in the population. By 1980, it is expected that aging women will outnumber older men by 4.7 million, and by the year 1985, by 5.3 million (Table 17-1).

Now that more men and women live into their 70s and 80s, more die of cardiovascular-renal disease and cancer (Figure 17-1). Of the roughly 2 million deaths each year in the United States, 113,000 are due to accidents, 24,000 to suicide, 18,000 to homicide, and 210,000 to fatal cerebrovascular episodes (Gaylin 1974:30). Death is no stranger to the aging, and comes to infants, children and young people as well.

Metropolitan Life Insurance Company-Standard Ordinary Policyholders

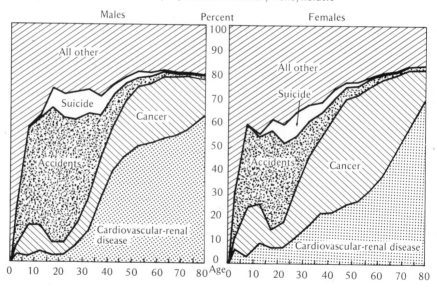

Figure 17-1
Percent of Death From Specified Causes by Sex and Age 1974
Source: "Leading Causes of Death Among Insured Lives." *Statistical Bulletin* 56 (August 1975): 11.

Table 17-1
Population at Ages 65 and Over, by Sex and Age
United States, 1960–1985

Sex and age	Population in 1,000's					Percent increase		
	April 1 1960	April 1 1970	July 1 1974	July 1 1980	July 1 1985	1960 to 1970	1970 to 1980	1980 to 1985
Male								
65 and over	7,503	8,366	8,966	9,914	10,684	11.5	18.5	7.8
65–69	2,931	3,124	3,473	3,827	4,040	6.6	22.5	5.6
70–74	2,185	2,316	2,411	2,818	3,015	6.0	21.7	7.0
75 and over	2,387	2,926	3,082	3,269	3,629	22.6	11.7	11.0
Female								
65 and over	9,057	11,605	12,849	14,609	15,975	28.1	25.9	9.4
65–69	3,327	3,872	4,362	4,836	5,121	16.4	24.9	5.9
70–74	2,554	3,130	3,291	3,931	4,213	22.6	25.6	7.2
75 and over	3,176	4,603	5,196	5,842	6,641	44.9	26.9	13.7

Source of basic data: Various reports of the Bureau of the Census, in "Profile of Elders in the United States." *Statistical Bulletin* 56 (April 1975): 8.

Death of children and young adults

A family is sometimes stricken by the sudden death of one of its children in a highway accident, drowning, fire, poisoning, a fatal fall, or one of the other catastrophic events that can take the life of a child. Accidental death triggers blame, guilt, and remorse in the ones thought to be responsible, as well as grief over the premature snuffing out of a life. An infant's unexplained crib death adds a further factor of speculation to the family's sense of loss.

Thousands of families know the agony of having a child who is terminally ill. Leukemia, the form of cancer most prevalent in children, each year afflicts thousands of boys and girls under 15. Child psychologists advise parents to watch their fatally-ill child for cues that will alert them to the child's readiness to discuss his fears and fantasies. For instance, when a terminally-ill youngster draws a picture filled with dark shadows and holes, a perceptive adult can say, "That's a scary picture : shall we talk about it?" This tells the child that it is all right to talk about fear of death, if and when he is ready.

What children think about death depends on the individual child, on his or her family, and on the child's psychological development. Under the age of two, a child has no conception of death and reflects only the parents' reaction. Between two and four, a child sees death as separation, most often temporary. Between four and six, preschoolers have seen or heard of animals crushed by traffic, and think of death as punishment or mutilation. In the early school years, most children think of death as permanent and fear it as inevitable.

Parents are wise to work at resolving their guilt feelings and at achieving a new sense of the meaning of life after the loss of one of their children. One such mother says, "We realized time was passing us by, so we thought we'd better make the best of it" (Keebler 1975:18).

Most of the 30,000 adults who responded to a *Psychology Today* questionnaire about death said that they first became aware of death when they were between the ages of three and ten. Their first personal involvement was the death of grandparents or great-grandparents (43 percent), or of animals (18 percent). Only three out of ten recalled open discussion of death in their families when they were growing up (Table 17-2).

Nearly half of these respondents, predominantly young adults, recalled a "heaven-or-hell" concept of death when they were children (48 percent). Equal percentages (10 percent) conceived of death as sleep and as mysterious and unknowable, as children. As young adults, more than four times as many (43 percent) believe in life after death as they did as children (9 percent); and a majority (55 percent) strongly wish for life after death (Shneidman 1971:74). More than two out of three (68 per-

Table 17-2
Discussion of Death in the Family
(30,000 Adults Recall Their Childhood Experience)

My family's discussion of death when I was a child	Percentage of replies
Never recall any discussion	33%
Discussed death openly	30
Talked about death with some discomfort	20
Only when necessary, then excluded children	15
As though it were a taboo subject	2
	100%

Source: Edwin S. Shneidman, "You and Death," *Psychology Today* 5, no. 1 (June 1971): 44.

cent) would prefer their own death to be sudden, nonviolent, quiet, and dignified. Two-thirds of the respondents believe they will die in old age (69 percent), and if they could choose, that is what they would want (Shneidman 1971:77).

Until World War I more women died in childbirth than men in battle (Duvall and Hill 1945:311). Now maternal death is relatively rare (Chapter 10) and the number of Americans who may die in battle will depend on the success of peace-keeping efforts around the world. Highway accidents still take the lives of many young men and women. However, enforcement of laws requiring reduced driving speeds and programs aimed at the prevention of driving while intoxicated have helped to reduce the number of such accident victims.

Awareness of dying

Young adults magnify the "crisis of dying," but the aged tend to take it in stride. In one study of dying elderly patients, only three out of 80 found it difficult to discuss death. In spite of their recognition that death was imminent, there was no storminess, no disruptiveness—"It was as if they were dealing with a developmental task they were coping with adequately. . . ." It is the *rare* case for an individual to have lived into the seventh or eighth decade of life without having come to grips with his own death and without having developed some personal philosophical system—although possibly a primitive one—for accounting for and dealing with it" (Lieberman 1973:13). Most people sense that there is a time for living and a time for dying, and the process appears to be easier for those who feel that the timing is appropriate.

Many dying patients do not need to be told that their death is expected. They know it anyway, by the change in the people around them. They see it in their loved ones' tears, and in the too-brave smiles of those who cannot hide their true feelings. They sense it in the lowered voices of those who attend them, and in their doctors' less frequent calls when

Table 17-3
Five Stages in Dying Patients' Reaction to Impending Death

Stages	Emotional meanings
1. Denial and isolation	"No, not me."
2. Anger, rage, envy, resentment	"Why me?" "Why not someone else?"
3. Bargaining with death for time	"Just one more, then I'll be ready."
4. Preparatory grief and depression	"Losing everything and everyone."
5. Acceptance	"I'm ready now."

Source: Elizabeth Kübler-Ross, *On Death and Dying* (New York: Macmillan Publishing Co., Inc., 1970); PBS interview, 1976, and other appearances.

there is no hope of recovery. Dr. Elizabeth Kübler-Ross, a psychiatrist who has worked with dying patients since 1965, has observed a sequence of five reactions to the knowledge of impending death (Table 17-3).

When the end comes, the majority of the dying have reached a stage in which they are able to accept death without despair or fear—and with a sense of having come full circle in life. When the illness has lasted for a long time and has been marked by great pain and suffering, death may be a welcome relief and release for the patient and for the family. Dr. Kübler-Ross describes her own mother's death, which came after four years of total paralysis, as a blessing (Kübler-Ross 1976).

The dying person's family

Family and friends tend to avoid mentioning even to each other the imminent death of a loved one, except in somber whispers and veiled allusions to his "passing away." The tendency is to put up a bright, brave front with the dying person and to deny that his life is about to end. When the one whose life is ebbing away tries to talk with his family about his death, his relatives are quick to change the subject or to tell him not to speak of such things.

As soon as a patient becomes critically ill, he is sent to a hospital, where medical personnel take over, and where family visits are limited. Many a terminally-ill older person is in the care, however expert, of strangers; and the inevitable tubes and machines intensify the impression of strangeness. He may hear his case discussed as though he were not there. When he, or she, worries about what the hospital care is costing, he gets little reassurance from either the medical attendants or his nearest of kin, who try to spare him such worries on his deathbed.

The aging wife whose husband is desperately ill may be so frightened by the imagined effect on her of his death that she is unable to give him the support he needs. If she has always depended on him, her security is threatened, and she wonders how she can carry on without him. The elderly husband whose wife is about to die may have an even greater sense of loss in that he, who has always been waited on, is now expected to do the thoughtful, personal things for which he is unprepared. He may resent this reversal of roles. "Why did she have to get sick on me?" one such man asked (Kübler-Ross 1970:158). The couple may have fought like cat and dog over the years but, faced with final separation, the survivor is torn with anguished regret—"Why wasn't I nicer to him/her while there was yet time?"

Those who are about to be left often blame themselves for their loved one's condition: "If only I'd insisted . . ." "If only I hadn't let him . . ." "If only I'd looked after her better." Members of the family may try to assuage their guilt by spending all the time permitted at the dying person's bedside, rather than allowing him some time to be alone with his thoughts—and themselves the necessary intervals of rest to keep up their strength for the difficult days ahead.

The dying person's problems come to an end, but those of the family members left behind are just beginning. They are about to face a series of difficult decisions and tasks—the disposal of the body, the carrying out of the wishes of the newly deceased, the closing of ranks in the family circle, financing the terminal illness and death, and handling their own feelings. For the first few days the family are busy alerting relatives and friends, getting obituary material together, and going through the funeral or memorial service. Then comes the time for tangled emotions to surface—numbness, emptiness, grief for the loved one and for the loss in their own lives. Grown children and grandchildren cannot be expected to react to the death in the same way as one who has shared the life of the person who has died for many years. Yet, they can encourage the widowed to weep and to work through the feelings that should be ventilated at this time (Kübler-Ross 1970:178–179).

Experiencing the death of a beloved person is never easy: it can be a shattering experience, or one that, after a time, leads one to new levels of awareness of the quality of life itself. One particularly sensitive man shares some of the intensely personal experiences he had upon the death of his father, and the reaction of his children to the loss of their grandfather,

> One by one they [the children] came to me to say goodnight and to share some of their thoughts and concerns of the day [of the funeral], their inability to understand some of their own reactions and feelings. And I listened and heard them in a way that I had never known before. In some ways their loss was indeed greater than mine. And I mourned more for them than for myself. In my relationship with my children, that night has become a watershed. I think of it often. How glad I was that the children had come with us. They had gained, I later learned from them, a bit of their past and who they

were in relationship to it, even in this brief and seemingly disturbing experience. Their roots of self had sunk a bit deeper. (Gaylin 1975:253)

Death education and counseling, as part of ongoing family life education, do much to help individuals and families cope with the experience of dying. Death is universal and comes to tens of thousands of families each year. High school and college courses using examples from literature and drama are helping students and future teachers to gain insights into death as a family experience and to form wholesome attitudes toward dying (Somerville 1971). Adults attend seminars on death and dying in many communities. Nursing and medical personnel are learning how to ease the psychological suffering of dying patients in their care (Kübler-Ross 1975; Weisman 1972). Those responsible for counseling the families of dying persons aim at helping family members to achieve three goals: (1) accepting death and their feelings about it; (2) mourning their loss; and (3) facing the stress of functioning as a family in new and different ways (Krieger and Bascue 1975:354).

The tragedy of suicide

Suicide is a tragedy for the individual and for the family. It leaves hurt, disgrace, remorse, and bitterness in its wake in many cases. Because of the stigma attached to suicide, family members often feel shame in addition to their grief. They feel that somehow they must be responsible for not having prevented one of their own from reaching such a point of desolation. They find it difficult, if not impossible, to collect the suicide's insurance. If they are Christians, they have been taught that the taking of one's life is a sin. As human beings, they have been reared to see suicide as a crime, immoral, and taboo. Yet, thousands of Americans commit suicide each year. Counting only recorded suicides—and excluding many questionable "accidents"—there are twice as many deaths by suicide as from homicide in the United States each year, according to the Center for Studies of Suicide Prevention of The National Institute of Mental Health (Frederick and Lague 1972:4).

The suicide rate is highest among professional and business men and lowest among farmers and artisans, but the risk is still high among unskilled workers. Black urban young men kill themselves at a higher rate than white youths, apparently because so many more nonwhites are unemployed. They feel helpless, useless, and hopeless because they are unable to make their own way (Seiden 1970:26). American Indians have twice as high a suicide rate as the national average in the United States, due probably to their poverty, unemployment, isolation, culture-conflict, and confused identity as tribal structures are weakened. Comparable figures for Spanish Americans are not available, but it is assumed that they are high because of poverty and the lack of father figures. In recent years suicide has risen to fourth place as the cause of death among teenagers and young adults, for a multitude of reasons: family problems, failure in school, love and friendship problems, loneliness, drugs, and alcoholism.

People commit suicide for any number of personal reasons: to get attention, as an act of aggression, to escape pain or to avoid expected suffering; or because of loneliness, hopelessness, disappointment, or the loss of some significant person. Nearly everyone loses a loved one or is disappointed by someone close to him or her at one time or another. Most people struggle through their pain and problems; others "just can't take any more." Experts classify the motives for suicide in four main categories (Table 17-4).

The high rate of suicide among the elderly is attributed to their isolation, loss of close relatives and friends, poor physical health, dwindling financial resources, and lack of involvement in the life around them (Bock 1972:71-79). Suicide prevention centers operate in many communities, maintaining round-the-clock telephone contact with individuals who are threatening to kill themselves. These efforts are expanding, developing into outreach programs in which lonely, discouraged people are visited, their needs explored, and their contact with the community reestablished when possible.

When healthy young adults were asked, "Has there ever been a time in your life when you wanted to die?" 60 percent replied in the affirmative, mostly because of emotional upsets (37 percent) or to escape an intolerable social or interpersonal situation (18 percent). When asked to speculate on the reason most likely for their committing suicide at

Table 17-4
Personal "Reasons" for Committing Suicide

Category	Illustrations and examples
1. Impulse	In the heat of anger, frustration, disappointment: a jilted lover walks into traffic, or takes sleeping pills
2. Depression	"Why go on living?" "Life has no meaning anymore; no one needs me."
3. Serious illness	Constant pain, long suffering, high costs of terminal illness make suicide seem like an escape for the invalid and the family
4. Communication attempt	A woman begs her husband to be faithful; a man asks his wife to come back to him in suicide attempts

Source: Calvin J. Frederick and Louise Lague, *Dealing with the Crisis of Suicide* (New York: Public Affairs Committee, 1972), pp. 12–14.

some time in the future these 30,000 young adults gave a number of possible motivations (Table 17-5).

An American priest says, "Suicide is admissible. Why? Because in today's tumultuous world of bitter politics and broken dreams, one does not know quite how he or she will die. Any one of us may be stricken with a terminal illness in a culture which has learned to prolong existence . . . but which has *not* learned to affirm death" (Leach 1973:14). A Roman Catholic theologian concedes that at times suicide may be moral, even though like war it is tragic. "There are times when the ending of life is the best that life offers" (Maguire 1974:85). When a world-renowned religious leader, a former president of Union Theological Seminary, and his wife ended their lives by their own hands, Norman Cousins devoted a full-page editorial to "The Right to Die," in which he concluded, "Death is not the greatest loss in life. The greatest loss is what dies inside us while we live. The unbearable tragedy is to live without dignity or sensitivity" (Cousins 1975:4).

Death with dignity

"Isn't there some way to end her suffering?" The family had watched their beloved mother endure pain month after month. She faced the amputation of a gangrenous leg. The suffering woman had said goodbye to her family when she was fully conscious. Now her groans and whimpers were her wordless testimony to her readiness to die.

Modern medicine has greatly increased man's power over life and death. Blood transfusions, drugs, intravenous feeding, mechanical respirators, heart stimulants, dialysis, organ transplants, and many other heroic measures can prolong life long after a patient is capable of fully human

Table 17-5
Most Likely Motivation for Committing Suicide
(Suppositions of 30,000 Adults)

Most likely motivation for committing suicide, personally	Percentage
Loneliness or abandonment	31%
Physical illness or pain	24
Death or loss of a loved one	9
Atomic war	8
Fear of insanity	6
Failure or disgrace	5
To get even or to hurt someone	2
Family strife	1
Other	14
	100%

Source: Edwin S. Shneidman, "You and Death," *Psychology Today* 5, no. 1 (June 1971): 79.

responses. An individual's greatest fear is not of death but of long, lingering, painful dying. The family stands helplessly by, unless some measures are taken to provide the death with dignity that all would prefer (Russell 1975:17).

Physicians are not deaf to those begging to die, but their training has been to preserve life as long as they possibly can. One physician questions traditional practice with the position, "At the end of life, the point is what the *patient* wants, not what the doctor wants. Most patients, I am sure, would gladly trade three days of being unconscious in an oxygen tent for one day of consciousness in which to say goodbye" (Barnard 1973:62). Doctors increasingly are respecting their patients' desire that no "heroic measures" be used to prolong life beyond the point where it has meaning (Mannes 1974). A woman in her eighties writes,

Hold Not My Life

When Death shall draw my number from the Ebon bowl
And there can be no question of His *sure* approach,
I trust no doctor's skilled hands will hold me back
With modern methods and techniques at his command.
I do not wish intake of food except by nature's way;
Prolong not an already finished life to suffer on awhile.
But pray keep me from agonizing pain or mental aberration
And help me pass into whatever Realm may lie beyond.

Evelyn M. Shafer, with permission

Euthanasia, a term derived from the Greek words for "a good death," is being widely discussed. *Active euthanasia* is an action taken to end mercifully the life of one who is enduring suffering or a meaningless existence. It is illegal under present law in most countries. *Negative euthanasia* is letting a hopelessly ill patient die without the use of extraordinary measures to prolong life. There is confusion about the legal status of this approach at the present writing. Legislatures are considering bills to make death with dignity legal in various states (Van Gieson 1974); and the United Nations has had a proposal under study ever since the International Conference on Human Rights in 1968 ("Medically Prolonging" release 1970).

Theologians generally affirm a patient's right to life and death. A pronouncement by Pope Pius XII in 1957 advised that it is in accord with the Gospel to use narcotics to relieve suffering in terminal cases even if by so doing life will be shortened and that it is not always necesary to use extraordinary means to prolong life. Years ago a professor of Christian ethics said decisively, "Death control, like birth control, is a matter of human dignity. Without it persons become puppets (Fletcher 1964:83).

Table 17-6
Most Clergymen and Lawyers Approve Negative Euthanasia

Item	Clergymen N = 100 Percentage			Lawyers N = 104 Percentage			Total N = 204 Percentage		
	Yes	No	?	Yes	No	?	Yes	No	?
1. Negative euthanasia for member/client	89	8	3	91	7	2	90	7	
2. Negative euthanasia for spouse	86	11	3	76	20	4	81	16	
3. Positive euthanasia for member/client	30	62	8	50	47	3	40	54	
4. Positive euthanasia for spouse	27	64	9	37	59	4	32	62	
5. Pain medication	93	4	3	93	1	6	93	2	
6. Autopsy/Transplant	98	0	2	99	1	0	99	1	
7. Have been involved in such decisions	69	28	3	26	69	5	47	49	
8. Religion is important in such matters	96	1	3	22	70	8	58	36	

Source: Caroline E. Preston and John Horton, "Attitudes among Clergy and Lawyers toward Euthanasia," *The Journal of Pastoral Care* 26, no. 2 (June 1972): 111.

A poll of randomly selected clergymen and lawyers found that the great majority of both ministers and attorneys approve of negative euthanasia (Table 17-6).

A number of arguments against death with dignity have been advanced. The Governor of Oregon refuted these as follows: (1) "It's suicide."—The motive for the action and the purpose served justify the action. (2) "The hospitals and the doctors will be subject to lawsuits."—This is a legalism that can be dealt with. (3) "A doctor declining to use heroic measures violates the Hippocratic oath."—The progress of medical science has outstripped both the laws that control it and the moral and ethical concepts upon which it was founded; and (4) "God has appointed the time for man to die."—If that is so, then it is as immoral to prolong life as it is to shorten it (McCall 1972:6). There is general agreement that adequate controls will have to be established to prevent political and personal abuse of the practice of euthanasia, either negative or positive.

Gallup pollsters (1973) reported that a majority of Americans said that doctors should be allowed by law to painlessly end the life of a person with an incurable disease if the patient and his family request it. A similar percentage (62 percent) of the public questioned in a Harris Poll (1973) believed that a terminally-ill patient ought to be able to tell his doctor to let him die rather than to extend life unduly when no cure is in sight. The eminent historian Will Durant wrote some years ago, "Life's final tragedy is unwilling continuance—to outlive one's self and be forbidden to die" (Durant 1944:231). Dr. Elizabeth Kübler-Ross (1976), when asked her views on euthanasia, responded that neither "euthanasia" nor "mercy killing" are appropriate terms for what she advocates—allowing a person to die a natural death without prolonging the process in a way that exacts heavy tolls, both emotional and financial.

Special hospitals for the terminally ill have been successful in relieving the physical, mental, spiritual and social distress of dying patients and their families. The name of such a facility is *hospice*, which means "a way station," a place of refuge for travelers on a journey—life's journey in the case of the dying patient. Most of the dying people in such hospices are comforted by the knowledge that they are meeting death with dignity and in peace (Barnard 1973).

More than 50 thousand Americans in one recent year wrote to the Euthanasia Educational Fund in New York for copies of "A Living Will," a short testament addressed to one's family, physician, clergyman, and lawyer, that says, in part, "If there is no reasonable expectation of my recovery from mental or physical disability, I request that I be allowed to die and not be kept alive by artificial means or heroic measures." Such a living will has no legal weight, but few can ignore it in good conscience. A Catholic theologian asks the basic ethical question, "Is merely physical, vegetative life sacred, or is it life that is actually and potentially personal that is sacred?" (Maguire 1974:62). A Miami physician, who has been active in promoting death with dignity legislation, told the White House Conference on Aging, "The prolongation of life, through modern medical miracles, is more inhumane than the peaceful natural end of such a life . . . when my own time comes, give me a death . . . in keeping with Carl Sandburg's words (my version), 'Death, like birth, can be glorious'" (Sackett 1971).

Laws in all 50 states make it easy for a person to will his or her body or any part of it for scientific and medical use. Ninety-nine out of a hundred lawyers and clergy would support a client in his decision to donate his body for autopsy or for transplantation of organs (Table 17-6, item 6). Morticians in many communities have forms that their future clients may sign, indicating their wish to have their human material donated to nearby medical facilities for teaching, research, or transplant. Surveys find that most people favor the donation of organs such as corneas, kidneys, etc. (Webster 1975).

Funeral arrangements

Immediately after a death in a family, there are many decisions to be made and many things to do. The funeral director is called. The hospital releases the body to him after the doctor has signed the death certificate. Vital statistics and biographical materials are gathered for the obituary and sent to newspapers in places where the deceased has lived. If flowers are to be omitted, the family may suggest some charity for memorial gifts. When the time for the funeral has been set, family members and friends are alerted and plans are made to extend hospitality to those coming from a distance. Neighbors and friends express their sympathy, and someone in the family may be assigned to answer the telephone and doorbell, if the most bereaved person wishes it.

If there is to be a traditional funeral, the mortician needs to know whether there will be viewing of the body, at times that he and the family set. The casket must be chosen by the widowed, with the help of some close friend or family member. Choices are made of the location of the funeral (usually church or funeral parlor), pallbearers, ushers, flowers, burial garments, and arrangements for burial or cremation. If the deceased has been a member of a fraternal or military order, their leaders are informed.

When death occurs under certain conditions (accidental death, death from other than natural causes, or sudden death of a person not under a doctor's care) the coroner's services are required. It is up to him to determine whether an autopsy is indicated. When arrangements have been made for the donation of the body for medical purposes, it is sent at once to the facility accepting it. When the funeral is to be held at a distance, arrangements are made for shipping the body and for its reception by a funeral director in that community.

More and more families are choosing cremation in place of burial of the body. When arrangements have already been made with a cremation society, the body is turned over to them as soon as it has been released; or the funeral director may arrange for cremation at the request of the family. The ashes may then be scattered or preserved at the discretion of the family. Memorial societies offer their members simple, dignified, and economical care and disposal of the dead, with or without a memorial service. Such a service usually takes place after the body has been cremated or interred, to emphasize the spiritual rather than the physical aspects of death, and to celebrate the life of the person who has departed.

Costs of dying

Death is financially fatal to many an American family. Costs for the funeral service and care of the body range from a few hundred to many thousands of dollars, depending on the cost of the casket, the funeral director's expenses, the vault or cemetery lot, and the simplicity of the plans. A government study estimates an average cost of $624 for the lowest quoted cemetery charges (Harmer 1974:61). If the body is to be donated to science or cremated, neither embalming nor an expensive casket are needed, and there are no costs for burial plot, vault, or funeral.

Prefinanced plans are available through funeral directors in most places. When making such arrangements, it is wise to know just what is included, the terms of the contract, the itemized costs of the various items and services, and the estimates for additional charges, if any.

Widows spend more on funerals than do men at all economic levels, perhaps because their insurance benefits tend to be greater, or because women react more emotionally to the loss of a mate than do men (Pine and Phillips 1971:133). In situations where death is expected, costs are higher at the upper social class levels, but in cases of unexpected death more working-class families spend in excess of $800 (Table 17-7). The costs of the long illness that leads to death often deplete a family's reserves, so that economy in funerals is sought by families with limited means. Whatever the socioeconomic status of the family, it is wise to wait a few months before buying expensive markers or monuments for the grave.

Most couples carry life insurance that helps with funeral costs and the expenses of the widowed for a while thereafter. All persons receiving Social Security are eligible for a lump sum death benefit up to $255. Widows of honorably discharged veterans are paid a basic $250 allowance toward the burial expenses of their veteran husbands. Service-connected death allowances can be as high as $800 (Porter 1975:753). As more Americans freely discuss death and plan for their own dying and for the security of those they leave behind, reasonable funeral costs may become the norm.

Death traps and widows' rackets

The recently bereaved are vulnerable to exploitation by con men who slip into town, register under assumed names, and set about trying to bilk widows mentioned in the obituary columns of the local paper. Sylvia Porter (1975:753-754) tells of hearse chasers indicted for mailing, C.O.D., bibles priced at many times their worth; of small loan company operators claiming payment and interest on purportedly unpaid loans made to the deceased; and even of persons posing as representatives having life in-

Table 17-7
Funeral Costs by Social Status and Mode of Death
Percent spending more than $800

Mode of death	Lower-class	Working-class	Middle-class	Upper-class	Total
Expected	12.5%	38.8%	56.1%	55.5%	45.5%
Unexpected	25.0	61.7	56.0	57.1	54.3

Source: Vanderlyn R. Pine and Derek L. Phillips, "The Cost of Dying: A Sociological Analysis of Funeral Expenditures," in Frances G. Scott and Ruth M. Brewer, eds., *Confrontations of Death* (Eugene, Ore.: Oregon Center for Gerontology, 1971), p. 135.

surance policies on the deceased, which, having lapsed, require the final premium of $30 or $40 for the face amount of the policy. The widow pays the supposedly lapsed premium and never sees it, her insurance money, or the man again.

Unscrupulous investment counselors, speculators, and seemingly trustworthy "friends" look for windfalls in the legacies of untold numbers of widows each year. Widows as well as widowers are advised to avoid hasty decisions about their money until they have recovered from their first grief, and until they have had a chance to check on any "offer too good to miss." A hardheaded member of the family, a lawyer, or some other person in whom the widow and her husband have had confidence may be worth his weight in gold in checking into some of the details a widow may overlook in her bereavement.

Grief and bereavement

Our society is not comfortable with grief, yet grief is an inevitable reaction to severe personal loss. The bereaved is at first numb and unbelieving, then despairing, angry, guilty, and restless as he or she seeks release from distress (Marris 1975:31). Grief is most intense and longest lasting when death comes unexpectedly. Studies in England, Sweden, and at Harvard University find that whereas a long illness prepares survivors for the loss of a loved one, sudden death leaves the widowed still struggling with grief two to four years after their loss ("Study Is Made of Bereavement" 1973). When the grieving person does not recover from the loss, he or she may go into a depression, which is indicated by such signs as: (1) feelings of hopelessness, (2) inability to concentrate, (3) change in physical activities, (4) loss of self-esteem, (5) withdrawal from others, (6) threats of suicide, (7) oversensitivity, (8) misdirected anger, (9) guilt, and (10) extreme dependence on others (National Association for Mental Health 1975:67).

The immediate effects and the secondary reactions to bereavement range from total failure to readjust to conspicuous success in the task of coping with bereavement (Table 17–8).

Widowhood

The widowed die sooner than the married, and while living they are more susceptible to suicide, social isolation, and mental illness. The death of a spouse is a crisis that strains the family's emotional and financial resources and that requires new ways of carrying out family operations. "The influence of the event travels through the family like a bowling ball through a set of tenpins—as one set of habits is disrupted, other sets are

Table 17-8
Individual Effects of Bereavement

A. Total failure to readjust
    1. Suicide
    2. Early death
    3. Insanity
    4. Moral disintegration
    5. Obsession

B. Partial failure
    1. Eccentricities
    2. Physical illness or prostration
    3. Aboulia, purposelessness
    4. Isolation
    5. Embitterment, misanthropy, cynicism
    6. Reversion to or recurrence of grief
    7. Self-blame or personal hates
    8. Fears
    9. Loneliness

C. Partial success
    1. Resignation, "God's will," etc.
    2. Stoicism
    3. Stereotyped formulae of immortality, misery escaped, etc.
    4. Sentimental memorials
    5. Effective repression of memories
    6. Intensification of affections
    7. Extension of affections
    8. Deliberate absorption in distractions or duties
    9. New or fantasied love objects

D. Conspicuous success
    1. New love object
    2. Thoroughgoing religious rationalization
    3. Spontaneous forgetting, relaxation of tensions
    4. Devotion to lifework
    5. Identification with role of deceased
    6. Creation of constructive memorials
    7. Transmutation of the experience into a productive reintegration of the personality

Source: Thomas D. Eliot, "The Bereaved Family," *Annals of the American Academy of Political and Social Science* (1932): 4.

affected and there arises the objective possibility of family paralysis" (Waller and Hill 1951:457).

Widowhood necessitates a reorganization of social roles suitable for the new status. An American widow is often uncertain about how long to mourn, how to make others aware of her readiness to resume normal social activities, how to manage her affairs as a lone woman, and whether to remarry. When death breaks a marriage of many decades, ways of living have been so intertwined that it is not easy to rebuild one's life without the lost mate.

Four times as many women (16 percent) as men (4 percent) in the United States had been widowed at the time of the 1970 census (Carter and Glick 1976:438). Women over 65 are much more likely to be widowed than married, and they outnumber men their age in increasing numbers. Forty years ago the American population was made up of about equal numbers of men and women 65 years of age and older; in 1976 there were 69 men for every 100 women, and by the year 2000 the ratio will be only 65 males to 100 females who are 65 or more years old. Dr. Jacob Siegel, senior statistician of the census bureau's population division, states that the coping competence of widows is increasing. "The world of 2000 will have a population of fairly sophisticated, educated, elderly women, many of whom have had outside work and have held managerial and professional positions" (Siegel 1976:12-A).

Dr. Helena Lopata's study of widowhood (1973) finds widows sharing the characteristics of other minority groups in that they are: (1) female in a male-dominated society; (2) old in a society that venerates youth; (3) lonely in a country that prefers to ignore such unhappy emotions; (4) without mates in a social network of couples; and (5) poor and uneducated in a wealthy, sophisticated land. In addition, one and one-half million are members of ethnic or racial minorities who already face discrimination (Lopata 1973:92). Lower-class widows have few relatives or longtime friends to help them. Two-thirds of the Chicago widows Lopata studied said that their in-laws did not even help them with their husband's funeral arrangements; less than one in four had been visited by their in-laws since the funeral. Twice as many black as white widows were accustomed to making their own decisions before they were widowed (Lopata 1970).

Surveys find that the widowed have lower morale and fewer affiliations than the married, because they are less affluent, usually (Hutchison 1975). The median income for families headed by people 65 years of age and over in 1974 was $7,298, less than three-fifths of the median of $12,836 for all families (Siegel 1976). America's two million widowers, who average 71.6 years of age, have a median income of less than $3,000 at the latest count. More than married men, widowers smoke, drink, and eat too much, and rarely get enough exercise. Some of them complain of matchmaking friends and neighbors; others welcome such overtures as a chance to spruce up and go out. Dr. Daniel Gianturco of Duke University's Center for the Study of Aging, finds that the death rate is twice as high among widowers as among married men over 65—or 113.5 vs 57.4 per 1,000 deaths a year ("The Plight of America's 2 Million Widowers" 1974).

A study of remarriage in old age found that widowers tend to remarry in about three years, and widows in seven years, if at all. Over half had known their new spouse a long while before they were widowed, many for most of their lives. The new partner often resembled the first wife or husband, and remarriage was more likely when the first marriage had been good. Three out of four remarriages were rated successful, an outcome that was most likely when: (1) the wife was younger (by less than 14 years); (2) the new couple engaged in many courtship activities; (3) there was a mutuality of interests; (4) the couple was motivated by love or companionship rather than by material goals; (5) both were able to find great satisfaction in life; (6) relations with the respective families (especially with their children) were good; (7) their children approved the marriage; and (8) they had sufficient income (McKain 1969).

When a widow is able to relate well to others, she may be helped by the kind of group discussion that takes place at widows' consultation centers, guidance services, and the like (Hiltz 1975). Talking with others and a willingness to consider all the aspects of one's situation are two mature coping devices that are useful for successful recovery from widowhood (Rosenbaum 1975).

Surviving widowhood is a major developmental task for the aging. Those who are most successful have autonomy as persons, enjoy continuing personal interests, have a backlog of economic security, possess a comforting philosophy of life, maintain concern for others, and are blessed with meaningful friendships that have lasted over the years.

The meaning of death

The individual dies, but mankind continues. Death in the family brings heartbreak, but in the larger context death is inevitable and necessary, for it makes a place for yet another generation (Whitman 1972:27). Without death there could be no new life, for each generation gives up its place to those that are to follow.

Death opens the human heart to the meaning of life itself. When a family loses a beloved member with whom life has been shared for years, memories of past experiences crowd in upon those that remain. They celebrate the life of the departed, renewing their sense of identity as a family and as individuals. "Death is inextricably woven into all that makes life rich, noble, and triumphant. To conceal it is to cheat one's self of what might give meaning to life. Indeed, one cannot accept life without knowing that it must end. Death is not the scissors that cuts the thread of our lives. It is rather one of the threads that is woven into the design of existence" (Elliott 1971:15).

Religious people are taught to believe that the human spirit lives on, on another plane of being. Many who do not consider themselves particularly devout join in the belief that there is something that lives on long after the physical body is gone. When Dr. Elizabeth Kübler-Ross was asked if she believed that there is life after death, she replied without a moment's hesitation, "Sure there is, without the shadow of a doubt." She went on to tell of her intensive research and clinical work with dying patients over the years. Not infrequently an individual who had been officially pronounced dead came back to life and reported having been aware of floating up out of the physical body and of having been met by some loved person "on the other side" (Kübler-Ross 1976).

Most Americans are hopefully optimistic about death. Responses from a representative cross-section of 1,467 people found that 58 percent view death with hope or optimism, that 24 percent are pessimistic, and that the remaining 18 percent are vague about their beliefs concerning death. Religious faith was related to optimism about death in most instances (National Opinion Research Center 1976). Meanwhile, scientists explore ways of delaying death by slowing the "clock of aging," the genetically based program that determines each individual's rate of aging and dying (Rosenfeld 1976).

The mystery of what happens after death has intrigued mankind through the centuries. It has been expressed in some of the world's great art, music, and literature. "Secluded behind her father's hemlock hedges, she found the 'polar privacy' she needed to probe the meaning of life and death. Death is the high voltage current that charges her most powerful poetry," writes Nardi Campion (1973) of Emily Dickinson, whose writing she uses to illustrate her point:

> Because I could not stop for Death
> He kindly stopped for me—
> The carriage held but just
>   Ourselves—
> And immortality.
>
>   Emily Dickinson

Death's mystery is no greater than the miracle of birth and of life itself in its myriad forms, its continuing development, and its many expressions of creativity, not the least of which is found in the heart of family living. In the end there are two great mysteries—death and life itself.

To have and to hold from this day forward, For better, for worse, for richer, for poorer, In sickness, and in health, to love and to cherish, Till death us do part.

Book of Common Prayer

for better or for worse

part six

Love the quest; marriage the conquest; divorce, the inquest.

Helen Rowland

Broken and rebuilt marriages

chapter eighteen

When a marriage breaks up, urgent tasks confront everyone in the family—husband, wife, children, and kinfolk. The couple sever their marriage contract and all of their intertwined habits of living together. They must adjust to living apart and to financing two households. They must go about healing the wounds of their broken marriage, helping their children to adjust to disrupted family patterns and their relatives to accept their changed status. Their social life must be adapted to the new situation, which is awkward in that it is one that calls for neither congratulations nor condolences. Mixed feelings of failure, defensiveness, guilt, regret, recrimination, and relief are expressed or repressed. Relatives are informed—but not in the happy mood of the original wedding announcements. Some take sides with one or the other of the partners. Often there is speculation about which is the injured party and why the union broke up.

Society expresses its concern for the preservation of family life in laws regulating the establishment and the termination of marriage. Legal regulation of marriage attempts to (1) promote public morality; (2) ensure family stability; (3) assure support obligations; and (4) assign child support and responsibility (Weitzman 1974:1243).

Marital dissolution

A marriage may be terminated in any of five ways: by the death of one or both of the partners (Chapter 17), or legally by annulment, desertion, separation, or divorce. *Annulment* is the legal erasure of a marriage for reasons of force, fraud, bigamy, insanity, falsified age at marriage, or any gross misrepresentation by either party that voids the contract. Annulment means in effect that there never has been a marriage, so that both parties return to their previous situation. Fewer than 5 percent of all legal terminations of marriage are annulments, and these occur mainly in religious groups in which divorce is not permitted, notably the Roman Catholic Church.

Desertion occurs when either the husband or the wife abandons the spouse and leaves the home. Estimates of the number of mates that run away each year range up to one million. Some runaways never return; others stay away only until they get over being "fed up" with conditions at home. Men have traditionally outnumbered women in deserting their families. A New York agency specializing in locating missing persons describes the typical runaway husband as 44 to 51 years old, college-educated, a salesman or middle-level executive, amiable, outgoing, and earning about $25,000 a year, with a liberal expense account.

Since 1974, however, missing persons' firms have been asked to find more runaway wives than deserting husbands (Ogg 1975:3). Typically, the woman who deserts her family is well-educated, about 35 years old; she married at 18 or 19 and had her first two children during the first two years of her marriage. Now, after 15 years or so of marriage, her husband and children no longer seem to need her, and she feels unappreciated and useless. Desertion is a form of escape. Some people take drugs, others drink or have nervous breakdowns; a few commit suicide; more simply run away (Hampton 1975:1, 12).

Desertion is known popularly as "the poor man's divorce." However, Kephart's classic work (1955:462) found that percentage figures for both divorce and desertion are similar in all occupational groups and that marital instability in general is most prevalent at the lowest economic levels. Nonwhites and Catholics are overrepresented in the lower classes, which have the highest divorce and desertion rates, reflecting the struggle to support their families on inadequate incomes (Monahan and Kephart 1954). Desertion occurs most often in families that have been established for ten or more years, at a time when the children have already come (Duberman 1974:170) and the burdens of child-rearing are heaviest, especially in low-income families. Children may be a precipitating factor in desertion, especially when a mother finds public support more readily available if she is rearing children alone.

Separation differs from desertion in that the couple has agreed to separate, and each spouse knows where the other is. Separation provides the time some couples need either to become reconciled or to proceed with a formal divorce. Marital dissolution has been increasing rapidly in recent years. In 1975, ten percent of married Americans between 25 and 54 years of age had either separated or divorced and had not remarried. The parallel figure five years earlier, in 1970, was 6.9 percent (U.S. Bureau of the Census 1976:1). The legally separated couple live apart, do not have sexual access to each other, continue to be responsible for the care and support of their children, and are not free to marry anyone else. A separation may be officially recorded, but more frequently it is an informal arrangement in which the pair live apart (Carter and Glick 1976:222). Separation is the dominant form of marital disruption among blacks, whereas divorce is the "dominant current form among whites" (U.S. Bureau of the Census 1975:5).

Divorce in the United States

The prevalence of divorce is widely discussed in both popular and professional literature. There is general agreement that there is more divorce now than formerly, but widespread confusion exists about how great the increase is. This uncertainty arises in part from the different ways of measuring the incidence of divorce.

Divorce ratios and rates

The divorce-marriage ratio is a popular way of referring to the prevalence of divorce in a community, in a state, or in the nation at large. It is a simple ratio of the number of divorces filed per number of recorded marriages in any given year. This is misleading, in that it draws from two different populations and does not include the many couples who remain married throughout the year in question and are thus not counted among the married in the ratio. An example of the divorce-marriage ratio is found in a graphic portrayal of the increase in divorce prepared by the U.S. News & World Report Economic Unit. The graph shows 26 divorces for every 100 marriages in 1960, 48 divorces for every 100 marriages in 1975, and an estimated 63 divorces for every 100 marriages in 1990 (*U.S. News & World Report* 1975:32).

The crude divorce rate is the number of divorces per 1,000 population. This is a general indicator of the prevalence of divorce. It is crude in that the general population includes many children and others who are not married and who therefore do not risk divorce. In 1974, the crude divorce rate for the United States was estimated to be 4.6 divorces per 1,000 population—up from 3.5 in 1970 and from 2.9 in 1968 (U.S. Department of Health, Education, and Welfare 1975:1).

The refined divorce rate is the number of divorces per 1,000 married persons. This measure confines itself to the already married and is superior to the crude divorce rate because it excludes those in the population for whom divorce is not applicable. The major problem with the refined divorce rate is that it is insensitive to variations in the age composition of the married population (England and Kunz 1975:41). Thus, a retirement community having an aging population would have a lower refined divorce rate than an area of young marrieds, among whom divorce is more prevalent. Divorce rates per 1,000 married persons in the United States increased from 3.0 in 1890 to 9.2 in 1960, and have been rising sharply since (Carter and Glick 1976:54 and Chapter 13).

The age-specific divorce rate is the number of divorces per 1,000 married women in each age group from 14 to 85+ by 5-year intervals. Since more divorces occur among younger than among older people, this method compares populations with different age distributions without the distortion of the age factor. The problem with age-specific divorce rates is that they do not give a single summary figure for comparison purposes.

A standardized divorce rate starts with the age-specific divorce rate of a given population. The expected number of divorces in each age category is added, the total divided by the population size, and the result multiplied by 1,000. This makes possible the construction of a single summary statistic for each population unit for comparison purposes, based on age-specific divorce rates and age distribution. However, in reaching such a summary figure, some valuable detail information is lost (England and Kunz 1975:42–3).

The number of divorces granted in any given year is still another measure of the prevalence of divorce in the United States. According to provisional reports, there were 970,000 divorces granted in 1974—more than double the number granted ten years earlier (U.S. Department of Health, Education and Welfare 1975:10). The sheer number of divorces granted may be deceiving because it does not take into account the size of the population and the number of married persons in the two or more time periods being compared.

Divorce rates by states is a measure employed to show the wide variation in incidence of divorce between two or more of the 50 states. Thus, in 1974, Nevada had a high divorce rate of 17.2 per 1,000 population, as compared with Wisconsin's low rate of 2.3 per 1,000 population. What such comparisons do not show is the many Nevada divorces involving nonresidents and the relative ease or difficulty in obtaining divorces in the several states (U.S. Department of Health, Education, and Welfare 1975:10).

The proportion of people currently divorced in the population is small. Between 2 and 4 percent are recorded as divorced persons in any given census. This measure disregards the fact that three-fourths of the women and five-sixths of the men remarry after having been divorced, and may thus not show up as divorced in a given census. The 1970 census, for instance, found that 10 percent of the men and 11 percent of the women had at some time in their lives been divorced (U.S. Bureau of the Census 1974:65).

Estimates of eventual divorce have been used in recent attempts to throw light on the marital history of adults in the United States. Glick and Norton (1973) estimated that 25 to 29 percent of the women who were 30 years old in 1971 would eventually divorce. Then, with the sharp increase in divorce in the 1970s, this estimate was upped, since "it seems reasonable to expect that somewhere between one-fourth and one-third of the women in the United States about 30 years old in 1973 may eventually end a marriage in divorce" (U.S. Bureau of the Census 1974: 66).

The divorce-prone

"Earliest married are soonest divorced" is a truism. The probability of divorce is high for those who marry young, as is clearly shown in 1970 census data (Table 18-1).

As the age at first marriage rises, a smaller percentage of men and women are divorced. This was true in 1970, when 7.9 percent of the men and 7.3 percent of the women who first married in their late twenties had been divorced—in contrast to 18.6 and 19.7 percent of men and women, respectively, who had married as teenagers (Table 18-1). As more men and women delay getting married until they have become mature and have established themselves financially, occupationally, and personally, their chances for greater marital stability should improve, other things being equal.

Blacks and other nonwhite races are more divorce-prone than are whites. Members of the white race in 1974 divorced at the rate of 58 per 1,000, as compared with 112 per 1,000 persons of the black and other races (U.S. Bureau of the Census 1974:4–5). The number of divorced persons per 1,000 of the married has been going up steadily in recent years, the sharpest rise occurring among nonwhite racial groups (Table 18-2).

The likelihood of divorce declines as income and educational levels

Table 18-1

Percentage of Married and Divorced Men and Women Who Married 1901–1970 by Age at First Marriage, United States, 1970

All races	Years of age at first marriage						
	14-19	20-24	25-29	30-34	35 and over	Total %
Total men	100.0%	100.0%	100.0%	100.0%	100.0%	100.0%
Married once	77.6	85.5	88.4	89.2	89.5	85.5
Married more than once	22.4	14.5	11.6	10.8	10.5	14.5
Divorced after first marriage	18.6	11.2	7.9	6.9	6.1	10.9
Total women	100.0%	100.0%	100.0%	100.0%	100.0%	100.0%
Married once	73.8	83.1	89.0	90.6	89.6	85.2
Married more than once	26.2	16.9	11.0	9.4	10.4	14.8
Divorced after first marriage	19.7	12.6	7.3	5.4	5.3	10.4

Source: U.S. Bureau of the Census, "Age at First Marriage," *1970 Census of the Population*, PC (2)–4D (Washington, D.C.: U.S. Government Printing Office, April 1973), Table 4.

Table 18-2

Number of Divorced Men and Women per 1,000 Married Persons, by Race, 1960, 1965, 1970, 1974

Year and sex	White race	Black and other races	Total
Total			
1974	58	112	63
1970	44	79	47
1965	39	70	41
1960	33	63	35
Men			
1974	46	87	49
1970	32	61	35
1965	32	56	34
1960	27	37	28
Women			
1974	71	136	77
1970	56	98	60
1965	46	85	49
1960	38	89	42

Source: U.S. Bureau of the Census, "Marital Status and Living Arrangements: March 1974," *Current Population Reports*, P-20, no. 271 (Washington, D.C.: Government Printing Office, October 1974), p. 5.

rise. When neither husband nor wife were college graduates, 75 percent had been married only once, in contrast to 90.4 percent of the couples both of whom were college graduates. "The higher the family income and the educational level of the husband and wife, the greater the likelihood of both partners having been married only once" (U.S. Bureau of the Census 1972:2). The relationship between education and divorce is complex, especially for women. As Glick (1975:7) points out, women college graduates 35 to 44 years of age held the record for the smallest percent divorced (3.0 percent in 1960 and 3.9 percent in 1970). But women in the same age group with one or more years of graduate schooling in the same period hold the record among educational groups for the largest percent divorced (4.8 percent in 1960 and 7.3 percent in 1970). One may speculate that the impact of the movement for equal rights for women is reflected in these figures. Better jobs, offering higher pay and greater freedom to women with graduate and professional training, made such women less dependent on marriage than women without such salable skills.

People with low incomes have more divorces than do those in more comfortable circumstances. For instance, 71.7 percent of husbands and wives with family incomes lower than $5,000 a year, compared with 83 percent of couples with annual incomes of $15,000 or more, have been married only once (U.S. Bureau of the Census 1972:2). As educational and income levels of blacks continue to rise, the gap that exists between

Broken and rebuilt marriages   439

racial groups in terms of incidence of divorce may be expected to narrow, unless other factors (early childbearing, babies out of wedlock, declining religiosity, etc.) intervene.

Children may increase a couple's divorce-proneness. Wives who had children during the first two years of their marriage had twice the divorce rate of wives who did not (24 vs 12 per 1,000 married women) in one recent year (U.S. Bureau of the Census 1971:3). Premarital conception adds to divorce-proneness, as do age differences, lack of religious deterrents, easy divorce laws, and a liberal attitude toward divorce (Schoen 1975:548). Protestants divorce more than do Jews or Catholics, and people with no religious ties more than the devout; inter-faith marriages are especially vulnerable to marital disruption (Bell 1971:489).

The increase in divorce

There are many complex and interrelated factors behind the increase in divorce. First is the rise of individualism, which emphasizes the rights of the individual to seek fulfillment and personal growth. Individualism lessens the sense of obligation to "do one's duty" when family responsibilities become too burdensome. Other societal changes contributing to the increase in divorce are: (2) wives' more advanced education, employability, and independence; (3) rising family incomes (enable more unhappy couples to afford a divorce and separate households); (4) free legal aid (allows more impoverished couples to obtain divorces); (5) social disruption such as the Vietnam war, inflation, and urban unrest (contributes to marital disruption); (6) greater acceptance of divorce as a way of resolving marital problems; (7) secularization of life (dilutes the influence of organized religion in discouraging divorce); (8) churches' relaxation of their stand against divorce; (9) education for marriage and family life in churches, schools and colleges (fosters more objective evaluation of marriage and divorce); (10) marriage and divorce counseling (assist incompatible couples to dissolve intolerable, conflict-ridden marriages); (11) increased equality of the sexes (makes living alone as a single or divorced man or woman more tolerable); and (12) legal reforms, especially the adoption of no-fault divorce laws, (make divorce easier in many states) (Glick 1975:8). While one or more of these factors persist, divorce may be expected to be a part of the American scene.

Divorce laws

Each of the 50 states enacts and enforces its own divorce laws. As a result, there are wide variations among the different states in the relative ease or difficulty of obtaining a divorce. States with the most permissive divorce laws have the most divorces, as might be expected (Stetson and Wright 1975). In states with tough divorce laws a disenchanted spouse who is able to finance an expensive lawyer or a trip to Nevada or Mexico can get a divorce—but such a solution is beyond the reach of a less affluent pair.

Grounds and reasons for divorce

Each state has its own grounds for divorce, and these vary widely. New Jersey, for instance, has only three, whereas some other states recognize a dozen or more grounds for divorce. Across the country there are some 45 legal grounds for divorce, "cruelty" accounting for most of the divorces granted. Desertion for varying lengths of time, nonsupport, adultery, habitual drunkenness, drug addiction, impotence, conviction of a crime, insanity, and other grounds are recognized in some states and not in others. At one time New York state recognized only adultery as grounds for divorce. When in 1966 the grounds were extended, New York's divorce rate trebled within two years (Clayton 1975:499). Generally, the easier it is to get a divorce in a given state, the higher its incidence of divorce.

The grounds for divorce are what the law requires and not necessarily the reasons why a couple find their marriage intolerable. Grievances cited by divorcing husbands and wives range from physical and verbal abuse and financial problems—most commonly given by lower-class wives—to sexual incompatibility—most frequent among middle-class husbands (Levinger 1966:805). Marriage and divorce counselors report that some other complaints impelling couples to seek divorce are neglect of the home and children, drinking, in-law problems, mental cruelty, lack of love, and incompatibility.

When 1,000 divorced men and women across the country were asked the question, "What do you feel was the underlying reason for your divorce?" more than four out of five (81.7 percent) said that they had married at too young an age and "were immature when married" (Addeo and Burger 1975). This is in accord with what professional researchers have been finding for many years (as summarized in Chapter 9). A good marriage requires maturity—a quality most often lacking in the unions of youngsters ill-prepared for the responsibilities of married life. This is the truth behind the wise observation that "the chief reason for divorce is marriage"—for too much is expected of marriage, and too little personal investment is made in it.

The process of alienation

Within a conflict-torn marriage alienation proceeds to the point where it cannot easily be stopped. Each additional crisis or conflict redefines the relationship in a way that precipitates it towards even greater alienation. Destructive quarrels, characteristic of marriages that end in divorce, alternate with intervals of peace during which there may be efforts to continue to live together. Then the conflict resumes around another sore point and continues until separation is more bearable than continuing to live together. The process of alienation proceeds through a series of crises that bring the couple to the final break (Table 18–3).

No-fault divorce

The traditional adversary system of proving in the courts the innocence of the injured party led to abuses, collusion, and inequities. Conflicting couples did what they could to dissolve their marriages, whether or not grounds for divorce were allowed in their state. Divorce legislation reforms attempt to make possible the termination of a marriage that is no longer viable without prevarication, collusion, and undue cost to the courts or to the families involved. No-fault divorce allows the estranged couple to terminate an intolerable marriage without assigning blame and without being required to prove that one of the partners is at fault. Divorces are granted on such grounds as "irreconcilable differences," "irremediable breakdown of the marriage," or separation for a specified length of time. Wheeler (1974) maintains that "true" no-fault divorce is based on prior separation for the period prescribed in a given state (ranging from one year or less to five years).

At the present writing, half of the 50 states have some form of no-fault divorce on their books, and legislators in nearly all other states are considering how to incorporate this feature in their divorce legislation. Legal scholars who are studying the question believe that no-fault divorce reforms are not as far-reaching as their advocates would like. In several states in which the no-fault feature was added to other grounds for divorce, one spouse may still blame the other and then agree to a more favorable property or support settlement under the no-fault legislation. "Under a 'true' no-fault divorce law, a couple may terminate its marriage

Table 18–3
The Process of Alienation Leading to Divorce

Steps	Progressive alienation from destructive quarreling to divorce
1.	Mutually destructive quarreling weakens the marriage
2.	Affection is withheld and loving responses decline
3.	Possibility of divorcing is mentioned and considered
4.	Others discover the couple's marital trouble
5.	The married pair admit failure to themselves and others
6.	Moving to separate bedrooms accentuates the break
7.	Husband and wife break up housekeeping and establish separate households
8.	Efforts at reconciliation are unsuccessful
9.	Divorce action is undertaken

Source: Adapted from Evelyn Millis Duvall and Reuben Hill, *When You Marry* (Boston, Mass.: D.C. Heath & Co., 1953), pp. 285–288; and based on formulations of Willard Walter, *The Old Love and the New: Divorce and Readjustment* (New York: Liveright, 1930), pp. 131–132.

without any expectation of punitive consequences resulting from the action" (Glick 1975:9).

Attitudes toward divorce

Individuals caught up in the turmoil of their own divorce are apt to be bewildered about how it came about. When Ann Landers, after 36 years of marriage and 20 years of writing her popular personal advice column, announced her own divorce, she wrote of the strange irony of her broken home as she asked, "How did it happen that something so good for so long didn't last forever? The lady with all the answers does not know the answer to this one" (Landers 1975).

A Roper survey of a national sample of 3000 women and 1000 men found that 60 percent of them felt that "bad marriages should be terminated by divorce" (Martin 1974:B3). The 340,374 middle-Americans surveyed by *Better Homes and Gardens* responded by an overwhelming 84 percent that they did not feel it wrong for a couple who can't get along to divorce. An even larger percentage thought that some marriages are so bad that they should be broken (Table 18–4).

When asked if they approved or disapproved of divorce simply by mutual consent, a much smaller percentage (60 percent) responded in the affirmative (*Better Homes and Gardens* 1972:58). There is widespread recognition that when divorce is too easy, many otherwise good marriages are irretrievably broken by impulse, anger, and ill-advised haste.

Alimony, property settlements, and child support

The financial arrangements surrounding divorce are rarely easy, especially for families already having money problems. The Family Service Association of America finds that hard times produce "an across the board increase in anxiety and irritability" in both husbands and wives. Financial problems are more pronounced among middle-class couples who have not previously felt such pressures; among the poor and the underemployed the money struggle is an old story (Stevens 1975:17). When families already under financial strain are broken, their money problems are compounded.

Alimony is derived from a Latin word meaning "sustenance." The idea behind it is that the husband as head of the family is responsible for the support of his wife and children no matter how able they are to support themselves independently through their own resources. Alimony is granted by court order, and if it is not paid the offending ex-spouse is guilty of contempt of court. Usually the husband pays the alimony designated by the court on the basis of his income, the duration of the

Table 18-4

Americans Say Some Marriages Should be Terminated

(Percentages of 340,374 respondents to the question, "Do you feel
that some marriages are so bad that they should be broken up,
for the children's sake, for everybody's?" by education and sex of household head)

| | Total | Education of household head | | | | | |
		High school	College	Graduate work	Male head	Female head	Both
Yes	86%	84%	87%	89%	79%	87%	87%
No	13	14	12	10	20	11	12
No reply	1	2	1	1	1	2	1

Source: Better Homes and Gardens, *A Report on the American Family* (Des Moines, Iowa: Meredith Corporation, 1972), p. 56.

marriage, and other factors in the case. Occasionally a well-to-do woman is held responsible for her husband's support through alimony payments to him after their divorce. Either spouse may petition to change the alimony arrangements as their financial conditions change. Alimony stops when the ex-spouse remarries, in most cases (Bohannan 1970:483). Alimony is hard to collect and rarely is sufficient to meet expenses without some supplementation. Some see alimony as "severance pay" for the wife who has worked for years as an unpaid domestic. Others view alimony as rehabilitative in that it enables the ex-wife to gain the salable skills she needs to become self-supporting (Ogg 1975:11). Alimony is actually awarded in less than 10 percent of divorce cases (Weitzman 1974: 1186).

Property settlements are made at the time of divorce to divide the material assets (and liabilities) built up during the marriage between the two spouses. Marital property includes those assets that belong jointly to husband and wife and that are divided between the two when they divorce. Separate property belongs solely to one of the partners, and is therefore not divided unless the court decides that it is in fact jointly held (Warner 1974:87). Occasionally a man holds in his name alone all of the accumulated assets of his career. His wife, who assisted in the growth of her husband's business, career, property, and income may find that her contribution to the partnership is unrecognized upon dissolution of the marriage (Weitzman 1974:1192). It can happen the other way around, too. For tax and liability purposes, a man may have put most of his assets in his wife's name, only to find at the time of their divorce that she has full title to the wealth he has accumulated.

In most divorce settlements, the wife receives from one-third to one-half of the property, depending on how diligent her lawyer is, how indulgent the court, and how she feels about it. Some wives insist on getting all they can out of their ex-husbands, as a form of retaliation; others quite as vehemently want nothing that reminds them of the man and of their life together. When it comes to dividing family pets and things of sentimental value, the issues become emotionally charged—to a degree quite unrelated to the actual value of the objects in question.

Child support and custody are awarded on the basis of parental competence, the age, sex, and wishes of the child(ren), and the preferences of the two parents. Children under 14 years of age are usually in the mother's custody, although there have been notable exceptions in recent years. Visitation rights are agreed on for the parent not having custody. Child support amounts are determined by the education, health, and earning power of the husband and wife, the length of the marriage, the ages and special requirements of the children, and any other factors that may pertain to a particular case.

Legally and morally a man is responsible for his children's support. The court sets an amount corresponding to the father's financial capability and the needs of his children. The man who reneges on child support payments is in contempt of court; but many a mother finds it hard to support the children without their father's willing cooperation, once the divorce is final and he lives elsewhere.

Children of divorce

Divorce creates a chasm for every member of the family. A psychiatrist who sees children of broken homes says that there are two ways to make the transition from pre-divorce to post-divorce living. One is to "jump the gap" by radically cutting off contact with the other parent and with the life of the family before it broke. The second, and preferable, way to make the shift is to bridge the gap by keeping in touch directly and through the children with the absent parent.

In some ways children of divorce have a more difficult time than do their parents, because they must adjust to the two new situations that both of their parents are establishing. Children of divorced parents must learn to live with their mother in her new setting and to adjust to their father and his new relationships. Divorced parents are advised to help their children talk about and share things about each other so that the children can integrate the two parents' lives and life-styles into a wholesome, meaningful system of living (Williams 1974:24–28). Anger, hurt, jealousy, and other negative emotions may make such an adjustment hard for both adults and children.

Interpreting divorce to children

"How can I tell the children why we are divorcing when I don't fully understand myself?" This father puts into words the confusion of many divorcing adults, who are so torn with conflicting feelings that rational analysis is well nigh impossible. Many parents try to be honest with their children about divorce. They know that they should prepare them for the two separate households being established by their mother and father. They sense that the children need to be reassured that they are still loved by both parents. The youngsters need reassurance, too, that they are not responsible for their parents' inability to continue to live together. Many a child fears that his naughtiness may have been the cause of the parents' breakup.

Parents are wise not to denigrate each other in order to justify their divorce in the eyes of the children. The divorced husband is still the children's father and is entitled to their love and respect no matter what transpired between him and their mother. The divorced woman will always be her children's mother regardless of her marital status. Explaining all the reasons for the divorce is not necessary, even if it were possible. It suffices to tell a young child that from now on Mother and Daddy will each have their own homes where the child will be welcome, and that they both will always love him no matter what. Older children who have been aware of the marital rift that has been widening before their eyes may understand what has happened without long explanations of the nature of the conflict. Children today are aware of the reality of divorce long before they are personally involved in it.

Divorce need not warp a child, even though he suffers severely during his family's breakup. Child specialists find that some children are actually relieved when the uneasiness at home ends and some peace and quiet are established after the divorce. As soon as they sense that the break in the family circle is final, they can adjust to it with the attitudes they see reflected in their parents' behavior. Review of many studies of the ways in which divorce affects children leads to the conclusion that "children from happy marriages are better adjusted than children from divorced marriages, but those of divorced parents are better adjusted than those of parents whose marriages are intact but unhappy" (Udry 1974:400).

Custody and living arrangements

Mothers are awarded custody of their children in an overwhelming majority of cases. This poses a number of problems: (1) it increases the wife's dependence on her husband for support; (2) it puts the greater personal and financial burden on the mother—who usually has lower earning potential than the father; (3) it may not fully take into account the needs of the children and the qualifications of the two parents (Weitzman 1974:1194); and (4) it deprives the husband of his full rights and preferences as the children's father. In many cases the divorce demotes the father from parent to visitor. Traditionally the father is awarded custody of the children only if the mother is an unfit parent.

Dr. Lee Salk, eminent child psychologist, was awarded custody of his two children not because their mother was incompetent, but because the judge held that the children's father in this case better met their emotional and cultural needs. Dr. Salk told an interviewer that although the usual practice is for the father to move out of the home, he remained in the large brownstone house with the children, who wanted to be there with him (Dullea 1975:44). General acceptance of flexible family roles may one day allow children to be placed with either parent, based on the merits of the particular case. In the meantime, most children of divorce live with their mothers.

The proportion of children living with only one parent (usually the mother) almost doubled between 1960 (when it was 8 percent) and 1974, when 14 percent of the nation's children under 18 lived with their mothers. (Glick 1975:2). The proportion of children living with a divorced or widowed parent rises sharply with the age of the child—from 2.7 percent under the age of three to 6.2 percent between 14 and 17 years of age (Table 18-5). Thus we see in Table 18-5 that of the nation's more than 10 million children living in one-parent homes (10,482,000), more than one-third (3,591,000) live with a divorced parent—almost twice the number living in a home broken by death (1,873,000).

Nearly half of all white children in single-parent families live with a divorced parent, as compared with about one-fifth of the black children in single-parent homes. Proportionally more black children (15 percent) than white (1 percent) under 3 years of age in 1974 were living with a parent who had never married. Another 15 percent of all black children under three years of age live with neither parent. One out of every four white preschoolers and half of all black schoolchildren live with only one parent, or with a parent who has either remarried or has never been married. "In other words, being a school child with parents who are not in an intact first marriage is far from a unique experience today" (Glick 1975:3). Furthermore, according to the 1970 census, white children living with both parents were in families with three times as much income as black children of the same age in families with only the mother present (Glick 1975:5).

The proportion of divorced women family-heads increased while that of divorced men family-heads declined between 1970 and 1974, although some fathers were awarded custody of their children. More young divorced men than women were "going home to Mother" between 1970 and 1974. Jessie Bernard (1975:587) speculates that "the presence of children may have made the women less welcome than the men in either the parental home or in the home of other relatives." Living arrangements change drastically for the children and for their parents as a result of both the divorce and the remarriage of either or both of the parents.

Both the divorce and the remarriage rate have risen sharply since the early 1930s. Especially sharp increases occurred during the 1960s, when these rates reached the highest levels ever reported for the United States. Since 1970, the divorce rate has continued to climb, while the remarriage rate has leveled off (Figure 18-1). The earlier the age at divorce, the greater the probability of remarriage (Carter and Glick 1976: 392).

Remarriage

Most divorced persons eventually remarry. Five out of six men and three out four women remarry after having been divorced, and the divorced of both sexes are much more likely to get married again than are the widowed (U.S. Bureau of the Census 1972:10-13). With such large

Table 18-5
Children by Age, and by Sex of Parent with Whom They Live

Sex and marital status of parents with whom children under 18 live	Total under 18		Age of child in years				
	Number	Percent	Under 3	3 to 5	6 to 9	10 to 13	14 to 18
All children	67,047	100.0%	9,489	10,363	14,340	16,473	16,382
Living with two parents	54,561	81.4	84.2%	82.4%	81.7%	81.1%	79.1%
Living with one parent	10,482	15.6	12.4	15.1	15.8	16.5	16.9
Mother only	9,647	14.4	11.9	14.3	14.8	15.0	14.9
Father only	842	1.3	0.5	0.8	1.0	1.5	2.0
Parent never married	986	1.5	3.2	2.4	1.3	0.8	0.6
Parent married:							
Not separated	748	1.1	1.7	1.1	1.1	1.0	1.0
Separated	3,284	4.9	4.2	5.4	5.5	5.2	4.2
Parent divorced	3,591	5.4	2.7	5.0	5.8	5.9	6.2
Parent widowed	1,873	2.8	0.5	1.2	2.0	3.6	5.0
Living with neither parent	1,997	3.0	3.4	2.5	2.5	2.5	4.0

(Numbers in thousands, for the United States, 1974)
Source: U.S. Bureau of the Census, *Current Population Reports*, Series P-20, No. 271, "Marital Status and Living Arrangements" (Washington, D.C.: U.S. Government Printing Office, October 1974), Tables 4, 5.

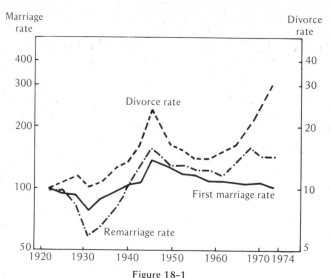

Figure 18-1

Rate of First Marriages, Divorces, and Remarriages: United States, Three-Year Averages, 1921 to 1974

Note: First marriages are per 1000 single women 14–44 years old; divorces—per 1000 married women 14–44 years old; remarriages—per 1000 widowed and divorced women 14–54 years old. Data sources: Glick and Norton, 1973; U.S. National Center for Health Statistics, 1975a; U.S. Bureau of the Census, 1973a.
Source: Arthur J. Norton; and Paul C. Glick, "Marital Instability: Past, Present, and Future," *Journal of Social Issues* 32, no. 1, (Winter 1976).

proportions of divorced husbands and wives remarrying, being a single parent is usually a temporary arrangement (Glick 1975:13).

Reasons for remarrying

Most Americans like to be married. Many of them try again after the failure of one marriage to contract another. Most men and women enjoy the emotional satisfaction and companionship that marriage offers. They grow accustomed to marital intimacy and sexual access and prefer it to "playing around." Divorced parents find it hard to fill both the mother's and the father's roles in the home, even if only one of them is the biological parent. Social life is organized around couples, as the lone adult soon finds after the dissolution of his or her marriage. Financially, two can manage better than one, even if the new partners have obligations for child support in a previous marriage. The formerly married have become used to paired living and feel incomplete without it. New mates are available for divorced husbands and wives who are attractive and resourceful. In fact, the presence of the person who is now the new mate may have been the precipitating factor in the dissolution of the marriage. Those whose marriages have failed usually attribute their failure to their immaturity, to faults in the mate, or to other problems in the earlier marriage that are not expected to be repeated in the next. In certain subcultures, remarriage is the expected thing to do—for instance, the widely publicized multiple marriages of some Hollywood personalities.

Reasons for not remarrying

One marriage is enough for some men and for even more women who do not remarry after their first marriage has been dissolved. There are several reasons why some divorced people do not remarry: (1) they are embittered about the opposite sex and disenchanted about marriage; (2) they are afraid to risk failure again; (3) they are perfectionists who demand so much of a marriage partner that they can find no one who meets their requirements; (4) they are rejected, since they have so few desirable physical, social, and psychological traits that they are passed over as marriage partners; (5) they are independent and adjusted to living alone as divorced persons, which they prefer to being married again (Bell 1971:527-529); (6) some have children so resistant to their marrying again that they discourage any likely prospect who comes around—so that the divorced parent refrains from a remarriage to satisfy the children; and (7) other personal, family, social, or occupational factors make it difficult to consider remarriage in some situations.

Remarriage success and failure

The likelihood of a successful second marriage after the failure of the first has been argued both pro and con. Psychiatrists like Bergler (1948) have warned that second marriages only repeat the problems of the first, because the reasons for failure lie deep within the personalities of the people involved. The pair may think that they have learned a lot from their mistakes and that their next marriage may be better, but this is an illusion. Why? Because the individual's neuroses cause him or her to fall in love for the wrong reasons and to repeat the same mistakes in second, third, or more marriages.

Psychiatrists, marriage counselors, and sociologists who believe in growth throughout adulthood tend to take a more positive view of remarriage. They see men and women growing in their capacity to cope with marital problems, learning about themselves from their experiences in intimate relationships, and acquiring the deeper understanding that can help them succeed in remarriage. Some see the second marriage as benefiting from the first—in the sense that the first has served as a training ground. William Goode (1956) found that 88 percent of the couples in his study rated their second marriage much better than their first and felt that their first marital experience had made things easier in the remarriage. Other experts speak of "team factors" and of the way that two mismated persons may fail in one marriage without necessarily hurting their chance for success in a second. Seven out of eight of the 2,009 remarriages studied by Jessie Bernard (1956) were rated as satisfactory. Similarly, Harvey Locke (1951) found three out of four of the remarrieds he studied to be happy or very happy.

Statistically, the remarriages of divorced people are somewhat more likely to end in divorce than are first marriages, but this does not mean that a given marriage is any less happy than the first. A flow-chart method of following the lifetime marriage career finds remarriages of divorced persons no more likely to end in divorce or separation than first marriages (Riley and Spreitzer 1974:67). Remarried divorced individuals have more problems than they had in their first marriages: self-doubt, the skepticism of relatives and friends, additional financial burdens, haunting comparisons with first spouses, and the complications of children by a former marriage. Yet, most of them rate their rebuilt marriages "very happy," and most of them stay married (Duberman 1974:203).

Stepchildren

His children, her children, and their children may all be part of the reconstituted families of the formerly married. Brothers and sisters, half brothers, half sisters, "own" children and stepchildren all share the home of the parent who has been married before. Some of the stepchildren may be only occasionally present—according to the visiting privileges of the parent and the age of the child. This adds to the accordion-like quality of rebuilt families.

Stepchildren necessarily have at least three parents and sometimes more, which makes for divided authority and the "you're not my father" type of rebellion of the older child. The "mean old stepmother" of fairy tales reflects not only the difficulty of mothering another woman's child, but also the youngster's resistance to any woman who occupies the mother's place through marriage to the child's father.

Attitudes of stepchildren and stepparents

Jessie Bernard says that she finds such terms as "stepchildren," "stepmother," and "stepfather" abhorrent because their negative emotional content makes them "smear words." She goes on to point out that the establishment of good relations between acquired parents and children has traditionally been considered one of the most difficult of all human assignments (Bernard 1956:14). Yet, her monumental study of divorced men and women in 2,009 cases of remarriage finds predominantly accepting attitudes toward one another on the part of both stepparents and stepchildren (Table 18-6).

Table 18-6

Attitudes of Stepchildren and Stepparents toward One Another

	Divorced women N = 849	Widowed women N = 445	Divorced men N = 809	Widowed men N = 543
Children's attitude toward parent's remarriage:				
Favorable	58.7%	71.2%	36.3%	64.8%
No attitude, indifferent	25.9	16.8	40.5	20.1
Unfavorable	15.4	12.0	23.2	15.1
Children's attitude toward parent's new spouse:				
Friendly	82.8	78.1	53.8	69.3
Neutral	12.2	16.5	34.4	21.6
Unfriendly	5.0	5.4	11.5	9.1
New husband's attitude toward wife's children:				
Affectionate	64.6	67.2	64.3	64.2
Neither fond nor rejecting	31.3	28.8	30.9	30.9
Rejecting	4.1	4.0	4.8	4.9
New wife's attitude toward husband's children:				
Affectionate	55.0	59.8	51.3	60.1
Neither fond nor rejecting	37.4	35.7	41.0	35.1
Rejecting	6.8	4.8	7.7	4.8

Source: Excerpted and adapted from Jessie Bernard, *Remarriage: A Study of Marriage* (New York: The Dryden Press, 1956), Table I-2, p. 11.

The summary data in Table 18-6 show clearly that generally the children are pleased with the idea of their mother's remarriage and that they like their new father, who returns their affection. The new stepmother likes her husband's children, but not quite as much as he likes hers. The second husband's relations with his wife's children are affectionate and hers with his children are only slightly less so. There is relatively little rejection of the stepchildren on the part of either of the spouses, and unfriendly attitudes on the part of the children toward their new stepparents are uncommon. "The general consensus among remarried parents seems to be that very young or quite grown-up children tend to assimilate a new parent more easily than do adolescents" (Bernard 1956:216).

A scholarly review of several studies of stepchildren and their new parents concludes that such families experience more stress and ambivalence and less cohesiveness than do families unbroken by divorce. Stepmothers have more difficult roles to play than do stepfathers, especially when there are adolescents in the family. Stepdaughters tend to have more extreme reactions toward their parents than do stepsons. And, the presence of stepparents affects the adjustment of the children to their natural parents somewhat negatively (Bowerman and Irish 1973:500).

How stepchildren fare

Stepchildren generally fare as well in the rebuilt families of divorced parents as do children in unbroken homes. Studies over the years find no significant differences between children with stepfathers and those who have their natural parents. Youngsters in either situation can have predominantly positive, predominantly negative, or mixed family experiences depending on a wide array of preexisting, transitional, and adaptive factors (Wilson, Zurcher, McAdams and Curtis 1975:535). Research findings that corroborate this view have been surfacing during recent decades (Bernard 1956; Goode 1956; Bohannan 1970; Walters and Stinnett 1971). Bernreuter Personality Inventory scores of college students from families in which there had been a remarriage, compared with standardized norms of college students, show that children of remarried divorced parents are quite as stable as college students in general. This does not mean that the stepchildren have not been affected, but rather that there is no measurable effect of their having grown up in rebuilt families (Bernard 1956:310–311).

Recovery from divorce

Getting over a divorce is like learning to walk with one leg after the other has been cut off. Divorce is the amputation of a marriage. No matter how necessary it is, it hurts; and there must be a period of recovery before the formerly married can go it alone again. At first one feels crippled, helpless, and/or free of a former part of oneself. It takes time to get one's bearings as a lone man or woman after having shared one's life with another person, even in a marriage marked by conflict.

One new divorcee tells of writing herself a list of all the things she now must learn to do by herself. It is a tragicomic list that includes such items as: opening bottles, carrying heavy things, going home alone, eating alone, entertaining alone, fighting with service companies alone, being sick alone, getting old alone, sleeping alone (O'Sullivan 1975:51). Even when some new mate is already on the horizon, there may be many dark clouds to be swept away before the skies of one's life clear once again.

Family functions after divorce

When a family breaks, major changes take place in basic family tasks and functions. One review of the way divorce changes family functioning lists four activities and relationships of major concern for the single parent: (1) economic functioning; (2) authority assignments; (3) household responsibilities; and (4) social and psychological support (Brandwein, Brown, and Fox 1974:499).

Economic functioning of a family is severely handicapped by its dissolution (Lake 1976). Since the mother usually has custody of the children, the parent least able to support them is left with the major economic responsibility. More divorced women than men receive financial help from both their parents and their parents-in-law (Spicer and Hampe 1975:118). The father who keeps his children faces ever-increasing expenditures for housekeeping and child care services, in addition to possible alimony for his divorced wife. Two family units now live, at least for a while, on a single income—one that may have been inadequate even before the break.

Authority patterns undergo change when a family breaks up. The head of the family is its representative in the community and its source of power in the home. Without a father the family is disorganized, unless and until the mother takes on the role of major disciplinarian. In trying to be both mother and father, the divorced woman tends to use more direct controls than do mothers who are not divorced (Kriesberg 1970). Conversely, women who have felt dominated by their husbands find new freedom, independence, and power in their roles as divorced heads of their own households (Brandwein, Brown, and Fox 1974:504).

Household responsibilities such as housework and childcare often find the divorced man more inept than his former wife, because of the usual division of family roles. If he can afford it, and if he can find a suitable person, he may hire someone to perform the domestic chores. His mother or some other female relative may help out, especially when young children are involved. The divorced mother may be reluctant to get a job for fear that her children will not be well cared for, especially in neighborhoods with few if any childcare facilities. More divorced women go it alone instead of going home to Mother than once was the case (U.S. Bureau of the Census, October 1974: Table 2), even though in general divorced mothers tend to rely on their kin (Goode 1956; Bohannan 1970).

Social and psychological supports are provided to both partners in intact marriages. The two adults lean on one another in meeting crises, making everyday decisions, and serving as emotional rehabilitators during each other's mood swings. After divorce each former mate must find other adults to serve as confidants and as replacements during illness and absence from the home, and to supply the comfort every adult needs from time to time. Depression is a common problem, especially among divorced parents of young children (Radloff 1974). Emotional support is found in the kin network, in friendship, and in nonfamily living arrangements (Table 18-7).

The process of divorce recovery

The process of recovering from a divorce takes place in three steps: (1) dealing with the complex feelings and decisions preceding the dissolution of the marriage; (2) riding out the storm of the divorce itself; and (3) picking up the pieces of life after the final decree. Each of the steps of the process is apt to be painful. The trauma can be eased somewhat by effective marriage and divorce counseling continuing throughout the process (Fisher 1974). Transition groups have been found to be valuable in relieving the pain of people suffering from post-partnership anguish (Morris and Prescott 1975). Divorcees in some communities band together in nonprofit service and social associations to help people recover from the trauma of a new divorce. Parents Without Partners associations meet regularly in many places to give group support to the parents and children

Table 18-7
Divorced Men's and Women's Living Arrangements, 1970, 1974

	Women		Men	
	1974	1970	1974	1970
Household head	81.4%	78.2%	61.2%	64.2%
Family	50.6	46.2	12.4	13.0
Nonfamily	1.9	2.1	5.5	4.6
Alone	28.9	29.9	43.3	46.5
Nonhead	18.6	21.8	38.8	35.8
Family	14.4	18.9	26.4	24.3
Nonfamily	4.2	3.0	12.3	11.5

Source: U.S. Bureau of the Census, *Marital Status and Living Arrangements: March 1974* (Washington, D.C.: U.S. Government Printing Office, October 1974), Table G.

of families broken by death or marital dissolution. Other helpful groups are being formed to help the formerly married reestablish themselves both as self-sufficient individuals and as productive members of society (Ogg 1975:19–21).

How serious is America's divorce problem?

No one questions the seriousness of divorce to the individuals involved. But what is happening to America's families is a perennial question. Professor Amitai Etzioni of Columbia University asks why there is more concern over the depletion of our oil reserves than over the exhaustion of our families and claims that "faced with the progressive crumbling of the American family, our society does little to react" (Phillips 1976). Many concerned people feel that divorce is a sign of a general disintegration of family life that threatens the stability of society and endangers future generations. Child development specialist Urie Bronfenbrenner told a joint Congressional hearing that the breakup of American families is responsible for a trebling of suicides among adolescents in the last two decades. Quoting census data showing that two-thirds of all children in families earning less than $4,000 a year live with only one parent, Professor Bronfenbrenner warns that youngsters growing up in broken, low-income families risk being damaged physically, emotionally, and socially (Hicks 1975). Many others claim that rising divorce rates so threaten American families that few will survive.

Another view is that divorce is an honest and realistic way to cope with marriages that should be terminated to free the partners and their children from intolerable situations. This point of view recognizes that modern families are changing in many respects: marriage at later ages—in addition to greater sexual freedom and experience; more flexible, egalitarian family roles; fewer (if any) children; and more opportunities for fulfilling relationships than have been possible in the past (Gordon 1973). More humane uniform divorce laws, family counseling and reconciliation services, comprehensive family courts, cooling-off periods to discourage impulsive premature divorce action, preparation-for-marriage programs, and marriage and family counseling are only a few of the efforts being made to strengthen family life in a period of rapid social change.

It is because Americans care so much about their families that they are willing to undergo such long and often wretched divorce experiences in order to find fulfillment within marriage and family life. "The wide use of divorce today is not a sign of a diminished desire to be married, but of an increased desire to be happily married" (Hunt 1966:233).

Now that more adults are remaining single, perhaps only those who truly want to will marry. Now that more married couples are choosing not to have children, only those who really want children will have them. Now that divorce is becoming a generally accepted way of dissolving a conflict-ridden marriage, fewer unhappy families become a possibility. Such selective factors could, in time, strengthen the American home. Many of the externally applied rules, taboos, laws, conventions, and economic necessities that once held families together have been weakened in our post-industrial society. It is high time that the cohesive forces within family relationships be given the chance to supply the inner strength and flexibility that marriage needs to flourish in the modern world.

The satisfactions of normal married life do not decline, but mount.

Charles W. Eliot

The crisis of yesterday is the joke of tomorrow.

H.G. Wells

Developmental crises and satisfactions

chapter nineteen

The dynamic quality of family development constitutes an ever present challenge. There are rarely two days that are alike in most families. The family no sooner get nicely settled into one stage of the family life cycle than another is upon them—with new demands, stresses, and satisfactions. It may seem that anything can happen, at any time, to a family. But certain crises are more likely, and some statisfactions are more prevalent, at some stages of the family life cycle than at others. So knowledge of family development helps us know what to expect throughout the life cycle.

Statistical probabilities over the family life cycle

At certain stages of the family life cycle, families typically feel the pinch of particular pressures more keenly than at others. During some life cycle stages, families tend to be more vulnerable to conflict, disruption, and disenchantment than at others. Families are more likely to be content with their lives at some periods than they are at others. The ability to see ahead and to plan for the near and distant future is facilitated by knowing some of the statistical probabilities in the various areas that affect family life.

Moving is most frequent
early in marriage

Every year, millions of families move from one home to another. The chance of a family's moving is four times greater in the early stages of the family life cycle than in the middle or later years. High mobility in the early years of marriage has been characteristic of American families for generations. Grandparent, parent, and married child generations all follow similar patterns—mobility peaks in the marriage's second year and declines rapidly thereafter, reaching a low after 40 years of marriage (Table 19-1).

American families typically live in a number of places over the years. Nine out of ten people in the United States move at least once in their lives, usually in their young adult years. More than three out of five men and women in their twenties moved in a recent four-year period. Families with school children move less often than those with little children (U.S. Bureau of the Census 1974; Long 1973). The pattern is generally:

1. Young people move as they complete their education and job training
2. New workers move to take advantage of occupational opportunities
3. Young adults leave their parental home for a place of their own
4. Newly married couples settle temporarily near their work
5. When children come, young parents move into larger living space
6. The presence of school children curtails family mobility

Costs are high when income is low

Family costs reach a peak during the first and last years of marriage, when incomes are low. Young couples on starting wages or salaries have the expense of establishing, furnishing and equipping their first home. Financial pressures remain high during the childbearing and child-rearing years, when full-time work is difficult for the mother and the father has not yet reached his full earning power. By the time a husband and wife have launched their children, their expenses decline and both may be working at jobs that pay better than those open to less experienced workers. Since middle-aged couples have fewer money problems, they can relax and prepare for their later years, when their income will predictably decline and their expenses increase. Many aging men and women

Table 19-1
High Mobility Comes Early in Marriage

Generation	Percentage of moving by year of marriage			
	1st year of marriage	2nd year of marriage	7th year of marriage	40th year of marriage
Grandparent	12%	42%	14%	4%
Parent	21	48	15	—
Married child	24	50	15	—

Source: Reuben Hill, *Family Development in Three Generations* (Cambridge, Mass.: Schenkman Publishing Company, 1970), Chap. 5.

have low incomes, usually accompanied by poor morale and dissatisfaction with their lives (Hutchison 1975; Chapter 16).

Wives work when their income is needed

Typically, the young wife works until the first child arrives and then drops out of the labor force until the children are in school. She may then return to work to help meet family costs and to assure the children of adequate schooling and of the standard of living to which she and her family aspire. More low-income mothers work, as do those who are heads of their households, out of sheer necessity (Carter and Glick 1976:424–430). When the children are old enough to work, the strain may be eased for less affluent families. But the teenage and launching stages bring further strains to middle-class families, who usually support their children throughout the college years and until they are in homes of their own. Middle-class wives tend to go back to work to relieve the financial pressure on their husbands and to give their children the advantages to which they are accustomed.

Marital power shifts over the years of marriage

Husband and wife make their decisions jointly more often in the early years, when full-time work is difficult for the mother and the father has differentiation develops as couples assign decisions to one or the other instead of assuming them jointly. As parents busy themselves with the many tasks of raising, supporting, and releasing their children, their time and energy are depleted, and it becomes easier to divide their responsibilities than to carry them together. They each become increasingly expert in the areas of their competence and take charge of those things that they do best. The wife's responsibility for homemaking increases as the husband's decision-making decreases—from a peak early in marriage to a low in the aging family stage. Older women generally are more vigorous, assertive, and competent than are their husbands.

Time spent in homemaking

The larger the family, the younger the children, and the greater the dependence of family members, the more time is spent in homemaking tasks. Many individual and family factors call for more housework in some families than in others, as is seen in Table 19-2.

Conflicting loyalties and burdens of guilt

During the establishment of a marriage, the young wife may be torn between her loyalty to her husband and her devotion to her parents; and she is apt to feel guilty about neglecting her mother. When she becomes pregnant, her husband sometimes feels guilty at having "gotten her that way," especially if she has some discomfort during the pregnancy. When the young mother becomes engrossed in childcare procedures that are new and demanding, she may feel guilty; and her husband may resent her neglect of him. All children disobey their parents from time to time and have subsequent feelings of guilt, while their parents undergo periods of anxiety, insecurity, and doubt about their parental competence.

Divided loyalties can be expected when adolescents pull away from earlier dependence on their parents and form close relationships with their peers. Youthful sex practices, hidden from their parents, bring a further burden of guilt to young adolescents. The father may feel guilty about neglecting his family while he pursues his career, more at some times than at others.

While older children are being launched, the mother may feel neglected and taken for granted. The emancipation of older teenagers must be accomplished, but it can involve a painful and anxious period for both parents and young people. Shifting loyalties throughout the family life cycle inevitably bring some feelings of guilt to various family members at times that can be predicted only in part.

In-law problems decline in time

Difficulties with relatives decline throughout the family life cycle. Early in the marriage husband and wife are getting used to their roles as members of each other's families. They must leave their own parents and give their first loyalty to their mates. Thus, in-law problems loom larger early in marriage than they ever will again in the family life cycle (Blood and Wolfe 1960:247).

There are several reasons for the decline of in-law problems in time: (1) the softening effect that becoming a grandmother has on the mother-

Table 19-2
Factors Determining Time Spent in Homemaking Activities

Classification of factors	Illustrative items
Household complexity	Number of persons in the household Size of the home being maintained Nature and condition of household equipment Proximity to shopping areas, medical, dental, and cultural facilities, etc.
Life cycle stage	Stage of the family life cycle Number and ages of children Career involvement of adult family members
Individual needs and interests	Special physical, emotional, educational, social, and personal needs of members Expectations of family members Flexibility of routines allowed
Husband's needs	Career expectations and demands Hostess roles and required entertaining Travel and leisure companionship expected Personal needs for wife and helpmate
Standard of living	Quality of life family aspires to Levels of competence homemaker expects Financial support—level and nature
Community involvement	Organizational demands on the family Expectations of children's school and neighborhood groups Homemaker's job, volunteer activities, civic responsibilities, personal enrichment
Available resources	Homemaker's management skills Qualifications of other helpers Type of assistance provided by others Frequency of others' assistance Availability of special services

Source: An elaboration and adaptation of Helena Znaniecki Lopata's "The Life Cycle of Social Roles of Housewife," Midwest Sociological Society meetings, Spring 1965, mimeographed paper, p. 7.

in-law relationship—found to be the most difficult in families with in-law problems (Duvall 1954:70–88); (2) the maturing of the young husband and wife as they themselves become parents; (3) the wearing off of stereotyped fears of in-laws; (4) growing appreciation for the help older family members give the younger; and (5) the gradual acceptance of the marriage by parents who previously may have disapproved.

Analysis of the views of husbands and wives on effective ways of working out harmonious relationships with their in-laws reveals two significant factors: acceptance ("They accept me, they are friendly, close, understanding . . .") and mutual respect ("We respect each other's personalities"). Out of 748 reasons (given by 345 married persons) why their in-law relationships had worked out harmoniously, items involving either acceptance or mutual respect were mentioned spontaneously 563 times, or in 75.2 percent of the cases (Duvall 1954:331–336).

Illness and death

All families know what it means to lose a family member in death (Chapter 17). Sickness is no stranger to most families at some time or other. Families with young children and with aging members go through bouts of sickness more often than do those in the middle stages of the family life cycle. Accidents are most common in families with young adults (highway and industrial accidents) and with fragile older members (falls due to failing sight and unsteady legs). Death strikes families with newborn babies more often than those with older children. Aging families inevitably terminate with the death of the older members, as time goes on. Illness and death can come at any time, to any family, but statistically they occur more often at some stages of the family life cycle than at others.

Critical periods in family development

Child development specialists recognize critical periods in human development when basic changes are taking place. Comparable periods of developmental crisis occur in families; these can be recognized, planned for, and met with understanding and courage.

No one can predict with certainty what any given family will go through in the years—or even the days—ahead. There are too many unknown factors and far too many contingencies to allow precise prediction in anything as complex as family life. But enough is known about families in general to forecast what to expect throughout the family life cycle. The stages of the family life cycle differ in length, in activity, in intensity of family interaction, and in the relative difficulty of their family developmental tasks.

The critical first stage of marriage

Since no two people ever grow up in identical families, each brings to marriage his or her own conceptions of what is appropriate behavior, what should and should not be done, how roles are conceived, and what a family should be like. These differences may be assimilated; they may partially coexist; one may dominate over the others; or they may remain in conflict. The powerful forces that brought the two persons together in marriage must now be channeled to resolve differences and achieve unity. This stage in marriage is thus not only important, but potentially explosive.

The crisis of first parenthood

The coming of the first child is a crisis, in that it calls for reorganization of the family. Roles must be reassigned; new needs must be met in new ways; and family values must be reoriented. The parents may want babies, but be dismayed to discover what they are like. Studies of hundreds of couples over the years concur that parenthood is a critical experience and that marital satisfaction drops sharply with the coming of the first baby (Chapter 10).

One interpretation is that their first child forces the young parents to take a major step into the adult world, as they encounter the developmental tasks of being responsible for another human being. Thus it is parenthood even more than marriage that demands maturity in both husband and wife.

Child-rearing stresses

Studies find that children are hard on marriage. Burr (1970), studying 116 middle-class couples representing all eight stages of the family life cycle, found the school-age stage to be a low point for both husbands and wives in such areas as finances, task performance, companionship, sex, and relationships with children. Random samples in three states showed that married couples' marital adjustment was at its lowest point during the school-age stage in the families of one state; and that it was rated near the bottom of all eight stages in the two other states (Spanier, Lewis, and Cole 1975). A national study underwritten by the Russell Sage Foundation explored adult Americans' perceived quality of life. Six of the questions posed to the 2,164 men and women interviewed inquired about their sense of being under pressure or stress. This research found that parents experienced the highest levels of stress when they had young children in the family (Figure 19–1).

Mothers trying to raise their children alone have the hardest lot. In a study of Americans' sense of well-being, Andrews and Withey surveyed more than 5000 men and women from all walks of life and in all stages of the family life cycle. They found the poorest quality of life among women with children, but without a husband. These parents without partners reported economic dissatisfactions, resentments, unhappiness, interpersonal crises, mixed feelings about their neighborhoods, and "abysmal evaluations" of their lost marriages (Andrews and Withey 1976; Chapter 9).

Attitudes toward family stress

Husbands and wives vary greatly in the ways in which they view what happens in their families. Some attitudes are negative and self-defeating:

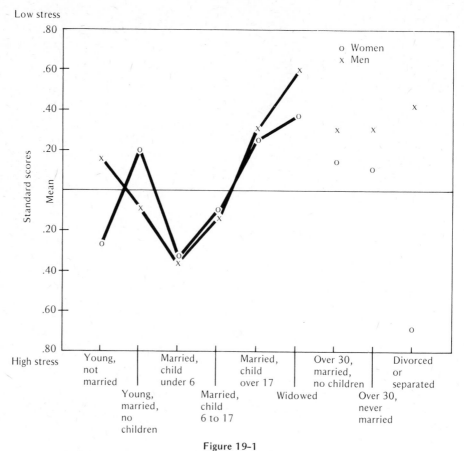

Figure 19-1
Perceived Stress Reported by Women and Men at Stages of the Life Cycle
Source: Angus Campbell, "Are Women's Lives More Frustrating and Less Rewarding then Men's?"
(Ann Arbor, Mich.: Institute of Social Research, University of Michigan, November 1974), mimeo-
graphed.

(1) "This is the last straw; I can't take any more" (defeatism); (2) "Why does this have to happen to me?" (self-pity). Attitudes more conducive to successful assimilation of the stresses occurring at critical periods of family development are (1) "This too will pass" (philosophical acceptance); (2) "It's only a stage we are going through" (recognition of the dynamic nature of family development); and (3) "Let's work it out" (positive action).

Family crises

A family crisis is any situation that cannot be coped with adequately by the usual patterns of living. Family crises may be classified as those resulting from the loss of one or more members (dismemberment); those resulting from the loss of face and status (demoralization); those resulting from the addition of one or more members (accession); and those that result from a combination of demoralization and dismemberment or accession (Table 19-3).

Weathering family crises

Families with few resources (economic, educational, personal, marital, familial) may be expected to weather crises less well than do more fortunate families. A crisis that breaks one family strengthens another, depending on how able they are to survive and to grow through it (Selig 1976). Families that have not completed their earlier developmental tasks are more susceptible to trouble related to specific unaccomplished tasks later in the life cycle. A first pregnancy that comes before an immature couple has established their marriage may be a real crisis; whereas pregnancy and the birth of the first child are taken more in stride by a mature

Table 19-3
Types of Family Crises

Dismemberment
Hospitalization
Loss of child
Loss of spouse
Orphanhood
Separation (military service, work, etc.)

Demoralization
Disgrace (alcoholism, crime, delinquency, drug addiction, etc.)
Infidelity
Nonsupport
Progressive dissension

Accession
Adoption
Birth (and possibly pregnancy)
Deserter returns
Relative moves in
Reunion after separation
Stepmother, stepfather marries in

Demoralization plus dismemberment or accession
Annulment
Desertion
Divorce
Illegitimacy
Imprisonment
Institutionalization
Runaway
Suicide or homicide

Source: Evelyn Millis Duvall and Reuben Hill, *Being Married* (Boston, Mass.: D.C. Heath & Co., 1960), pp. 298–299.

couple whose marriage is soundly established and who are ready for childbearing.

Typically, a crisis is not an isolated event. There is an initial cause that precipitates tensions that may become critical. For example, cultural disparity may result in sexual dissatisfaction because of the pair's differing attitudes toward sexual behavior. This leads to suspicion of the mate and resistance as breadwinner or homemaker, which in turn creates crises in reciprocal roles in the family, drawing some family members into new positions of power and responsibility at the expense of other members. All this may so weaken family integration that the members are unable to meet even a simple departure from their everyday routines. The result, when an out-of-the-ordinary event occurs, is a crisis.

Social pressures on families

Every family is to some extent vulnerable to anxiety and harassment and beset with complexities that arise both from within the family and from the social forces that impinge upon it. Modern families are under constant pressure from various agencies, industries, professions, and programs to modify, change, and reorganize one or more of their living habits in accordance with others' norms, values, and interests. Ever-present television commercials, multimillion dollar advertising campaigns, governmental policies, and neighborhood norms maintain a steady bombardment of demands upon families.

In times of social unrest (crime in the streets, or war at home or abroad, for instance), families are called upon to protect themselves and to safeguard the nation's security. In periods of unemployment, inflation, depression, or all three together, some families are unable to tighten their belts and deal with the realities of the times. Hard times lead to self-doubt, depression, alcoholism, and marital discord in many families, according to community health and family agencies (Crittenden 1976). A recent study of a national probability sample of American family members found that many of them were worried about money, especially when they had minor children in the home (Figure 19-2).

How families cope with their problems

A study of families subjected to the stresses of living in a rapidly urbanizing southern community found that good family adjustment was closely associated with family philosophy and outlook, with family policies and practices, and with the personal resources of individual family members. Families coped best with the rapid social changes they were undergoing when they possessed the characteristics listed as statistically significant in Table 19-4.

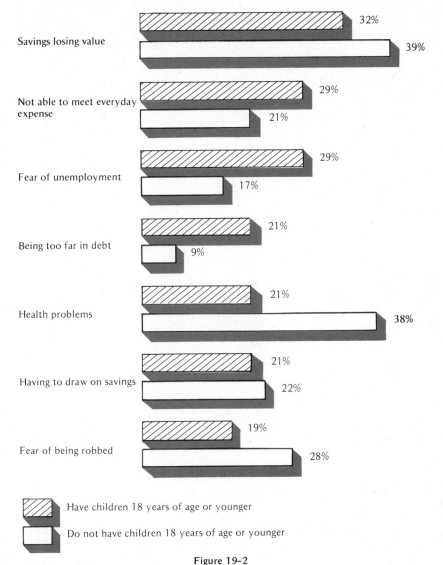

Savings losing value — 32% / 39%

Not able to meet everyday expense — 29% / 21%

Fear of unemployment — 29% / 17%

Being too far in debt — 21% / 9%

Health problems — 21% / 38%

Having to draw on savings — 21% / 22%

Fear of being robbed — 19% / 28%

Have children 18 years of age or younger

Do not have children 18 years of age or younger

Figure 19-2
Family Problems by Age of Children
Source: Yankelovich, Skelly, and White, Inc., *The General Mills American Family Report* (A Study of the American Family and Money) (Minneapolis, Minn.: General Mills, Inc., 1975), p. 52.

Table 19-4
Factors Affecting Family Adjustment to Rapid Social Change

1. Nonmaterialistic philosophy of life	7. Perception of emotional problems as family concern
2. Family orientation to trouble	
3. Developmental conceptions of parenthood	8. Diffusion of leadership in family problem-solving
4. Number of tasks shared by husband and wife	
5. Family adaptability	9. Problem-solving skill of wife
6. Accuracy of family perception of problems	10. Personal adjustment of husband and wife

Source: Reuben Hill, Joel Moss, and Claudine Wirths, "Eddysville's Families" (Chapel Hill, N.C.: University of North Carolina, 1953), mimeographed.

Conflict as crisis

Conflict can shatter a family in one violent outburst or erode it over a period of time. Depending on how it is handled, conflict between husband and wife can destroy or strengthen their relationship. Family conflict can help relieve the inevitable tensions that come from learning new habits and attempting new developmental tasks. Conflict, constructively managed, exposes the growing edge of a relationship so that it can be dealt with productively. It can redefine a situation and leave the marriage stronger than it was before. Constructive quarreling is directed at the issues, problems, and dilemmas facing the pair, rather than at one another's egos. As time goes on, a couple learn what to expect of one another and how to solve their problems, so that conflict is neither so frequent nor so painful.

Normal conflict throughout the family life cycle

Tradition, which once dictated the roles of husbands and wives, no longer serves as a guide to what the partners may expect of one another. Men and women come to marriage today with divergent goals and needs that frequently clash. Their differing beliefs, dreams, habits, and moods must be reconciled if their marriage is to survive.

The newly-married couple face tasks of role-defining, planning, and decision-making that must be accomplished to establish the marriage. In time they learn to mesh their personalities, to reconcile their differences, and to pull together as a team. Childbearing brings new possibilities for conflict, for the young couple must undertake their unfamiliar parental roles while confronted by the ever-present demands of the new baby. The little child soon asserts his independence in ways that threaten parental authority. The toddler's exploration of potentially dangerous situations brings on confrontations with protective parents. Preschoolers and school-agers bring home alien demands, expressions, and habits that conflict with family patterns and values.

Adolescent-parent conflict is widely recognized as a corollary of teenagers' struggle for autonomy. The pressures felt and exerted by young adults for lives of their own conflict with parental concern about their grown children's choice of mates (leading to in-law problems), of careers, and of differing life styles. The discontent felt by both sexes during the middle years must be dealt with anew by the couple in the empty nest. Even retirement is a mixed blessing, since some conflict between the two aging mates is inevitable. Finally, death itself is fraught with conflict—between letting-go and hanging-on attitudes and between death-affirming and death-denying stances—as well as with an inner struggle with the guilt and frustration accumulated over years of intimate association.

Development is inevitably accompanied by conflict. As each successive stage is sloughed off and a new stage begun, the individual, the marriage, and the family as a whole are in a crisis situation. These are the growing pains of life that are to be expected in development. The challenge is not to avoid problems, but to solve them one by one as they come along.

Desperation and disintegration

Desperation in families living beyond their means may break forth in disintegrating ways. A working-class husband can become abusive and domineering, while contributing neither material nor emotional support to the family. His wife, carrying more than her share of family responsibility, becomes discouraged, then desperate. Insufficient income causes unhappiness, dissatisfaction, worry, and hopelessness, and can lead to physical symptoms that are actually an expression of anxiety. Lower-class families have less access to professional help because: (1) they do not recognize their real problems; (2) they do not know where to go for help; and (3) help is not readily available for them (Gurin, Veroff, and Feld 1960:374–376). Destructive quarreling and chronic complaints build up until the man leaves home or the couple separates. Statistically, separation and divorce are most prevalent in lower-class families.

Relatively affluent couples also become discouraged in their efforts to find satisfaction with one another (Cuber and Harroff 1965). Today, since men and women demand happiness as their right; since divorce is more acceptable; and since employment is a possibility for the wife, and the pair can afford to maintain two separate households, disintegration of middle- and upper-class marriages is increasing (Chapter 18).

Destructive conflict is rightly feared as harmful to the participants and to their relationship. Explosive outbursts or aggressive silences that attack another's ego are threatening and belittling. They leave the marriage weaker than it was and the spouses farther apart than ever. In time, the two become alienated and break up, unless they have the will and the ability to strengthen their union.

Divorce probability

The probability of divorce rises rapidly in the first few years of marriage and declines thereafter through the years, as is seen in Figure 19-3. Men who marry in their teens are more divorce-prone than all others throughout their marriages. The line at the top of the chart shows that these men are four times as likely to divorce as men who marry in their

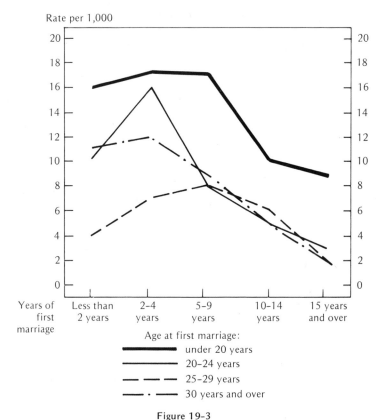

Figure 19-3
Probabilities of Divorce per 1,000 White Males by Age at First Marriage and Duration of First Marriage: 1960-1966

Source: U.S. Bureau of the Census, unpublished data from the 1967 Survey of Economic Opportunity, presented by Paul C. Glick and Arthur J. Norton, "Probabilities of Marriage, Divorce, Widowhood, and Remarriage," at the annual meeting of the Population Association of America, Atlanta, Ga., April 16-18, 1970, mimeographed. Figure 3.

middle to late twenties—both at the beginning of marriage and after 15 or more years of marriage.

Coping with conflict constructively

Three widely used ways of coping with conflict are generally ineffective:

1. Escape—the husband deserts; the wife goes home to mother or files for divorce. This settles nothing, but merely relieves the immediate pressure. The original imbalance between what the individual gets and gives in the relationship is ignored rather than renegotiated (Goode 1971)
2. Submission to domination—may keep up the appearance of peace for a while; but when the submission is reluctant and resentful, as it often is, anger rages beneath the surface until it erupts in open conflict
3. Physical force—the husband beats his wife when he is failing as a provider in an effort to assert his superior status as head of the house (O'Brien 1971). Open warfare in the home or beyond is death-defying, as is seen in the high proportion of homicides that are family-related (Boudouris 1971). Violence settles nothing, but leaves the partners and their children battered in body and spirit.

Coping with conflict effectively involves using such approaches as: (1) open two-way communication of feelings and wishes; (2) willingness and ability to empathize with each other; (3) competency in role-playing and role-reversal; (4) negotiation until both are satisfied with the new situation; (5) mental health maintenance for the family as a whole and for its members; (6) consultation with one or more competent resource persons and following through with their recommendations; (7) consolidation of the couple's joint goals—each partner internalizes the new roles to which he or she is newly committed. Each now rewards the other for progress made and is pleased with his own improvement (Duvall and Hill 1960:273–293).

Successful conflict resolution can leave a marriage stronger than it was before. Husband and wife realize that, having weathered the storms they have come through, they can take anything. They get to the place where they no longer fear their differences, but can relax and enjoy them for the satisfactions they bring.

Satisfactions over the family life cycle

Married men and women are more likely to be satisfied with their lives than are the single, the divorced, or the widowed. These conclusions are based on research underwritten by the Russell Sage Foundation. The study sought to learn how American men and women feel about their lives (Campbell 1974). One question in this national interview survey asked 2,164 adult Americans to rate their satisfaction with life as a whole on a seven-point scale. Satisfactions of both men and women peak at the same stages—first, the young married with no children; and second, the married with children over the age of 17. Lowest life satisfaction was reported by the divorced or separated and by the never-married men and women. A simple conclusion to be drawn from this research is that general life satisfaction tends to be enhanced by marriage, but to be reduced by parenthood (Campbell 1974).

Parental role strains and satisfactions

Rollins and Feldman (1970), in a review of 12 studies conducted in the United States over several decades, found a consistent decline in marital satisfaction during the first ten years of marriage. Their own study of 799 couples, classified into Duvall's eight-stage family life cycle, found 80 percent of both husbands and wives reporting that things were going well in their marriages most of or all of the time. However, their data suggest that childbearing and rearing have a negative effect on wives' marital satisfaction and feeling of self-worth in their marriages. For both husbands and wives there is a decline in general marital satisfaction following the coming of children; and there is a marked increase in satisfaction during the last stage of the family life cycle (Tables 19-5 and 19-6).

During the child-rearing years, husbands and wives are so absorbed in their separate roles as fathers and mothers that they may stop doing things together and grow apart. Then, when the children have grown and the couple might enjoy one another's company, they may have become strangers under a common roof with little to share with one another. This is not inevitable. Half of the older wives are still satisfied with or enthusiastic about their husband's companionship. Others become so dissatisfied that they either look elsewhere for companionship, or become resigned to loneliness (Blood and Wolfe 1960).

Rollins and Cannon (1974:281) suggest that role strain is least and marital satisfaction greatest at both ends of the family life cycle. In addition to role strain, such other variables as communication, commitment, emotional maturity, age of the two partners, length of the marriage, and companionship may account for variation in marital satisfaction more than does stage of the family life cycle (Spanier, Lewis, and Cole 1975: 265). Two of these variables (age and length of marriage) are easy to determine. Questions might be raised about the relative ease of ascertaining the stage of the family life cycle, as compared with such "slippery" variables as communication, commitment, emotional maturity, or companionship. It is agreed that "the best solution to these methodological

Table 19-5

Marital Satisfaction by Stage of the Family Life Cycle—Wives

Measure and level of marital satisfaction	Stage of family life cycle									Statistical evaluation
	1 N = 51	2 N = 51	3 N = 82	4 N = 244	5 N = 227	6 N = 64	7 N = 30	8 N = 50	Total N = 799	
General marital satisfaction										
All the time	41%	31%	22%	11%	14%	20%	17%	38%	20%	$\chi^2 = 55.8$
Most of the time	47	51	58	63	55	56	43	50	56	df = 14
Less often	12	18	20	26	31	24	40	12	24	$p < .001$
										C = .31
Negative feelings										
Never	10%	4%	4%	8%	12%	25%	13%	28%	11%	$\chi^2 = 61.9$
Once-twice a year	41	37	40	36	49	42	54	44	42	df = 21
Once-twice a month	35	41	45	39	26	20	30	18	33	$p < .001$
More often	14	18	11	17	13	13	3	10	14	C = .31
Positive companionship										
More than once a day	16%	10%	7%	5%	5%	5%	10%	12%	7%	$\chi^2 = 46.0$
About once a day	55	39	29	31	36	38	27	24	35	df = 21
Once-twice a week	25	39	49	46	34	45	40	44	50	$p < .001$
Less often	4	12	25	18	25	12	23	20	18	C = .27
Present family life cycle stage										
Very satisfying	74%	76%	50%	35%	17%	8%	17%	82%	45%	$\chi^2 = 242.2$
Quite satisfying	22	18	33	44	38	16	13	14	33	df = 14
Less satisfying	4	6	17	21	15	76	70	4	22	$p < .001$
										C = .59

Source: Boyd C. Rollins and Harold Feldman, "Marital Satisfaction over the Family Life Cycle," *Journal of Marriage and the Family* 32, no. 1 (February 1970): 24.

Table 19-6
Marital Satisfaction by Stage of the Family Life Cycle—Husbands

Measure and level of marital satisfaction	Stage of family life cycle								Total N = 799	Statistical evaluation
	1 N = 51	2 N = 51	3 N = 82	4 N = 244	5 N = 227	6 N = 64	7 N = 30	8 N = 50		
General marital satisfaction										
All the time	27%	22%	17%	14%	18%	27%	27%	42%	20%	$\chi^2 = 32.5$
Most of the time	61	62	59	63	60	55	40	52	60	df = 14
Less often	12	16	24	23	22	18	33	6	20	$p < .01$
										C = .24
Negative feelings										
Never	10%	10%	7%	15%	19%	12%	10%	32%	15%	$\chi^2 = 32.4$
Once-twice a year	41	47	54	50	44	63	43	40	48	df = 21
Once-twice a month	31	31	28	25	28	17	37	22	27	$p > .05$
More often	18	12	11	10	9	8	10	6	10	C = .23
Positive companionship										
More than once a day	22%	8%	4%	6%	8%	10%	10%	6%	8%	$\chi^2 = 42.2$
About once a day	49	43	34	35	34	31	40	26	36	df = 21
Once-twice a week	27	37	38	41	39	45	33	60	40	$p < .01$
Less often	2	12	24	18	19	14	17	8	16	C = .26
Present family life cycle stage										
Very satisfying	55%	69%	61%	39%	44%	9%	24%	66%	44%	$\chi^2 = 184.7$
Quite satisfying	39	23	31	45	41	25	13	30	37	df = 14
Less satisfying	6	8	8	16	15	66	63	4	19	$p < .001$
										C = .53

Source: Boyd C. Rollins and Harold Feldman, "Marital Satisfaction over the Family Life Cycle," *Journal of Marriage and the Family* 32, no. 1 (February 1970): 24.

problems is the collection of longitudinal data which, at the very least, follow a given couple from one stage to the next. If a sample of respondents stratified by stage of the family life cycle could be followed for at least a few years, to allow for a transition to the next stage, one might better understand the impact of each transition" (Spanier, Lewis, and Cole 1975:274).

Separating respondents of the 1973 and 1974 General Social Surveys (conducted by the National Opinion Research Center) into age groups, Glenn (1975:597) found that significantly more men and women over (rather than under) the age of 40 said that they were "very happy." From analysis of data drawn from three national surveys this sociologist concludes that women generally experience both greater stresses and greater satisfactions in marriage than do men (Glenn 1975:599).

Marital satisfactions increase after the children have grown

Women whose children have grown and gone report substantially happier marriages than do mothers of the same age with children still at home, according to data from six national surveys in recent years (Glenn 1975). Larger percentages of postparental than of parental wives living with a husband or some other adult say that they are "very happy" in answer to the question, "Taken all together, how would you say things are these days—would you say that you are very happy, pretty happy, or not too happy?" (Glenn 1975:106). Apparently the empty nest is not as bleak as folklore has had it, for many middle-aged and older women report marital happiness and general satisfaction once their children have left home.

Significantly more men report being happy when they are married, with grown children out of the home, than at earlier stages in the family life cycle. This finding comes from an analysis of data from the 1973 NORC General Social Survey, a self-weighting national probability sample of United States population 18 years of age and older. Only fully-employed single or married men were included in this analysis, which used the family life cycle as the principal independent variable. Married men are happier than single men, and happiness increases with age for those husbands who follow the typical family life cycle without significant detours (divorce, separation, widowerhood), and who have their children on schedule (Table 19-7).

Andrews and Withey (1976) of the University of Michigan's Institute for Social Research found that regardless of age, race, sex, education, or other factors, "people seem to arrive at a sense of global well-being by simply adding up life's pluses and minuses" (*ISR Newsletter* 1976). It appears from these several substantial studies that family experience contributes to more than it detracts from life's satisfactions.

Table 19-7
Happiness by Life Cycle Stage Among Men

Stage of the family life cycle	Percentage reporting being happy
Single	20%
Married, no children	29
Married, preschool children	35
Married, school-age children	39
Married, teenage children	41
Married, children grown and gone	46

Source: Excerpted from Joseph Harry and Edmund Doherty, "Evolving Sources of Happiness for Men over the Life Cycle: A Structural Analysis" (Detroit, Mich.: Wayne State University, 1976), mimeographed, Table 1.

Husband-wife enjoyment of leisure and marital satisfaction

Having fun together is significantly associated with the satisfaction husbands and wives find in marriage. One recent study finds that in some activities more than half the enjoyment is found to be due to the spouses' enjoying the same things. "The enjoyment of activities by husbands and wives may be separate, [but] they resemble one another, and they not only influence one another but overall the influence tends to increase the spouse's enjoyment" (Rapoport, Rapoport, and Thiessen 1974:589).

Enjoying leisure activities together is especially important in the first five years of marriage, when the relationship is being established, and again after the two have been married 18-23 years, when they are adjusting to being a pair again after releasing their grown children. Individual activities requiring no communication tend to be negatively related to marital satisfaction. Parallel leisure activities providing some interaction are somewhat positively related to husband-wife satisfaction, but their influence is not as great as that of joint activities. Joint activities requiring a high degree of interaction and role interchange are positively related to marital satisfaction for both husbands and wives (Orthner 1975).

More time off for vacations and sabbaticals for workers has a positive influence on marital interaction (Klausner 1968). Family camping trips may give a marriage a new sense of solidarity, especially when the members have been experiencing a sense of low cohesiveness (West and Merriam 1970). It may be that the slogan "The family that plays together, stays together" contains more truth than some of its detractors recognize.

Successful families

Families may become better than ever now that multiple options allow women and men who prefer individual freedom to remain unmarried and childless. Successful marriage depends on the willingness of mature adults to work toward a lasting commitment to each other and to their union. Marriage involves the risk of failure and the loss of some privacy and autonomy in exchange for the warmth of companionship with a familiar mate over the years. Those who would rather "be safe than sorry" today can opt to forego the satisfactions of marriage in favor of single-hood, which offers neither the risks nor the rewards of marriage. Meanwhile, the casualties of broken marriages—unwanted children and bruised persons of both sexes and of all ages, who have been caught in the cross-fire of conflicting male and female roles and confused by new, untried patterns of marriage and family life—continue to challenge the best preventive and remedial efforts of modern society (DeMott 1976).

Parenthood has become a courageous leap of faith into the future that only the brave should attempt. Its reponsibilities frighten the immature, who prefer pursuing their own personal goals to taking on the burden of dependent youngsters. This means that in time, only those who want to have children may bear and rear them. Couples who enjoy their nurturing roles, who know what to expect of their children and of themselves, and who have positive attitudes about the developmental crises that come to all families, may be expected to raise their children with less stress than do so many less competent parents. The satisfactions more than outweigh the stresses for those who want a stake in creating the culture of the future through their own sons and daughters.

The future is built in families. There the citizens of tomorrow are nurtured, and the culture is translated into action. "Apart from millions of decisions by couples . . . to bring forth children they will nourish, teach, and launch against the void, the human race has no future—no wisdom, no advance, no community, no grace . . . It is the destiny of flesh and blood to be familial" (Novak 1976:46).

Developing strong families

Family strength is at best relative. There are few absolutes or ideal situations in family development. Families are pulsing, dynamic units of interpersonal interaction with great potential for change, growth, and development. As family members become aware of their potential strengths and weaknesses, they can be helped to accomplish their developmental tasks effectively, thereby advancing their personal and family development.

Every individual, every family, is doing well or not so well in the developmental tasks of the moment. Doing well, the person or the family as a whole is happy, well-adjusted, competent, strong, and self-assured. The challenge to families, and to those who care about them, is to increase the incidence of success and to diminish the frequencies of failure in the developmental tasks of life, throughout the entire family life cycle.

Families function at the frontiers of modern life. Today we push our way through the wilderness of family confusion and cultural conflict, but some day our children's children may experience smooth, established ways of family living. Road-building is strenuous work, but the dream of a nation of vital, happy families producing generation after generation of strong, creative people is a worthy one, and a goal worth the struggle.

glossary*

Adaptability: ability of a person to modify his roles, attitudes, and behavior

Adaptation: process of adjusting to new and different conditions

Affect: emotional feeling tone; emotion

*Selected and adapted from sources representing various disciplines, including: U.S. Bureau of the Census; *A Psychiatric Glossary* (Washington, D.C.: American Psychiatric Association, 1969); Harold T. Christensen, ed., *Handbook of Marriage and the Family* (Chicago: Rand McNally and Company, 1964); F. Ivan Nye and Felix M. Berardo, eds., *Emerging Conceptual Frameworks in Family Analysis* (New York: Macmillan Company, 1966); American Home Economics Association, "Report of a National Project," in *Concepts and Generalizations* (Washington, D.C.: American Home Economics Association, 1967); and a number of sources of terms in child, adolescent, and adult human development. Omitted are many terms and concepts dealt with in detail in the various chapters of this text, as well as those to be found in any standard dictionary that provides general rather than technical definitions.

Affluence: wealthy; a state of plenty; comfortable living

Age and Sex Grades (categories, sets): ways of classifying the members of a society by age and sex

Alienation: being estranged and cut off from others

Ambivalence: simultaneous presence of opposite feelings (e.g., love and hate) toward the same person, thing, or possibility

Androgyny: having the characteristics of both sexes (biological and/or psychological)

Annulment: legally rescinding a marriage and returning the husband and wife to the same legal status they had before they married

Autonomy: ability of a person to be self-governing

Basic Needs: those things felt to be essential for the individual, family, or society

Birth Cohorts: group of persons who were born in a specified calendar period

Birth Order: sequence of children borne alive by the mother (first, second, etc.)

Career: set of role clusters in sequence; a position in the family consisting of role clusters in sequence over time; see positional career

Chauvinism: boastful devotion to one's own sex, race, or country

Cohabitation: living intimately with a member of the opposite sex to whom one is not married

Commitment: intent to follow a given course of action; unreserved devotion to a person or a cause

Communication: network for transmitting information, ideas, and feelings between members of a group; exchange of meaningful symbols (words and gestures)

Companionship: association of two or more persons based on common interests and mutual acceptance

Compatibility: condition of getting along well together

Complementarity: meeting one another's needs in an intimate relationship

Compulsion: insistent, repetitive, irrational urge to perform an act or ritual

Condonation: action that erases the grounds for divorce in most states

Conflict: opposing interests, ideas, drives, drives, or impulses within an individual or between two or more persons

Conjugal Family: family unit in which the husband-wife relationship is given preponderant importance

Conjugal Roles: behavioral expectations of husbands and wives

Consanguineal Family: family unit in which blood relatives take precedence over marriage partners

Consumption: use of economic resources by the ultimate consumer

Copes: behaves in a purposeful, problem-solving manner

Coverture: legal rights of and status of a wife

Creativity: ability to invent or improvise new roles or alternative lines of action in problematic situations

Crisis: any decisive change that creates a condition for which habitual patterns of behavior are inadequate

Cultural Conflict: inconsistencies arising out of incompatible elements in a culture or between cultures

Cultural Inconsistency: discrepancy or contradiction existing between various aspects of a culture

Cultural Lag: discrepancy in a culture resulting from some aspects changing more slowly than others

Cultural Patterns: standardized behavioral forms, practices, rules, and sentiments in a society

Cultural Variation: cross-cultural or historical differences in institutional behavioral patterns in societies corresponding to the different cultures and values represented in the society

Culture: way of life; the patterned behaviors, knowledge, and attitudes that members of a society learn and teach to their children

Culture of Poverty: distinguishing folkways of the very poor

Customs: standardized ways of doing, knowing, thinking, and feeling that are valued in a given group at a given time

Cycle of Poverty: poverty extending from generation to generation

Definition of the Situation: interpreting, making judgments, and representing the elements in a situation to oneself and others

Deprivation: inadequate standard of living; lacking essential or needed care and attention

Development: process leading toward fulfillment and realization of potential of an individual, family, or group over time

Developmental Task: growth responsibility that arises at or about a certain time in the life of an individual, successful accomplishment of which leads to success in later tasks

Differential Change: condition in which one mate outgrows the other, emotionally, intellectually, or socially

Disenchantment: decline in satisfaction and adjustment

Disengagement: decline in the number and quality of relationships between a person and other individuals, groups, and associations

Disorganization: loss of common objectives and functioning roles and tasks

Dissolution: dissolving of marriage by death, divorce, or separation

Dyadic Relation: interaction between two partners

Dysfunction: negative consequences of an activity; impaired functioning

Economic Stratification: levels in society ordered by differences in income and wealth

Efficiency: effective use of resources to obtain goals

Electra Complex: girl's attachment to her father, accompanied by aggressive feelings toward her mother

Empathy: subtle interpersonal sensitivity enabling a person to step into another's experience and to think and feel as he does

Endogamy: the tendency to marry within one's own group (race, religion, social class, etc.); as opposed to *exogamy*, marrying outside one's group

Erogenous Zones: areas of the body susceptible to sexual stimulation

Ethnic: of human groups sharing a common culture (language, customs, etc.)

Evaluation: appraising actions, decisions, and results in relation to goals

Expressed Culture: that part of the cultural content that operates on the surface, with activities and words taken at their face value

Expressive Feelings: emotions that reveal personal feeling states

Family: two or more persons related by marriage, blood, birth, or adoption; structurally a family is a set of positions each of which is composed of roles, which in turn are composed of norms; dynamically a family is a system of role complexes played sequentially to form a set of related careers

Family Developmental Tasks: growth responsibilities that arise at certain stages in the life of a family, achievement of which leads to success with later tasks; sequential functional prerequisites

Family Functions: what a family does to meet the needs of its members, to survive, and to make a contribution to the larger society

Family Integration: bonds of unity including affection, common interests, and economic interdependence within a family

Family Life Cycle: sequence of characteristic stages beginning with family formation and continuing through the life of the family to its dissolution

Family Life Education: systematic study or guidance in the development of knowledge, skills, attitudes, and values concucive to effective functioning as a family member of any age or status

Family Life-style: unique patterning of an individual family seen in its goals and in the way it goes about achieving them

Family of Orientation: family into which one is born and from which one gets most basic socialization

Family of Procreation: family one establishes through marriage and reproduction

Family Ritual: established procedure in a family, involving patterned behavior that is valued for itself

Family Structure: regular, routinized characteristics of the family as a whole, observable in style, pattern of interaction, and power hierarchy, established as properties of the group

Family Subculture: complex of family habits, attitudes, and relationships that aid family members in selecting, interpreting, and evaluating the various cultural patterns to which they are exposed

Family Types: classification of families by descent, location of residence, authority, and life-style

Family Values: what a family appreciates, considers desirable and of worth

Femininity: the quality of being feminine as defined with a given society

Feminism: the belief that women should have equal rights with men; the movement to secure economic, political, and social rights for women equal to those of men; popularly known as "Women's Liberation" or "Women's Lib"

Fidelity: faithful devotion to one's vows; loyalty to one's spouse; exclusiveness in sexual behavior of monogamous mates

Firm Discipline: child-rearing that allows freedom within limits, allowing the child to know clearly what is expected of him without undue harshness

Fixation: intense attachment to an object; arrest of psychosexual maturation

Functional Prerequisites: conditions necessary for the survival and continuation of a family group, or society; social imperatives;

"Gay": popular term used in describing homosexual behavior or individuals

Gender Roles: behavioral expectations specific to members of either sex

Generation Spiral: continuous overlapping of family life cycles in one generation after another in a family

Generative: pertaining to the production of offspring; procreative

Genetic: determined by heredity

Genital: pertaining to the reproductive organs

Goals: the ends toward which an individual, family, group, or society directs its efforts in the pursuit of values

Group Marriage: three or more individuals pair-bonded (having sexual access) to one another

Growth: change in amount, degree, or function of bodily structure, personality feature, or of a group as a whole (like a family), over time

Growth and Development: increasing amount or complexity, or both, of and in living things

Habit: acquired disposition to act in a certain way when in a given situation

Health: positive realization of physical and emotional potentialities

Heredity: characteristics and potentialities attributable to the genes

Home Management: making decisions and utilizing resources to attain goals in the family

Homogamy: tendency of courting and married couples to resemble each other; choosing a marriage partner who is like oneself in many respects

Household: all persons living in the same residence

Human Development: sum total of processes of change in a person from conception through old age

Idealization: consciously or unconsciously overestimating an admired attribute of another person; a mental mechanism

Ideal Mate: preconceived combination of characteristics embodied in one's image of the kind of person he or she would like to marry

Identification: unconscious endeavor to pattern oneself after another; defense mechanism playing a major role in personality development

Identity Confusion: uncertainty as to what one wants to do with his life

Identity Crisis: loss of the sense of continuity within oneself and inability to accept, or adopt the role expected of one

Individual: sum total of qualities that make each person unique among all others

Insight: self-understanding; a person's awareness of the origins, nature, and dynamics of his attitude and behavior

Instinct: a natural, inborn drive, such as self-preservation

Institution: reasonably enduring complex pattern of behavior by which social control is exerted and through which social needs can be met

Integration: effective incorporation of new experience, knowledge, and emotional capacities into the personality or into a relationship; e.g., marital integration is the unity between husband and wife that brings mutual satisfaction

Intelligence: capacity to learn and to use appropriately what one has learned

Interaction: mutual stimulation and response between persons, or between individuals and groups, or between families and other institutions in the society

Interpersonal Competence: skills contributing to effective social interaction

Interpersonal Relationship: system of interaction between two or more persons

Intimacy: quality of a personal relationship that satisfies desires for love, affection, understanding, appreciation, and security

Judgment: capacity to evaluate a number of alternatives in a given situation

Kinship: relationships within the larger family to which all the members belong; kinship may be traced through the father's line (patrilineal), through the mother's line (matrilineal), or through both family lines (bilineal) in "lineage tracing"

Libido: psychic drive or energy stemming from the life instinct, or the sexual drive, broadly defined

Love: strong attachement, affection, or devotion to a person or object; active concern for the life and growth of the beloved

Machismo: accentuated or exaggerated masculinity

Macho: popular term for extreme emphasis on being and acting masculine

Manifest Function: recognized and intended consequences of an activity (in contrast to *latent* function, which is unrecognized and unintended)

Marital Adjustment: relation between husband and wife on the major issues of their marriage

Marital Roles: behavioral expectations of husbands and wives

Marital Status: condition of being single, married, widowed, or divorced

Marriage: socially sanctioned union of

husband and wife with the expectation that they will assume the responsibilities and play the roles of married partners

Marriageability: readiness for marriage based on such factors as adaptability, interpersonal competence, preparation for marital roles, and maturity

Marriage Cohorts: a group of persons first married in a specified calendar period

Masculinity: the quality of being masculine as defined in a given society

Mate Selection: process of choosing and being chosen by one's future marriage partner

Maturation: coming to full growth and development

Median: a value that divides a distribution into two equal parts (the midpoint)

Mental Health: having relatively good personal integration so that one can love, work, and play with satisfaction; emotional health and well-being

Mental Hygiene: prevention and early treatment of mental disorders

Minimum Standard of Living: material resourses in the least amounts consistent with health and decency

Mobility: moving; changing status (upward or downward)

Modeling: process by which an individual incorporates into his behavior the perceived behavior of another with whom he identifies intentionally or unintentionally

Norm: a patterned or commonly held behavior expectation; a learned response held in common by members of a group; i.e., ways in which a family member is expected to play one of his roles

Normality: usual, healthy, conforming to expected standards

Nuclear Family: husband, wife, and their immediate children

Nurturance: ministering to the vital processes and emotional needs of another person

Obsession: persistent, unwanted impulse or idea that cannot be eliminated by reasoning

Oedipus Complex: attachment of the child for the parent of the opposite sex, accompanied by aggressive and envious feelings toward the parent of the same sex

Orgasm: sexual climax that relieves physical and emotional tension

Parsimony: saving rather than spending money on consumable items; the "law of parsimony" is choosing the simplest of several interpretations of a phenomenon

Personality: the whole person, embodying all of his physiological, psychological, and social characteristics; distinctive, individual qualities of a person seen collectively; composite of inborn capacities molded and expressed through cultural conditioning

Personification: images a person holds of himself or of another person

Pleasure Principle: tendency to seek gratification independent of all other considerations; striving for pleasure

Position: location in a social structure that is associated with a set of social norms; socially recognized category; the location of a family member in the family structure, i.e., husband-father, wife-mother, son-brother, daughter-sister

Positional Career: longitudinal history of an individual family position composed of an ever-changing cluster of roles

Power: actions that control, initiate, change, or modify the behavior of others

Primary Group: face-to-face relationships involving a high degree of intimacy and communication; e.g., the family is a primary group

Puberal: pertaining to puberty, the

period of rapid development in which boys begin to mature into men, and girls begin to mature toward womanhood

Readiness: physical, emotional, and intellectual capacity to learn a particular thing at a particular time

Recreation: activities voluntarily engaged in during leisure, primarily motivated by the pleasure they bring or the satisfaction inherent in them

Recrimination: action that nullifies the ground for divorce in most states; both partners have committed acts that would be grounds for divorce, thus nullifying the original suit

Residence Rules: a society's regulations for the residence of newly married couples: the husband leaves his parental home to live with his bride's family (matrilocal); the bride leaves her parental home to live with or near her husband's family (patrilocal); the young couple live with or near either of the parental homes (bilocal); the newly married couple establish their own independent home (neolocal)

Resources: means available for meeting needs, implementing wishes, and attaining desired goals

Role: part of a social position consisting of a more or less integrated or related set of social norms, which is distinguishable from other sets of norms forming the same position; i.e., father plays many roles: breadwinner, companion, disciplinarian, etc.; generally institutionalized social expectations, obligations, and rights imposed on an individual and arising from the status accorded to him (status roles)

Role Behavior: actual behavior of the occupant of a position with reference to a particular role, i.e., how father performs in the role of breadwinner

Role Cluster: set of roles being played by an occupant of a position at any one time; concurrent roles of a family member

Role Complex: two or more sets of role clusters

Role Differentiation: differences between individuals that affect the role distribution in a family or other group group

Role-making: creation and modification of existing roles

Role-playing: acting out assigned roles; living up to obligations because of one's commitments

Role Reversal: swapping roles; e.g., the wife works and the husband cares for the children

Role Sequence: series of roles an occupant of a position plays throughout the life cycle; longitudinal expression of roles

Role-taking: modification of one's behavior in anticipation of the responses of others; imagining how one looks from another person's viewpoint

Sanctions: institutionalized ways of constraining individuals or groups to conform to accepted norms; role behavior having reward or punishment implications

Self: way one describes his relationships with others; consciously recognized pattern of perceptions pertaining to an individual; composte of the individual's thoughts, feelings, values, and perceptions of his roles

Self-concept: who a person thinks he is; how an individual perceives himself

Self-consciousness: ability to call out in ourselves a set of definite responses that belong to the others of the group; awareness of inner reality

Sentiments: complex combination of feelings and opinions as a basis for action or judgment

Sequential Roles: series of roles an occupant of a position (e.g., family member) plays over time

Sex Education: guiding individuals of

any age or status to achieve a wholesome awareness of what it means to be a male or female person, of the process of individual development, and of the responsible use of sexuality for personal fulfillment and social well-being; the knowledge, skills, attitudes, and values that have to do with healthy, effective relationships with persons of the same and opposite sex

Sexism: prejudicial restriction of personal roles by gender

Sexuality: recognition of what it means to be a sexual being with the capacity for interacting with members of the same and opposite sex

Sex Role Transcendence: flexible expression of differences in persons regardless of their sex

Sibling Rivalry: competition between brothers and sisters for their parent's love, attention, and favors

Significant Others: persons of special importance in the life of an individual

Singlehood: remaining unmarried

Situation Content: attitudes, ideas, words, and gestures thought of as culture

Social Act: any behavior in which the appropriate object is another person; a social act involves at least two individuals, each of whom takes the other into account in the processes of satisfying impulses and achieving goals

Social Context: complex of interpersonal relationships that help to shape the personality for life

Social Control: ways in which a society or group maintains its integrity, through folkways, mores, customs, sanctions, etc., either coercive or persuasive

Social Functions: ways in which individuals and groups serve society's purposes and serve given ends

Social Imperatives: functional pre-requisites; the things that must be done in any society if it is to continue

Social Interest: concern for the welfare of a group

Socialization: process by which the individual is taught the ways of a given culture, the cultural expectations related to his age, sex, and other roles, and the means by which he seeks to conform to those expectations

Socialized Person: one who has learned to participate effectively in social groups

Social Patterns: attitudes, values, and behavior ascribed by a society to its members through various roles and statuses

Social Process: operation of the social life; the multitude of actions and interactions of human beings, acting as individuals or in groups

Social Relations: ties by which persons and groups are bound to one another in the activities of social life

Social Relationship: interaction occurring between two or more partners in a relationship

Social Status: place in a particular system occupied by a given individual at a given time

Social Structure: division of society into social groups, based on conventionally standardized social relations between individuals; social organization

Society: set of individuals organized in a given way of life; an aggregate of social relations; a social system that survives its original members, replaces them through biological reproduction, and is relatively self-sufficient

Solidarity: mutual affection, value consensus, and interdependence of roles, as in a family

Standard: measure of quality and/or quantity that reflects reconciliation of resources with demands

Standard of Living: an ideal or desired

norm of consumption, usually defined in terms of quantity and quality of goods and services

Status: social position defined by society; the position a person or a group (family) maintains in society because of the way he (or they) are evaluated

Stimulus: any action or agent that causes or changes an activity in an organism or group

Swinging: married couples swapping partners with one or more couples

Symptom: specific manifestation of an unhealthy physical or mental state

Syndrome: combination of symptoms that constitutes a recognizable condition

Task Behavior: interaction directed towards the completion of group or individual tasks

Thinking: internalized manipulation of symbols by which solutions are found

Two-way Communication: process of understanding each others' thoughts and feelings as well as the implications involved in such thoughts and feelings

Utility: the want-satisfying power of goods; i.e., time, place, form, or possession utility

Value: the power of one good to command other goods (or money) in exchange; that which is cherished, appreciated, and sought after

Volition: the process of selecting among alternatives symbolically present in the experiences of the individual

References

Chapter 1
Sex differences and gender roles

Bem, Sandra. "Sex-Role Adaptability: One Consequence of Psychological Androgyny." *Journal of Personality and Social Psychology* 31 (1975): 634–643.

Bernard, Jessie. *Women, Wives, Mothers: Values and Options.* Chicago: Aldine Publishing Co., 1975.

Biller, Henry B. "Masculine Development: An Integrative Review." *The Merrill-Palmer
Quarterly of Behavior and Development* 13, no. 4 (October 1967).

Brenton, Myron. *The American Male.* New York, N.Y.: Coward-McCann, Inc., 1966.

Brim, Orville G., Jr. "The Parent-Child Relation as a Social System: I. Parent and Child
Roles." *Child Development* 28 (1957): 344–364.

Brim, Orville G., Jr. "Family Structure and Sex Role Learning by Children." Pp. 43–
47 in Marcia E. and Thomas E. Lasswell, eds., *Love—Marriage—Family: A Developmental Approach.* Glenview, Ill.: Scott, Foresman & Co., 1973.

Bronfenbrenner, Urie. *Two Worlds of Childhood.* New York, N.Y.: Russell Sage Foundation, 1970.

Christensen, Harold T. "Are Sex Roles Necessary?" Paper read at Purdue University, Layfayette, Ind. 4 April 1975.

Feldman, Harold, and Feldman, Margaret. "Beyond Sex Role Differentiation." Paper read at International Seminary on Changing Sex Roles in Family and Society. Dubrovnik, Yugoslavia, 18 June 1975.

Fling, S., and Manosevitz, M. "Sex Typing in Nursery School Children's Play Interests." *Developmental Psychology* 7 (1972): 146-152.

Gagnon, John H., and Simon, William. *Sexual Conduct: The Social Sources of Human Sexuality.* Chicago: Aldine Publishing Co., 1973.

Hartley, Ruth E. "Sex-Role Pressures and the Socialization of the Male Child." *Psychological Reports* 5 (1959).

Hefner, Robert; Meda, Rebecca; and Oleshansky, Barbara. "The Development of Sex-Role Transcendence." Preprint, 1975.

Heilbrun, Carolyn G. *Toward a Recognition of Androgyny.* New York, N.Y.: Alfred A. Knopf, 1973.

Hill, Reuben. "Family Implications of Changing Sex Roles." Paper read at Purdue University, Lafayette, Ind., June 1975.

Horner, M. "Toward an Understanding of Achievement Related Conflicts in Women." *Journal of Social Issues* 28, no. 2 (1972): 157-175.

Kagan, Jerome. Quoted in *Sexuality*, booklet prepared in cooperation with the National Association for Mental Health. New York, N.Y. (1975): 2.

Koch, Helen L. "Some Personality Correlates of Sex, Sibling Position, and Sex of Sibling among Five- and Six-Year-Old Children." *Genetic Psychology Monographs* 52 (1955): 3-50.

Koch, Helen L. "Sissiness and Tomboyishness in Relation to Sibling Characteristics." *Journal of Genetic Psychology* 88 (1956): 231-244.

Laws, Judith. "Work Motivation and Work Behavior of Women: Future Perspectives, Signs." In J. Sherman and F. Denmark, *Psychology of Women: Future Direction in Research.* New York, N.Y.: Psychological Dimensions, Inc., 1976.

Lee, P. and Groper, N. "Sex-Role Culture and Educational Practice." *Harvard Educational Review* 44, no. 3 (August 1974).

Lynn, David B. "The Process of Learning Parental and Sex-Role Identification." *Journal of Marriage and the Family* 28, no. 4 (November 1966): 466-470.

Maccoby, Eleanor Emmons, and Jacklin, Carol Nagy. *The Psychology of Sex Differences.* Stanford, Calif.: Stanford University Press, 1975.

Macmillan Guidelines for Creating Positive Sexual and Racial Images in Educational Materials. New York, N.Y.: Macmillan Publishing Co., 1975.

Mahan, Charles S., and Broderick, Carlfred B. "Human Reproduction." Chap. 12 in Carlfred B. Broderick and Jessie Bernard, *The Individual, Sex, and Society.* Baltimore, Md.: Johns Hopkins University Press, 1969.

Mariani, John. "The Enlightened Stud." *Harper's Magazine* (July 1975): 5.

Meixel, C. "Female Adolescents' Sex Role Stereotypes and Competence Motivation." Ph.D. dissertation, Cornell University, 1976.

Money, John, and Ehrhardt, Anke. *Man and Woman, Boy and Girl.* Baltimore, Md.: Johns Hopkins University Press, 1972.

Money, John, and Tucker, Pat. *Sexual Signatures: On Being a Man or a Woman.* Boston, Mass.: Little, Brown & Co., 1975.

Nye, Ivan F., ed. *Role Structure and Analysis of the Family.* Beverly Hills, Calif.: Sage Publications, Inc., 1976.

Sawhill, Isabel; Ross, Heather L.; and MacIntosh, Anita. *The Family in Transition.* Washington, D.C.: Urban Institute, 1973.

Schwenn, M. "Arousal of the Motive to Avoid Success." Unpublished paper, Harvard University, 1970.

Secor, C. "The Androgyny Papers." *Women's Studies* 2 (1974).

Sex Roles: A Research Bibliography. Philadelphia, Pa.: Public Documents Distribution Center, 1975.

Sexuality. Booklet prepared in cooperation with the National Association for Mental Health, Rosslyn, Va., 1975.

Shaw, M., and McCuen, C. "The Onset of Academic Underachievement and Sex-Role Preference on Three Determinants of Achievement Motivation." *Developmental Psychology* 4 (1971): 219-231.

Skolnick, Arlene. *The Intimate Environment: Exploring Marriage and the Family.* Boston, Mass.: Little, Brown & Co., 1973.

Smart, Mollie S., and Smart, Russell C. *Children: Development and Relationships.* 2nd ed. New York, N.Y.: Macmillan Publishing Co., 1972.

Udry, J. Richard. *The Social Context of Marriage.* 3rd ed. Philadelphia, Pa.: J.B. Lippincott Co., 1974.

Chapter 2
Sexual attitudes and behavior in the
United States

Bell, Robert R., and Chaskes, Jay B. "Premarital Sexual Experience among Coeds." *Journal of Marriage and the Family* 32, no. 1 (February 1970): 81-84.

Bernard, Jessie. *The Sex Game.* Englewood Cliffs, N.J.: Prentice-Hall, 1968.

Bernard, Jessie. *Women, Wives, Mothers: Values and Options.* Chicago: Aldine Publishing Co., 1975.

Better Homes and Gardens. A Report on the American Family. Des Moines, Iowa: Meredith Corp., 1972.

Broderick, Carlfred B., and Bernard, Jessie, eds. *The Individual, Sex & Society.* Baltimore Md., Johns Hopkins University Press, 1969.

Christensen, Harold T., and Gregg, Christina F. "Changing Sexual Norms in America and Scandinavia." *Journal of Marriage and the Family* 32, no. 4 (November 1970): 616-627.

Cuber, John. "How New Ideas about Sex Are Changing Our Lives." *Redbook* (March 1971): 85, 173-177.

Cuber, John, and Harroff, Peggy B. *The Significant Americans: A Study of Sexual Behavior among the Affluent.* New York: Appleton-Century-Crofts, 1965.

Duberman, Lucile. "Sexual Attitudes and Behavior." *Marriage and Its Alternatives.* New York: Praeger Publications, 1974, pp. 41-77.

Duvall, Evelyn M., and Duvall, Sylvanus M., eds. *Sex Ways—In Fact and Faith.* New York: Association Press, 1961.

Edwards, John N., and Booth, Alan. "Sexual Behavior In and Out of Marriage: An Assessment of Correlates." *Journal of Marriage and the Family* 38, no. 1 (February 1976): 73-81.

Gallup, George. "Sex Revolution in U.S.?" *The Gallup Poll*, Part 1 (22 June 1969), Part 3 (23 June 1969).

Gordon, Michael, and Bernstein, M. Charles. "Mate Choice and Domestic Life in the 19th Century Marriage Manual." *Journal of Marriage and the Family* 32, no. 4 (November 1970): 665-674.

Hendin, Herbert. "The Revolt against Love." *Harper's* (August 1975): 20, 22, 26, 27.

Hill, Reuben. "Family Implications of Changing Sex Roles." Paper presented at Purdue University, Lafayette, Ind., June 1975.

Hooker, Evelyn. "Homosexuality—Summary of Studies." Pp. 166-183 in Evelyn M. Duvall and Sylvanus M. Duvall, eds., *Sex Ways—In Fact and Faith*. New York: Association Press, 1961.

Joint Committee on Health Problems in Education of the N.E.A.-A.M.A. Resolutions: Schools and Problems Relating to Sex. March 30-31, April 1, 1964.

Kantner, John F., and Zelnik, Melvin. "Sexual Experience of Young Unmarried Women in the United States." *Family Planning Perspectives* 4, no. 4 (October 1972): 9-18.

Kantner, John F., and Zelnik, Melvin. "Contraception and Pregnancy: Experience of Young Unmarried Women in the United States." *Family Planning Perspectives* 5, no. 1 (Winter 1973): 21-35.

Katz, Barbara J. "Plebiscite Vote Says, 'Keep Abortion Legal.'" *The National Observer*, week ending 13 March 1976, p. 1.

Katz, Joseph, "Women Report Higher Degrees of Satisfaction." *Sarasota Herald-Tribune*, 10 February 1974, p. 4-E.

Kerckhoff, Richard K., and panel. "Community Experiences with the 1969 Attack on Sex Education." *The Family Coordinator* 19, no. 1 (January 1970): 104-110.

Kinsey, Alfred, et al. *Sexual Behavior in the Human Female*. Philadelphia, Pa.: W.B. Saunders Co., 1953.

Lantz, Herman R.; Keyes, Jane; and Schultz, Martin. "The American Family in the Preindustrial Period: From Base Lines in History to Change." *American Sociological Review* 40, no. 1 (February 1975): 21-36.

LeMasters, E.E.; Lewis, Robert; Burt, John R.; Osmond, Marie W.; and Smith, Rebecca M. "A Cool Look at Sex Education: A Forum in Print." *The PTA Magazine* 65, no. 4 (December 1970): 2-5.

Levin, Robert J. "The Redbook Report on Premarital and Extramarital Sex—The End of the Double Standard?" *Redbook* (October 1975).

Levin, Robert J., and Levin, Amy. "Sexual Pleasure: The Surprising Preferences of 100,000 Women." *Redbook* (September 1975): 52-58.

Masters, William, and Johnson, Virginia E. *Human Sexual Response*. Boston, Mass.: Little, Brown & Co., 1966.

Masters, William, and Johnson, Virginia E. *The Pleasure Bond: A New Look at Sexuality and Commitment*. Boston, Mass.: Little, Brown & Co., 1975a.

Masters, William, and Johnson, Virginia E. "What Women Don't Understand about Men." *Redbook* (July 1975b): 42, 51, 52.

Miller, Patricia Y., and Simon, William. "Adolescent Sexual Behavior: Context and Change." *Social Problems* 22, no. 2 (1974): 58-76.

Mirande, Alfred M., and Hammer, Elizabeth L. "Premarital Sexual Permissiveness: A Research Note." *Journal of Marriage and the Family* 36 no. 2 (May 1974): 356-358.

Moore, James E. "Problematic Sexual Behavior." Pp. 343-372 in Carlfred B. Broderick and Jessie Bernard, eds., *The Individual, Sex and Society*. Baltimore, Md.: Johns Hopkins University Press, 1969.

Pilpel, Harriet F.; Zuckerman, Jane; and Ogg, Elizabeth. *Abortion: Public Issue, Private Decision*. New York, N.Y.: Public Affairs Committee, 1975.

Planned Parenthood of New York City. *Abortion, A Woman's Guide*. New York: Abelard-Schuman, Ltd., 1973.

Reiss, Ira L. *The Social Context of Premarital Permissiveness*. New York: Holt, Rinehart & Winston, 1967.

Reiss, Ira L. "Premarital Sexual Standards." Chap. 7 in Carlfred B. Broderick and Jessie Bernard, eds., *The Individual, Sex and Society*. Baltimore, Md.: Johns Hopkins University Press, 1969.

Reiss, Ira. L. *Heterosexual Relationships Inside and Outside of Marriage*. Morristown, N.J.: General Learning Press, 1973.

Reiss, Ira L.; Banwart, Albert; and Foreman, Harry. "Premarital Contraceptive Usage: A Study of Some Theoretical Explorations." *Journal of Marriage and the Family* 37, no. 3 (August 1975): 619-630.

Richardson, James T., and Fox, Sandie Wightman. "Religion and Voting on Abortion: A Follow-Up Study." *Journal for the Scientific Study of Religion* 14, no. 2 (June 1975): 159-164.

Robinson, Ira E.; King, Karl; and Balswick, Jack O. "The Premarital Sexual Revolution Among Females." *The Family Coordinator* 37, no. 2 (April 1972): 189-194.

Ryser, P.E.; Cutler, J.C.; and Grice, J.E., Jr. "Changes in Attitudes Toward Abortions: 1965-1973." Paper presented at the Annual Meeting of the American Public Health Association, New Orleans, La., 21 October 1974.

Silver, Roy R. "L.I. Parents Protest Deletion of Sex Section from Health Textbook." *New York Times*, 17 October 1970, p. 30.

Simon, William; Berger, Alan S.; and Gagnon, John H. "Beyond Anxiety and Fantasy: The Coital Experiences of College Youth." *Journal of Youth and Adolescence* 1, no. 3 (1972): 203-222.

Simon, William, and Gagnon, John H. "Homosexuality: The Formulation of a Sociological Perspective." *Journal of Health & Social Behavior* 8, no. 3 (September 1967): 177-185.

Skolnick, Arlene. "Sexual Destiny, Sexual Knowledge and Social Change." *The Intimate Environment*. Boston, Mass.: Little, Brown & Co., 1973, pp. 151-192.

Smothers, Ronald. "Bill on Homosexuals Is Debated." *New York Times*, 12 September 1975, p. 33.

Somerville, Rose M. "Family Life and Sex Education in the Turbulent Sixties." *Journal of Marriage and the Family* 33, no. 1 (February 1971): 11-35.

Spock, Benjamin. *Decent and Indecent*. Greenwich, Conn.: Fawcett Crest Publications, 1971.

"Teen-Age Sex: Letting the Pendulum Swing." *Time*, 21 August 1972, pp. 34-40.

"The Homosexual: Newly Visible, Newly Understood." *Time*, 31 October 1969, pp. 56-67.

Whitehurst, Robert N. "Violence Potential in Extramarital Sexual Responses." *Journal of Marriage and the Family* 33, no. 4 (November 1971): 683-691.

Zelnik, Melvin, and Kantner, John F. "Sexuality, Contraception and Pregnancy among Young Unwed Females in the United States." Pp. 358-374 in Charles F. Westoff and Robert Parke, Jr., eds., *Demographic and Social Aspects of Population Growth*, vol. 1. Washington, D.C.: Commission on Population Growth and the American Future, 1972a.

Zelnik, Melvin, and Kantner, John F. "The Probability of Premarital Intercourse." *Social Science Research* 1, no. 3 (September 1972b): 335-341.

Zelnik, Melvin, and Kantner, John F. "The Resolution of Teenage First Pregnancies." *Family Planning Perspectives* 6, no. 2 (Spring 1974): 74-80.

Zelnik, Melvin, and Kantner, John F. "Attitudes of American Teenagers Toward Abortion." *Family Planning Perspectives* 7, no. 2 (March-April 1975): 89-91.

Chapter 3
Changing families in a changing world

Bengtson, Vern L. "Generation and Family Effects in Value Socialization." *American Sociological Review* 40, no. 3 (June 1975): 358-371.

Bengtson, Vern L., and Laufer, Robert S., eds. "Youth, Generations, and Social Change: Part II." *The Journal of Social Issues* 30, no. 3 (1974).

Bernard, Jessie. *Remarriage: A Study of Marriage*. New York: Dryden Press, 1956.

Bernard, Jessie. *The Future of Marriage*. New York: World Publishing Co., 1972.

Better Homes and Gardens. A Report on the American Family. Des Moines, Iowa: Meredith Corp., 1972.

Boulding, Kenneth. "There's a Challenge in Changing Things." *America and the Future of Man: No. 10*. Developed by the University of South Florida and the National Endowment for the Humanities. *Sarasota Herald-Tribune*, 2 December 1973, p. 5-F.

Carter, Hugh, and Glick, Paul C. *Marriage and Divorce: A Social and Economic Study*. Cambridge, Mass.: Harvard University Press, 1970.

Duvall, Evelyn Millis. "Conceptions of Parenthood." *American Journal of Sociology* 52, no. 3 (November 1946): 193-203.

Elder, Rachel Ann. "Traditional and Developmental Conceptions of Fatherhood." Master's thesis, Iowa State University, 1947, p. 21.

Epstein, Joseph. *Divorced in America: Marriage in an Age of Possibility*. New York: Penguin Books, Inc., 1974.

Fendrich, James M. "Activists: Ten Years Later: A Test of Generational Unit Continuity." *The Journal of Social Issues* 30, no. 3 (1974): 95-118.

Forbes Magazine. March 1, 1975 feature; reprinted as "Is Depression the Only Cure for Inflation?" *The National Observer*, week ending 7 June 1975, p. 14.

Freeman, Richard, and Hollomon, J. Herbert. Quoted in Robert W. Merry, "Downward Mobility . . . Diplomas No Longer Are Tickets to Higher Pay—Or Even to Jobs." *The National Observer*, week ending 23 August 1975, p. 10.

Friedman, Milton, "Where Has the 'Hot' Summer Gone?" *Newsweek*, 4 August 1975, p. 63.

Gagnon, John H., and Simon, William. "Prospects for Change in American Sexual Patterns." Chap. 12 in Gordon F. Streib, ed., *The Changing Family: Adaptation and Diversity*. Reading, Mass.: Addison-Wesley Publishing Co., 1973, p. 144.

Glick, Paul C. "A Demographer Looks at American Families." *Journal of Marriage and the Family* 37, No. 1 (February 1975a): 15-26.

Glick, Paul C. *Some Recent Changes in American Families*. Bureau of the Census, Current Population Reports Special Studies, Series P-23, no. 52, 1975b.

Gordon, Michael. "Infant Care Revisited." *Journal of Marriage and the Family* 30, no. 4 (November 1968): 578-583.

Gribbin, August. "Americans Making More and Enjoying It Less." *The National Observer*, week ending 2 August 1975, p. 7.

Hill, Reuben, et al. *Family Development in Three Generations*. Cambridge, Mass.: Schenkman Publishing Co., 1970.

Jondrow, Marjean, ed. *Focus on Poverty Research*. Madison: University of Wisconsin, Institute for Research on Poverty, Spring-Summer 1976.

Kell, Leone, and Aldous, Joan, "Trends in Child Care over Three Generations," *Marriage and Family Living* 22, no. 2 (May 1960): 176-177.

Kessler, Sheila. *The American Way of Divorce: Prescription for Change*. Chicago: Nelson-Hall, 1975.

Laufer, Robert S., and Bengtson, Vern L. "Generations, Aging, and Social Stratification: on the Development of Generational Units." *Journal of Social Issues* 30, no. 3 (1974): 181-205.

Merry, Robert W. "Downward Mobility . . . Diplomas No Longer Are the Tickets to Higher Pay—or Even to Jobs." *The National Observer*, week ending 23 August 1975, p. 10.

Miller, Daniel R., and Swanson, Guy E. *The Changing American Parent*. New York: John Wiley & Sons, 1958.

Monthly Vital Statistics Report, *Annual Summary for the United States, 1974*. Rockville, Md.: U.S. Department of Health, Education, and Welfare, 30 May 1975.

National Center for Education Statistics, American Association of University Professors. In *U.S. News & World Report*, 1 September 1975, p. 45.

O'Riley, John. "Prices . . . Putting the High Cost of Living in Perspective." *The National Observer*, week ending 1 October 1975., p. 11-A.

Porter, Sylvia. *Sylvia Porter's Money Book*. Garden City, N.Y.: Doubleday & Co., 1975, Chap. 10, pp. 373-405.

Riesman, David; Glazer, Nathan; and Denney, Reuel. *The Lonely Crowd: A Study of the Changing American Character*. New Haven, Conn.: Yale University Press, 1950.

Staples, Ruth, and Smith, June Warden. "Attitudes of Grandmothers and Mothers toward Child-rearing Practices." *Child Development* 25 (1954): 91-97.

Statistical Abstract of the United States. Washington, D.C.: U.S. Bureau of the Census, 1957, 1958, 1960, 1961, 1962, 1963, 1973, 1974, 1975.

Statistical Abstract Supplement. *Historical Statistics of the United States: Colonial Times to 1957*. Washington, D.C.: U.S. Bureau of the Census, with the cooperation of the Social Science Research Council, 1960.

Statistical Bulletin. "Trends in Expected Family Size in the United States." New York: Metropolitan Life, January 1975, vol. 56, pp. 8-11.

Stendler, Celia B. "Sixty Years of Child Training Practices." *Journal of Pediatrics* 36, no. 1 (January 1950): 122-134.

Streib, Gordon F., ed. *The Changing Family: Adaptation and Diversity.* Reading, Mass.: Addison-Wesley Publishing Co., 1973.

Toffler, Alvin. *Future Shock.* New York: Bantam Books, 1970.

Toynbee, Arnold J. "We Must Pay for Freedom." *Woman's Home Companion* (March 1955): 52-53, 133-136.

U.S. Bureau of the Census. *Age at First Marriage*, PC(2)-4D, 1970 Census of Population. Washington, D.C.: U.S. Department of Commerce, April 1973.

U.S. Bureau of the Census. "Educational Attainment in the United States: March 1973 and 1974." *Current Population Reports*, Series P-20, no. 274. Washington, D.C.: U.S. Department of Commerce, December 1974a.

U.S. Bureau of the Census. "Population of the United States Trends and Prospects: 1950-1990." *Current Population Reports Special Studies*, Series P-23, no. 49. Washington, D.C.: U.S. Department of Commerce, December 1974b.

U.S. Bureau of the Census. "Estimates of the Population of the United States and Components of Change: 1974 (with Annual Data from 1930)." *Current Population Reports*, Series P-25, no. 545. Washington, D.C.: U.S. Department of Commerce, April 1975a.

U.S. Bureau of the Census. "Household and Family Characteristics: March 1974." *Current Population Reports*, Series P-20, no. 276. Washington, D.C.: U.S. Department of Commerce, February 1975b.

U.S. Bureau of the Census. "Projections of the Population of the United States by Age and Sex, 1975 to 2000, with Extensions of Total Population to 2025." *Current Population Reports*, Series P-25, no. 541. Washington, D.C.: U.S. Department of Commerce, February 1975c.

U.S. Department of Labor. *Children of Working Mothers, March 1974.* Washington, D.C.: Special Labor Force Report, 1975a.

U.S. Department of Labor. *Marital and Family Characteristics of the Labor Force, March 1974.* Washington, D.C.: Special Labor Force Report 173, 1975b.

U.S. News & World Report. "Labor: For 5 Million—An 'Inflation Cushion.'" 29 September 1975a, p. 89.

U.S. News & World Report. "New Era: A Look at Americans in Year 2000." 3 March 1975b, p. 35.

U.S. News & World Report. "The Shrinking Dollar." 6 October 1975c, p. 62.

U.S. News & World Report. Special Section, "Crisis in the Schools." 1 September 1975d, pp. 42-55.

Waldman, Elizabeth. *Children of Working Mothers, March 1974.* Washington, D.C.: U.S. Department of Labor, 1975.

Wattenberg, Ben J. *The Real America: A Surprising Examination of the State of the Union.* Garden City, N.Y.: Doubleday & Co., 1974.

Westoff, Leslie Aldridge. "Two-time winners." *New York Times Magazine*, 10 August 1975, pp. 9-14.

Yankelovich, Skelly and White, Inc. *The American Family Report: A Study of the American Family and Money.* Minneapolis, Minn.: General Mills, Inc., 1975.

Chapter 4
Marital roles and conjugal options

Aldous, Joan. "Occupational Characteristics and Males' Role Performance in the Family." *Journal of Marriage and the Family* 31, no. 4 (November 1969): 707-712.

Aldous, Joan. "The Conceptual Approach." *The Developmental Approach to Family Analysis*, vol. 1. Athens: University of Georgia Press, 1974.

American Council on Education, Office of Research. *Summary of Data on Entering Freshmen*. Fall 1968, 1969, 1970, 1971, 1972.

Associated Press. "Women Graduate Students Increasing." *Sarasota Herald-Tribune*, 3 July 1975, p. 16-A.

Astin, Helen S.; Suniewick, Nancy; and Dwock, Susan. *Women: A Bibliography on Their Education and Careers*. New York: Behavioral Publications, Inc., 1974.

Axelson, Leland. "The Marital Adjustment and Role Definitions of Husbands of Working and Nonworking Wives." *Journal of Marriage and the Family* 25, no. 2 (May 1963): 189-195.

Bahr, Stephen J. "Competence, Authority, and Conjugal Control." Paper read at the Annual Meeting of the American Sociological Association, San Francisco, Calif. August 1975. Mimeographed.

Bahr, Stephen J., and Rollins, Boyd. "Crisis and Conjugal Power." *Journal of Marriage and the Family* 33, no. 2 (May 1971).

Bayer, A.E.; Royer, J.T.; and Webb, R.M. *Four Years After College Entry*. American Council on Education, Research Report, vol. 8, 1973.

Bernard, Jessie. *The Sex Game*. Englewood Cliffs, N.J.: Prentice-Hall, 1968.

Bernard, Jessie. *Women, Wives, Mothers: Values and Options*. Chicago: Aldine Publishing Co. 1975.

Better Homes and Gardens. A Report on the American Family. Des Moines, Iowa: Meredith Corp., 1972.

Blau, Peter. *Exchange and Power in Social Life*. New York: John Wiley & Sons, 1964.

Brenton, Myron. *The American Male*. New York: Coward-McCann, Inc., 1966.

Bronfenbrenner, Urie. Quoted in Barbara Freeman, *Free and Female*. New York: Fawcett World Library, 1973.

Cavan, Ruth Shonle, and Ranck, Katherine Howland. *The Family and the Depression*. Chicago: The University of Chicago Press, 1938.

Chase Manhattan Bank of New York. Quoted in Sylvia Porter, "Housewife: 12 Occupations," syndicated feature in *Sarasota Herald-Tribune*, 14 February 1972, p. 9-B.

Christensen, Harold T. "Are Sex Roles Necessary?" Paper read at Purdue University, Lafayette, Ind., 4 April 1975. Mimeographed.

Cogswell, Betty E., and Sussman, Marvin B. "Changing Roles of Women, Family Dynamics, and Fertility." Pp. 9-26 in H. Yuan Tien and Frank D. Bean, eds., *Comparative Family and Fertility Research*. Leiden: E.J. Brill, 1974.

Cromwell, Ronald E., and Olson, David H., eds. *Power in Families*. New York: John Wiley & Sons, 1975.

Deckard, Barbara. *The Women's Movement: Political, Socioeconomic, and Psychological Issues*. New York: Harper & Row, Publishers, 1975.

Dullea, Georgia. "Families Are Going to School—for Vacation." *New York Times*, 15 July 1975, p. 24.

Educational Communications, Inc. *1974 Survey.* Quoted in *The Sounding Board* 22, no. 9 (September 1975):2.

Farkas, George. "Education, Wage Rates, and the Division of Labor between Husband and Wife." Paper read at the Annual Meeting of the American Sociological Association, August 1975. Mimeographed.

Feldman, Harold, and Feldman, Margaret. "The Effect of Father Absence on Adolescents." Paper read at the Annual Meeting of the National Council on Family Relations, Salt Lake City, Utah, August 1975. Mimeographed.

Fiske, Edward B. "Women Get Backing as Rhodes Scholars." *New York Times*, 17 September 1975, pp. 1, 36.

Freeman, Barbara. *Free and Female.* Greenwich, Conn.: Fawcett Publications, 1973.

Gage, M. Geraldine. "Economic Roles of Wives and Family Economic Development." *Journal of Marriage and the Family* 37, no. 1 (February 1975): 121-128.

Glenn, Norval D. "The Contribution of Marriage to the Psychological Well-Being of Males and Females." Analysis of National Opinion Research Center and Roper Public Opinion Research Center data. 1975. Mimeographed.

Green, Maureen. *Fathering.* New York: McGraw-Hill Book Co. 1976.

Hazleton, Lesley. Special to the New York Times from Kibbutz Harel, Israel. *New York Times*, 4 March 1976, p. 26.

Horner, Matina. "Femininity and Successful Achievement: A Basic Inconsistency." P. 117 in Michele Hoffnung Garskof, ed., *Roles Women Play.* Belmont, Calif.: Brooks/Cole Publishing Co., 1971.

Kolb, Trudy M., and Strauss, Murray A. "Marital Power and Marital Happiness in Relation to Problem-Solving Ability." *Journal of Marriage and the Family* 36, no. 4 (November 1974): 756-766.

Komarovsky, Mirra. *Dilemmas of Masculinity: A Study of College Youth.* New York: W.W. Norton & Co., 1976.

LeMasters, Ersel E. *Parents in Modern America: A Sociological Analysis.* Homewood, Ill.: The Dorsey Press, 1970.

Levin, Robert J. "The Redbook Report on Premarital and Extramarital Sex—The End of the Double Standard?" *Redbook* (October 1975): 38-44, 190-192.

Levin, Robert J., and Levin, Amy. "Sexual Pleasure: The Surprising Preferences of 100,000 Women." *Redbook* (September 1975): 51-58.

Lewis, Robert A. "Satisfaction with Conjugal Power Over the Family Life Cycle." Paper read at the meetings of the National Council on Family Relations, Portland, Ore., 31 October 1972. Mimeographed.

McGrady, Mike. "Let 'Em Eat Leftovers." *Newsweek*, 2 February 1976, p. 13.

Martin, Thomas W.; Berry, Kenneth J.; and Jacobsen, R. Brooke. "The Impact of Dual-Career Marriages on Female Professional Careers: An Empirical Test of a Parsonian Hypothesis." *Journal of Marriage and the Family* 37, no. 4 (November 1975): 734-742.

Meier, Harold C. "Mother-Centeredness and College Youths' Attitudes toward Social Equality for Women: Some Empirical Findings." *Journal of Marriage and the Family* 34, no. 1 (February 1972): 115-121.

"More Women to Become Executives." *Family News and Features*. New York: Institute of Life Insurance, 30 July 1973, p. 1.

Mott, Paul E., et al. *Shift Work: The Social, Psychological and Physical Consequences.* Ann Arbor: University of Michigan Press, 1975.

Nye, Ivan F., ed. *Role Structure and Analysis of the Family.* Beverly Hills, Calif.: Sage Publications, Inc., 1976.

Orden, Susan, and Bradburn, Norman M. "Working Wives and Marriage Happiness." *American Journal of Sociology* 74 (January 1969). Reprinted in Marcia Lasswell and Thomas Lasswell, eds., *Love—Marriage—Family: A Developmental Approach.* Glenview, Ill.: Scott, Foresman & Co., 1973, pp. 384-395.

Osmond, Marie Withers, and Martin, Patricia Yancey. "Sex and Sexism: A Comparison of Male and Female Sex-Role Attitudes." *Journal of Marriage and the Family* 37, no. 4 (November 1975): 744-758.

Parelius, Ann P. "Change and Stability in College Women's Orientations Toward Education, Family, and Work." Paper read at Montclair State College, Montclair, N.J., 17 May 1974. Mimeographed.

Parelius, Ann P. "Emerging Sex-Role Attitudes, Expectations, and Strains Among College Women." *Journal of Marriage and the Family* 37, no. 1 (February 1975): 146-153.

Porter, Sylvia. "Housewife: 12 Occupations." Syndicated feature in *Sarasota Herald-Tribune*, 14 February 1972, p. 9-B.

Rossi, Alice S. "Sex Equality: The Beginnings of Ideology." Chap. 36 in Ira L. Reiss, ed., *Readings on the Family System.* New York: Holt, Rinehart & Winston, 1972.

Scanzoni, Letha, and Scanzoni, John. *Men, Women, and Change: A Sociology of Marriage.* New York: McGraw-Hill Book Co., 1976.

Smart, Mollie S., and Smart, Russell C. *Children: Development and Relationships.* 2nd ed. New York: Macmillan Publishing Co., 1972.

"Taking Homemakers' Pulses." *The Sounding Board*. New York, N.Y.: Public Relations Board, September 1975, p. 2.

Treiman, Donald J., and Terrell, Kermit. "Sex and the Process of Status Attainment: A Comparison of Working Women and Men." *American Sociological Review* 40 (April 1975): 174-200.

Trice, Harrison M. *Alcoholism in America.* New York: McGraw-Hill Book Co., 1966.

Turk, James L., and Bell, Normal W. "Measuring Power in Families." *Journal of Marriage and the Family* 34, no. 2 (May 1972): 215-234.

Udry, J. Richard. *The Social Context of Marriage.* 3rd ed. Philadelphia: J.B. Lippincott Co. 1974.

UPI release. "Both Husband, Wife Work in Typical American Family." *Sarasota Herald-Tribune*, 23 May 1976, p. 7-A.

U.S. Bureau of the Census and other federal agencies. "A Close-Up Look at Women in U.S. . . . and Ways Their Status is Changing." *U.S. News & World Report*, 8 December 1975, pp. 56-57.

Waldman, Elizabeth. "Changes in Labor Force Activity of Women." *Monthly Labor Review* 93 (1970): 10-17.

Walker, Kathryn. "Household Work Time: Its Implication for Family Decisions." *Journal of Home Economics* 65, no. 1 (October 1973): 11.

"Women Graduate Students Increasing." Associated Press release, 3 July 1975.

Yankelovich, Skelly and White, Inc. *The General Mills American Family Report.* Minneapolis, Minn.: General Mills, Inc., 1975.

Chapter 5
Ethnic, racial, and social class differences

Andrews, Frank M., and Withey, Stephen B. *Social Indicators of Well-Being in America: The Development and Measurement of Perceptual Indicators.* New York: Plenum Publishing Corp., 1976.

Bachman, Jerald. *Youth in Transition, Volume II: The Impact of Family Background and Intelligence on Tenth-Grade Boys.* Ann Arbor: Institute for Social Research, University of Michigan, 1970.

Bernard, Jessie. *Marriage and Family Among Negroes.* Englewood Cliffs, N.J.: Prentice-Hall, 1966.

Billingsley, Andrew. *Black Families in White America.* Englewood Cliffs, N.J.: Prentice-Hall, 1968.

Blakeslee, Sandra. "Study Refutes View of Minority Learning." *New York Times,* 25 October 1975, p. 48.

Blood, Robert O., Jr., and Wolfe, Donald M. "Negro-White Differences in Blue-Collar Marriages in a Northern Metropolis." *Social Forces* 48, no. 1 (September 1969): 59-64.

Blumberg, Paul M., and Paul, P.W. "Continuities and Discontinuities in Upper-Class Marriages." *Journal of Marriage and the Family* 37, no. 1 (February 1975): 63-77.

Brown, Les. "Study Finds Nonwhite TV Viewers Exceed Whites." *New York Times,* 30 September 1975, p. 67.

Carter, Hugh, and Glick, Paul C. *Marriage and Divorce: A Social and Economic Study.* Rev. ed. Cambridge, Mass.: Harvard University Press, 1976.

Chilman, Catherine S. *Growing Up Poor.* Washington, D.C.: U.S. Government Printing Office, 1966.

Chilman, Catherine S. "Families in Poverty in the Early 1970's: Rates, Associated Factors, Some Implications." *Journal of Marriage and the Family* 37, no. 1 (February 1975): 49-60.

Christensen, Harold T., and Gregg, Christina F. "Changing Sex Norms in America and Scandanavia." *Journal of Marriage and the Family* 32 (1970): 616-627.

Coles, Robert. *Uprooted Children: The Early Life of Migrant Farm Workers.* Pittsburgh, Pa.: University of Pittsburgh Press, 1970.

Cutright, Phillips. "Income and Family Events: Marital Stability." *Journal of Marriage and the Family* 33, no. 2 (May 1971).: 291-306.

Davis, Allison. "Socioeconomic Influences upon Children's Learning." *School Life* 33, no. 6 (March 1951): 87.

Dornbusch, Sanford M.; Massey, Grace Carroll; and Scott, Mona Vaughn. "Racism without Racists, Institutional Racism in Urban Schools." Stanford University unpublished study summarized in "Study Refutes View of Minority Learning." *New York Times,* 15 October 1975, p. 48.

Duncan, Otis Dudley. "Social Stratification and Mobility: Problems in the Measurement of Trend." Pp. 675-719 in E.B. Sheldon and W. Moore, eds., *Indicators of Social Change.* New York: Russell Sage Foundation, 1968.

Duvall, Evelyn Millis. "Conceptions of Parenthood." *American Journal of Sociology* 52, no. 3 (November 1946): 193-203.

Erlanger, Howard D. "Social Class and Corporal Punishment in Childbearing: A Reassessment." *American Sociological Review* 39 (February 1974): 68-85.

Feinberg, Lawrence. "Study Shows Academic Achievement Depends on Family Background." *Los Angeles Times/Washington Post Service*, 19 March 1972.

Feuer, Lewis S. *The Conflict of Generations: The Character and Significance of Student Movements.* New York: Basic Books, 1969.

Flaim, Paul O.; Bradshaw, Thomas F.; and Gilroy, Curtis L. "Employment and Unemployment in 1974." *Monthly Labor Review* (February 1975): 3-14.

Fuchs, Estelle, and Havighurst, Robert J. *To Live on This Earth: American Indian Education.* New York: Doubleday & Co., 1972.

Gagnon, John, and Simon, William. Unpublished analysis of 1967 national college student sample, 1972.

Gatlin, Fred. "Educational Gap between Blacks and Whites Continues to Narrow, Census Bureau Study Indicates." Washington, D.C.: *United States Department of Commerce News*, 31 December 1974, pp. 1-2.

Glick, Paul C. "A Demographer Looks at American Families." *Journal of Marriage and the Family* 37, no. 1 (February 1975): 15-26.

Glick, Paul C., and Mills. Karen M. "Black Families: Marriage Patterns and Living Arrangements." Proceedings of the W.E. DuBois Conference on American Blacks, Atlanta, Ga., October 1974, in press.

Hammond, Boone E., and Ladner, Joyce A. "Socialization into Sexual Behavior in a Negro Slum Ghetto." Pp. 41-51 in Carlfred B. Broderick and Jessie Bernard, eds., *The Individual, Sex, and Society.* Baltimore, Md.: Johns Hopkins University Press, 1969.

Hayghe, Howard. "Marital and Family Characteristics of the Labor Force, March 1974." *Monthly Labor Review* (January 1975): 60-63.

Hechinger, Grace, and Hechinger, Fred M. "The Ebb and Flow of Student Rebellion." *Saturday Review,* 6 September 1975, pp. 46-49.

Heath, Linda L.; Roper, Brent S.; and King Charles D. "A Research Note on Children Viewed as Contributors to Marital Stability: The Relationship to Birth Control Use, Ideal and Expected Family Size." *Journal of Marriage and the Family* 36, no. 2 (May 1974): 304-306.

Institute for Social Research. "Cross-Racial Contact Increases in Seventies; Attitude Gap Narrows for Blacks and Whites." *ISR Newsletter* (Autumn, 1975): 4-7.

Iutaka, Sugiyama; Bock, E. Wilbur; and Berardo, Felix. "Social Status, Mobility, Illegitimacy and Subsequent Marriage." *Journal of Marriage and the Family* 37, no. 3 (August 1975): 643-654.

Jencks, Christopher. *Inequality: A Reassessment of the Effect of Family and Schooling in America.* New York: Basic Books, Inc., 1972.

Kantner, John F., and Zelnik, Melvin. "Sexual Experience of Young Unmarried Women in the United States." *Family Planning Perspectives* 4, no. 4 (October 1972):9-18.

Keniston, Kenneth. *Young Radicals: Notes on Committed Youth.* New York: Harcourt, Brace & World, 1968.

Koller, Marvin R. *Families: A Multigenerational Approach.* New York: McGraw-Hill Book Co., 1974, Chap. 7.

Komarovsky, Mirra. *Blue-Collar Marriage.* New York: Random House, Inc., 1964.

Komarovsky, Mirra. "Response." P. 29 in Kathryn P. Johnson, *Changing Roles in Sex and Marriage: A Symposium.* West Lafayette, Ind.: Institute for the Study of Social Change, Department of Sociology and Anthropology, Purdue University, 1976.

Kriesberg, Louis. *Mothers in Poverty: A Study of Fatherless Families.* Chicago: Aldine Publishing Co., 1970.

Laufer, Robert S., and Bengtson, Vern L. "Generations, Aging, and Social Stratification: On the Development of Generational Units." In Vern L. Bengtson and Robert S. Laufer, eds., "Youth, Generations, and Social Change: Part II." *The Journal of Social Issues* 30, no. 3 (1974):181-205.

Levin, Herman. "Income Alternatives for Poor Families." *The Family Coordinator* 24, no. 3 (July 1975):312.

McEaddy, Beverly J. "Educational Attainment of Workers, March 1974." *Monthly Labor Review* (February 1975):64-69.

Malloy, Michael. "The Black Kids' Burden." *The National Observer*, week ending 15 November 1975, pp. 1, 18.

Malloy, Michael. "'We Don't Want Your Melting Pot.'" *The National Observer*, week ending 7 August 1976, pp. 1, 12.

Morgan, James N.; Dickson, Katherine; Dickson, Jonathan; Benus, Jacob; and Duncan, Greg. *Five Thousand American Families—Patterns of Economic Progress.* Ann Arbor: Institute for Social Research, University of Michigan, 1974.

Mosteller, Frederick, and Moynihan, Daniel P. *On Equality of Educational Opportunity.* New York: Random House, Inc., 1972.

Moynihan, Daniel P. *The Negro Family: A Case for National Action.* Washington, D.C.: U.S. Department of Labor, Office of Planning Policy and Research, 1965.

Neugarten, Bernice. "The Relation Between Family Social Position and the Social Development of the Child." Ph.D. dissertation, University of Chicago, 1943.

Novak, Michael. "White Ethnic." *Harper's Magazine* (September 1971):44-50.

Otto, Luther B. "Class and Status in Family Research." *Journal of Marriage and the Family* 37, no. 2 (May 1975):315-332.

Pearlin, Leonard I. "Status Inequality and Stress in Marriage." *American Sociological Review* 40 (June 1975): 344-357.

Pope, Hallowell. "Negro-White Differences in Decisions Regarding Illegitimate Children." *Journal of Marriage and the Family* 31, no. 4 (November 1969):756-764.

Porter, Sylvia. *Sylvia Porter's Money Book.* New York: Doubleday & Company, 1975.

Rainwater, Lee. *Behind Ghetto Walls: Black Family Life in a Federal Slum.* Chicago: Aldine Publishing Co., 1970.

Rainwater, Lee. "Sex in the Culture of Poverty." Pp. 129-140 in Carlfred B. Broderick and Jessie Bernard, eds., *The Individual, Sex, and Society.* Baltimore, Md.: Johns Hopkins University Press, 1969.

Rainwater, Lee, and Yancey, William L. *The Moynihan Report and the Politics of Controversy.* Cambridge, Mass.: The M.I.T. Press, 1967.

Reiss, Ira L. *Heterosexual Relationships Inside and Outside of Marriage.* Morristown, N.J.: General Learning Press, 1973.

Renne, Karen S. "Correlates of Dissatisfaction in Marriage." Pp. 395-406 in Marcia E. Lasswell and Thomas E. Lasswell, eds., *Love—Marriage—Family: A Developmental Approach.* Glenview, Ill.: Scott, Foresman & Co., 1973.

Scanzoni, John. "Sex Roles, Economic Factors, and Marital Solidarity in Black and White Marriages." *Journal of Marriage and the Family* 37, no. 1 (February 1975): 130-144.

Schulz, David A. *Coming Up Black.* Englewood Cliffs, N.J.: Prentice-Hall, 1969.

Sears, Robert R.; Maccoby, Eleanor E.; and Levin, Harry. *Patterns of Child-Rearing.* Evanston, Ill.: Row, Peterson & Co., 1957.

Sewell, William H.; Haller, Archibald O.; and Ohlendorf, George, "The Educational and Early Occupational Attainment Process: Replications and Revisions." *American Sociological Review* 35 (December 1970): 1014-1027.

Sørensen, Aage B. "The Structure of Intragenerational Mobility." *American Sociological Review* 40, no. 4 (August 1975): 456-471.

Stack, Carol B. *All Our Kin: Strategies for Survival in a Black Community.* New York: Harper & Row, Publishers, Inc., 1974.

Staples, Robert. "Research on Black Sexuality: Its Implication for Family Life, Sex Education, and Public Policy." *The Family Coordinator* 21, no. 2 (April 1972): 183-188.

Staples, Robert. "Research on the Negro Family: A Source for Family Practitioners." *The Family Coordinator* 18, no. 3 (July 1969): 202-209.

Stinnett, Nick; Talley, Sharon; and Walters, James. "Parent-Child Relationships of Black and White High School Students: A Comparison." *The Journal of Social Psychology* 91 (1973): 349-350.

Thernstrom, Stephan. "Poverty in Historical Perspective." Pp. 110-155 in Daniel P. Moynihan, ed., *On Understanding Poverty.* New York: Basic Books Inc., 1968.

U.S. Bureau of the Census. Data quoted in "Whites Keep Fleeing to Suburbs—and Negroes Crowd into Cities." *U.S. News & World Report*, 1 March 1971, p. 24.

U.S. Bureau of the Census. "Characteristics of Low-Income Population 1971." *Current Population Reports*, Series P-60, no. 86. Washington, D.C.: U.S. Government Printing Office, 1972.

U.S. Bureau of the Census. "Marital Status and Living Arrangements: March 1974." *Current Population Reports*, Series P-20, no. 271, 1974, Tables 4 and 5.

U.S. Bureau of the Census. "Educational Attainment in the United States: March 1973 and 1974." *Current Population Reports*, Series P-20, no. 274, December 1974a.

U.S. Bureau of the Census. "Estimates of the Population of the United States, by Age, Sex, and Race: July 1, 1974 and April 1, 1970." *Current Population Reports*, Series P-25, no. 529, September 1974b.

U.S. Bureau of the Census. "Social and Economic Status of the Black Population." Quoted in "How Blacks Are Faring: Latest Official Report." *U.S. News & World Report*, 11 August 1975a.

U.S. Bureau of the Census. "Money Income in 1973 of Families and Persons in the United States." *Current Population Reports*, Series P-20, no. 97, January 1975b.

U.S. Bureau of the Census. "Population Profile of the United States." *Current Population Reports*, Series P-20, no. 279, March 1975c. Table 10.

U.S. Bureau of the Census. *Social and Economic Status of the Black Population.* Washington, D.C.: U.S. Department of Commerce, 28 July 1975d.

U.S. Department of Labor, Bureau of Labor Statistics. *Employment and Earnings* 21, no. 12 (June 1975).

U.S. Immigration and Naturalization Service. Quoted in "More Asians Pour into U.S.

Melting Pot." *U.S. News & World Report*, 13 October 1975, pp. 70-71.

Waldman, Elizabeth. "Children of Working Mothers, March 1974." *Monthly Labor Review* (January 1975): 64-67.

Wattenberg, Ben J. *The Real America*. Garden City, N.Y.: Doubleday & Co., 1974.

Winch, Robert F., et al. *Familial Organization: A Quest for determinants*, forthcoming.

Zelnik, Melvin, and Kantner, John F. "Sexuality, Contraception and Pregnancy among Young Unwed Females in the United States." *Research Reports, Vol. 1, Demographic and Social Aspects of Population Growth*. Commission on Population Growth and the American Future. Baltimore, Md.: Johns Hopkins University Press, 1972, pp. 358-374.

Zelnik, Melvin, and Kantner, John F. "The Resolution of Teenage First Pregnancies." *Family Planning Perspectives* 6, no. 4 (Spring 1974):74-80.

Chapter 6
Families and family study

Aldous, Joan. "Intergenerational Visiting Patterns: Variations in Boundary Maintenance as an Explanation." *Family Process* 6, no. 2 (September 1967): 235-251.

Aldous, Joan. *The Developmental Approach to Family Analysis, Volume One: The Conceptual Approach*. Athens: University of Georgia Press, 1974.

Barthel, Joan. "Old-Fashioned Marriage Is Back in Style." *Ladies' Home Journal* (January 1976): 93, 132-148.

Better Homes and Gardens. A Report on the American Family. Des Moines, Iowa: Meredith Corp., 1972.

Billingsley, Andrew. Quoted in "Shaky Family Life Style Suffers Strong Winds of Change, Stress." *Sarasota Herald-Tribune*, 25 May 1975, p. F-1.

Blood, Robert O., Jr. *Impact of Urbanization on American Family Structure and Functioning*. An Arbor: Center for Research on Social Organization, University of Michigan, 1964.

Brazelton, T. Berry. "The Father Alone: Eighteen Months." *Redbook* (September 1975): 22-26.

Broderick, Carlfred B. "Reaction to 'Familial Development, Selective Needs, and Predictive Theory.'" *Journal of Marriage and the Family* 29, no. 2 (May 1967): 237-240.

Brozan, Nadine. "Ex-Addicts in a Lonely World Create Their Own 'Family.'" *New York Times* 17 July 1975, p. 34.

Burgess, Ernest W. and Locke, Harvey J. *The Family: From Institution to Companionship*. New York: American Book Co. 1953.

Cavan, Ruth Shonle, ed. "Special Issue: Communes, Historical and Contemporary." *The International Review of Modern Sociology*, 1976.

Chilman, Catherine S. *Growing Up Poor*. Washington, D.C.: Welfare Administration Publication no. 13, 1966.

Cogswell, Betty E., and Sussman, Marvin B. "Changing Family and Marriage Forms: Complications for Human Service Systems." *The Family Coordinator* 21, no. 4 (October 1972): 505-516.

Constantine, Larry L., and Constantine, Joan M. "Report on Ongoing Research in

Group Marriage." Paper read at the Society for the Scientific Study of Sex, New York, N.Y., January 1971.

David, Deborah. *Career Patterns and Values: A Study of Men and Women in Science and Engineering*. New York, N.Y.: Bureau of Applied Social Science, Columbia University, 1973.

Denfield, Duane, and Gordon, Michael. "The Swingers." Pp. 87-94 in G. Streib, ed., *The Changing Family: Adaptation and Diversity*. Reading, Mass.: Addison-Wesley Publishing Co., 1973.

Edwards, Maxine, and Stinnett, Nick. "Perceptions of College Students Concerning Alternate Life Styles." *The Journal of Psychology* 87 (1974): 143-156.

Ellis, Albert. "Group Marriage: A Possible Alternative?" P. 82 in G. Streib, ed., *The Changing Family: Adaptation and Diversity*. Reading, Mass.: Addison-Wesley Publishing Co., 1973.

Etzioni, Amitai. "The American Family." *Sarasota Herald-Tribune* 29 December 1975, p. C-1.

Gilmartin, Brian G. "That Swinging Couple Down the Block." *Psychology Today* 8, no. 9 (February 1975): 58.

Glick, Paul C. "Updating the Life Cycle of the Family." Paper read at the Annual Meeting of the Population Association of America, Montreal, 30 April 1976.

Goode, William J. *The Family*. Englewood Cliffs, N.J.: Prentice-Hall, 1964.

Gordon, Suzanne. *Lonely in America*. New York, N.Y.: Simon & Schuster, 1976.

Hagestad, Gunhild. Quoted in "For Singles, Life Isn't All 'Swinging.'" *U.S. News & World Report*, 8 December 1975, pp. 67-68.

Havens, E.M. "Women, Work, and Wedlock: A Note on Female Marital Patterns in the United States." *American Journal of Sociology* 78 (January 1973): 975-981.

Hazleton, Lesley. "Israel's Founding Mothers Look at Kibbutz Women Today with Resignation and Disillusionment." *New York Times*, 4 March 1976, p. 26.

Henze, Lura F., and Hudson, John W. "Personal and Family Characteristics of Cohabiting and Noncohabiting College Students." *Journal of Marriage and The Family* 36, no. 4 (November 1974): 722-727.

Hill, Reuben, et al. *Family Development in Three Generations*. Cambridge, Mass.: Schenkman Publishing Co., 1970.

Hill, Reuben, and Hansen, Donald A. "The Identification of Conceptual Frameworks Utilized in Family Study." *Marriage and Family Living* 22, no. 4 (November 1960): 308.

Hooker, Evelyn. Interviewed in "Facts that Liberated the Gay Community." *Psychology Today* 9, no. 7 (December 1975): 52-55, 99.

Hudson, R. Lofton. *A Conversation with R. Lofton Hudson on Marriage and Family*. Austin, Texas: Hogg Foundation for Mental Health, The University of Texas, 1975, p. 8.

Kanter, Rosabeth Moss. "Communes." *Psychology Today* 4, no. 2 (July 1970): 53-57, 78.

Kirkpatrick, Clifford. "Familial Development, Selective Needs, and Predictive Theory." *Journal of Marriage and the Family* 22, no. 2 (May 1967): 229-236.

LeMasters, Ersel E. "Parents Without Partners." P. 56 in G. Streib, ed., *The Changing Family: Adaptation and Diversity*. Reading, Mass.: Addison-Wesley Publishing Co., 1973.

Lewis, Robert A.; Spanier, Graham B.; Storm, Virginia L.; and LeHecka, Charlotte F.

"Commitment in Married and Unmarried Cohabitation." Paper read at the American Sociological Association annual meeting, San Francisco, Calif. 27 August 1975.

Lindsay, Ben B. "The Companionate Marriage." *Redbook* (October 1926).

Litwak, Eugene. "Extended Kin Relations in an Industrial Democratic Society." In E. Shanas and G. Streib, eds., *Social Structure and the Family*. Englewood Cliffs, N.J.: Prentice-Hall, 1965.

Lyness, Judith L.; Lipetz, Milton E.; and Davis, Keith E. "Living Together: an Alternative to Marriage." *Journal of Marriage and the Family* 34, no. 2 (May 1972): 305–312.

McCormack, Patricia. "New Family Definitions from Future Leaders." UPI release. *Sarasota Herald-Tribune*, 4 August 1974, p. 6-E.

Macklin, Eleanor D. "Cohabitation in College." *Psychology Today* 8, no. 6 (November 1974): 53–59.

McWhirter, William A. "'The Arrangement' at College: Part I." Pp. 203–207 in M.E. Lasswell and T.E. Lasswell, eds., *Love—Marriage—Family: A Developmental Approach*. Glenview, Ill.: Scott, Foresman & Co., 1973.

Mead, Margaret. "Every Home Needs Two Adults." *Redbook* (May 1976): 38–42.

Mead, Margaret. "Marriage in Two Steps." *Redbook* 127 (1966): 48–49.

Mead, Margaret. Presentation at the 1975 American Orthopsychiatric Association's Symposium on Family Research. Reported in K. Schaar, "Mead, Bronfenbrenner Critique Family Research." *APA Monitor* 6, no. 5 (May 1975): 8.

Murdock, George. *Social Structure*. New York, N.Y.: Macmillan Publishing Co., 1949.

Peterman, Dan J.; Ridley, Carl A.; and Anderson, Scott M. "A Comparison of Cohabiting and Noncohabiting College Students." *Journal of Marriage and the Family* 36, no. 2 (May 1974): 344–354.

Rabkin, Leslie Y. "In Israel's Radical Communes . . . The Institution of the Family is Alive and Well." *Psychology Today* 9, no. 9 (February 1976): 66–73.

Ramey, James W. "Emerging Patterns of Innovative Behavior in Marriage." *The Family Coordinator* 21, no. 4 (October 1972): 435–456.

"'Singleness' Is on the Rise Among Women." *Family News and Features*, 24 December 1975, p. 1.

Spiegel, John. *Transactions: The Interplay between Individual, Family, and Society*. New York, N.Y.: Science House, 1971.

Spreitzer, Elmer, and Riley, Lawrence E. "Factors Associated with Singlehood." *Journal of Marriage and the Family* 36, no. 3 (August 1974): 533–542.

Stein, Peter J. "Singlehood: An Alternative to Marriage." *The Family Coordinator* 24, no. 4 (October 1975): 489–503.

Streib, Gordon F., ed. *The Changing Family: Adaptation and Diversity*. Reading, Mass.: Addison-Wesley Publishing Co., 1973.

Sussman, Marvin B. "Marriage Contracts: Social and Legal Consequences." Paper read at the 1975 International Workshop on Changing Sex Roles in Family and Society, 17 June 1975. Mimeographed.

Sussman, Marvin B., and Burchinal, Lee. "Kin Family Network: Unheralded Structure in Current Conceptualizations of Family Functioning." *Marriage and Family Living* 24, no. 2 (August 1962): 231–240.

U.S. Bureau of the Census. "Household and Family Characteristics: March 1974." *Current Population Reports*, Series P–20, no. 276. Washington, D.C.: U.S. Department of Commerce, 1975.

Veysey, Laurence. "Communal Sex and Communal Survival: Individualism Busts the Commune Boom." *Psychology Today* 8, no. 7 (December 1974): 73-78.

Weitzman, Lenore J. "Legal Regulation of Marriage: Tradition and Change." *California Law Review* 62, no. 4 (July-September) 1974.

Wells, J. Gipson. "A Critical Look at Personal Marriage Contracts." *The Family Coordinator* 25, no. 1 (January 1976): 33-37.

Winch, Robert F., et al. *Familial Organization: A Quest for Determinants*, forthcoming.

Yorburg, Betty. P. 396 in *Contemporary Sociology* 4, no. 4 (July 1975). Review of James R. Smith, and Lynn G. Smith. *Beyond Monogamy: Recent Studies of Sexual Alternatives to Marriage*. Baltimore, Md.: Johns Hopkins University Press.

Yost, Edwin D., and Adamek, Raymond J. "Parent-Child Interaction and Changing Values: A Multivariate Analysis." *Journal of Marriage and the Family* 36, no. 1 (February 1974): 115-121.

Zablocki, B. *The Joyful Community: An Account of the Bruderhof, a Communal Movement Now in Its Third Generation*. Baltimore, Md.: Penguin Books, 1971.

Chapter 7
The family life cycle

Albrecht, Ruth. "Intergeneration Parent Patterns." *Journal of Home Economics* 46, no. 1 (1954): 31.

Aldous, Joan. *The Developmental Approach to Family Analysis, Volume One: The Conceptual Framework*. Unpublished manuscript. Athens: University of Georgia, 1974.

Bigelow, Howard F. Pp. 382-386, Chap. 17, in Howard Becker and Reuben Hill, eds., *Marriage and the Family*. Boston, Mass.: D.C. Heath & Co., 1942.

Blood, Robert O., Jr., and Wolfe, Donald M. *Husbands and Wives: The Dynamics of Married Living*. New York: The Free Press, Division of Macmillan Publishing Co., 1960.

Bossard, James H.S. "The Law of Family Interaction." *American Journal of Sociology* (January 1945): 292.

Cavan, Ruth Shonle. "The Cycle of Family Life." *The American Family*. 4th ed. New York: Thomas Y. Crowell Co., 1969, pp. 231-512.

Cavan, Ruth Shonle, ed. *Marriage and Family in the Modern World: A Book of Readings*. 3rd ed. Chap. 13 "Nuclear Family and Kinship Web," pp. 353-369. New York: Thomas Y. Crowell Co., 1969.

Clayton, Richard R. "The Developmental Framework." *The Family, Marriage and Social Change*. Lexington, Mass.: D.C. Heath & Co., 1975, pp. 21-26.

Duvall, Evelyn Millis. "Family Development Applications: An Essay Review." *The Family Coordinator* 21, no. 3 (July 1972): 331-333.

Duvall, Evelyn Millis. *In-Laws: Pro and Con*. New York: Association Press, 1954.

Duvall, Evelyn Millis, and Hill, Reuben, cochairmen. "Report of the Committee on the Dynamics of Family Interaction." Prepared at the request of the National Conference on Family Life, Washington, D.C., 1948. Mimeographed.

Feldman, Harold. *Development of the Husband-Wife Relationship: A Research Report*. Ithaca, N.Y.: Cornell University, 1965.

Feldman, Harold, and Feldman, Margaret. "The Family Life Cycle: Some Suggestions for Recycling." *Journal of Marriage and the Family* 37, no. 2 (May 1975): 277-284.

Glick, Paul C. "Updating the Life Cycle of the Family." Paper read at the annual meeting of the Population Association of America, Montreal, 30 April 1976.

Glick, Paul C., and Parke, Robert Jr. "New Approaches in Studying the Life Cycle of the Family." *Demography* (1965): 187-202.

Goode, William. "Family Cycle and Theory Construction." In M. Jean Cuisenier, ed., *Family Life Cycle in European Societies*. Paris, France: Mouton, in press.

Hareven, T.K. "The Family as Process: The Historical Study of the Family Cycle." *Journal of Social History* 7, no. 3 (1974): 322-329.

Hill, Reuben. "Interdependence among the Generations." *Family Development in Three Generations*. Cambridge, Mass.: Schenkman Publishing Co., 1970, Chap. 3.

Kaluger, George, and Kaluger, Meriem Fair. *Human Development: The Span of Life*. St. Louis, Mo.: C.V. Mosby Co., 1974.

Kirkpatrick, Clifford. "Life Cycle of Family Experience." *The Family as Process and Institution*. 2nd ed. New York: Ronald Press, 1963, Part 3, pp. 175-535.

Kirkpatrick, E.L., et al. *The Life Cycle of the Farm Family in Relation to Its Standard of Living*. Agricultural Experiment Station Research Bulletin no. 121. Madison: University of Wisconsin, 1934.

Lansing, John B., and Kish, Leslie. "Family Life Cycle as an Independent Variable." *American Sociological Review* 22, no. 5 (October 1957): 512-519.

Lidz, Theodore. "The Life Cycle." *The Person: His Development throughout the Life Cycle*. New York: Basic Books, Inc., 1968, Part 2, pp. 93-506.

Litwak, Eugene. "The Use of Extended Family Groups in the Achievement of Social Goals: Some Policy Implications." *Social Problems* 7 (Winter 1959-1960): 177-187.

Lurie, Elinor. "Sex and Stage Differences in Perceptions of Marital and Family Relationships." *Journal of Marriage and the Family* 36, no. 2 (May 1974): 260-269.

Neugarten, Bernice L. "Introduction to the Symposium Models and Methods for the Study of the Life Cycle." *Human Development* 14, no. 2 (1971): 81-86.

Norton, Arthur J. "The Family-Life Cycle Updated." Pp. 162-170 in Robert F. Winch and Graham B. Spanier, eds., *Selected Studies in Marriage and the Family*. New York: Holt, Rinehart & Winston, 1974.

Ogren, Evelyn H., "Family Dynamics for Paraprofessional Workers." *The Family Coordinator* 20, no. 1 (January 1971): 11-16.

Parke, Robert Jr., and Glick, Paul C. "Prospective Changes in Marriage and the Family." *Journal of Marriage and the Family* 29, no. 2 (May 1967): 249-256.

Rodgers, Roy H. *Family Interaction and Transaction: The Developmental Approach*. Englewood Cliffs, N.J.: Prentice-Hall, 1973.

Rodgers, Roy H. "Improvements in the Construction and Analysis of Family Life Cycle Categories." Ph.D. dissertation, University of Minnesota, 1962.

Rodgers, Roy H. "Proposed Modification of Duvall Family Life Cycle Stages." Paper read at the American Sociological Association Meetings, New York City, 31 August 1960.

Segalen, Martine. "Research and Discussion Around Family Life Cycle: An Account of the 13th Seminar on Family Research." *Journal of Marriage and the Family* 36, no. 4 (November 1974): 814-818.

Shanas, Ethel, and Streib, Gordon F., eds. *Social Structure and the Family: Generational Relations*. Englewood Cliffs, N.J. Prentice-Hall, 1965.

Sorokin, Pitrim; Zimmerman, Carle C.; and Galpin, C.J. *A Systematic Source Book in Rural Sociology*. Minneapolis: University of Minnesota Press, 1931, vol. 2, p. 31.

Sussman, Marvin B. "Family Sociology." Chap. 2 in Margaret S. Archer, ed., *Current Research in Sociology*. Paris, France: Mouton, 1974, pp. 27-65.

Sussman, Marvin B. "Relationships of Adult Children with Their Parents in The United States." Chap. 4 in Ethel Shanas and Gordon F. Streib, eds., *Social Structure and the Family: Generational Relations*. Englewood Cliffs, N.J.: Prentice-Hall, 1965.

Sussman, Marvin B., and Burchinal, Lee. "Kin Family Network: Unheralded Structure in Current Conceptualizations of Family Functioning." *Marriage and Family Living* 24, no. 3 (August 1962): 231-240.

Uhlenberg, Peter. "Cohort Variations in Family Life Cycle Experiences of U.S. Females." *Journal of Marriage and the Family* 36, no. 2 (May 1974): 284-292.

U.S. Bureau of the Census. "Projections of the Population of the United States, by Age and Sex, 1975 to 2000, with Extensions of Total Population to 2025 (Advance Report)." *Current Population Reports*, Series P-25, no. 541. Washington, D.C.: U.S. Government Printing Office, February 1975.

Chapter 8
Developmental tasks: individual and family

Aldous, Joan. *The Developmental Approach to Family Analysis, Volume One: The Conceptual Framework*. Athens: University of Georgia, 1974. Mimeographed.

Bloom, Benjamin S. *Stability and Change in Human Characteristics*. New York: John Wiley & Sons, 1964.

Broderick, Carlfred B. "Beyond the Five Conceptual Frameworks: A Decade of Development of Family Theory." *Journal of Marriage and the Family* 33, no. 1 (February 1971): 139-159.

Close, Kathryn. "Youth and the Life Cycle." (Interview with Erik H. Erikson.) *Children* (March–April 1960).

Erikson, Erik H. *Childhood and Society*. New York: W.W. Norton & Co., 1950.

Freud, Sigmund. *New Introductory Lectures on Psychoanalysis*. Edited by James Stachey. New York: W.W. Norton & Co., 1965.

Havighurst, Robert J. *Developmental Tasks and Education*. 3rd ed. New York: David McKay Co., 1972.

Hill, Reuben. "Interdisciplinary Workshop on Marriage and Family Research." *Marriage and Family Living* 13, no. 1 (February 1951): 13-28.

Hill, Reuben, et al. *Family Development in Three Generations*. Cambridge, Mass.: Schenkman Publishing Co., 1970.

Hunt, J. McV. *Intelligence and Experience*. New York: Ronald Press Co., 1961.

Lidz, Theodore. *The Person: His Development throughout the Life Cycle*. New York: Basic Books, Inc., 1968.

McCandless, Boyd R. *Children: Behavior and Development*. New York: Holt, Rinehart & Winston, 1967.

Magrabi, Frances M., and Marshall, William H. "Family Developmental Tasks: A Research Model." *Journal of Marriage and the Family* 27, no. 4 (November 1965): 454-461.

Piaget, Jean, and Inhelder, Bärbel. *The Psychology of the Child*. New York: Basic Books, Inc., 1969.

Rodgers, Roy H. *Family Interaction and Transaction: The Developmental Approach*. Englewood Cliffs, N.J.: Prentice-Hall, 1973.

Sanford, Nevitt, ed. *The American College*. New York: John Wiley & Sons, 1962.

Smart, Mollie S., and Smart, Russell C. *Children: Development and Relationships*. New York: Macmillan Publishing Co., 1972.

Thurstone, L.I. *The Differential Growth of Mental Abilities*. Chapel Hill: University of North Carolina Psychometric Laboratory, 1955.

White, Burton L. "The Initial Coordination of Sensorimotor Schemas in Human Infants—Piaget's Ideas and the Role of Experience." Pp. 237-256 in David Elkind and John H. Flavell, eds., *Studies in Cognitive Development*. New York: Oxford University Press, 1969.

Chapter 9
Married couples

Aldous, Joan. *The Developmental Approach to Family Analysis: Volume One: The Conceptual Framework*. Athens: University of Georgia, 1974. Mimeographed.

Better Homes and Gardens. A Report on the American Family. Des Moines, Iowa: Meredith Corp., 1972.

Blood, Robert O., Jr., and Wolfe, Donald M. *Husbands and Wives: The Dynamics of Married Living*. New York: The Free Press, 1961.

Burchinal, Lee G., and Chancellor, Loren E. "Survival Rates among Religiously Homogamous and Interreligious Marriages." *Social Forces* 41, (May 1963): 353-362.

Campbell, Angus. "The American Way of Mating, Marriage Sí, Children Only Maybe." *Psychology Today* 8, no. 12 (May 1975): 37-43.

Centers, Richard; Ravan, Bertram H.; and Rodrigues, Aroldo. "Conjugal Power Structure: A Reexamination." *American Sociological Review* 36 (1971): 264-278.

Cutright, Phillips. "Income and Family Events: Getting Married." *Journal of Marriage and the Family* 32, no. 4 (November 1970): 628-637.

Duvall, Evelyn Millis. *In-Laws: Pro and Con*. New York: Association Press. 1954.

Elder, Glen H. "Role Orientations, Marital Age and Life Patterns in Adulthood." *Merrill-Palmer Quarterly* 18 (1972): 3-24.

Elder, Glenn H., Jr., and Rockwell, Richard C. "Marital Timing in Women's Life Patterns." *Journal of Family History* 1, no. 1 (Autumn 1976): 34-53.

Eshleman, J. Ross, and Hunt, Chester L. "Social Class Influences and Family Adjustment Patterns of Married College Students." *Journal of Marriage and the Family* 29, no. 3 (August 1967): 485-491.

Glick, Paul C. "A Demographer Looks at American Families." *Journal of Marriage and the Family* 37, no. 1 (February 1975): 15-26.

Glick, Paul C. "Updating the Life Cycle of the Family." Paper read at the annual meeting of the Population Association of America, Montreal, 30 April 1976.

Goodrich, Wells; Ryder, Robert G.; and Raush, Harold L. "Patterns of Newlywed Marriage." *Journal of Marriage and the Family* 30, no. 3 (August 1968): 383-391.

Gribbin, August. "Abortion. . . New Scientific Report Shows Drop in Risk of Death." *The National Observer*, week ending 10 June 1975, p. 10.

Handler, Philip. Interview in "Overpopulation." *This Week Magazine*, 29 June 1969, pp. 14-15.

Hill, Reuben, et al. *Family Development in Three Generations*. Cambridge, Mass.: Schenkman Publishing Co., 1970.

Jackson, D., and Lederer, W. *Mirages of Marriage*. New York: W.W. Norton & Company, 1969.

Komarovsky, Mirra. *Blue-Collar Marriage*. New York: Random House, Inc., 1964.

Levin, Robert J., and Levin, Amy. "Sexual Pleasure: The Surprising Preferences of 100,000 Women." *Redbook* (September 1975): 51-58.

Levy, John, and Munroe, Ruth. *The Happy Family*. New York: Alfred A. Knopf, 1962.

Lopata, Helena Z. *Occupation: Housewife*. New York: Oxford University Press, 1971.

Neugarten, Bernice L., ed. *Middle Age and Aging*. Chicago: University of Chicago Press, 1968, p. 143.

Porter, Sylvia. Syndicated column. 24 November 1972.

Rapoport, Rhona. "Normal Crises, Family Structure and Mental Health." *Family Process* 2, no. 1 (March 1963): 68-80.

Rapoport, Rhona. *The Study of Marriage as a Critical Transition for Personality and Family Development*. Cambridge, Mass.: Harvard Medical School, January 1965. Mimeographed.

Rapoport, Robert; and Rapoport, Rhona, "Work and Family in Contemporary Society." *American Sociological Review* 30, no. 3 (June 1965): 381-394.

Raush, Harold L.; Goodrich, Wells; and Campbell, John D. "Adaptation to the First Years of Marriage." *Psychiatry* 26, no. 4 (November 1963): 368-380.

Reiss, Ira L. *Heterosexual Relationships Inside and Outside of Marriage*. Morristown, N.J.: General Learning Press, 1973.

Ryder, Robert G. "Husband-Wife Dyads versus Married Strangers." *Family Process* 7, no. 2 (September 1968): 233-238.

Ryder, Robert G., and Goodrich, Wells. "Married Couples' Responses to Disagreement." *Family Process* 5, no. 1 (March 1966): 30-42.

Shope, David F., and Broderick, Carlfred B. "Level of Sexual Experience and Predicted Adjustment in Marriage." *Journal of Marriage and the Family* 29, no. 3 (August 1967): 424-433.

Stilley, Joy. "Kids Don't Easily Accept Stepparents." Associated Press release, 16 November 1975.

Tietze, Christopher; Bongartz, John; and Schearer, Bruce. "Population Study Reported." *Family Planning Perspectives* (July 1976).

U.S. Bureau of the Census. "Social and Economic Variations in Marriage, Divorce and Remarriage: 1967." *Current Population Reports*, Series P-20, no. 233. Washington, D.C.: U.S. Government Printing Office, 1971.

U.S. Bureau of the Census. "Marriage, Divorce, and Remarriage by Year of Birth: June 1971." *Current Population Reports*. Series P-20, no. 239. Washington, D.C.: U.S. Government Printing Office, 1972.

U.S. Bureau of the Census. "Marital Status and Living Arrangements: March 1974." *Current Population Reports*, Series P-20, no. 271. Washington, D.C.: U.S. Government Printing Office, October 1974a.

U.S. Bureau of the Census. "Mobility of the Population of the United States March 1970 to March 1974." *Current Population Reports*, Series P-20, no. 273. Washington, D.C.: U.S. Government Printing Office, December 1974b.

U.S. Bureau of the Census. "Population of the United States Trends and Prospects: 1950-1990." *Current Population Reports*, Series P-23, no. 49. Washington, D.C.: U.S. Government Printing Office, May 1974c.

U.S. Bureau of the Census. "Projections of the Population of the United States by Age and Sex, 1975-2000, with Extensions of Total Population to 2025 (Advance Report)." *Current Population Reports*, Series P-25, no. 541, February 1975, p. 1.

U.S. Department of Health, Education, and Welfare. "Births, Deaths, Marriages, and Divorces, Annual Summary for the United States, 1974." *Monthly Vital Statistics Report* 23, no. 13 (May 30, 1975a): 4.

U.S. Department of Health Education, and Welfare. "Births, Marriages, Divorces, and Deaths for July 1975." *Monthly Vital Statistics Report* 24, no. 7 (September 29, 1975b): 3.

U.S. Office of Education. Release on University of Texas study of the knowledges and skills of the adult population, 29 October 1975, as reported in "Modern Life Is Too Much for 23 Million Americans." *U.S. News & World Report*, 10 November 1975, p. 84.

Westoff, Charles F.; Moore, Emily C.; and Ryder, Norman B. "The Structure of Attitudes toward Abortion." *Milbank Memorial Quarterly* (January 1969).

Chapter 10
Childbearing families

"Accident Mortality Among Infants." *Statistical Bulletin* 56, no. 10 (July 1975).

Arms, Suzanne. *Immaculate Deception*. Boston: Houghton Mifflin Co., 1975.

Associated Press. "New Legal Abortions Reducing Adoptions." 11 February 1971.

Bell, Richard Q. "Level of Arousal in Breast-fed and Bottle-fed Human Newborns." *Psychosomatic Medicine* 28, no. 2 (March-April 1966): 177-180.

Berry, Warren. "Latest Estimates Peg Cost of Raising Child at $70,000." *Sarasota Herald-Tribune*, 14 September 1975, p. 9-E.

Blood, Robert O., Jr., and Wolfe, Donald M. *Husbands and Wives: The Dynamics of Married Living*. New York: The Free Press, 1960, pp. 156, 174.

Brozan, Nadine. "The Adoption Law: When Should Mother Lose Rights to a Child?" *New York Times*, 24 March 1971, p. 42M.

Chilman, Catherine S. *Growing Up Poor*. Welfare Administration Publication no. 13. Washington, D.C., 1966, pp. 81-87.

deHartog, Jan. *The Children*. New York: Atheneum, 1969.

Duvall, Evelyn Millis. *In-Laws: Pro and Con*. New York: Association Press, 1954.

Dyer, Everett D. "Parenthood as Crisis: A Restudy." *Marriage and Family Living* 25, no. 2 (May 1963): 196-201.

Feldman, Harold. "The Development of the Husband-Wife Relationship." Study supported in part by the National Institute of Mental Health; unpublished data received through personal correspondence, 24 March 1961, with permission.

Feldman, Harold. "Parent and Marriage: Myths and Realities." Address presented at Merrill-Palmer Institute Conference on the Family. 1969. Mimeographed.

Feldman, Harold, and Rogoff, Michael. "Correlates of Changes in Marital Satisfaction with the Birth of the First Child." Paper read at the American Psychological Association meetings, 3 September 1968.

Flaste, Richard. "American Childbirth Practices: Time of Change." *New York Times*, 7 November 1975, p. 43.

Flavell, John H. *The Developmental Psychology of Jean Piaget*. Princeton, N.J.: Van Nostrand, 1963.

Goldberg, Susan, and Lewis, Michael. "Play Behavior in the Year-Old Infant: Early Sex Differences." *Child Development* 40, no. 1 (March 1969): 21-31.

Gordon, Ira J. "Stimulation via Parent Education." *Children* 16, no. 2 (April 1969): 57-59.

Haire, Doris. *The Cultural Warping of Childbirth*. Seattle, Wash.: International Childbirth Education Association Supplies Center, 1975.

Hill, Reuben, et al. *Family Development in Three Generations*. Cambridge, Mass.: Schenkman Publishing Co., 1970.

Leboyer, Frederick. *Birth Without Violence*. New York: Alfred A. Knopf. 1975.

LeMasters, Ersel E. "Parenthood as Crisis." *Marriage and Family Living* 19, no. 4 (November 1957): 352-355.

Leo, John. "I.Q.s of Underprivileged Infants Raised Dramatically by Tutors." *New York Times*, 26 December 1968.

Lidz, Theodore. *The Person: His Development throughout the Life Cycle*. New York: Basic Books, Inc., 1968, pp. 93-158.

McCandless, Boyd R. *Children: Behavior and Development*. New York: Holt, Rinehart & Winston, 1967.

Moss, Howard A. "Methodological Issues in Studying Mother-Infant Interaction." *American Journal of Orthopsychiatry* 35, no. 3 (April 1965): 482-486.

Moss, Howard A. "Sex, Age, and State as Determinants of Mother-Infant Interaction." *Merrill-Palmer Quarterly* 13, no. 1 (1967): 19-36.

Moss, Howard A; Ryder, Robert C.; and Robson, Kenneth S. "The Relationships between Pre-Parental Variables Assessed at the Newlywed Stage and Later Maternal Behavior." Paper read at the meetings of the Society for Research in Child Development, 1967.

Murphy, Lois Barclay. "Children under Three. . . Finding Ways to Stimulate Development." *Children* 16, no. 2 (March-April 1969): 48-49.

Newton, Niles. Review of "Putting the Child Back in Childbirth." *Psychology Today* 9, no. 3 (August 1975): 24-25.

Piaget, Jean. *The Origins of Intelligence in Children*. Translated by Margaret Cook. New York: International Universities Press, 1966.

Pomeroy, Margaret R. "Sudden Death Syndrome." *American Journal of Nursing* (September 1969).

Porter, Sylvia. *Sylvia Porter's Money Book*. Garden City, N.Y.: Doubleday & Co., 1975, pp. 697-700.

Raush, Harold L.; Marshall, Karol A.; and Featherman, Jo-Anna M. "Relations at Three Early Stages of Marriage as Reflected by the Use of Personal Pronouns." National Institute of Mental Health. n.d. mimeographed. Pp. 11, 20.

Time. "Maternity: Back to the Breast." *Time*, 19 July 1968, pp. 53-54.

U.S. Bureau of the Census. "Mobility of the Population of the United States March

1970 to March 1974." *Current Population Reports*, Series P-20, no. 273, December 1974, p. 2.

U.S. Department of Health, Education, and Welfare. "Births, Marriages, Divorces, and Deaths for May 1975." *Monthly Vital Statistics Report* 24, no. 5. Washington, D.C.: National Center for Health Statistics, 24 July 1975.

"Vaccination Action. . .Are Your Children Protected?" *National Observer*, 25 October 1975, p. 8.

Walker, Kathryn E. "Time Spent in Household Work by Homemakers." *Family Economics Review* (September 1969): 5-6.

Wiegand, Elizabeth, and Gross, Irma H. *Fatigue of Homemakers with Young Children.* East Lansing, Mich.: Agricultural Experiment Station Technical Bulletin no. 265, 1958.

White, Burton L. *The First Three Years of Life.* Englewood Cliffs, N.J.: Prentice-Hall, 1975.

Chapter 11
Families with preschool children

Abernethy, E.M. *Relationships between Physical and Mental Growth.* Monograph of the Society for Research in Child Development, vol. 1, no. 7, 1936.

Bijou, Sidney W. "Development in the Preschool Years." *American Psychologist* 30, no. 8 (August 1975): 829-837.

Biller, Henry B. "Masculine Development: An Integrative Review." *Merrill-Palmer Quarterly* 13, no. 4 (October 1967): 253-294.

Bloom, Benjamin S. "Early Learning in the Home." First B.J. Paley lecture, University of California at Los Angeles, 18 July 1965. Mimeographed, pp. 23-24.

Bloom, Benjamin S. *Stability and Change in Human Characteristics.* New York: John Wiley & Sons, 1964.

Bronfenbrenner, Urie. "The Split-Level American Family." *Saturday Review*, 7 October 1967, pp. 60-66.

Cater, Douglass, and Strickland, Stephen. *TV Violence and the Child: The Evolution and Fate of the Surgeon General's Report.* New York: Russell Sage Foundation and Basic Books, Inc., 1975.

Comer, James P., and Poussaint, Alvin F. Interview in Richard Flaste, "Child-Rearing from a Black Viewpoint," *New York Times*, 30 May 1975, p. 36-C.

Daley, Eliot A. "Is TV Brutalizing Your Child?" *Look*, 2 December 1969, pp. 99-100.

Feldman, Harold. "The Development of the Husband-Wife Relationship." Study supported in part by the National Institute of Mental Health; unpublished data received through personal correspondence, 24 March 1961, with permission.

Feldman, Harold. "Parent and Marriage: Myths and Realities." Paper read at the Merrill-Palmer Institute Conference on the Family, 21 November 1969. Mimeographed, pp. 18-19.

Flaste, Richard. "Child-Rearing from a Black Viewpoint." *New York Times*, 30 May 1975, p. 36.

Glick, Paul C. "Living Arrangements of Children and Young Adults." Paper read at the annual meeting of the Population Association of America, Seattle, Wash., 17-19 April 1975. Mimeographed.

Hickey, Neil. "Does America Want Family Viewing Time?" *TV Guide Magazine*, 6 December 1975.

Jones, Mary Cover, and Mussen, P.H. "Self-Conceptions, Motivations, and Interpersonal Attitudes of Early- and Late-Maturing Girls." *Child Development* 19 (1958): 492-501.

Ketcham, W.A. "Relationship of Physical and Mental Traits in Intellectually Gifted and Mentally Retarded Boys." *Merrill-Palmer Quarterly* 6 (1960): 171-177.

Kiester, Edwin, Jr. "TV Violence: What Can Parents Do?" *Better Homes and Gardens* (September 1975): 4-16.

Kirkpatrick, Clifford. *The Family as Process and Institution.* 2nd ed. New York: Ronald Press Company, 1963.

Kraft, Ivor; Fuschillo, Jean; and Herzog, Elizabeth. *Prelude to School: An Evolution of an Inner-City Preschool Program.* Washington, D.C.: Children's Bureau Research Reports no. 3, 1968.

Lasko, J.K. "Parent Behavior toward First and Second Children." *Genetic Psychology Monograph* 49, no. 1 (February 1954): 99-137.

Leslie, Gerald; Christensen, Harold; and Pearman, Glenn. "Studies in Child Spacing: The Time-Interval Separating All Children in Completed Families of Purdue University Graduates." *Social Forces* 34, no. 1 (October 1955): 77-82.

McCarthy, D. "Language Development in Children." Pp. 492-630 in L. Carmichael, ed., *Manual of Child Psychology*. New York: John Wiley & Sons, 1954.

Masters, William H., and Johnson, Virginia E. "Teaching Your Children About Sex." *Redbook* (September 1975): 68-71.

Mitscherlich, Alexander. *Society without Father.* New York: Harcourt, Brace & World, 1969.

Mussen, Paul H., and Jones, Mary Cover. "The Behavior-Inferred Motivations of Late- and Early-Maturing Boys." *Child Development* 29 (1958): 61-67.

Popenoe, Paul. "Fathers In and Out of the Home." *Family Life* 28, no. 2 (February 1968): 1-2.

Smith, Ruth H.; Downer, Donna Beth; and Lynch, Mildred T. "The Man in the House." *Family Coordinator* 18, no. 2 (April 1969): 107-111.

Tanner, J.M. "The Regulation of Human Growth." *Child Development* 34, (1963): 817-847.

Terman, Lewis, et al. *Psychological Factors in Marital Happiness.* New York: McGraw-Hill Book Co., 1938, Chap. 5.

Tobin, Richard L. "When Violence Begets Violence." *Saturday Review*, 11 October 1969, pp. 69-70.

"TV Violence 'Appalling.'" *U.S. News and World Report*, 6 October 1969, pp. 55-56.

U.S. Bureau of the Census. "Nursery School and Kindergarten Enrollment: October 1973." *Current Population Reports*, Series P-20, no. 268, August 1974.

U.S. News & World Report Economic Unit. "Smaller Families: A Growing Trend." *U.S. News & World Report*, 27 October 1975, p. 32.

Waldman, Elizabeth. "Children of Working Mothers, March 1974." *Monthly Labor Review*. Washington, D.C.: Bureau of Labor Statistics, U.S. Department of Labor, January 1975, pp. 64-67.

Walters, James, ed. *Special Issue: Fatherhood. The Family Coordinator* 25, no. 2 (October 1976).

Chapter 12
Families with schoolchildren

Ackerson, Luton D. Quoted in *Junior Guidance Newsletter*. Chicago: Science Research Associates, 1952.

Baldigo, Jeanne. "Parental Role Reversals: Elementary School Children's Conceptions and Assessments." Paper read at the annual meeting of the American Sociological Association, San Francisco, August 1975.

Blood, Robert O., Jr., and Wolfe, Donald M. *Husbands and Wives: The Dynamics of Married Living*. New York: The Free Press, 1960.

Bloom, Benjamin S. "Early Learning in the Home." First B.J. Paley Lecture, University of California, Los Angeles, 18 July 1965. Mimeographed.

Bloom, Benjamin S. *Stability and Change in Human Characteristics*. New York: John Wiley & Sons, 1964.

Blum, Sam, "The Perfect Parent." *McCall's* (August 1969): 51, 95-98.

Bossard, James H.S., and Boll, Elizabeth S. *The Large Family System*. Philadelphia: University of Pennsylvania Press, 1956.

Bowerman, Charles E., and Kinch, John W. "Changes in Family and Peer Orientation of Children between the Fourth and Tenth Grades." *Social Forces* 37, no. 3 (March 1959): 206-211.

Brenton, Myron. *Playmates: The Importance of Childhood Friendships*. New York: Public Affairs Committee, Inc., 1975.

Broderick, Carlfred B., and Fowler, Stanley E. "New Patterns of Relationships between the Sexes among Preadolescents." *Marriage and Family Living* 23, no. 1 (February 1961): 27-30.

Burr, Wesley R. "Satisfaction with Various Aspects of Marriage over the Life Cycle: A Random Middle Class Sample." *Journal of Marriage and the Family* 32, no. 1 (February 1970): 29-37.

Dillin, John. "Racial Balance in U.S. Schools: Will 'Desegregation' Mean '90 Percent Black'?" *The Christian Science Monitor*, 19 June 1975, p. 15.

Duvall, Evelyn Millis. "Conceptions of Parenthood." *The American Journal of Sociology* 52, no. 3 (November 1946): 193-203.

Duvall, Evelyn Millis. *In-Laws: Pro and Con*. New York: Association Press, 1954, pp. 89-99.

Etaugh, Claire. "Effects of Maternal Employment on Children, a Review of Current Research." *Merrill-Palmer Quarterly* 20, no. 2 (1974). 71-98.

Feldman, Harold. "The Development of the Husband-Wife Relationship." Personal Communication, 24 March 1961, with permission.

Fulcomer, David. Personal communication, with permission.

Gallup International survey for the Institute for Development of Educational Activities, an affiliate of the Charles F. Kettering Foundation. In "How to Help Your Child Do Well in School." *U.S. News & World Report*, 6 October 1969, pp. 49-50.

Hammel, Lisa. "'When I Grow Up I'm Going to Be. . .'—An Old Game, New Ideas," *New York Times*, 12 June 1975, p. 43.

Harris, Dale B., and Tseng, S.C. "Children's Attitudes toward Peers and Parents as Revealed by Sentence Completions." *Child Development* 28 (1957): 401-411.

Hartley, Ruth E. "Sex Role Pressures and the Socialization of the Male Child." *Psychological Reports* 5 (1959): 457-468.

Hartley, Ruth E., and Hardesty, F.P. "Children's Perceptions of Sex Roles in Childhood." *Journal of Genetic Psychology* 105 (1964): 48.

Havighurst, Robert J. *Developmental Tasks and Education*. 3rd ed. New York: David McKay Co., 1972.

Hawkes, Glenn R.; Burchinal, Lee G.; and Gardner, Bruce. "Preadolescents' Views of Some of Their Relations with Their Parents." *Child Development* 28, no. 4 (December 1957): 393-399.

Hoffman, Lois Wladis; Rosen, Sidney; and Lippitt, Ronald. "Parental Coerciveness, Child Autonomy, and Child's Role at School." *Sociometry* 23, no. 1 (March 1960): 15-22.

Kelly, John R. "Life Styles and Leisure Choices." *The Family Coordinator* 24, no. 2 (April 1975): 185-190.

Koch, Helen L. *The Relation of Certain Formal Attributes of Siblings to Attitudes Held Toward Each Other and Toward Their Parents*. Monograph of the Society for Research in Child Development, serial no. 78, vol. 25, no. 4, 1960.

Kohlberg, Lawrence. "The Child as a Moral Philosopher." *Psychology Today* 2, no. 4 (September 1968): 25-30.

Lewis, Gertrude M. *Educating Children in Grades Four, Five and Six*. Washington, D.C.: U.S. Office of Education, 1960.

Macfarlane, Jean W.; Allen, Lucile; and Honzik, Marjorie P. *A Developmental Study of the Behavior Problems of Normal Children between Twenty-one Months and Fourteen Years*. Berkeley: University of California Press, 1954, pp. 146-186.

Marcus, Irwin, et al. *An Interdisciplinary Approach to Accident Patterns in Children*. Monograph of the Society for Reasearch in Child Development, serial no. 76, vol. 25, no. 2, 1960, pp. 53-54.

Miller, Daniel R., and Swanson, Guy E. *The Changing American Parent*. New York: John Wiley & Sons, 1958.

Moss, Howard A., and Kagan, Jerome. "Stability of Achievement and Recognition Seeking Behaviors from Early Childhood through Adulthood." Yellow Springs, Ohio: Fels Institute, n.d. Mimeographed, p. 21.

Packard, Vance. "First, Last, or Middle Child—The Surprising Differences." *Reader's Digest* (December 1969): 25-32.

Porter, Blaine M. "Measurement of Parental Acceptance of Children." *Journal of Home Economics* 46, no. 3 (March 1954): 176-182.

Rollins, Boyd C., and Feldman, Harold. "Marital Satisfaction over the Family Life Cycle." *Journal of Marriage and the Family* 32, no. 1 (February 1970): 20-28.

Rosenblatt, Paul C., and Russell, Martha G. "The Social Psychology of Potential Problems in Family Vacation Travel." *The Family Coordinator* 24, no. 2 (April 1975): 209-215.

Survey Research Center. *A Study of Boys Becoming Adolescents*. Ann Arbor: University of Michigan, 1960, p. 215.

Sussman, Marvin B. "The Help Pattern in the Middle Class Family." *American Sociological Review* 18, no. 1 (February 1953): 22-28.

Toman, Walter. *Family Constellation*. New York: Springer Publishing Co., 1961.

VanBortel, Dorothy G. "Conception of Woman's Role in the Home in Two Social Classes." Paper read at the Seventh Annual Symposium, Committee on Human Development, University of Chicago, 25 February 1956.

Waldman, Elizabeth. "Children of Working Mothers, March 1974." *Monthly Labor Review* (January 1975): 64–67.

Williams, James H. "Close Friendship Relations of Housewives Residing in an Urban Community." *Social Forces* 36, no. 4 (May 1958): 358–362.

Zimmerman, Carle C., and Cervantes, Lucius F. *Successful American Families.* New York: Pageant Press, 1960.

Chapter 13
Families with teenagers

Allen, Donald E., and Sandhu, H.S. "Alienation, Hedonism, and Life Vision of Delinquents." *Journal of Criminal Law, Criminology and Police Science* 58 (September 1967): 325–329.

Bengtson, Vern L. "Generation and Family Effects in Value Socialization." *American Sociological Review* 40, no. 3 (June 1975): 358–371.

Bengtson, Vern L. "Inter-Age Perceptions and the Generation Gap." *The Gerontologist, Part 2.* 11, no. 4 (Winter 1971): 85–89.

Bengtson, Vern L., and Lovejoy, M.C. "Values, Personality, and Social Structure: An Integenerational Analysis." *American Behavioral Scientist* 16, no. 6 (1973): 880–912.

Benson, Leonard G. "Family Social Status and Parental Authority Evaluations among Adolescents." *Southwest Social Science Quarterly* 36, no. 1 (June 1955): 46–54.

Bienvenu, Millard J., Sr. *Parent-Teen-ager Communication.* Public Affairs Pamphlet no. 438. New York: Public Affairs Committee, 1969.

Blood, Linda, and D'Angelo, Rocco. "A Progress Research Report on Value Issues in Conflict Between Runaways and Their Parents." *Journal of Marriage and the Family* 36, no. 3 (August 1974): 486–491.

Blood, Robert O., Jr.; and Wolfe, Donald M. *Husbands and Wives: The Dynamics of Married Living.* New York: The Free Press, 1960.

Bloom, Martin. "The Money Problems of Adolescents in the Secondary Schools of Springfield, Massachusetts." Ed. D. dissertation, New York University, 1955.

Blos, Peter. "The Child Analyst Looks at the Young Adolescent." *Daedalus* 100, no. 4 (Fall 1971): 961–978.

Bowerman, Charles E, and Kinch, John W. "Changes in Family and Peer Orientation of Children between the Fourth and Tenth Grades." *Social Forces* 37, no. 3 (March 1959): 206–211.

Briggs, Vivian, and Schulz, Lois R. "Parental Response to Concepts of Parent-Adolescent Relationships." *Child Development* 26, no. 4 (December 1955): 279–284.

Brittain, C.V. "Adolescent Choices and Parent-Peer Cross-Pressure." *American Sociological Review* 28 (1963): 385–391.

Butler, Ruth M. "Mothers' Attitudes toward the Social Development of Their Adolescents." *Social Casework* (May-June 1956).

Byler, Ruth; Lewis, Gertrude; and Totman, Ruth. *Teach Us What We Want to Know.* Published for the Connecticut State Board of Education by the Mental Health Materials Center, New York: N.Y., 1969.

Conger, John Janeway. "A World They Never Knew: The Family and Social Change." *Daedalus* 100, 4 (Fall 1971): 1105–1138.

Cooperative Institutional Research Program. *The American Freshman: National Norms for Fall 1974.* American Council on Education, University of California at Los Angeles, 1975.

Dales, Ruth J. "A Method for Measuring Developmental Tasks: Scales for Selected Tasks at the Beginning of Adolescence." *Child Development* 26, no. 2 (June 1955): 111-122.

Dickens, Helen O.; Mudd, Emily Hartshorne; and Huggins, George R. "Teenagers, Contraception, and Pregnancy." *Journal of Marriage and Family Counseling* 1, no. 2 (April 1975): 175-181.

Dickinson, George E. "Dating Behavior of Black and White Adolescents Before and After Desegregation." *Journal of Marriage and the Family* 37, no. 3 (August 1975): 602-608.

Dubbe, Marvin C. "What Young People Can't Talk over with Their Parents." *National Parent-Teacher* 52, no. 2 (October 1957): 18-20.

Duvall, Evelyn Millis. "Conceptions of Parenthood." *American Journal of Sociology* 52, no. 3 (November 1946): 193-203.

Duvall, Evelyn Millis. "Family Dilemmas with Teen-Agers." *Family Life Coordinator* 14, no. 2 (April 1965): 35-38.

Duvall, Evelyn Millis. *Parent and Teenager: Living and Loving.* Nashville, Tenn.: Broadman Press, 1976.

Duvall, Evelyn Millis. *Today's Teenagers.* New York: Association Press, 1966.

Dynes, Russell R.; Clarke, Alfred C.; and Dinitz, Simon. "Levels of Occupational Aspiration: Some Aspects of Family Experiences as a Variable." *American Sociological Review* 21, no. 2 (April 1956): 212-215.

Feldman, Harold. "Development of the Husband-Wife Relationship: A Research Report." Ithaca, N.Y.: Cornell University, 1965. Mimeographed, p. 41.

Fiske, Edward B. "Writing Ability Found Slipping." *New York Times*, 19 November 1975, p. 42.

Fortune-Yankelovich Survey. "American Youth: Its Outlook Is Changing the World." *Fortune* (January 1969): 70-71; 179-181.

Getzels, Jacob W., and Jackson, Philip W. "Family Environment and Cognitive Style: A Study of the Sources of Highly Intelligent and Highly Creative Adolescents." *American Sociological Review* 26, no. 3 (June 1961): 351-359.

"Girls Lag in Tests: Unequal Education?" *U.S. News & World Report*, 20 October 1975, p. 54.

Havighurst, Robert J. "Adolescence and the Postponement of Adulthood." *School Review* (Spring 1960): 52-62.

Havighurst, Robert J. *Developmental Tasks and Education.* 3rd ed. New York: David McKay Co., 1972.

Havighurst, Robert J., ed. *Youth.* Yearbook of the National Society for the Study of Education. Chicago: University of Chicago Press, 1975.

Henderson, Patricia Maxwell; Connor, Ruth; and Walters, James. "Family Member Perceptions of Parent Role Performance." *Merrill-Palmer Quarterly* 7, no. 1 (1961): 31-37.

Hess, Robert D., and Goldblatt, Irene. "The Status of Adolescents in American Society: A Problem in Social Identity." *Child Development* 28, no. 4 (December 1957): 459-468.

Hill, Margaret. *Parents and Teenagers.* Public Affairs Pamphlet no. 490. New York: Public Affairs Committee, 1973.

Jessen, Margaret S. "Factors in Parents' Understanding of Adolescent Attitudes." Unpublished Research report. Woodland, Calif., 1975.

Johannis, Theodore B., Jr. "Participation by Fathers, Mothers, and Teenage Sons and Daughters in Selected Household Tasks." *Coordinator* 6, no. 4 (June 1958): 61-62.

Johannis, Theodore B., Jr., and Rollins, James M. "Teenager Perception of Family Decision Making and Social Activity." *Family Life Coordinator* 8, no. 3 (March 1960): 59-60.

Jones, Mary Cover. "Psychological Correlates of Somatic Development." *Child Development* 36, no. 4 (December 1965): 899-911.

Kagan, Jerome. "A Conception of Early Adolescence." *Daedalus* 11, no. 4 (Fall 1971): 997-1012.

Kandel, D., and Lesser, G. *Youth in Two Worlds*. San Francisco, Calif.: Jossey-Bass, 1972.

King, Karl; McIntyre, Jennie; and Axelson, Leland. "Adolescents' Views of Maternal Employment as a Threat to the Marital Relationship." *Journal of Marriage and the Family* 30, no. 4 (November 1968): 633-637.

Kohlberg, Lawrence, and Gilligan, Carol. "The Adolescent as a Philosopher: The Discovery of the Self in a Postconventional World." *Daedalus* 100, no. 4 (Fall 1971): 1051-1086.

Kohn, Melvin. "Social Class and Parental Authority." *American Sociological Review* 24, no. 3 (June 1959): 352-366.

Kvaraceus, William C., et al. *Delinquent Behavior*, vol. 1. Washington, D.C.: National Education Association, 1959, pp. 24-31.

Leidy, Thomas R., and Starry, Allan R. "Contemporary Youth Culture." *N.E.A. Journal* 56 (October 1967): 8.

LeMasters, E.E. "Parents, Mass Media, and the Youth Peer Group." *Parents in Modern America*. Homewood, Ill.: Dorsey Press, 1969, Chap. 10, pp. 176-191.

Lorenz, Konrad. "The Enmity Between the Generations and Its Probable Ethological Causes." *The Psychoanalytic Review* 57 (1970): 333-377.

Maas, Henry S. "Some Social Class Differences in the Family Systems and Group Relations of Pre- and Early Adolescents." *Child Development* 22, no. 2 (June 1951): 145-152.

McClelland, David C. "Cultural Variation and Achievement Motivation." Paper read at the Twelfth Annual Symposium of the Committee on Human Development, University of Chicago, Chicago, Ill., April 1961.

National Assessment of Eductional Progress. Report in "Those Dropping Test Scores— Experts Grope for the Reasons." *U.S. News & World Report*, 24 November 1975, pp. 33-34.

National Institute of Alcohol Abuse and Alcoholism. Report in "School Study Calls 28% of Teen-Agers 'Problem' Drinkers." *New York Times*, 21 November 1975, p. 41.

National Institute on Drug Abuse. Report in "Alcohol and Marijuana Spreading Menace Among Teen-Agers." *U.S. News & World Report*, 24 November 1975, pp. 28-30.

Nye, Ivan. "Adolescent-Parent Adjustment: Age, Sex, Sibling Number, Broken Homes, and Employed Mothers as Variables." *Marriage and Family Living* 14, no. 4 (November 1952): 331.

Nye, Ivan. "Adolescent-Parent Adjustment—Socio-Economic Level as a Variable." *American Sociological Review* 16, no. 3 (June 1951): 341-349.

Porter, Sylvia. *Sylvia Porter's Money Book.* Garden City, N.Y.: Doubleday & Co., 1975.

Robey, A.; Rosenwald, Small; and Rosenwald, Lee. "The Runaway Girl, A Reaction to Family Stress." *American Journal of Orthopsychiatry* 34 (1964): 762-767.

Sheils, Merrill. "Why Johnny Can't Write." *Newsweek*, 8 December 1975, pp. 58-65.

Slocum, W.L., and Stone, Carol L. "A Method for Measuring Family Images Held by Teen-Agers." *Marriage and Family Living* 21, no. 3 (August 1959): 245-250.

Smart, Mollie S., and Smart, Russell C. *Children: Development and Relationships.* 2nd ed. New York: Macmillan Publishing Co., 1972.

Sørensen, R.C. *Adolescent Sexuality in Contemporary America, Personal Values and Sexual Behavior Ages 13-19.* New York: World Publishing Co., 1973.

Stinnett, Nick; Farris, Joe Ann; and Walters, James. "Parent-Child Relationships of Male and Female High School Students." *The Journal of Genetic Psychology* 125 (1974): 99-106.

Stinnett, Nick, and Walters, James. "Parent-Peer Orientation of Adolescents from Low-Income Families." *Journal of Home Economics* 59, no. 1 (January 1967): 37-40.

"Teen-Agers' Writing Ability Impaired by Telephone, TV." AP release, *Sarasota Herald-Tribune*, 18 November 1975. p. 15-A.

Thurnher, Majda; Spence, Donald; and Lowenthal, Marjorie Fiske. "Value Confluence and Behavioral Conflict in Intergenerational Relations." *Journal of Marriage and the Family* 36, no. 2 (May 1974): 308-319.

Tuma, Elias, and Livson, Norman. "Family Socioeconomic Status and Adolescent Attitudes toward Authority." *Child Development* 31, no. 2 (June 1961): 387-399.

U.S. Department of Health, Education, and Welfare data for various years.

U.S. Department of Labor. Report in "A Half Billion Dollars to Put Restless Kids to Work" *U.S. News & World Report*, 30 June 1975. p. 67.

Wattenberg, Ben J. *The Real America.* Garden City, N.Y.: Doubleday & Co., 1974, p. 80.

Withrow, Jerre L., and Trotter, Virginia Y. "Space for Leisure Activities of Teen-Agers." *Journal of Home Economics* 53, no. 5 (May 1961): 359-362.

Yankelovich, Daniel. "How Students Control Their Drug Crisis." *Psychology Today* 9, no. 5 (October 1975): 39-42.

Yankelovich, Daniel. *The New Morality: A Profile of American Youth in the Seventies.* New York: McGraw-Hill Book Co., 1974.

Chapter 14
Families launching young adults

Adams, Margaret. "The Single Woman in Today's Society." *The American Journal of Orthopsychiatry* 41 (1971): 776-786.

Baker, Russell. "Observer: Youth as a Tiresome Old Windbag." *New York Times*, 17 October 1967, p. 46.

Bell, Robert. *Marriage and Family Interaction.* Homewood, Ill.: Dorsey Press, 1971.

Bengtson, Vern L., and Kuypers, Joseph A. "Generational Differences and the Developmental Stake." *Aging and Human Development* 2 (1971): 249-259.

Bernard, Jessie. "Note on Changing Life Styles, 1970-1974." *Journal of Marriage and the Family* 37, no. 3 (August 1975): 582-593.

Bigelow, Howard F. *Family Finance.* Philadelphia: J.B. Lippincott Co., 1953, p. 333.

Bird, Caroline. *Is College Necessary?* New York: David McKay Co., 1975.

Blumberg, Paul M., and Paul, P.W. "Continuities and Discontinuities in Upper-Class Marriages." *Journal of Marriage and the Family* 37, no. 1 (February 1975): 63-77.

Borland, Dolores M. "An Alternative Model of the Wheel Theory." *The Family Coordinator* 24, no. 3 (July 1975): 289-292.

Bossard, James H.S. "Residential Propinquity as a Factor in Marriage Selection." *American Journal of Sociology* (1932-1933): 219-224.

Brim, Orville G., and Forer, Raymond. "A Note on the Relation of Values and Social Structure to Life Planning." *Sociometry* 19, no. 1 (March 1956): 54-60.

Burgess, Ernest W., and Wallin, Paul. *Engagement and Marriage.* Philadelphia: J.B. Lippincott Co., 1953, p. 547.

Catton, William R., Jr., and Smircich, R.J. "A Comparison of Mathematical Models for the Effect of Residential Propinquity on Mate Selection." *American Sociological Review* 29, (1964): 522-529.

Cavan, Ruth Shonle. "Concepts and Terminology in Interreligious Marriage." *Journal for the Scientific Study of Religion* 9, no. 4 (1970): 314.

Center Magazine, "No Silence Please." Vol. 2, no. 2 (March 1969): 83-86.

Chilman, Catherine S. "Families in Development at Mid-Stage of the Family Life Cycle." *The Family Coordinator* 17, no. 4 (October 1968): 297-312.

Clarke, Alfred C. "An Examination of the Operation of Residential Propinquity as a Factor in Mate Selection." *American Sociological Review* 27, (1952): 17-22.

Clayton, Richard R. *The Family, Marriage, and Social Change.* Lexington, Mass.: D.C. Heath & Co., 1975, p. 280.

Cooperative Institutional Research Program. *The American Freshman: National Norms for Fall 1974.* University of California at Los Angeles: American Council on Education, 1975.

David, Deborah. *Career Patterns and Values: A Study of Men and Women in Science and Engineering.* New York: Columbia University, Bureau of Applied Social Research, 1973.

Davidson, Bill. "Nothing's Too Good for My Daughter." *Saturday Evening Post,* 13 August 1966, pp. 28-35.

Davie, Maurice R., and Reeves, Ruby Jo. "Propinquity of Residence before Marriage." *American Journal of Sociology* 44 (1938-1939): 510-517.

Duberman, Lucile. *Marriage and Its Alternatives.* New York: Praeger Publishers, 1974.

Duvall, Evelyn Millis. *In-Laws: Pro and Con.* New York: Association Press, 1954, pp. 278-279.

Duvall, Evelyn Millis. *Love and the Facts of Life.* New York: Association Press, 1963.

Duvall, Evelyn Millis, and Hill, Reuben. *Being Married.* Boston, Mass.: D.C. Heath & Co., 1960.

Duvall, Evelyn Millis, and Hill, Reuben. *When You Marry.* Rev. ed. Boston, Mass.: D.C. Heath & Co., 1967.

Dynes, Russell R.; Clarke, Alfred C.; and Dinitz, Simon. "Levels of Occupational Aspiration: Some Aspects of Family Experience as a Variable." *American Sociological Review* 21, no. 2 (April 1956): 212-215.

Ellis, Evelyn. "Social Psychological Correlates of Upward Social Mobility among Unmarried Career Women." *American Sociological Review* 17, no. 5 (October 1952): 558-563.

Freeman, Richard. *The Overeducated American.* New York: Academic Press, 1976.

Fortune-Yankelovich Survey. "What They Believe." *Fortune* (January 1969): 70–71; 179–181.

Glick, Paul C. "Living Arrangements of Children and Young Adults." Paper read at the annual meeting of the Population Association of America, Seattle, Wash., 17–19 April 1975.

Glick, Paul C. "Some Recent Changes in American Families." *Current Population Reports.* Special Studies, Series P-23, no. 52. Washington, D.C.: U.S. Government Printing Office, 1975.

Hacker, David W. "Jobs for New Grads: The Hunting Is Still Tough." *The National Observer*, week ending 3 January 1976, p. 4.

Havens, E.M. "Women, Work, and Wedlock: A Note on Female Marital Patterns in the United States." *American Journal of Sociology* 78 (January 1973):975–981.

Havighurst, Robert J. *Developmental Tasks and Education.* New York: David McKay Co., 1972.

Hechinger, Grace, and Hechinger, Fred M. "The Ebb and Flow of Student Rebellion." *The Saturday Review*, 6 September 1975, pp. 46–49.

Henze, Lura F., and Hudson, John W. "Personal and Family Characteristics of Cohabiting and Noncohabiting Students." *Journal of Marriage and the Family* 36, no. 4 (November 1974): 722–727.

Hollingshead, August B. "Cultural Factors in the Selection of Marriage Mates." *American Sociological Review* 15, no. 5 (October 1950): 619–627.

Johnston, Lloyd; O'Malley, Patrick; and Eveland, Leslie. *Drugs and American Youth.* Institute for Social Research, Ann Arbor: University of Michigan, 1975.

Kennedy, Ruby Jo Reeves. "Premarital Residential Propinquity and Ethnic Endogamy." *American Journal of Sociology* 48 (1942-1943): 580–584.

Krain, Mark. "Communication Among Premarital Couples at Three Stages of Dating." *Journal of Marriage and the Family* 37, no. 3 (August 1975): 609–618.

Kuhn, Manford H. "How Mates Are Sorted." Chap. 8, pp. 246–275, in Howard Becker and Reuben Hill, eds., *Family, Marriage, and Parenthood.* Boston, Mass.: D.C. Heath & Co., 1948.

Landis, Judson T. "Functional and Dysfunctional Aspects of Stress in Happy and Unhappy Marriages." Paper read at the annual meeting of the National Council on Family Relations, Washington, D.C., October 22-25 1969.

Lewis, Robert A. "A Longitudinal Test of a Developmental Framework for Premarital Dyadic Formation." *Journal of Marriage and the Family* 35, no. 1 (February 1973): 16–25.

Lewis, Robert A. "Social Reaction and the Formation of Dyads: An Interactionist Approach to Mate Selection." *Sociometry* 36, no. 3 (1973): 409–418.

McClusky, Howard Y., and Zander, Alvin. "Residential Propinquity and Marriage in Branch County, Michigan." *Social Forces* (1940): 79–81.

McGuire, Carson. "Conforming, Mobile, and Divergent Families." *Marriage and Family Living* 14, no. 2 (May 1952): 113.

Marriage Council Newsletter. Philadelphia, Pa.: Marriage Council of Philadelphia, September 1969, p. 1.

Mitchell, Donald, "Residential Propinquity and Marriage in Carver and Scott Counties, Minnesota." *Social Forces* 20 (1941): 256–259.

Mueller, Kate Hevner. "The Marriage Trap." *Mademoiselle*, pp. 1–2 of release, Spring 1955.

National Broadcasting Company National News Poll, Network Report, 4 January 1976.

National Center for Education Statistics: American Association of University Professors. "Zooming Prices on the Campus." *U.S. News & World Report*, 1 September 1975, p. 45.

National Center for Education Statistics. "That Slack Year in Colleges—Why It Isn't Happening." *U.S. News & World Report*, 10 November 1975, pp. 45–46.

Oppenheimer, Valerie Kincade. "The Life-Cycle Squeeze: The Interaction of Men's Occupational and Family Life Cycles." *Demography* 11 (1974): 227–245.

Parelius, Ann P. "Emerging Sex-Role Attitudes, Expectations, and Strains Among College Women." *Journal of Marriage and Family Living* 37, no. 1 (February 1975): 146–153.

Perlman, Daniel. "Self-Esteem and Sexual Permissiveness." *Journal of Marriage and the Family* 36, no. 3 (August 1974): 470–473.

Peterman, Dan J.; Ridley, Carl A.; and Anderson, Scott M. "A Comparison of Cohabiting and Noncohabiting College Students." *Journal of Marriage and the Family* 36, no. 2 (May 1974): 344–354.

Porter, Sylvia. *Sylvia Porter's Money Book*. Garden City, N.Y.: Doubleday & Co., 1975, pp. 393–397.

Rapoport, Rhona. "The Transition from Engagement to Marriage." *Acta Sociologica* 9 (1964).

Reiss, Ira L. "Toward a Sociology of the Heterosexual Love Relationship." *Journal of Marriage and the Family* 22, no. 2 (May 1960): 139–145.

Reiss, Ira L.; Banwart, Albert; and Foreman, Harry. "Premarital Contraceptive Usage: A Study of Some Theoretical Explorations." *Journal of Marriage and the Family* 37, no. 3 (August 1975): 619–630.

Seligson, Marcia. *The Eternal Bliss Machine: America's Way of Wedding*. New York: William Morrow & Co., 1973.

Spreitzer, Elmer, and Riley, Lawrence E. "Factors Associated with Singlehood." *Journal of Marriage and the Family* 36, no. 3 (August 1974): 533–542.

Stein, Peter J. "Singlehood: An Alternative to Marriage." *The Family Coordinator* 24, no. 4 (October 1975): 489–503.

Stein, Peter J. *Single in America*. Englewood Cliffs, N.J.: Prentice-Hall. 1976.

U.S. Bureau of the Census. "Annual Mean Income, Lifetime Income, and Educational Attainment of Men in the United States, for Selected Years, 1956 to 1972." *Current Population Reports*, Series P-60, no. 92. Washington, D.C.: U.S. Government Printing Office, March 1974.

U.S. Bureau of the Census. *Marital Status*, PC(2)-4C. Washington, D.C.: U.S. Government Printing Office, 1970, Table 12, p. 262.

U.S. Bureau of the Census. "Marital Status and Family Status, March 1968." *Current Population Reports*, Series P-20, no. 187. Washington, D.C.: U.S. Government Printing Office, August 11, 1969, p. 2.

Wilkes, Paul. *Trying Out the Dream: A Year in the Life of an American Family*. Philadelphia: J.B. Lippincott Co. 1975.

Yankelovich, Daniel. "Drug Users Vs. Drug Abusers." *Psychology Today* 9, no. 5 (October 1975): 39–42.

Chapter 15
Middle-aged parents in an empty nest

Anderson, Wayne J. *Challenges for Successful Family Living.* Minneapolis, Minn.: T.S. Denison & Co., 1974.

Axelson, Leland J. "Personal Adjustment in the Postparental Period." *Marriage and Family Living* 22, no. 1 (February 1960): 66-68.

Bengtson, Vern L. "Generation and Family Effects in Value Socialization." *American Sociological Review* 40, no. 3 (June 1975): 358-371.

Bengtson, Vern L.; Furlong, Michael J.; and Laufer, Robert S. "Time, Aging, and the Continuity of Social Structure: Themes and Issues in Generational Analysis." *Journal of Social Issues* 30, no. 2 (1974): 1-30.

Better Homes and Gardens. A Report on the American Family. Des Moines, Iowa: Meredith Corp., 1972.

Blood, Robert O. Jr., and Wolfe, Donald M. *Husbands and Wives: The Dynamics of Married Living.* New York: The Free Press, 1960.

Bossard, James H.S., and Boll, Elizabeth S. "Marital Unhappiness in the Life Cycle." *Marriage and Family Living* 17, no. 1 (February 1955): 10-14.

Brady, Dorothy A., and Froeder, Marsha. "Influence of Age on Saving and Spending Patterns." *Monthly Labor Review* 78, no. 11 (November 1955): 1240-1244.

Cavan, Ruth Shonle. "Family Tensions between the Old and the Middle-Aged." *Marriage and Family Living* 18, no. 4 (November 1956): 323-327.

Chilman, Catherine S. "Families in Development at Mid-Stage of the Family Life Cycle." *The Family Coordinator* 17, no. 4 (October 1968): 297-312.

Cumming, Elaine; Dean, Lois R.; Newell, David; and McCaffrey, Isabel. "Disengagement—A Tentative Theory of Aging." *Sociometry* 23, no. 1 (March 1960): 23-35.

Davidoff, Ida Fisher, and Markewich, May Elish. "The Postparental Phase in the Life-Cycle of Fifty College-Educated Women." Doctor of Education Project Report, Teachers College, Columbia University, 1961.

Deutscher, Irwin. "Husband-Wife Relations in Middle-Age: An Analysis of Sequential Roles among the Urban Middle Classes." Unpublished manuscript, Department of Sociology, University of Missouri, July 1954, pp. 122-130.

Deutscher, Irwin. "Married Life in the Middle Years." *Community Studies.* Kansas City, Mo., 1959.

Deutscher, Irwin. "The Quality of Postparental Life: Definitions of the Situation." *Journal of Marriage and the Family* 26, no. 1 (February 1964): 52-59.

Dizard, J. "Social Change and the Family." Chicago: University of Chicago, Family Study Center, 1968.

Duvall, Evelyn Millis. *In-Laws: Pro and Con.* New York: Association Press, 1954.

Feldman, Harold. *Development of the Husband-Wife Relationship.* Ithaca, N.Y. Cornell University, 1965.

Gallup, George. "Church-Going Holds Firm." *Gallup Poll.* Princeton, N.J., 17 January 1976.

Glenn, Norval D. "Psychological Well-Being in the Postparental Stage: Some Evidence from National Surveys." *Journal of Marriage and the Family* 37, no. 1 (February 1975): 105-110.

Glick, Paul C. "The Life Cycle of the Family." *Marriage and Family Living* 17, no. 1 (February 1955): 3-9.

Glick, Paul C., and Parke, Robert, Jr. "New Approaches in Studying the Life Cycle of the Family." *Demography* 2 (1965).

Gurin, Gerald; Veroff, Joseph; and Feld, Sheila. *Americans View Their Mental Health: A Nationwide Interview Study.* New York: Basic Books Inc., 1960.

Hartley, Eugene L., and Hartley, Ruth E. *Fundamentals of Social Psychology.* New York: Alfred A. Knopf, 1952, pp. 495-496.

Havighurst, Robert J. *Developmental Tasks and Education.* 3rd ed. New York: David McKay Co., 1972.

Havighurst, Robert J. "Life Style Transitions Related to Personality Type after Age Fifty." Unpublished manuscript, University of Chicago, Chicago, Ill., March 1975.

Havighurst, Robert J. "The Social Competence of Middle-Aged People." *Genetic Psychology Monographs* 56 (1957): 297-375.

Havighurst, Robert J., and Feigenbaum, Kenneth. "Leisure and Life-Style." *American Journal of Sociology* 64, no. 4 (January 1959): 396-404.

Havighurst, Robert J., and Orr, Betty. *Adult Education and Adult Needs: A Report.* Chicago, Ill.: Center for the Study of Liberal Education for Adults, 1956.

Hayes, Maggie Parks, and Stinnett, Nick. "Life Satisfaction of Middle-Aged Husbands and Wives." *Journal of Home Economics* 63, no. 9 (December 1971): 669-674.

Hill, Reuben, et al. *Family Development in Three Generations.* Cambridge, Mass.: Schenkman Publishing Co., 1970.

Irwin, Theodore. *Male "Menopause" Crisis in the Middle Years.* Public Affairs Pamphlet no. 526. New York: Public Affairs Committee, 1975.

Janeway, Elizabeth. "In Praise of Middle Age." *McCall's* (October 1971): 112, 174.

Johnson, Ralph E. Jr. *Marital Patterns During the Middle Years.* Ph.D. dissertation, University of Minnesota, 1968.

Kinsey, Alfred C., et al. *Sexual Behavior in the Human Female.* Philadelphia, Pa.: W.B. Saunders Co., 1953.

Komarovsky, Mirra. "Functional Analysis of Sex Roles." *American Sociological Review* 15, no. 4 (August 1950).

Kupperman, Herbert S. "The So-Called 'Male Menopause,'" *Modern Maturity* (August-September 1975): 61-62.

Lansing, John B., and Kish, Leslie. "Family Life Cycle as an Independent Variable." *American Sociological Review* 22, no. 5 (October 1957): 512-519.

Levin, Robert J. "The Redbook Report on Premarital and Extramarital Sex." *Redbook* (October 1975): 38-44, 190-192.

Levin, Robert J., and Levin, Amy. "Sexual Pleasure: The Surprising Preferences of 100,000 Women." *Redbook* (September 1975): 51-58.

Ligon, Ernest M. "Some Modern Skills of Grandparenthood." Address given at the Annual Conference of District 710, Rotary International, 28 April 1973.

Lowenthal, Marjorie F., and Chiriboga, David. "Transition to the Empty Nest: Crisis, Challenge, or Relief?" *Archives of General Psychiatry* 26 (1972): 8-14.

Masters, William H., and Johnson, Virginia E. *Human Sexual Response.* Boston, Mass.: Little, Brown & Co., 1966.

Masters, William H., and Johnson, Virginia E. "Human Sexual Response: The Aging Female and the Aging Male. Chap. 30, pp. 271-275 in Bernice L., Neugarten, ed., *Middle Age and Aging.* Chicago: University of Chicago Press, 1968.

Mead, Margaret. "What Is Modern Grandparent's Role?" *Redbook* (June 1966): 28, 30.

Neugarten, Bernice L. "Adult Personality: A Developmental View." *Human Development* 9 (1966): 61-73.

Neugarten, Bernice L. "Dynamics of Transition of Middle Age to Old Age Adaptation and the Life Cycle." *Journal of Geriatric Psychiatry* IV, no. 1 (Fall 1970): 71-87.

Neugarten, Bernice L., and Gutmann, David L. "Age-Sex Roles and Personality in Middle Age: A Thematic Apperception Study." *Psychological Monographs* 72, no. 17 (1958): 32-33.

Neugarten, Bernice L.; Havighurst, Robert J.; and Tobin, Sheldon S. "The Measurement of Life Satisfaction." *Journal of Gerontology* 16, no. 2 (April 1961): 134-143.

Neugarten, Bernice L., and Peterson, Warren A. "A Study of the American Age-Grade System." *Proceedings of the Fourth Congress of the International Association of Gerontology*, vol. 3, Sociological Division, Merano, Italy, 14-19 July 1957, pp. 497-502.

Neugarten, Bernice L., and Weinstein, Karol K. "The Changing American Grandparent." *Journal of Marriage and the Family* 26, no. 2 (May 1964): 199-204.

Orthner, Dennis K. "Leisure Activity Patterns and Marital Satisfaction Over the Marital Career." *Journal of Marriage and the Family* 37, no. 1 (February 1975): 91-102.

Peterson, James A. *Married Love in the Middle Years.* New York: Association Press, 1968.

Petranek, Charles Frank. "The Forgotten Phase of Life—The Postparental Period of Marriage." Unpublished manuscript, 1971.

Petranek, Charles Frank. *Postparental Spouses' Perception of Their Dyadic Interaction as Related to Their Life Satisfaction.* Tallahassee, Fla.: Department of Sociology, Florida State University, 1970.

Pineo, Peter C. "Disenchantment in the Later Years of Marriage." *Marriage and Family Living* 23, no. 1 (February 1961): 3-11.

Rollins, Boyd C., and Feldman, Harold. "Marital Satisfaction over the Family Life Cycle." *Journal of Marriage and the Family* 32, no. 1 (February 1970): 24.

Rose, Arnold M. "Factors Associated with the Life Satisfaction of Middle-Class, Middle-Aged Persons." *Marriage and Family Living* 17, no. 1 (February 1955): 15-19.

Saunders, LaVell E. *Social Class and Postparental Perspective.* Ph.D. dissertation, University of Minnesota, 1969.

Stanford University. "Study Shows Career Women Happiest." UPI release, 8 November 1975.

Statistical Bulletin. "Accident Mortality Among Men at the Working Ages." New York: Metropolitan Life, September 1975.

Sussman, Marvin B. "Activity Patterns of Postparental Couples and Their Relationship to Family Continuity." *Marriage and Family Living* 17, no. 4 (November 1955): 338-341.

Sussman, Marvin B. "The Help Pattern in the Middle Class Family." *American Sociological Review* 18, no. 1 (February 1953): 27-28.

Sussman, Marvin B. "Kin Relations and Social Roles in Middle Age." 1959. Mimeographed.

U.S. News & World Report. "A Look at Americans in Year 2000." U.S. Bureau of the Census and *U.S. News & World Report* Economic Unit, 3 March 1975, p. 35.

References   531

Chapter 16
Aging family members

AD. "Study Refutes Ideas about the Elderly." *AD* 5, no. 2 (February 1976): 39.

Adams, Bert N. "Isolation, Function, and Beyond: American Kinship in the 1960s." *Journal of Marriage and the Family* 32, no. 4 (November 1970): 575-597.

Albrecht, Ruth. "Relationships of Older Parents with Their Children." *Marriage and Family Living* 16, no. 1 (February 1954): 33.

Aldous, Joan. "Intergenerational Visiting Patterns: Variation in Boundary Maintenance as an Explanation." *Family Process* 6, no. 2 (1967): 235-251.

Bahr, Howard M. "Aging and Religious Disaffiliation." *Social Forces* 49, no. 1 (September 1970): 59-71.

Ballweg, John A. "Resolution of Conjugal Role Adjustment after Retirement." *Journal of Marriage and the Family* 29, no. 2 (1967): 277-281.

Beard, Belle Boone. "Religion at 100." *Modern Maturity* 12 (1969): 1-4.

Blenkner, Margaret. "Social Work and Family Relationships in Later Life with Some Thoughts on Filial Maturity." In Ethel Shanas and Gordon Streib, eds., *Social Structure and the Family: Generational Relations.* Englewood Cliffs, N.J.: Prentice-Hall, 1965.

Booth, Alan, and Hess, Elaine. "Cross-Sex Friendship." *Journal of Marriage and the Family* 36, no. 1 (February 1974): 38-47.

Burr, Wesley R. "Satisfaction with Various Aspects of Marriage Over the Life Cycle: A Random Middle Class Sample." *Journal of Marriage and the Family* 32, no. 1 (February 1970): 29-37.

Burr, Wesley R. *Theory Construction and the Sociology of the Family.* New York: John Wiley & Sons, 1973.

Butler, Robert N. "Old People Don't Lose Sex Drives." Report on address to American Medical Association. UPI release, 4 April 1974.

Butler, Robert N. "Psychiatry and the Elderly: An Overview." *American Journal of Psychiatry* 132, no. 9 (September 1975): 893-900.

Butler, Robert N. Public Interest Report, Number 9: "How to Grow Old and Poor in an Affluent Society." *International Journal of Aging and Human Development* 4 (1973): 277-279.

Cavan, Ruth S.; Burgess, Ernest W.; and Goldhammer, Herbert. *Personal Adjustment in Old Age.* Science Research Associates, 1949, p. 58.

Crampton, C. Ward. *Live Long and Like It.* New York: Public Affairs Committee, 1948, p. 19.

Cumming, Elaine, and Henry, William. *Growing Old.* New York: Basic Books, Inc., 1961.

Darnley, Fred J. "Adjustment to Retirement: Integrity or Despair." *The Family Coordinator* 24, no. 2 (April 1975): 217-226.

Duke University Aging Research Study. *AD* 5, no. 2 (February 1976): 39-40.

Duvall, Evelyn Millis. *In-Laws: Pro and Con.* New York: Association Press, 1954, pp. 323-324.

Eisdorfer, C., and Lawton, M.P., eds. *The Psychology of Adult Development and Aging.* Washington, D.C.: American Psychological Association, 1973.

Feigenbaum, Eliott; Lowenthal, Marjorie F.; and Trier, Mella L. "Sexual Attitudes in the Elderly." Paper read at the Gerontological Society, New York, 1966.

Felix, Robert H. *Ready for Retirement?* Hogg Foundation for Mental Health, Austin: University of Texas, 1975.

Folsom, James. "Reversing Senility." Interview in *Newsweek*, 4 September 1972, p. 68.

Glick, Paul C. "Some Recent Changes in American Families." *Current Population Reports: Special Studies*, Series P-23, no. 52, Washington, D.C.: Superintendent of Documents, 1975.

Golant, Stephen M. "Residential Concentrations of the Future Elderly." In Bernice L. Neugarten, ed., *"Aging in the Year 2000: A Look at the Future." The Gerontologist* 15, no. 1 (February 1975): 16-23.

Goldfarb, Alvin "Improved Care Urged for Aged." Interview in *L.A. Times. Washington Post News Service* release, 29 September 1972.

Havighurst, Robert J. *Developmental Tasks and Education.* New York: David McKay Co., 1972.

Havighurst, Robert J., and Albrecht, Ruth. *Older People.* New York: Longmans, Green & Co., 1953.

Havighurst, Robert J.; Munnicks, M.A.; Joep, Thomas; and Neugarten, Bernice L., *Adjustment to Retirement: A Cross-National Study.* Assen, Netherlands: Van Goscum, 1969.

Heschel, Abraham J. "The Older Person and the Family in the Perspective of Jewish Tradition." Paper read at the White House Conference on Aging, 9 January 1961, pp. 15-16.

Hill, Reuben. "Decision Making and the Family Life Cycle." P. 123 in Ethel Shanas and Gordon F. Streib, eds., *Social Structure and the Family: Generational Relations.* Englewood Cliffs, N.J.: Prentice-Hall, 1965.

Hill, Reuben, et al. *Family Development in Three Generations.* Cambridge, Mass.: Schenkman Publishing Co., 1970.

Hochschild, A.R. *The Unexpected Community.* Englewood Cliffs, N.J.: Prentice-Hall, 1973.

Jackson, Jacquelyne Johnson. "Marital Life Among Aging Blacks." *The Family Coordinator* 21, no. 1 (January 1972): 21-27.

Jarvik, Lissy F. "Thoughts on the Psychobiology of Aging." *American Psychologist* 30, no. 5 (May 1975): 576-583.

Kahn, Robert L. "The Mental Health System and the Future Aged," In Bernice L. Neugarten, ed., "Aging in the Year 2000: A Look at the Future." *The Gerontologist* 15, no. 1 (February 1975): 24-31.

Keller, Helen "My Luminous Universe." *Guideposts* (June 1956): 2.

Koller, Marvin R. "Studies in Three-Generation Households." *Marriage and Family Living* 16, no. 3 (August 1954): 206.

Lasswell, Marcia E. "Looking Ahead in Aging: Love After Fifty." Pp. 518-524 in Marcia E. Lasswell and Thomas E. Lasswell, eds., *Love—Marriage—Family: A Developmental Approach.* Glenview, Ill.: Scott, Foresman & Co., 1973.

Lewis, Charles N. "Reminiscing and Self-Concept in Old Age." *Journal of Gerontology* 26 (1971): 240-243.

Lobsenz, Norman M. *Sex after Sixty-Five.* Public Affairs Pamphlet No. 519. New York: Public Affairs Committee, 1975.

Maas, Henry S., and Kuypers, Joseph A. *From Thirty to Seventy* (A Forty-Year Longitudinal Study of Adult Life Styles and Personality). San Francisco, Calif.: Jossey-Bass, Inc., 1974.

Maddox, George L. "Persistence of Life Style among the Elderly: A Longitudinal Study of Patterns of Social Activity in Relation to Life Satisfaction." In Bernice L. Neugarten, ed., *Middle Age and Aging.* Chicago: University of Chicago Press, 1968.

Martin, Clyde E. "Aging and Society Study." Reported by Jack Gourlay in *Sarasota Herald-Tribune*, 1 March 1974, p. 10-A.

Maynard, J., *Growing Up Old in the Sixties.* Garden City, N.Y.: Doubleday & Co., 1973.

Medicaid, Medicare: Which Is Which? Washington, D.C.: Superintendent of Documents, 1969.

Moberg, David O. "Religion and the Aging Family." *The Family Coordinator* 21, no. 1 (January 1972): 47-60.

Montgomery, James E. "The Housing Patterns of Older Families." *The Family Coordinator* 21, no. 1 (January 1972): 37-46.

Neugarten, Bernice L. "The Future and the Young-Old." *The Gerontologist* 15, no. 1 (February 1975): 4-9.

Neugarten, Bernice L., ed. *Middle Age and Aging.* Chicago: University of Chicago Press, 1968.

Neugarten, Bernice L. "The Old and the Young in Modern Societies." *American Behavioral Scientist* 14, no. 1 (September–October 1970): 13-24.

Neugarten, Bernice L. "The Young-Old." *The University of Chicago Magazine* 68, no. 1 (Autumn 1975): 22-23.

Neugarten, Bernice L., and Weinstein, Karol K. "The Changing American Grandparent." *Journal of Marriage and the Family* 26, no. 2 (May 1964): 199-204.

Perera, George A. "Finding Golden Threads Among the Silver." *New York Times*, 6 March 1974, p. 33.

Peterson, James A. "Anticipation of Things to Come," Pp. 524-531 in Marcia E. Lasswell and Thomas E. Lasswell, eds., *Love-Marriage-Family: A Developmental Approach.* Glenview, Ill.: Scott, Foresman & Co., 1973.

Pfeiffer, Eric. "Successful Aging." Paper read at meeting of the American Medical Association, Chicago, Ill., 1-3 April 1974.

Pincus, Allen. "Reminiscence in Aging and Its Implications for Social Work Practice." *Social Work* 15, no. 3 (1970): 47-53.

Renne, Karen S. "Correlates of Dissatisfaction in Marriage." *Journal of Marriage and the Family* 32, no. 1 (February 1970): 54-67.

Riesman, David. "Some Clinical and Cultural Aspects of Aging." *American Journal of Sociology* 59, no. 4 (January 1954): 379-383.

Rollins, Boyd C., and Cannon, Kenneth L. "Marital Satisfaction over the Family Life Cycle: A Reevaluation." *Journal of Marriage and the Family* 36, no. 2 (May 1974): 271-282.

Rollins, Boyd C., and Feldman, Harold. "Marital Satisfaction over the Family Life Cycle." *Journal of Marriage and the Family* 32, no. 1 (February 1970): 20-28.

Sarason, Seymour B.; Sarason, Esther K.; and Cowden, Peter. "Aging and the Nature of Work." *American Psychologist* 30, no. 5 (May 1975): 584-592.

Schorr, Alvin L. *Filial Responsibility in the Modern American Family.* Washington, D.C.: Superintendent of Documents, 1960.

Shanas, Ethel. "Family Help Patterns and Social Class in Three Countries." *Journal of Marriage and the Family* 29, no. 2 (May 1967): 257-266.

Shanas, Ethel, and Streib, Gordon F., eds. *Social Structure and the Family: Generational Relations.* Englewood Cliffs, N.J.: Prentice-Hall, 1965.

Sheldon, Alan; McEwan, Peter J.M.; and Ryser, Carol Pierson. *Retirement Patterns and Predictions.* Washington, D.C.: Superintendent of Documents, 1975.

Smith, Bert Kruger. *Mental Health in Nursing Homes.* The Hogg Foundation for Mental Health, Austin: University of Texas, 1975.

Statistical Bulletin. "Expectation of Life in the United States at New High." New York: Metropolitan Life, April 1975, Vol. 56, pp. 5-7.

Stinnett, Nick; Carter, Linda Mittelstet; and Montgomery, James E. "Older Persons' Perceptions of Their Marriages." *Journal of Marriage and the Family* 34, no. 4 (November 1972): 665-670.

Streib, Gordon F. "Intergenerational Relations: Perspectives of the Two Generations on the Older Parent." *Journal of Marriage and the Family* 27, no. 4 (November 1965): 469-476.

Streib, Gordon F. "Older Families and Their Troubles: Familial and Social Responses." *The Family Coordinator* 21, no. 1 (January 1972): 5-19.

Streib, Gordon F., and Schneider, Clement J. *Retirement in America.* Ithaca, N.Y.: Cornell University Press, 1971.

Streib, Gordon F., and Thompson, Wayne E. "The Older Person in a Family Context." P. 476 in Clark Tibbitts, ed., *Handbook of Social Gerontology.* Chicago: University of Chicago Press, 1960.

Sussman, Marvin, and Burchinal, Lee. "Kin Family Network: Unheralded Structure in Current Conceptualizations of Family Functioning." *Marriage and Family Living* 24, no. 3 (August 1962): 231-240.

The Older American. Washington, D.C.: Superintendent of Documents, 1963.

Troll, Lillian E. "The Family of Later Life: A Decade Review." *Journal of Marriage and the Family* 33, no. 2 (May 1971): 263-290.

U.S. Bureau of the Census. "Income of Families in the United States." *Current Population Reports,* Series P-60, no. 59, 18 April 1969.

U.S. Bureau of the Census. "Mobility of the Population of the United States March 1970 to March 1974." *Current Population Reports,* Series P-20, no. 273, December 1974, p. 12.

U.S. Bureau of the Census. "A Look at Americans in Year 2000." *U.S. News & World Report,* 3 March 1975, p. 35.

U.S. Bureau of the Census. "Men Over 65 Retiring at a More Rapid Rate." UPI release, 27 November 1975.

U.S. Bureau of the Census release, 1 August 1976.

U.S. Department of Health, Education and Welfare. *Monthly Vital Statistics Reports* 18, no. 5 (23 June 1969): 1.

U.S. News & World Report. "An Aging Population." 3 March 1975, p. 35.

Warren, Roland L. "Old Age in a Rural Township." P. 156 in *Age Is No Barrier.* Albany, New York: New York State Joint Legislative Committee on Problems of the Aging, 1952.

Whitworth, Rick. "Nursing Home Care in the United States." United States Senate, Subcommittee on Long Term Care, report of 19 May 1975.

Young, Patrick. "For a Zestier Life...R Sex Over Sixty." *The National Observer,* 1 February 1975, pp. 1, 18.

Chapter 17
Death in the family

Barnard, Charles N. "A Good Death." *Family Health* (April 1973): 41-42, 60-62.

Berardo, Felix M. "Widowhood Status in the United States: Perspective on a Neglected Aspect of the Family Life Cycle." *The Family Coordinator* 17, no. 3 (July 1968): 191-203.

Bock, E. Wilbur. "Aging and Suicide: The Significance of Marital, Kinship, and Alternative Relations." *The Family Coordinator* 21, no. 1 (January 1972): 71-79.

Campion, Nardi Reeder. "A Delayed 'Obituary.'" *New York Times*, 22 May 1973, p. 39.

Carter, Hugh, and Glick, Paul C. *Marriage and Divorce: A Social and Economic Study.* Rev. ed. Cambridge, Mass.: Harvard University Press, 1976.

Cousins, Norman. "The Right to Die." *Saturday Review*, 14 June 1975, p. 4.

Durant, Will. *Caesar and Christ.* The Story of Civilization: Part III. New York: Simon & Schuster, 1944, p. 231.

Duvall, Evelyn Millis, and Hill, Reuben. *When You Marry.* Boston, Mass.: D.C. Heath & Co., 1945, p. 311.

Eliot, Thomas D. "The Bereaved Family." *Annals of the Academy of Political and Social Science* (March 1932): 4.

Elliot, Grace Loucks. *To Come Full Circle Toward an Understanding of Death.* New York: Union Seminary Book Store, 1971, p. 15.

Fletcher, Joseph F. "Anti-Dysthanasia: The Problem of Prolonging Death." *The Journal of Pastoral Care* 18 (Summer 1964): 77.

Frederick, Calvin J., and Lague, Louise. *Dealing with the Crisis of Suicide.* New York: Public Affairs Committee, 1972.

Gallup Poll. "Euthanasia Backed in Terminal Illness by 53% in a Poll." *New York Times*, 2 August 1973.

Gaylin, Ned L. "On the Quality of Life and Death." *The Family Coordinator* 24, no. 3 (July 1975): 247-255.

Gaylin, Willard. "Harvesting the Dead." *Harper's* (September 1974): 23-30.

Gubrium, Jaber F. "Marital Desolation and the Evaluation of Everyday Life in Old Age." *Journal of Marriage and the Family* 36, no. 1 (February 1974): 107-113.

Harmer, Ruth Mulvey. "Funerals That Make Sense." *Modern Maturity* (June-July 1974): 59-61.

Harris, Louis. "The Harris Poll." *Sarasota Herald-Tribune*, 23 April 1973, p. 5-B.

Harvey, Carol D., and Bahr, Howard M. "Widowhood, Morale, and Affiliation." *Journal of Marriage and the Family* 36, no. 1 (February 1974): 97-106.

Hiltz, S. Roxanne. "Helping Widows: Group Discussions as a Therapeutic Technique." *The Family Coordinator* 24, no. 3 (July 1975): 331-336.

Hutchison, Ira W, III. "The Significance of Marital Status for Morale and Life Satisfaction Among Low-Income Elderly." *Journal of Marriage and the Family* 35, no. 2 (May 1975): 287-293.

Keebler, Nancy. "When a Child Might Die." *The National Observer*, week ending 12 April 1975, p. 1.

Kitagawa, Evelyn M. "Socioeconomic Differences in Mortality in the United States and Some Implications for Population Policy." *U.S. Commission on Population Growth and the American Future* (1972): 85-110.

Krieger, G.W., and Bascue, L.O. "Terminal Illness: Counseling with a Family Perspective." *The Family Coordinator* 24, no. 3 (July 1975): 351–355.

Kübler-Ross, Elizabeth. *Death and Dying.* Interview on Public Broadcasting System. 8 January 1976.

Kübler-Ross, Elizabeth. *Death: The Final Stage of Growth.* Englewood Cliffs, N.J.: Prentice-Hall, 1975.

Kübler-Ross, Elizabeth. *On Death and Dying.* New York: Macmillan Publishing Co., 1970.

Leach, Norman E. "Suicide and Life." *PHP* 4, no. 11 (November 1973): 13–16.

"Leading Causes of Death Among Insured Lives." *Statistical Bulletin* 56 (August 1975): 11.

Lieberman, E. James. "Americans No Longer Know How to Mourn." *The Washington Post/Potomac*, 20 December 1970, pp. 7–10, 17, 25.

Lieberman, Morton A. "New Insights into Crises of Aging." *University of Chicago Magazine* 66, no. 1 (July–August 1973): 11–14.

Lopata, Helena Znaniecki. "Living Through Widowhood." *Psychology Today* 7, no. 2 (July 1973): 86–92.

Lopata, Helena Znaniecki. *Widowhood in an American City.* Cambridge, Mass.: Schenkman Publishing Co., 1970.

McCall, Tom. "The Argument for 'Death with Dignity.'" *AARP News Bulletin* 8 (September 1972): 6.

McKain, Walter C. "A New Look at Older Marriages." *The Family Coordinator* 21, no. 1 (January 1972): 61–69.

McKain, Walter C. *Retirement Marriages.* Agriculture Experiment Station Monograph 3. Storrs, Conn.: University of Connecticut, 1969.

Maguire, Daniel C. "Death by Chance, Death by Choice." *The Atlantic* (January 1974): 57–65.

Maguire, Daniel C. "Death, Legal and Illegal." *The Atlantic* (February 1974): 72–85.

Mannes, Marya. *Last Rights: A Case for the Good Death.* New York: William Morrow & Co., 1974.

Marris, Peter. "The Meaning of Grief." *New York Times*, 10 March 1975, p. 31.

"'Medically Prolonging Life' Studied." AP release from United Nations, New York, 6 April 1970.

Mitford, Jessica. *The American Way of Death.* New York: Simon & Schuster 1963.

National Association for Mental Health. "Depression Danger Signals." *U.S. News & World Report*, 1 December 1975, p. 67.

National Opinion Research Center. AP release, "Majority of U.S. 'Optimistic' About Death." *Sarasota Herald-Tribune*, 12 June 1976, p. 5-B.

Pine, Vanderlyn R., and Phillips, Derek L. "The Cost of Dying: A Sociological Analysis of Funeral Expenditures." Pp. 130–139 in Frances G. Scott and Ruth M. Brewer, eds., *Confrontations of Death.* Eugene, Ore.: Oregon Center for Gerontology, 1971.

"The Plight of America's 2 Million Widowers." *U.S. News & World Report*, 15 April 1974, pp. 59–60.

Porter, Sylvia. *Sylvia Porter's Money Book.* New York: Doubleday & Co., 1975, pp. 753–754.

Preston, Caroline E., and Horton, John. "Attitudes among Clergy and Lawyers toward Euthanasia." *The Journal of Pastoral Care* 26, no. 2 (June 1972): 108–115.

"Profile of Elders in the United States." *Statistical Bulletin* 56 (April 1975): p. 8.

Rosenbaum, Veryl. "How to Cope with Crises." *Modern Maturity* (August-September 1975): 51-52.

Rosenfeld, Albert. "Are We Programmed to Die?" *Saturday Review*, 2 October 1976, pp. 10-17.

Russell, O. Ruth. "Freedom to Choose Death." *PHP* 6, no. 6 (June 1975): 17-19.

Sackett, Walter W. "Death with Dignity." White House Conference on Aging, Washington, D.C., 29 November 1971.

Seiden, Richard H. "We're Driving Young Blacks to Suicide." *Psychology Today* 4, no. 3 (August 1970): 24-28.

Shafer, Evelyn M. "Hold Not My Life." Personal communication, with permission, 1975.

Shneidman, Edwin S. "You and Death." *Psychology Today* 5, no. 1 (June 1971): 43-45, 74-80.

Siegel, Jacob S. U.S. Bureau of the Census release. "Over-65 Population Continues to Grow Rapidly." *Sarasota Herald-Tribune*, 1 June 1976, p. 12-A.

Somerville, Rose M. "Death Education as Part of Family Life Education: Using Imaginative Literature for Insights into Family Crises." *The Family Coordinator* 20, no. 3 (July 1971): 209-224.

"Study Is Made of Bereavement as an Illness." AP release, *Sarasota Herald-Tribune*, 5 November 1973, p. 10-A.

U.S. Bureau of the Census. "Population of the United States Trends and Prospects: 1950-1990." *Current Population Reports*, Series P-23, no. 49, "Differential Mortality." May 1974, pp. 41-50.

U.S. Department of Health, Education, and Welfare. "Annual Summary for the United States, 1974." *Monthly Vital Statistics Report, Provisional Statistics* 23, no. 13 (30 May 1975): 4.

Van Gieson, John. "Doctor Wages Two Fights." AP release, *Sarasota Herald-Tribune*, 13 January 1974, p. 7-B.

Waller, Willard, and Hill, Reuben. *The Family: A Dynamic Interpretation*. New York: Dryden Press, 1951, p. 457.

Webster, Bayard, "Survey Indicates Most Persons Favor Donation of Human Organs and Tissue." *New York Times*, 22 November 1975.

Weisman, Avery D. *On Dying and Denying: A Psychiatric Study of Terminality*. New York: Behavioral Publications, 1972.

Wessel, Morris A. "Children Cope with Facts of Death." Interview in AP release, New Haven, Conn., 5 January 1976.

Whitman, Alden. "Reflections of an Obituary Writer." *Modern Maturity* (June-July 1972): 26-27.

Chapter 18
Broken and rebuilt marriages

Addeo, Edmond G., and Burger, Robert E. *Ironside Divorce—Is It What You Really Want?* New York: McGraw-Hill Book Co., 1975.

Bell, Robert R. *Marriage and Family Interaction*. 3rd ed. Homewood, Ill.: Dorsey Press, 1971.

Bergler, Edmund. *Divorce Won't Help*. New York: Harper & Brothers, 1948.

Bernard, Jessie. "Note On Changing Life Styles, 1970-1974." *Journal of Marriage and the Family* 37, no. 3 (August 1975): 582-593.

Bernard, Jessie. *Remarriage: A Study of Marriage.* New York: The Dryden Press, 1956.

Better Homes and Gardens. A Report on the American Family. Des Moines, Iowa: Meredith Corp., 1972.

Bohannan, Paul, ed. *Divorce and After.* Garden City, N.Y.: Doubleday & Co., 1970.

Bohannan, Paul. "The Six Stations of Divorce." Pp. 475-489 in Marcia E. Lasswell and Thomas E. Lasswell, eds., *Love—Marriage—Family: A Developmental Approach.* Glenview, Ill.: Scott, Foresman & Co., 1973.

Bowerman, Charles E., and Irish, Donald P. "Some Relationships of Stepchildren to Their Parents." Pp. 495-501 in Marcia E. Lasswell and Thomas E. Lasswell. eds., *Love—Marriage—Family: A Developmental Approach.* Glenview, Ill.: Scott, Foresman & Co., 1973.

Brandwein, Ruth A.; Brown, Carol A.; and Fox, Elizabeth Maury. "Women and Children Last: The Social Situation of Divorced Mothers and Their Families." *Journal of Marriage and the Family* 36, no. 3 (August 1974): 498-514.

Carter, Hugh, and Glick, Paul C. *Marriage and Divorce: A Social and Economic Study.* Rev. ed. Cambridge, Mass.: Harvard University Press, 1976.

Clayton, Richard R. *The Family, Marriage, and Social Change.* Lexington, Mass.: D.C. Heath & Co., 1975.

Duberman, Lucile. *Marriage and Its Alternatives.* New York: Praeger Publishers, 1974.

Dullea, Georgia. "Who Gets Custody of Children? Fathers Now Being Heeded." *New York Times*, 14 October 1975, p. 44.

Duvall, Evelyn Millis, and Hill, Reuben. Rev. ed. *When You Marry.* Lexington, Mass.: D.C. Heath & Co., 1953.

England, J. Lynn, and Kunz, Phillip R. "The Application of Age-Specific Rates to Divorce." *Journal of Marriage and the Family* 37, no. 1 (February 1975): 40-46.

Etzioni, Amitai. "Breaking Up the Family—The Newest In Thing?" *San Francisco Chronicle*, 5 February 1976, p. 21.

Family Service Association of America. Survey quoted in William E. Stevens. "If Recession Comes in the Door, Love May Fly Out the Window." *New York Times*, 28 July 1975, p. 17.

Fisher, Esther Oshiver. *Divorce: The New Freedom, A Guide to Divorcing and Divorce Counseling.* New York: Harper & Row Publishers, Inc., 1974.

Glenn, Norval D. "The Contribution of Marriage to the Psychological Well-Being of Males and Females." *Journal of Marriage and the Family* 37, no. 3 (August 1975): 594-600.

Glick, Paul C. "Living Arrangements of Children and Young Adults." Paper read at the annual meeting of the Population Association of America, Seattle, Washington, 17-19 April 1975.

Glick, Paul C. "Some Recent Changes in American Families." *Current Population Reports: Special Studies*, Series P-23, no. 52. Washington, D.C.: U.S. Government Printing Office, 1975.

Glick, Paul C., and Norton, Arthur J. "Perspectives on the Recent Upturn in Divorce and Remarriage." *Demography* 10, no. 3 (1973): 301-314.

Goode, William J. *After Divorce.* New York: The Free Press, 1956.

Gordon, Michael. *The American Family: Past, Present, and Future.* New York: Random House, 1973.

Hampton, Hartley. "When the Millstone Gets Too Heavy. . .They Cut and Run." *The National Observer*, week ending 6 September 1975, p. 1.

Hicks, Nancy. "Economy Held Key to Child Suicides." *New York Times*, 20 June 1975, p. 34.

Hunt, Morton M. *The World of the Formerly Married.* New York: McGraw-Hill Book Co., 1966.

Kephart, William M. "Occupational Level and Marital Disruption." *American Sociological Review* 20 (1955): 460-462.

Kriesberg, Louis. *Mothers in Poverty.* Chicago, Ill.: Aldine-Atherton, Inc., 1970.

Lake, Alice. "Divorcees: The New Poor." *McCall's* (September 1976): 18-24, 152.

Landers, Ann. "A Sad and Personal Message." Syndicated column, 2 July 1975.

Levinger, George. "Sources of Marital Dissatisfaction among Applicants for Divorce." *American Journal of Orthopsychiatry* 36 (1966): 803-807.

Locke, Harvey J. *Predicting Adjustment in Marriage.* New York: Holt, Rinehart & Winston, 1951.

Martin, J. "Surveying Attitudes on Marriage, Divorce, the Family and Sex." *The Washington Post*, 3 October 1974, p. B3.

Monahan, Thomas P., and Kephart, William M. "Divorce and Desertion by Religious and Mixed Religious Groups." *American Journal of Sociology* 59 (1954).

Morris, James D., and Prescott, Mary R. "Transition Groups: An Approach to Dealing with Post-Partnership Anguish." *The Family Coordinator* 24, no. 3 (July 1975): 325-330.

Norton, Arthur J., and Glick, Paul C. "Marital Instability: Past, Present, and Future." *Journal of Social Issues* 32, no. 1 (Winter 1976): 5-20.

Ogg, Elizabeth. *Divorce.* New York: Public Affairs Committee, 1975.

O'Sullivan, Sonya. "Single Life in a Double Bed." *Harper's Magazine* (November 1975): 45-52.

Phillips, Kevin P. "Politicians, Awake! Family Is Ideal Political Issue." *Philadelphia Evening Bulletin*, 9 February 1976.

Radloff, Lenore. "Sex Differences in Mental Health: The Effects of Marital and Occupational Status." Paper read at meeting of the American Public Health Association, October 1974.

Riley, Lawrence E., and Spreitzer, Elmer A. "A Model for the Analysis of Lifetime Marriage Patterns." *Journal of Marriage and the Family* 36, no. 1 (February 1974): 64-70.

Schoen, Robert. "California Divorce Rates by Age at First Marriage and Duration of First Marriage." *Journal of Marriage and the Family* 37, no. 3 (August 1975): 548-555.

Spicer, Jerry W., and Hampe, Gary D. "Kinship Interaction after Divorce." *Journal of Marriage and the Family* 37, no. 1 (February 1975): 113-119.

Stetson, Dorothy M., and Wright, Gerald C., Jr. "The Effects of Laws on Divorce in American States." *Journal of Marriage and the Family* 37, no. 3 (August 1975): 537-547.

Stevens, William K. "If Recession Comes in the Door, Love May Fly Out the Window." *New York Times*, 28 July 1975, p. 17.

Udry, J. Richard. *The Social Context of Marriage.* Philadelphia: J.B. Lippincott Co., 1974.

U.S. Bureau of the Census. "Age at First Marriage." *1970 Census of Population.* PC (2)-4D. Washington, D.C.: U.S. Government Printing Office, April 1973.

U.S. Bureau of the Census. "Census Bureau Reports Growth in Singlehood." Release in *The National Observer,* 17 January 1976, p. 1.

U.S. Bureau of the Census. "Marital Status." *1970 Census of Population,* PC (2)-4C. Washington, D.C.: U.S. Government Printing Office, 1972.

U.S. Bureau of the Census. "Marital Status and Living Arrangements: March 1974." *Current Population Reports,* P-20, no. 271. Washington, D.C.: U.S. Government Printing Office, October 1974.

U.S. Bureau of the Census. "Marital Status and Living Arrangements: March 1975." *Current Population Reports,* Series P-20, no. 287, Washington D.C.: U.S. Government Printing Office, December 1975.

U.S. Bureau of the Census. "Marriage, Divorce, and Remarriage by Year of Birth: June 1971." *Current Population Reports,* Series P-20, no. 239. Washington, D.C.: U.S. Government Printing Office, 1972.

U.S. Bureau of the Census. "Population of the United States Trends and Prospects: 1950-1990." *Current Population Reports,* Series P-23, no. 49. Washington, D.C.: U.S. Government Printing Office, May 1974.

U.S. Bureau of the Census. "Social and Economic Variations in Marriage, Divorce and Remarriage." *Current Population Reports,* Series P-20, no. 223. Washington, D.C.: U.S. Government Printing Office, 1971.

U.S. Bureau of the Census. "Unwed Mothers Have Less Stable Marriages." UPI release, 17 August 1976.

U.S. Department of Health, Education, and Welfare. "Annual Summary for the United States, 1974 Birth, Deaths, Marriages, and Divorces." *Monthly Vital Statistics Report* 23, no. 13 (30 May 1975).

U.S. News & World Report Economic Unit. "Family Trends Now Taking Shape." *U.S. News & World Report,* 27 October 1975, p. 32.

Waller, Willard. *The Old Love and the New.* New York: Liveright, 1930.

Walters, James, and Stinnett, Nick. "Parent-Child Relationships: A Decade Review of Research." *Journal of Marriage and the Family* 33, no. 1 (February 1971): 70-111.

Warner, Julian R. "Arriving at a Property Settlement." *Marriage & Divorce* 1, no. 1 (March–April 1974): 86-91.

Weitzman, Lenore J. "Legal Regulation of Marriage: Tradition and Change." *California Law Review* 62, no. 4 (July-September 1974): 1169-1288.

Wheeler, Michael. *No-Fault Divorce.* Boston, Mass.: Beacon Press, 1974.

Williams, Frank S. "Children of Divorce. . .Detectives, Diplomats or Despots?" *Marriage & Divorce* 1, no. 1 (March–April 1974): 24-28.

Wilson, Kenneth L. Zurcher, Louis A.; McAdams, Diana Claire; and Curtis, Russell L. "Stepfathers and Stepchildren: An Exploratory Analysis from Two National Surveys." *Journal of Marriage and the Family* 37, no. 3 (August 1975): 526-536.

Chapter 19
Developmental crises and satisfactions

Andrews, Frank M., and Withey, Stephen B. *Social Indicators of Well-Being.* New York: Plenum Publishing Corp., 1976.

Blood, Robert O., Jr., and Wolfe, Donald M. *Husbands and Wives: The Dynamics of Married Living.* New York: The Free Press, 1960.

Boudouris, James. "Homicide and the Family." *Journal of Marriage and the Family* 33, no. 4 (November 1971): 667–676.

Burr, Wesley R. "Satisfaction with Various Aspects of Marriage over the Life Cycle: A Random Middle Class Sample." *Journal of Marriage and the Family* 32, no. 1 (February 1970): 29–37.

Campbell, Angus. "Are Women's Lives More Frustrating and Less Rewarding than Men's?" Ann Arbor, Mich.: Institute for Social Research, The University of Michigan, November 1974. Mimeographed.

Carter, Hugh, and Glick, Paul C. *Marriage and Divorce: A Social and Economic Study.* Rev. ed. Cambridge, Mass.: Harvard University Press, 1976.

Crittenden, Ann. "The Recession Takes Its Toll: Family Discord, Mental Illness." *New York Times*, 19 April 1976, p. 32.

Cuber, John F., and Harroff, Peggy B. *The Significant Americans: A Study of Sexual Behavior Among the Affluent.* New York: Appleton-Century 1965.

DeMott, Benjamin. "After the Sexual Revolution." *Atlantic Monthly* (November 1976): 71–93.

Duvall, Evelyn Millis. *Handbook for Parents.* Nashville, Tenn.: Broadman Press, 1974.

Duvall, Evelyn M. *In-Laws: Pro and Con.* New York: Association Press, 1954.

Duvall, Evelyn Millis. *Parent and Teenager Living and Loving.* Nashville, Tenn.: Broadman Press, 1976.

Duvall, Evelyn M., and Hill, Reuben. *Being Married.* Boston, Mass.: D.C. Heath & Co., 1960.

Glenn, Norval D. "The Contribution of Marriage to the Psychological Well-Being of Males and Females." *Journal of Marriage and the Family* 37, no. 3 (August 1975a): 594–600.

Glenn, Norval D. "Psychological Well-Being in the Postparental Stage: Some Evidence from National Surveys." *Journal of Marriage and the Family* 37, no. 1 (February 1975b): 105–110.

Goode, William J. "Force and Violence in the Family." *Journal of Marriage and the Family* 33, no. 4 (November 1971): 624–636.

Gurin, Gerald; Veroff, Joseph; and Feld, Sheila. *Americans View Their Mental Health: A Nationwide Interview Study.* New York: Basic Books, 1960.

Harry, Joseph; and Doherty, Edmund. "Evolving Sources of Happiness for Men over the Life Cycle: A Structural Analysis." Research report, Wayne State University, 1976. Mimeographed.

Hill, Reuben; Moss, Joel; and Wirths, Claudine. "Eddyville's Families." Chapel Hill: Institute for Research in Social Science, University of North Carolina, 1953.

Hill, Reuben, with chapters in collaboration with Foote, Nelson; Aldous, Joan; Carlson, Robert; and Macdonald, Robert. *Family Development in Three Generations: A Longitudinal Study of Changing Family Patterns of Planning and Achievement.* Cambridge, Mass.: Schenkman Publishing Co., 1970.

Hutchison, Ira W., III. "The Significance of Marital Status for Morale and Life Satisfaction Among Lower-Income Elderly." *Journal of Marriage and the Family* 37, no. 2 (May 1975): 287–293.

ISR Newsletter. "Americans' View of Life's Satisfactions Charted in New Volume on Social Indicators." Ann Arbor, Mich.: Institute for Social Research, The University of Michigan, Spring, 1976, pp. 6–7.

Joint Commission on Mental Illness and Health. *Action for Mental Health.* New York: Basic Books, Inc., 1961, p. 107.

Klausner, W.J. "An Experiment in Leisure." *Science Journal* 4 (1968): 81–85.

Long, Larry H. "New Estimates of Migration Expectancy in the United States." *Journal of the American Statistical Association* 68, no. 341 (1973): 37–43.

Lopata, Helena Z. "The Life Cycle of Social Roles of Housewife." Paper read at Midwest Sociological Society, Spring, 1965. Mimeographed.

Mudd, Emily H., and Hill, Reuben. "Memorandum on Strengthening Family Life in the United States." Prepared for Commissioners Charles I. Schottland and William L. Mitchell of the United States Department of Health, Education and Welfare. Washington, D.C.: Social Security Administration, 1956. Mimeographed.

Novak, Michael. "The Family Out of Favor." *Harper's Magazine* (April 1976): 37–46.

O'Brien, John. "Violence in Divorce Prone Families." *Journal of Marriage and the Family* 33, no. 4 (November 1971): 692–698.

Orthner, Dennis K. "Leisure Activity Patterns and Marital Satisfaction over the Marital Career." *Journal of Marriage and the Family* 37, no. 1 (February 1975): 91–102.

Rapoport, Rhona; Rapoport, Robert; and Thiessen, Victor. "Couple Symmetry and Enjoyment." *Journal of Marriage and the Family* 36, no. 3 (August 1974): 588–591.

Rollins, Boyd C., and Feldman, Harold. "Marital Satisfaction Over the Family Life Cycle." *Journal of Marriage and the Family* 32, no. 1 (February 1970): 24.

Rollins, Boyd C., and Cannon, Kenneth L. "Marital Satisfaction Over the Family Life Cycle: A Reevaluation." *Journal of Marriage and the Family* 36, no. 2 (May 1974): 271–282.

Selig, Andrew L. "Crisis Theory and Family Growth." *The Family Coordinator* 25, no. 3 (July 1976): 291–295.

Shaver, Phillip, and Freedman, Jonathan. "Your Pursuit of Happiness." *Psychology Today* 10, no. 3 (August 1976): 26–32, 75.

Spanier, Graham B.; Lewis, Robert A.; and Cole, Charles L. "Marital Adjustment Over the Family Life Cycle: The Issue of Curvilinearity." *Journal of Marriage and the Family* 37, no. 2 (May 1975): 263–275.

U.S. Bureau of the Census. "Mobility of the Population of the United States March 1970-March 1974." *Current Population Reports*, Series P-20, no. 273 (December 1974).

West, Patrick, and Merriam, L.C., Jr. "Outdoor Recreation and Family Cohesiveness: A Research Approach." *Journal of Leisure Research* 2 (1970): 251–259.

Yankelovich, Skelly and White, Inc. *The General Mills American Family Report: A Study of the American Family and Money.* Minneapolis, Minn.: General Mills. Inc., 1975, p. 52.

index of names

Downer, Donna Beth, 262
Dubbe, Marvin C., 313
Duberman, Lucile, 25, 331, 435, 452
Dullea, Georgia, 78, 447
Durant, Will, 110, 421
Duvall, Evelyn Millis, 65, 81, 101, 143,
  145, 153, 157, 193, 200, 242, 278,
  282, 301, 302, 311, 313, 314, 333,
  341, 348, 377, 379, 392, 400, 465,
  466, 475
Dyer, Everett D., 215
Dynes, Russell R., 298

Edwards, Maxine, 121, 122, 123, 124
Ehrhardt, Anke, 4
Elder, Glenn H., Jr., 186
Elliott, Grace Loucks, 427
Ellis, Albert, 123
Ellis, Evelyn, 324
England, J. Lynn, 436
Erikson, Erik, 11, 160, 162, 166
Erlanger, Howard D., 104
Eshleman, J. Ross, 186
Etaugh, Claire, 275
Etzioni, Amitai, 118, 457
Eveland, Leslie, 323

Farkas, George, 78
Farris, Joe Ann, 313
Featherman, Jo-Anna M., 240
Feigenbaum, Kenneth, 381
Feld, Sheila, 373, 379
Feldman, Harold, 19, 80, 152-153, 157,
  215, 239, 240, 260, 266, 281, 286,
  312, 373, 401, 476
Feldman, Margaret, 19, 80, 152-153
Felix, Robert H., 390
Fendrich, James M., 67
Feuer, Lewis S., 96
Fisher, Esther Oshiver, 456
Fiske, Edward B., 73, 297
Flaste, Richard, 214
Fletcher, Joseph F., 419
Fling, S., 8
Folsom, James, 399
Foreman, Harry, 38, 333
Forer, Raymond, 323
Fowler, Stanley E., 275
Fox, Elizabeth Maury, 455
Fox, Sandie Wightman, 38
Frederick, Calvin J., 416
Freeman, Barbara, 80
Freeman, Richard, 52, 328
Freud, Sigmund, 10, 160
Friedman, Milton, 56
Froeder, Marsha, 368
Fromm, Erich, 19
Fuchs, Estelle, 90

Fulcomer, David, 279
Furlong, Michael J., 382
Fuschillo, Jean, 257

Gage, M. Geraldine, 72
Gagnon, John H., 15, 25, 28, 39, 67
Gallup, George, 382
Gardner, Bruce, 277
Gatlin, Fred, 97
Gaylin, Ned L., 415-416
Gaylin, Willard, 410
Gebhard, Paul H., 375
Getzels, Jacob W., 298
Gianturco, Daniel, 426
Gilligan, Carol, 299, 318
Gilmartin, Brian G., 123
Gilmore, John V., 19
Glazer, Nathan, 64
Glenn, Norval D., 361, 479
Glick, Paul C., 61, 62, 93, 96, 120, 121,
  124, 152, 186, 204-205, 258, 330,
  332, 391, 426, 435, 436, 437, 439,
  440, 442-443, 447, 448, 450, 463
Golant, Stephen M., 391
Goldberg, Susan, 217
Goldblatt, Irene, 301
Goldfarb, Alvin, 399
Goldhammer, Herbert, 406
Goode, William, 116, 156, 451, 454,
  456, 475
Goodrich, Wells, 189, 195, 197, 199
Gordon, Ira J., 217
Gordon, Michael, 24, 64, 123, 457
Gordon, Suzanne, 121
Green, Maureen, 80
Gregg, Christina F., 28, 104
Gribbin, August, 52, 204
Grice, J.E., Jr., 39
Groper, N., 15
Gross, Irma H., 226
Gurin, Gerald, 373, 379
Gutmann, David L., 371

Hacker, David W., 327
Hagestad, Gunhild, 121
Haire, Doris, 214
Haller, Archibald O., 92
Hammel, Lisa, 275
Hammer, Elizabeth L., 27
Hampe, Gary D., 455
Hampton, Hartley, 434
Handler, Philip, 200
Hardesty, F.P., 274
Harmer, Ruth Mulvey, 422
Harris, Dale B., 275
Harroff, Peggy B., 35
Hartley, Eugene L., 370
Hartley, Ruth E., 8, 274, 275, 370

index of subjects

553